MW01492291

The Annotated

JOSEPH AND HIS FRIEND

THE ANNOTATED
JOSEPH AND HIS FRIEND

The Story of America's First Gay Novel

BAYARD TAYLOR
ANNOTATED BY
L.A. FIELDS

LETHE PRESS
Maple Shade, New Jersey

Published by Lethe Press
lethepressbooks.com

'Joseph and his Friend' by Bayard Taylor
is a public domain text

Annotations copyright © 2017 L.A. Fields

A list of citations and references
appears on pages 365-369

ISBN: 978-1-59021-642-2

No part of this work may be reproduced or
utilized in any form or by any means, electronic
or mechanical, including photocopying,
microfilm, and recording, or by any information
storage and retrieval system, without permission
in writing from the Author or Publisher.

*

Cover art
by Ben Baldwin

Cover and interior design
by Inkspiral Design

"The better angel is a man right fair;
The worser spirit a woman colour'd ill."

SHAKESPEARE: *Sonnets.*

CONTENTS

To THOSE WHO prefer quiet pictures of life to startling incidents, the attempt to illustrate the development of character to the mysteries of an elaborate plot, and the presentation of men and women in their mixed strength and weakness to the painting of wholly virtuous ideals and wholly evil examples: who are as interested in seeing moral and intellectual forces at work in a simple country community as on a more conspicuous plane of human action: who believe in the truth and tenderness of man's love for man, as of man's love for woman: who recognize the trouble which confused ideas of life and the lack of high and intelligent culture bring upon a great portion of our country population,—to all such, no explanation of this volume is necessary. Others will not read it.

AMERICA'S FIRST
GAY NOVEL?

THE QUESTION OF America's first gay novel is a layered one. As far as glimmers of masculine fixation before it, there is *The Private Memoirs and Confessions of a Justified Sinner* (1824), which has the same element of 'brotherly love' found in Bayard Taylor's "Twin-Love"[A.3] and Ambrose Bierce's "The Mocking-Bird" (see <u>Chapter 3: Twin-Love</u> for more detail), but it's Scottish in author and setting, and so out of the running. There is Charles Brockden Brown's *Edgar Huntly, Or, Memoirs of a Sleepwalker* (1799), which is American, and like *Joseph and His Friend* (1870), set on a farm in Pennsylvania (just outside of Philadelphia), but the obsessive male fixation is on Edgar's murdered friend Clithero, and the solving of that mystery by way of sleep-walking, barehanded panther-killing, and the rescuing of a white damsel from Indian attacks, is the more overwhelming plot of the story.

Here is the argument for *Joseph*:

Joseph and His Friend, considered the first American gay novel, was produced a century before Stonewall would mark the rise of America's modern gay rights movement and was introduced by lines from a Shakespearean sonnet: "The better angel is a man right fair" (Sonnet 144). In spite of Coleridge's editing of pronouns in Shakespeare's sonnets, they have long served as a rich source for homosexual allusion. Halleck, who was "a close student of Shakespeare," did not believe that Shakespeare wrote the sonnets, arguing that they were "quite out of his straightforward character." Taylor's novel may have inspired Richard Meeker's *Better Angel* (1933), republished as *Torment*, in which the plot echoes the brother-sister motif of Taylor's *Joseph*. Hubert Kennedy's estimation of *Better Angel* as the first homosexual American novel with a positive ending does not account for *Joseph and His Friend*. In time, the word "angel" came to connote a masculine male who kept a more effeminate male partner. [...] Taylor's novel pitted individual sexual freedom against mob morality.[22]

And yet, *Joseph and His Friend* is not always the apparent first of a homosexual novel in the United States. Though Taylor's book is dedicated to those "who believe in the truth and tenderness of man's love for man, as of man's love for woman" (a dedication omitted from the British edition)[30], Roger Austen, author of *Playing the Game: The Homosexual Novel in America*, considers it a false start:

> A little noticed nineteenth-century novel that exalted male friendship at the expense of heterosexual hearth and home was *Joseph and His Friend* (1870) by the "Laureate of the Gilded Age," Bayard Taylor. Although some of his poetry conveys homoerotic touches, the details of his life present no conclusive evidence that Taylor was any more overtly homosexual than he should have been. He was born in Kennett Square, Pennsylvania, in 1825, became a sailor, wrote travel books and "household" poems, mixed with the Nathaniel Parker Willis "Bohemian" set in New York, but married twice and died in Germany in 1878. What is clear, though, is that in at least one of his six novels (which include a juvenile, *Boys of Other Countries*), Taylor set out to celebrate "manly love" as boldly as possible within the conventions of genteel fiction.
>
> *Joseph and His Friend* is prefaced by a dedication to "those . . . who believe in the truth and tenderness of man's love for man, as of man's love for woman . . ." and by two lines from a Shakespeare sonnet: "The better angel is a man right fair;/The worser spirit a woman colour'd ill." The hero is a handsome blue-eyed twenty-two-year-old Pennsylvania farmer, Joseph Asten, who is "different"—he shrinks from "all display of rude manners" and hungers for the taste of "higher things." Joseph broods over the facts that love must be "hidden as if it were a reproach; friendship watched, lest it express its warmth too frankly . . . ," and he wanly concludes that in his search for companionship there is only "one gate . . . free to me,—that leading to the love of woman."
>
> The woman that Taylor provides for Joseph is a dreadful thirty-year-old city girl, ironically named Julia Blessing, who secretly takes arsenic to improve her fading complexion [see <u>Chapter 30: Arsenic and Face</u>]. But just before Joseph married Julia, he meets his "friend" on a train, a twenty-eight-year-old with "all the charm of early manhood": golden hair, dark gray eyes, and a mouth at once firm and full. Joseph gazes at Philip Held, and Philip answers his gaze with a look implying "We are men, let us know each other!"—with Taylor adding that this sort of look "is, alas! too rare in this world." A convenient train wreck throws Joseph at Philip, who happens to be on his way to Joseph's very neighborhood to inspect a forge and furnace for his company. The night before Joseph's wedding, Philip tells him that "a man's perfect friendship is rarer than a woman's love," and he promises: "I can be nearer than a brother. I know that I am in your heart as you are in mine.

There is no faith between us that need be limited, there is no truth too secret to be veiled."

Taylor's novel goes on to belie Philips's final vow, of course. The marriage is disastrous, but even as Joseph drifts away from Julia toward Philip, the author stops short of lifting the veil to show that the men's love for each other is more sexual than brotherly. The nearest that Taylor comes to candor is midway through the novel when Joseph is "ruined" (because of his father-in-law's chicanery) and Philip soothes him with an alternative to suicide. They could both go to a great valley, Philip says, "dotted with groves of orange and olive" and be free from the "distorted laws of men." Joseph suggests they wait, and the author closes the chapter with this set-piece paragraph, significant for its repetition of the word "alas!": "They took each other's hands. The day was fading, the landscape was silent, and only the twitter of nesting birds was heard in the boughs above them. Each gave way to the impulse of his manly love, rarer, alas! but as tender and true as the love of woman, and they drew nearer and kissed each other. As they walked back and parted on the highway, each felt that life was not wholly unkind, and that happiness was not yet impossible."

In the last few chapters of the novel, Taylor sets the stage for what could conceivably be a genuinely gay denouement. With "the worser spirit" dead from an overdose of arsenic, the two men are finally free to go out West together to find that homoerotic happiness for which they seem to yearn. Indeed, Joseph does go out to California on a trip and thinks he recognizes the paradisiacal valley that Philip described. The two exchange "manly love" letters, but in the final paragraph we learn that Philip will have to content himself with the role of brother-in-law rather than lover—Joseph returns to take a sudden and almost inexplicable interest in Philip's look-alike sister, Madeline Held.[1]

Austen volunteers another book, written by an American but set and published abroad, as the real deal:

So far as is known, the first American male to write and publish a sympathetic and explicitly gay novel was Edward Prime-Stevenson, and that novel was *Imre: A Memorandum*, published in Naples in 1906, when the author was thirty-eight [under the pseudonym "Xavier Mayne"]. Some of the games Stevenson played in regard to *Imre* were no doubt necessary—this is not a novel that American publishers would touch, and the author probably felt he was forced to rely on non-English speaking (Neapolitan) typesetters and private publication (125 copies) in a foreign country. In the preface he states that he is not really the author but merely the editor of a manuscript sent to him by a British friend named Oswald. This fact, coupled with his

expatriate status—he moved to Europe in 1901 and died there in 1942—
suggests that the game-playing was motivated by more than just caution:
Stevenson had a healthy dislike for homophobic America. In *Imre* all the
allusions to the United States are negative—there is an American specialist
in "nervous diseases" whose invariable advice to urnings is marriage, and a
whole paragraph is devoted to the comparatively benighted aspects of Yankee
civilization [...].

Imre is written from the gentlemanly point of view of thirty-year-old
Oswald, who is spending a leisurely summer of language study in Hungary, and
Stevenson has created a simple plot to serve as the framework for his apologia.
In the first chapter, "Masks," Oswald meets Imre, a twenty-five-year-old
Hungarian army officer, at an outdoor café and falls in love with him. During
the long evening walk which comprises most of the middle chapter, "Masks
and—a Face," Oswald confesses and defends his urningism [a 19th-century
term that referred to a person of a third sex, originally, someone with "a female
psyche in a male body" who is sexually attracted to men; variations are Urning
and Uranist] to Imre but receives no definite response in return. This talky
chapter is dominated by Stevenson, who argues the case for homosexuality
with the well-organized thoroughness one might expect from a former law
student. In the last chapter, "Faces—Hearts—Souls," Imre finally makes a
similar confession to Oswald, and the novel ends with them in each other's
arms and on the verge of going to bed together for the first time. [...] *Imre* is
the first, the best, the brightest and in a sense the only novel of its time written
by a male American which reflects the same spirit of exaltation that moved
Carpenter to write so positively about "the Noble Uranian" in England. *Imre* is
the felicitous result of Stevenson finding himself at the right place at the right
time—away from the killjoy culture of Middle America and before the shadow
of Freud darkened the consciousness of the gay novelist and gay novel.[1]

The only other contender rests between *Joseph* and *Imre*, essentially sitting on the
fence in all categories:

Three years after the appearance of *Joseph and His Friend*, a Boston firm
published a more widely read book, *South-Sea Idyls*, by Charles Warren
Stoddard, a thirty-year-old bachelor who had grown up in California to
become an actor, a bookstore clerk, and a traveling newspaper correspondent.
This novel is almost as gay as Edward Stevenson's *Imre*, which was to be
published three years later in Italy; the key difference is that while Stevenson
discusses homosexuality per se, Stoddard persists in the use of such
euphemisms as "chum" and "pal."[1]

For more on Stoddard, see <u>Chapter 3: Twin Love</u>, <u>Chapter 15: Avowals to Walt Whitman</u>, and <u>Chapter 20: Contemporary Camerados</u>, as well as [A.14] for some of his correspondence with Walt Whitman.

The contemporary thoughts on *Joseph and His Friend* were as equally mixed as they continue to be today. In his correspondence, Taylor responded to a bit of praise for *Joseph* with his own thoughts:

> What you say of "Joseph" delights me, for you have recognized exactly what I attempted to do,—that is, to throw some indirect light on the great questions which underlie civilized life, and the existence of which is only dimly felt, not intelligently perceived, by most Americans. I allowed the plot to be directed by these cryptic forces; hence, a reader who does not feel them will hardly be interested in the external movement of the story. The book is not what it might be, if I could have given more time and study to it; but I would rather miss a high mark than hit a low one in the bull's eye. I will tell you, now, that I consider it my best novel, with all its deficiencies. So do a few others; but the blessed half-educated public sees nothing in the book but dullness.[24]

Taylor's first biographer, Albert Henry Smyth, considered it Taylor's worst book (it was in fact his "least successful and most disliked novel" according to his 1975 biographer, Wermuth). Smyth writes:

> The fourth and last of Bayard Taylor's novels, "Joseph and his Friend: A Story of Pennsylvania," was begun in January, 1869, at Cedarcroft, contributed serially to the "Atlantic," and published by Putnam, November 24, 1870. It is an unpleasant story of mean duplicity and painful mistakes. The characters are shallow and their surroundings shabby. There is not a single pleasing situation or incident in the book. Bismarck told Bayard Taylor that he had read the novel twice and was sure that it contained one serious defect. He said, "You let your villain escape too easily; that is not poetic justice, nor any kind of justice, in my opinion."[45]

Wermuth is no more comfortable with *Joseph* than Smyth:

> [T]he suggestions of homosexuality can hardly be overlooked. Certainly, the relationship between Joseph and his friend has such overtones. Scenes of their embracing and kissing each other make the reader somewhat uncomfortable. Yet it is by no means certain that the book should be interpreted this way.
>
> Still, there are many odd passages in this book. After Philip prevented Joseph's suicide, "he led him to the bank, sat down beside him, and laid his arm about his neck. The silence and the caress were more soothing to Joseph than

any words." In another scene, "their hands closed upon each other, and they were entirely happy in the tender and perfect manly love which united them." One of the climactic scenes reads: "They took each other's hands. The day was fading, the landscape was silent, and only the twitter of nesting birds was heard in the boughs above them. Each gave way to the impulse of his manly love, rarer, alas! but as tender and true as the love of woman, and they drew nearer and kissed each other. As they walked back and parted on the highway, each felt that life was not wholly unkind, and that happiness was not yet impossible."

The emphasis on "manly" love suggests Whitman, and perhaps Taylor derived the idea, or the encouragement to write about it, from Whitman, to whom there are many references in his books, though most are unfavorable. It is interesting to note that Whitman, like Taylor, had a Quaker background; for the repressions of Quakerism probably had something to do with this question. Taylor evidently felt that Quakerism led to the stigmatizing of feelings with which there was nothing wrong; and Quakerism was one of the things from which he was escaping [see Chapter 31: The Society of Friends for more]. *Joseph and His Friend* may be Taylor's outcry against this repression. "Why do men so carefully conceal what is deepest and strongest in their natures?" asks Joseph. And elsewhere, Philip says to him: "A man's perfect friendship is rarer than a woman's love, and most hearts are content with one or the other . . ."

Taylor had many close relationships with men ([August] Bufleb springs immediately to mind [see Chapter 2: Taylor's Relationships]); and the type of relationship that is depicted in the novel was more normal in the nineteenth century than today. Male friendships were closer and more casual because relationships with women were more formal and artificial. Benjamin Franklin could offer health as a reason for practicing "venery," but a man of Taylor's time could not openly offer that or any other excuse; for attitudes toward marriage, women, and family life forbade it.

[. . .] Whatever Taylor's motive, the book is somewhat confused. But one thing is clear: although the story has much of the usual relationships between men and women, its real center is that between two men. Friendship and love are, after all, different degrees of the same feeling, not different feelings. In the 1970's, such a theme would hardly excite notice, but for 1896 it seems daring.

Even post-Stonewall there was a hesitation to say *Joseph and His Friend* was a homosexual novel, let alone America's first, but it is still the strongest candidate.

I

JOSEPH

RACHEL MILLER WAS not a little surprised when her nephew Joseph came to the supper-table, not from the direction of the barn and through the kitchen, as usual, but from the back room upstairs, where he slept. His work-day dress had disappeared; he wore his best Sunday suit, put on with unusual care, and there were faint pomatum odors in the air when he sat down to the table.

Her face said—and she knew it—as plain as any words, "What in the world does this mean?" Joseph, she saw, endeavored to look as though coming down to supper in that costume were his usual habit; so she poured out the tea in silence. Her silence, however, was eloquent; a hundred interrogation-marks would not have expressed its import; and Dennis, the hired man, who sat on the other side of the table, experienced very much the same apprehension of something forthcoming, as when he had killed her favorite speckled hen by mistake.

Before the meal was over, the tension between Joseph and his aunt had so increased by reason of their mutual silence, that it was very awkward and oppressive to both; yet neither knew how to break it easily. There is always a great deal of unnecessary reticence in the intercourse of country people, and in the case of these two it had been specially strengthened by the want of every relationship except that of blood. They were quite ignorant of the fence, the easy thrust and parry of society, where talk becomes an art; silence or the bluntest utterance were their alternatives, and now the one had neutralized the other. Both felt this, and Dennis, in his dull way, felt it too. Although not a party concerned, he was uncomfortable, yet also internally conscious of a desire to laugh.

The resolution of the crisis, however, came by his aid. When the meal was finished and Joseph betook himself to the window, awkwardly drumming upon the pane, while his aunt gathered the plates and cups together, delaying to remove them as was her wont, Dennis said, with his hand on the door-knob: "Shall I saddle the horse right off?"

"I guess so," Joseph answered, after a moment's hesitation.

Rachel paused, with the two silver spoons in her hand. Joseph was still drumming upon the window, but with very irregular taps. The door closed upon Dennis.

"Well," said she, with singular calmness, "a body is not bound to dress particularly fine for watching, though I would as soon show him that much respect, if need be, as anybody else. Don't forget to ask Maria if there's anything I can do for her."

Joseph turned around with a start, a most innocent surprise on his face.

"Why, aunt, what are you talking about?"

"You are not going to Warne's to watch? They have nearer neighbors, to be sure, but when a man dies, everybody is free to offer their services. He was always strong in the faith."

Joseph knew that he was caught, without suspecting her manœuvre. A brighter color ran over his face, up to the roots of his hair. "Why, no!" he exclaimed; "I am going to Warriner's to spend the evening. There's to be a little company there,—a neighborly gathering. I believe it's been talked of this long while, but I was only invited today. I saw Bob, in the road-field."

Rachel endeavored to conceal from her nephew's eye the immediate impression of his words. A constrained smile passed over her face, and was instantly followed by a cheerful relief in his.

"Isn't it rather a strange time of year for evening parties?" she then asked, with a touch of severity in her voice.

"They meant to have it in cherry-time, Bob said, when Anna's visitor had come from town."

"That, indeed! I see!" Rachel exclaimed. "It's to be a sort of celebration for—what's-her-name? Blessing, I know,—but the other? Anna Warriner was there last Christmas, and I don't suppose the high notions are out of her head yet. Well, I hope it'll be some time before they take root here! Peace and quiet, peace and quiet, that's been the token of the neighborhood; but town ways are the reverse."

"All the young people are going," Joseph mildly suggested, "and so—"

"O, I don't say you shouldn't go, *this* time," Rachel interrupted him; "for you ought to be able to judge for yourself what's fit and proper, and what is not. I should be sorry, to be sure, to see you doing anything and going anywhere that would make your mother uneasy if she were living now. It's so hard to be conscientious, and to mind a body's bounden duty, without seeming to interfere."

She heaved a deep sigh, and just touched the corner of her apron to her eyes. The mention of his mother always softened Joseph, and in his earnest desire to live so that his life might be such as to give her joy if she could share it, a film of doubt spread itself over the smooth, pure surface of his mind. A vague consciousness of his inability to express himself clearly upon the question without seeming to slight her memory affected his thoughts.

"But, remember, Aunt Rachel," he said, at last, "I was not old enough, then, to go into society. She surely meant that I should have some independence, when the time came. I am doing no more than all the young men of the neighborhood."

"Ah, yes, I know," she replied, in a melancholy tone; "but they've got used to it by degrees, and mostly in their own homes, and with sisters to caution them; whereas you're younger according to your years, and innocent of the ways and wiles of men, and—and girls."

Joseph painfully felt that this last assertion was true. Suppressing the impulse to exclaim, "Why am I younger 'according to my years?' why am I so much more 'innocent'— which is, ignorant—than others?" he blundered out, with a little display of temper, "Well, how am I ever to learn?"

"By patience, and taking care of yourself. There's always safety in waiting. I don't mean you shouldn't go this evening, since you've promised it, and made yourself smart. But, mark my words, this is only the beginning. The season makes no difference; townspeople never seem to know that there's such things as hay-harvest and corn to be worked. They come out for merry-makings in the busy time, and want us country folks to give up everything for their pleasure. The tired plough-horses must be geared up for 'em, and the cows wait an hour or two longer to be milked while they're driving around; and the chickens killed half-grown, and the washing and baking put off when it comes in their way. They're mighty nice and friendly while it lasts; but go back to 'em in town, six months afterwards, and see whether they'll so much as ask you to take a meal's victuals!"

Joseph began to laugh. "It is not likely," he said, "that I shall ever go to the Blessings for a meal, or that this Miss Julia—as they call her—will ever interfere with our harvesting or milking."

"The airs they put on!" Rachel continued. "She'll very likely think that she's doing you a favor by so much as speaking to you. When the Bishops had boarders, two years ago, one of 'em said,—Maria told me with her own mouth,—'Why don't all the farmers follow your example? It would be so refining for them!' They may be very well in their place, but, for my part, I should like them to stay there."

"There comes the horse," said Joseph. "I must be on the way. I expect to meet Elwood Withers at the lane-end. But—about waiting, Aunt—you hardly need—"

"O, yes, I'll wait for you, of course. Ten o'clock is not so very late for me."

"It might be a little after," he suggested.

"Not much, I hope; but if it should be daybreak, wait I will! Your mother couldn't expect less of me."

When Joseph whirled into the saddle, the thought of his aunt, grimly waiting for his return, was already perched like an imp on the crupper, and clung to his sides with claws of steel. She, looking through the window, also felt that it was so; and, much relieved, went back to her household duties.

He rode very slowly down the lane, with his eyes fixed on the ground. There was a rich orange flush of sunset on the hills across the valley; masses of burning cumuli hung, self-suspended, above the farthest woods, and such depths of purple-gray opened beyond them as are wont to rouse the slumbering fancies and hopes of a young man's heart; but the beauty and fascination and suggestiveness of the hour could not lift his downcast, absorbed glance. At last his horse, stopping suddenly at the gate, gave a whinny of recognition, which was answered.

Elwood Withers laughed. "Can you tell me where Joseph Asten lives?" he cried,—"an old man, very much bowed and bent."

Joseph also laughed, with a blush, as he met the other's strong, friendly face. "There is plenty of time," he said, leaning over his horse's neck and lifting the latch of the gate.

"All right; but you must now wake up. You're spruce enough to make a figure to-night."

"O, no doubt!" Joseph gravely answered; "but what kind of a figure?"

"Some people, I've heard say," said Elwood, "may look into their looking-glass every day, and never know how they look. If you appeared to yourself as you appear to me, you wouldn't ask such a question as that."

"If I could only not think of myself at all, Elwood,—if I could be as unconcerned as you are—"

"But I'm not, Joseph, my boy!" Elwood interrupted, riding nearer and laying a hand on his friend's shoulder. "I tell you, it weakens my very marrow to walk into a room full o' girls, even though I know every one of 'em. They know it, too, and, shy and quiet as they seem, they're unmerciful. There they sit, all looking so different, somehow,—even a fellow's own sisters and cousins,—filling up all sides of the room, rustling a little and whispering a little, but you feel that every one of 'em has her eyes on you, and would be *so* glad to see you flustered. There's no help for it, though; we've got to grow case-hardened to that much, or how ever could a man get married?"

"Elwood!" Joseph asked, after a moment's silence, "were you ever in love?"

"Well,"—and Elwood pulled up his horse in surprise,—"well, you *do* come out plump. You take the breath out of my body. Have I been in love? Have I committed murder? One's about as deadly a secret as the other!"

The two looked each other in the face. Elwood's eyes answered the question, but Joseph's,—large, shy, and utterly innocent,—could not read the answer.

"It's easy to see *you*'ve never been," said the former, dropping his voice to a grave gentleness. "If I should say Yes, what then?"

"Then, how do you know it,—I mean, how did you first begin to find it out? What is the difference between that and the feeling you have towards any pleasant girl whom you like to be with?"

"All the difference in the world!" Elwood exclaimed with energy; then paused, and knitted his brows with a perplexed air; "but I'll be shot if I know exactly what else to say; I never thought of it before. How do I know that I am Elwood Withers? It seems just as plain as that,—and yet—well, for one thing, she's always in your mind, and you think and dream of just nothing but her; and you'd rather have the hem of her dress touch you than kiss anybody else; and you want to be near her, and to have her all to yourself, yet it's hard

JOSEPH AND HIS FRIEND

work to speak a sensible word to her when you come together,—but, what's the use? A fellow must feel it himself, as they say of experiencing religion; he must get converted, or he'll never know. Now, I don't suppose you've understood a word of what I've said!"

"Yes!" Joseph answered; "indeed, I think so. It's only an increase of what we all feel towards some persons. I have been hoping, latterly, that it might come to me, but— but—"

"But your time will come like every man's," said Elwood; "and, maybe, sooner than you think. When it does, you won't need to ask anybody; though I think you're bound to tell me of it, after pumping my own secret out of me."

Joseph looked grave.

"Never mind; I wasn't obliged to let you have it. I know you're close-mouthed and honest-hearted, Joseph; but I'll never ask your confidence unless you can give it as freely as I give mine to you."

"You shall have it, Elwood, if my time ever comes. And I can't help wishing for the time, although it may not be right. You know how lonely it is on the farm, and yet it's not always easy for me to get away into company. Aunt Rachel stands in mother's place to me, and maybe it's only natural that she should be over-concerned; any way, seeing what she has done for my sake, I am hindered from opposing her wishes too stubbornly. Now, to-night, my going didn't seem right to her, and I shall not get it out of my mind that she is waiting up, and perhaps fretting, on my account."

"A young fellow of your age mustn't be so tender," Elwood said. "If you had your own father and mother, they'd allow you more of a range. Look at me, with mine! Why, I never as much as say 'by your leave.' Quite the contrary; so long as the work isn't slighted, they're rather glad than not to have me go out; and the house is twice as lively since I bring so much fresh gossip into it. But then, I've had a rougher bringing up."

"I wish I had had!" cried Joseph. "Yet, no, when I think of mother, it is wrong to say just that. What I mean is, I wish I could take things as easily as you,—make my way boldly in the world, without being held back by trifles, or getting so confused with all sorts of doubts. The more anxious I am to do right, the more embarrassed I am to know what is the right thing. I don't believe you have any such troubles."

"Well, for my part, I do about as other fellows; no worse, I guess, and likely no better. You must consider, also, that I'm a bit rougher made, besides the bringing up, and that makes a deal of difference. I don't try to make the scales balance to a grain; if there's a handful under or over, I think it's near enough. However, you'll be all right in a while. When you find the right girl and marry her, it'll put a new face on to you. There's nothing like a sharp, wide-awake wife, so they say, to set a man straight. Don't make a mountain of anxiety out of a little molehill of inexperience. I'd take all your doubts and more, I'm sure, if I could get such a two-hundred-acre farm with them."

"Do you know," cried Joseph eagerly, his blue eyes flashing through the gathering dusk, "I have often thought very nearly the same thing! If I were to love,—if I were to marry—"

"Hush!" interrupted Elwood; "I know you don't mean others to hear you. Here come two down the branch road."

The horsemen, neighboring farmers' sons, joined them. They rode together up the knoll towards the Warriner mansion, the lights of which glimmered at intervals through the trees. The gate was open, and a dozen vehicles could be seen in the enclosure between the house and barn. Bright, gliding forms were visible on the portico.

"Just see," whispered Elwood to Joseph; "what a lot of posy-colors! You may be sure they're every one watching us. No flinching, mind; straight to the charge! We'll walk up together, and it won't be half as hard for you."

1. BAYARD TAYLOR

According to an autobiographic sketch which Bayard Taylor himself gave to a German magazine, he has this to say of his ancestry and birth:

> Robert Taylor, a rich Quaker, who came to Pennsylvania in 1681, with William Penn, settled near the Brandywine Creek, and part of the land which his eldest son inherited from him is in my possession [at Cedarcroft]. His descendants clung to the soil with a Saxon tenacity. I have not, thus far, followed my family-tree beyond Robert; but if I should discover that Bishop Jeremy Taylor sprang from the same stock, I should be prouder of him than of a possible descent from Tudor or Plantagenet. I suspect that Joseph Taylor, the friend of Shakespeare and the first interpreter of Hamlet, was one of my ancestors, for the family has preserved his name. My grandfather, who had married a Lutheran of pure German blood, was excommunicated by his brother Quakers, and none of his children ever returned to the Society. I was born the 11th of January, 1825, the year when the first locomotive successfully performed its trial trip; I am therefore just as old as the railroad. [23]

The first born after three miscarriages, Bayard Taylor took an interest in poetry and literature at a young age. At the age of fifteen, Taylor wrote "Byron is dead!" on a rock in grief upon hearing the news (the inspiration for *Joseph and His Friend*, poet Fitz-Greene Halleck, had a similar reaction to the death of Lord Byron, long before the two would ever meet; see <u>Chapter 8: Halleck and the Death of Byron</u> for more). At the age of seventeen, Taylor successfully solicited an autograph from Halleck[22], and also wrote to Charles Dickens, from whom he was overwhelmed to receive an autographed reply[45]:

> I went to the Academy, where I received a letter that had come on Saturday. It was from Hartford; I knew instantly it was from Dickens. It was double, and sealed neatly with a seal bearing the initials C. D. In the inside was a sheet of

satin note-paper, on which was written, 'Faithfully yours, Charles Dickens, City Hotel, Hartford, Feb. 10, 1842;' and below, 'With the compliments of Mr. Dickens.' I can long recollect the thrill of pleasure I experienced on seeing the autograph of one whose writings I so ardently admired, and to whom, in spirit, I felt myself attached; and it was not without a feeling of ambition that I looked upon it that as he, an humble clerk, had risen to be the guest of a mighty nation, so I, an humble pedagogue, might by unremitted and arduous intellectual and moral exertion become a light, a star, among the names of my country. May it be![23]

Bayard Taylor did indeed receive a great deal of recognition in his own life. Taylor grew up in Quaker Pennsylvania (the setting for *Joseph and His Friend*), and was famous as an author for traveling and writing his way through nearly the whole of Europe, Mexico, Egypt, Palestine, Abyssinia, Syria, Turkey, Russia, India, Japan, and China. He is the traveler in John Greenleaf Whittier's poem "The Tent on the Beach." He was also the first to translate Goethe's *Faust* into English.[30]

Although Taylor had an enviable amount of esteem in his lifetime, his name has not had the permanence Charles Dickens, nor has he gained the posthumous fame and high regard of Walt Whitman, who was once quite envious of the accolades Taylor received (for more detail, see <u>Chapter 10: Taylor and Whitman</u>). In fact, according to *The Unionville Times* on February 13, 2015, Bayard Taylor Library was recently renamed Kennett Public Library with the explanation: "The change isn't just change for the sake of change, they say, but signals a desire to keep with the times."[34] Taylor's memory is fading.

II

MISS BLESSING

To consider the evening party at Warriner's a scene of "dissipation"—as some of the good old people of the neighborhood undoubtedly did—was about as absurd as to call butter-milk an intoxicating beverage. Anything more simple and innocent could not well be imagined. The very awkwardness which everybody felt, and which no one exactly knew how to overcome, testified of virtuous ignorance. The occasion was no more than sufficed for the barest need of human nature. Young men and women must come together for acquaintance and the possibilities of love, and, fortunately, neither labor nor the severer discipline of their elders can prevent them.

Where social recreation thus only exists under discouraging conditions, ease and grace and self-possession cannot be expected. Had there been more form, in fact, there would have been more ease. A conventional disposition of the guests would have reduced the loose elements of the company to some sort of order; the shy country nature would have taken refuge in fixed laws, and found a sense of freedom therein. But there were no generally understood rules; the young people were brought together, delighted yet uncomfortable, craving yet shrinking from speech and jest and song, and painfully working their several isolations into a warmer common atmosphere.

On this occasion, the presence of a stranger, and that stranger a lady, and that lady a visitor from the city, was an additional restraint. The dread of a critical eye is most keenly felt by those who secretly acknowledge their own lack of social accomplishment. Anna Warriner, to be sure, had been loud in her praises of "dear Julia," and the guests were prepared to find all possible beauty and sweetness; but they expected, none the less, to be scrutinized and judged.

Bob Warriner met his friends at the gate and conducted them to the parlor, whither the young ladies, who had been watching the arrival, had retreated. They were disposed along the walls, silent and cool, except Miss Blessing, who occupied a rocking-chair in front of the mantel-piece, where her figure was in half-shadow, the lamplight only touching some roses in her hair. As the gentlemen were presented, she lifted her face and smiled upon each, graciously offering a slender hand. In manner and attitude, as in dress, she seemed a different being from the plump, ruddy, self-conscious girls on the sofas. Her dark hair fell about her neck in long, shining ringlets; the fairness of her face heightened the brilliancy of her eyes, the lids of which were slightly drooped as if kindly veiling their beams; and her lips, although thin, were very sweetly and delicately curved. Her dress, of some white, foamy texture, hung about her like a trailing cloud, and the cluster of rosebuds on her bosom lay as if tossed there.

The young men, spruce as they had imagined themselves to be, suddenly felt that their clothes were coarse and ill-fitting, and that the girls of the neighborhood, in their neat gingham and muslin dresses, were not quite so airy and charming as on former occasions. Miss Blessing, descending to them out of an unknown higher sphere, made their deficiencies unwelcomely evident; she attracted and fascinated them, yet was none the less a disturbing influence. They made haste to find seats, after which a constrained silence followed.

There could be no doubt of Miss Blessing's amiable nature. She looked about with a pleasant expression, half smiled—but deprecatingly, as if to say, "Pray, don't be offended!"—at the awkward silence, and then said, in a clear, carefully modulated voice: "It is beautiful to arrive at twilight, but how charming it must be to ride home in the moonlight; so different from our lamps!"

The guests looked at each other, but as she had seemed to address no one in particular, so each hesitated, and there was no immediate reply.

"But is it not awful, tell me, Elizabeth, when you get into the shadows of the forests? we are so apt to associate all sorts of unknown dangers with forests, you know," she continued.

The young lady thus singled out made haste to answer: "O, no! I rather like it, when I have company."

Elwood Withers laughed. "To be sure!" he exclaimed; "the shade is full of opportunities."

Then there were little shrieks, and some giggling and blushing. Miss Blessing shook her fan warningly at the speaker.

"*How* wicked in you! I hope you will have to ride home alone to-night, after that speech. But you are all courageous, compared with *us*. We are really so restricted in the city, that it's a wonder we have any independence at all. In many ways, we are like children."

"O Julia, dear!" protested Anna Warriner, "and *such* advantages as you have! I shall never forget the day Mrs. Rockaway called—her husband's cashier of the Commercial Bank" (this was said in a parenthesis to the other guests)—"and brought you all the news direct from head-quarters, as she said."

"Yes," Miss Blessing answered, slowly, casting down her eyes," there must be two sides to everything, of course; but how much we miss until we know the country! Really, I quite envy you."

Joseph had found himself, almost before he knew it, in a corner, beside Lucy Henderson. He felt soothed and happy, for of all the girls present he liked Lucy best. In the few meetings of the young people which he had attended, he had been drawn towards her by an instinct founded, perhaps, on his shyness and the consciousness of it; for she alone had the power, by a few kindly, simple words, to set him at ease with himself. The straightforward glance of her large brown eyes seemed to reach the self below the troubled surface. However much his ears might have tingled afterwards, as he recalled how frankly and freely he had talked with her, he could only remember the expression of an interest equally frank, upon her face. She never dropped one of those amused side-glances, or uttered one of those pert, satirical remarks, the recollection of which in other girls stung him to the quick.

Their conversation was interrupted, for when Miss Blessing spoke, the others became silent. What Elwood Withers had said of the phenomena of love, however, lingered in Joseph's mind, and he began, involuntarily, to examine the nature of his feeling for Lucy Henderson. Was she not often in his thoughts? He had never before asked himself the question, but now he suddenly became conscious that the hope of meeting her, rather than any curiosity concerning Miss Blessing, had drawn him to Warriner's. Would he rather touch the edge of her dress than kiss anybody else? That question drew his eyes to her lips, and with a soft shock of the heart, he became aware of their freshness and sweetness as never before. To touch the edge of her dress! Elwood had said nothing of the lovelier and bolder desire which brought the blood swiftly to his cheeks. He could not help it that their glances met,—a moment only, but an unmeasured time of delight and fear to him,—and then Lucy quickly turned away her head. He fancied there was a heightened color on her face, but when she spoke to him a few minutes afterwards it was gone, and she was as calm and composed as before.

In the meantime there had been other arrivals; and Joseph was presently called upon to give up his place to some ladies from the neighboring town. Many invitations had been issued, and the capacity of the parlor was soon exhausted. Then the sounds of merry chat on the portico invaded the stately constraint of the room; and Miss Blessing, rising gracefully and not too rapidly, laid her hands together and entreated Anna Warriner,—

"O, *do* let us go outside! I think we are well enough acquainted now to sit on the steps together."

She made a gesture, slight but irresistibly inviting, and all arose. While they were cheerfully pressing out through the hall, she seized Anna's arm and drew her back into the dusky nook under the staircase.

"Quick, Anna!" she whispered; "who is the roguish one they call Elwood? *What* is he?"

"A farmer; works his father's place on shares."

"Ah!" exclaimed Miss Blessing, in a peculiar tone; "and the blue-eyed, handsome one, who came in with him? He looks almost like a boy."

"Joseph Asten? Why, he's twenty-two or three. He has one of the finest properties in the neighborhood, and money besides, they say; lives alone, with an old dragon of an aunt as housekeeper. Now, Julia dear, there's a chance for you!"

"Pshaw, you silly Anna!" whispered Miss Blessing, playfully pinching her ear; "you know I prefer intellect to wealth."

"As for that"—Anna began, but her friend was already dancing down the hall towards the front door, her gossamer skirts puffing and floating out until they brushed the walls on either side. She hummed to herself, "O Night! O lovely Night!" from the *Désert*, skimmed over the doorstep, and sank, subsiding into an ethereal heap, against one of the pillars of the portico. Her eyelids were now fully opened, and the pupils, the color of which could not be distinguished in the moonlight, seemed wonderfully clear and brilliant.

"Now, Mr. Elwood—O excuse me, I mean Mr. Withers," she began, "you must repeat your joke for my benefit. I missed it, and I feel so foolish when I can't laugh with the rest."

Anna Warriner, standing in the door, opened her eyes very wide at what seemed to her to be the commencement of a flirtation; but before Elwood Withers could repeat his rather stupid fun, she was summoned to the kitchen by her mother, to superintend the preparation of the refreshments.

Miss Blessing made her hay while the moon shone. She so entered into the growing spirit of the scene and accommodated herself to the speech and ways of the guests, that in half an hour it seemed as if they had always known her. She laughed with their merriment, and flattered their sentiment with a tender ballad or two, given in a veiled but not unpleasant voice, and constantly appealed to their good nature by the phrase: "Pray, don't mind me at all; I'm like a child let out of school!" She tapped Elizabeth Fogg on the shoulder, stealthily tickled Jane McNaughton's neck with a grass-blade, and took the roses from her hair to stick into the buttonholes of the young men.

"Just see Julia!" whispered Anna Warriner to her half-dozen intimates; "didn't I tell you she was the life of society?"

Joseph had quite lost his uncomfortable sense of being watched and criticized; he enjoyed the unrestraint of the hour as much as the rest. He was rather relieved to notice that Elwood Withers seemed uneasy, and almost willing to escape from the lively circle around Miss Blessing. By and by the company broke into smaller groups, and Joseph again found himself near the pale pink dress which he knew. What was it that separated him from her? What had slipped between them during the evening? Nothing, apparently; for Lucy Henderson, perceiving him, quietly moved nearer. He advanced a step, and they were side by side.

"Do you enjoy these meetings, Joseph?" she asked.

"I think I should enjoy everything," he answered, "if I were a little older, or—or—"

"Or more accustomed to society? Is not that what you meant? It is only another kind of schooling, which we must all have. You and I are in the lowest class, as we once were,—do you remember?"

"I don't know why," said he, "—but I must be a poor scholar. See Elwood, for instance!"

"Elwood!" Lucy slowly repeated; "he is another kind of nature, altogether."

There was a moment's silence. Joseph was about to speak when something wonderfully soft touched his cheek, and a delicate, violet-like odor swept upon his senses. A low, musical laugh sounded at his very ear.

"There! Did I frighten you?" said Miss Blessing. She had stolen behind him, and, standing on tiptoe, reached a light arm over his shoulder, to fasten her last rosebud in the upper buttonhole of his coat.

"I quite overlooked you, Mr. Asten," she continued. "Please turn a little towards me. Now!—has it not a charming effect? I do like to see some kind of ornament about the gentlemen, Lucy. And since they can't wear anything in their hair, —but, tell me, wouldn't a wreath of flowers look well on Mr. Asten's head?"

"I can't very well imagine such a thing," said Lucy.

"No? Well, perhaps I am foolish: but when one has escaped from the tiresome conventionalities of city life, and comes back to nature, and delightful natural society, one feels so free to talk and think! Ah, you don't know what a luxury it is, just to be one's true self!"

Joseph's eyes lighted up, and he turned towards Miss Blessing, as if eager that she should continue to speak.

"Lucy," said Elwood Withers, approaching; "you came with the McNaughtons, didn't you?"

"Yes: are they going?"

"They are talking of it now; but the hour is early, and if you don't mind riding on a pillion, you know my horse is gentle and strong—"

"That's right, Mr. Withers!" interrupted Miss Blessing. "I depend upon you to keep Lucy with us. The night is at its loveliest, and we are all just fairly enjoying each other's society. As I was saying, Mr. Asten, you cannot conceive what a new world this is to *me*: oh, I begin to breathe at last!"

Therewith she drew a long, soft inspiration, and gently exhaled it again, ending with a little flutter of the breath, which made it seem like a sigh. A light laugh followed.

"I know, without looking at your face, that you are smiling at me," said she. "But you have never experienced what it is to be shy and uneasy in company; to feel that you are expected to talk, and not know what to say, and when you do say something, to be startled at the sound of your voice; to stand, or walk, or sit, and imagine that everybody is watching you; to be introduced to strangers, and be as awkward as if both spoke different languages, and were unable to exchange a single thought. Here, in the country, you experience nothing of all this."

"Indeed, Miss Blessing," Joseph replied, "it is just the same to us—to me—as city society is to you."

"How glad I am!" she exclaimed, clasping her hands. "It is very selfish in me to say it, but I can't help being sincere towards the Sincere. I shall now feel ever so much more freedom in talking with you, Mr. Asten, since we have *one* experience in common. Don't you think, if we all knew each other's natures truly, we should be a great deal more at ease, —and consequently happier?"

She spoke the last sentence in a low, sweet, penetrating tone, lifted her face to meet his gaze a moment, the eyes large, clear, and appealing in their expression, the lips parted like those of a child, and then, without waiting for his answer, suddenly darted away, crying, "Yes, Anna dear!"

"What is it, Julia?" Anna Warriner asked.

"O, didn't you call me? Somebody surely called some Julia, and I'm the only one, am I not? I've just arranged Mr. Asten's rosebud so prettily, and now all the gentlemen are decorated. I'm afraid they think I take great liberties for a stranger, but then, you all make me forget that I am strange. Why is it that everybody is so good to me?"

She turned her face upon the others with a radiant expression. Then there were earnest protestations from the young men, and a few impulsive hugs from the girls, which latter Miss Blessing returned with kisses.

Elwood Withers sat beside Lucy Henderson, on the steps of the portico. "Why, we owe it to you that we're here to-night, Miss Blessing!" he exclaimed. "We don't come together half often enough as it is; and what better could we do than meet again, somewhere else, while you are in the country?"

"O, how delightful! how kind!" she cried. "And while the lovely moonlight lasts! Shall I really have another evening like this?"

The proposition was heartily seconded, and the only difficulty was, how to choose between the three or four invitations which were at once proffered. There was nothing better to do than to accept all, in turn, and the young people pledged themselves to attend. The new element which they had dreaded in advance, as a restraint, had shown itself to be the reverse: they had never been so free, so cheerfully excited. Miss Blessing's unconscious ease of manner, her grace and sweetness, her quick, bright sympathy with country ways, had so warmed and fused them, that they lost the remembrance of their stubborn selves and yielded to the magnetism of the hour. Their manners, moreover, were greatly improved, simply by their forgetting that they were expected to have any.

Joseph was one of the happiest sharers in this change. He eagerly gave his word to be present at the entertainments to come: his heart beat with delight at the prospect of other such evenings. The suspicion of a tenderer feeling towards Lucy Henderson, the charm of Miss Blessing's winning frankness, took equal possession of his thoughts; and not until he had said good night did he think of his companion on the homeward road. But Elwood Withers had already left, carrying Lucy Henderson on a pillion behind him.

"Is it ten o'clock, do you think?" Joseph asked of one of the young men, as they rode out of the gate.

The other answered with a chuckle: "Ten? It's nigher morning than evening!"

The imp on the crupper struck his claws deep into Joseph's sides. He urged his horse into a gallop, crossed the long rise in the road and dashed along the valley-level, with the cool, dewy night air whistling in his locks. After entering the lane leading upward to his home, he dropped the reins and allowed the panting horse to choose his own gait. A light, sparkling through the locust-trees, pierced him with the sting of an unwelcome external conscience, in which he had no part, yet which he could not escape.

Rachel Miller looked wearily up from her knitting as he entered the room. She made a feeble attempt to smile, but the expression of her face suggested imminent tears.

"Aunt, why did you wait?" said he, speaking rapidly. "I forgot to look at my watch, and I really thought it was no more than ten—"

He paused, seeing that her eyes were fixed. She was looking at the tall old-fashioned clock. The hand pointed to half-past twelve, and every cluck of the ponderous pendulum said, distinctly, "Late! late! late!"

He lighted a candle in silence said, "Good night, Aunt!" and went up to his room.

"Good night, Joseph!" she solemnly responded, and a deep, hollow sigh reached his ear before the door was closed.

2. TAYLOR'S RELATIONSHIPS

Twice married, but under peculiar circumstances each time, Bayard Taylor's life was dominated by masculine friendships. The first significant gentleman was a lifetime friend of Taylor's along with Henry Richard Stoddard, George Boker. George Henry Boker was a wealthy Philadelphian, served as ambassador to Turkey (1871-1875) and Russia (1875), and is best known for *Francesca da Rimini* (staged 1855), a popular play about adultery among the Italian nobility. Boker was dissatisfied with his theatrical career and desperately wanted a following for his *Plays and Poems* (1856). Boker's suppressed *Sonnets: A Sequence on Profane Love* (1929) are thought to be inspired by his wife, Julia, and a mistress, Angie King Hicks. In contrast to Walt Whitman's concept of manly love, Boker's conception of comradeship was feminine rather than masculine, as is indicated in a letter to his friend Bayard Taylor: "We have both . . . an almost feminine tenderness for those we love . . . are you laughing at me for making love to you, as if you were a green girl?"[31]

Taylor's first marriage was to Mary Agnew, whom he'd known in his youth, and with whom he entered into a long, distant engagement. The volumes of his letters put out in 1895 (seventeen years after his death, in part by his second wife) describe how difficult their time apart was on both parties. The volumes point out that Mary "was not so much the inspiration of special poems addressed to her, as she was the guiding star to Bayard Taylor's passion and thought," while Taylor himself was described by a Kennett neighbor as, at the time, "a bright, blushing, diffident youth, just entering manhood."[23] A six year engagement culminated in marriage only after Mary Agnew came down with tuberculosis, of which she died only two months into their wedded life. Taylor wrote to his friend R.H. Stoddard of her loss:

> Kennett Square, Pa., December 27, 1850. It is over. Perhaps you may already know it, but I wish to tell you so before we meet. She died on Saturday last, and was buried in the midst of that cruel storm on Monday. She is now a saint in heaven. She had no foes to pardon and no sins to be forgiven. God help me to be worthy of her guarding care through life and her welcome after death! My dear friend, I cannot now write to you more. I will not attempt to tell you all the anguish I have suffered. I have submitted myself to God's

will, and neither hope for nor desire consolation. The blow has shaken me terribly, but I have been strengthened to bear it. I shall return to New York on Monday night or Tuesday morning, and hope to see you in better hopes and spirits. God give you a happier fate than mine![23]

After his wife's death, and while engaged in the travel-writing that made him famous, Taylor met the greatest friend of his life, Mr. August Bufleb, a German land-owner and business man. Writing in 1973, Paul C. Wermuth characterizes their intense, sudden friendship by saying, "August Bufleb [...] became so enamored of Taylor that it is embarrassing."[55] The *Life and Letters of Bayard Taylor* speaks of Mr. Bufleb as well:

It was on the steamer, when passing from Smyrna to Alexandria, that Bayard Taylor fell in with this gentleman, Mr. August Bufleb, and thus began an acquaintance which ripened into an ardent friendship. Mr. Bufleb, in his letters to his wife at this time, speaks in the strongest terms of his new-found friend. "A glorious young man," he says. "If it were not for you I would go with him." "His company is a gain to me in every respect. He, with his clear head and pure heart has preferred to travel with me, while many of his countrymen are following or sailing ahead of us. . . . He has won my love by his amiability, his excellent heart, his pure spirit, in a degree of which I did not believe myself capable."[23]

Taylor's letters home to his mother speak about his new friend with the same passion:

Near Korosko, Nubia, December 19, 1851: I want to speak of the friend from whom I have just parted, because I am very much moved by his kindness, and the knowledge may be grateful to you. His friendship for me is something wonderful, and it seems like a special Providence that in Egypt, where I anticipated the want of all near sympathy and kindness, I should find it in such abundant measure. He is a man of totally different experience from myself; accustomed all his life to wealth, to luxury, and to the exercise of authority. He was even prejudiced against America and the Americans, and he confessed to me that he was by nature stubborn and selfish. Yet few persons have ever placed such unbounded confidence in me, or treated me with such devotion and generosity. He gave me his pistols for the journey, his medicines, and everything which he thought I would need. Besides this, he purchased a number of supplies in Assouan, pretending they were for his return journey, and then persuaded Achmet to pack them secretly in my boxes. He also told Achmet he was going to leave a handsome present for him with a merchant in Cairo, but he (Achmet) would not receive it unless he had served me faithfully. For two days before our parting he could scarcely eat or sleep, and when the time drew near he was so pale and agitated that

I almost feared to leave him. I have rarely been so moved as when I saw a strong, proud man exhibit such an attachment for me. He told me he could scarcely account for it, but he felt almost ready to give up all his engagements to return home and accompany me. I told him all my history, and showed him the portrait I have with me [of Mary Agnew]. He went out of the cabin after looking at it, and when he returned I saw that he had been weeping. . . . Almost the last thing he asked of me was to look at it once more before leaving. And he knew so well how to speak to me, soothing, but without offering consolation, that I feel stronger than for a long time past. The last three days have been very lonely, but they would have been more so had I not met with him. I shall pursue my travels in a far more happy and courageous mood than I anticipated. Besides, I have promised to spend two or three weeks with him next summer in Germany, and shall keep my promise. I owe him far more than I can lightly repay, and it is some satisfaction to confess the debt to you.[23]

Taylor did meet his friend again in Germany, going to Gotha to pay the promised visit to Bufleb, who received him with open arms. Taylor wrote of the trip his mother:

Indeed, he had not dared to leave Gotha for four weeks beforehand, fearing I should arrive in his absence. Every kindness that friendship could invent has been heaped upon me. All his relatives and friends received me like a lost member of the family; every door was open for me, and there was a place already prepared at every table. Two days after I arrived, as the weather was fine, we started on a tour through the Thuringian Forest, which we made partly on foot, partly in B.'s carriage.[23]

In the following three years, August Bufleb would go so far as to build Taylor a permanent residence at his home:

A. BUFLEB TO BAYARD TAYLOR. Gotha, July 27, 1855. A short time ago I bought a piece of property adjoining my estate, a garden with a small, modest house. This house is to be Taylor's home, when he keeps his promise next year, and visits us, I said to myself. All arrangements are made with this in view. The upper part of the garden, a genuine French establishment of the last century, with its statues and fountains, its densely shaded beech-alleys and smoothly shorn box trees, is in readiness and awaits my distant friend. A smaller house near the fountain, covered with bark, is to be the bath-house. The lower part of the garden, a little grove with beautiful large forest trees covering an acre or so, is to refresh you with its cool shade, and will I hope become for you a snug sanctuary of nature. The little salon in the house will serve for us when we gather around you at your pleasure. You see how I have written to you, my dear Taylor. In spite of our long separation and remoteness from each other, your heart I know could never tell you of any change in my feelings and thoughts. On the contrary, this rapport which we enjoy has for me a profound meaning; whilst you were dedicating your glorious work on Central Africa to me, I was setting in order for you the most cherished part of my possessions.[23]

While visiting that house in Gotha with his family (his two sisters and youngest brother), Taylor wrote to his mother:

Gotha, August 20, 1856. I write to you from my house, sitting in my room, with my fountain playing before the window. I reached here last Thursday, and was received with open arms. My house adjoins Bufleb's residence, and the gardens are thrown into one. It is one of the most charming little places I ever saw. The house is a story and a half high, with a large room and two side boudoirs on the first floor, a little cellar, a study and bed-room above, and no end to the closets and queer little nooks. It is furnished in antique style with high-backed red velvet chairs, Brussels rugs, sofas, mirrors, flower-stands, matches and cigars on the table, tea, sugar, etc., in the cupboard, and beer in the cellar. Nothing was forgotten; the smallest things were all in their places, and here I live like a prince. The house stands on a raised terrace covered with flowers. A flight of stone steps, with statues at the foot, leads to a broader terrace, in the middle of which is a fountain, always playing. The basin is deep, and I have three big fish which come to be fed. From this terrace commences an arched avenue of the dwarf beech, making a comfortable shade. It opens into a large circular arbor, and then continues a hundred feet farther, to a garden walk bordered with flowers. Then you come to a pool surrounded with water-lilies, then more flower-beds, and finally a sort of triumphal arch ushers you into the grove,—two acres of wood, with winding paths, statues, fountains, a hermitage of bark, and numerous stone seats and tables. At the end of the wood is the Duke's tree, a large walnut planted by Ernest II. in 1760. The house was built in the same year by his prime minister. Fred and I sleep in the house, which will hold only two, and the girls in Bufleb's house. We spend the day here, and take our meals (except supper) with them. . . . We have made two excursions,—to Eisenach and the Wartburg, and to the Thüringian Forest. Although it rained a little both days, we had delightful trips, and the Buflebs enjoyed them as much as the rest of us. They have taken quite a fancy to Fred and the girls, and this relieves me from all feeling of uneasiness at taxing them with so many guests. Everybody knew me on my return, and they all seemed truly glad to see me.[23]

After the visit to the Buflebs, Bayard Taylor took his party to Switzerland and Italy, and returning to Switzerland, left his sisters and brother in Lausanne for the winter. He then went to Gotha, where he made a month's stay before going to the north. During that stay he wrote to his mother (on October 20, 1856) of Bufleb's "great rejoicing over my return," and a few days later he announced to his mother his engagement to "Marie Hansen, (daughter of [Peter Andreas Hansen, the eminent astronomer and director of the Ducal Observatory], and niece of Mrs. Bufleb," writing, "I hope you will be satisfied with a step which makes us all so happy and my future so bright."[23]

Taylor married Marie Hansen in Gotha October 27, 1857. They stayed married for the rest of his life (twenty-one years), so long that in 1872 he noted in another letter from Gotha that Bufleb's life was waning:

> Gotha, Germany, July 3, 1872. There is one sad figure in the merry family circle. M.'s uncle [Mr. August Bufleb], who traveled with me in Egypt twenty years ago, and through whose friendship I was first brought here to find the best of my life's fortunes, has been so lamed and maimed, bodily and mentally, by paralysis, that he is almost lost to us. I could get used to his helplessness, his half-incoherent words (the tongue being also lamed); but the indifference to everything in which he once took an interest, the death or sleep of all his finer qualities of mind and heart, makes a very painful impression.[24]

Bufleb died in 1874. After Taylor's death in 1878, his widow collected his large correspondence, and with Horace E. Scudder, edited *Life and Letters of Bayard Taylor*[45]. That collection, incidentally, does not include Taylor's letters to Walt Whitman.

III

THE PLACE AND PEOPLE

JOSEPH ASTEN'S NATURE was shy and sensitive, but not merely from a habit of introversion. He saw no deeper into himself, in fact, than his moods and sensations, and thus quite failed to recognize what it was that kept him apart from the society in which he should have freely moved. He felt the difference of others, and constantly probed the pain and embarrassment it gave him, but the sources wherefrom it grew were the last which he would have guessed.

A boy's life may be weakened for growth, in all its fibres, by the watchfulness of a too anxious love, and the guidance of a too exquisitely nurtured conscience. He may be so trained in the habits of goodness, and purity, and duty, that every contact with the world is like all abrasion upon the delicate surface of his soul. Every wind visits him too roughly, and he shrinks from the encounters which brace true manliness, and strengthen it for the exercise of good.

The rigid piety of Joseph's mother was warmed and softened by her tenderness towards him, and he never felt it as a yoke. His nature instinctively took the imprint of hers, and she was happy in seeing so clear a reflection of herself in his innocent young heart. She prolonged his childhood, perhaps without intending it, into the years when the unrest of approaching manhood should have led him to severer studies and lustier sports. Her death transferred his guardianship to other hands, but did not change its character. Her sister Rachel was equally good and conscientious, possibly with an equal capacity for tenderness, but her barren life had restrained the habit of its expression. Joseph could not but confess that she was guided by the strictest sense of duty, but she seemed to him cold, severe, unsympathetic. There were times when the alternative presented itself to his mind, of either allowing her absolute control of all his actions, or wounding her to the heart by asserting a moderate amount of independence.

He was called fortunate, but it was impossible for him consciously to feel his fortune. The two hundred acres of the farm, stretching back over the softly swelling hills which enclosed the valley on the east, were as excellent soil as the neighborhood knew; the stock was plentiful; the house, barn, and all the appointments of the place were in the best order, and he was the sole owner of all. The work of his own hands was not needed, but it was a mechanical exhaustion of time,—an enforced occupation of body and mind, which he followed in the vague hope that some richer development of life might come afterwards. But there were times when the fields looked very dreary,—when the trees, rooted in their places, and growing under conditions which they were powerless to choose or change, were but tiresome types of himself,—when even the beckoning heights far down the valley failed to touch his fancy with the hint of a broader world. Duty said to him, "You must be perfectly contented in your place!" but there was the miserable, ungrateful, inexplicable fact of discontent.

Furthermore, he had by this time discovered that certain tastes which he possessed were so many weaknesses—if not, indeed, matters of reproach—in the eyes of his neighbors. The delight and the torture of finer nerves—an inability to use coarse and strong phrases, and a shrinking from all display of rude manners—were peculiarities which he could not overcome, and must endeavor to conceal. There were men of sturdy intelligence in the community; but none of refined culture, through whom he might have measured and understood himself; and the very qualities, therefore, which should have been his pride, gave him only a sense of shame.

Two memories haunted him, after the evening at Warriner's; and, though so different, they were not to be disconnected. No two girls could be more unlike than Lucy Henderson and Miss Julia Blessing; he had known one for years, and the other was the partial acquaintance of an evening; yet the image of either one was swiftly followed by that of the other. When he thought of Lucy's eyes, Miss Julia's hand stole over his shoulder; when he recalled the glossy ringlets of the latter, he saw, beside them, the faintly flushed cheek and the pure, sweet mouth which had awakened in him his first daring desire.

Phantoms as they were, they seemed to have taken equal possession of the house, the garden, and the fields. While Lucy sat quietly by the window, Miss Julia skipped lightly along the adjoining hall. One lifted a fallen rose-branch on the lawn, the other snatched the reddest blossom from it. One leaned against the trunk of the old hemlock-tree, the other fluttered in and out among the clumps of shrubbery; but the lonely green was wonderfully brightened by these visions of pink and white, and Joseph enjoyed the fancy without troubling himself to think what it meant.

The house was seated upon a gentle knoll, near the head of a side-valley sunk like a dimple among the hills which enclosed the river-meadows, scarcely a quarter of a mile away. It was nearly a hundred years old, and its massive walls were faced with checkered bricks, alternately red and black, to which the ivy clung with tenacious feet wherever it was allowed to run. The gables terminated in broad double chimneys, between which a railed walk, intended for a lookout, but rarely used for that or any other purpose, rested on the peak of the roof. A low portico paved with stone extended along the front, which was further shaded by two enormous sycamore-trees as old as the house itself. The evergreens and ornamental shrubs which occupied the remainder of the little lawn denoted the taste of a later generation. To the east, an open turfy space, in the centre of which stood a superb weeping-willow, divided the house from the great stone barn with its flanking cribs and "overshoots;" on the opposite side lay the sunny garden, with gnarled grape-vines clambering along its walls, and a double row of tall old box-bushes, each grown into a single solid mass, stretching down the centre.

The fields belonging to the property, softly rising and following the undulations of the hills, limited the landscape on three sides; but on the south there was a fair view of the valley of the larger stream, with its herd-speckled meadows, glimpses of water between the fringing trees, and farm-houses sheltered among the knees of the farther hills. It was a region of peace and repose and quiet, drowsy beauty, and there were few farms which were not the ancestral homes of the families who held them. The people were satisfied, for they lived upon a bountiful soil; and if but few were notably rich, still fewer were absolutely poor. They had a sluggish sense of content, a half-conscious feeling that their lines were cast in pleasant places; they were orderly, moral, and generally honest, and their own types were so constantly reproduced and fixed, both by intermarriage and intercourse, that any variation therein was a thing to be suppressed if possible. Any sign of an unusual taste, or a different view of life, excited their suspicion, and the most of them were incapable of discriminating between independent thought on moral and social questions, and "free-thinking" in the religious significance which they attached to the word. Political excitements, it is true, sometimes swept over the neighborhood, but in a mitigated form; and the discussions which then took place between neighbors of opposite faith were generally repetitions of the arguments furnished by their respective county papers.

To one whose twofold nature conformed to the common mould,—into whom, before his birth, no mysterious element had been infused, to be the basis of new sensations, desires, and powers,—the region was a paradise of peaceful days. Even as a boy the probable map of his life was drawn: he could behold himself as young man, as husband, father, and comfortable old man, by simply looking upon these various stages in others.

If, however, his senses were not sluggish, but keen; if his nature reached beyond the ordinary necessities, and hungered for the taste of higher things; if he longed to share in that life of the world, the least part of which was known to his native community; if, not content to accept the mechanical faith of passive minds, he dared to repeat the long struggle of the human race in his own spiritual and mental growth; then,—why, then, the region was not a paradise of peaceful days.

Rachel Miller, now that the dangerous evening was over, was shrewd enough to resume her habitual manner towards her nephew. Her curiosity to know what had been done, and how Joseph had been affected by the merry-making, rendered her careful not to frighten him from the subject by warnings or reproaches. He was frank and communicative, and Rachel found, to her surprise, that the evening at Warriner's was much, and not wholly unpleasantly, in her thoughts during her knitting-hours. The farm-work was briskly forwarded; Joseph was active in the field, and decidedly brighter in the house; and when he announced the new engagement, with an air which hinted that his attendance was a matter of course, she was only able to say:—

"I'm very much mistaken if *that's* the end. Get agoing once, and there's no telling where you'll fetch up. I suppose that town's girl won't stay much longer,—the farm-work of the neighborhood couldn't stand it,—and so she means to have all she can while her visit lasts."

"Indeed, Aunt," Joseph protested, "Elwood Withers first proposed it, and the others all agreed."

"And ready enough they were, I'll be bound."

"Yes, they were," Joseph replied, with a little more firmness than usual. "All of them. And there was no respectable family in the neighborhood that wasn't represented."

Rachel made an effort and kept silence. The innovation might be temporary, and in that case it were prudent to take no further notice; or it might be the beginning of a change in the ways of the young people, and if so, she needed further knowledge in order to work successfully against it in Joseph's case.

She little suspected how swiftly and closely the question would be brought to her own door.

A week afterwards the second of the evening parties was held, and was even more successful than the first. Everybody was there, bringing a cheerful memory of the former occasion, and Miss Julia Blessing, no longer dreaded as an unknown scrutinizing element, was again the life and soul of the company. It was astonishing how correctly she retained the names and characteristics of all those whom she had already met, and how intelligently she seemed to enjoy the gossip of the neighborhood. It was remarked that her dress was studiously simple, as if to conform to country ways, yet the airy, graceful freedom of her manner gave it a character of elegance which sufficiently distinguished her from the other girls.

Joseph felt that she looked to him, as by an innocent natural instinct, for a more delicate and intimate recognition than she expected to find elsewhere. Fragments of sentences, parenthetical expressions, dropped in her lively talk, were always followed by a quick glance which said to him: "We have one feeling in common; I know that *you* understand me." He was fascinated, but the experience was so new that it was rather bewildering. He was drawn to catch her seemingly random looks,—to wait for them, and then, shrink timidly when they came, feeling all the while the desire to be in the quiet corner, outside the merry circle of talkers, where sat Lucy Henderson.

When, at last, a change in the diversions of the evening brought him to Lucy's side, she seemed to him grave and preoccupied. Her words lacked the pleasant directness and self-possession which had made her society so comfortable to him. She no longer turned her full face towards him while speaking, and he noticed that her eyes were wandering over the company with a peculiar expression, as if she were trying to listen with them. It seemed to him, also, that Elwood Withers, who was restlessly moving about the room, was watching someone, or waiting for something.

"I have it!" suddenly cried Miss Blessing, floating towards Joseph and Lucy; "it shall be *you*, Mr. Asten!"

"Yes," echoed Anna Warriner, following; "if it could be, how delightful!"

"Hush, Anna dear! Let us keep the matter secret!" whispered Miss Blessing, assuming a mysterious air; "we will slip away and consult; and, of course, Lucy must come with us."

"Now," she resumed, when the four found themselves alone in the old-fashioned dining-room, "we must, first of all, explain everything to Mr. Asten, The question is, where we shall meet, next week. McNaughtons are building an addition (I believe you call it) to their barn, and a child has the measles at another place, and something else is wrong somewhere else. We cannot interfere with the course of nature; but neither should we give up these charming evenings without making an effort to continue them. Our sole hope and reliance is on you, Mr. Asten."

She pronounced the words with a mock solemnity, clasping her hands, and looking into his face with bright, eager, laughing eyes.

"If it depended on myself—" Joseph began.

"O, I know the difficulty, Mr. Asten!" she exclaimed; "and really, it's unpardonable in me to propose such a thing. But isn't it possible—just possible—that Miss Miller might be persuaded by us?"

"Julia dear!" cried Anna Warriner, "I believe there's nothing you'd be afraid to undertake."

Joseph scarcely knew what to say. He looked from one to the other, coloring slightly, and ready to turn pale the next moment, as he endeavored to imagine how his aunt would receive such an astounding proposition.

"There is no reason why she should be asked," said Lucy. "It would be a great annoyance to her."

"Indeed?" said Miss Blessing; "then I should be *so* sorry! But I caught a glimpse of your lovely place the other day as we were driving up the valley. It was a perfect picture,— and I have such a desire to see it nearer!"

"Why will you not come, then?" Joseph eagerly asked. Lucy's words seemed to him blunt and unfriendly, although he knew they had been intended for his relief.

"It would be a great pleasure; yet, if I thought your aunt would be annoyed—"

"I am sure she will be glad to make your acquaintance," said Joseph, with a reproachful side-glance at Lucy.

Miss Blessing noticed the glance. "I am more sure," she said, playfully, "that she will be very much amused at my ignorance and inexperience. And I don't believe Lucy meant to frighten me. As for the party, we won't think of that now; but you will go with us, Lucy, won't you,—with Anna and myself, to make a neighborly afternoon call?"

Lucy felt obliged to accede to a request so amiably made, after her apparent rudeness. Yet she could not force herself to affect a hearty acquiescence, and Joseph thought her singularly cold.

He did not doubt but that Miss Blessing, whose warm, impulsive nature seemed to him very much what his own might be if he dared to show it, would fulfil her promise. Neither did he doubt that so much innocence and sweetness as she possessed would make a favorable impression upon his aunt; but he judged it best not to inform the latter of the possible visit.

3. TWIN LOVE

Joseph and His Friend is not the only work of homoerotic note from Bayard Taylor. Along with a couple of poems that linger on male and masculine beauty ("To A Persian Boy"[A.1] on the sensuous sighting of a Persian youth, and "On the Headland"[A.2], which has a narrator yearning for the touch of sea-faring men), there is also his short story "Twin-Love"[A.3]. In it, the twins are David and Jonathan, referencing the biblical relationship between David and Jonathan and their love "passing the love of women." That pair is a shorthand often used when implying homosexuality, the same way the legend of Damon and Pythias is used in describing real-life friendships like that between Fitz-Greene Halleck and Joseph Rodman Drake (see Chapter 5: Halleck and Drake and Chapter 9: Joseph and His Fitz-Greene), as well as fictional homosexual couples, as in 1889's *A Marriage Below Zero* (see Chapter 32: On Women, and A Marriage Below Zero). After Oscar Wilde's conviction for gross indecency in 1895, his name becomes the same sort of watch-word for the next century (see Chapter 19: Calamus as Cruising Apparatus for more detail).

In "Twin-Love," twins David and Jonathan are deemed by their ailing mother to be one soul in two bodies. She urges them with her dying breath, "Be one, always!" and so that is how they exist, obsessively intertwined, until their father insists they learn independence by spending some time apart. During that time, Jonathan meets a girl, Ruth, and becomes engaged. He brings her kiss to his brother, "pressing his lips to David's," to transfer said kiss, and they attempt to continue 'being one' until the marriage itself forces them apart. Then David disappears, and Jonathan and his wife have children. It's only the terminal sickness of the wife which brings them back together, when Ruth tells her husband to call out telepathically to his brother so they can all be reunited before she dies (channeling their mother's motives). Once Ruth dies, in perfect peace because she reunited the twin-hearts, her children call both David and Jonathan "father," an ending not unlike the conclusion of *Joseph and His Friend*, where Philip decides that he can accept Joseph marrying his sister, because their children will belong to him too.

"Twin-Love" (1871) has its own brother in a story by Ambrose Bierce, described in *Pages Passed from Hand to Hand: The Hidden Tradition of Homosexual Literature in English from 1748 to 1914*:

Ambrose Bierce's best-known works are surely *The Devil's Dictionary* (1911) and the *Tales of Soldiers and Civilians* (1891; the most famous being "An Occurrence at Owl Creek Bridge"). "The Mocking-Bird" [1891] is very different from the rest of Bierce's work, for though the story describes an episode of the Civil War, and was published at the beginning of the 1890s, it reads as a pastiche of fiction from the end of that decade. Death is poeticized to an extraordinary degree, as it is in some Stenbock, or Wilde. And yet, there is a fairy-tale quality to the story: when the soldier fighting for the Union troops discovers the body of his twin brother who fought for the Confederacy ("to whom he gave his heart and soul in love"), one is forcibly reminded of the Prince's discovery of Sleeping Beauty, or of Narcissus (whose story Wilde reinvents to make the pool love Narcissus back because "in the mirror of his eyes I saw ever my own beauty mirrored"). Bierce further participates in the tradition of naming a homosexual utopia; in his case a place that is not merely homosexual, but incestuous. In the end, the soldier who has slain his brother cannot bear the song of the mockingbird that sings over the youth whose body is warm and whose gray uniform is stained only by a spot of blood on the breast—the song that was to him "the meaning and interpretation to sense of the mysteries of life and love." Like Isolde, life without his Tristan is impossible.[30]

However, it is also interesting to note that like Bayard Taylor's changing opinions on Walt Whitman (whom he admired as a younger man for the representation of manly love in *Leaves of Grass*, but openly mocked as he 'matured,' see <u>Chapter 10: Taylor and Whitman</u>), Bierce's opinions on honest homosexuality can be seen as a struggle through his friendship with Charles Warren Stoddard, a life-long devotee of Whitman's and author of homosexual novels himself (see <u>Chapter 15: Avowals to Walt Whitman</u> and <u>Chapter 20: Contemporary Camerados</u> for more on Stoddard). From Robert L. Gale's *An Ambrose Bierce Companion*:

> Bierce was familiar enough with [Charles Warren] Stoddard, and his sexual inclinations, to query him crudely by letter (29 December 1872) about loving "'nigger' boy[s]" in Hawaii. ["Tell me all about everybody, won't you, and about your last voyage. Did you fall in love with another nigger boy."] When Stoddard first arrived in London, Bierce warned him by letter to "avoid any appearance of eccentricity" (28 September 1873). Stoddard naturally ignored the advice. During his stay in England, Bierce wrote Stoddard, often absent, a few letters in which he commented about his wife—this, contrary to his reticence about her in letters. Stoddard returned to San Francisco in 1878, and he and his "Biercy" had a permanent falling out, doubtlessly owing to Bierce's dislike of Stoddard's homosexuality.[16]

In these instances, the suggestion of incest is more palatable than the idea of physical affection between unrelated men, perhaps with the permission granted by the fact that identical twin brothers would have once literally shared one another's bodies. Add to that permission the preternatural aid of some same-minded telepathy, which assures each twin that his brother thinks and desires the same thing does, and you have a form of perfectly failsafe, like-knows-like, unmistakable gaydar (see <u>Chapter 22: Whitman's Peter</u> for just how like fiction a real life instance of gaydar could be).

IV

MISS BLESS CALLS ON RACHEL MILLER

ON THE FOLLOWING Saturday afternoon, Rachel Miller sat at the front window of the sitting-room, and arranged her light task of sewing and darning, with a feeling of unusual comfort. The household work of the week was over; the weather was fine and warm, with a brisk drying breeze for the hay on the hill-field, the last load of which Joseph expected to have in the barn before his five o'clock supper was ready. As she looked down the valley, she noticed that the mowers were still swinging their way through Hunter's grass, and that Cunningham's corn sorely needed working. There was a different state of things on the Asten place. Everything was done, and well done, up to the front of the season. The weather had been fortunate, it was true; but Joseph had urged on the work with a different spirit. It seemed to her that he had taken a new interest in the farm; he was here and there, even inspecting with his own eyes the minor duties which had been formerly entrusted to his man Dennis. How could she know that this activity was the only outlet for a restless heart?

If any evil should come of his social recreation, she had done her duty; but no evil seemed likely. She had always separated his legal from his moral independence; there was no enactment establishing the period when the latter commenced, and it could not be made manifest by documents, like the former. She would have admitted, certainly, that her guardianship must cease at some time, but the thought of making preparation for that time had never entered her head. She only understood conditions, not the adaptation of characters to them. Going back over her own life, she could recall but little difference between the girl of eighteen and the woman of thirty. There was the same place in her home, the same duties, the same subjection to the will of her parents—no exercise of independence or self-reliance anywhere, and no growth of those virtues beyond what a passive maturity brought with it.

Even now she thought very little about any question of life in connection with

Joseph. Her parents had trained her in the discipline of a rigid sect, and she could not dissociate the idea of morality from that of solemn renunciation. She could not say that social pleasures were positively wrong, but they always seemed to her to be enjoyed on the outside of an open door labelled "Temptation;" and who could tell what lay beyond? Some very good people, she knew, were fond of company, and made merry in an innocent fashion; they were of mature years and settled characters, and Joseph was only a boy. The danger, however, was not so imminent: no fault could be found with his attention to duty, and a chance so easily escaped was a comfortable guaranty for the future.

In the midst of this mood (we can hardly say train of thought), she detected the top of a carriage through the bushes fringing the lane. The vehicle presently came into view: Anna Warriner was driving, and there were two other ladies on the back seat. As they drew up at the hitching-post on the green, she recognized Lucy Henderson getting out; but the airy creature who sprang after her—the girl with dark, falling ringlets,— could it be the stranger from town? The plain, country-made gingham dress, the sober linen collar, the work-bag on her arm—could they belong to the stylish young lady whose acquaintance had turned Anna's head?

A proper spirit of hospitality required her to meet the visitors at the gate; so there was no time left for conjecture. She was a little confused, but not dissatisfied at the chance of seeing the stranger.

"We thought we could come for an hour this afternoon, without disturbing you," said Anna Warriner. "Mother has lost your receipt for pickling cherries, and Bob said you were already through with the hay-harvest; and so we brought Julia along—this is Julia Blessing."

"How do you do?" said Miss Blessing, timidly extending her hand, and slightly dropping her eyelids. She then fell behind Anna and Lucy, and spoke no more until they were all seated in the sitting-room.

"How do you like the country by this time?" Rachel asked, feeling that a little attention was necessary to a new guest.

"So well that I think I shall never like the city again," Miss Blessing answered. "This quiet, peaceful life is such a rest; and I really never before knew what order was, and industry, and economy."

She looked around the room as she spoke, and glanced at the barn through the eastern window.

"Yes, your ways in town are very different," Rachel remarked.

"It seems to me, *now*, that they are entirely artificial. I find myself so ignorant of the proper way of living that I should be embarrassed among you, if you were not all so very kind. But I am trying to learn a little."

"O, we don't expect too much of town's-folks," said Rachel, in a much more friendly tone, "and we're always glad to see them willing to put up with our ways. But not many are."

"Please don't count *me* among those!" Miss Blessing exclaimed.

"No, indeed, Miss Rachel!" said Anna Warriner; "you'd be surprised to know how Julia gets along with everything—don't she, Lucy?"

"Yes, she's very quick," Lucy Henderson replied.

Miss Blessing cast down her eyes, smiled, and shook her head.

Rachel Miller asked some questions which opened the sluices of Miss Warriner's gossip—and she had a good store of it. The ways and doings of various individuals were discussed, and Miss Blessing's occasional remarks showed a complete familiarity with them. Her manner was grave and attentive, and Rachel was surprised to find so much unobtrusive good sense in her views. The reality was so different from her previously assumed impression, that she felt bound to make some reparation. Almost before she was aware of it, her manner became wholly friendly and pleasant.

"May I look at your trees and flowers?" Miss Blessing asked, when the gossip had been pretty well exhausted.

They all arose and went out on the lawn. Rose and woodbine, phlox and verbena, passed under review, and then the long, rounded walls of box attracted Miss Blessing's eye. This was a feature of the place in which Rachel Miller felt considerable pride, and she led the way through the garden gate. Anna Warriner, however, paused, and said:—

"Lucy, let us go down to the spring-house. We can get back again before Julia has half finished her raptures."

Lucy hesitated a moment. She looked at Miss Blessing, who laughed and said, "O, don't mind me!" as she took her place at Rachel's side.

The avenue of box ran the whole length of the garden, which sloped gently to the south. At the bottom the green walls curved outward, forming three fourths of a circle, spacious enough to contain several seats. There was a delightful view of the valley through the opening.

"The loveliest place I ever saw!" exclaimed Miss Blessing, taking one of the rustic chairs. "How pleasant it must be, when you have all your neighbors here together!"

Rachel Miller was a little startled; but before she could reply, Miss Blessing continued:—

"There is such a difference between a company of young people here in the country, and what is called 'a party' in the city. There it is all dress and flirtation and vanity, but here it is only neighborly visiting on a larger scale. I have enjoyed the quiet company of all your folks *so* much the more, because I felt that it was so very innocent. Indeed, I don't see how anybody *could* be led into harmful ways here."

"I don't know," said Rachel: "we must learn to mistrust our own hearts."

"You are right! The best are weak—of themselves; but there is more safety where all have been brought up unacquainted with temptation. Now, you will perhaps wonder at me when I say that I could trust the young men—for instance, Mr. Asten, your nephew—as if they were my brothers. That is, I feel a positive certainty of their excellent character. What they say they mean: it is otherwise in the city. It is delightful to see them all together, like members of one family. You must enjoy it, I should think, when they meet here."

Rachel Miller's eyes opened wide, and there was both a puzzled and a searching expression in the look she gave Miss Blessing. The latter, with an air of almost infantine simplicity, her lips slightly parted, accepted the scrutiny with a quiet cheerfulness which seemed the perfection of candor.

"The truth is," said Rachel, slowly, "this is a new thing. I hope the merry-makings are as innocent as you think; but I'm afraid they unsettle the young people, after all."

"Do you, really?" exclaimed Miss Blessing. "What have you seen in them which leads you to think so? But no—never mind my question; you may have reasons which I have no right to ask. Now, I remember Mr. Asten telling Anna and Lucy and myself, how much he should like to invite his friends here, if it were not for a duty which prevented it; and a duty, he said, was more important to him than a pleasure."

"Did Joseph say that?" Rachel exclaimed.

"O, perhaps I oughtn't to have told it," said Miss Blessing, casting down her eyes and blushing in confusion: "in that case, *please* don't say anything about it! Perhaps it was a duty towards you, for he told me that he looked upon you as a second mother."

Rachel's eyes softened, and it was a little while before she spoke. "I've tried to do my duty by him," she faltered at last, "but it sometimes seems an unthankful business, and I can't always tell how he takes it. And so he wanted to have a company here?"

"I am so sorry I said it!" cried Miss Blessing. "I never thought you were opposed to company, on principle. Miss Chaffinch, the minister's daughter, you know, was there the last time; and, really, if you could see it— But it is presumptuous in me to say anything. Indeed, I am not a fair judge, because these little gatherings have enabled me to make such pleasant acquaintances. And the young men tell me that they work all the better after them."

"It's only on *his* account," said Rachel.

"Nay, I'm sure that the last thing Mr. Asten would wish would be your giving up a principle for his sake! I know, from his face, that his own character is founded on principle. And, besides, here in the country, you don't keep count of hospitality, as they do in the city, and feel obliged to return as much as you receive. So, if you will try to forget what I have said—"

Rachel interrupted her. "I meant something different. Joseph knows why I objected to parties. He must not feel under obligations which I stand in the way of his repaying. If he tells me that he should like to invite his friends to this place, I will help him to entertain them."

"You *are* his second mother, indeed," Miss Blessing murmured, looking at her with a fond admiration. "And now I can hope that you will forgive my thoughtlessness. I should feel humiliated in his presence, if he knew that I had repeated his words. But he will not ask you, and this is the end of any harm I may have done."

"No," said Rachel, "he will not ask me; but won't I be an offence in his mind?"

"I can understand how you feel—only a woman can judge a woman's heart. Would you think me too forward if I tell you what might be done, this once?"

She stole softly up to Rachel as she spoke, and laid her hand gently upon her arm.

"Perhaps I am wrong—but if *you* were first to suggest to your nephew that if he wished to make some return for the hospitality of his neighbors,—or put it in whatever form you think best,—would not that remove the 'offence' (though he surely cannot look at it in that light), and make him grateful and happy?"

"Well," said Rachel, after a little reflection, "if anything is done, that would be as good a way as any."

"And, of course, you won't mention me?"

"There is no call to do it—as I can see."

"Julia, dear!" cried Anna from the gate; "come and see the last load of hay hauled into the barn!"

"I should like to see it, if you will excuse me," said Miss Blessing to Rachel; "I have taken quite an interest in farming."

As they were passing the porch, Rachel paused on the step and said to Anna: "You'll bide and get your suppers?"

"I don't know," Anna replied: "we didn't mean to; but we stayed longer than we intended—"

"Then you can easily stay longer still."

There was nothing unfriendly in Rachel's blunt manner. Anna laughed, took Miss Blessing by the arm, and started for the barn. Lucy Henderson quietly turned and entered the house, where, without any offer of services, she began to assist in arranging the table.

The two young ladies took their stand on the green, at a safe distance, as the huge fragrant load approached. The hay overhung and concealed the wheels, as well as the hind quarters of the oxen, and on the summit stood Joseph, in his shirt-sleeves and leaning on a pitch-fork. He bent forward as he saw them, answering their greetings with an eager, surprised face.

"O, take care, take care!" cried Miss Blessing, as the load entered the barn-door; but Joseph had already dropped upon his knees and bent his shoulders. Then the wagon stood upon the barn-floor; he sprang lightly upon a beam, descended the upright ladder, and the next moment was shaking hands with them.

"We have kept our promise, you see," said Miss Blessing.

"Have you been in the house yet?" Joseph asked, looking at Anna.

"O, for an hour past, and we are going to take supper with you."

"Dennis!" cried Joseph, turning towards the barn, "we will let the load stand to-night."

"How much better a man looks in shirt-sleeves than in a dress-coat!" remarked Miss Blessing aside to Anna Warriner, but not in so low a tone as to prevent Joseph from hearing it.

"Why, Julia, you are perfectly countrified! I never saw anything like it!" Anna replied.

Joseph turned to them again, with a bright flush on his face. He caught Miss Blessing's eyes, full of admiration, before the lids fell modestly over them.

"So you've seen my home, already?" he said, as they walked slowly towards the house.

"O, not the half yet!" she answered, in a low, earnest tone. "A place so lovely and quiet as this cannot be appreciated at once. I almost wish I had not seen it: what shall I do when I must go back to the hot pavements, and the glaring bricks, and the dust, and the hollow, artificial life?" She tried to check a sigh, but only partially succeeded; then, with a sudden effort, she laughed lightly, and added: "I wonder if everybody doesn't long for something else? Now, Anna, here, would think it heavenly to change places with me."

"Such privileges as you have!" Anna protested.

"Privileges?" Miss Blessing echoed. "The privilege of hearing scandal, of being judged by your dress, of learning the forms and manners, instead of the good qualities, of men and women? No! give me an independent life."

"Alone?' suggested Miss Warriner.

Joseph looked at Miss Blessing, who made no reply. Her head was turned aside, and he could well understand that she must feel hurt at Anna's indelicacy.

In the house Rachel Miller and Lucy had, in the meantime, been occupied with domestic matters. The former, however, was so shaken out of her usual calm by the conversation in the garden, that in spite of prudent resolves to keep quiet, she could not restrain herself from asking a question or two.

"Lucy," said she, "how do you find these evening parties you've been attending?"

"They are lively and pleasant,—at least every one says so."

"Are you going to have any more?"

"It seems to be the wish," said Lucy, suddenly hesitating, as she found Rachel's eyes intently fixed upon her face.

The latter was silent for a minute, arranging the tea-service; but she presently asked again: "Do you think Joseph would like to invite the young people here?"

"She has told you!" Lucy exclaimed, in unfeigned irritation. "Miss Rachel, don't let it trouble you a moment: nobody expects it of you!"

Lucy felt, immediately, that her expression had been too frankly positive; but even the consciousness thereof did not enable her to comprehend its effect.

Rachel straightened herself a little, and said "Indeed?" in anything but an amiable tone. She went to the cupboard and returned before speaking again. "I didn't say anybody told me," she continued; "it's likely that Joseph might think of it, and I don't see why people should expect me to stand in the way of his wishes."

Lucy was so astonished that she could not immediately reply; and the entrance of Joseph and the two ladies cut off all further opportunity of clearing up what she felt to be an awkward misunderstanding.

"I must help, too!" cried Miss Blessing, skipping into the kitchen after Rachel. "That is one thing, at least, which we can learn in the city. Indeed, if it wasn't for housekeeping, I should feel terribly useless."

Rachel protested against her help, but in vain. Miss Blessing had a laugh and a lively answer for every remonstrance, and flitted about in a manner which conveyed the impression that she was doing a great deal.

Joseph could scarcely believe his eyes, when he came down from his room in fresh attire, and beheld his aunt not only so assisted, but seeming to enjoy it. Lucy, who appeared to be ill at ease, had withdrawn from the table, and was sitting silently beside the window. Recalling their conversation a few evenings before, he suspected that she might be transiently annoyed on his aunt's account; she had less confidence, perhaps, in Miss Blessing's winning, natural manners. So Lucy's silence threw no shadow upon his cheerfulness: he had never felt so happy, so free, so delighted to assume the character of a host.

After the first solemnity which followed the taking of seats at the table, the meal proceeded with less than the usual decorum. Joseph, indeed, so far forgot his duties, that his aunt was obliged to remind him of them from time to time. Miss Blessing was enthusiastic over the cream and butter and marmalade, and Rachel Miller found it exceedingly pleasant to have her handiwork appreciated. Although she always did her best, for Joseph's sake, she knew that men have very ignorant, indifferent tastes in such matters.

When the meal was over, Anna Warriner said: "We are going to take Lucy on her way as far as the cross-roads; so there will not be more than time to get home by sunset."

Before the carriage was ready, however, another vehicle drove up the lane. Elwood Withers jumped out, gave Joseph a hearty grip of his powerful hand, greeted the others rapidly, and then addressed himself specially to Lucy: "I was going to a township-meeting at the Corner," said he; "but Bob Warriner told me you were here with Anna, so I thought I could save her a roundabout drive by taking you myself."

"Thank you; but I'm sorry you should go so far out of your road," said Lucy. Her face was pale, and there was an evident constraint in the smile which accompanied the words.

"O, he'd go twice as far for company," Anna Warriner remarked. "You know I'd take you, and welcome, but Elwood has a good claim on you, now."

"I have no *claim*, Lucy," said Elwood, rather doggedly.

"Let us go, then," were Lucy's words.

She rose, and the four were soon seated in the two vehicles. They drove away in the low sunshine, one pair chatting and laughing merrily as long as they were within hearing, the other singularly grave and silent.

4. HALLECK THE INSPIRATION

The inspiration for *Joseph and His Friend* came from poet Fitz-Greene Halleck and his passionate friendship with Joseph Rodman Drake. According to John W.M. Hallock, a distant relative of Fitz-Greene, in his book *The American Byron: Homosexuality and the Fall of Fitz-Greene Halleck*, this is how Halleck and Taylor came to know one another:

> As a confident seventeen-year-old, Taylor had solicited Halleck's autograph. The teenaged Taylor apologized for his boldness and closed his letter, "By sending [your autograph] with the bearer you will confer a lasting favour on yours truly." The favor was repaid with interest: Taylor would fictionalize Halleck's love for Drake. [...] Halleck had met both his biographer James Grant Wilson and Taylor at Bixby's Hotel in New York City in 1851. [...] Although the hotel catered to the bachelor, Taylor, who was a married man, found himself there. Taylor had remarkable insight into both the expression and oppression of homosexuality in nineteenth-century America. Taylor's widow did not give Wilson the impression that her husband had been happy, and Taylor's sexuality has been questioned by at least three scholars who treat him as homosexual.[22]

John W.M. Hallock begins his book on the poet Halleck with this star-studded introduction to Fitz-Greene:

> President Jackson had dined twice with the man [...], President Lincoln had complimented him, and John Quincy Adams had alluded to one of his poems in a speech delivered to the House of Representatives in 1836. [...] He was a favorite of Charles Dickens and William Thackeray as well as of the American literary giants, Bryant, James Fenimore Cooper, Washington Irving, and Edgar Allan Poe.[22]

The man who would become so distinguished and lauded started small:

Halleck [...] suffered from partial deafness since the age of two. The hearing loss was traceable to a prank two drunken soldiers had played on Halleck. Planning to startle the toddler, the men discharged their guns near his left ear. The assault resulted in a number of public embarrassments and ultimately an almost total loss of hearing in the years following an unsuccessful and excruciating remedy Halleck underwent when he was thirty years old.[22]

Of Fitz-Greene's boyhood it may be said, as would be true of his whole career, that it was uneventful. As a lad he was noticeable for the same quiet, studious, refined habits and associations which characterized his mature years. He had no taste for the rough sports and adventures in which most boys find delight, but preferred to wander alone in the fields and woods, by the river's banks, or on the shores of Long Island Sound, with a copy of Campbell's poems or some other favorite volume, with which he would beguile the hours. The only boyish pastime in which he took part with the other lads was in a mild game of marbles, or a quiet fishing excursion in one of the streams that wind their tortuous course through Guilford. He was the best scholar in the school, and a very great favorite with the teacher, Samuel Johnson, a gentleman by birth and a graduate of Yale College. During Fitz-Greene's whole career at school, he invariably knew his lessons, and was never on any occasion called up for misconduct or delinquency of any description. Many a pleasant ramble did the master and scholar take together after school-hours, the gentle and diffident boy drinking in with eagerness the teacher's conversation about poetry and other literary topics.[62]

Quick to misogyny (see Chapter 32: On Women, and A Marriage Below Zero for more) once he started losing his good-looking friends to marriages and family life, Halleck did still keep a friendly correspondence with his sister Maria, writing to her of the men he met in New York after leaving his hometown of Guilford, Connecticut:

New York, Aug. 3, 1811 [...] James is a fine young fellow, very pretty-looking—I say pretty, for he has quite a boyish appearance—has a peculiar talent for attracting the good graces of the females of his acquaintance, and is, properly speaking, a "ladies' man." He stutters a little, and is very agreeable, of an excellent disposition, open, frank, and generous to a fault; but, alas, he has one crime, which no repentance can atone for—"he is poor." On my first entrance into the office, he appeared very anxious to form an intimacy with me; his condescending and amiable manners soon endeared him to *me*, and we vowed eternal friendship when we had hardly seen each other an hour.
    [...]

New York, Aug. 20, 1811 [...] B——s is about twenty-two, and the handsomest man, without exception, I ever saw. His dress is very neat, and he always looks as though he had just been lifted out of a bandbox. He is a clerk to Cairns & Lord, dry goods dealers, Pearl Street. His disposition appears very good, and his conduct and character are unimpeachable. He is intimate with B——d in the belles' parties, but in my opinion there is a great dissimilarity between them. B——s is from Hartford, Conn.[62]

And yet he was worried that he would never find the man he was looking for. Near the end of one of his letters to his sister, after pages and pages of listing men he'd met, their looks, temperaments, and ultimately their failings, he wrote:

New York, Aug. 20, 1811 [...] Thus have I effaced a large quantity of paper in detailing the persons and characters of my fellow-boarders. To conclude. There is not one of them whose acquaintance I would wish to cultivate, nor with whom I would be willing to intrust my secrets, or place that confidence in which the name and character of a *friend* may claim. It is very difficult, I find, to discover, among the numerous fellow-mortals I meet with, a person whose disposition and ideas are congenial with my own, and whose friendship I might cherish as a valuable acquisition, nor do I expect to find one. G——d, one of my fellow-clerks, would in most respects be worthy one's esteem and confidence, but it requires a longer acquaintance to form a just conclusion.[62]

John W.M. Hallock clarifies further, using one previously mentioned man as a specific example:

[Halleck] was especially smitten with one of his coworkers whom he sketched for Maria. James B——r was "a fine young fellow, very pretty-looking—I say pretty, for he has quite a boyish appearance." Perhaps moved by wishful thinking, Halleck claimed, "On my first entrance into the office, [James] appeared very anxious to form an intimacy with me; his condescending and amiable manners soon endeared him to *me*, and we vowed eternal friendship when we had hardly seen each other an hour." [...] In April 1812, he wrote that James had "become a candidate for offering an oblation on the alter of Hymen." Inverting gender roles, Halleck described the groom as sexually sacrificed to the bride. He would recurrently denigrate women as duplicitous and aggressive and the men who married them as passive but greedy. [...] Halleck advanced his theory: "Miss Somebody," James's new fiancé, had "a fortune of 12,000 dollars [which] obliterated the remembrance of Rebecca from his mind, and induced him to make proposals of marriage.... So much for James B——r." In these few words, Halleck negates the bride's identity

("Miss Somebody"), cancels James's sincerity toward either woman (one being obliterated for the other's fortune), emasculates the groom (who is induced to propose), and ascribes calculated exploitation to the friend he writes off ("so much for James B——-r"). Maria would trace this formula time and again in her brother's correspondence.[22]

Halleck set himself up in society to meet as many eligible bachelors as he could:

[Halleck] was elected poet laureate of the Ugly Club, a fraternity of the city's best-looking men, and [...] Halleck was increasingly courted by New York's most elite social circles. Privately, he had begun a series of erratic romances with foreign men, but these did not eclipse his persistent doubt that he would ever find his ideal partner.[22]

"Of the 'Ugly Club,'" Halleck wrote to his sister, "I have no further information than that its members consisted of the handsomest young men of that day to be found in New-York City, and that they had frequent convivial meetings at their headquarters in Wall Street, a few doors from Broadway."[62] He was in position to find happiness, and yet of all the acquaintances he made, he did not come across the man he was looking for until 1813:

Halleck's search for a soul mate was delayed by the War of 1812 when he served in the Iron Grays, a metropolitan military unit consisting of wealthy boys. By his mid-twenties, his muse finally materialized in the figure of Joseph Rodman Drake, a young doctor and the most desirable man in town. Halleck was physically and emotionally drawn to Drake, but the powerful attraction was not completely mutual. The two men did collaborate, however, on a series of comic social commentaries. An over-night sensation, their Croaker poems initiated a form of social dialogue unprecedented in American periodicals. In the spring of 1819, more than thirty-five of these satirical Pindaric odes appeared anonymously in the New York Evening Post and later in the National Advocate. This venture of "Croaker" (Drake) and "Croaker Jr." (Halleck) awoke Halleck's poetic strength and permanently linked him with Drake.[22]

Drake was everything he admired and wanted, and through Drake, Halleck revealed his own talent and found success.

V

ELWOOD'S EVENING,
AND JOSEPH'S

FOR HALF A mile Elwood Withers followed the carriage containing Anna Warriner and her friend; then, at the curve of the valley, their roads parted, and Lucy and he were alone. The soft light of the delicious summer evening was around them; the air, cooled by the stream which broadened and bickered beside their way, was full of all healthy meadow odors, and every farm in the branching dells they passed was a picture of tranquil happiness. Yet Lucy had sighed before she was aware of it,— a very faint, tremulous breath, but it reached Elwood's sensitive ear.

"You don't seem quite well, Lucy," he said.

"Because I have talked so little?" she asked.

"Not just that, but—but I was almost afraid my coming for you was not welcome. I don't mean—" But here he grew confused, and did not finish the sentence.

"Indeed, it was very kind of you," said she. This was not an answer to his remark, and both felt that it was not.

Elwood struck the horse with his whip, then as suddenly drew the reins on the startled animal. "Pshaw!" he exclaimed, in a tone that was almost fierce, "what's the use o' my beating about the bush in this way?"

Lucy caught her breath, and clenched her hands under her shawl for one instant. Then she became calm, and waited for him to say more.

"Lucy!" he continued, turning towards her, "you have a right to think me a fool. I can talk to anybody else more freely than to you, and the reason is, I want to say more to you than to any other woman! There's no use in my being a coward any longer; it's a desperate venture I'm making, but it must be made. Have you never guessed how I feel towards you?"

"Yes," she answered, very quietly.

"Well, what do you say to it?" He tried to speak calmly, but his breath came thick and hard, and the words sounded hoarsely.

"I will say this, Elwood," said she, "that because I saw your heart, I have watched your ways and studied your character. I find you honest and manly in everything, and so tender and faithful that I wish I could return your affection in the same measure."

A gleam, as of lightning, passed over his face.

"O, don't misunderstand me!" she cried, her calmness forsaking her, "I esteem, I honor you, and that makes it harder for me to seem ungrateful, unfeeling,—as I must. Elwood, if I could, I would answer you as you wish, but I cannot."

"If I wait?" he whispered.

"And lose your best years in a vain hope! No, Elwood, my friend,—let me always call you so,—I have been cowardly also. I knew an explanation must come, and I shrank from the pain I should feel in giving you pain. It is hard; and better for both of us that it should not be repeated!"

"There's something wrong in this world!" he exclaimed, after a long pause. "I suppose you could no more force yourself to love me than I could force myself to love Anna Warriner or that Miss Blessing. Then what put it into my heart to love you? Was it God or the Devil!"

"Elwood!"

"How can I help myself? Can I help drawing my breath? Did I set about it of my own will? Here I see a life that belongs to my own life,—as much a part of it as my head or heart; but I can't reach it,—it draws away from me, and maybe joins itself to someone else forever! O my God!"

Lucy burst into such a violent passion of weeping, that Elwood forgot himself in his trouble for her. He had never witnessed such grief, as it seemed to him, and his honest heart was filled with self-reproach at having caused it.

"Forgive me, Lucy!" he said, very tenderly encircling her with his arm, and drawing her head upon his shoulder; "I spoke rashly and wickedly, in my disappointment. I thought only of myself, and forgot that I might hurt you by my words. I'm not the only man who has this kind of trouble to bear; and perhaps if I could see clearer—but I don't know; I can only see one thing."

She grew calmer as he spoke. Lifting her head from his shoulder, she took his hand, and said: "You are a true and a noble man, Elwood. It is only a grief to me that I cannot love you as a wife should love her husband. But my will is as powerless as yours."

"I believe you, Lucy," he answered, sadly. "It's not your fault,—but, then, it isn't mine, either. You make me feel that the same rule fits both of us, leastways so far as helping the matter is concerned. You needn't tell me I may find another woman to love; the very thought of it makes me sick at heart. I'm rougher than you are, and awkward in my ways—"

"It is not that! O, believe me, it is not that!" cried Lucy, interrupting him. "Have you ever sought for reasons to account for your feeling toward me? Is it not something that does not seem to depend upon what I am,—upon any qualities that distinguish me from other women?"

"How do you know so much?" Elwood asked. "Have you—" He commenced, but did not finish the question. He leaned silently forward, urged on the horse, and Lucy could see that his face was very stern.

"They say," she began, on finding that he was not inclined to speak,—"they say that women have a natural instinct which helps them to understand many things; and I think it must be true. Why can you not spare me the demand for reasons which I have not? If I were to take time, and consider it, and try to explain, it would be of no help to you: it would not change the fact. I suppose a man feels humiliated when this trouble comes upon him. He shows his heart, and there seems to be a claim upon the woman of his choice to show hers in return. The sense of injustice is worse than humiliation, Elwood. Though I cannot, cannot do otherwise, I shall always have the feeling that I have wronged you."

"O Lucy," he murmured, in a very sad, but not reproachful voice, "every word you say, in showing me that I must give you up, only makes it more impossible to me. And it *is* just impossible,—that's the end of the matter! I know how people talk about trials being sent us for our good, and its being the will of God, and all that. It's a trial, that's true: whether it's for my good or not, I shall learn after a while; but I can find out God's will only by trying the strength of my own. Don't be afeared, Lucy! I've no notion of saying or doing anything from this time on to disturb you, but *here* you are" (striking his breast with his clenched hand), "and here you will be when the day comes, as I feel that it must and *shall* come, to bring us together!"

She could see the glow of his face in the gathering dusk, as he turned towards her and offered his hand. How could she help taking it? If some pulse in her own betrayed the thrill of admiring recognition of the man's powerful and tender nature, which suddenly warmed her oppressed blood, she did not fear that he would draw courage from the token. She wished to speak, but found no words which, coming after his, would not have seemed either cold and unsympathetic, or too near the verge of the hope which she would gladly have crushed.

Elwood was silent for a while, and hardly appeared to be awaiting an answer. Meanwhile the road left the valley, climbing the shoulders of its enclosing hills, where the moist meadow fragrance was left behind, and dry, warm breezes, filled with the peculiar smell of the wheat-fields, blew over them. It was but a mile farther to the Corner, near which Lucy's parents resided.

"How came you three to go to Joseph's place this afternoon?" he asked. "Wasn't it a dodge of Miss Blessing's?"

"She proposed it,—partly in play, I think; and when she afterwards insisted on our going, there seemed to be no good reason for refusing."

"O, of course not," said Elwood; "but tell me now, honestly, Lucy, what do you make out of her?"

Lucy hesitated a moment. "She is a little willful in her ways, perhaps, but we mustn't judge too hastily. We have known her such a short time. Her manner is very amiable."

"I don't know about that," Elwood remarked. "It reminds me of one of her dresses,—so ruffled, and puckered, and stuck over with ribbons and things, that you can't rightly tell what the stuff is. I'd like to be sure whether she has an eye to Joseph."

"To *him*!" Lucy exclaimed.

"Him first and foremost! He's as innocent as a year-old baby. There isn't a better fellow living than Joseph Asten, but his bringing up has been fitter for a girl than a boy. He hasn't had his eye-teeth cut yet, and it's my opinion that she has."

"What do you mean by that?"

"No harm. Used to the world, as much as anything else. He don't know how to take people; he thinks th' outside color runs down to the core. So it does with him; but *I* can't see what that girl is, under her pleasant ways, and he won't guess that there's anything else of her. Between ourselves, Lucy,—you don't like her. I saw that when you came away, though you were kissing each other at the time."

"What a hypocrite I must be!" cried Lucy, rather fiercely.

"Not a bit of it. Women kiss as men shake hands. You don't go around, saying, 'Julia dear!' like Anna Warriner."

Lucy could not help laughing. "There," she said, "that's enough, Elwood! I'd rather you would think yourself in the right than to say anything more about her this evening."

She sighed wearily, not attempting to conceal her fatigue and depression.

"Well, well!" he replied; "I'll pester you no more with disagreeable subjects. There's the house, now, and you'll soon be rid of me. I won't tell you, Lucy, that if you ever want for friendly service, you must look to me,—because I'm afeared you won't feel free to do it; but you'll take all I can find to do without your asking."

Without waiting for an answer he drew up his horse at the gate of her home, handed her out, said "Good night!" and drove away.

Such a singular restlessness took possession of Joseph, after the departure of his guests, that the evening quiet of the farm became intolerable. He saddled his horse and set out for the village, readily inventing an errand which explained the ride to himself as well as to his aunt.

The regular movements of the animal did not banish the unquiet motions of his mind, but it relieved him by giving them a wider sweep and a more definite form. The man who walks is subject to the power of his Antæus of a body, moving forwards only by means of the weight which holds it to the earth. There is a clog upon all his thoughts, an ever-present sense of restriction and impotence. But when he is lifted above the soil, with the air under his foot-soles, swiftly moving without effort, his mind, a poising Mercury, mounts on winged heels. He feels the liberation of new and nimble powers; wider horizons stretch around his inward vision; obstacles are measured or overlooked; the brute strength under him charges his whole nature with a more vigorous electricity.

The fresh, warm, healthy vital force. which filled Joseph's body to the last embranchment of every nerve and vein—the hum of those multitudinous spirits of life, which, while building their glorious abode, march as if in triumphant procession through its secret passages, and summon all the fairest phantoms of sense to their completed chambers—constituted, far more than he suspected, an element of his disturbance. This was the strong pinion on which his mind and soul hung balanced, above the close atmosphere which he seemed to ride away from, as he rode. The great joy of human life filled and thrilled him; all possibilities of action and pleasure and emotion swam before his sight; all he had read or heard of individual careers in all ages, climates, and conditions of the race—dazzling pictures of the myriad-sided earth, to be won by whosoever dared arbitrarily to seize the freedom waiting for his grasp—floated through his brain.

Hitherto a conscience not born of his own nature,—a very fair and saintly-visaged jailer of thought, but a jailer none the less,—had kept strict guard over every outward movement of his mind, gently touching hope and desire and conjecture when they reached a certain line, and saying, "No; no farther: it is prohibited." But now, with one strong, involuntary throb, he found himself beyond the line, with all the ranges ever trodden by man stretching forward to a limitless horizon. He rose in his stirrups, threw out his arms, lifted his face towards the sky, and cried, "God! I see what I am!"

It was only a glimpse,—like that of a landscape struck in golden fire by lightning, from the darkness. "What is it," he mused, "that stands between me and this vision of life? Who built a wall of imaginary law around these needs, which are in themselves inexorable laws? The World, the Flesh, and the Devil, they say in warning. Bright, boundless world, my home, my play-ground, my battle-field, my kingdom to be conquered! And this body they tell me to despise,—this perishing house of clay, which is so intimately myself that its comfort and delight cheer me to the inmost soul: it is a dwelling fit for an angel to inhabit! Shall not its hungering senses all be fed? Who shall decide for me—if not myself —on their claims?—who can judge for me what strength requires to be exercised, what pleasure to be enjoyed, what growth to be forwarded? All around me, everywhere, are the means of gratification,—I have but to reach forth my hand and grasp; but a narrow cell, built ages ago, encloses me wherever I go!"

Such was the vague substance of his thoughts. It was the old struggle between life— primitive, untamed life, as the first man may have felt it—and its many masters: assertion and resistance, all the more fierce because so many influences laid their hands upon its forces. As he came back to his usual self, refreshed by this temporary escape, Joseph wondered whether other men shared the same longing and impatience; and this turned his musings into another channel. "Why do men so carefully conceal what is deepest and strongest in their natures? Why is so little of spiritual struggle and experience ever imparted? The convert publicly admits his sinful experience, and tries to explain the entrance of grace into his regenerated nature; the reformed drunkard seems to take a positive delight in making his former condition degraded and loathsome; but the opening of the individual life to the knowledge of power and passion and all the possibilities of the world is kept more secret than sin. Love is hidden as if it were a reproach; friendship watched, lest it express its warmth too frankly; joy and grief and doubt and anxiety repressed as much as possible. A great lid is shut down upon the human race. They must painfully stoop and creep, instead of standing erect with only God's heaven over their heads. I am lonely, but I know not how to cry for companionship; my words would not be understood, or, if they were, would not be answered. Only one gate is free to me,—that leading to the love of woman. There, at least, must be such an intense, intimate sympathy as shall make the reciprocal revelation of the lives possible!"

Full of this single certainty, which, the more he pondered upon it, seemed to be his nearest chance of help, Joseph rode slowly homewards. Rachel Miller, who had impatiently awaited his cowing, remarked the abstraction of his face, and attributed it to a very different cause. She was thereby wonderfully strengthened to make her communication in regard to the evening company; nevertheless, the subject was so slowly approached and so ambiguously alluded to, that Joseph could not immediately understand it.

"That is something! That is a step!" he said to himself; then turning towards her with a genuine satisfaction in his face, added: "Aunt, do you know that I have never really felt until now that I am the owner of this property? It will be more of a home to me after I have received the neighborhood as my guests. It has always controlled me, but now it must serve me."

He laughed in great good-humor, and Rachel Miller, in her heart, thanked Miss Julia Blessing.

5. HALLECK AND DRAKE

The exact moment of meeting between Halleck and Drake is practically mired in legends:

> Charles P. Clinch compared the two men and declared, "Drake was the handsomest man in New York." Halleck had finally "met a man after his own heart" whose poetical mind corresponded to his physical beauty. Accounts of the Halleck-Drake meeting in the spring of 1813 are varied but universally idealized. Speculating that it was a spectacular sunset or sudden rainbow that ignited discussion about Thomas Campbell between the two young men, biographical materials have variously placed their initial introduction at the Ugly Club, via a formal intervention by James DeKay on another occasion, through an accidental encounter during a summer afternoon on a muddy pathway in New York's Battery Park, or in a mixture of circumstance on a boat excursion on New York Bay. Perhaps Drake overheard Halleck wish aloud "to lounge upon the rainbow" and read Campbell "and from that moment took Halleck to his heart." Or maybe the wish was Drake's, the response Halleck's who "grasped [Drake's] arm cordially, and said 'We must know each other.'" The rainbow may have been seen during a September ride down the bay, or possibly when the two men first went sailing together. Perhaps DeKay simply invited both friends over in that winter of 1812-1813. Adkins wrote that whatever the account of the meeting, Halleck "discovered in the sensitive and poetic Drake the true companion for which he longed." Both early and late critics described the immediate friendship, which had been delayed nearly three years by the War of 1812, as "romantic." Others called the connection "sweet companionship," adding that the poets aspired to a "romantic youthful friendship, not common."[22]

James Grant Wilson in 1869's *Life and Letters of Fitz-Greene Halleck* went so far as to say that from the hour of their meeting, "the two poets maintained a friendship only severed by death."[62] That sounds like marriage vows, but it was a marriage that ultimately came between them, even before Drake's young death:

> The two men appeared inseparable, but their flowering intimacy was to be interrupted by Drake's marriage. If the military had kept Halleck from Drake's side, this more powerful force would surely separate them and turn Halleck's hot hopes cold by summer's end. He was defeated again by his most constant adversary, marriage. Within a year of finding Drake, Halleck had to give him away.
>
> [...]
>
> [T]he reality of the Drakes' honeymoon jarred Halleck from the emotional shock of the wedding and [Walter] Franklin's suicide [see <u>Chapter 20: Contemporary Camerados</u>]. A honeymoon was meant to seal the legal agreement with sexual consummation.
>
> Maria was perhaps less surprised at the diagnosis than Halleck who "really thought myself the last man in the world for such a disorder." He relates the condition poignantly: "a total loss of appetite, or rather—for I know not what to call it—a total indifference whether I ate or drank any thing or not; a sort of ague all day and a violent fever all night, have continued to worry me and wear me out. I felt no pain or feebleness. I was not miserable, but my mind felt a kind of indifference toward every thing like emotion, whether of pain or pleasure; in short I was a complete stoic, and could have received the most unexpected delight without a smile, and heard some unlooked-for stroke of ruin without a pang. . . . I then fancied all was over with me." Halleck provides a textbook account of an eating disorder, insomnia, and the mental numbness symptomatic of a clinical depression, but his prognosis is good [...] Apparently unaware of the connection between Drake's absence and his hypochondria, he nevertheless ties the events up in one neat stroke: "I really am better this week, and intend to recover. The Drakes . . . have returned."[22]

While feeling abandoned, Halleck wrote of the marriage to Maria, trying to excuse it:

> New York, Ja. 29, 1817 [...] He was poor, as poets, of course, always are, and offered himself a sacrifice at the shrine of Hymen to shun the "pains and penalties" of poverty. I officiated as groomsman, though much against my will. His wife is good-natured, and loves him to distraction. He is, perhaps, the handsomest man in New York—a face like an angel, a form like an Apollo, and, as I well knew that his person was the true index of his mind, I felt myself during the ceremony as committing a crime in aiding and assisting in such a sacrifice.[62]

The misery was not completely one-sided:

> Drake's "Life and Love" expressed his disillusionment with marriage and mourned a past friendship. The "delusive sleep" of romance is shaken off: "Love is an empty name, / That leads to pain and woe, / And friendship's holy flame, / Hath ceased to glow." The narrator envies Halleck's "visioned eye" in an allusion to *Fanny*: "Ne'er may his fairy dream, / Vanish like mine." [...] Beginning in December 1818, Drake took extraordinary measures to close the gap with Halleck. In January 1819, he made the consolatory gesture of christening his only child, a daughter, Halleck. Named for her father's best friend, Janet Halleck Drake was nicknamed Joe after her father, and Drake referred to Janet as his son.[22]

Drake's efforts to win back his jilted friend worked, and after their reconciliation, they began writing and publishing satirical poems under the pseudonyms "Croaker" and "Croaker Jr.," which made them the talk of the town and blissfully happy:

> Halleck gushed about the unexpected and dramatic results of his reconciliation with Drake in a letter to his sister written on April Fool's Day in 1819. He rhetorically asked, "Can you believe it, Maria, Joe and I have become authors?" Halleck believed that he was winning Drake back from [his wife] Sarah Eckford and basked in the victory. He divulged Drake's response to receiving Croaker proof sheets indiscriminately: Drake "laid his cheek down upon the lines he had written, and, looking at me with beaming eyes, said, 'O, Halleck, isn't this happiness!'"[22]

VI

IN THE GARDEN

RACHEL MILLER was not a woman to do a thing by halves. As soon as the question was settled, she gave her heart and mind to the necessary preparations. There might have been a little surprise in some quarters, when the fact became known in the neighborhood through Joseph's invitation, but no expression of it reached the Asten place. Mrs. Warriner, Anna's mother, called to inquire if she could be of service, and also to suggest, indirectly, *her* plan of entertaining company. Rachel detected the latter purpose, and was a little more acquiescent than could have been justified to her own conscience, seeing that at the very moment when she was listening with much apparent meekness, she was mentally occupied with plans for outdoing Mrs. Warriner. Moreover, the Rev. Mr. Chaffinch had graciously signified his willingness to be present, and the stamp of strictest orthodoxy was thus set upon the entertainment. She was both assured and stimulated, as the time drew near, and even surprised Joseph by saying: "If I was better acquainted with Miss Blessing, she might help me a good deal in fixing everything just as it should be. There are times, it seems, when it's an advantage to know something of the world."

"I'll ask her!" Joseph exclaimed.

"You! And a mess you'd make of it, very likely; men think they've only to agree to invite a company, and that's all! There's a hundred things to be thought of that women must look to; you couldn't even understand 'em. As for speaking to her,—she's one of the *invites*, and it would never do in the world."

Joseph said no more, but he silently determined to ask Miss Blessing on her arrival; there would still be time. She, with her wonderful instinct, her power of accommodating people to each other, and the influence which she had already acquired with his aunt, would certainly see at a glance how the current was setting, and guide it in the proper direction.

But, as the day drew near, he grew so restless and uneasy that there seemed nothing better to do than to ride over to Warriner's in the hope of catching a moment's conference with her, in advance of the occasion.

He was entirely fortunate. Anna was apparently very busy with household duties, and after the first greetings left him alone with Miss Blessing. He had anticipated a little difficulty in making his message known, and was therefore much relieved when she said: "Now, Mr. Asten, I see by your face that you have something particular to say. It's about to-morrow night, isn't it? You must let me help you, if I can, because I am afraid I have been, without exactly intending it, the cause of so much trouble to you and your aunt."

Joseph opened his heart at once. All that he had meant to say came easily and naturally to his lips, because Miss Blessing seemed to feel and understand the situation, and met him half-way in her bright, cheerful acquiescence. Almost before he knew it, he had made her acquainted with what had been said and done at home. How easily she solved the absurd doubts and difficulties which had so unnecessarily tormented him! How clearly, through her fine female instinct, she grasped little peculiarities of his aunt's nature, which he, after years of close companionship, had failed to define! Miss Rachel, she said, was both shy and inexperienced, and it was only the struggle to conceal these conscious defects which made her seem—not unamiable, exactly, but irregular in her manner. Her age, and her character in the neighborhood, did not permit her to appear incompetent to any emergency; it was a very natural pride, and must be treated very delicately and tenderly.

Would Joseph trust the matter entirely to her, Miss Blessing? It was a great deal to ask, she knew, comparative stranger as she was; but she believed that a woman, when her nature had not been distorted by the conventionalities of life, had a natural talent for smoothing difficulties, and removing obstacles for others. Her friends had told her that she possessed this power; and it was a great happiness to think so. In the present case, she was *sure* she should make no mistake. She would endeavor not to seem to suggest anything, but merely to assist in such a way that Miss Rachel would of herself see what else was necessary to be done.

"Now," she remarked, in conclusion, "this sounds like vanity in me; but I really hope it is not. You must remember that in the city we are obliged to know all the little social arts,—and artifices; I am afraid. It is not always to our credit, but then, the heart *may* be kept fresh and uncorrupted."

She sighed, and cast down her eyes. Joseph felt the increasing charm of a nature so frank and so trustful, constantly luring to the surface the maiden secrets of his own. The confidence already established between them was wholly delightful, because their sense of reciprocity increased as it deepened. He felt so free to speak that he could not measure the fitness of his words, but exclaimed, without a pause for thought:—

"Tell me, Miss Julia, did you not suggest this party to Aunt Rachel?"

"Don't give me too much credit!" she answered; "it was talked about, and I couldn't help saying Ay. I longed so much to see you—all—again before I go away."

"And Lucy Henderson objected to it?"

"Lucy, I think, wanted to save your aunt trouble. Perhaps she did not guess that the real objection was inexperience, and not want of will to entertain company. And very likely she helped to bring it about, by seeming to oppose it; so you must not be angry with

Lucy,—promise me!"

She looked at him with an irresistibly entreating expression, and extended her hand, which he seized so warmly as to give her pain. But she returned the pressure, and there was a moment's silence, which Anna Warriner interrupted at the right time.

The next day, on the Asten farm, all the preparations were quietly and successfully made long in advance of the first arrivals. The Rev. Mr. Chaffinch and a few other specially chosen guests made their appearance in the afternoon. To Joseph's surprise, the Warriners and Miss Blessing speedily joined them. It was, in reality, a private arrangement which his aunt had made, in order to secure at the start the very assistance which he had been plotting to render. One half the secret of the ease and harmony which he felt was established was thus unknown to him. He looked for hints or indications of management on Miss Blessing's part, but saw none. The two women, meeting each other half-way, needed no words in order to understand each other, and Miss Rachel, gradually made secure in her part of hostess, experienced a most unaccustomed sense of triumph.

At the supper-table Mr. Chaffinch asked a blessing with fervor; a great, balmy dish of chickens stewed in cream was smoking before his nostrils, and his fourth cup of tea made Rachel Miller supremely happy. The meal was honored in silence, as is the case where there is much to eat and a proper desire and capacity to do it; only towards its close were the tongues of the guests loosened, and content made them cheerful.

"You have entertained us almost too sumptuously, Miss Miller," said the clergyman. "And now let us go out on the portico, and welcome the young people as they arrive."

"I need hardly ask you, then, Mr. Chaffinch," said she, "whether you think it right for them to come together in this way."

"Decidedly!" he answered; "that is, so long as their conversation is modest and becoming. It is easy for the vanities of the world to slip in, but we must watch,—we must watch."

Rachel Miller took a seat near him, beholding the gates of perfect enjoyment opened to her mind. Dress, the opera, the race-course, literature, stocks, politics, have their fascination for so many several classes of the human race; but to her there was nothing on this earth so delightful as to be told of temptation and backsliding and sin, and to feel that she was still secure. The fact that there was always danger added a zest to the feeling; she gave herself credit for a vigilance which had really not been exercised.

The older guests moved their chairs nearer, and listened, forgetting the sweetness of sunset which lay upon the hills down the valley. Anna Warriner laid her arm around Miss Chaffinch's waist, and drew her towards the mown field beyond the barn; and presently, by a natural chance, as it seemed, Joseph found himself beside Miss Blessing, at the bottom of the lawn.

All the western hills were covered with one cool, broad shadow. A rich orange flush touched the tops of the woods to the eastward, and brightened as the sky above them deepened into the violet-gray of coming dusk. The moist, delicious freshness which filled the bed of the valley slowly crept up the branching glen, and already tempered the air about them. Now and then a bird chirped happily from a neighboring bush, or the low of cattle was heard from the pasture-fields.

"Ah!" sighed Miss Blessing, "this is too sweet to last: I must learn to do without it."

She looked at him swiftly, and then glanced away. It seemed that there were tears in her eyes.

Joseph was about to speak, but she laid her hand on his arm. "Hush!" she said; "let us wait until the light has faded."

The glow had withdrawn to the summits of the distant hills, fringing them with a thin, wonderful radiance. But it was only momentary. The next moment it broke on the irregular topmost boughs, and then disappeared, as if blown out by a breeze which came with the sudden lifting of the sky. She turned away in silence, and they walked slowly together towards the house. At the garden gate she paused.

"That superb avenue of box!" she exclaimed; "I must see it again, if only to say farewell."

They entered the garden, and in a moment the dense green wall, breathing an odor seductive to heart and senses, had hidden them from the sight—and almost from the hearing—of the guests on the portico. Looking down through the southern opening of the avenue, they seemed alone in the evening valley.

Joseph's heart was beating fast and strong; he was conscious of a wild fear, so interfused with pleasure, that it was impossible to separate the sensations. Miss Blessing's hand was on his arm, and he fancied that it trembled.

"If life were as beautiful and peaceful as this," she whispered, at last, "we should not need to seek for truth and—and—sympathy: we should find them everywhere."

"Do you not think they are to be found?" he asked.

"O, in how few hearts! I can say it to *you*, and you will not misunderstand me. Until lately I was satisfied with life as I found it: I thought it meant diversion, and dress, and gossip, and common daily duties, but now —now I see that it is the union of kindred souls!"

She clasped both her hands over his arm as she spoke, and leaned slightly towards him, as if drawing away from the dreary, homeless world. Joseph felt all that the action expressed, and answered in an unsteady voice:—

"And yet—with a nature like yours—you must surely find them."

She shook her head sadly, and answered: "Ah, a woman cannot seek. I never thought I should be able to say—to any human being—that I have sought, or waited for recognition. I do not know why I should say it now. I try to be myself—my true self—with all persons; but it seems impossible: my nature shrinks from some and is drawn towards others. Why is this? What is the mystery that surrounds us?"

"Do you believe," Joseph asked, "that two souls may be so united that they shall dare to surrender all knowledge of themselves to each other, as we do, helplessly, before God?"

"O," she murmured, "it is my dream! I thought I was alone in cherishing it! Can it ever be realized?"

Joseph's brain grew hot: the release he had invoked sprang to life and urged him forward. Words came to his lips, he knew not how.

"If it is my dream and yours,—if we both have come to the faith and the hope we find in no others, and which alone will satisfy our lives, is it not a sign that the dream is over and the reality has begun?"

She hid her face in her hands. "Do not tempt me with what I had given up, unless you can teach me to believe again?" she cried.

"I do not tempt you," he answered breathlessly. "I tempt myself. I believe."

She turned suddenly, laid a hand upon his shoulder, lifted her face and looked into his eyes with an expression of passionate eagerness and joy. All her attitude breathed of the pause of the wave that only seems to hesitate an instant before throwing itself upon the waiting strand. Joseph had no defense, knew of none, dreamed of none. The pale-brown eyes, now dark, deep, and almost tearful, drew him with irresistible force: the sense of his own shy reticent self was lost, dissolved in the strength of an instinct which possessed him body and soul,—which bent him nearer to the slight form, which stretched his arms to answer its appeal, and left him, after one dizzy moment, with Miss Blessing's head upon his breast.

"I should like to die now," she murmured: "I never can be so happy again."

"No, no," said he, bending over her; "live for me!"

She raised herself, and kissed him again and again, and this frank, almost childlike betrayal of her heart seemed to claim from Joseph the full surrender of his own. He returned her caresses with equal warmth, and the twilight deepened around them as they stood, still half-embracing.

"Can I make you happy, Joseph?"

"Julia, I am already happier than I ever thought it possible to be."

With a sudden impulse she drew away from him. "Joseph!" she whispered, "will you always bear in mind what a cold, selfish, worldly life mine has been? You do not know me; you cannot understand the school in which I have been taught. I tell you, now, that I have had to learn cunning and artifice and equivocation. I am dark beside a nature so pure and good as yours! If you must ever learn to hate me, begin now! Take back your love: I have lived so long without the love of a noble human heart, that I can live so to the end!"

She again covered her face with her hands, and her frame shrank, as if dreading a mortal blow. But Joseph caught her back to his breast, touched and even humiliated by such sharp self-accusation. Presently she looked up: her eyes were wet, and she said, with a pitiful smile:—

"I believe you *do* love me."

"And I will not give you up," said Joseph, "though you should be full of evil as I am, myself."

She laughed, and patted his cheek: all her frank, bright, winning manner returned at once. Then commenced those reciprocal expressions of bliss, which are so inexhaustibly fresh to lovers, so endlessly monotonous to everybody else; and Joseph, lost to time, place, and circumstance, would have prolonged them far into the night, but for Miss Julia's returning self-possession.

"I hear wheels," she warned; "the evening guests are coming, and they will expect you to receive them, Joseph. And your dear, good old aunt will be looking for *me*. O, the world, the world! We must give ourselves up to it, and be as if we had never found each other. I shall be wild unless you set me an example of self-control. Let me look at you once,—one full, precious, perfect look, to carry in my heart through the evening!"

Then they looked in each other's faces; and looking was not enough; and their lips, without the use of words, said the temporary farewell. While Joseph hurried across the bottom of the lawn, to meet the stream of approaching guests which filled the lane, Miss Julia, at the top of the garden, plucked amaranth leaves for a wreath which would look well upon her dark hair, and sang, in a voice loud enough to be heard from the portico:—

> "Ever be happy, light as thou art,
> Pride of the pirate's heart!"

Everybody who had been invited—and, quite a number who had not been, availing themselves of the easy habits of country society—came to the Asten farm that evening. Joseph, as host, seemed at times a little confused and flurried, but his face bloomed, his blue eyes sparkled, and even his nearest acquaintances were astonished at the courage and cordiality with which he performed his duties. The presence of Mr. Chaffinch kept the gayety of the company within decorous bounds; perhaps the number of detached groups appeared to form too many separate circles, or atmospheres of talk, but they easily dissolved, or gave to and took from each other. Rachel Miller was not inclined to act the part of a moral detective in the house which she managed; she saw nothing which the strictest sense of propriety could condemn.

Early in the evening, Joseph met Lucy Henderson in the hall. He could not see the graver change in her face; he only noticed that her manner was not so quietly attractive as usual. Yet on meeting her eyes he felt the absurd blood rushing to his cheeks and brow, and his tongue hesitated and stammered. This want of self-possession vexed him; he could not account for it; and he cut short the interview by moving abruptly away.

Lucy half turned, and looked after him, with an expression rather of surprise than of pain. As she did so she felt that there was an eye upon her, and by a strong effort entered the room without encountering the face of Elwood Withers.

When the company broke up, Miss Blessing, who was obliged to leave with the Warriners, found an opportunity to whisper to Joseph: "Come *soon!*" There was a long, fervent clasp of hands under her shawl, and then the carriage drove away. He could not see how the hand was transferred to that of Anna Warriner, which received from it a squeeze conveying an entire narrative to that young lady's mind.

Joseph's duties to his many guests prevented him from seeing much of Elwood during the evening; but, when the last were preparing to leave, he turned to the latter, conscious of a tenderer feeling of friendship than he had ever before felt, and begged him to stay for the night. Elwood held up the lantern, with which he had been examining the harness of a carriage that had just rolled away, and let its light fall upon Joseph's face.

"Do you really mean it?" he then asked.

"I don't understand you, Elwood."

"Perhaps I don't understand myself." But the next moment he laughed, and then added, in his usual tone: "Never mind; I'll stay."

They occupied the same room; and neither seemed inclined to sleep. After the company had been discussed, in a way which both felt to be awkward and mechanical, Elwood said: "Do you know anything more about love, by this time?"

Joseph was silent, debating with himself whether he should confide the wonderful secret. Elwood suddenly rose up in his bed, leaned forward, and whispered: "I see,—you need not answer. But tell me this one thing: is it Lucy Henderson?"

"No; O, no!"

"Does she know of it? Your face told some sort of a tale when you met her to-night."

"Not to her,—surely not to her!" Joseph exclaimed.

"I hope not," Elwood quietly said: "I love her."

With a bound Joseph crossed the room and sat down on the edge of his friend's bed. "Elwood!" he cried; "and you are happy, too! O, now I can tell you all,—it is Julia Blessing!"

"Ha! ha!" Elwood laughed,—a short, bitter laugh, which seemed to signify anything but happiness. "Forgive me, Joseph!" he presently added, "but there's a deal of difference between a mitten and a ring. You will have one and I have the other. I did think for a little while that you stood between Lucy and me; but I suppose disappointment makes men fools."

Something in Joseph's breast seemed to stop the warm flood of his feelings. He could only stammer, after a long pause: "But I am not in your way."

"So I see,—and perhaps nobody is, except myself. We won't talk of this any more; there's many a roundabout road that comes out into the straight one at last. But you,—I can't understand the thing at all. How did she—did you come to love her?"

"I don't know; I hardly guessed it until this evening."

"Then, Joseph, go slowly, and feel your way. I'm not the one to advise, after what has happened to me; but maybe I know a little more of womankind than you. It's best to have a longer acquaintance than yours has been; a fellow can't always tell a sudden fancy from a love that has the grip of death."

"Now I might turn your own words against you, Elwood, for you tried to tell me what love is."

"I did; and before I knew the half. But come, Joseph: promise me that you won't let Miss Blessing know how much you feel until—"

"Elwood," Joseph breathlessly interrupted, "she knows it now! We were together this evening."

Elwood fell back on the pillow with a groan. "I'm a poor friend to you," he said: "I want to wish you joy, but I can't,—not to-night. The way things are fixed in this world stumps me, out and out. Nothing fits as it ought, and if I didn't take my head in my own hands and hold it towards the light by main force, I'd only see blackness, and death, and hell."

Joseph stole back to his bed, and lay there silently. There was a subtle chill in the heart of his happiness, which all the remembered glow of that tender scene in the garden could not thaw.

6. THE DEATH OF DRAKE

SHORTLY AFTER THEIR "Croaker" success, Joseph Rodman Drake came down with consumption:

> In spring 1820 [...] Halleck realized just how dire Drake's condition had become. Halleck stayed close by for the rest of that summer and watched over Drake's bedside "with more than a brother's love." Assuming a wife's position, Halleck "smoothed [Drake's] pillow" and appears to have tended to Drake by himself at the end. Halleck stayed up through the entire night. Exhausted and helplessly alone, he ended his vigil just minutes before dawn when Drake gasped his last breath of air. Halleck's bedside remonstrations against death were not enough to save Drake, who died on September 21, 1820, at the age of twenty-five. In that moment of agony, Halleck's own faith in life ended. He was only thirty.[22]

From the death of Drake comes Halleck's most well-known and highly regarded poem:

"On the Death of Joseph R. Drake" is prefaced by William Wordsworth's searing words: "The Good die first, / And they, whose hearts are dry as summer dust, / Burn to the socket." Poe observed that Halleck's elegy for Drake was a rewriting of Wordsworth's "She Dwelt Among the Untrodden Ways." Richard Stoddard provided a second sexually curious literary cross-reference by claiming that Halleck's elegy imitated Wordsworth's poems to women and may have intended a clever sexual pun on living among "untrodden ways." The poem begins with Halleck's most famous quatrain:

> Green be the turf above thee,
> Friend of my better days!
> None knew thee but to love thee,
> Nor named thee but to praise.

Drake's gravestone was inscribed with these lines. When the Bronx graveyard became Joseph Rodman Drake Park in 1915, a bronze tablet bearing more lines was added to the original epitaph in marble. The addition conveyed Halleck's utter anguish:

> Tears fell, when thou wert dying,
> From eyes unused to weep,
> And long where thou art lying,
> Will tears the cold turf steep.

The poem ends by expressing Halleck's sense of displacement at the funeral, where he could not assume the role of widower:

> And I, who woke each morrow
> To clasp thy hand in mine,
> Who shared thy joy and sorrow,
> Whose weal and woe were thine:

> It should be mine to braid it [the wreath]
> Around thy faded brow,
> But I've in vain essayed it,
> And feel I can not now.

> While memory bids me weep thee,
> Nor thoughts nor words are free,
> The grief is fixed too deeply
> That mourns a man like thee.

The first of these last three stanzas implies a physical consummation with Drake and refutes the limits that society imposes on male friendship. To no avail, the narrator has "essayed" his claim to the widow's rights, which "should be mine." This vain effort yields confusion as the speaker consciously controls his restricted tears. Not free to share his thoughts or feelings in public, his pain becomes as fixed as a statue.

The narrator, who once felt Drake's "weal and woe," feels nothing now. The emotional numbness that Halleck felt during Drake's honeymoon recurs even as he claims a love for Drake superior to that of Drake's wife, who is alone entitled to the privilege of dressing her husband's corpse. Like modern survivors of gay partners with AIDS, Halleck's own needs are subordinate to the legal and social prerogative of the American nuclear family.

[... Edgar Allan] Poe preferred the poem above all others by Halleck, as did others. One critic deemed four lines of the elegy "worth all of [Halleck's]

Byronizing," while another commented on its display of "the tender regret that is usually the slow result of time."[22]

For the full poem see [A.5]. For Poe's criticisms on Halleck, see [A.7] and Chapter 7: Poe and Taylor on Halleck. For more on Halleck's 'Byronizing,' see Chapter 8: Halleck and the Death of Byron.

It is interesting to note that Chapter 7 from *Marius the Epicurean* is included in *Pages Passed from Hand to Hand*, alongside passages from *Joseph and His Friend*, solely to point out this form of care-taking:

> [I]nsofar as it is one of the earliest—if not the earliest—(proto-)homosexual 'nursing scenes' in literature: a scene that, with the advent of AIDS, has become a fixture of homosexual fiction. Among other such notable pre-AIDS scenes: Wilde's *De Profundis*, when Lord Alfred Douglas abandons him in Brighton, and writes, '*When you are not on your pedestal you are not interesting. The next time you are ill I will go away at once*'; and Forster's *Maurice*, where Clive Durham has a relapse of influenza at the Hallses the night he tells Maurice of his determination to travel to Greece.[30]

The same the same impulse is seen surrounding Walt Whitman's work as a hospital helper during the Civil War:

> Whitman's narrator kisses an enemy's corpse in "Reconciliation," [see Chapter 11: Leaves of Grass] and, as Halleck recalled Perth Amboy's platoon kissing ["I delight in recollecting" the account that had "long been a favorite of mine," wrote Halleck, of Amboy and "his comrades" and the "*as one man*' kiss of affection with which they greeted kneeling their 'Mother Land' [being] the only instance of kissing by *Platoons* within my memory." Halleck's deliberate emphases on "as one man" and "platoons" suggest that the soldiers may have been kissing not only American soil but one another.], Whitman praises homoerotic relations in the army: "The chief encircles their necks with his arm and kisses." Whitman responded to war by nursing strangers; Halleck responded to the threat of death by nursing Drake.[22]

At least one of "the boys" Whitman nursed he became quite enamored of (see Chapter 25: The Civil War), the common thread being that between Halleck and so many others, if they are refused the role of lovers, they become mothers in a sense, care-takers and nurses. Byron displayed this behavior as well (see Chapter 8: Halleck and the Death of Byron).

Halleck himself would die in 1867, at the age of seventy-seven, living with his sister. His last words to her were, "Marie, hand me my pantaloons, if you please,"[22] and when she turned around with them she found he had died without another sound.

VII

THE BLESSING FAMILY

JOSEPH'S SECRET WAS not suspected by any of the company. Elwood's manner towards him next morning was warmer and kinder than ever; the chill of the past night had been forgotten, and the betrothal, which then almost seemed like a fetter upon his future, now gave him a sense of freedom and strength. He would have gone to Warriner's at once, but for the fear lest he should betray himself. Miss Blessing was to return to the city in three days more, and a single farewell call might be made with propriety; so he controlled his impatience and allowed another day to intervene.

When, at last, the hour of meeting came, Anna Warriner proved herself an efficient ally. Circumstances were against her, yet she secured the lovers a few minutes in which they could hold each other's hands, and repeat their mutual delight, with an exquisite sense of liberty in doing so. Miss Blessing suggested that nothing should be said until she had acquainted her parents with the engagement; there might be some natural difficulties to overcome; it was so unexpected, and the idea of losing her would possibly be unwelcome, at first. She would write in a few days, and then Joseph must come and make the acquaintance of her family.

"*Then*," she added, "I shall have no fear. When they have once seen you all difficulties will vanish. There will be no trouble with ma and sister Clementina; but pa is sometimes a little peculiar, on account of his connections. There! don't look so serious, all at once; it is *my* duty, you know, to secure you a loving reception. You must try to feel already that you have two homes, as I do."

Joseph waited very anxiously for the promised letter, and in ten days it came; it was brief, but satisfactory. "Would you believe it, dear Joseph," she commenced, "pa makes no difficulty! he only requires some assurances which you can very easily furnish. Ma, on the other hand, don't like the idea of giving me up. I can hardly say it without seeming to praise myself; but Clementina never took very kindly to housekeeping and managing, and even if I were only indifferent in those branches, I should be missed. It really went to my heart when ma met me at the door, and cried out, 'Now I shall have a little rest!' You may imagine how hard it was to tell her. But she is a dear, good mother, and I know she will be *so* happy to find a son in you—as she certainly will. Come, soon,—soon! They are all anxious to know you."

The city was not so distant as to make a trip thither an unusual event for the young farmers of the neighborhood. Joseph had frequently gone there for a day in the interest of his sales of stock and grain, and he found no difficulty in inventing a plausible reason for the journey. The train at the nearest railway station transported him in two or three hours to the commencement of the miles of hot, dusty, rattling, pavements, and left him free to seek for the brick nest within which his love was sheltered.

Yet now, so near the point whence his new life was to commence, a singular unrest took possession of him. He distinctly felt the presence of two forces, acting against each other with nearly equal power, but without neutralizing their disturbing influence. He was developing faster than he guessed, yet, to a nature like his, the last knowledge that comes is the knowledge of self. Some occult instinct already whispered that his life thenceforth would be stronger, more independent, but also more disturbed; and this was what he had believed was wanting. If the consciousness of loving and being loved were not quite the same in experience as it had seemed to his ignorant fancy, it was yet a positive happiness, and wedlock would therefore be its unbroken continuance. Julia had prepared for his introduction into her family; he must learn to accept her parents and sister as his own; and now the hour and the opportunity were at hand.

What was it, then, that struck upon his breast almost like a physical pressure, and mysteriously resisted his errand? When he reached the cross-street, in which, many squares to the northward, the house was to be found, he halted for some minutes, and then, instead of turning, kept directly onward toward the river. The sight of the water, the gliding sails, the lusty life and labor along the piers, suddenly refreshed him. Men were tramping up and down the gangways of the clipper-ships; derricks were slowly swinging over the sides the bales and boxes which had been brought up from the holds; drays were clattering to and fro: wherever he turned he saw a picture of strength, courage, reality, solid work. The men that went and came took life simply as a succession of facts, and if these did not fit smoothly into each other, they either gave themselves no trouble about the rough edges, or drove them out of sight with a few sturdy blows. What Lucy Henderson had said about going to school was recalled to Joseph's mind. Here was a class where he would be apt to stand at the foot for many days. Would any of those strapping forms comprehend the disturbance of his mind?—they would probably advise him to go to the nearest apothecary-shop and purchase a few blue-pills. The longer he watched them, the more he felt the contagion of their unimaginative, face-to-face grapple with life; the manly element in him, checked so long, began to push a vigorous shoot towards the light.

"It is only the old cowardice, after all," he thought. "I am still shrinking from the encounter with new faces! A lover, soon to be a husband, and still so much of a green youth! It will never do. I must learn to handle my duty as that stevedore handles a barrel,—take hold with both hands, push and trundle and guide, till the weight becomes a mere plaything. There!—he starts a fresh one,—now for mine!"

Therewith he turned about, walked sternly back to the cross-street, and entered it without pausing at the corner. It was still a long walk; and the street, with its uniform brick houses, with white shutters, green interior blinds, and white marble steps, grew more silent and monotonous. There was a mixed odor of salt-fish, molasses, and decaying oranges at every corner; dark wenches lowered the nozzles of their jetting hose as he passed, and girls in draggled calico frocks turned to look at him from the entrances of gloomy tunnels leading into the back yards. A man with something in a cart uttered from time to time a piercing unintelligible cry; barefooted youngsters swore over their marbles on the sidewalk; and, at rare intervals, a marvelous moving fabric of silks and colors and glosses floated past him. But he paused for none of these. His heart beat faster, and the strange resistance seemed to increase with the increasing numbers of houses, now rapidly approaching The One—then it came!

There was an entire block of narrow three-storied dwellings, with crowded windows and flat roofs. If Joseph had been familiar with the city, he would have recognized the air of cheap gentility which exhaled from them, and which said, as plainly as if the words had been painted on their fronts, "Here we keep up appearances on a very small capital." He noticed nothing, however, except the marble steps and the front doors, all of which were alike to him until he came upon a brass plate inscribed "B. Blessing." As he looked up a mass of dark curls vanished with a start from the window. The door suddenly opened before he could touch the bell-pull, and two hands upon his own drew him into the diminutive hall.

The door instantly closed again, but softly: then two arms were flung around his neck, and his willing lips received a subdued kiss. "Hush!" she said; "it is delightful that you have arrived, though we didn't expect you so immediately. Come into the drawing-room, and let us have a minute together before I call ma."

She tripped lightly before him, and they were presently seated side by side, on the sofa.

"What could have brought me to the window just at that moment?" she whispered; "it must have been presentiment."

Joseph's face brightened with pleasure. "And I was long on the way," he answered. "What will you think of me, Julia? I was a little afraid."

"I know you were, Joseph," she said. "It is only the cold, insensible hearts that are never agitated."

Their eyes met, and he remarked, for the first time, their peculiar pale-brown, almost tawny clearness. The next instant her long lashes slowly fell and half concealed them; she drew away slightly from him, and said: "I should like to be beautiful, for your sake; I never cared about it before."

Without giving him time to reply, she rose and moved towards the door, then looked back, smiled, and disappeared.

Joseph, left alone, also rose and walked softly up and down the room. To his eyes it seemed an elegant, if rather chilly apartment. It was long and narrow, with a small, delusive fireplace of white marble (intended only for hot air) in the middle, a carpet of many glaring colors on the floor, and a paper brilliant with lilac-bunches on the walls. There was a centre-table, with some lukewarm literature cooling itself on the marble top; an *étagère*, with a few nondescript cups and flagons, and a cottage piano, on which lay several sheets of music by Verdi and Balfe. The furniture, not very abundant, was swathed in a nankeen summer dress. There were two pictures on the walls, portraits of a gentleman and lady, and when once Joseph had caught the fixed stare of their lusterless eyes, he found it difficult to turn away. The imperfect light which came through the bowed window shutters revealed a florid, puffy-faced young man, whose head was held up by a high black satin stock. He was leaning against a fluted pillar, apparently constructed of putty, behind which fell a superb crimson curtain, lifted up at one corner to disclose a patch of stormy sky. The long locks, tucked in at the temples, the carefully-delineated whiskers, and the huge signet-ring on the second finger of the one exposed hand, indicated that a certain "position" in society was either possessed or claimed of right by the painted person. Joseph could hardly doubt that this was a representation of "B. Blessing," as he appeared twenty or thirty years before.

He turned to the other picture. The lady was slender, and meant to be graceful, her head being inclined so that the curls on the left side rolled in studied disorder upon her shoulder. Her face was thin and long, with well-marked and not unpleasant features. There was rather too positive a bloom upon her cheeks, and the fixed smile on the narrow mouth scarcely harmonized with the hard, serious stare of the eyes. She was royally attired in purple, and her bare white arm—much more plumply rounded than her face would have given reason to suspect—hung with a listless grace over the end of a sofa.

Joseph looked from one face to the other with a curious interest, which the painted eyes seemed also to reflect, as they followed him. They were strangers, out of a different sphere of life, yet they must become, nay, were already, a part of his own! The lady scrutinized him closely, in spite of her smile; but the indifference of the gentleman, blandly satisfied with himself, seemed less assuring to his prospects.

Footsteps in the hall interrupted his revery, and he had barely time to slip into his seat when the door opened and Julia entered, followed by the original of one of the portraits. He recognized her, although the curls had disappeared, the dark hair was sprinkled with gray, and deep lines about the mouth and eyes gave them an expression of care and discontent. In one respect she differed from her daughter: her eyes were gray.

She bent her head with a stately air as Joseph rose, walked past Julia, and extended her hand, with the words,—

"Mr. Asten, I am glad to see you. Pray be seated."

When all had taken seats, she resumed: "Excuse me if I begin by asking a question. You must consider that I have only known you through Julia, and her description could not, under the circumstances, be very clear. What is your age?"

"I shall be twenty-three next birthday," Joseph replied.

"Indeed! I am happy to hear it. You do not look more than nineteen. I have reason to dread *very* youthful attachments and am therefore reassured to know that you are fully a man and competent to test your feelings. I trust that you *have* so tested them. Again I say, excuse me if the question seems to imply a want of confidence. A mother's anxiety, you know—"

Julia clasped her hands and bent down her head.

"I am quite sure of myself," Joseph said, "and would try to make you as sure, if I knew how to do it."

"If you were one of us,—of the city, I mean,—I should be able to judge more promptly. It is many years since I have been outside of our own select circle, and I am therefore not so competent as once to judge of men in general. While I will never, without the most sufficient reason, influence my daughters in their choice, it is my duty to tell you that Julia is exceedingly susceptible on the side of her affections. A wound *there* would be incurable to her. We are alike in that; I know her nature through my own."

Julia hid her face upon her mother's shoulder: Joseph was moved, and vainly racked his brain for some form of assurance which might remove the maternal anxiety. "There," said Mrs. Blessing; "we will say no more about it now. Go and bring your sister!"

"There are some other points, Mr. Asten," she continued, "which have no doubt already occurred to your mind. Mr. Blessing will consult with you in relation to them. I make it a rule never to trespass upon his field of duty. As you were not positively expected to-day, he went to the Custom House as usual; but it will soon be time for him to return. Official labors, you understand, cannot be postponed. If you have ever served in a government capacity, you will appreciate his position. I have sometimes wished that we had not become identified with political life; but, on the other hand, there are compensations."

Joseph, impressed more by Mrs. Blessing's important manner than the words she uttered, could only say, "I beg that my visit may not interfere in any way with Mr. Blessing's duties."

"Unfortunately," she replied, "they cannot be postponed. His advice is more required by the Collector than his special official services. But, as I said, he will confer with you in regard to the future of our little girl. I call her so, Mr. Asten, because she is the youngest, and I can hardly yet realize that she is old enough to leave me. Yes: the youngest, and the first to go. Had it been Clementina, I should have been better prepared for the change. But a mother should always be ready to sacrifice herself, where the happiness of a child is at stake."

Mrs. Blessing gently pressed a small handkerchief to the corner of each eye, then heaved a sigh, and resumed her usual calm dignity of manner. The door opened, and Julia re-entered, followed by her sister.

"This is Miss Blessing," said the mother.

The young lady bowed very formally, and therewith would have finished her greeting, but Joseph had already risen and extended his hand. She thereupon gave him the tips of four limp fingers, which he attempted to grasp and then let go.

Clementina was nearly a head taller than her sister, and amply proportioned. She had a small, petulant mouth, small gray eyes, a low, narrow forehead, and light brown hair. Her eyelids and cheeks had the same puffy character as her father's, in his portrait on the wall; yet there was a bloom and brilliancy about her complexion which suggested beauty.

A faint expression of curiosity passed over her face, on meeting Joseph, but she uttered no word of welcome. He looked at Julia, whose manner was suddenly subdued, and was quick enough to perceive a rivalry between the sisters. The stolidity of Clementina's countenance indicated that indifference which is more offensive than enmity. He disliked her from the first moment.

Julia kept modestly silent, and the conversation, in spite of her mother's capacity to carry it on, did not flourish. Clementina spoke only in monosyllables, which she let fall from time to time with a silver sweetness which startled Joseph, it seemed so at variance with her face and manner. He felt very much relieved when, after more than one significant glance had been exchanged with her mother, the two arose and left the room. At the door Mrs. Blessing said: "Of course you will stay and take a family tea with us, Mr. Asten. I will order it to be earlier served, as you are probably not accustomed to our city hours."

Julia looked up brightly after the door had closed, and exclaimed: "Now! when ma says *that*, you may be satisfied. Her housekeeping is like the laws of the Medes and Persians. She probably seemed rather formal to you, and it is true that a certain amount of form has become natural to her; but it always gives way when she is strongly moved. Pa is to come yet, but I am sure you will get on very well with him; men always grow acquainted in a little while. I'm afraid that Clementina did not impress you very—very genially; she is, I may confess it to you, a little peculiar."

"She is very quiet," said Joseph, "and very unlike you."

"Every one notices that. And we seem to be unlike in character, as much so as if there were no relationship between us. But I must say for Clementina, that she is above personal likings and dislikings; she looks at people abstractly. You are only a future brother-in-law to her, and I don't believe she can tell whether your hair is black or the beautiful golden brown that it is."

Joseph smiled, not ill-pleased with Julia's delicate flattery. "I am all the more delighted," he said, "that you are different. I should not like you, Julia, to consider me an abstraction."

"You are very real, Joseph, and very individual," she answered, with one of her loveliest smiles.

Not ten minutes afterwards, Julia, whose eyes and ears were keenly on the alert, notwithstanding her gay, unrestrained talk, heard the click of a latch-key. She sprang up, laid her forefinger on her lips, gave Joseph a swift, significant glance, and darted into the hall. A sound of whispering followed, and there was no mistaking the deep, hoarse murmur of one of the voices.

Mr. Blessing, without the fluted pillar and the crimson curtain, was less formidable than Joseph had anticipated. The years had added to his body and taken away from his hair; yet his face, since high stocks were no longer in fashion, had lost its rigid lift, and expressed the chronic cordiality of a popular politician. There was a redness about the rims of his eyes, and a fullness of the under lid, which also denoted political habits. However, despite wrinkles, redness, and a general roughening and coarsening of the features, the resemblance to the portrait was still strong; and Joseph, feeling as if the presentation had already been made, offered his hand as soon as Mr. Blessing entered the room.

"Very happy to see you, Mr. Asten," said the latter. "An unexpected pleasure, sir."

He removed the glove from his left hand, pulled down his coat and vest, felt the tie of his cravat, twitched at his pantaloons, ran his fingers through his straggling gray locks, and then threw himself into a chair, exclaiming: "After business, pleasure, sir! My duties are over for the day. Mrs. Blessing probably informed you of my official capacity; but you can have no conception of the vigilance required to prevent evasion of the revenue laws. We are the country's watch-dogs, sir."

"I can understand," Joseph said, "that an official position carries with it much responsibility."

"Quite right, sir, and without adequate remuneration. Figuratively speaking, we handle millions, and we are paid by dimes. Were it not for the consciousness of serving and saving for the nation—but I will not pursue the subject. When we have become better acquainted, you can judge for yourself whether preferment always follows capacity. Our present business is to establish a mutual understanding,— as we say in politics, to prepare a platform,—and I think you will agree with me that the circumstances of the case require frank dealing, as between man and man."

"Certainly!" Joseph answered; "I only ask that, although I am a stranger to you, you will accept my word until you have the means of verifying it."

"I may safely do that with you, sir. My associations—duties, I may say—compel me to know many persons with whom it would *not* be safe. We will forget the disparity of age and experience between us. I can hardly ask you to imagine yourself placed in my situation, but perhaps we can make the case quite as clear if I state to you, without reserve, what *I* should be ready to do, if our present positions were reversed: Julia, will you look after the tea?"

"Yes, pa," said she, and slipped out of the drawing-room.

"If I were a young man from the country, and had won the affections of a young lady of—well, I may say it to you—of an old family, whose parents were ignorant of my descent, means, and future prospects in life, I should consider it my first duty to enlighten those parents upon all these points. I should reflect that the lady must be removed from their sphere to mine; that, while the attachment was, in itself, vitally important to her and to me, those parents would naturally desire to compare the two spheres, and assure themselves that their daughter would lose no material advantages by the transfer. You catch my meaning?"

"I came here," said Joseph, "with the single intention of satisfying you—at least, I came hoping that I shall be able to do so—in regard to myself. It will be easy for you to test my statements."

"Very well. We will begin, then, with the subject of Family. Understand me, I mention this solely because, in our old communities, Family is the stamp of Character. An established name represents personal qualities, virtues. It is indifferent to me whether my original ancestor was a De Belsain (though beauty and health have always been family characteristics); but it *is* important that he transmitted certain traits which—which others, perhaps, can better describe. The name of Asten is not usual; it has, in fact, rather a distinguished sound; but I am not acquainted with its derivation."

Joseph restrained a temptation to smile, and replied: "My great-grandfather came from England more than a hundred years ago: that is all I positively know. I have heard it said that the family was originally Danish."

"You must look into the matter, sir: a good pedigree is a bond for good behavior. The Danes, I have been told, were of the same blood as the Normans. But we will let that pass. Julia informs me you are the owner of a handsome farm, yet I am so ignorant of values in the country,—and my official duties oblige me to measure property by such a different standard,—that, really, unless you could make the farm evident to me in figures, I—"

He paused, but Joseph was quite ready with the desired intelligence. "I have two hundred acres," he said, "and a moderate valuation of the place would be a hundred and thirty dollars an acre. There is a mortgage of five thousand dollars on the place, the term of which has not yet expired; but I have nearly an equal amount invested, so that the farm fairly represents what I own."

"H'm," mused Mr. Blessing, thrusting his thumbs into the arm-holes of his waistcoat," that is not a great deal here in the city, but I dare say it is a handsome competence in the country. It doubtless represents a certain annual income!"

"It is a very comfortable home, in the first place," said Joseph; "the farm ought to yield, after supplying nearly all the wants of a family, an annual return of a thousand to fifteen hundred dollars, according to the season."

"Twenty-six thousand dollars!—and five per cent!" Mr. Blessing exclaimed. "If you had the farm in money, and knew how to operate with it, you might pocket ten—fifteen—twenty per cent. Many a man, with less than that to set him afloat, has become a millionaire in five years' time. But it takes pluck and experience, sir!"

"More of both than I can lay claim to," Joseph remarked; "but what there is of my income is certain. If Julia were not so fond of the country, and already so familiar with our ways, I might hesitate to offer her such a plain, quiet home, but—"

"O, I know!" Mr. Blessing interrupted. "We have heard of nothing but cows and spring-houses and willow-trees since she came back. I hope, for your sake, it may last; for I see that you are determined to suit each other. I have no inclination to act the obdurate parent. You have met me like a man, sir: here's my hand; I feel sure that, as my son-in-law, you will keep up the reputation of the family!"

7. POE AND TAYLOR ON HALLECK

Several years after the publication of *Joseph and His Friend*, Bayard Taylor wrote a paper entitled "Fitz-Greene Halleck" that was published in *The North American Review* in 1877. In it he speaks of Halleck and Drake, their friendship and the impact of their work:

> His friendship with Joseph Rodman Drake, which began about the close of the year 1813, and continued until the latter's death in 1820, was the spell which awoke his true powers, and gave him a swift and delightful fame. Drake was a born singer,—almost an *improvvisatore*,—whose imaginative faculty, although of rather flimsy texture, was always rapid, joyous, and infectious. He wrote in the ardor of his first conceptions, and seems to have rarely retouched or elaborated his work. Halleck, who, I suspect, composed more slowly, resembled Drake in the unstudied ease, grace, and sweetness of his lines. Before "The Croakers" and "Fanny," there was no American verse that was not either pompously solemn or coarsely farcical: hence this new fountain, wilfully casting forth its pure sparkling, capricious jets of song, was welcomer to the public than poetry can ever be again. If to readers of this day the sentiment may now and then appear conventional, or the humor dull, or the political allusions obscure, it must be remembered that Halleck was first read by a generation which had never before been refreshed by sentiment and humor and cleverness of allusion. The light abandon of his stanzas was as new as their racy local flavor. The mock American Muse seemed suddenly to have come down from her clattering *cothurni*, thrown away her grim Minerva-mask, and shown herself in young and breathing beauty, with the elastic step of a mountain maiden.[50]

For Bayard Taylor's dedication of the Halleck Monument at Guilford, Connecticut, July 8th, 1869, "Fitz-Greene Halleck," see [A.6].

Edgar Allan Poe too wrote a critical piece on Halleck's work, and for the full essay see [A.7]. Halleck's letters also reveal that Poe was one of the younger poets who received substantial assistance from Halleck. In answer to the following appeal, Halleck loaned Poe one hundred dollars, "a sum which the gifted but unfortunate young singer, like many others of the rhyming fraternity, who received aid from the generous Halleck, was never able to repay"[62]:

> New York, Dec. 1, 1845. My dear Mr. Halleck: On the part of one or two persons who are much imbittered against me, there is a deliberate attempt now being made to involve me in ruin, by destroying The Broadway Journal. I could easily frustrate them, but for my total want of money, and of the necessary time in which to procure it: the knowledge of this has given my enemies the opportunities desired. In this emergency without leisure to think whether I am acting improperly I venture to appeal to you. The sum I need is $100. If you could loan me for three months any portion of it, I will not be ungrateful. Truly yours, Edgar A. Poe.[62]

From another essay a Mr. Rufus W. Griswold requested from Poe, he had this to say about Halleck's work after the death of Drake (keeping in mind that before Drake's death, their collaborations on the "Croaker" satires never received compensation, and were done more as a labor of love). Poe wrote of Halleck:

> His usual pursuits have been commercial; but, for many years, he has been the principal superintendent of John Jacob Astor's monetary and general business affairs. Of late days, consequently, he has nearly abandoned the Muses much to the regret of his friends and to the neglect of his reputation. He is now in the maturity of his powers, and might redeem America from an imputation to which she has been too frequently subjected—the imputation of inability to produce a *great* poem. A few brief translations, at rare intervals, and chiefly from vapid German or Spanish originals, are now all that remind us of 'Marco Bozzaris,' or that, as a poet, its author still lives.[62]

It so happens that Horace Traubel (see <u>Chapter 14: Bucke, Traubel, and The Multitudes of Whitman</u>) once asked Walt Whitman if he liked Edgar Allan Poe. Whitman had this to say about Poe:

> "At the start, for many years, not: but three or four years ago I got to reading him again, reading and liking, until at last—yes, now—I feel almost convinced that he is a star of considerable magnitude, if not a sun, in the literary firmament. Poe was morbid, shadowy, lugubrious—seemed to suggest dark nights, horrors, spectralities—I could not originally stomach him at all. . . . I was a young man of about thirty, living in New York, when 'The Raven'

appeared—created its stir: everybody was excited about it—every reading body: somehow it did not enthuse me." [...] Poor Poe! Poor Poe! who shall not say he did not have failings, defects, weaknesses: serious weaknesses— grave, oh! so grave!—from which he suffered? [...] I have seen Poe—met him: he impressed me very favorably: was dark, quiet, handsome—Southern from top to toe: languid, tired out, it is true, but altogether ingratiating.

Note: On November 17, 1875, Whitman was the only literary figure present for the reburial of Poe and dedication of a Poe memorial in Baltimore.[39]

VIII

A CONSULTATION

THE FAMILY TEA was served in a small dining-room in the rear. Mr. Blessing, who had become more and more cordial with Joseph after formally accepting him, led the way thither, and managed to convey a rapid signal to his wife before the family took their seats at the table. Joseph was the only one who did not perceive the silent communication of intelligence; but its consequences were such as to make him speedily feel at ease in the Blessing mansion. Even Clementina relented sufficiently to say, in her most silvery tones, "May I offer you the butter, Mr. Asten?"

The table, it is true, was very unlike the substantial suppers of the country. There was a variety of diminutive dishes, containing slices so delicate that they mocked rather than excited the appetite; yet Julia (of course it was she!) had managed to give the repast an air of elegance which was at least agreeable to a kindred sense. Joseph took the little cup, the thin tea, the five drops of milk, and the fragment of sugar, without asking himself whether the beverage were palatable: he divided a leaf-like piece of flesh and consumed several wafers of bread, blissfully unconscious whether his stomach were satisfied. He felt that he had been received into The Family. Mr. Blessing was magnificently bland, Mrs. Blessing was maternally interested, Clementina recognized his existence, and Julia,—he needed but one look at her sparkling eyes, her softly flushed cheeks, her bewitching excitement of manner, to guess the relief of her heart. He forgot the vague distress which had preceded his coming, and the embarrassment of his first reception, in the knowledge that Julia was so happy, and through the acquiescence of her parents, in his love.

It was settled that he should pass the night there. Mrs. Blessing would take no denial; he must now consider their house as his home. She would also call him "Joseph," but not now,—not until she was entitled to name him "son." It had come suddenly upon her, but it was her duty to be glad, and in a little while she would become accustomed to the change.

All this was so simply and cordially said, that Joseph quite warmed to the stately woman, and unconsciously decided to accept his fortune, whatever features it might wear. Until the one important event, at least; after that it would be in his own hands—and Julia's.

After tea, two or three hours passed away rather slowly. Mr. Blessing sat in the pit of a back yard and smoked until dusk; then the family collected in the "drawing-room," and there was a little music, and a variety of gossip, with occasional pauses of silence, until Mrs. Blessing said: "Perhaps you had better show Mr. Asten to his room, Mr. Blessing. We may have already passed over his accustomed hour for retiring. If so, I know he will excuse us; we shall soon become familiar with each other's habits."

When Mr. Blessing returned, he first opened the rear window, drew an arm-chair near it, took off his coat, seated himself, and lit another cigar. His wife closed the front shutters, slipped the night-bolts of the door, and then seated herself beside him. Julia whirled around on her music-stool to face the coming consultation, and Clementina gracefully posed herself in the nearest corner of the sofa.

"How do you like him, Eliza?" Mr. Blessing asked, after several silent, luxurious whiffs.

"He is handsome, and seems amiable, but younger than I expected. Are you sure of his—his feelings, Julia?"

"O ma!" Julia exclaimed; "what a question! I can only judge them by my own."

Clementina curled her lip in a singular fashion, but said nothing.

"It seems like losing Julia entirely," Mrs. Blessing resumed. "I don't know how she will be able to retain her place in our circle, unless they spend a part of the winter in the city, and whether he has means enough—"

She paused, and looked inquisitively at her husband.

"You always look at the establishment," said he, "and never consider the chances. Marriage is a deal, a throw, a sort of kite-flying, in fact (except in *our* case, my dear), and, after all I've learned of our future son-in-law, I must say that Julia hasn't a bad hand."

"I knew you'd like him, pa!" cried the delighted Julia. Mr. Blessing looked at her steadily a moment, and then winked; but she took no notice of it.

"There is another thing," said his wife. "If the wedding comes off this fall, we have but two months to prepare; and how will you manage about the—the money? We can save afterwards, to be sure, but there will be an immediate and fearful expense. I've thought, perhaps, that a simple and private ceremony,—married in travelling-dress, you know, just before the train leaves, and no cards,—it is sometimes done in the highest circles."

"It won't do!" exclaimed Mar. Blessing, waving his right hand. "Julia's husband must have an opportunity of learning our standing in society. I will invite the Collector, and the Surveyor, and the Appraiser. The money *must* be raised. I should be willing to pawn—"

He looked around the room, inspecting the well-worn carpet, the nankeen-covered chairs, the old piano, and finally the two pictures.

"—Your portrait, my dear; but, unless it were a Stuart, I couldn't get ten dollars on it. We must take your set of diamonds, and Julia's rubies, and Clementina's pearls."

He leaned back, and laughed with great glee. The ladies became rigid and grave.

"It is wicked, Benjamin," Mrs. Blessing severely remarked, "to jest over our troubles at such a time as this. I see nothing else to do, but to inform Mr. Asten, frankly, of our condition. He is yet too young, I think, to be repelled by poverty."

"Ma, it would break my heart," said Julia. "I could not bear to be humiliated in his eyes."

"Decidedly the best thing to do," warbled Clementina, speaking for the first time.

"That's the way with women,—flying from one extreme to the other. If you can't have white, you turn around and say there's no other color than black. When all devices are exhausted, a man of pluck and character goes to work and constructs a new one. Upon my soul, I don't know where the money is to come from; but give me ten days, and Julia shall have her white satin. Now, girls, you had better go to bed."

Mr. Blessing smoked silently until the sound of his daughters' footsteps had ceased on the stairs; then, bringing down his hand emphatically upon his thigh, he exclaimed, "By Jove, Eliza, if I were as sharp as that girl, I'd have had the Collectorship before this!"

"What do you mean? She seems to be strongly attached to him."

"O, no doubt! But she has a wonderful talent for reading character. The young fellow is pretty green wood still; what he'll season into depends on her. Honest as the day,— there's nothing like a country life for that. But it's a pity that such a fund for operations should lie idle; he has a nest-egg that might hatch out millions!"

"I hope, Benjamin, that after all your unfortunate experience—"

"Pray don't lament in advance, and especially now, when a bit of luck comes to us. Julia has done well, and I'll trust her to improve her opportunities. Besides, this will help Clementina's chances; where there is one marriage in a family, there is generally another. Poor girl! she has waited a long while. At thirty-three, the market gets v-e-r-y flat."

"And yet Julia is thirty," said Mrs. Blessing; "and Clementina's complexion and manners have been considered superior."

"There's just her mistake. A better copy of Mrs. Halibut's airs and attitudes was never produced, and it was all very well so long as Mrs. Halibut gave the tone to society; but since she went to Europe, and Mrs. Bass has somehow crept into her place, Clementina is quite—I may say—obsolete. I don't object to her complexion, because that is a standing fashion, but she is expected to be chatty, and witty, and instead of that she stands about like a Venus of Milo. She looks like me, and she can't lack intelligence and tact. Why couldn't she unbend a little more to Asten, whether she likes him or not?"

"You know I never seemed to manage Clementina," his wife replied; "if she were to dispute my opinion sometime, I might, perhaps, gain a little influence over her: but she won't enter into a discussion."

"Mrs. Halibut's way. It was new, then, and, with her husband's money to back it, her 'grace' and 'composure' and 'serenity' carried all before her. Give me fifty thousand a year, and I'll put Clementina in the same place! But, come,—to the main question. I suppose we shall need five hundred dollars!"

"Three hundred, I think, will be ample," said Mrs. Blessing.

"Three or five, it's as hard to raise one sum as the other. I'll try for five, and if I have luck with the two hundred over—small, careful operations, you know, which always succeed—I may have the whole amount on hand, long before it's due."

Mrs. Blessing smiled in a melancholy, hopeless way, and the consultation came to an end.

When Joseph was left alone in his chamber, he felt no inclination to sleep. He sat at the open window, and looked down into the dim, melancholy street, the solitude of which was broken about once every quarter of an hour by a forlorn pedestrian, who approached through gloom and lamplight, was foreshortened to his hat, and then lengthened away on the other side. The new acquaintances he had just made remained all the more vividly in his thoughts from their nearness; he was still within their atmosphere. They were unlike any persons he knew, and therefore he felt that he might do them injustice by a hasty estimate of their character. Clementina, however, was excluded from this charitable resolution. Concentrating his dislike on her, he found that her parents had received him with as much consideration as a total stranger could expect. Moreover, whatever they might be, Julia was the same here, in her own home, as when she was a guest in the country. As playful, as winning, and as natural; and he began to suspect that her present life was not congenial to such a nature. If so, her happiness was all the more assured by their union.

This thought led him into a pictured labyrinth of anticipation, in which his mind wandered with delight. He was so absorbed in planning the new household, that he did not hear the sisters entering the rear room on the same floor, which was only separated by a thin partition from his own.

"White satin!" he suddenly heard Clementina say: "of course I shall have the same. It will become *me* better than you."

"I should think you might be satisfied with a light silk," Julia said; "the expenses will be very heavy."

"We'll see," Clementina answered shortly, pacing up and down the room.

After a long pause, he heard Julia's voice again. "Never mind," she said, "I shall soon be out of your way."

"I wonder how much he knows about you!" Clementina exclaimed. "Your arts were new there, and you played an easy game." Here she lowered her voice, and Joseph only distinguished a detached word now and then. He rose, indignant at this unsisterly assault, and wishing to hear no more; but it seemed that the movement was not noticed, for Julia replied, in smothered, excited tones, with some remark about "complexion."

"Well, there is one thing," Clementina continued,—"one thing you will keep very secret, and that is your birthday. Are you going to tell him that you are—"

Joseph had seized the back of a chair, and with a sudden impulse tilted it and let it fall on the floor. Then he walked to the window, closed it, and prepared to go to rest,—all with more noise than was habitual with him. There were whispers and hushed movements in the next room, but not another audible word was spoken. Before sleeping he came to the conclusion that he was more than Julia's lover: he was her deliverer. The idea was not unwelcome: it gave a new value and significance to his life.

However curious Julia might have been to discover how much he had overheard, she made no effort to ascertain the fact. She met him next morning with a sweet unconsciousness of what she had endured, which convinced him that such painful scenes must have been frequent, or she could not have forgotten so easily. His greeting to Clementina was brief and cold, but she did not seem to notice it in the least.

It was decided, before he left, that the wedding should take place in October.

8. HALLECK AND THE DEATH OF BYRON

On Byron's death, Halleck was even more overcome than the young Bayard Taylor who carved "Byron is dead!" on a rock:

> In almost the only eyewitness account of his ever having wept, Halleck's old friend, Mrs. John Rush, saw that he was "quite overcome, and could not restrain his tears." As "a great admirer of the poet [Byron], if not of the man," Halleck "walked up and down the drawing-room wringing his hands, saying, with brief pauses between each remark: 'What a terrible loss to literature!—and 'Byron dead, and I did not see him!'" For a moment, Halleck regretted his European solitude [when after Drake's death he had many introductions to literary figures in Europe but could only bear to travel alone]. Rush's account conveyed alarm. Her stoic friend was crying over a stranger. He paced, wrung his hands, stammered, and wailed that "poor Byron" could "be taken away at thirty-six!" Halleck's poetry rarely aspired to the dramatic pitch of his real-life reaction to the loss of Byron.
>
> Halleck's distress was exaggerated by a profound connection with the British poet turned sexual outlaw. Both men were survivors of younger men whom they could not satisfactorily eulogize despite multiple attempts. Byron's love for John Edlestone, who was born in the same year as Halleck but died at age twenty-one, was expressed and reexpressed in a poetic series that conveyed Byron's same-sex desire as well as his tragic loss. Halleck's love for Drake was not returned in kind, and similarly, in the last year of his life, Byron was rumored to have suffered unrequited love for his Greek page, Lukas Chalandrutsanos. Byron's attempt to personally nurse Chalandrutsanos for fear of the boy's death shortly before dying himself stands out as one of the few selfless acts of Byron's existence. Chalandrutsanos survived his benefactor, and a Greek commemorative statue depicts Byron "expiring in the arms of his Greek page." Halleck [...] denied the rights of a widow, related to Byron's exile as well as his role as nurse. Both scoffed at matrimonial oaths: Byron by

breaking them and Halleck by refusing to take them. Byron's marriage lasted less than one year before Byron's wife was granted divorce; she had hoped to "marry a poet and reform a rake" who turned out to be "a Caligula." Halleck said that he had "lost on Byron's death a brother," and Drake, a love object also referred to by Halleck as a brother, was inseparably meshed with Byron, an icon of sexual and literary liberation.[22]

Halleck had his say on Byron in the end, as Taylor eventually had on Halleck, which (in John W.M. Hallock's opinion) served to set an important part of each man's life free after his death: "As Halleck had done for Byron, Taylor liberated Halleck's sexual content from the metaphor."[22] That occasion:

Halleck was contracted to edit anonymously the first complete edition of Lord Byron's work and letters; it appeared in 1832. Halleck's text contained many suppressed letters and boldly incorporated bisexual aspects of Byron's life. As in the case of his coauthorship with Drake, Halleck's allegiance to Byron was simultaneously artistic and erotic. [...] Halleck included some of the materials [in his *Works of Lord Byron*] that Byron's sibling, Thomas Moore, and John Murray found too distasteful to publish. Byron's recollection of greeting male friends with kisses and of painted Turkish boys ("the prettiest little animals I ever saw") are faithfully preserved. Halleck includes Byron's enthusiasm for Turkish pederasty but omits the actual word "sodomy" from one of Byron's letters: "Was [Perry] ever in a Turkish bath— that marble paradise of sherbet and * * [sodomy]?" Byron's familiarity with homosexual allusion is evidenced by letters to Murray on nude wrestling and by his observation that historical and literary men often had emotional propensities "natural in an effeminate character."[22]

Byron is not the only one to take very careful note of homosexuality and pederasty abroad. Bayard Taylor's poem "To A Persian Boy"[A.1] does the same, and even more so T.E. Lawrence in the next century, known also as Lawrence of Arabia, whose dedication of the book *Seven Pillars of Wisdom* about his role in the Arab Revolt against the Ottoman Turks (1916-1918) is to an S.A., thought to be Selim Ahmed (called Dahoum or "little dark one"), his young companion in the desert. Dahoum came to live with Lawrence in an expedition hut in Carchemish, where Lawrence had the young man pose naked for a sculpture that he carved out of soft limestone and set on display outside of the hut.[63] In the introduction to *Seven Pillars of Wisdom*, Lawrence writes:

The Arab was by nature continent; and the use of universal marriage had nearly abolished irregular courses in his tribes. The public women of the rare settlements we encountered in our months of wandering would have been nothing to our numbers, even had their raddled meat been palatable to a man of healthy parts. In horror of such sordid commerce our youths began indifferently to slake one another's few needs in their own clean bodies—a cold convenience that, by comparison, seemed sexless and even pure. Later, some began to justify this sterile process, and swore that friends quivering together in the yielding sand with intimate hot limbs in supreme embrace, found there hidden in the darkness a sensual co-efficient of the mental passion which was welding our souls and spirits in one flaming effort. Several, thirsting to punish appetites they could not wholly prevent, took a savage pride in degrading the body, and offered themselves fiercely in any habit which promised physical pain or filth.[29]

Lawrence, upon his return to England, was known to hire men to whip and beat him under the ruse of an elaborate story about it being punishment required by an uncle who did not exist[61], a predilection he either brought with him to the desert or came home with after his experiences in Arabia. One experience he reports in *Seven Pillars of Wisdom* is of a flogging and sexual assault upon himself from soldiers in Deraa, the truth of which is often questioned by scholars. As it was in life, when it comes to suspicion of homosexuality in literature, Roger Austen points out that the young, the uneducated, and the foreign were more likely to get you a social pass:

> It was also all the more acceptable if the attractive male was a member of one of the more picturesque darker (Polynesian, Indian, Algerian) or more passionate, impulsive (French) races or one of the lower class (Whitman's workmen). When, however, a sexual attraction was suggested between two white gentleman behind closed doors of a drawing room, fresh air naturalness often gave way to hothouse unnaturalness and produced the decadent atmosphere that characterized Oscar Wilde's *The Picture of Dorian Gray* and Jean Lorrian's *Monsier de Phocas*, a 1901 novel full of depraved artists, circus acrobats, duchesses addicted to morphine, and pimps.[1]

Returning to Byron, Walt Whitman had an occasion to remark upon him as well:

> Byron has enough fire to burn forever. Byron deserves one great point to be made for him—this point, namely—that his alleged wickedness, queernesses are no more than the doctor's enumeration of diseases. The whole spirit of the persecution of Byron is the spirit of the town police—just as the spirit of the obscenity hunter anywhere (in mails and whatnot)—the spirit that will ignore all the gigantic evils—steal a way down to the shore—lay low—pull in a lot of little naked boys, there to take a bath—snake 'em in! It well pictures for me what is too commonly called the greatness and majesty of the law.[39]

IX

JOSEPH AND HIS FRIEND

The train moved slowly along through the straggling and shabby suburbs, increasing its speed as the city melted gradually into the country; and Joseph, after a vain attempt to fix his mind upon one of the volumes he had procured for his slender library at home, leaned back in his seat and took note of his fellow-travellers. Since he began to approach the usual destiny of men, they had a new interest for him. Hitherto he had looked upon strange faces very much as on a strange language, without a thought of interpreting them but now their hieroglyphics seemed to suggest a meaning. The figures around him were so many sitting, silent histories, so many locked-up records of struggle, loss, gain, and all the other forces which give shape and color to human life. Most of them were strangers to each other, and as reticent (in their railway conventionality) as himself; yet, he reflected, the whole range of passion, pleasure, and suffering was probably illustrated in that collection of existences. His own troublesome individuality grew fainter, so much of it seemed to be merged in the common experience of men.

There was the portly gentleman of fifty, still ruddy and full of unwasted force. The keenness and coolness of his eyes, the few firmly marked lines on his face, and the color and hardness of his lips, proclaimed to everybody: "I am bold, shrewd, successful in business, scrupulous in the performance of my religious duties (on the Sabbath), voting with my party, and not likely to be fooled by any kind of sentimental nonsense." The thin, not very well-dressed man beside him, with the irregular features and uncertain expression, announced as clearly, to any who could read: "I am weak, like others, but I never consciously did any harm. I just manage to get along in the world, but if I only had a chance, I might make something better of myself." The fresh, healthy fellow, in whose lap a child was sleeping, while his wife nursed a younger one,—the man with ample mouth, large nostrils, and the hands of a mechanic,—also told his story: "On the whole, I find life a comfortable thing. I don't know much about it, but I take it as it comes, and never worry over what I can't understand."

The faces of the younger men, however, were not so easy to decipher. On them life was only beginning its plastic task, and it required an older eye to detect the delicate touches of awakening passions and hopes. But Joseph consoled himself with the thought that his own secret was as little to be discovered as any they might have. If they were still ignorant of the sweet experience of love, he was already their superior; if they were sharers in it, though strangers, they were near to him. Had he not left the foot of the class, after all?

All at once his eye was attracted by a new face, three or four seats from his own. The stranger had shifted his position, so that he was no longer seen in profile. He was apparently a few years older than Joseph, but still bright with all the charm of early manhood. His fair complexion was bronzed from exposure, and his hands, graceful without being effeminate, were not those of the idle gentleman. His hair, golden in tint, thrust its short locks as it pleased about a smooth, frank forehead; the eyes were dark gray, and the mouth, partly hidden by a mustache, at once firm and full. He was moderately handsome, yet it was not of that which Joseph thought; he felt that there was more of developed character and a richer past history expressed in those features than in any other face there. He felt sure—and smiled at himself, notwithstanding, for the impression—that at least some of his own doubts and difficulties had found their solution in the stranger's nature. The more he studied the face, the more he was conscious of its attraction, and his instinct of reliance, though utterly without grounds, justified itself to his mind in some mysterious way.

It was not long before the unknown felt his gaze, and, turning slowly in his seat, answered it. Joseph dropped his eyes in some confusion, but not until he had caught the full, warm, intense expression of those that met them. He fancied that he read in them, in that momentary flash, what he had never before found in the eyes of strangers,—a simple, human interest, above curiosity and above mistrust. The usual reply to such a gaze is an unconscious defiance: the unknown nature is on its guard: but the look which seems to answer, "We are men, let us know each other!" is, alas! too rare in this world.

While Joseph was fighting the irresistible temptation to look again, there was a sudden thud of the car-wheels. Many of the passengers started from their seats, only to be thrown into them again by a quick succession of violent jolts. Joseph saw the stranger springing towards the bell-rope; then he and all others seemed to be whirling over each other; there was a crash, a horrible grinding and splintering sound, and the end of all was a shock, in which his consciousness left him before he could guess its violence.

After a while, out of some blank, haunted by a single lost, wandering sense of existence, he began to awaken slowly to life. Flames were still dancing in his eyeballs, and waters and whirlwinds roaring in his ears; but it was only a passive sensation, without the will to know more. Then he felt himself partly lifted and his head supported, and presently a soft warmth fell upon the region of his heart. There were noises all about him, but he did not listen to them; his effort to regain his consciousness fixed itself on that point alone, and grew stronger as the warmth calmed the confusion of his nerves.

"Dip this in water!" said a voice, and the hand (as he now knew it to be) was removed from his heart.

Something cold came over his forehead, and at the same time warm drops fell upon his cheek.

"Look out for yourself: your head is cut!" exclaimed another voice.

"Only a scratch. Take the handkerchief out of my pocket and tie it up; but first ask yon gentleman for his flask!"

Joseph opened his eyes, knew the face that bent over his, and then closed them again. Gentle and strong hands raised him, a flask was set to his lips, and he drank mechanically, but a full sense of life followed the draught. He looked wistfully in the stranger's face.

"Wait a moment," said the latter; "I must feel your bones before you try to move. Arms and legs all right,—impossible to tell about the ribs. There! now put your arm around my neck, and lean on me as much as you like, while I lift you."

Joseph did as he was bidden, but he was still weak and giddy, and after a few steps, they both sat down together upon a bank. The splintered car lay near them upside down; the passengers had been extricated from it, and were now busy in aiding the few who were injured. The train had stopped and was waiting on the track above. Some were very pale and grave, feeling that Death had touched without taking them; but the greater part were concerned only about the delay to the train.

"How did it happen?" asked Joseph: "where was I? how did you find me?"

"The usual story,—a broken rail," said the stranger. "I had just caught the rope when the car went over, and was swung off my feet so luckily that I somehow escaped the hardest shock. I don't think I lost my senses for a moment. When we came to the bottom you were lying just before me; I thought you dead until I felt your heart. It is a severe shock, but I hope nothing more."

"But you,—are you not badly hurt?"

The stranger pushed up the handkerchief which was tied around his head, felt his temple, and said: "It must have been one of the splinters; I know nothing about it. But there is no harm in a little blood-letting except"—he added, smiling—"except the spots on your face."

By this time the other injured passengers had been conveyed to the train; the whistle sounded a warning of departure.

"I think we can get up the embankment now," said the stranger. "You must let me take care of you still: I am travelling alone."

When they were seated side by side, and Joseph leaned his head back on the supporting arm, while the train moved away with them, he felt that a new power, a new support, had come to his life. The face upon which he looked was no longer strange; the hand which had rested on his heart was warm with kindred blood. Involuntarily he extended his own; it was taken and held, and the dark-gray, courageous eyes turned to him with a silent assurance which he felt needed no words.

"It is a rough introduction," he then said: "my name is Philip Held. I was on my way to Oakland Station; but if you are going farther—"

"Why, that is my station also!" Joseph exclaimed, giving his name in return.

"Then we should have probably met, sooner or later, in any case. I am bound for the forge and furnace at Coventry, which is for sale. If the company who employ me decide to buy it,—according to the report I shall make,—the works will be placed in my charge."

"It is but six miles from my farm," said Joseph, "and the road up the valley is the most beautiful in our neighborhood. I hope you can make a favorable report."

"It is only too much to my own interest to do so. I have been mining and geologizing in Nevada and the Rocky Mountains for three or four years, and long for a quiet, ordered life. It is a good omen that I have found a neighbor in advance of my settlement. I have often ridden fifty miles to meet a friend who cared for something else than horse-racing or *monte*; and your six miles,—it is but a step!"

"How much you have seen!" said Joseph. "I know very little of the world. It must be easy for you to take your own place in life.

A shade passed over Philip Held's face. "It is only easy to a certain class of men," he replied,—"a class to which I should not care to belong. I begin to think that nothing is very valuable, the right to which a man don't earn,—except human love, and that seems to come by the grace of God."

"I am younger than you are,—not yet twenty-three," Joseph remarked. "You will find that I am very ignorant."

"And I am twenty-eight, and just beginning to get my eyes open, like a nine-days' kitten. If I had been frank enough to confess my ignorance, five years ago, as you do now, it would have been better for me. But don't let us measure ourselves or our experience against each other. That is one good thing we learn in Rocky Mountain life; there is no high or low, knowledge or ignorance, except what applies to the needs of men who come together. So there are needs which most men have, and go all their lives hungering for, because they expect them to be supplied in a particular form. There is something," Philip concluded, "deeper than that in human nature."

Joseph longed to open his heart to this man, every one of whose words struck home to something in himself. But the lassitude which the shock left behind gradually overcame him. He suffered his head to be drawn upon Philip Held's shoulder, and slept until the train reached Oakland Station. When the two got upon the platform, they found Dennis waiting for Joseph, with a light country vehicle. The news of the accident had reached the station, and his dismay was great when he saw the two bloody faces. A physician had already been summoned from the neighboring village, but they had little need of his services. A prescription of quiet and sedatives for Joseph, and a strip of plaster for his companion, were speedily furnished, and they set out together for the Asten place.

It is unnecessary to describe Rachel Miller's agitation when the party arrived; or the parting of the two men who had been so swiftly brought near to each other; or Philip Held's farther journey to the forge that evening. He resisted all entreaty to remain at the farm until morning, on the ground of an appointment made with the present proprietor of the forge. After his departure Joseph was sent to bed, where he remained for a day or two, very sore and a little feverish. He had plenty of time for thought,—not precisely of the kind which his aunt suspected, for out of pure, honest interest in his welfare, she took a step which proved to be of doubtful benefit. If he had not been so innocent,—if he had not been quite as unconscious of his inner nature as he was over-conscious of his external self,—he would have perceived that his thoughts dwelt much more on Philip Held than on Julia Blessing. His mind seemed to run through a swift, involuntary chain of reasoning, to account to himself for his feeling towards her, and her inevitable share in his future; but towards Philip his heart sprang with an instinct beyond his control. It was impossible to imagine that the latter also would not be shot, like a bright thread, through the web of his coming days.

On the third morning, when he had exchanged the bed for an arm-chair, a letter from the city was brought to him. "Dearest Joseph," it ran, "what a fright and anxiety we have had! When pa brought the paper home, last night, and I read the report of the accident, where it said, '*J. Asten*, severe contusions,' my heart stopped beating for a minute, and I can only write now (as you see) with a trembling hand. My first thought was to go directly to you; but ma said we had better wait for intelligence. Unless our engagement were generally known, it would give rise to remarks,—in short, I need not repeat to you all the *worldly* reasons with which she opposed me; but, oh, how I longed for *the right* to be at your side, and assure myself that the dreadful, dreadful danger has passed! Pa was quite shaken with the news: he felt hardly able to go to the Custom-House this morning. But he sides with ma about my going, and now, when my time as a daughter with them is growing so short, I dare not disobey. I know you will understand my position, yet, dear and true as you are, you cannot guess the anxiety with which I await a line from your hand, the hand that was so nearly taken from me forever!"

Joseph read the letter twice and was about to commence it for the third time, when a visitor was announced. He had barely time to thrust the scented sheet into his pocket; and the bright eyes and flushed face with which he met the Rev. Mr. Chaffinch convinced both that gentleman and his aunt, as she ushered the latter into the room, that the visit was accepted as an honor and a joy.

On Mr. Chaffinch's face the air of authority which he had been led to believe belonged to his calling had not quite succeeded in impressing itself; but melancholy, the next best thing, was strongly marked. His dark complexion and his white cravat intensified each other; and his eyes, so long uplifted above the concerns of this world, had ceased to vary their expression materially for the sake of any human interest. All this had been expected of him, and he had simply done his best to meet the requirements of the flock over which he was placed. Any of the latter might have easily been shrewd enough to guess, in advance, very nearly what the pastor would say, upon a given occasion; but each and all of them would have been both disappointed and disturbed if he had not said it.

After appropriate and sympathetic inquiries concerning Joseph's bodily condition, he proceeded to probe him spiritually.

"It was a merciful preservation. I hope you feel that it is a solemn thing to look Death in the face."

"I am not afraid of death," Joseph replied.

"You mean the physical pang. But death includes what comes after it,—judgment. That is a very awful thought."

"It may be to evil men; but I have done nothing to make me fear it."

"You have never made an open profession of faith; yet it may be that grace has reached you," said Mr. Chaffinch. "Have you found your Saviour?"

"I believe in him with all my soul!" Joseph exclaimed; "but you mean something else by 'finding' him. I will be candid with you, Mr. Chaffinch. The last sermon I heard you preach, a month ago, was upon the nullity of all good works, all Christian deeds; you called them 'rags, dust, and ashes,' and declared that man is saved by faith alone. I *have* faith, but I can't accept a doctrine which denies merit to works; and you, unless I accept it, will you admit that I have 'found' Christ?"

"There is but One Truth!" exclaimed Mr. Chaffinch, very severely.

"Yes, Joseph answered, reverently, "and that is only perfectly known to God."

The clergyman was more deeply annoyed than he cared to exhibit. His experience had been confined chiefly to the encouragement of ignorant souls, willing to accept *his* message, if they could only be made to comprehend it, or to the conflict with downright doubt and denial. A nature so seemingly open to the influences of the Spirit, yet inflexibly closed to certain points of doctrine, was something of a problem to him. He belonged to a class now happily becoming scarce, who, having been taught to pace a reasoned theological round, can only efficiently meet those antagonists who voluntarily come inside of their own ring.

His habit of control, however, enabled him to say, with a moderately friendly manner, as he took leave: "We will talk again when you are stronger. It is my duty to give spiritual help to those who seek it."

To Rachel Miller he said: "I cannot say that he is dark. His mind is cloudy, but we find that the vanities of youth often obscure the true light for a time."

Joseph leaned back in his arm-chair, closed his eyes, and meditated earnestly for half an hour. Rachel Miller, uncertain whether to be hopeful or discouraged by Mr. Chaffinch's words, stole into the room, but went about on tiptoe, supposing him to be asleep. Joseph was fully conscious of all her movements, and at last startled her by the sudden question:—

"Aunt, why do you suppose I went to the city?"

"Goodness, Joseph! I thought you were sound asleep. I suppose to see about the fall prices for grain and cattle."

"No, aunt," said he, speaking with determination, though the foolish blood ran rosily over his face, "I went to get a wife!"

She stood pale and speechless, staring at him. But for the rosy sign on his cheeks and temples she could not have believed his words.

"Miss Blessing?" she finally uttered, almost in a whisper. Joseph nodded his head. She dropped into the nearest chair, drew two or three long breaths, and in an indescribable tone ejaculated, "Well!"

"I knew you would be surprised," said he; "because it is almost a surprise to myself. But you and she seemed to fall so easily into each other's ways, that I hope—"

"Why, you're hardly acquainted with her!" Rachel exclaimed. "It is so hasty! And you are so young!"

"No younger than father was when he married mother; and I have learned to know her well in a short time. Isn't it so with you, too, aunt?—you certainly liked her?"

"I'll not deny that, nor say the reverse now: but a farmer's wife should be a farmer's daughter."

"But suppose, aunt, that the farmer doesn't happen to love any farmer's daughter, and *does* love a bright, amiable, very intelligent girl, who is delighted with country life, eager and willing to learn, and very fond of the farmer's aunt (who can teach her everything)?"

"Still, it seems to me a risk," said Rachel; but she was evidently relenting.

"There is none to you," he answered, "and I am not afraid of mine. You will be with us, for Julia couldn't do without you, if she wished. If she were a farmer's daughter, with different ideas of housekeeping, it might bring trouble to both of us. But now you will have the management in your own hands until you have taught Julia, and afterwards she will carry it on in your way."

She did not reply; but Joseph could see that she was becoming reconciled to the prospect. After awhile she came across the room, leaned over him, kissed him upon the forehead, and then silently went away.

9. JOSEPH AND HIS FITZ-GREENE

According to John W.M. Hallock, here is what Taylor accomplished with *Joseph and His Friend*:

> Halleck's love for Drake inspired Bayard Taylor to challenge the conventional heterosexual novel with his homosexual romance *Joseph and His Friend*, published shortly after Halleck's death. [...] Halleck escaped the exiles suffered by Byron and Oscar Wilde and avoided the desperate denial of homosexuality such as that Whitman made to John Addington Symonds [see Chapter 20: Contemporary Camerados] in 1890 when he claimed six illegitimate children.
>
> [...]
>
> With Drake and Halleck both dead, the story of their friendship could finally be told. [...] Taylor was preparing his dedicatory address for [Halleck's Guilford monument ceremony in July 1869, see: (A.6)] and was writing his version of Goethe's *Faust* when he arrived in Guilford. Taylor was also outlining his manuscript for America's first homosexual novel, *Joseph and His Friend* (1870). [...] Halleck had had an excellent friend in Taylor, who also attended the unveiling of Halleck's statue eight years later.
>
> [...]
>
> It seems remarkable that Taylor had contracted *Joseph and His Friend* for publication in the *Atlantic Monthly* in 1869, more than a century before Gore Vidal's *Burr* (1973), which barely alludes to Halleck's homosexuality at all. [...] Vidal presented Halleck and Drake as minor characters in *Burr* and embellished their relationship in ways fitting the genre of historical fiction. Halleck and Drake live and work together in Vidal's novel. Regarding himself as an enemy of the people, Vidal's Halleck acknowledges his outsider status, telling a young admirer that he is a monarchist and a Catholic. After Halleck departs from one scene, Irving gossips to an attractive young man: "You look so much like his friend Joseph Rodman Drake [who died fifteen years ago]

. . . Halleck has not recovered to this day." Later, Irving refers to the poetic duo as Jonathan and David. A teary, rum-soaked Halleck recalls the Croaker project with Drake and makes a reference to his membership in the Ugly Club. As with biographies of Halleck, the earlier novel discloses his sexuality more forthrightly, and like Wilson, Taylor knew his subject personally.[22]

For more connection to Gore Vidal, see <u>Chapter 19: Calamus as Cruising Apparatus</u>.

Taylor probably read Wilson's *The Life and Letters of Fitz-Greene Halleck* (published in 1869) as a source for his Guilford speech. Joseph's monologue in Taylor's *Joseph and His Friend* echoes Halleck's early New York letters to Maria confessing his fear that he was unique and would never find a compatible partner. Joseph "wondered whether other men shared the same longing" and pondered the social injustice of reformed drunkards being praised while a man discovering all the possibilities of passion "is kept more secret than sin. Love is hidden as if it were a reproach; friendship watched, lest it express its warmth too frankly." Coming out to himself, he is baffled by the revelation: "I am lonely, but I know not how to cry for companionship; my words would not be understood, or, if they were, would not be answered. Only one gate is free to me,—that leading to the love of woman." Joseph arrives at the same conclusion that his real-life model, Joseph Drake, had drawn.

[...]

The novel's protagonist, Joseph Asten, is an innocent, twenty-three-year-old man who is associated with cherry-time and cherries, which symbolize his sexual naiveté. Joseph Asten takes Joseph Drake's first name while his surname is reminiscent of Astor, Halleck's famous employer and friend, whom Taylor accused of hindering Halleck's artistic development. (Taylor's father was also named Joseph.) Joseph has several flirtatious exchanges with men, especially Elwood Withers who may be modeled on Halleck's friend, Daniel Embury, before being seduced by a deceptive woman, ironically named Julia Blessing. She prefers intellect to wealth, but her father does not. It is probable that Henry Eckford [Sarah Eckford's father] fathered both Halleck's Fanny and Taylor's Julia. [...] An exhilarating horseback ride unleashes Joseph's "jailor of thought" beyond the boundaries that had prohibited personal freedom: [...] "God! I see what I am!" Cloaked in Halleck's metaphor of criminal as hero, Joseph embarks on his sexual awakening. The horseback ride, a common romantic metaphor for sex, had figured as well in Drake's poem "To Croaker, Junior." Taylor's wording is also suspiciously close to that of Whitman's "Hours Continuing Long" wherein the narrator abandons self-doubt and shame, declaring, "I am what I am."[22]

For "Hours Continuing Long" see <u>Chapter 11: Leaves of Grass</u>. For more of that self-realization and revelation, see <u>Chapter 15: Avowals to Walt Whitman</u>. There are hints of his nature that Joseph does not heed before his marriage in Chapter 6:

> As the last guests leave Joseph's "coming-out" party, he is "conscious of a tenderer feeling of friendship than he had ever before felt, and begged [Elwood] to stay for the night." Elwood reluctantly agrees and the two swap secrets about women before "Joseph stole back to his bed, and lay there silently." "Stole" hints at sexual crime in this silent bedroom scene. Later, on his way to ask for Julia's hand, Joseph is perplexed by a chest pang that "mysteriously resisted his errand." The pain is temporarily relieved by the sight of sailors and blue-collar men. The omen is not heeded and Joseph's marriage is set for October, the same month as Drake's real-life wedding.[22]

Once the Halleck figure arrives, Taylor's novel begins rewriting the real-life story of Halleck and Drake, correcting it:

> Joseph's introduction to the friend of the book's title, Philip Held, immediately establishes him as a Halleck figure. Joseph literally falls into the arms of Philip, who is studying hieroglyphics, an interest that suggests words must be open to interpretation. Philip Held's initials echo Fitz-Greene Halleck's initials and *Held* is "hero" in German, a language with which Taylor was well acquainted. Like Fitz-Greene Halleck, Philip Held alone never submits to marriage. In addition to his name, other details establish Philip as the reincarnation of Halleck. / Philip is twenty-eight, five years older than Joseph. Halleck was five years Drake's senior. Philip is allowed to act on the private feelings that Halleck had conveyed to his sister and attempts to talk Joseph out of his engagement, refusing the honor of best man, as Halleck had also wished to do. The similarity extends to physical appearance. Philip has "a smooth, frank forehead," hands "graceful without being effeminate," and dark gray eyes that provide contrast to Joseph's sparkling blue pair. The description fits the gray-eyed Halleck who was smitten by "the light of [Drake's] young blue eyes."
> [...]
> Joseph bashfully beholds Philip. Experiencing the equivalent of contemporary gaydar, an instinctive gaze of recognition between gay men, Joseph eyes the stranger who provides a resolution to his self-doubt. Whitman also noted this phenomenon, writing: "O Manhattan—your frequent and swift flash of eyes offering me love." One narrator celebrates the "curious questioning glances—glints of love!" as he cruises Broadway, which is one big "unspeakable show," and another speaker finds "one picking me out by secret and divine signs" in the anonymous multitude in which "some are baffled,

but that one is not—that one knows me. Ah lover and perfect equal, . . . to discover you by the like in you." In Taylor's novel, Philip "felt his [Joseph's] gaze," "answered it," and Joseph "dropped his eyes in some confusion" until a "momentary flash" of self-recognition strikes. The narrator comments that Philip's gaze carries the nonverbal response: "'We are men, let us know each other!' [which] is, alas! too rare in this world." The words mimic Halleck's exclamation that he and Drake must know each other, allegedly blurted out upon their first introduction. Joseph is "fighting the irresistible temptation to look again" when the train they are riding in crashes. Knocked unconscious, Joseph literally awakens to a new life with his head in Philip's lap.

In one of the most romantic scenes ever devised, Joseph is baptized into a new love by fire and ice: the cold water of a cloth Philip presses to his forehead as Philip's hot tears simultaneously drop on Joseph's cheeks. Discovering new power, Joseph finds familiarity in Philip's face and "the hand which had rested on his heart was warm with kindred blood." Philip insists on nursing Joseph, lifts him up, and takes the hand involuntarily offered by the injured man "with a silent assurance which he felt need no words." Philip nurses Joseph, a role that Halleck in life fulfilled with "more than a brother's love" in Drake's last days.[22]

For more of Whitman's poems including the above "Among the Multitude," see Chapter 11: Leaves of Grass and [A.13]. See Chapter 22: Whitman's Peter for a real life instance of Whitman and gaydar. John W.M. Hallock's analysis of *Joseph* continues:

Chapter 20, "A Crisis," provides the climax of homosexual emancipation in the novel. Like Walter Franklin [the friend of Drake and Halleck who committed suicide by gunshot after spending his last day in the company of Drake; for more on Franklin, see Chapter 20: Contemporary Camerados], Joseph, who had considered suicide the day before his wedding, reconsiders self-destruction. Julia has convinced Chaffinch to reproach Joseph with blasphemy, but the tables turn on the startled minister. Joseph accuses him of "pious impertinence" by blackmailing "this most sacred part of his nature" and leaves "crying aloud: 'I will go to Philip! . . . I must have a word of love from a friend, or I shall go mad!'" He stumbles into the hemlocks of the forest where Philip intuitively finds him contemplating death. Reading Joseph's thoughts, "Philip took his hand, drew him nearer, and flinging his arms around him, held him to his heart." Philip assures Joseph that rather than feeling inferior he can take absolute confidence that his special design places him above the average laws of the human race.[22]

In the fictional rendering of this relationship, the Halleck figure gets what he wants. "Unlike Halleck's unfulfilled wish to remove Sarah Eckford Drake, Philip's desire for Julia

Blessing Asten's death is granted,"[22] and Taylor reveals it to us plainly: on learning of
Julia's death, "Philip's heart [gives] a single leap of joy" before he forces himself to think
first "of Joseph and the exigencies of the situation."[51] He is happy to know that Joseph's
wife is dead and his affections free again, just as Halleck would have been. However, Taylor
pulls short of giving them their ideal happy ending together in Philip's "great valley."[51]
Instead, Joseph finds another wife:

> Philip feels "a little sting of pain somewhere" when Joseph and Madeline
> announce plans to wed and believes that "they have destroyed my life." As
> Halleck had been unable to do for Drake and Sarah Eckford, Philip pledges
> to be "vicariously happy" for the newlyweds but warns couples that "God's
> wonderful system is imperfect." He claims his place in society by adopting
> their future offspring: "myself in their children, nay, claiming and making
> them *mine* as well." The scene reminds the reader of Halleck's namesake,
> Janet Halleck Drake, and his role as godfather to Drake's grandchild.
> [...]
> In Halleck's poems and collected letters, Taylor heard Halleck's
> "repressed sobs." His criminal act of officiating as Drake's best man was
> turned upside down in Taylor's novel. Unlike Halleck, Philip does not
> compromise his integrity by acting as Joseph's groomsman. Joseph's wedding
> is itself the criminal act. Philip insists that Joseph's last full day as a single
> man be shared alone with him in the city. There, Philip begs Joseph not to
> marry and articulates what Halleck could not say fifty years before.[22]

All that being done, the ending of the book is not all that different than the reality of
Halleck's life, it is only more out in the open, more honest.

X

APPROACHING FATE

ONLY TWO MONTHS intervened until the time appointed for the marriage, and the days rolled swiftly away. A few lines came to Joseph from Philip Held, announcing that he was satisfied with the forge and furnace, and the sale would doubtless be consummated in a short time. He did not, however, expect to take charge of the works before March, and therefore gave Joseph his address in the city, with the hope that the latter would either visit or write to him.

On the Sunday after the accident Elwood Withers came to the farm. He seemed to have grown older in the short time which had elapsed since they had last met; after his first hearty rejoicing over Joseph's escape and recovery, he relapsed into a silent but not unfriendly mood. The two young men climbed the long hill behind the house and seated themselves under a noble pin-oak on the height, whence there was a lovely view of the valley for many miles to the southward.

They talked mechanically, for a while, of the season, and the crops, and the other usual subjects which farmers never get to the end of discussing; but both felt the impendence of more important themes, and, nevertheless, were slow to approach them. At last Elwood said: "Your fate is settled by this time, I suppose?"

"It is arranged, at least," Joseph replied. "But I can't yet make clear to myself that I shall be a married man in two months from now."

"Does the time seem long to you?"

"No," Joseph innocently answered; "it is very short." Elwood turned away his head to conceal a melancholy smile; it was a few minutes before he spoke again.

"Joseph," he then said, "are you sure, quite sure, you love her?"

"I am to marry her."

"I meant nothing unfriendly," Elwood remarked, in a gentle tone. "My thought was this,—if you should ever find a still stronger love growing upon you,—something that would make the warmth you feel now seem like ice compared to it,—how would you be able to fight it? I asked the question of myself for you. I don't think I'm much different from most soft-hearted men,—except that I keep the softness so well stowed away that few persons know of it,—but if I were in your place, within two months of marriage to the girl I love, I should be miserable!"

Joseph turned towards him with wide, astonished eyes.

"Miserable from hope and fear," Elwood went on; "I should be afraid of fever, fire, murder, thunderbolts! Every hour of the day I should dread lest something might come between us; I should prowl around her house day after day, to be sure that she was alive! I should lengthen out the time into years; and all because I'm a great, disappointed, soft-hearted fool!"

The sad, yearning expression of his eyes touched Joseph to the heart. "Elwood," he said, "I see that it is not in my power to comfort you; if I give you pain unknowingly, tell me how to avoid it! I meant to ask you to stand beside me when I am married; but now you must consider your own feelings in answering, not mine. Lucy is not likely to be there."

"That would make no difference," Elwood answered. "Do you suppose it is a pain for me to see her, because she seems lost to me? No; I'm always a little encouraged when I have a chance to measure myself with her, and to guess—sometimes this and sometimes that—what it is that she needs to find in me. Force of will is of no use; as to faithfulness,—why, what it's worth can't be shown unless something turns up to try it. But you had better not ask me to be your groomsman. Neither Miss Blessing nor her sister would be overly pleased."

"Why so?" Joseph asked; "Julia and you are quite well acquainted, and she was always friendly towards you."

Elwood was silent and embarrassed. Then, reflecting that silence, at that moment, might express even more than speech, he said: "I've got the notion in my head; maybe it's foolish, but there it is. I talked a good deal with Miss Blessing, it's true, and yet I don't feel the least bit acquainted. Her manner to me was very friendly, and yet I don't think she likes me."

"Well!" exclaimed Joseph, forcing a laugh, though he was much annoyed, "I never gave you credit for such a lively imagination. Why not be candid, and admit that the dislike is on your side? I am sorry for it, since Julia will so soon be in the house there as my wife. There is no one else whom I can ask, unless it were Philip Held—"

"Held! To be sure, he took care of you. I was at Coventry the day after, and saw something of him." With these words, Elwood turned towards Joseph and looked him squarely in the face. "He'll have charge there in a few months, I hear," he then said, "and I reckon it as a piece of good luck for you. I've found that there are men, all, maybe, as honest and outspoken as they need be; yet two of 'em will talk at different marks and never fully understand each other, and other two will naturally talk right straight at the same mark and never miss. Now, Held is the sort that can hit the thing in the mind of the man they're talking to; it's a gift that comes o' being knocked about the world among all classes of people. What we learn here, always among the same folks, isn't a circumstance."

"Then you think I might ask him?" said Joseph, not fully comprehending all that Elwood meant to express.

"He's one of those men that you're safe in asking to do anything. Make him spokesman of a committee to wait on the President, arbitrator in a crooked lawsuit, overseer of a railroad gang, leader in a prayer-meeting (if he'd consent), or whatever else you choose, and he'll do the business as if he was used to it! It's enough for you that I don't know the town ways, and he does; it's considered worse, I've heard, to make a blunder in society than to commit a real sin."

He rose, and they loitered down the hill together. The subject was quietly dropped, but the minds of both were none the less busy. They felt the stir and pressure of new experiences, which had come to one through disappointment and to the other through success. Not three months had passed since they rode together through the twilight to Warriner's, and already life was opening to them,—but how differently! Joseph endeavored to make the most kindly allowance for his friend's mood, and to persuade himself that his feelings were unchanged. Elwood, however, knew that a shadow had fallen between them. It was nothing beside the cloud of his greater trouble: he also knew the cost of his own justification to Joseph, and prayed that it might never come.

That evening, on taking leave, he said: "I don't know whether you meant to have the news of your engagement circulated; but I guess Anna Warriner has heard, and that amounts to—"

"To telling it to the whole neighborhood, doesn't it?" Joseph answered. "Then the mischief is already done, if it is a mischief. It is well, therefore, that the day is set: the neighborhood will have little time for gossip."

He smiled so frankly and cheerfully, that Elwood seized his hand, and with tears in his eyes, said: "Don't remember anything against me, Joseph. I've always been honestly your friend, and mean to stay so."

He went that evening to a homestead where he knew he should find Lucy Henderson. She looked pale and fatigued, he thought; possibly his presence had become a restraint. If so, she must bear his unkindness: it was the only sacrifice he could not make, for he felt sure that his intercourse with her must either terminate in hate or love. The one thing of which he was certain was, that there could be no calm, complacent friendship between them.

It was not long before one of the family asked him whether he had heard the news; it seemed that they had already discussed it, and his arrival revived the flow of expression. In spite of his determination, he found it impossible to watch Lucy while he said, as simply as possible, that Joseph Asten seemed very happy over the prospect of the marriage; that he was old enough to take a wife; and if Miss Blessing could adapt herself to country habits, they might get on very well together. But later in the evening he took a chance of saying to her: "In spite of what I said, Lucy, I don't feel quite easy about Joseph's marriage. What do you think of it?"

She smiled faintly, as she replied: "Some say that people are attracted by mutual unlikeness. This seems to me to be a case of the kind; but they are free choosers of their own fates."

"Is there no possible way of persuading him—them—to delay?"

"No!" she exclaimed, with unusual energy; "none whatever!"

Elwood sighed, and yet felt relieved.

Joseph lost no time in writing to Philip Held, announcing his approaching marriage, and begging him—with many apologies for asking such a mark of confidence on so short an acquaintance—to act the part of nearest friend, if there were no other private reasons to prevent him.

Four or five days later the following answer arrived:—

> MY DEAR ASTEN:—Do you remember that curious whirling, falling sensation, when the car pitched over the edge of the embankment? I felt a return of it on reading your letter; for you have surprised me beyond measure. Not by your request, for that is just what I should have expected of you; and as well now, as if we had known each other for twenty years; so the apology is the only thing objectionable— But I am tangling my sentences; I want to say how heartily I return the feeling which prompted you to ask me, and yet how embarrassed I am that I cannot unconditionally say, "Yes, with all my heart!" My great, astounding surprise is, to find you about to be married to Miss Julia Blessing,—a young lady whom I once knew. And the embarrassment is this: I knew her under circumstances (in which she was not personally concerned, however) which might possibly render my presence now, as your groomsman, unwelcome to the family: at least, it is my duty—and yours, if you still desire me to stand beside you—to let Miss Blessing and her family decide the question. The circumstances to which I refer concern them rather than myself. I think your best plan will be simply to inform them of your request and my reply, and add that I am entirely ready to accept whatever course they may prefer. Pray don't consider that I have treated your first letter to me ungraciously. I am more grieved than you can imagine that it happens so. You will probably come to the city a day before the wedding, and I insist that you shall share my bachelor quarters, in any case. Always your friend, PHILIP HELD.

This letter threw Joseph into a new perplexity. Philip a former acquaintance of the Blessings! Formerly, but not now; and what could those mysterious "circumstances" have been, which had so seriously interrupted their intercourse? It was quite useless to conjecture; but he could not resist the feeling that another shadow hung over the aspects of his future. Perhaps he had exaggerated Elwood's unaccountable dislike to Julia, which had only been implied, not spoken; but here was a positive estrangement on the part of the man who was so suddenly near and dear to him. He never thought of suspecting Philip of blame; the candor and cheery warmth of the letter rejoiced his heart. There was evidently nothing better to do than to follow the advice contained in it, and leave the question to the decision of Julia and her parents.

Her reply did not come by the return mail, nor until nearly a week afterwards; during which time he tormented himself by imagining the wildest reasons for her silence. When the letter at last arrived, he had some difficulty in comprehending its import.

"Dearest Joseph," she said, "you must *really* forgive me this long trial of your patience. Your letter was *so* unexpected,—I mean its contents—and it seems as if ma and pa and Clementina would never agree what was best to be done. For that matter, I cannot say that they agree now; we had *no idea* that you were an intimate friend of Mr. Held, (I can't think how ever you should have become acquainted!) and it seems to break open old wounds,—none of mine, fortunately, for I have none. As Mr. Held leaves the question in our hands, there is, you will understand, all the more necessity that we should be careful. Ma thinks he has said nothing to you about the unfortunate occurrence, or you would have expressed an opinion. You never can know how happy your fidelity makes me; but I felt that, the first moment we met.

"Ma says that at *very private* (what pa calls informal) weddings there need not be bridesmaids or groomsmen. Miss Morrisey was married that way, not long ago; it is true that she is not of our circle, nor strictly a *first* family (this is ma's view, not mine, for I understand the hollowness of society); but we could very well do the same. Pa would be satisfied with a reception afterwards; he wants to ask the Collector, and the Surveyor, and the Appraiser. Clementina won't say anything now, but I know what she thinks, and so does ma; however, Mr. Held has so dropped out of city life that it is not important. I suppose everything must be dim in his memory now; you do not write to me much that he related. How strange that he should be your friend! They say my dress is lovely, but I am sure I should like a plain muslin just as well. I shall only breathe freely when I get back to the quiet of the country, (and your—*our* charming home, and dear, good Aunt Rachel!) and away from all these conventional forms. Ma says if there is one groomsman there ought to be two; either very simple, or according to custom. In a matter so delicate, perhaps, Mr. Held would be as competent to decide as we are; at least *I* am quite willing to leave it to *his* judgment. But how trifling is all this discussion, compared with the importance of the day to us! It is now drawing very near, but I have no misgivings, for I confide in you wholly and forever!"

After reading the letter with as much coolness as was then possible to him, Joseph inferred three things: that his acquaintance with Philip Held was not entirely agreeable to the Blessing family; that they would prefer the simplest style of a wedding, and this was in consonance with his own tastes; and that Julia clung to him as a deliverer from conditions with which her nature had little sympathy. Her incoherence, he fancied, arose from an agitation which he could very well understand, and his answer was intended to soothe and encourage her. It was difficult to let Philip know that his services would not be required, without implying the existence of an unfriendly feeling towards him; and Joseph, therefore, all the more readily accepted his invitation. He was assured that the mysterious difficulty did not concern Julia; even if it were so, he was not called upon to do violence, without cause, to so welcome a friendship.

The September days sped by, not with the lingering, passionate uncertainty of which

Elwood Withers spoke, but almost too swiftly. In the hurry of preparation, Joseph had scarcely time to look beyond the coming event and estimate its consequences. He was too ignorant of himself to doubt: his conscience was too pure and perfect to admit the possibility of changing the course of his destiny. Whatever the gossip of the neighborhood might have been, he heard nothing of it that was not agreeable. His aunt was entirely reconciled to a wife who would not immediately, and probably not for a long time, interfere with her authority; and the shadows raised by the two men whom he loved best seemed, at last, to be accidentally thrown from clouds beyond the horizon of his life. This was the thought to which he clung, in spite of a vague, utterly formless apprehension, which he felt lurking somewhere in the very bottom of his heart.

Philip met him on his arrival in the city, and after taking him to his pleasant quarters, in a house looking on one of the leafy squares, good-naturedly sent him to the Blessing mansion, with a warning to return before the evening was quite spent. The family was in a flutter of preparation, and though he was cordially welcomed, he felt that, to all except Julia, he was subordinate in interest to the men who came every quarter of an hour, bringing bouquets, and silver spoons with cards attached, and pasteboard boxes containing frosted cakes. Even Julia's society he was only allowed to enjoy by scanty instalments; she was perpetually summoned by her mother or Clementina, to consult about some indescribable figment of dress. Mr. Blessing was occupied in the basement, with the inspection of various hampers. He came to the drawing-room to greet Joseph, whom he shook by both hands, with such incoherent phrases that Julia presently interposed. "You must not forget, pa," she said, "that the man is waiting: Joseph will excuse you, I know." She followed him to the basement, and he returned no more.

Joseph left early in the evening, cheered by Julia's words: "We can't complain of all this confusion, when it's for our sakes; but we'll be happier when it's over, won't we?"

He gave her an affirmative kiss, and returned to Philip's room. That gentleman was comfortably disposed in an armchair, with a book and a cigar. "Ah!" he exclaimed, "you find that a house is more agreeable any evening than that before the wedding?"

"There is one compensation," said Joseph; "it gives me two or three hours with you."

"Then take that other arm-chair, and tell me how this came to pass. You see I have the curiosity of a neighbor, already."

He listened earnestly while Joseph related the story of his love, occasionally asking a question or making a suggestive remark, but so gently that it seemed to come as an assistance. When all had been told, he rose and commenced walking slowly up and down the room. Joseph longed to ask, in turn, for an explanation of the circumstances mentioned in Philip's letter; but a doubt checked his tongue.

As if in response to his thought, Philip stopped before him and said: "I owe you my story, and you shall have it after a while, when I can tell you more. I was a young fellow of twenty when I knew the Blessings, and I don't attach the slightest importance, now, to anything that happened. Even if I did, Miss Julia had no share in it. I remember her distinctly; she was then about my age, or a year or two older; but hers is a face that would not change in a long while."

Joseph stared at his friend in silence. He recalled the latter's age, and was startled by the involuntary arithmetic which revealed Julia's to him. It was unexpected, unwelcome, yet inevitable.

"Her father had been lucky in some of his 'operations,'" Philip continued, but I don't think he kept it long. I hardly wonder that she should come to prefer a quiet country life to such ups and downs as the family has known. Generally, a woman don't adapt herself so readily to a change of surroundings as a man: where there is love, however, everything is possible."

"There is! there is!" Joseph exclaimed, certifying the fact to himself as much as to his friend. He rose and stood beside him.

Philip looked at him with grave, tender eyes.

"What can I do?" he said.

"What should you do?" Joseph asked.

"This!" Philip exclaimed, laying his hands on Joseph's shoulders,—"this, Joseph! I can be nearer than a brother. I know that I am in your heart as you are in mine. There is no faith between us that need be limited, there is no truth too secret to be veiled. A man's perfect friendship is rarer than a woman's love, and most hearts are content with one or the other: not so with yours and mine! I read it in your eyes, when you opened them on my knee: I see it in your face now. Don't speak: let us clasp hands."

But Joseph could not speak.

10. TAYLOR AND WHITMAN

Near the end of Walt Whitman's life, Horace Traubel began visiting Whitman almost daily, taking copious notes in preparation for what became a nine-volume biography of Whitman's final four years, *With Walt Whitman in Camden*. (For more on Traubel, see: Chapter 14: Bucke, Traubel, and the Multitudes of Whitman.) He attempted to record and preserve everything he could about Whitman's life, his thoughts, and his correspondence, while Whitman still hoped to censor some aspects of his life from his legacy. He teased Traubel about his desire to keep and record every scrap, going so far as to tell him he had surprise information (that was never ultimately revealed). From Traubel:

> Said again to W: "I am still waiting for that surprise." "Why, so you are—I had almost forgotten. A day or two more and you may come to your own." Four days later: I reminded W that I was losing sleep and meals in my anxiety over the 'surprise' that he still held back. "Still harping on my daughter?" he exclaimed and said no more. Three days later Walt says, "And by the way, our 'surprise' that we have talked so much about has threatened to be a boomerang." I pricked up my ears. Was the revelation about to come? He saw my interested face. "Are you ready for it?" I laughingly replied: "I'm leanin' up against myself strong!" But on this occasion the "surprise" is only a few old letters from Bayard Taylor expressing his affinity for *Leaves of Grass*.[39]

Bayard Taylor's letters to Whitman can be read in [A.8]. The letters Taylor sent to Whitman at age forty-one are full of gratitude for the sincerity of his poems, going so far as to be specific, saying, "There is one quality I recognize in you, which warmly and constantly attracts me. That is, your deep and tender reverence for Man—your unwearied, affectionate, practical fraternity. There is too little of this quality in the world, and the race will be better and happier in proportion as it is manifested," but his positive regard for Whitman did not last long, for by 1871 Taylor would start writing public parodies of Whitman and speaking against his work (which can be read in [A.9] and [A.10]. From Traubel's *With Walt Whitman in Camden*, Volume 2:

After a bit he suddenly said: "And, now, Horace, what about the Taylor letter? Did you read it? There was no ahem and ahaw in that letter, do you think? Have you got the letter in your pocket? Yes? Read it to me." The letter was addressed to W. at Washington. W. endorsed the envelope: "from Bayard Taylor Nov. 16, 1866." As I finished reading W. asked: "Well—what do you say to that? That don't sound like the note of a man who was in great doubt, does it? I don't make too much of such things. They come and go—or they don't come: and if they don't come, that is right too. But I find the Taylor of that time interesting because people say (the gossips say) the Taylor of today won't have me on any terms—hates to hear my name mentioned. I don't know about it all: men do change their minds: the Taylor who did like me may be wrong, the Taylor who does not like me (if there is such a Taylor) may be right. Who knows? Who knows? I wish I had the other letter now for you to read—it puts a finish on the little story. Damn it, I wonder where that letter got to? Sometimes I'm all in a heap here—goods, chattels, anything, myself with everything, all in a heap." After a laugh he added: "No matter what the fellers said, didn't say—no matter for the curses, the blessings—no matter for anything, I had to stick to my business. If I had stopped to dispute with my enemies, even to dally or luxuriate with my friends, the book would have gone begging. The book—the book: that was always the thing!"[14]

Bayard Taylor is not the only man who had a change of heart over Whitman. In Gary Schmidgall's *Walt Whitman: A Gay Life*, he notes another:

Thinking of many readers like Edmund Gosse and Bayard Taylor, who idolized him in their youth and then fell away, Whitman observed: "The young fellows seem rather bowled over by me: [then] they get respectable or something and I will no longer do. . . . I suppose I don't wear well—that's what's the matter: I fool 'em for a time, when they're in their teens, but when they grow up they can no longer be deceived." [...] Whitman dug up a gushing letter of Taylor's written more than twenty years before. Amid its purple prose: "There is not one word of your large and beautiful sympathy for men which I cannot take into my own heart, nor one of those subtle and wonderful physical affinities you describe which I cannot comprehend *etc.*" After Traubel read it aloud, Whitman remarked that Taylor, who for years had been writing very genteel lavender-tinged poetry and fiction, had lately been "quoted against me—especially against the sex poems."[40]

Below are details of Gosse's curious falling out with Whitman. For more on Gosse's correspondence with Whitman, see <u>Chapter 15: Avowals to Walt Whitman</u>.

Sir Edmund Gosse was a popular British poet, critic, and literary biographer who wrote more than sixty books between 1873 and 1928. He is best remembered for his personal memoir, *Father and Son* (1908). In 1873 Gosse had sent Walt Whitman a copy of his own first book of poems, *On Viol and Flute* (1873), together with an effusive letter in which he declared himself to be "the new person drawn toward you . . . I draw only closer and closer to you." It was signed, "your sincere disciple." Some years later, in the 1880s, Gosse was on a lecture tour in the United States and was able to visit with Whitman for several hours in his Camden home. By the time of the interview Gosse had apparently become much less enthusiastic about Whitman's poetry. In his essay about their interview, however, Gosse presented a clear and favorable picture of Whitman. He said that he had gone to see him as a "stiff necked unbeliever" but that he left with "a heart full of affection for the beautiful old man." Gosse chose not to reveal much about their conversation. He devoted much of the essay to his theory that Whitman's poetry is "[l]iterature in the condition of protoplasm, an intellectual organism so simple that it takes the instant impression of whatever mood approaches it." Gosse saw this as explaining why some readers liked Whitman while they were young but became less enthusiastic as they aged. The essay was not published during Whitman's lifetime. It first appeared in April of 1894 and was included by Gosse in his *Critical Kit-Kats* (1896). In a conversation with Horace Traubel in 1888 Whitman included Gosse in a list of several British critics who "seem to understand me," but in a letter to Richard Bucke in 1889 he characterized Gosse as "one of the amiable conventional wall-flowers of literature." Gosse's last word on Whitman was not until 1927. In the last of his books, he concluded a review of John Bailey's new *Walt Whitman* by saying, "that is really the one subject of Walt Whitman, the masculinity of other men. . . . It is best not to inquire too closely about all this, but to accept Walt Whitman for what he gives . . . the undeniable beauty and originality of his strange unshackled rhapsody."[14]

Another of Walt Whitman's early literary executors was Canadian physician Richard Maurice Bucke, who became one of Walt Whitman's most devoted friends and supporters in the poet's later years, and the editor of several books on Whitman. He wrote in defense of Whitman against Taylor and others:

> This ridiculous notion of *Leaves of Grass* as a sort of rowdy amplification of Emerson, began twenty years ago with some amusing persiflage in "Putnam's Magazine"—the harmless fancy of my old friend Mr. George William Curtis, who sometimes softly, sweetly, slips into ad captandums with irresponsible indolent grace. It was taken up again, and enforced, not at all harmlessly, but with malicious iteration, by Mr. Bayard Taylor, in a series

of gratuitous and inappropriate editorials, published seven years ago in the "New York Tribune," with the object of breaking down a certain movement in behalf of Mr. Whitman, and it gave me then, in conjunction with some of his other representations, a new idea of what might be meant by the old saying that "a tailor is the ninth part of a man."[4]

For more on Whitman's involvement with Emerson, see <u>Chapter 12: Whitman and Emerson</u>. For more information on Dr. Bucke, see <u>Chapter 14: Bucke, Traubel, and the Multitudes of Whitman</u>.

Mitch Gould writing in *The Routledge Encyclopedia of Walt Whitman* describes the nature of Taylor's parodies and how his associations with Whitman ultimately ended:

> In *John Godfrey's Fortunes* (1864), Taylor portrays Whitman as the Bohemian poet Mr. Smithers, who prefers "the fireman, in his red flannel shirt, with the sleeves rolled up to his shoulders" over fools with "the morbid sensitiveness which follows culture." Taylor's "Echo Club" parodies, published in *The Atlantic Monthly* in 1872, called *Leaves of Grass* a "modern, half-Bowery-boy, half-Emersonian apprehension of the old Greek idea of physical life . . . A truer sense of art would have prevented . . . offensive frankness."
>
> Whitman noted that Taylor's *Poems of the Orient* (1854) "indirectly has a meaning," which, according to Byrne Fone, was Whitman's way of indicating a homosexual discourse [see: (A.1) for an excerpt]. Thus Whitman was hardly surprised when Taylor confided that he found in his own nature both Whitman's "physical attraction" and "tender and noble love of man for man." Taylor offered his suspicious Quaker neighbors *The Story of Kennett* (1866) as an alternative to the fad of "exceptional or morbid" kinds of "psychological problems," and his two male characters avoided a tender embrace because that "was the custom of the neighborhood." However, his odd novel *Joseph and His Friend* (1870) showed heroes holding hands and kissing, as dictated by "a loftier faith, a juster law," and "instincts, needs, knowledge, and rights—ay, rights! of their own."
>
> In 1856, George Boker, who was married, wrote Taylor, who was widowed, that he had "never loved anything human as I love you. It is a joy and a pride to my heart to know that this feeling is truly returned." In the years after 1874, Whitman may have intruded upon their Philadelphia turf, when the "florid, almost effusive" Boker invited him to dine "two or three times." By 1876, Taylor was blasting Whitman in the New York Tribune, and after that, the two never reconciled.[31]

John W.M. Hallock suggests another element at play in the Taylor-Whitman fallout, writing, "Whitman and Taylor had been good friends before their 1876 estrangement that was possibly caused by Whitman's professional jealousy of Taylor,"[22] a sentiment that Gould suggests Taylor nearly shared when he pointed out that "[Taylor's] poetic style, rooted in the classics and Victorian sentiment, brought him so little acclaim that he began to resent the mass appeal of his travel writing. Only his *Faust* translation is well known today."[31] Whitman has surely out-famed Taylor posthumously.

In conclusion, on one occasion Whitman had this to say, not about Taylor specifically, but about the type of man Taylor and others turned out to be when it came to their preoccupation with himself:

"I don't mind the fellows who say without a tremor: 'Here, damn you, Walt Whitman, what do you mean by all this nonsense. To hell with you, Walt Whitman: to hell with you! to hell with you!' That don't sound bad—on the contrary it sounds very good—it is tonic. But when a fellow comes along, convinced and not convinced, hungry for your society and afraid of your society, blowing hot and cold, with praise on his lips that had better be blame, you are at your wit's end to know how to meet him."[39]

XI

A CITY WEDDING

THERE WAS NOT much of the happy bridegroom to be seen in Joseph's face when he arose the next morning. To Philip's eyes he appeared to have suddenly grown several years older; his features had lost their boyish softness and sweetness, which would thenceforth never wholly come back again. He spoke but little, and went about his preparation with an abstracted, mechanical air, which told how much his mind was preoccupied. Philip quietly assisted, and when all was complete, led him before the mirror.

"There!" he said; "now study the general effect; I think nothing more is wanting."

"It hardly looks like myself," Joseph remarked, after a careless inspection.

"In all the weddings I have seen," said Philip, "the bridegrooms were pale and grave, the brides flushed and trembling. You will not make an exception to the rule; but it is a solemn thing, and I—don't misunderstand me, Joseph—I almost wish you were not to be married to-day."

"Philip!" Joseph exclaimed, "let me think, now, at least,—now, at the last moment,—that it is best for me! If you knew how cramped, restricted, fettered, my life has been, and how much emancipation has already come with this—this love! Perhaps my marriage is a venture, but it is one which must be made; and no consequence of it shall ever come between us!"

"No; and I ought not to have spoken a word that might imply a doubt. It may be that your emancipation, as you rightly term it, can only come in this way. My life has been so different, that I am unconsciously putting myself in your place, instead of trying to look with your eyes. When I next go to Coventry Forge, I shall drive over and dine with you, and I hope your Julia will be as ready to receive me as a friend as I am to find one in her. There is the carriage at the door, and you had better arrive a little before the appointed hour. Take only my good wishes, my prayers for your happiness, along with you,—and now, God bless you, Joseph!"

The carriage rolled away. Joseph, in full wedding costume, was painfully conscious of the curious glances which fell upon him, and presently pulled down the curtains. Then, with an impatient self-reprimand, he pulled them up again, lowered the window, and let the air blow upon his hot cheeks. The house was speedily reached, and he was admitted by a festive waiter (hired for the occasion) before he had been exposed for more than five seconds to the gaze of curious eyes in all the windows around.

Mrs. Blessing, resplendent in purple, and so bedight that she seemed almost as young as her portrait, swept into the drawing-room. She inspected him rapidly, and approved, while advancing; otherwise he would scarcely have received the thin, dry kiss with which she favored him.

"It lacks half an hour," she said; "but you have the usual impatience of a bridegroom. I am accustomed to it. Mr. Blessing is still in his room; he has only just commenced arranging his cambric cravat, which is a work of time. He cannot forget that he was distinguished for an elegant tie in his youth. Clementina,"—as that young lady entered the room,—"is the bride completely attired?"

"All but her gloves," replied Clementina, offering three-fourths of her hand to Joseph. "And she don't know what ear-rings to wear."

"I think we might venture," Mrs. Blessing remarked, "as there seems to be no rule applicable to the case, to allow Mr. Asten a sight of his bride. Perhaps his taste might assist her in the choice."

Thereupon she conducted Joseph upstairs, and, after some preliminary whispering, he was admitted to the room. He and Julia were equally surprised at the change in each other's appearance: he older, paler, with a grave and serious bearing; she younger, brighter, rounder, fresher, and with the loveliest pink flush on her cheeks. The gloss of her hair rivalled that of the white satin which draped her form and gave grace to its outlines; her neck and shoulders were slight, but no one could have justly called them lean; and even the thinness of her lips was forgotten in the vivid coral of their color, and the nervous life which hovered about their edges. At that moment she was certainly beautiful, and a stranger would have supposed her to be young.

She looked into Joseph's face with a smile in which some appearance of maiden shyness yet lingered. A shrewder bridegroom would have understood its meaning, and would have said, "How lovely you are!" Joseph, it is true, experienced a sense of relief, but he knew not why, and could not for his life have put it into words. His eyes dwelt upon and followed her, and she seemed to be satisfied with that form of recognition. Mrs. Blessing inspected the dress with a severe critical eye, pulling out a fold here and smoothing a bit of lace there, until nothing further could be detected. Then, the adornment of the victim being completed, she sat down and wept moderately.

"O ma, try to bear up!" Julia exclaimed, with the very slightest touch of impatience in her voice; "it is all to come yet."

There was a ring at the door.

"It must be your aunt," said Mrs. Blessing, drying her eyes. "My sister," she added, turning to Joseph,—"Mrs. Woollish, with Mr. Woollish and their two sons and one daughter. He's in the—the leather trade, so to speak, which has thrown her into a very different circle; but, as we have no nearer relations in the city, they will be present at the ceremony. He is said to be wealthy. I have no means of knowing; but one would scarcely think so, to judge from his wedding-gift to Julia."

"Ma, why should you mention it?"

"I wish to enlighten Mr. Asten. Six pairs of shoes!—of course all of the same pattern; and the fashion may change in another year!"

"In the country we have no fashions in shoes," Joseph suggested.

"Certainly!" said Julia. "I find Uncle Woollish's present very practical indeed."

Mrs. Blessing looked at her daughter, and said nothing.

Mr. Blessing, very red in the face, but with triumphant cambric about his throat, entered the room, endeavoring to get his fat hands into a pair of No. 9 gloves. A strong smell of turpentine or benzine entered with him.

"Eliza" said he, "you must find me some eau de cologne. The odor left from my—my rheumatic remedy is still perceptible. Indeed, patchouly would be better, if it were not the scent peculiar to *parvenus*."

Clementina came to say that the clergyman's carriage had just reached the door, and Mr. Blessing was hurried down stairs, mopping his gloves and the collar of his coat with liquid fragrance by the way. Mrs. Blessing and Clementina presently followed.

"Julia," said Joseph when they were quite alone, "have you thought that this is for life?"

She looked up with a tender smile, but something in his face arrested it on her lips.

"I have lived ignorantly until now," he continued,—"innocently and ignorantly. From this time on I shall change more than you, and there may be, years hence, a very different Joseph Asten from the one whose name you will take to-day. If you love me with the love I claim from you,—the love that grows with and through all new knowledge and experience,—there will be no discord in our lives. We must both be liberal and considerate towards each other; it has been but a short time since we met, and we have still much to learn."

"O, Joseph!" she murmured, in a tone of gentle reproach, "I knew your nature at first sight."

"I hope you did," he answered gravely, "for then you will be able to see its needs, and help me to supply them. But, Julia, there must not the shadow of concealment come between us: nothing must be reserved. I understand no love that does not include perfect trust. I must draw nearer, and be drawn nearer to you, constantly, or—"

He paused; it was no time to utter the further sentence in his mind. Julia glided to him, clasped her arms about his waist, and laid her head against his shoulder. Although she said nothing, the act was eloquent. It expressed acquiescence, trust, fidelity, the surrender of her life to his, and no man in his situation could have understood it otherwise. A tenderness, which seemed to be the something hitherto lacking to his love, crept softly over his heart, and the lurking unrest began to fade from his face.

There was a rustle on the stairs; Clementina and Miss Woollish made their appearance. "Mr. Bogue has arrived," whispered the former, "and ma thinks you should come down soon. Are you entirely ready? I don't think you need the salts, Julia; but you might carry the bottle in your left hand: brides are expected to be nervous."

She gave a light laugh, like the purl and bubble of a brook; but Joseph shrank, with an inward chill, from the sound.

"So! shall we go? Fanny and I—(I beg pardon; Mr. Asten—Miss Woollish)—will lead the way. We will stand a little in the rear, not beside you, as there are no groomsmen. Remember, the farther end of the room!"

They rustled slowly downward, in advance, and the bridal pair followed. The clergyman, Mr. Bogue, suddenly broke off in the midst of an oracular remark about the weather, and, standing in the centre of the room, awaited them. The other members of the two families were seated, and very silent.

Joseph heard the introductory remarks, the ceremony, and the final benediction, as in a dream. His lips opened mechanically, and a voice which did not exactly seem to be his own uttered the "I will!" at the proper time; yet, in recalling the experience afterwards, he was unable to decide whether any definite thought or memory or hope had passed through his mind. From his entrance into the room until his hand was violently shaken by Mr. Blessing, there was a blank.

Of course there were tears, but the beams of congratulation shone through them, and they saddened nobody. Miss Fanny Woollish assured the bridal pair, in an audible whisper, that she had never seen a *sweeter* wedding; and her mother, a stout, homely little body, confirmed the opinion with, "Yes, you both did beautifully!" Then the marriage certificate was produced and signed, and the company partook of wine and refreshments to strengthen them for the reception.

Until there had been half a dozen arrivals, Mrs. Blessing moved about restlessly, and her eyes wandered to the front window. Suddenly three or four carriages came rattling together up the street, and Joseph heard her whisper to her husband: "There they are! it will be a success!" It was not long before the little room was uncomfortably crowded, and the presentations followed so rapidly that Joseph soon became bewildered. Julia, however, knew and welcomed every one with the most bewitching grace, being rewarded with kisses by the gorgeous young ladies and compliments by the young men with weak mouths and retreating chins.

In the midst of the confusion Mr. Blessing, with a wave of his hand, presented "Mr. Collector Twining" and "Mr. Surveyor Knob" and "Mr. Appraiser Gerrish," all of whom greeted Joseph with a bland, almost affectionate, cordiality. The door of the dining-room was then thrown open, and the three dignitaries accompanied the bridal pair to the table. Two servants rapidly whisked the champagne bottles from a cooling-tub in the adjoining closet, and Mr. Blessing commenced stirring and testing a huge bowl of punch. Collector Twining made a neat little speech, proposing the health of bride and bridegroom, with a pun upon the former's name, which was received with as much delight as if it had never been heard before. Therefore Mr. Surveyor Knob repeated it in giving the health of the bride's parents. The enthusiasm of the company not having diminished, Mr. Appraiser Gerrish improved the pun in a third form, in proposing "the Ladies." Then Mr. Blessing, although his feelings overcame him, and he was obliged to use a handkerchief smelling equally of benzine and eau de cologne, responded, introducing the collector's and surveyor's names with an ingenuity which was accepted as the inspiration of genius. His peroration was especially admired.

"On this happy occasion," he said, "the elements of national power and prosperity are represented. My son-in-law, Mr. Asten, is a noble specimen of the agricultural population,—the free American yeomanry; my daughter, if I may be allowed to say it in the presence of so many bright eyes and blooming cheeks, is a representative child of the city, which is the embodiment of the nation's action and enterprise. The union of the two is the movement of our life. The city gives to the country as the ocean gives the cloud to the mountain-springs: the country gives to the city as the streams flow back to the ocean. ["Admirable!" Mr. Collector Twining exclaimed.] Then we have, as our highest honor, the representatives of the political system under which city and country flourish alike. The wings of our eagle must be extended over this fortunate house today, for here are the strong Claws which seize and guard its treasures!"

The health of the Claws was drunk enthusiastically. Mr. Blessing was congratulated on his eloquence; the young gentlemen begged the privilege of touching their glasses to his, and every touch required that the contents be replenished; so that the bottom of the punch-bowl was nearly reached before the guests departed.

When Joseph came down in his travelling-dress, he found the drawing-room empty of the crowd; but leaves, withered flowers, crumbs of cake, and crumpled cards scattered over the carpet, indicated what had taken place. In the dining-room Mr. Blessing, with his cravat loosened, was smoking a cigar at the open window.

"Come, son-in-law!" he cried, "take another glass of punch before you start."

Joseph declined, on the plea that he was not accustomed to the beverage.

"Nothing could have gone off better!" said Mr. Blessing. "The collector was delighted: by the by, you're to go to the St. Jerome, when you get to New York this evening. He telegraphed to have the bridal-chamber reserved for you. Tell Julia: she won't forget it. That girl has a deuced sharp intellect: if you'll be guided by her in your operations—"

"Pa, what are you saying about me?" Julia asked, hastily entering the room.

"Only that you have a deuced sharp intellect, and to-day proves it. Asten is one of us now, and I may tell him of his luck."

He winked and laughed stupidly, and Joseph understood and obeyed his wife's appealing glance. He went to his mother-in-law in the drawing-room.

Julia lightly and swiftly shut the door. "Pa," she said, in a strong, angry whisper; "if you are not able to talk coherently, you must keep your tongue still. What will Joseph think of *me*, to hear you?"

"What he'll think anyhow, in a little while," he doggedly replied. "Julia, you have played a keen game, and played it well; but you don't know much of men yet. He'll not always be the innocent, white-nosed lamb he is now, nibbling the posies you hold out to him. Wait till he asks for stronger feed, and see whether he'll follow you!"

She was looking on the floor, pale and stern. Suddenly one of her gloves burst, across the back of the hand. "Pa," she then said, "it's very cruel to say such things to me, now when I'm leaving you."

"So it is!" he exclaimed, tearfully contrite; "I am a wretch! They flattered my speech so much,—the collector was so impressed by me,—and said so many pleasant things, that—I don't feel quite steady. Don't forget the St. Jerome; the bridal-chamber is ordered, and I'll see that Mumm writes a good account for the 'Evening Mercury.' I wish you could be here to remember my speech for me. O, I shall miss you! I shall miss you!"

With these words, and his arm lovingly about his daughter, they joined the family. The carriage was already at the door, and the coachman was busy with the travelling-trunks. There were satchels, and little packages,—an astonishing number it seemed to Joseph,—to be gathered together, and then the farewells were said.

As they rolled through the streets towards the station, Julia laid her head upon her husband's shoulder, drew a long, deep breath, and said, "Now all our obligations to society are fulfilled, and we can rest awhile. For the first time in my life I am a free woman,—and you have liberated me!"

He answered her in glad and tender words; he was equally grateful that the exciting day was over. But, as they sped away from the city through the mellow October landscapes, Philip's earnest, dark gray eyes, warm with more than brotherly love, haunted his memory, and he knew that Philip's faithful thoughts followed him.

II. LEAVES OF GRASS

The following section includes notable poems from Walt Whitman's *Leaves of Grass*, with their years and editions noted, as Whitman would often add to or censor his poems with each new edition. The excerpts have been pulled from the online Walt Whitman Archive (accessed 2017), maintained by chief editors Ed Folsom and Kenneth M. Price.

9. [HOURS CONTINUING LONG]

Hours continuing long, sore and heavy-hearted,
Hours of the dusk, when I withdraw to a lonesome and unfrequented spot,
        seating myself, leaning my face in my hands;
Hours sleepless, deep in the night, when I go forth, speeding swiftly the
        country roads, or through the city streets, or pacing miles and
        miles, stifling plaintive cries;
Hours discouraged, distracted—for the one I cannot content myself
        without, soon I saw him content himself without me;
Hours when I am forgotten, (O weeks and months are passing, but I
        believe I am never to forget!)
Sullen and suffering hours! (I am ashamed—but it is useless—I am what I
        am;)
Hours of my torment—I wonder if other men ever have the like, out of the
        like feelings?
Is there even one other like me—distracted—his friend, his lover, lost to
        him?
Is he too as I am now? Does he still rise in the morning, dejected, thinking
        who is lost to him? and at night, awaking, think who is lost?
Does he too harbor his friendship silent and endless? harbor his anguish
        and passion?

Does some stray reminder, or the casual mention of a name, bring the fit
        back upon him, taciturn and deprest?
Does he see himself reflected in me? In these hours, does he see the face of
        his hours reflected?

(*Leaves of Grass*, 1860; 3rd Edition)
http://whitmanarchive.org/published/LG/1860/poems/85

WHOEVER YOU ARE HOLDING ME NOW IN HAND.

1
Whoever you are, holding me now in hand,
Without one thing, all will be useless,
I give you fair warning, before you attempt me further,
I am not what you supposed, but far different.

2
Who is he that would become my follower?
Who would sign himself a candidate for my affections?

3
The way is suspicious—the result uncertain, perhaps destructive;
You would have to give up all else—I alone would expect to be your God,
        sole and exclusive,
Your novitiate would even then be long and exhausting,
The whole past theory of your life, and all conformity to the lives around
        you, would have to be abandoned;
Therefore release me now, before troubling yourself any further—Let go
        your hand from my shoulders,
Put me down, and depart on your way.

4
Or else, by stealth, in some wood, for trial,
Or back of a rock, in the open air,
(For in any roof'd room of a house I emerge not—nor in company,
And in libraries I lie as one dumb, a gawk, or unborn, or dead,)
But just possibly with you on a high hill—first watching lest any person, for
        miles around, approach unawares,
Or possibly with you sailing at sea, or on the beach of the sea, or some quiet
        island,
Here to put your lips upon mine I permit you,

With the comrade's long-dwelling kiss, or the new husband's kiss,
For I am the new husband, and I am the comrade.

5

Or, if you will, thrusting me beneath your clothing,
Where I may feel the throbs of your heart, or rest upon your hip,
Carry me when you go forth over land or sea;
For thus, merely touching you, is enough—is best,
And thus, touching you, would I silently sleep and be carried eternally.

6

But these leaves conning, you con at peril,
For these leaves, and me, you will not understand,
They will elude you at first, and still more afterward—I will certainly elude you,
Even while you should think you had unquestionably caught me, behold!
Already you see I have escaped from you.

7

For it is not for what I have put into it that I have written this book,
Nor is it by reading it you will acquire it,
Nor do those know me best who admire me, and vauntingly praise me,
Nor will the candidates for my love, (unless at most a very few,) prove
        victorious,
Nor will my poems do good only—they will do just as much evil, perhaps
        more;
For all is useless without that which you may guess at many times and not
        hit—that which I hinted at;
Therefore release me, and depart on your way.

(*Leaves of Grass*, 1867; 5th Edition)
http://whitmanarchive.org/published/LG/1867/clusters/23

IN PATHS UNTRODDEN.

IN paths untrodden,
In the growth by margins of pond-waters,
Escaped from the life that exhibits itself,
From all the standards hitherto publish'd—from the
        pleasures, profits, eruditions, conformities,
Which too long I was offering to feed my soul;
Clear to me, now, standards not yet publish'd—clear to me that my Soul,

That the Soul of the man I speak for, feeds, rejoices most in comrades;
Here, by myself, away from the clank of the world,
Tallying and talk'd to here by tongues aromatic,
No longer abash'd—for in this secluded spot I can respond as I would not
          dare elsewhere,
Strong upon me the life that does not exhibit itself, yet contains all the rest,
Resolv'd to sing no songs to-day but those of manly attachment,
Projecting them along that substantial life,
Bequeathing, hence, types of athletic love,
Afternoon, this delicious Ninth-month, in my forty-first year,
I proceed, for all who are, or have been, young men,
To tell the secret of my nights and days,
To celebrate the need of comrades.

(*Leaves of Grass*, 1871; 6th Edition)
http://whitmanarchive.org/published/LG/1871/poems/38

AMONG THE MULTITUDE.

AMONG the men and women the multitude,
I perceive one picking me out by secret and divine signs,
Acknowledging none else, not parent, wife, husband, brother, child, any
          nearer than I am,
Some are baffled, but that one is not—that one knows me.

Ah lover and perfect equal,
I meant that you should discover me so by faint indirections,
And I when I meet you mean to discover you by the like in you.

(*Leaves of Grass*, 1881-1882; 8th Edition)
http://whitmanarchive.org/published/LG/1881/poems/81

GODS

Lover divine and perfect Comrade,
Waiting content, invisible yet, but certain,
Be thou my God.

Thou, thou, the Ideal Man,
Fair, able, beautiful, content, and loving,
Complete in body and dilate in spirit,
Be thou my God.

O Death, (for Life has served its turn,)
Opener and usher to the heavenly mansion,
Be thou my God.

Aught, aught of mightiest, best I see, conceive, or know,
(To break the stagnant tie—thee, thee to free, O soul,)
Be thou my God.

All great ideas, the races' aspirations,
All heroisms, deeds of rapt enthusiasts,
Be ye my Gods.

Or Time and Space,
Or shape of Earth divine and wondrous,
Or some fair shape I viewing, worship,
Or lustrous orb of sun or star by night,
Be ye my Gods.

(*Leaves of Grass*, 1881-1882; 8th Edition)
http://whitmanarchive.org/published/LG/1881/clusters/122

THE WOUND-DRESSER.

1

An old man bending I come among new faces,
Years looking backward resuming in answer to children,
Come tell us old man, as from young men and maidens that love me,
(Arous'd and angry, I'd thought to beat the alarum, and urge relentless war,
But soon my fingers fail'd me, my face droop'd and I resign'd myself,
To sit by the wounded and soothe them, or silently watch the dead;)
Years hence of these scenes, of these furious passions, these chances,
Of unsurpass'd heroes, (was one side so brave? the other was equally brave;)
Now be witness again, paint the mightiest armies of earth,
Of those armies so rapid so wondrous what saw you to tell us?
What stays with you latest and deepest? of curious panics,
Of hard-fought engagements or sieges tremendous what deepest remains?

2

O maidens and young men I love and that love me,
What you ask of my days those the strangest and sudden your talking
      recalls,
Soldier alert I arrive after a long march cover'd with sweat and dust,
In the nick of time I come, plunge in the fight, loudly shout in the rush of
      successful charge,
Enter the captur'd works—yet lo, like a swift-running river they fade,
Pass and are gone they fade—I dwell not on soldiers' perils or soldiers' joys,
(Both I remember well—many the hardships, few the joys, yet I was
      content.)

But in silence, in dreams' projections,
While the world of gain and appearance and mirth goes on,
So soon what is over forgotten, and waves wash the imprints off the sand,
With hinged knees returning I enter the doors, (while for you up there,
Whoever you are, follow without noise and be of strong heart.)

Bearing the bandages, water and sponge,
Straight and swift to my wounded I go,
Where they lie on the ground after the battle brought in,
Where their priceless blood reddens the grass the ground,
Or to the rows of the hospital tent, or under the roof'd hospital,
To the long rows of cots up and down each side I return,
To each and all one after another I draw near, not one do I miss,
An attendant follows holding a tray, he carries a refuse pail,
Soon to be fill'd with clotted rags and blood, emptied, and fill'd again.

I onward go, I stop,
With hinged knees and steady hand to dress wounds,
I am firm with each, the pangs are sharp yet unavoidable,
One turns to me his appealing eyes—poor boy! I never knew you,
Yet I think I could not refuse this moment to die for you, if that would save
      you.

3

On, on I go, (open doors of time! open hospital doors!)
The crush'd head I dress, (poor crazed hand tear not the bandage away,)
The neck of the cavalry-man with the bullet through and through I
      examine,
Hard the breathing rattles, quite glazed already the eye, yet life struggles
      hard,
(Come sweet death! be persuaded O beautiful death! In mercy come quickly.)

From the stump of the arm, the amputated hand,
I undo the clotted lint, remove the slough, wash off the matter and blood,
Back on his pillow the soldier bends with curv'd neck and side-falling head,
His eyes are closed, his face is pale, he dares not look on the bloody stump,
And has not yet look'd on it.

I dress a wound in the side, deep, deep,
But a day or two more, for see the frame all wasted and sinking,
And the yellow-blue countenance see.

I dress the perforated shoulder, the foot with the bullet-wound,
Cleanse the one with a gnawing and putrid gangrene, so sickening, so
      offensive,
While the attendant stands behind aside me holding the tray and pail.

I am faithful, I do not give out,
The fractur'd thigh, the knee, the wound in the abdomen,
These and more I dress with impassive hand, (yet deep in my breast a fire, a
      burning flame.)

4

Thus in silence in dreams' projections,
Returning, resuming, I thread my way through the hospitals,
The hurt and wounded I pacify with soothing hand,
I sit by the restless all the dark night, some are so young,
Some suffer so much, I recall the experience sweet and sad,
(Many a soldier's loving arms about this neck have cross'd and rested,
Many a soldier's kiss dwells on these bearded lips.)

(*Leaves of Grass*, 1881-1882; 8th Edition)
http://whitmanarchive.org/published/LG/1881/poems/169

NATIVE MOMENTS.

Native moments—when you come upon me—ah you are here now,
Give me now libidinous joys only,
Give me the drench of my passions, give me life coarse and rank,
To-day I go consort with Nature's darlings, to-night too,
I am for those who believe in loose delights, I share the midnight orgies of
      young men,
I dance with the dancers and drink with the drinkers,
The echoes ring with our indecent calls, I pick out some low person for my
      dearest friend,
He shall be lawless, rude, illiterate, he shall be one condemn'd by others for
      deeds done,
I will play a part no longer, why should I exile myself from my companions?
O you shunn'd persons, I at least do not shun you,
I come forthwith in your midst, I will be your poet,
I will be more to you than to any of the rest.

(*Leaves of Grass*, 1891-1892; 9th Edition)
http://whitmanarchive.org/published/LG/1891/poems/40

THIS MOMENT YEARNING AND THOUGHTFUL.

This moment yearning and thoughtful sitting alone,
It seems to me there are other men in other lands yearning and thoughtful,
It seems to me I can look over and behold them in Germany, Italy, France,
      Spain,
Or far, far away, in China, or in Russia or Japan, talking other dialects,
And it seems to me if I could know those men I shouldbecome attached to
      them as I do to men in my own lands,
O I know we should be brethren and lovers,
I know I should be happy with them.

(*Leaves of Grass*, 1891-1892; 9th Edition)
http://whitmanarchive.org/published/LG/1891/poems/64

WE TWO BOYS TOGETHER CLINGING.

We two boys together clinging,
One the other never leaving,
Up and down the roads going, North and South excursions making,
Power enjoying, elbows stretching, fingers clutching,
Arm'd and fearless, eating, drinking, sleeping, loving,
No law less than ourselves owning, sailing, soldiering, thieving, threatening,
Misers, menials, priests alarming, air breathing, water drinking, on the turf
        or the sea-beach dancing,
Cities wrenching, ease scorning, statutes mocking, feebleness chasing,
Fulfilling our foray.

(*Leaves of Grass*, 1891-1892; 9th Edition)
http://whitmanarchive.org/published/LG/1891/poems/68

VIGIL STRANGE I KEPT ON THE FIELD ONE NIGHT.

Vigil strange I kept on the field one night;
When you my son and my comrade dropt at my side that day,
One look I but gave which your dear eyes return'd with a look I shall never
        forget,
One touch of your hand to mine O boy, reach'd up as you lay on the
        ground,
Then onward I sped in the battle, the even-contested battle,
Till late in the night reliev'd to the place at last again I made my way,
Found you in death so cold dear comrade, found your body son of
        responding kisses, (never again on earth responding,)
Bared your face in the starlight, curious the scene, cool blew the moderate
        night-wind,
Long there and then in vigil I stood, dimly around me the battle-field
        spreading,
Vigil wondrous and vigil sweet there in the fragrant silent night,
But not a tear fell, not even a long-drawn sigh, long, long I gazed,
Then on the earth partially reclining sat by your side leaning my chin in my
        hands,
Passing sweet hours, immortal and mystic hours with you dearest
        comrade—not a tear, not a word,
Vigil of silence, love and death, vigil for you my son and my soldier,
As onward silently stars aloft, eastward new ones upward stole,
Vigil final for you brave boy, (I could not save you, swift was your death,

I faithfully loved you and cared for you living, I think we shall surely meet
        again,)
Till at latest lingering of the night, indeed just as the dawn appear'd,
My comrade I wrapt in his blanket, envelop'd well his form,
Folded the blanket well, tucking it carefully over head and care-fully under
        feet,
And there and then and bathed by the rising sun, my son in his grave, in his
        rude-dug grave I deposited,
Ending my vigil strange with that, vigil of night and battle-field dim,
Vigil for boy of responding kisses, (never again on earth responding,)
Vigil for comrade swiftly slain, vigil I never forget, how as day brighten'd,
I rose from the chill ground and folded my soldier well in his blanket,
And buried him where he fell.

(*Leaves of Grass*, 1891-1892; 9th Edition)
http://whitmanarchive.org/published/LG/1891/clusters/163

RECONCILIATION.

Word over all, beautiful as the sky!
Beautiful that war, and all its deeds of carnage, must in time be utterly lost;
That the hands of the sisters Death and Night, incessantly softly wash
        again, and ever again, this soil'd world;
For my enemy is dead—a man divine as myself is dead;
I look where he lies, white-faced and still, in the coffin—I draw near;
I bend down, and touch lightly with my lips the white face in the coffin.

(*Leaves of Grass*, 1891-1892; 9th Edition)
http://whitmanarchive.org/published/LG/1891/poems/182

O CAPTAIN! MY CAPTAIN!

O Captain! my Captain! our fearful trip is done,
The ship has weather'd every rack, the prize we sought is won,
The port is near, the bells I hear, the people all exulting,
While follow eyes the steady keel, the vessel grim and daring;
                But O heart! heart! heart!
                    O the bleeding drops of red,
                            Where on the deck my Captain lies,
                                Fallen cold and dead.

O Captain! my Captain! rise up and hear the bells;
Rise up—for you the flag is flung—for you the bugle trills,
For you bouquets and ribbon'd wreaths—for you the shores a-crowding,
For you they call, the swaying mass, their eager faces turning;
      Here Captain! dear father!
          This arm beneath your head!
            It is some dream that on the deck,
              You've fallen cold and dead.

My Captain does not answer, his lips are pale and still,
My father does not feel my arm, he has no pulse nor will,
The ship is anchor'd safe and sound, its voyage closed and done,
From fearful trip the victor ship comes in with object won;
      Exult O shores, and ring O bells!
          But I with mournful tread,
            Walk the deck my Captain lies,
              Fallen cold and dead.

(*Leaves of Grass*, 1891-1892; 9th Edition)
http://whitmanarchive.org/published/LG/1891/poems/194

For the much lengthier "Poem of Walt Whitman, An American" from the 2nd Edition (1856) of *Leaves of* Grass, which was later reworked into "Song of Myself," see [A.13]. It includes (as the title might suggest) the multitudes of Walt Whitman, with lines so provocative that they're missing from some of the later editions, like, "Dash me with amorous wet, I can repay you." It also includes fellatio imagery such as, "How you settled your head athwart my hips, and gently turn'd over upon me, / And parted the shirt from my bosom-bone, and plunged your tongue to my bare-stript heart, / And reach'd till you felt my beard, and reach'd till you held my feet." There is even a line somewhat prophetic, considering that he would not meet the omnibus conductor Peter Doyle (with whom he had a long and caring relationship, see <u>Chapter 22: Whitman's Peter</u> for more details) until around 1869: "young fellow drives the express-wagon (I love him, though I do not know him)."

Whitman was also once bold with the artwork for *Leaves*, on the title page of the 3rd Edition (1860):

On the title page, the words *Leaves of Grass* are rendered with little spermatozoa swimming among the letters. Plenty of risqué content can be found in the poems, some of which were carried over from the earlier two editions. There's "love-flesh swelling and deliciously aching" and a "slow rude muscle" and "delirious juice" and "limitless limpid jets of love hot and enormous" and "bellies pressed and glued together with love."[33]

Whitman himself had this to say about the angry squeamishness that met his ever-evolving book and its subject matter:

"We have got so in our civilization (which is no civilization at all) that we are afraid to face the body and its issues—when we shrink from the realities of our bodily life: when we refer the functions of the man and the woman, their sex, their passion, their normal necessary desires, to something which is to be kept in the dark and lied about instead of being avowed and gloried in. . . . Sex: sex: sex: whether you sing or make a machine, or go to the North Pole, or love your mother, or build a house, or black shoes, or anything—anything at all—it's sex, sex, sex: sex is the root of it all: sex—the coming together of men and women: sex, sex. . . . always immanent: here with us discredited—not suffered: rejected from our art: yet still sex, sex: the root of roots: the life below the life! . . . It is the thing in my work which has been most misunderstood—that has excited the roundest opposition, the sharpest venom, the unintermitted slander, of the people who regard themselves as the custodians of the morals of the world. Horace [Traubel], you are too young to know the fierceness, the bitterness, the vile quality of this antagonism—how it threw aside all reserves and simply tore me to pieces metaphorically without giving me half a chance to make my meanings clear. You have only heard the echoes of that uproar."[39]

XII

CLOUDS

THERE ARE SOME days when the sun comes slowly up, filling the vapory air with diffused light, in advance of his coming; when the earth grows luminous in the broad, breezeless morning; when nearer objects shine and sparkle, and the distances melt into dim violet and gold; when the vane points to the southwest, and the blood of man feels neither heat nor cold, but only the freshness of that perfect temperature wherein the limits of the body are lost; and the pulses of its life beat in all the life of the world. But ere long the haze, instead of thinning into blue, gradually thickens into gray; the vane creeps southward, swinging to southeast in brief, rising flaws of the air; the horizon darkens; the enfranchised life of the spirit creeps back to its old isolation, shorn of all its rash delight, and already foreboding the despondency which comes with the east wind and the chilly rains.

Some such variation of the atmospheric influences attended Joseph Asten's wedding-travel. The mellow, magical glory of his new life diminished day by day; the blue of his sky became colder and grayer. Yet he could not say that his wife had changed: she was always ready with her smiles, her tender phrases, her longings for quiet and rest, and simple, natural life, away from the conventionalities and claims of Society. But, even as, looking into the pale, tawny-brown of her eyes, he saw no changing depth below the hard, clear surface, so it also seemed with her nature; he painfully endeavored to penetrate beyond expressions, the repetition of which it was hard not to find tiresome, and to reach some spring of character or feeling; yet he found nothing. It was useless to remember that he had been content with those expressions before marriage had given them his own eager interpretation, independent of her will and knowledge; that his duty to her remained the same, for she had not deceived him.

On the other hand, she was as tender and affectionate as he could desire. Indeed, he would often have preferred a less artless manifestation of her fondness; but she playfully insisted on his claiming the best quarters at every stopping-place, on the ground of their bridal character, and was sometimes a little petulant when she fancied that they had not been sufficiently honored. Joseph would have willingly escaped the distinction, allowing himself to be confounded with the prosaic multitude, but she would not permit him to try the experiment.

"The newly married are always detected," she would say, "and they are only laughed at when they try to seem like old couples. Why not be frank and honest, and meet half-way the sympathy which I am sure everybody has for us?"

To this he could make no reply, except that it was not agreeable to exact a special attention.

"But it is our right!" was her answer.

In every railway-car they entered she contrived, in a short time, to impress the nature of their trip upon the other travellers; yet it was done with such apparent unconsciousness, such innocent, impulsive manifestations of her happiness in him, that he could not, in his heart, charge her with having intentionally brought upon him the discomfort of being curiously observed. He could have accustomed himself to endure the latter, had it been inevitable; the suspicion that he owed it to her made it an increasing annoyance. Yet, when the day's journey was over, and they were resting together in their own private apartment, she would bring a stool to his feet, lay her head on his knee, and say: "Now we can talk as we please,—there are none watching and listening."

At such times he was puzzled to guess whether some relic of his former nervous shyness were not remaining, and had made him over-sensitive to her ways. The doubt gave him an additional power of self-control; he resolved to be more slow and cautious of judgment, and observe men and women more carefully than he had been wont to do. Julia had no suspicion of what was passing in his mind: she took it for granted that his nature was still as shallow and transparent as when she first came in contact with it.

After nearly a fortnight this flying life came to an end. They returned to the city for a day, before going home to the farm. The Blessing mansion received them with a hearty welcome; yet, in spite of it, a depressing atmosphere seemed to fill the house. Mrs. Blessing looked pinched and care-worn, Clementina discontented, and Mr. Blessing as melancholy as was possible to so buoyant a politician.

"What's the matter? I hope pa hasn't lost his place," Julia remarked in an undertone to her mother.

"Lost my place!" Mr. Blessing exclaimed aloud; "I'd like to see how the collection of customs would go on without me. But a man may keep his place, and yet lose his house and home."

Clementina vanished, Mrs. Blessing followed, with her handkerchief to her eyes, and Julia hastened after them, crying: "Ma! dear ma!"

"It's only on *their* account," said Mr. Blessing, pointing after them and speaking to Joseph. "A plucky man never desponds, sir; but women, you'll find, are upset by every reverse."

"May I ask what has happened?"

"A delicate regard for you," Mr. Blessing replied, "would counsel me to conceal it, but my duty as your father-in-law leaves me no alternative. Our human feelings prompt us to show only the bright side of life to those whom we love; principle, however,—conscience, commands us not to suppress the shadows. I am but one out of the many millions of victims of mistaken judgment. The case is simply this; I will omit certain legal technicalities touching the disposition of property, which may not be familiar to you, and state the facts in the most intelligible form; securities which I placed as collaterals for the loan of a sum, not a very large amount, have been very unexpectedly depreciated, but only temporarily so, as all the market knows. If I am forced to sell them at such an untoward crisis, I lose the largest part of my limited means; if I retain them, they will ultimately recover their full value."

"Then why not retain them?" Joseph asked.

"The sum advanced upon them must be repaid, and it so happens—the market being very tight—that every one of my friends is short. Of course, where their own paper is on the street, I can't ask them to float mine for three months longer, which is all that is necessary. A good indorsement is the extent of my necessity; for any one who is familiar with the aspects of the market can see that there must be a great rebound before three months."

"If it were not a very large amount," Joseph began.

"Only a thousand! I know what you were going to say it is perfectly natural: I appreciate it, because, if our positions were reversed, I should have done the same thing. But, although it is a mere form, a temporary fiction, which has the force of reality, and, therefore, so far as you are concerned, I should feel entirely easy, yet it might subject me to very dishonoring suspicions! It might be said that I had availed myself of your entrance into my family to beguile you into pecuniary entanglements; the amount might be exaggerated, the circumstance misrepresented,—no, no! rather than that, let me make the sacrifice like a man! I'm no longer young, it is true; but the feeling that I stand on principle will give me strength to work."

"On the other hand, Mr. Blessing," said Joseph, "very unpleasant things might be said of me, if I should permit you to suffer so serious a loss, when my assistance would prevent it."

"I don't deny it. You have made a two-horned dilemma out of a one-sided embarrassment. Would that I had kept the secret in my own breast! The temptation is strong, I confess, for the mere use of your name for a few months is all I should require. Either the securities will rise to their legitimate value, or some of the capitalists with whom I have dealings will be in a position to accommodate me. I have frequently tided over similar snags and sand-bars in the financial current; they are familiar even to the most skillful operators,—navigators, I might say, to carry out the figure,—and this is an instance where an additional inch of water will lift me from wreck to flood-tide. The question is, should I allow what I feel to be a just principle, a natural suggestion of delicacy, to intervene between my necessity and your generous proffer of assistance?"

"Your family—" Joseph began.

"I know! I know!" Mr. Blessing cried, leaning his head upon his hand. "There is my vulnerable point,—my heel of Achilles! There would be no alternative,—better sell this house than have my paper dishonored! Then, too, I feel that this is a turning-point in my fortunes: if I can squeeze through this narrow pass, I shall find a smooth road beyond. It is not merely the sum which is at stake, but the future possibilities into which it expands. Should I crush the seed while it is germinating? Should I tear up the young tree, with an opening fruit-bud on every twig? You see the considerations that sway me: unless you withdraw your most generous proffer, what can I do but yield and accept it?"

"I have no intention of withdrawing it," Joseph answered, taking his words literally; "I made the offer freely and willingly. If my indorsement is all that is necessary now, I can give it at once."

Mr. Blessing grasped him by the hand, winked hard three or four times, and turned away his head without speaking. Then he drew a large leather pocket-book from his breast, opened it, and produced a printed promissory note.

"We will make it payable at your county bank," said he, "because your name is known there, and upon acceptance—which can be procured in two days—the money will be drawn here. Perhaps we had better say four months, in order to cover all contingencies."

He went to a small writing-desk, at the farther end of the room, and filled the blanks in the note, which Joseph then endorsed. When it was safely lodged in his breast-pocket, he said: "We will keep this entirely to ourselves. My wife, let me whisper to you, is very proud and sensitive, although the De l'Hotels (Doolittles now) were never quite the equals of the De Belsains; but women see matters in a different light. They can't understand the accommodation of a name, but fancy that it implies a kind of humiliation, as if one were soliciting charity."

He laughed and rubbed his hands. "I shall soon be in a position," he said, "to render you a favor in return. My long experience, and, I may add, my intimate knowledge of the financial field, enables me to foresee many splendid opportunities. There are, just now, some movements which are not yet perceptible on the surface. Mark my words! we shall shortly have a new excitement, and a cool, well-seasoned head is a fortune at such times."

"In the country," Joseph replied, "we only learn enough to pay off our debts and invest our earnings. We are in the habit of moving slowly and cautiously. Perhaps we miss opportunities; but if we don't see them, we are just as contented as if they had not been. I have enough for comfort, and try to be satisfied."

"Inherited ideas! They belong to the community in which you live. Are you satisfied with your neighbors' ways of living and thinking? I do not mean to disparage them, but have you no desire to rise above their level? Money,—as I once said at a dinner given to a distinguished railroad man,—money is the engine which draws individuals up the steepest grades of society; it is the lubricating oil which makes the truck of life run easy; it is the safety-break which renders collision and wreck impossible! I have long been accustomed to consider it in the light of power, not of property, and I classify men according as they take one or the other view. The latter are misers; but the former, sir, are philosophers!"

Joseph scarcely knew how to answer this burst of eloquence. But there was no necessity for it; the ladies entered the room at that moment, each one, in her own way, swiftly scrutinizing the two gentlemen. Mrs. Blessing's face lost its woe-worn expression, while a gleam of malicious satisfaction passed over Clementina's.

The next day, on their journey to the country, Julia suddenly said, "I am sure, Joseph, that pa made use of your generosity; pray don't deny it."

There was the faintest trace of hardness in her voice, which he interpreted as indicating dissatisfaction with his failure to confide the matter to her.

"I have no intention of denying anything, Julia," he answered. "I was not called upon to exercise generosity; it was simply what your father would term an 'accommodation.'"

"I understand. How much?"

"An endorsement of his note for a thousand dollars, which is little, when it will prevent him from losing valuable securities."

Julia was silent for at least ten minutes; then, turning towards him with a sternness which she vainly endeavored to conceal under a "wreathed smile," she said: "In future, Joseph, I hope you will always consult me in any pecuniary venture. I may not know much about such matters, but it is my duty to learn. I have been obliged to hear a great deal of financial talk from pa and his friends, and could not help guessing some things which I think I can apply for your benefit. We are to have no secrets from each other, you know."

His own words! After all, what she said was just and right, and he could not explain to himself why he should feel annoyed. Perhaps he missed a frank expression of delight in the assistance he had so promptly given; but why should he suspect that it was unwelcome to her? He tried to banish the feeling, to hide it under self-reproach and shame, but it clung to him most uncomfortably.

Nevertheless, he forgot everything in the pleasure of the homeward drive from the station. The sadness of late autumn lay upon the fields, but spring already said, "I am coming!" in the young wheat; the houses looked warm and cosey behind their sheltering fir-trees; cattle still grazed on the meadows, and the corn was not yet deserted by the huskers. The sun gave a bright edge to the sombre colors of the landscape, and to Joseph's eyes it was beautiful as never before. Julia leaned back in the carriage, and complained of the cold wind.

"There!" cried Joseph, as a view of the valley opened below them, with the stream flashing like steel between the leafless sycamores,—"there is home-land! Do you know where to look for our house?"

Julia made an effort, leaned forward, smiled, and pointed silently across the shoulder of a hill to the eastward. "You surely didn't suppose I *could* forget," she murmured.

Rachel Miller awaited them at the gate, and Julia had no sooner alighted than she flung herself into her arms. "Dear Aunt Rachel!" she cried: "you must now take my mother's place; I have so much to learn from you! It is doubly a home since you are here. I feel that we shall all be happy together!"

Then there were kisses, of which Joseph received his share, and the first evening lapsed away in perfect harmony. Everything was delightful: the room, the furniture, the meal, even the roar of the wind in the dusky trees. While Julia lay in the cushioned rocking-chair, Rachel gave her nephew an account of all that had been done on the farm; but Joseph only answered her from the surface of his mind. Under the current of his talk ran a graver thought, which said: "You wanted independence and a chance of growth for your life; you fancied they would come in this form. Lo, now! here are the conditions which you desired to establish; from this hour begins the new life of which you dreamed. Whether you have been wise or rash, you can change nothing. You are limited, as before, though within a different circle. You may pace it to its fullest extent, but all the lessons you have yet learned require you to be satisfied within it."

12. WHITMAN AND EMERSON

Walt Whitman and Ralph Waldo Emerson had as strange an association as that between Whitman and Taylor:

Back in the 1830s, Ralph Waldo Emerson had emerged as the leading light of transcendentalism, the profoundly influential movement centered in New England and dedicated to such precepts as the infinite potential of humankind and the need for self-reliance. Arguably, Emerson remained *the* arbiter of literary taste in America. He had a very different response to Whitman's work than the critics. On July 21, 1855, Emerson wrote Whitman a five-page letter that contained the following: "I am not blind to the worth of the wonderful gift of 'Leaves of Grass.' I find it the most extraordinary piece of wit and wisdom that America has yet contributed. . . . I find incomparable things said incomparably well, as they must be." And the kicker: "I greet you at the beginning of a great career." On receiving the letter, Whitman was wonderstruck. For several months, he carried the folded letter around in his pocket, secret confirmation of his singular talent. [...] For the second edition [of *Leaves of Grass*], the most striking change appeared on the book's spine, where the following was stamped in gold: "I Greet You at the Beginning of a Great Career R. W. Emerson." Inside the volume, Whitman reprinted Emerson's letter in full. [See (A.11) for Emerson's letter as reprinted by Whitman.] Taking matters still further, Whitman crafted a kind of open letter to Emerson. He didn't mail it to him; rather, the letter was simply published in the book, where it served as a canny device to help position the new volume. Whitman's open letter begins: "Here are thirty-two Poems, which I send you, dear Friend and Master." The implication was clear: not only had Emerson endorsed the twelve poems in the first edition, but his blessing extended to the new poems as well. Upon receiving a copy of the new edition in the mail, the cold, fastidious Emerson was overcome with hot passion. Friends reported that they had never seen him so angry.

Whitman had overstepped his boundaries and succeeded in pushing away his benefactor.[33]

In similar outrageous fashion, Whitman also anonymously reviewed his own book in *The New York Saturday Press* for September of 1855 (see [A.12]). For his part, Emerson would state that he had "great hopes of Whitman until he became Bohemian,"[33] but there is proof that Emerson's greats hopes were always hedged:

From "The Press," Philadelphia, March 18th, 1883: Ralph Waldo Emerson's cordial letter to Walt Whitman "at the beginning of a great career," has become familiar in American literature. Of scarcely less interest is Emerson's frank personal estimate of the new poet in a letter written to Carlyle in 1856, when the flat, thin quarto was unknown to the general, or for that matter, to any reader. "One book came out last summer in New York," Emerson writes, "a nondescript monster, which yet had terrible eyes and buffalo strength, and was indisputably American. It is called *Leaves of Grass*. After you have looked into it, if you think, as you may, that it is only an auctioneer's inventory of a warehouse, you can light your pipe with it."[4]

Emerson still liked Whitman for the type of man he was, however, though he consistently advised against Whitman's choices in poetry (see <u>Chapter 13: Perceptions of Whitman</u> for more detail). Whitman told Traubel:

"Emerson said when we were out together in New York and Boston—said it more than once: 'I envy you your capacity for being at home with anybody in any crowd.' Then he asked me on another occasion: 'Don't you fear now and then that your freedom, your ease, your nonchalance, with men may be misunderstood?' I asked him: 'Do you misunderstand it?' He put his hand on my arm and said: 'No: I see it for what it is: it is beautiful.' Then I said to him: 'Misunderstood? Yes: it will be misunderstood. But what is there I do that is not misunderstood?' He smiled in his sweet gentle way and murmured: 'True! true!'"[39]

Traubel records that Whitman returned Emerson's admiration:

"I loved Emerson for his personality and I always felt that he loved me for something I brought him from the rush of the big cities and the mass of men. We used to walk together, dine together, argue, even, in a sort of a way, though neither of one of us was much of an arguer. We were not much for repartee or sallies or what people ordinarily call humor, but we got along together beautifully—the atmosphere was always sweet, I don't mind saying it, both on Emerson's side and mine: we had no friction—there was no kind of fight in us for each other—we were like two Quakers together."[39]

XIII

PRESENTIMENTS

THE AUTUMN LAPSED into winter, and the household on the Asten farm began to share the isolation of the season. There had been friendly visits from all the nearest neighbors and friends, followed by return visits, and invitations which Julia willingly accepted. She was very amiable, and took pains to confirm the favorable impression which she knew she had made in the summer. Everybody remarked how she had improved in appearance, how round and soft her neck and shoulders, how bright and fresh her complexion. She thanked them, with many grateful expressions to which they were not accustomed, for their friendly reception, which she looked upon as an adoption into their society; but at home, afterwards, she indulged in criticisms of their manners and habits which were not always friendly. Although these were given in a light, playful tone, and it was sometimes impossible not to be amused, Rachel Miller always felt uncomfortable when she heard them.

Then came quiet, lonely days, and Julia, weary of her idle life, undertook to master the details of the housekeeping. She went from garret to cellar, inspecting every article in closet and pantry, wondering much, censuring occasionally, and only praising a little when she found that Rachel was growing tired and irritable. Although she made no material changes, it was soon evident that she had very stubborn views of her own upon many points, and possessed a marked tendency for what the country people call "nearness." Little by little she diminished the bountiful, free-handed manner of provision which had been the habit of the house. One could not say that anything needful was lacking, and Rachel would hardly have been dissatisfied, had she not felt that the innovation was an indirect blame.

In some directions Julia seemed the reverse of "near," persuading Joseph into expenditures which the people considered very extravagant. When the snow came, his new and elegant sleigh, with the wolf-skin robe, the silver-mounted harness, and the silver-sounding bells, was the envy of all the young men, and an abomination to the old. It was a splendor which he could easily afford, and he did not grudge her the pleasure; yet it seemed to change his relation to the neighbors, and some of them were very free in hinting that they felt it so. It would be difficult to explain why they should resent this or any other slight departure from their fashions, but such had always been their custom.

In a few days the snow vanished and a tiresome season of rain and thaw succeeded. The south-eastern winds, blowing from the Atlantic across the intervening lowlands, rolled interminable gray masses of fog over the hills and blurred the scenery of the valley; dripping trees, soaked meadows, and sodden leaves were the only objects that detached themselves from the general void, and became in turn visible to those who travelled the deep, quaking roads. The social intercourse of the neighborhood ceased perforce though the need of it were never so great: what little of the main highway down the valley was visible from the windows appeared to be deserted.

Julia, having exhausted the resources of the house, insisted on acquainting herself with the barn and everything thereto belonging. She laughingly asserted that her education as a farmer's wife was still very incomplete; she must know the amount of the crops, the price of grain, the value of the stock, the manner of work, and whatever else was necessary to her position. Although she made many pretty blunders, it was evident that her apprehension was unusually quick, and that whatever she acquired was fixed in her mind as if for some possible future use. She never wearied of the most trivial details, while Joseph, on the other hand, would often have willingly shortened his lessons. His mind was singularly disturbed between the desire to be gratified by her curiosity, and the fact that its eager and persistent character made him uncomfortable.

When an innocent, confiding nature begins to suspect that its confidence has been misplaced, the first result is a preternatural stubbornness to admit the truth. The clearest impressions are resisted, or half-consciously misinterpreted, with the last force of an illusion which already foresees its own overthrow. Joseph eagerly clung to every look and word and action which confirmed his sliding faith in his wife's sweet and simple character, and repelled—though a deeper instinct told him that a day would come when it *must* be admitted—the evidence of her coldness and selfishness. Yet, even while almost fiercely asserting to his own heart that he had every reason to be happy, he was consumed with a secret fever of unrest, doubt, and dread.

The horns of the growing moon were still turned downwards, and cold, dreary rains were poured upon the land. Julia's patience, in such straits, was wonderful, if the truth had been known, but she saw that some change was necessary for both of them. She therefore proposed, not what she most desired, but what her circumstances prescribed,—a visit from her sister Clementina. Joseph found the request natural enough: it was an infliction, but one which he had anticipated; and after the time had been arranged by letter, he drove to the station to meet the westward train from the city.

Clementina stepped upon the platform, so cloaked and hooded that he only recognized her by the deliberate grace of her movements. She extended her hand, giving his a cordial pressure, which was explained by the brass baggage-checks thus transferred to his charge.

"I will wait in the ladies' room," was all she said.

At the same moment Joseph's arm was grasped.

"What a lucky chance!" exclaimed Philip: then, suddenly pausing in his greeting, he lifted his hat and bowed to Clementina, who nodded slightly as she passed into the room.

"Let me look at you!" Philip resumed, laying his hands on Joseph's shoulders. Their eyes met and lingered, and Joseph felt the blood rise to his face as Philip's gaze sank more deeply into his heart and seemed to fathom its hidden trouble; but presently Philip smiled and said: "I scarcely knew, until this moment, that I had missed you so much, Joseph!"

"Have you come to stay?" Joseph asked.

"I think so. The branch railway down the valley, which you know was projected, is to be built immediately; but there are other reasons why the furnaces should be in blast. If it is possible, the work—and my settlement with it—will begin without any further delay. Is she your first family visit?"

He pointed towards the station.

"She will be with us a fortnight; but you will come, Philip?"

"To be sure!" Philip exclaimed. I only saw her face indistinctly through the veil, but her nod said to me, 'A nearer approach is not objectionable.' Certainly, Miss Blessing; but with all the conventional forms, if you please!"

There was something of scorn and bitterness in the laugh which accompanied these words, and Joseph looked at him with a puzzled air.

"You may as well know now," Philip whispered, "that when I was a spoony youth of twenty, I very nearly imagined myself in love with Miss Clementina Blessing, and she encouraged my greenness until it spread as fast as a bamboo or a gourd-vine. Of course, I've long since congratulated myself that she cut me up, root and branch, when our family fortune was lost. The awkwardness of our intercourse is all on her side. Can she still have faith in her charms and my youth, I wonder? Ye gods! that would be a lovely conclusion of the comedy!"

Joseph could only join in the laugh as they parted. There was no time to reflect upon what had been said. Clementina, nevertheless, assumed a new interest in his eyes; and as he drove her towards the farm, he could not avoid connecting her with Philip in his thoughts. She, too, was evidently preoccupied with the meeting, for Philip's name soon floated to the surface of their conversation.

"I expect a visit from him soon," said Joseph. As she was silent, he ventured to add: "You have no objections to meeting with him, I suppose?"

"Mr. Held is still a gentleman, I believe," Clementina replied, and then changed the subject of conversation.

Julia flew at her sister with open arms, and showered on her a profusion of kisses, all of which were received with perfect serenity, Clementina merely saying, as soon as she could get breath: "Dear me, Julia, I scarcely recognize you! You are already so countrified!"

Rachel Miller, although a woman, and notwithstanding her recent experience, found herself greatly bewildered by this new apparition. Clementina's slow, deliberate movements and her even-toned, musical utterance impressed her with a certain respect;

yet the qualities of character they suggested never manifested themselves. On the contrary, the same words, in any other mouth, would have often expressed malice or heartlessness. Sometimes she heard her own homely phrases repeated, as if by the most unconscious purposeless imitation, and had Julia either smiled or appeared annoyed her suspicions might have been excited; as it was, she was constantly and sorely puzzled.

Once only, and for a moment, the two masks were slightly lifted. At dinner, Clementina, who had turned the conversation upon the subject of birthdays, suddenly said to Joseph: "By the way, Mr. Asten, has Julia told you her age?"

Julia gave a little start, but presently looked up, with an expression meant to be artless.

"I knew it before we were married," Joseph quietly answered.

Clementina bit her lip. Julia, concealing her surprise, flashed a triumphant glance at her sister, then a tender one at Joseph, and said: "We will both let the old birthdays go; we will only have one and the same anniversary from this time on!"

Joseph felt, through some natural magnetism of his nature rather than from any perceptible evidence, that Clementina was sharply and curiously watching the relation between himself and his wife. He had no fear of her detecting misgivings which were not yet acknowledged to himself, but was instinctively on his guard in her presence.

It was not many days before Philip called. Julia received him cordially, as the friend of her husband, while Clementina bowed with an impassive face, without rising from her seat. Philip, however, crossed the room and gave her his hand, saying cheerily: "We used to be old friends, Miss Blessing. You have not forgotten me?"

"We cannot forget when we have been asked to do so," she warbled.

Philip took a chair. "Eight years!" he said: "I am the only one who has changed in that time."

Julia looked at her sister, but the latter was apparently absorbed in comparing some zephyr tints.

"The whirligig of time!" he exclaimed: "who can foresee anything? Then I was an ignorant, petted young aristocrat,—an expectant heir; now behold me, working among miners and puddlers and forgemen! It's a rough but wholesome change. Would you believe it, Mrs. Asten, I've forgotten the mazurka!"

"I wish to forget it," Julia replied: "the spring-house is as important to me as the furnace to you."

"Have you seen the Hopetons lately?" Clementina asked.

Joseph saw a shade pass over Philip's face, and he seemed to hesitate a moment before answering: "I hear they will be neighbors of mine next summer. Mr. Hopeton is interested in the new branch down the valley, and has purchased the old Calvert property for a country residence."

"Indeed? Then you will often see them."

"I hope so: they are very agreeable people. But I shall also have my own little household: my sister will probably join me."

"Not Madeline!" exclaimed Julia.

"Madeline," Philip answered. "It has long been her wish, as well as mine. You know the little cottage on the knoll, at Coventry, Joseph! I have taken it for a year."

"There will be quite a city society," murmured Clementina, in her sweetest tones. "You will need no commiseration, Julia. Unless, indeed, the country people succeed in changing you all into their own likeness. Mrs. Hopeton will certainly create a sensation. I am told that she is very extravagant, Mr. Held?"

"I have never seen her husband's bank account," said Philip, dryly.

He rose presently, and Joseph accompanied him to the lane. Philip, with the bridle-rein over his arm, delayed to mount his horse, while the mechanical commonplaces of speech, which, somehow, always absurdly come to the lips when graver interests have possession of the heart, were exchanged by the two. Joseph felt, rather than saw, that Philip was troubled. Presently the latter said: "Something is coming over both of us,— not between us. I thought I should tell you a little more, but perhaps it is too soon. If I guess rightly, neither of us is ready. Only this, Joseph, let us each think of the other as a help and a support!"

"I do, Philip!" Joseph answered. "I see there is some influence at work which I do not understand, but I am not impatient to know what it is. As for myself, I seem to know nothing at all; but you can judge,—you see all there is."

Even as he pronounced these words Joseph felt that they were not strictly sincere, and almost expected to find an expression of reproof in Philip's eyes. But no: they softened until he only saw a pitying tenderness. Then he knew that the doubts which he had resisted with all the force of his nature were clearly revealed to Philip's mind.

They shook hands, and parted in silence; and Joseph, as he looked up to the gray blank of heaven, asked himself: "Is this all? Has my life already taken the permanent imprint of its future?"

13. PERCEPTIONS OF WHITMAN

From family, friends, foes, and fellow poets, here are some assorted criticisms and perceptions of Walt Whitman and his work throughout the years:

Mother
Whitman's father died too soon to read *Leaves of Grass*, for example, and Horace asked if "not one in the bunch" of his relatives was "in touch with what you have written." Walt replied, "Not one of them, from my dear mother down—not one of them: on the contrary, they are dead set against my book and what it stands for." On another occasion he said of his mother, "She stood before *Leaves of Grass* mystified, defeated."[40]

The Critic
[A] London publication called the *Critic* in 1855: "Walt Whitman is as unacquainted with art, as a hog is with mathematics. His poems—we must call them so for convenience—twelve in number, are innocent of rhythm and resemble nothing so much as the war-cry of Red Indians."[33]

Swinburne
"He is a writer of something occasionally like English, and a man of something occasionally like genius." – Algernon Charles Swinburne, English poet and critic, *Whitmania* (1887)[2]

John Ruskin was Slade Professor of Fine Arts at Oxford University, 1870-78, at the time that Oscar Wilde was a student, and he is one of two major influences on Wilde's formative years at Oxford (the other being Walter Pater). Wilde would later meet Whitman in 1882 (see Chapter 18: Whitman and Wilde for more detail).

Ruskin
In this letter, the prolific Victorian essayist and art critic John Ruskin voices

his surprise and delight upon first encountering Whitman's poetry. A lyrical and omnivorously curious writer himself, Ruskin shows how Whitman's poetry was well received by an English audience generally unprejudiced by negative American reviews.

"These are quite glorious things you have sent me. Who is Walt (Walter?) Whitman, and is much of him like this?" – John Ruskin, Letter to William Harrison Riley (1879)[2]

A Jesuit priest and formal poet, Gerard Manley Hopkins, confesses his admiration for Whitman's poetry and his dislike of his character, which Hopkins regrets resembles his own. Given that both poets were likely homosexual, it may be safe to assume just what he found to worry about in Whitman's poems; as with Bayard Taylor (see Chapter 10: Taylor and Whitman), one gets the impression that certain men with certain private feelings are uncomfortable looking into mirrors.

Hopkins

"I may as well say what I should not otherwise have said, that I always knew in my heart Walt Whitman's mind to be more like my own than any other man's living. As he is a very great scoundrel this is not a pleasant confession. And this also makes me the more desirous to read him and the more determined that I will not. . . . His 'savage' style has advantages, and he has chosen it; he says so. But you cannot eat your cake and keep it: he eats his offhand, I keep mine. It makes a very great difference." – Gerard Manley Hopkins, Letter to Robert Bridges (October 18, 1882)[2]

Whitman's proponents take a similar stance, that if a reader finds something filthy in Whitman, they have brought it there themselves:

Purity Test

Anonymous, "Innate Vulgarity," *Fourteen Thousand Miles Afoot* (1859): "Nothing can more clearly demonstrate the innate vulgarity of our American people, their radical immodesty, their internal licentiousness, their unchastity of heart, their foulness of feeling, than the tabooing of Walt Whitman's *Leaves of Grass*. It is quite impossible to find a publisher for the new edition which has long since been ready for the press, so measureless is the depravity of public taste. There is not an indecent word, an immodest expression, in the entire volume; not a suggestion which is not purity itself, and yet it is rejected on account of its indecency! So much do I think of this work by the healthiest and most original poet America has produced, so valuable a means is it of rightly estimating character, that I have been accustomed to try with it of what quality was the virtue my friends possessed. How few stood the test I shall not say. Some did, and praised it beyond measure. These I set down without hesitation as radically pure, as 'born again,' and fitted for the society of heaven and the angels. And this test I would recommend to every one. Would you, reader, male or female, ascertain if you be actually modest, innocent, pure-minded? read the *Leaves of Grass*. If you find nothing improper there, you are one of the virtuous and pure. If, on the contrary, you find your sense of decency shocked, then is that sense of decency an exceedingly foul one, and you, man or woman, a very vulgar, dirty person."[2]

Nature Without Fig Leaves

Anonymous (1860): "The first and greatest objection brought against Walt Whitman and his *Leaves of Grass* is their indecency. Nature is treated here without fig leaves; things are called by their names, without any apparent sense of modesty or shame. Of this peculiarity—so shocking in an artificial era—the dainty reader should be especially warned. But it is a mistake to infer that the book is on this account necessarily immoral. It is the poet's design, not to entice to the perversion of Nature, which is vice, but to lead us back to Nature, which in his theory is the only virtue. His theory may be wrong, and the manner in which he carried it out repulsive, but no one who reads and understands him will question the sincerity of his motives, however much may be doubted the wisdom of attempting in this way to restore mankind to the days of undraped innocence."[2]

Dr. Bucke records another mention of the metaphorical fig leaf: "Let me suppose that Mr. Phillips, in his own enchanting fashion, really did say of *Leaves of Grass*, as our gossip reports him 'here be all sorts of leaves except fig leaves.'"[4] This same point is repeated back and forth for years, that Whitman's work is naked, and therefor it is good, or bad, or both, meaning neither:

They Find Themselves Obscene

Joseph B. Marvin in the Boston quarterly "Radical" for August, 1877: "A critic of our popular literary school avers that there is not an impure word in Shakespeare, but that Whitman is obscene. Such a declaration as this is the result of a literary glamour which renders moral discrimination simply impossible. Every line of Shakespeare is justified by the standard of supreme art; but whether the critic means to say that the great dramatist's writing are free from textual impurities, or from moral licentiousness, his assertion is equally untrue and absurd. There is not a play of Shakespeare in which the text is not altered upon the stage to suit the prudery of our time; and this critic himself could hardly be persuaded, not withstanding his assertion to read "Venus and Adonis" to a miscellaneous company. But Walt Whitman, though he is gross and rude, is always pure. His grossness is the grossness of Nature, of rude health. Shakespeare's treatment of the amorous passion is often that of the gallant and the voluptuary. Whitman's never; for, though he celebrates the sensuous, he never writes in the interest of sensuality, but of fatherhood and maternity. He avows and rejoices in the deliciousness of sex; but, like Plato in the 'Republic,' he demands sanity and health in it all, and as the result of it all. He is the one poet, in all time, who has celebrated sex in the interest of human progress; in the service of health,—physical and moral,—of equality, Democracy, religion. They who think they find him obscene, in truth find Nature obscene,—find themselves obscene."[4]

Oscar Wilde said the same thing of his own book, *The Picture of Dorian Gray*, in 1890 in writing to the editor of the *Scots Observer*: "Each man sees his own sin in Dorian Gray. What Dorian Gray's sins are no-one knows. He who finds them has brought them." Wilde even built his own 'purity test' into *The Picture of Dorian Gray* via the blackmail between Dorian and chemist Alan Campbell in Chapter Fourteen. Alan's secret is written on a piece of paper, folded carefully, and pushed across a table for him to read to himself. Any suspicion of what Alan might have done would have to come directly from the reader, as it is never revealed what secret is so shameful that it would make a man consent to chemically obliterating a murdered body. It is interesting to note that the arguments over Walt Whitman's purity continue on for so long that Whitman is tarred in comparison with the much younger Oscar Wilde himself:

Slop-Bucket
From the "New York Tribune," November 19, 1881: "After the dilettante indelicacies of William H. Mallock [accused of introducing "the beastly into literature"[14] by a critic] and Oscar Wilde, we are presented with the slop-bucket of Walt Whitman."[4]

For more about Whitman and Oscar Wilde, their correspondence and meeting, see Chapter 18: Whitman and Wilde. The debate carries on:

Venus de Milo
From the "Boston Herald," May 28th, 1882: "Suppressing Walt Whitman's poems is like putting the Venus of Milo in petticoats."[4]

A Sentimental Donkey
From the Boston "Intelligencer," May 3, 1856: "We were attracted by the very singular title of the work to seek the work itself, and what we thought ridiculous in the title is eclipsed in the pages of this heterogeneous mass of bombast, egotism, vulgarity, and nonsense. The beastliness of the author is set forth in his own description of himself, and we can conceive no better reward than the lash for such a violation of decency as we have before us. Speaking of 'this mass of stupid filth,' the 'Criterion' says: 'It is impossible to imagine

how any man's fancy could have conceived it, unless he were possessed of
the soul of a sentimental donkey that had died of disappointed love.' This
book should find no place where humanity urges any claim to respect, and
the author should be kicked from all decent society as below the level of
the brute. There is neither wit nor method in his disjointed babbling, and it
seems to us he must be some escaped lunatic raving in pitiable delirium."[4]

A Faun or A Satyr
William Sloane Kennedy, Massachusetts: "He is not immoral, but unmoral,
as a faun or a satyr; a dynamic force, an animate fragment of the universe, a
destroyer of shams, a live fighter upon the stage."[4]

The book's reputation precedes it in literary circles:

Disgraceful
In April 1862 [Emily Dickinson] wrote to Tomas Higginson, "You speak of
Mr Whitman—I never read his Book—but was told he was disgraceful."[40]

For more on Higginson's criticisms of Whitman, see Chapter 25: The Civil War. For a
long time, and long after Whitman's death, this question posed early on remained: *Can
America embrace its own?*

The Most Prudish Nation in the World
From "The Critic," London, England, 1855: "Is it possible that the most
prudish nation in the world will adopt a poet whose indecencies stink in the
nostrils?"[4]

It was the 3rd Edition of *Leaves of Grass* (1860) that first included the "Calamus" cluster
of poems as a companion to "The Children of Adam" sequence. Calamus is a plant native
to the United States featuring a long, phallic bloom, and the poems focus on man's love for
man (see Chapter 19: Calamus as Cruising Apparatus for more information on its uses).
Here is Whitman's later defense against "Calamus" being too 'Greek,' i.e. homosexual:

Greek culture also came up, unsurprisingly, apropos the Calamus poems.
Traubel reports of a discussion at a Whitman meeting: "There was the subject
of Calamus, which had been much discussed—Sulzberger questioning the
comradeship there announced as verging upon the licentiousness of the
Greek. W. took it seriously, saying thereto: 'He meant the handsome Greek
youth—the one for the other?—Yes I see! and indeed I can see how it might
be opened to such an interpretation. But I can say further, that in the ten
thousand who for many years now have stood ready to make any possible
charge against me—to seize any pretext or suspicion—none have raised this
objection. . . . "Calamus" is a Latin word. . . . I like it much—it is to me, for

my intentions, indispensable—the sun revolves about it, it is a timber of the ship.'"[39]

The timber or mast of a ship, of course, displays the same sort of phallic thrust as the plant's spadix. Shortly before publishing the 1860 edition, Whitman confided to a notebook, "I write with reference to being far better understood then [in "future ages"] than I can possibly be now."[40] Oscar Wilde once more shares nearly the same thought in a letter to Lord Alfred Douglas (see <u>Chapter 19: Calamus as Cruising Apparatus</u> for Whitman's connection to their meeting), saying of his and *Dorian Gray's* perception by the public, "Basil Hallward is what I think I am: Lord Henry is what the world thinks of me: Dorian is what I would like to be—in other ages, perhaps."

> In this [1860] edition those poems treating especially of sexual passions and acts are, for the first time, grouped together under one name, "Children of Adam." Walt Whitman was advised, urged, even implored by his friends to omit or at least modify these pieces. An old and intimate personal friend, urging him one day to leave them out, said to him, "What in the world do you want to put in that stuff for, that nobody can read?" He answered with a smile, "Well, John, if you need to ask that question, it is evident at any rate that the book was not written for you."
>
> In the course of the summer of 1860, while Walt Whitman was in Boston, putting that third edition through the press, Emerson came to see him, and presently said, "When people want to talk in Boston, they go to the Common; let us go there." So they went to the Common, and Emerson talked for something like two hours on the subject of "Children of Adam." He set forth the impolicy, the utter inadvisability of those poems. Walt Whitman listened to all he had to say; he did not argue the point, but when Emerson made an end, he said quietly, "My mind is not changed; I feel, if possible more strongly than ever, that those pieces should be retained." "Very well," said Emerson, "then let us go to dinner."[4]

Whitman's resistance to Emerson's advice continued after the publication of the 3rd Edition and beyond (for more details on the 3rd Edition, see <u>Chapter 11: Leaves of Grass</u>):

> Glowing though all of Whitman's subsequent public comments on Emerson were, in private he never ceased to rankle at Emerson's attempt, during a walk on Boston Common, to urge a taming of his more daring poems. Almost three decades later, Whitman summed up: "He did not see the significance of the sex element as I put it into the book and resolutely there stuck to it—he did not see that if I had cut sex out I might just as well have cut everything out—the full scheme would no longer exist—it would have been violated in

its most sensitive spot."

[...]

Traubel asked, "Don't you think that maybe Emerson was as glad in the end as you were that you refused to expurgate your book?" Whitman's response: "Horace, there—that's it: you've hit the nail on the head: I think he was—yes, just as glad: he liked me better for not accepting his advice. He must have known as well as I knew that it would have been decenter to throw the book away than to mutilate it."[39]

Other critics were not so even-handed:

The third edition of *Leaves* was both a demanding and a provocative work. Predictably, critics tended to focus on the controversial passages. The headlines speak volumes. "'Leaves of Grass'—Smut in Them."—*Springfield (MA) Daily Republican.* "Walt. Whitman's Dirty Book"—*Cincinnati Daily Commercial.* "Mr. Whitman sees nothing vulgar in that which is commonly regarded as the grossest obscenity," wrote a *New York Times* critic, adding that the poet "rejects the laws of conventionality so completely as to become repulsive; gloats over coarse images with the gusto of a Rabelais." In the *Boston Wide World*, a reviewer wrote, "Why, these 'poems' (prose run crazy) are the veriest trash ever written, and vulgar and disgusting to the last degree. There never was more unblushing obscenity presented to the public eye than is to be found in these prurient pages and how any respectable House could publish the volume is beyond my powers to comprehend."[33]

The criticism of Walt Whitman's work did not limit itself to written review, and continued after his death:

Whitman left his gold watch to Traubel in a final will three months before he died. The ultimate fate of the gold watch [...] is melancholy too—and sadly suggestive of how long Whitman has remained, as he said, "*non grata . . . not welcome in the world*" to some folks. When Traubel's transcripts and other manuscripts came to reside permanently in the Library of Congress, the gold watch was found among them and thought inappropriate for housing with the collection. It was forwarded to a Traubel family descendent. Shortly thereafter the disgusted relative returned it—smashed.[40]

Likewise, the criticism of sexual content did not limit itself to Walt Whitman's work, but came to include ill-informed speculation on his personal life as well (as it did in his lifetime, such as when Whitman was fired for being the author of *Leaves of Grass*, see <u>Chapter 24: The Good Gray Poet</u> for details). Assumptions abounded:

In 1913, for example, a Dr. W. C. Rivers published a pamphlet called *Walt Whitman's Anomaly*—its sale, said the title page, being restricted to "Members of the Legal and Medical Professions." Rivers boldly (for his day) concludes that Whitman was a homosexual. Among the dead giveaways: his delight in "cooking, not as a sportsman sometimes will, but for its own sake"; his ability to "talk about clothes with a woman's knowledge"; his "feminine pity for military suffering"; and the "rows of kisses marked upon the paper with crosses" in his "love letters" to Peter Doyle. When Rivers comes to ask "the question as to whether Whitman confined his feelings of affection for his own sex to the emotional sphere only, or whether they found physical vent," he is able to save the poet from *peccatum horrible* by emphasizing his "invariable" passivity. "Partly on account of the passivity noticed, there is no need to charge the poet with the grossest unnatural indulgence of an active kind, but that he experienced orgasm seems certain . . . probably masturbation." Rivers adds, with cheerful, mind-boggling effrontery, "For Whitman mere contact would suffice," and ends with the boast that his analysis is "as sound as an anvil."[40]

For more criticism of Whitman's sympathy for military suffering, see Chapter 25: The Civil War. In the meantime, know that the squeamishness over the subject of Whitman and sex, and the lack of any cognizant conviction about it, extends for over one hundred years after his work first appeared, to 1984:

Paul Zweig [...] allows his courage to weaken when he poses the crucial questions: "A century later, Whitman's sexual life is still a mystery. Was he homosexual? Did he become openly homosexual in the 1850s, his new poetry a celebration of erotic freedom?" Instead of boldly answering these questions with the obvious "yes," Zweig refers at some length to the "dozens" of names of young workingmen that Whitman listed in his notebooks of the 1850s and simply wonders, "Were these men Whitman's lovers? Possibly, but so many?" Then he backed away with charming equivocation, saying that these lists "do not tell us that he was homosexual or, if he was, that he performed athletic feats of intercourse and kept a score sheet." These lists, Zweig lamely adds, only tell us of Whitman's "collector's mentality."[40]

For more information on Whitman's lists of men he encountered, see: Chapter 21: Whitman's Boys. Walt Whitman was often criticized for thinking much more highly of himself than his critics deemed he ought to, and John W.M. Hallock points out that Whitman was once so bold as to officially review himself:

Whitman realized that if one did not like what critics had to say, one could anonymously review oneself. Byron had been destroyed by the media,

Halleck had evaded it, and Whitman manipulated it to an unconscionable degree.[22]

It is the same impulse that led Oscar Wilde to go onstage, after a performance of his play *Lady Windermere's Fan*, and review both himself and his audience very glowingly, or to tell people plainly that they should go see his play because, "It is genius!" (see <u>Chapter 18: Whitman and Wilde</u> for more detail). For what Whitman had to say about himself, see [A.12]. For what he had to say about his critics in return, see below:

[They were] Whitman's despised fancy, parlor-bound literary critics and custodians of morals—the prudes and puritans, as he wrote in his open letter to Emerson in 1856, who were wedded to "the fashionable delusion of the inherent nastiness of sex, and of the feeble and querulous modesty of deprivation."[40]

In response to bad reviews Walt said: "Better to have people stirred against you if they can't be stirred for you—better that than not to stir them at all."[33]

"The world at large might suppose I am sensitive. . . . But there are three or four of my very most intimate friends—those nearest, best understanding me—who thoroughly realize that my disposition is to hear all—the worst word that is said—the ignorantest—whatever."[39]

"Every whipper-snapper of a reviewer, instead of trying to get at the motive of a book or an incident, sets out sharply to abuse a fellow because he don't accomplish what he never aimed for and sometimes would not have if he could."[39]

In 1888 [...] he reported to Traubel, "A man was here the other day who asked me: 'Don't you feel rather sorry on the whole that you wrote the sex poems?' I answered him by asking another question: 'Don't you feel rather sorry on the whole that I am Walt Whitman?'"[40]

XIV

THE AMARANTH

CLEMENTINA RETURNED TO the city without having made any very satisfactory discovery. Her parting was therefore conventionally tender: she even thanked Joseph for his hospitality, and endeavored to throw a little natural emphasis into her words as she expressed the hope of being allowed to renew her visit in the summer.

During her stay it seemed to Joseph that the early harmony of his household had been restored. Julia's manner had been so gentle and amiable, that, on looking back, he was inclined to believe that the loneliness of her new life was alone responsible for any change. But after Clementina's departure his doubts were reawakened in a more threatening form. He could not guess, as yet, the terrible chafing of a smiling mask; of a restraint which must not only conceal itself, but counterfeit its opposite; of the assumption by a narrow, cold, and selfish nature of virtues which it secretly despises. He could not have foreseen that the gentleness, which had nearly revived his faith in her, would so suddenly disappear. But it was gone, like a glimpse of the sun through the winter fog. The hard, watchful expression came back to Julia's face; the lowered eyelids no longer gave a fictitious depth to her shallow, tawny pupils; the soft roundness of her voice took on a frequent harshness, and the desire of asserting her own will in all things betrayed itself through her affected habits of yielding and seeking counsel.

She continued her plan of making herself acquainted with all the details of the farm business. When the roads began to improve, in the early spring, she insisted in driving to the village alone, and Joseph soon found that she made good use of these journeys in extending her knowledge of the social and pecuniary standing of all the neighboring families. She talked with farmers, mechanics, and drovers; became familiar with the fluctuations in the prices of grain and cattle; learned to a penny the wages paid for every form of service; and thus felt, from week to week, the ground growing more secure under her feet.

Joseph was not surprised to see that his aunt's participation in the direction of the household gradually diminished. Indeed, he scarcely noticed the circumstance at all, but he was at last forced to remark her increasing silence and the trouble of her face. To all appearance the domestic harmony was perfect, and if Rachel Miller felt some natural regret at being obliged to divide her sway, it was a matter, he thought, wherein he had best not interfere. One day, however, she surprised him by the request:—

"Joseph, can you take or send me to Magnolia to-morrow?"

"Certainly, Aunt!" he replied. "I suppose you want to visit Cousin Phebe; you have not seen her since last summer."

"It was that,—and something more." She paused a moment, and then added, more firmly: "She has always wished that I should make my home with her, but I couldn't think of any change so long as I was needed here. It seems to me that I am not really needed now."

"Why, Aunt Rachel!" Joseph exclaimed, "I meant this to be your home always, as much as mine! Of course you are needed,—not to do all that you have done heretofore, but as a part of the family. It is your right."

"I understand all that, Joseph. But I've heard it said that a young wife should learn to see to everything herself, and Julia, I'm sure, doesn't need either my help or my advice."

Joseph's face became very grave. "Has she—has she—?" he stammered.

"No," said Rachel, "she has not said it—in words. Different persons have different ways. She is quick, O very quick!—and capable. You know I could never sit idly by, and look on; and it's hard to be directed. I seem to belong to the place and everything connected with it; yet there's times when what a body ought to do is plain."

In endeavoring to steer a middle course between her conscience and her tender regard for her nephew's feelings Rachel only confused and troubled him. Her words conveyed something of the truth which she sought to hide under them. She was both angered and humiliated; the resistance with which she had attempted to meet Julia's domestic innovations was no match for the latter's tactics; it had gone down like a barrier of reeds and been contemptuously trampled underfoot. She saw herself limited, opposed, and finally set aside by a cheerful dexterity of management which evaded her grasp whenever she tried to resent it. Definite acts, whereon to base her indignation, seemed to slip from her memory, but the atmosphere of the house became fatal to her. She felt this while she spoke, and felt also that Joseph must be spared.

"Aunt Rachel," said he, "I know that Julia is very anxious to learn everything which she thinks belongs to her place,—perhaps a little more than is really necessary. She's an enthusiastic nature, you know. Maybe you are not fully acquainted yet; maybe you have misunderstood her in some things: I would like to think so."

"It is true that we are different, Joseph,—*very* different. I don't say, therefore, that I'm always right. It's likely, indeed, that any young wife and any old housekeeper like myself would have their various notions. But where there can be only one head, it's the wife's place to be that head. Julia has not asked it of me, but she has the right. I can't say, also, that I don't need a little rest and change, and there seems to be some call on me to oblige Phebe. Look at the matter in the true light," she continued, seeing that Joseph remained silent, "and you must feel that it's only natural."

"I hope so," he said at last, repressing a sigh; "all things are changing."

"What can we do?" Julia asked, that evening, when he had communicated to her his aunt's resolution; "it would be so delightful if she would stay, and yet I have had a presentiment that she would leave us—for a little while only, I hope. Dear, good Aunt Rachel! I couldn't help seeing how hard it was for her to allow the least change in the order of housekeeping. She would be perfectly happy if I would sit still all day and let her tire herself to death; but how can I do that, Joseph? And no two women have exactly the same ways and habits. I've tried to make everything pleasant for her: if she would only leave many little matters entirely to me, or at least not think of them,—but I fear she cannot. She manages to see the least that I do, and secretly worries about it, in the very kindness of her heart. Why can't women carry on partnerships in housekeeping as men do in business? I suppose we are too particular; perhaps I am just as much so as Aunt Rachel. I have no doubt she thinks a little hardly of me, and so it would do her good—we should really come nearer again—if she had a change. If she *will* go, Joseph, she must at least leave us with the feeling that our home is always hers, whenever she chooses to accept it."

Julia bent over Joseph's chair, gave him a rapid kiss, and then went off to make her peace with Aunt Rachel. When the two women came to the tea-table the latter had an uncertain, bewildered air, while the eyelids of the former were red,—either from tears or much rubbing.

A fortnight afterwards Rachel Miller left the farm and went to reside with her widowed niece, in Magnolia.

The day after her departure another surprise came to Joseph in the person of his father-in-law. Mr. Blessing arrived in a hired vehicle from the station. His face was so red and radiant from the March winds, and perhaps some private source of satisfaction, that his sudden arrival could not possibly be interpreted as an omen of ill-fortune. He shook hands with the Irish groom who had driven him over, gave him a handsome gratuity in addition to the hire of the team, extracted an elegant travelling-satchel from under the seat, and met Joseph at the gate, with a breezy burst of feeling:—

"God bless you, son-in-law! It does my heart good to see you again! And then, at last, the pleasure of beholding your ancestral seat; really, this is quite—quite manorial!"

Julia, with a loud cry of "O pa!" came rushing from the house.

"Bless me, how wild and fresh the child looks!" cried Mr. Blessing, after the embrace. "Only see the country roses on her cheeks! Almost too young and sparkling for Lady Asten, of Asten Hall, eh? As Dryden says, 'Happy, happy, happy pair!' It takes me back to the days when I was a gay young lark; but I must have a care, and not make an old fool of myself. Let us go in and subside into soberness: I am ready both to laugh and cry."

When they were seated in the comfortable front room, Mr. Blessing opened his satchel and produced a large leather-covered flask. Julia was probably accustomed to his habits, for she at once brought a glass from the sideboard.

"I am still plagued with my old cramps," her father said to Joseph, as he poured out a stout dose. "Physiologists, you know, have discovered that stimulants diminish the wear and tear of life, and I find their theories correct. You, in your pastoral isolation and pecuniary security, can form no conception of the tension under which we men of office and of the world live. *Beatus ille*, and so forth,—strange that the only fragment of Latin which I remember should be so appropriate! A little water, if you please, Julia."

In the evening, when Mr. Blessing, slippered, sat before the open fireplace, with a cigar in his mouth, the object of his sudden visit crept by slow degrees to the light. "Have you been dipping into oil?" he asked Joseph.

Julia made haste to reply. "Not yet, but almost everybody in the neighborhood is ready to do so now, since Clemson has realized his fifty thousand dollars in a single year. They are talking of nothing else in the village. I heard yesterday, Joseph, that Old Bishop has taken three thousand dollars' worth of stock in a new company."

"Take my advice, and don't touch 'em!" exclaimed Mr. Blessing.

"I had not intended to," said Joseph.

"There is this thing about these excitements," Mr. Blessing continued: "they never reach the rural districts until the first sure harvest is over. The sharp, intelligent operators in the large cities—the men who are ready to take up soap, thimbles, hand-organs, electricity, or hymn-books, at a moment's notice—always cut into a new thing before its value is guessed by the multitude. Then the smaller fry follow and secure their second crop, while your quiet men in the country are shaking their heads and crying 'humbug!' Finally, when it really gets to be a humbug, in a speculative sense, they just begin to believe in it, and are fair game for the bummers and camp-followers of the financial army. I respect Clemson, though I never heard of him before as for Old Bishop, he may be a very worthy man, but he'll never see the color of his three thousand dollars again."

"Pa!" cried Julia, "how clear you do make everything. And to think that I was wishing—O, wishing *so* much!—that Joseph would go into oil."

She hung her head a little, looking at Joseph with an affectionate, penitent glance. A quick gleam of satisfaction passed over Mr. Blessing's face; he smiled to himself, puffed rapidly at his cigar for a minute, and then resumed: "In such a field of speculation everything depends on being initiated. There are men in the city—friends of mine—who know every foot of ground in the Alleghany Valley. They can smell oil, if it's a thousand feet deep. They never touch a thing that isn't safe,—but, then, they know *what's* safe. In spite of the swindling that's going on, it takes years to exhaust the good points; just so sure as your honest neighbors here will lose, just so sure will these friends of mine gain. There are millions in what they have under way, at this moment."

"What is it?" Julia breathlessly asked, while Joseph's face betrayed that his interest was somewhat aroused.

Mr. Blessing unlocked his satchel, and took from it a roll of paper, which he began to unfold upon his knee. "Here," he said, "you see this bend of the river, just about the centre of the oil region, which is represented by the yellow color. These little dots above the bend are the celebrated Fluke Wells; the other dots below are the equally celebrated Chowder Wells. The distance between the two is nearly three miles. Here is an untouched portion of the treasure,—a pocket of Pactolus waiting to be rifled. A few of us have acquired the land, and shall commence boring immediately."

"But," said Joseph, "it seems to me that either the attempt must have been made already, or that the land must command such an enormous price as to lessen the profits."

"Wisely spoken! It is the first question which would occur to any prudent mind. But what if I say that neither is the case? And you, who are familiar with the frequent eccentricities of old farmers, can understand the explanation. The owner of the land was one of your ignorant, stubborn men, who took such a dislike to the prospectors and speculators, that he refused to let them come near him. Both the Fluke and Chowder Companies tried their best to buy him out, but he had a malicious pleasure in leading them on to make immense offers, and then refusing. Well, a few months ago he died, and his heirs were willing enough to let the land go; but before it could be regularly offered for sale, the Fluke and Chowder Wells began to flow less and less. Their shares fell from 270 to 95; the supposed value of the land fell with them, and finally the moment arrived when we could purchase for a very moderate sum. I see the question in your mind; why should we wish to buy when the other wells were giving out? There comes in the secret, which is our veritable success. Consider it whispered in your ears, and locked in your bosoms,—torpedoes! It was not then generally exploded (to carry out the image), so we bought at the low figure, in the very nick of time. Within a week the Fluke and Chowder Wells were torpedoed, and came back to more than their former capacity; the shares rose as rapidly as they had fallen, and the central body we hold—to which they are, as it were, the two arms—could now be sold for ten times what it cost us!"

Here Mr. Blessing paused, with his finger on the lap, and a light of merited triumph in his eyes. Julia clapped her hands, sprang to her feet, and cried: "Trumps at last!"

"Ay," said he, "wealth, repose for my old days, wealth for us all, if your husband will but take the hand I hold out to him. You now know, son-in-law, why the endorsement you gave me was of such vital importance; the note, as you are aware, will mature in another week. Why should you not charge yourself with the payment, in consideration of the transfer to you of shares of the original stock, already so immensely appreciated in value? I have delayed making any provision, for the sake of offering you the chance."

Julia was about to speak, but restrained herself with an apparent effort.

"I should like to know," Joseph said, "who are associated with you in the undertaking?"

"Well done, again! Where did you get your practical shrewdness? The best men in the city!—not only the Collector and the Surveyor, but Congressman Whaley, E. D. Stokes, of Stokes, Pirricutt and Company, and even the Reverend Doctor Lellifant. If I had not been an old friend of Kanuck, the agent who negotiated the purchase, my chance would have been impalpably small. I have all the documents with me. There has been no more splendid opportunity since oil became a power! I hesitate to advise even one so near to me in such matters; but if you knew the certainties as I know them, you would go in with all your available capital. The excitement, as you say, has reached the country communities, which are slow to rise and equally slow to subside; all oil stock will be in demand, but the Amaranth,—'The Blessing,' they wished to call it, but I was obliged to decline, for official reasons,—the Amaranth shares will be the golden apex of the market!"

Julia looked at Joseph with eager, hungry eyes. He, too, was warmed and tempted by the prospect of easy profit which the scheme held out to him; only the habit of his nature resisted, but with still diminishing force. "I might venture the thousand," he said.

"It is no venture!" Julia cried. "In all the speculations I have heard discussed by pa and his friends, there was nothing so admirably managed as this. Such a certainty of profit may never come again. If you will be advised by me, Joseph, you will take shares to the amount of five or ten thousand."

"Ten thousand is exactly the amount I hold open," Mr. Blessing gravely remarked. "That, however, does not represent the necessary payment, which can hardly amount to more than twenty-five per cent before we begin to realize. Only ten per cent has yet been called, so that your thousand at present will secure you an investment of ten thousand. Really, it seems like a fortunate coincidence."

He went on, heating himself with his own words, until the possibilities of the case grew so splendid that Joseph felt himself dazzled and bewildered. Mr. Blessing was a master in the art of seductive statement. Even where he was only the mouthpiece of another, a few repetitions led him to the profoundest belief. Here there could be no doubt of his sincerity, and, moreover, every movement from the very inception of the scheme, every statistical item, all collateral influences, were clear in his mind and instantly accessible. Although he began by saying, "I will make no estimate of the profits, because it is not prudent to fix our hopes on a positive sum," he was soon carried far away from this resolution, and most luxuriously engaged, pencil in hand, in figuring out results which drove Julia wild with desire, and almost took away Joseph's breath. The latter finally said, as they rose from the session, late at night:—

"It is settled that I take as much as the thousand will cover; but I would rather think over the matter quietly for a day or two before venturing further."

"You must," replied Mr. Blessing, patting him on the shoulder. "These things are so new to your experience, that they disturb and—I might almost say—alarm you. It is like bringing an increase of oxygen into your mental atmosphere. (Ha! a good figure: for the result will be, a richer, fuller life. I must remember it.) But you are a healthy organization, and therefore you are certain to see clearly: I can wait with confidence."

The next morning Joseph, without declaring his purpose, drove to Coventry Forge to consult Philip. Mr. Blessing and Julia, remaining at home, went over the shining ground again, and yet again, confirming each other in the determination to secure it. Even Joseph, as he passed up the valley in the mild March weather, taking note of the crimson and gold of the flowering spice-bushes and maple-trees, could not prevent his thoughts from dwelling on the delights of wealth,—society, books, travel, and all the mellow, fortunate expansion of life. Involuntarily, he hoped that Philip's counsel might coincide with his father-in-law's offer.

But Philip was not at home. The forge was in full activity, the cottage on the knoll was repainted and made attractive in various ways, and Philip would soon return with his sister to establish a permanent home. Joseph found the sign-spiritual of his friend in numberless little touches and changes; it seemed to him that a new soul had entered into the scenery of the place.

A mile or two farther up the valley, a company of mechanics and laborers were apparently tearing the old Calvert mansion inside out. House, barn, garden, and lawn were undergoing a complete transformation. While he paused at the entrance of the private lane, to take a survey of the operations, Mr. Clemson rode down to him from the house. The Hopetons, he said, would migrate from the city early in May: work had already commenced on the new railway, and in another year a different life would come upon the whole neighborhood.

In the course of the conversation Joseph ventured to sound Mr. Clemson in regard to the newly formed oil companies. The latter frankly confessed that he had withdrawn from further speculation, satisfied with his fortune; he preferred to give no opinion, further than that money was still to be made, if prudently placed. The Fluke and Chowder Wells, he said, were old, well known, and profitable. The new application of torpedoes had restored their failing flow, and the stock had recovered from its temporary depreciation. His own venture had been made in another part of the region.

The atmosphere into which Joseph entered, on returning home, took away all further power of resistance. Tempted already, and impressed by what he had learned, he did what his wife and father-in-law desired.

14. BUCK, TRAUBEL, AND THE MULTITUDES OF WHITMAN

Some information regarding the two men who took up the task of archiving and cataloguing Walt Whitman during his lifetime:

Bucke

"His method is peaceful, uncoercive, quiet, though always firm—rather persuasive than anything else. Bucke is without brag or bluster. It is beautiful to watch him at his work—to see how he can handle difficult people with such an easy manner. Bucke is a man who enjoys being busy—likes to do things—is swift of execution—lucid, sure, decisive. Doctors are not in the main comfortable creatures to have around, but Bucke is helpful, confident, optimistic—has a way of buoying you up." Thus Whitman sums up his impressions of Richard Maurice Bucke, one of the most important friends of his last two decades. Though a constant and important presence at Mickle Street, he in fact lived hundreds of miles away in the Canadian province of Ontario. Here, in more formal terms, is how Whitman described him in June 1891 in a letter of introduction to Alfred Lord Tennyson: "let me introduce my good friend & physician Dr Bucke—He is Superintendent (medical and other) of the big Insane Canadian Asylum at London Ontario—he is an Englishman born but raised (as we say it) in America." Bucke, who visited Camden several times during the *With Walt Whitman* years, alone received an almost daily letter from Whitman in the poet's last years, and his advice on the management of Whitman's health care—and countless literary transactions—was much valued and often even followed. It was his recommendation that led to one of Walt's happiest male nurse experiences. [...] Bucke published his idolizing *Walt Whitman* in 1883 (Whitman actually wrote many of the passages); Walt said of the book in 1889 that it "has my cordial regard" but that "the book is guilty, like the dinner [that honored his seventieth birthday], of being too honeyish." Bucke became one of Whitman's literary executors and in that capacity published two volumes of Whitman

letters, *Calamus: A Series of Letters Written during the Years 1868–1880*
(1897; these were letters to Peter Doyle) and *The Wound Dresser: A Series of
Letters Written from the Hospitals in Washington* (1898).[39]

Traubel

Horace Logo Traubel was born in Camden on December 19, 1858, the
fifth of seven children of a Jewish immigrant father from Frankfurt and a
Christian mother (neither was practicing). Though an early schoolleaver,
Horace became an omnivorous reader on his own. Some of his tutelage was
at Whitman's side; as Traubel recalled, "My earliest memory of Whitman
leads me back to boyhood, when, sitting together on his doorstep, we spent
many a late afternoon or evening in review of books we had read." Like Walt,
Horace drifted into the publishing trade, becoming a printer's devil and later a
compositor, typesetter, and reporter for the Camden New Republic and later
for the Camden Evening Visitor. Subsequently, he was a factory paymaster,
then finally landed a clerical position at the Farmers' and Mechanics' Bank,
where he worked during his years of closest association with Whitman.

[...]

Young Traubel had first met Whitman in 1873, when he was a teenager
and the then more-notorious-than-celebrated poet was fifty-four, gray-
bearded, and already seriously incapacitated by various ailments. Traubel,
like Whitman, had left school at the age of twelve and was in 1888 a clerk in
the Farmers' and Mechanics' Bank on Chestnut Street in Philadelphia. As the
months of daily visits passed by, he became Whitman's alter ego, factotum,
and liaison with the local press and many a visiting stranger, as well as his
increasingly overworked amanuensis and, crucially, a manager of the poet's
financial and printing affairs. Traubel's loyalty and the regularity of his visits
to the little, ramshackle two-story house were staggering. A passing remark he
made toward the end of his four years of service—"Never miss a morning"—
was almost true: the days he records not appearing or being out of town are
extremely rare. When he did miss a day, it was usually a Sunday. After one
Sunday in which he had been absent, Traubel notes that Whitman "greeted
me as 'a stranger.'" Once, when he missed two consecutive days, Traubel
records that Whitman "called out 'Horace' with great cordiality—took and
held my hand—said, 'I had wondered what had become of you: was going to
send up to ask tomorrow.' I explained my absence—he assenting, 'I know—it
was all right—I am not disposed to question it. But we missed you.'" Traubel's
daily visits were frequently multiple. "Four times there today—8 a.m.—5:30
p.m.—8p.m. and again on return from Philadelphia at midnight," he records;
then, a week later: "The fourth time at W.'s at12:40." Gradually, however, he
concluded there was an ideal time to accost and record: "Eight o'clock is his
good hour invariably if there is a good hour in the day. For that reason I have

mostly made it the hour for consultation." Rarely did he arrive after 9 p.m. In the event that Walt was not in a consulting mood, Traubel knew well enough to beat a hasty retreat: "I did not prolong my stay," he notes of one April day, "W. not in good talking mood. In such cases I never linger."[39]

For Traubel, the dedication to Whitman and the defense of his work might have come from an deep understanding of his meaning:

Ed Folsom, a leading Whitman scholar and longtime editor of the *Walt Whitman Quarterly Review*, has discovered in correspondence in the Library of Congress that Traubel seems to have had a passionate relationship with a man five years younger than himself. This person, Gustave Percival Wiksell, became a dentist residing in Boston and for many years presided over the Whitman Fellowship there (he also presided over the secular memorial service for Traubel in 1919). In the introduction for the last volume of *With Walt Whitman in Camden*, Folsom describes a "heated correspondence spanning five years (1899–1905)" in which "Traubel and Wiksell poured out their love for each other, often expressing themselves in Whitman's Calamus terminology." "Percival, darling, my sweet camerado," wrote Traubel, for example, in a 1902 letter, recalling a recent meeting with Wiksell: "Definitely sweet was one hour & the next while we remained in love's carouse—That day will go with me into all eternities. Send me your words, dear love—your words live. They go into my veins. I do not put you away with a kiss. I hold you close, close, close!" [...] In the spring of 1895 came the sensational and (to homosexuals) intimidating trial and imprisonment of Oscar Wilde. The following November [Philip] Dalmas wrote Traubel something of a Dear John letter that appears to allude to the event: "in these days of subtle reasoning one's declarations of love can be turned into engines of hate by the loved one's lofty conception of what life is and since the unnatural has gone out of fashion." (Traubel devoted the first *Conservator* to appear after Wilde's May 25 conviction, the June issue, entirely to Whitman. It contains two remarkable defenses of Whitman against the charges of "morbid psychology" then associated with homosexuality: a damning review of Max Nordau's book *Degeneration*, which attacked both Whitman and Wilde, and a long essay by Bucke, "Was Whitman Mad?").[39]

The Critter

What follows are quaint curiosities of Walt Whitman, documented largely by Traubel, that have no other place but are worth including. These are the details Whitman told Traubel he most appreciated being preserved: "I see more value in the matter you are piling together in your little article—personal memorabilia, traits of character, incidents, habits—the pulse and throb of the critter himself!"[39] As Schmidgall puts it, these are "[s]ome of Whitman's paradoxes" that "leave not only a side-curved head but also a smile,"[40] like the dreadful temperance novel *Franklin Evans* which Whitman wrote early in life supposedly with the help of "gin cocktails" (incidentally, Whitman called New Jersey moonshine "lunar champagne"), or the fact that Whitman, so fond of democracy, never voted himself, telling Traubel, "I always refrain—yet advise everybody else not to forget."[40] Here are some of his stray thoughts and eccentricities regarding books and writing:

"Oh! I use ruled paper, but I don't write on the lines!" This was a tendency Whitman shared with Oscar Wilde, whose "huge and sprawling" hand at Oxford "took no notice of lines" in examination books.[39]

"I do not think even intelligent people know how much goes to the making of a book: worry, fret, anxiety—downright hard work—poverty—finally, nothingness! It is a story yet to be told."[39]

Traubel records: "Laughingly [Whitman] told me [David] McKay had been over a few days ago—'paid me royalties between 50 and 60 dollars: think of it!—for *Leaves of Grass* and *Specimen Days* both! It is a long story of woe—a catalogue of impecuniosities—this record of my printed labor!' But there were other ways in which he was 'compensated'—'in best friends: friends, few, but the better of which the world never saw.'" [39]

"Books are like men—the best of them have flaws. Thank God for the flaws!"[39]

"Literary men learn so little from life—borrow so much from the borrowers."[39]

"I do not value literature as a profession. I feel about literature what Grant did about war. He hated war. I hate literature. I am not a literary West Pointer."[39]

"What would we do without sinners? Take them out of literature and it would be barren."[39]

Whitman considered *Franklin Evans, or The Inebriate*—the lurid temperance novel he published in 1842 in the *New World*—one of the nastier skeletons in his literary closet. One day he reminisced about how he composed it. The publisher's "offer of cash payment was so tempting—I was so hard up at the time—that I set to work at once ardently on it (with the help of a bottle of port or what not). In three days constant work I finished the book. Finished the book? Finished myself. It was damned rot—rot of the worst sort. . . .

I never cut a chip off that kind of timber again."[39]

It is interesting to note that in 2017, while this book was being compiled, another anonymous novel written by Walt Whitman was discovered by Zachary Turpin, a grad student at the University of Houston:

It's a work of short fiction: a 36,000-word novella published anonymously, in six parts, in a New York newspaper in 1852. The discursive nature of the manuscript's full title—*Life and Adventures of Jack Engle: An Auto-Biography; In Which The Reader Will Find Some Familiar Characters*—places it squarely in its literary era, as does its subtitle, *A Story of New York at the Present Time.* [54]

XV

A DINNER PARTY

HAVING ASSUMED THE payment of Mr. Blessing's note, as the first instalment upon his stock, Joseph was compelled to prepare himself for future emergencies. A year must still elapse before the term of the mortgage upon his farm would expire, but the sums he had invested for the purpose of meeting it when due must be held ready for use. The assurance of great and certain profit in the meantime rendered this step easy; and, even at the worst, he reflected, there would be no difficulty in procuring a new mortgage whereby to liquidate the old. A notice which he received at this time, that a second assessment of ten per cent on the Amaranth stock had been made, was both unexpected and disquieting. Mr. Blessing, however, accompanied it with a letter, making clear not only the necessity, but the admirable wisdom of a greater present outlay than had been anticipated. So the first of April—the usual business anniversary of the neighborhood—went smoothly by. Money was plenty, the Asten credit had always been sound, and Joseph tasted for the first time a pleasant sense of power in so easily receiving and transferring considerable sums.

One result of the venture was the development of a new phase in Julia's nature. She not only accepted the future profit as certain, but she had apparently calculated its exact amount and framed her plans accordingly. If she had been humiliated by the character of Joseph's first business transaction with her father, she now made amends for it. "Pa" was their good genius. "Pa" was the agency whereby they should achieve wealth and social importance. Joseph now had the clearest evidence of the difference between a man who knew the world and was of value in it, and their slow, dull-headed country neighbors. Indeed, Julia seemed to consider the Asten property as rather contemptible beside the splendor of the Blessing scheme. Her gratitude for a quiet home, her love of country life, her disparagement of the shams and exactions of "society," were given up as suddenly and coolly as if she had never affected them. She gave herself no pains to make the transition gradual, and thus lessen its shock. Perhaps she supposed that Joseph's fresh, unsuspicious nature was so plastic that it had already sufficiently taken her impress, and that he would easily forget the mask she had worn. If so, she was seriously mistaken.

He saw, with a deadly chill of the heart, the change in her manner,—a change so complete that another face confronted him at the table, even as another heart beat beside his on the dishallowed marriage-bed. He saw the gentle droop vanish from the eyelids, leaving the cold, flinty pupils unshaded; the soft appeal of the half-opened lips was lost in the rigid, almost cruel compression which now seemed habitual to them; all the slight dependent gestures, the tender airs of reference to his will or pleasure, had rapidly transformed themselves into expressions of command or obstinate resistance. But the patience of a loving man is equal to that of a loving woman: he was silent, although his silence covered an ever-increasing sense of outrage.

Once it happened, that after Julia had been unusually eloquent concerning "what pa is doing for us," and what use they should make of "pa's money, as I call it," Joseph quietly remarked:—

"You seem to forget, Julia, that without my money not much could have been done."

An angry color came into her face; but, on second thought, she bent her head, and murmured in an offended voice: "It is very mean and ungenerous in you to refer to our temporary poverty. You might forget, by this time, the help pa was compelled to ask of you."

"I did not think of that!" he exclaimed. "Besides, you did not seem entirely satisfied with my help, at the time."

"O, how you misunderstand me!" she groaned. "I only wished to know the extent of his need. He is so generous, so considerate towards us, that we only guess his misfortune at the last moment."

The possibility of being unjust silenced Joseph. There were tears in Julia's voice, and he imagined they would soon rise to her eyes. After a long, uncomfortable pause, he said, for the sake of changing the subject: "What can have become of Elwood Withers? I have not seen him for months."

"I don't think you need care to know," she remarked. "He's a rough, vulgar fellow: it's just as well if he keeps away from us."

"Julia! he is my friend, and must always be welcome to *me*. You were friendly enough towards him, and towards all the neighborhood, last summer: how is it that you have not a good word to say now?

He spoke warmly and indignantly. Julia, however, looked at him with a calm, smiling face. "It is very simple," she said. "You will agree with me, in another year. A guest, as I was, must try to see only the pleasant side of people: that's our duty; and so I enjoyed— as much as I could—the rusticity, the awkwardness, the ignorance, the (now, don't be vexed, dear!)—the vulgarity of your friend. As one of the society of the neighborhood, as a resident, I am not bound by any such delicacy. I take the same right to judge and select as I should take anywhere. Unless I am to be hypocritical, I cannot—towards you, at least—conceal my real feelings. How shall I ever get you to see the difference between yourself and these people, unless I continually point it out? You are modest, and don't like to acknowledge your own superiority."

She rose from the table, laughing, and went out of the room humming a lively air, leaving Joseph to make the best of her words.

A few days after this the work on the branch railway, extending down the valley, reached a point where it could be seen from the Asten farm. Joseph, on riding over to inspect the operations, was surprised to find Elwood, who had left his father's place and become a sub-contractor. The latter showed his hearty delight at their meeting.

"I've been meaning to come up," he said, "but this is a busy time for me. It's a chance I couldn't let slip, and now that I've taken hold I must hold on. I begin to think this is the thing I was made for, Joseph."

"I never thought of it before," Joseph answered, "and yet I'm sure you are right. How did you hit upon it?"

"*I* didn't; it was Mr. Held."

"Philip?"

"Him. You know I've been hauling for the Forge, and so it turned up by degrees, as I may say. He's at home, and, I expect, looking for you. But, how *are* you now, really?"

Elwood's question meant a great deal more than he knew how to say. Suddenly, in a flash of memory, their talk of the previous year returned to Joseph's mind; he saw his friend's true instincts and his own blindness as never before. But he must dissemble, if possible, with that strong, rough, kindly face before him.

"O," he said, attempting a cheerful air, "I am one of the old folks now. You must come up—"

The recollection of Julia's words cut short the invitation upon his lips. A sharp-pang went through his heart, and the treacherous blood crowded to his face all the more that he tried to hold it back.

"Come, and I'll show you where we're going to make the cutting," Elwood quietly said, taking him by the arm. Joseph fancied, thenceforth, that there was a special kindness in his manner, and the suspicion seemed to rankle in his mind as if he had been slighted by his friend.

As before, to vary the tedium of his empty life, so now, to escape from the knowledge which he found himself more and more powerless to resist, he busied himself beyond all need with the work of the farm. Philip had returned with his sister, he knew, but after the meeting with Elwood he shrank with a painful dread from Philip's heart-deep, intimate eye. Julia, however, all the more made use of the soft spring weather to survey the social ground, and choose where to take her stand. Joseph scarcely knew, indeed, how extensive her operations had been, until she announced an invitation to dine with the Hopetons, who were now in possession of the renovated Calvert place. She enlarged, more than was necessary, on the distinguished city position of the family, and the importance of "cultivating" its country members. Joseph's single brief meeting with Mr. Hopeton—who was a short, solid man, in ripe middle age, of a thoroughly cosmopolitan, though not a remarkably intellectual stamp—had been agreeable, and he recognized the obligation to be neighborly. Therefore he readily accepted the invitation on his own grounds.

When the day arrived, Julia, after spending the morning over her toilet, came forth

resplendent in rosy silk, bright and dazzling in complexion, and with all her former grace
of languid eyelids and parted lips. The void in Joseph's heart grew wider at the sight of
her; for he perceived, as never before, her consummate skill in assuming a false character.
It seemed incredible that he should have been so deluded. For the first time a feeling
of repulsion, which was almost disgust, came upon him as he listened to her prattle of
delight in the soft weather, and the fragrant woods, and the blossoming orchards. Was
not, also, this delight assumed? he asked himself: false in one thing, false in all, was the
fatal logic which then and there began its torment.

The most that was possible in such a short time had been achieved on the Calvert
place. The house had been brightened, surrounded by light, airy verandas, and the lawn
and garden, thrown into one and given into the hands of a skillful gardener, were scarcely
to be recognized. A broad, solid gravel-walk replaced the old tan-covered path; a pretty
fountain tinkled before the door; thick beds of geranium in flower studded the turf and
veritable thickets of rose-trees were waiting for June. Within the house, some rooms lad
been thrown together, the walls richly yet harmoniously colored, and the sumptuous
furniture thus received a proper setting. In contrast to the houses of even the wealthiest
farmers, which expressed a nicely reckoned sufficiency of comfort, the place had an air of
joyous profusion, of a wealth which delighted in itself.

Mr. Hopeton met them with the frank, offhand manner of a man of business. His
wife followed, and the two guests made a rapid inspection of her as she came down
the hall. Julia noticed that her crocus-colored dress was high in the neck, and plainly
trimmed; that she wore no ornaments, and that the natural pallor of her complexion had
not been corrected by art. Joseph remarked the simple grace of her movement the large,
dark, inscrutable eyes, the smooth bands of her black hair, and the pure though somewhat
lengthened oval of her face. The gentle dignity of her manner more than refreshed, it
soothed him. She was so much younger than her husband that Joseph involuntarily
wondered how they should have come together.

The greetings were scarcely over before Philip and Madeline Held arrived. Julia, with
the least little gush of tenderness, kissed the latter, whom Philip then presented to Joseph
for the first time. She had the same wavy hair as her brother, but the golden hue was
deepened nearly into brown, and her eyes were a clear hazel. It was also the same frank,
firm face, but her woman's smile was so much the sweeter as her lips were lovelier than the
man's. Joseph seemed to clasp an instant friendship in her offered hand.

There was but one other guest, who, somewhat to his surprise, was Lucy Henderson.
Julia concealed whatever she might have felt, and made so much reference to their former
meetings as might satisfy Lucy without conveying to Mrs. Hopeton the impression of any
special intimacy. Lucy looked thin and worn, and her black silk dress was not of the latest
fashion: she seemed to be the poor relation of the company. Joseph learned that she had
taken one of the schools in the valley, for the summer. Her manner to him was as simple
and friendly as ever, but he felt the presence of some new element of strength and self-
reliance in her nature.

His place at dinner was beside Mrs. Hopeton, while Lucy—apparently by accident—

sat upon the other side of the hostess. Philip and the host led the conversation, confining it too exclusively to the railroad and iron interests; but these finally languished, and gave way to other topics in which all could take part. Joseph felt that while the others, except Lucy and himself, were fashioned under different aspects of life, some of which they shared in common, yet that their seeming ease and freedom of communication touched, here and there, some invisible limit, which they were careful not to pass. Even Philip appeared to be beyond his reach, for the time.

The country and the people, being comparatively new to them, naturally came to be discussed.

"Mr. Held, or Mr. Asten,—either of you know both,"—Mr. Hopeton asked, "what are the principal points of difference between society in the city and in the country?"

"Indeed, I know too little of the city," said Joseph.

"And I know too little of the country,—here, at least," Philip added. "Of course the same passions and prejudices come into play everywhere. There are circles, there are jealousies, ups and downs, scandals, suppressions, and rehabilitations: it can't be otherwise."

"Are they not a little worse in the country," said Julia, "because—I may ask the question here, among *us*—there is less refinement of manner?"

"If the external forms are ruder," Philip resumed, "it may be an advantage, in one sense. Hypocrisy cannot be developed into an art."

Julia bit her lip, and was silent.

"But are the country people, hereabouts, so rough?" Mrs. Hopeton asked. "I confess that they don't seem so to me. What do you say, Miss Henderson.?"

"Perhaps I am not an impartial witness," Lucy answered. "We care less about what is called 'manners' than the city people. We have no fixed rules for dress and behavior,—only we don't like any one to differ too much from the rest of us."

"That's it!" Mr. Hopeton cried; "the tyrannical levelling sentiment of an imperfectly developed community! Fortunately, I am beyond its reach."

Julia's eyes sparkled: she looked across the table at Joseph, with a triumphant air.

Philip suddenly raised his head. "How would you correct it? Simply by resistance?" he asked.

Mr. Hopeton laughed. "I should no doubt get myself into a hornet's-nest. No; by indifference!"

Then Madeline Held spoke. "Excuse me," she said; "but is indifference possible, even if it were right? You seem to take the levelling spirit for granted, without looking into its character and causes; there must be some natural sense of justice, no matter how imperfectly society is developed. We are members of this community,—at least, Philip and I certainly consider ourselves so,—and I am determined not to judge it without knowledge, or to offend what may be only mechanical habits of thought, unless I can see a sure advantage in doing so."

Lucy Henderson looked at the speaker with a bright, grateful face. Joseph's eyes wandered from her to Julia, who was silent and watchful.

"But I have no time for such conscientious studies," Mr. Hopeton resumed. "One can be satisfied with half a dozen neighbors, and let the mass go. Indifference, after all, is the best philosophy. What do you say, Mr. Held?"

"Indifference!" Philip echoed. A dark flush came into his face, and he was silent a moment. "Yes: our hearts are inconvenient appendages. We suffer a deal from unnecessary sympathies, and from imagining, I suppose, that others feel them as we do. These uneasy features of society are simply the effort of nature to find some occupation for brains otherwise idle—or empty. Teach the people to think, and they will disappear."

Joseph stared at Philip, feeling that a secret bitterness was hidden under his careless, mocking air. Mrs. Hopeton rose, and the company left the table. Madeline Held had a troubled expression, but there was an eager, singular brightness in Julia's eyes.

"Emily, let us have coffee on the veranda," said Mr. Hopeton, leading the way. He had already half forgotten the subject of conversation: his own expressions, in fact, had been made very much at random, for the sole purpose of keeping up the flow of talk. He had no very fixed views of any kind, beyond the sphere of his business activity.

Philip, noticing the impression he had made on Joseph, drew him to one side. "Don't seriously remember my words against me," he said; "you were sorry to hear them, I know. All I meant was, that an over-sensitive tenderness towards everybody is a fault. Besides, I was provoked to answer him in his own vein."

"But, Philip!" Joseph whispered, "such words tempt me! What if they were true?"

Philip grasped his arm with a painful force. "They never can be true to you, Joseph," he said.

Gay and pleasant as the company seemed to be, each one felt a secret sense of relief when it came to an end. As Joseph drove homewards, silently, recalling what had been said, Julia interrupted his reflections with: "Well, what do you think of the Hopetons?"

"She is an interesting woman," he answered.

"But reserved; and she shows very little taste in dress. However, I suppose you hardly noticed anything of the kind. She kept Lucy Henderson beside her as a foil: Madeline Held would have been damaging."

Joseph only partly guessed her meaning; it was repugnant, and he determined to avoid its further discussion.

"Hopeton is a shrewd business man," Julia continued, "but he cannot compare with her for shrewdness—either with her or—Philip Held!"

"What do you mean?"

"I made a discovery before the dinner was over, which you—innocent, unsuspecting man that you are—might have before your eyes for years, without seeing it. Tell me now, honestly, did you notice nothing?"

"What should I notice, beyond what was said?" he asked.

"That was the least!" she cried; "but, of course, I knew you couldn't. And perhaps you won't believe me, when I tell you that Philip Held,—your particular friend, your hero, for aught I know, your pattern of virtue and character, and all that is manly and noble,—that Philip Held, I say, is furiously in love with Mrs. Hopeton!"

Joseph started as if he had been shot, and turned around with an angry red on his brow. "Julia!" he said, "how dare you speak so of Philip!"

She laughed. "Because I dare to speak the truth, when I see it. I thought I should surprise you. I remembered a certain rumor I had heard before she was married,—while she was Emily Marrable,—and I watched them closer than they guessed. I'm certain of Philip: as for her, she's a deep creature, and she was on her guard; but they are near neighbors."

Joseph was thoroughly aroused and indignant. "It is your own fancy!" he exclaimed. "You hate Philip on account of that affair with Clementina; but you ought to have some respect for the woman whose hospitality you have accepted!

"Bless me! I have any quantity of respect both for her and her furniture. By the by, Joseph, our parlor would furnish better than hers; I have been thinking of a few changes we might make, which would wonderfully improve the house. As for Philip, Clementina was a fool. She'd be glad enough to have him now, but in these matters, once gone is gone for good. Somehow, people who marry for love very often get rich afterwards,—ourselves, for instance."

It was some time before Joseph's excitement subsided. He had resented Julia's suspicion as dishonorable to Philip, yet he could not banish the conjecture of its possible truth. If Philip's affected cynicism had tempted him, Julia's unblushing assumption of the existence of a passion which was forbidden, and therefore positively guilty, seemed to stain the pure texture of his nature. The lightness with which she spoke of the matter was even more abhorrent to him than the assertion itself; the malicious satisfaction in the tones of her voice had not escaped his ear.

"Julia," he said, just before they reached home, "do not mention your fancy to another soul than me. It would reflect discredit on you."

"You *are* innocent," she answered. "And you are not complimentary. If I have any remarkable quality, it is tact. Whenever I speak, I shall know the effect beforehand; even pa, with all his official experience, is no match for me in this line. I see what the Hopetons are after, and I mean to show them that we were first in the field. Don't be concerned, you good, excitable creature, you are no match for such well-drilled people. Let me alone, and before the summer is over *we* will give the law to the neighborhood!'

15. AVOWALS TO WALT WHITMAN

The following material was excerpted from letters Whitman received, with context provided by Gary Schmidgall in *Intimate with Walt, Selections from Whitman's Conversations with Horace Traubel, 1888-1892*. For greater exploration of relevant "avowal" letters, see <u>Chapter 10: Taylor and Whitman</u>, <u>Chapter 16: Whitman, Stoker, and Wilde</u> and <u>Chapter 20: Contemporary Camerados</u>.

The daily arrival of mail was perhaps second in importance only to the arrival of Horace [Traubel] himself at Mickle Street. "W. loves to receive letters," Traubel records, "any letters, provided they are in the true sense human documents. He is always disappointed if the postman passes without stopping." Upset of the mail's movement was one of the few events that could anger Whitman, as Traubel notes one day: "Mrs. Davis tells me of a minute's passion in W. yesterday because a letter he had thought mailed had been neglected; unusual."

[...]

The most eagerly perused letters were doubtless what came to be called "avowal" letters—missives variously expressing kindred-spiritedness, affection, or admiration for the poet and *Leaves of Grass*. On one occasion Whitman referred to these as "love letters": "I receive many queer letters—a couple of weeks ago there was one from an Englishman . . . it was very gushing, very. Yes, I have received love letters—many of them—especially years ago—plenty—even now, having one occasionally." Traubel told Walt, "O'Connor thinks you should collect all your comrade letters in a book: he says they exemplify your revolutionary sympathies." The idea was declined: "Ah! that is his idea? they seem so personal: it might be done but not by me: I would not be the best one for such a delicate task."

Sometimes there came avowals within avowals. One Hiram Ramsdell, for example, included a third party's expression of delight, and Walt wrote back to Ramsdell, reaching out in pure *Leaves* style for emotional contact with the reader-stranger: "I value George Alfred Townsend's appreciation of *L. of G*. It was magnificent. Where is Townsend now? I hope it may happen one day that I may have him near at hand, that we get to be friends—such is in my mind."

And sometimes the avowal letters went overboard. Whitman received such a letter from a consul in Colombia: "one of the enthusiastic sloppy letters I sometimes get." (Walt carefully removed its stamps for stampcollecting Ed Wilkins and a local boy.)

[...]

Drawn toward You: Edmund Gosse

Traubel includes a letter from twenty-four-year-old Edmund Gosse from London dated December 12, 1873. It includes this passage: "The *Leaves of Grass* have become part of my every-day thought and experience. I have considered myself as 'the new person drawn toward' you." After reading Gosse's letter aloud, Traubel asks Whitman if Gosse's enthusiasm lasted: "Who knows? I think he does—but I would not be surprised if he does not: I am used to defections—especially of the young enthusiasts that grow old—yes, old and cold." Gosse did indeed grow colder toward Whitman as he aged, writing a decidedly dubious essay on the poet the year after his death. In it Gosse asserted that "discomfort and perplexity" await anyone entering the "little room called 'Walt Whitman'" in the castle of literature. Whitman took his revenge for Gosse's lapse in admiration. When Gosse, thoroughly aristocratic, wrote on "Democracy in Literature," Walt said Gosse was "no more able to grasp [that] than a neat cockroach w'd one of Kepler's principal laws." Walt later said snippily, "It is dangerous for a man like Gosse, having so little butter, to attempt to spread it over so much bread—it comes up very thin."

For more on Gosse, see Chapter 10: Taylor and Whitman.

With Sugar in It: John Swinton

"This letter is almost like a love letter—it has sugar in it," Whitman said as he handed Traubel a letter from John Swinton dated January 23, 1884 and written from East 38th Street in Manhattan. "John, you know, is stormy, tempestuous," he adds; "raises a hell of a row over things—yet underneath all is nothing that is not noble, sweet, sane." The letter, included in full, contains this passage: "My beloved Walt. You know how I have worshipped you, without change or cessation, for twenty years. While my soul exists, that worship must be ever new. It was perhaps the very day of the publication of the first edition of the *Leaves of Grass* that I saw a copy of it at a newspaper stand in Fulton street, Brooklyn. I got it, looked into it with wonder, and felt that here was something that touched the depths of my humanity. Since then you have grown before me, grown around me, and grown into me."

One of the Just-comers: Lionel Johnson

An Englishman schoolboy, Lionel Johnson, wrote to Whitman in 1885: "I have lived as yet but eighteen years; yet in all the constant thoughts and acts of my last few years, your words have been my guides and true oracles . . . the help and exaltation I have won from [Leaves of Grass] have been won by many another boy and young man." The poet's response to hearing the letter read: "It's not the least flattering feature of my experience that I have been most successful with young people, the just-comers, and least successful with the full done and over done literary masters of ceremony."

Note: Johnson later became a friend of Oscar Wilde; he wrote of his first meeting with his fellow Oxford undergraduate: "He discoursed, with infinite flippancy, of everyone: lauded the Dial: laughed at Pater: and consumed all my cigarettes. I am in love with him."

For Johnson's full letter, see [A.18]. For more on Johnson's role in Wilde's life, see <u>Chapter 19: Calamus as Cruising Apparatus</u>.

A New World in the Old: W. C. Angus

In October 1888 W. C. Angus wrote from Glasgow: "When a young man I read your *Leaves of Grass* 1855 edition. It revealed a new world to me—the world within myself. Your *Specimen Days* I regard as the most humane book of the present century. . . . I regard your *Leaves of Grass* as being the most original of American books." He concludes with the request: "If you would write your name upon my 1855 edition, which I intend to present to a public library, I should send it to you. . . ."

A Leaf from the Inmost Bosom: Allen Upward

One of the lengthiest and most over-the-top avowal letters arrived in March 1884 from Allen Upward, an English resident of Dublin. It begins: "O Walt! Take this Calamus leaf at the hands of him thou hast sought for. Lo! I am he. What shall I say, or how shall I utter, the radiant feelings that gush from my heart at the magical words thou hast sung to the unknown?" He later prefaces some autobiographical pages: "Let me unroll the extensive panorama of my own personality." Upward says he has been a freethinker, Buddhist, and Darwinian, as well as a liberal, radical, socialist, and anarchist. Now he is a Whitmanite of startling passion, as the letter's closing paragraph suggests: "This is the Calamus leaf which the Englishman Allen Upward (Upward, ought I not to be proud of the name?) plucked from the soil of his inmost bosom to send to Walt Whitman, the American, poet, writer and lover." Horace remarks that this is "the biggest job you've ever given me in the reading line" and asks Walt what he makes of the letter. Whitman mulls a while, then: "Nothing: taking it as a whole, nothing definite: I have feelings about it but no conclusions: it's so youthful, so green, so little, so big, so spontaneous, so stagy, so bulging with vanity, so crowded with affection." The letter, he adds, reminds him of Stoker's performance: "The same impertinence, and pertinence, too? the same crude boy confidence, the same mix-up of instincts, magnetisms, revolts? In both cases there's the curious, beautiful self-deception of youth . . . they were really writing more definitely to themselves."

A Gaze: William Hawley
In August 1869 William Hawley wrote to Whitman from Syracuse, New York: "I would I could grasp your hand, look in your eyes and have you look in mine. Then you would see how much you have done for me. Yours with a brother's love."

Interrogating Enthusiast: Edward Carpenter
Edward Carpenter, the eminent English social reformer, author, and apologist for homosexuality, wrote Whitman several times. Handing a very long one to Traubel, dated January 3, 1876, to read aloud, Whitman called it "one of Carpenter's early fine letters. He was never nobler than then, in that period of interrogating enthusiasm." It included these passages: "Dear friend, you have so infused yourself that it is daily more and more possible for men to walk hand in hand over the whole earth. . . . What have we dreamed? a union which even now binds us closer than all thought high up above all individual gain or loss—an individual self which stands out free and distinct, most solid of all facts, commensurate with all existence—love disclosing each ever more and more. See, you have made the earth sacred for me. Meanwhile, they say that your writings are 'immoral.' . . . Need I say that I do not agree with them in the least. I believe on the contrary that you have been the first to enunciate the law of purity and health which sooner or later must assert itself. After ages perhaps man will return consciously to the innocent joyous delight in his own natural powers and instincts which characterized the earlier civilizations."

Earlier Traubel had received a Carpenter letter dated December 19, 1877 (Whitman had written "Splendid letter" on it). One reason for this assessment was doubtless Carpenter's singling out for praise the poems that had caused such a rumpus among American prudes: "I want to say how splendid I think your *Children of Adam*. I was reading those pieces again the other day, and of course they came back upon me, as your things always do, with new meaning. The freedom, the large spaces you make around one, fill me with continual delight."

[...]

Note: Edward Carpenter (1844–1929), who lived openly with his working-class male lover, published widely on a variety of reforming topics. He came to the United States twice, in 1877 and 1884, mainly to visit his idol, Whitman. In 1906 he published his reminiscences of these visits as *Days with Walt Whitman*. Among his titles are *Towards Democracy* (1905) and an exploration of homosexuality, *The Intermediate Sex* (1908).[39]

Carpenter paints a picture of the world that sounds like the "great valley" Philip talks of in *Joseph and His Friend*. In *Pages Passed from Hand to Hand*, it's pointed out:

In 1902, Edward Carpenter published what may have been the first English-language anthology with a homosexual theme, *Iolaus: An Anthology of Friendship*, which excerpted works by—among others—Lord Byron, Pindar, Plato, Plutarch, Saint Augustine, and August von Platen. In his preface, Carpenter wrote: "The degree to which Friendship, in the early history of the world, has been recognized as an institution, and the dignity ascribed to it, are things hardly realised to-day. Yet a very slight examination of the subject shows the important part it has played. In making the following connection I have been struck by the remarkable manner in which the customs of the various races and times illustrate each other, and the way in which they point to a solid and enduring body of human sentiment on a subject." That "Friendship," for Carpenter, meant specifically a bond between two men (or two women) is borne out by the book's epigraph, from Plutarch: "And as to the loves of Hercules it is difficult to record them because of their number. But some who think that Iolaus was one of them do to this day worship and honour him; and make their loved ones swear fidelity at his tomb." Like Damon and Pythias, Achilles and Patroclus, and the Ladies of Llangollen, Hurcules and Iolaus represented for Carpenter a high-minded, even exalted ideal of same-sex love, one that his contemporaries might emulate, and that he himself sought to embody in the rural utopia he shared with George Merrill.[30]

For more on how certain books operate as shorthand for coded communication, see Chapter 19: Calamus as Cruising Apparatus. For more on the legend of Damon and Pythias, see Chapter 32: On Women, and A Marriage Below Zero. Returning to Schmidgall's works:

Arc of Comradery: Charles Warren Stoddard
An old letter, dated March 2, 1869, written by Charles Warren Stoddard from Honolulu, is found among Whitman's papers and is re-read and discussed.

Leaves, Stoddard says, has had a liberating effect upon him: "for the first time I act as my nature prompts me. It would not answer in America, as a general principle, not even in California, where men are tolerably bold." He also tells of his experiences sleeping on mats at night with a Hawaiian "lad of eighteen or twenty years" with "his arm over my breast and around me." Whitman's reply says he was deeply touched to learn about "those tender and primitive personal relations away off there in the Pacific islands." Whitman sums up about such letters: "true it is that a man can't go anywhere without taking himself along and without finding love meeting him more than half way. It gives you a new intimation of the providences to become the subject of such an ingratiating hospitality: it makes the big world littler—it knits all the fragments together: it makes the little world bigger—it expands the arc of comradery."

In a later letter to Whitman dated April 2, 1870, and included by Traubel, Stoddard wrote from San Francisco of another trip he planned, this one to Tahiti; his allusion seems to be to that location's indifference to forbidden sexual behavior: "I must get in amongst people who are not afraid of instincts and who scorn hypocrisy. I am numbed with the frigid manners of the Christians; barbarism has given me the fullest joy of my life and I long to return to it and be satisfied." This leads Whitman to make a poignant and revealing comparison of Stoddard and Traubel (certainly glancing at Whitman's own self-image, perhaps glancing, implicitly, at the subject of sexuality identity): "I have had other letters from him: when they turn up you shall have them: he is your kind of a man some ways. . . . [H]e is of a simple direct naive nature—never seemed to fit in very well with things here: many of the finest spirits don't—seem to be born for another planet—seem to have got here by mistake: they are not too bad—no: they are too good: they take their stand on a plane higher than the average practice. You would think they would be respected for that, but they are not: they are almost universally agreed to be fools—they are derided rather than reverenced: why, Horace, you are a good sight such a sort of a fool yourself." Thinking this might hurt, Whitman laid his hand on Traubel's and added, "You know what I refer to in you? I mean your other worldliness, as they call it: you have that in you: the disposition to sacrifice yourself to others—ideas, ideals—all that: it means hell for you maybe here and there but heaven too for sure. Stoddard was, is, that sort of a man, they tell me: I have felt it in his letters."[39]

See [A.14] for more of Stoddard's communications with Walt Whitman, as well as Chapter 3: Twin Love and Chapter 20: Contemporary Camerados. Schmidgall identifies Stoddard as "a reader who gladly nominates himself a 'detected person'" by writing such a letter to Whitman. Whitman's response:

Whitman replied supportively but with a word of warning about being too emotive: "As to you, I do not of course object to your emotional & adhesive nature, & the outlet thereof, but warmly approve them—but do you know (perhaps you do,) how the hard, pungent, gritty, worldly experiences & qualities in American practical life, also serve? how they prevent extravagant sentimentalism?" Whitman adds, in closing, "I am not a little comforted when I learn that young men dwell in thought upon me & my utterances."[40]

For more on "adhesive" natures, see <u>Chapter 20: Contemporary Camerados</u>. The "avowals" go on:

Penetrating the Remotest Parts: Standish O'Grady
Traubel is handed a letter to Whitman from "a young man of great spirit." It is from Standish O'Grady in Dublin and is dated October 5, 1881. It includes this passage: "I find as I change I cannot so change as that I do not meet in you the expression of every changing ideal penetrating even the remotest parts of my nature with a profound sympathy as of his who knew what was in man."

Some Shucks: Louis Sullivan
A February 3, 1887, letter from the great architect, Louis Sullivan, then in his early thirties, arrived from Chicago. Its opening paragraph read: "It is less than a year ago that I made your acquaintance so to speak, quite by accident, searching among the shelves of a book store. I was attracted by the curious title: *Leaves of Grass*, opened the book at random and my eyes met the lines of 'Elemental Drifts.' You then and there entered my soul, have not departed, and never will depart." Walt's remarks on hearing the letter again: "Ain't that catchin'? It sounds like something good that comes along on the wind for them as know enough to suck in. I'd say that feller's some shucks himself. . . . He's an architect or something: and he's a man for sure."

Three of You, Walt: Logan Pearsall Smith
Whitman was close to the local family of Robert Pearsall Smith for several years but later (after the family moved to England) experienced an estrangement that troubled him. Only the son, Logan (1865–1946), who was gay and who became a prolific author and critic, remained "quite warm for Walt," as Bucke observed. Traubel reproduces a letter dated August 8, 1891, that Logan wrote from Haslemere, "We have just had a visit from Dr. Bucke, and we were so glad to hear from him all about you. In furnishing our house here we have got three of those New York photographs of you framed together, hanging in our dining room, and it almost feels as if you were with us sometimes." Much later, in 1938, Smith published a memoir, *Unforgotten*

Years, in which he alluded rather candidly to the liberating impact *Leaves of Grass* had for young homosexuals in the late nineteenth century: "Much that was suppressed in the young people of my generation found a frank avowal in *Leaves of Grass*; feelings and affections for each other, which we had been ashamed of, thoughts which we had hidden as unutterable, we found printed in its pages, discovering that they were not, as we had believed, the thoughts and feelings of young, guilty, half-crazy goblins, but portions of the Kingdom of Truth and the sane experience of mankind."

Whitman himself had this same need to be understood that all the men who wrote to him clearly felt:

> Whitman hands over to Traubel the draft of one of his chatty letters written from Washington to Hugo Fritsch, one of his New York circle, with these emotional words: "I want you some day to write, to talk, about me: to tell what I mean by Calamus: to make no fuss but to speak out of your own knowledge: these letters will help you: they will clear up some things that have been misunderstood: you know what: I don't need to say. The world is so topsy turvy, so afraid to love, so afraid to demonstrate, so good, so respectable, so aloof, that it sees two people or more people who really, greatly, wholly care for each other and say so—when they see such people they wonder and are incredulous or suspicious or defamatory, just as if they had somehow been the victims of an outrage. For instance, any demonstration between men— any: it is always misjudged: people come to conclusions about it: they know nothing, there is nothing to be known; nothing except what might just as well be known: yet they shake their wise heads—they meet, gossip, generate slander: they know what is not to be known—they see what is not to be seen: so they confide in each other, tell the awful truth: the old women men, the old men women, the guessers, the false-witnesses—the whole caboodle of liars and fools."[39]

It's easy enough to see why *Leaves of Grass* and the "Calamus" poems made men feel so known and grateful for the acknowledgement: Whitman himself wrote in a notebook from before his writing of *Leaves*, "A man is only interested in any thing when he identifies himself with it."[40] Some men write poems to reach out, some write letters, and many more use the works of others to find their own private intimacies (see <u>Chapter 19: Calamus as Cruising Apparatus</u>). In an 1890 conversation recorded by Traubel, Whitman remembered being struck by "a splendid thought" Wilde had expressed while in America, "that no first-class fellow wishes to be flattered, aureoled, set upon a throne—but craves to be understood, to be appreciated for his immediate active present power."[40] T.E. Lawrence, mentioned previously in <u>Chapter 8: Halleck and the Death of Byron</u>, said about the same thing in his *Seven Pillars of Wisdom* (1922):

There was my craving to be liked—so strong and nervous that never could I open myself friendly to another. The terror of failure in an effort so important made me shrink from trying; besides, there was the standard; for intimacy seemed shameful unless the other could make the perfect reply, in the same language, after the same method, for the same reasons. There was a craving to be famous; and a horror of being known to like being known. Contempt for my passion for distinction made me refuse every offered honour . . . .[29]

A.E. Housman, another homosexual poet and contemporary of Oscar Wilde's (they were students at Oxford at the same time), whose poems in *A Shropshire Lad* (1896) are used in much the same manner as *Leaves of Grass* for expressing 'manly love' to readers who seek the signs (see <u>Chapter 19: Calamus as Cruising Apparatus</u>), wrote in his personal copy of *Seven Pillars of Wisdom*, against the above passage, his own small avowal: "This is me."[25]

Walt Whitman did not say the following specifically about himself, but for his impact on the world, and the devotion expressed above by the men who read him, it is a fairly prophetic description of his influence. Speaking to Traubel, Whitman once said:

I anticipate the day when some wise man will start out to argue that two and two are not four but five or something else: history proving that two and two couldn't be four: and probability, too: yes, more than that, the wise man will prove it out of his own consciousness—prove it for somebody—for a few: they will believe in him—a body of disciples will believe: then, presto! you have a new religion![39]

For more in this vein, see <u>Chapter 19: Calamus as Cruising Apparatus</u> and <u>Chapter 20: Contemporary Camerados</u>.

XVI

JOSEPH'S TROUBLE, AND PHILIP'S

THE BARE, REPULSIVE, inexorable truth was revealed at last. There was no longer any foothold for doubt, any possibility of continuing his desperate self-deceit. From that day all the joy, the trust, the hope, seemed to fade out of Joseph's life. What had been lost was irretrievable: the delusion of a few months had fixed his fate forever.

His sense of outrage was so strong and keen—so burned upon his consciousness as to affect him like a dull physical pain—that a just and temperate review of his situation was impossible. False in one thing, false in all: that was the single, inevitable conclusion. Of course she had never even loved him. Her coy maiden airs, her warm abandonment to feeling, her very tears and blushes, were artfully simulated: perhaps, indeed, she had laughed in her heart, yea, sneered, at his credulous tenderness! Her assumption of rule, therefore, became an arrogance not to be borne. What right had she, guilty of a crime for which there is no name and no punishment, to reverse the secret justice of the soul, and claim to be rewarded?

So reasoned Joseph to himself, in his solitary broodings; but the spell was not so entirely broken as he imagined. Sternly as he might have resolved in advance, there was a glamour in her mask of cheerfulness and gentleness, which made his resolution seem hard and cruel. In her presence he could not clearly remember his wrongs: the past delusion had been a reality, nevertheless; and he could make no assertion which did not involve his own miserable humiliation. Thus the depth and vital force of his struggle could not be guessed by Julia. She saw only irritable moods, the natural male resistance which she had often remarked in her father,—perhaps, also, the annoyance of giving up certain "romantic" fancies, which she believed to be common to all young men, and never permanent. Even an open rupture could not have pushed them apart so rapidly as this hollow external routine of life.

Joseph took the earliest opportunity of visiting Philip, whom he found busy in forge and foundry. "This would be the life for you!" he said: "we deal only with physical forces, human and elemental: we direct and create power, yet still obey the command to put money in our purses."

"Is that one secret of your strength?" Joseph asked.

"Who told you that I had any?"

"I feel it," said Joseph; and even as he said it he remembered Julia's unworthy suspicion.

"Come up and see Madeline a moment, and the home she has made for me. We get on very well, for brother and sister—especially since her will is about as stubborn as mine."

Madeline was very bright and cheerful; and Joseph, certainly, saw no signs of a stubborn will in her fair face. She was very simply dressed, and busy with some task of needle-work, which she did not lay aside.

"You might pass already for a member of our community," he could not help saying.

"I think your most democratic farmers will accept me," she answered, "when they learn that I am Philip's housekeeper. The only dispute we have had, or are likely to have, is in relation to the salary."

"She is an inconsistent creature, Joseph," said Philip. "I was obliged to offer her as much as she earned by her music-lessons before she would come at all, and now she can't find work enough to balance it."

"How can I, Philip, when you tempt me every day with walks and rides, botany, geology, and sketching from nature?"

So much frank, affectionate confidence showed itself through the playful gossip of the two, that Joseph was at once comforted and pained. "If I had only had a sister!" he sighed to Philip, as they walked down the knoll.

The friends took the valley road, Joseph leading his horse by the bridle. The stream was full to its banks, and crystal clear: shoals of young fishes passed like drifted leaves over the pebbly ground, and the fragrant water-beetles skimmed the surface of the eddies. Overhead the vaults of the great elms and sycamores were filled with the green, delicious illumination of the tender foliage. It was a scene and a season for idle happiness.

Yet the first words Philip spoke, after a long silence, were: "May I speak now?" There was infinite love and pity in his voice. He took Joseph by the hand.

"Yes," the latter whispered.

"It has come," Philip continued; "you cannot hide it from yourself any longer. My pain is that I did not dare to warn you, though at the risk of losing your friendship. There was so little time—"

"You *did* try to warn me, Philip! I have recalled your words, and the trouble in your face as you spoke, a thousand times. I was a fool, a blind, miserable fool, and my folly has ruined my life!

"Strange," said Philip, musingly, "that only a perfectly good and pure nature can fall into such a wretched snare. And yet 'Virtue is its own reward,' is dinned into our ears! It is Hell for a single fault: nay, not even a fault, an innocent mistake! But let us see what can be done: is there no common ground whereon your natures can stand together? If there should be a child—"

Joseph shuddered. "Once it seemed too great, too wonderful a hope," he said, "but now, I don't dare to wish for it. Philip, I am too sorely hurt to think clearly: there is nothing to do but to wait. It is a miserable kind of comfort to me to have your sympathy, but I fear you cannot help me."

Philip saw that he could bear no more: his face was pale to the lips and his hands trembled. He led him to the bank, sat down beside him, and laid his arm about his neck. The silence and the caress were more soothing to Joseph than any words; he soon became calm, and remembered an important part of his errand, which was to acquaint Philip with the oil speculation, and to ask his advice.

They discussed the matter long and gravely. With all his questions, and the somewhat imperfect information which Joseph was able to give, Philip could not satisfy himself whether the scheme was a simple swindle or a well-considered business venture. Two or three of the names were respectable, but the chief agent, Kanuck, was unknown to him; moreover, Mr. Blessing's apparent prominence in the undertaking did not inspire him with much confidence.

"How much have you already paid on the stock?" he asked.

"Three instalments, which, Mr. Blessing thinks, is all that will be called for. However, I have the money for a fourth, should it be necessary. He writes to me that the stock has already risen a hundred per cent in value."

"If that is so," said Philip, "let me advise you to sell half of it, at once. The sum received will cover your liabilities, and the half you retain, as a venture, will give you no further anxiety."

"I had thought of that; yet I am sure that my father-in-law will oppose such a step with all his might. You must know him, Philip; tell me, frankly, your opinion of his character."

"Blessing belongs to a class familiar enough to me," Philip answered; "yet I doubt whether you will comprehend it. He is a swaggering, amiable, magnificent adventurer; never purposely dishonest, I am sure, yet sometimes engaged in transactions that would not bear much scrutiny. His life has been one of ups and downs. After a successful speculation, he is luxurious, open-handed, and absurdly self-confident; his success is soon flung away: he then good-humoredly descends to poverty, because he never believes it can last long. He is unreliable, from his over-sanguine temperament; and yet this very temperament gives him a certain power and influence. Some of our best men are on familiar terms with him. They are on their guard against his pecuniary approaches, they laugh at his extravagant schemes, but they now and then find him useful. I heard Gray, the editor, once speak of him as a man 'filled with available enthusiasms,' and I guess that phrase hits both his strength and his weakness."

On the whole, Joseph felt rather relieved than disquieted. The heart was lighter in his breast as he mounted his horse and rode homewards.

Philip slowly walked forwards, yielding his mind to thoughts wherein Joseph was an important but not the principal figure. Was there a positive strength, he asked himself, in a wider practical experience of life? Did such experience really strengthen the basis of character which must support a man, when some unexpected moral crisis comes upon him? He knew that he seemed strong, to Joseph; but the latter, so far, was bearing his terrible test with a patience drawn from some source of elemental power. Joseph had simply been ignorant: *he* had been proud, impatient, and—he now confessed to himself—weakly jealous. In both cases, a mistake had passed beyond the plastic stage where life may still be remoulded: it had hardened into an inexorable fate. What was to be the end of it all?

A light footstep interrupted his reflections. He looked up, and almost started, on finding himself face to face with Mrs. Hopeton.

Her face was flushed from her walk and the mellow warmth of the afternoon. She held a bunch of wild-flowers,—pink azaleas, delicate sigillarias, valerian, and scarlet painted-cup. She first broke the silence by asking after Madeline.

"Busy with some important sewing,—curtains, I fancy. She is becoming an inveterate housekeeper," Philip said.

"I am glad, for her sake, that she is here. And it must be very pleasant for you, after all your wanderings.

"I must look on it, I suppose," Philip answered, "as the only kind of a home I shall ever have,—while it lasts. But Madeline's life must not be mutilated because mine happens to be."

The warm color left Mrs. Hopeton's face. She strove to make her voice cold and steady, as she said: "I am sorry to see you growing so bitter, Mr. Held."

"I don't think it is my proper nature, Mrs. Hopeton, But you startled me out of a retrospect which had exhausted my capacity for self-reproach, and was about to become self-cursing. There is no bitterness quite equal to that of seeing how weakly one has thrown away an irrecoverable fortune."

She stood before him, silent and disturbed. It was impossible not to understand, yet it seemed equally impossible to answer him. She gave one glance at his earnest, dark gray eyes, his handsome manly face, and the sprinkled glosses of sunshine on his golden hair, and felt a chill strike to her heart. She moved a step, as if to end the interview.

"Only one moment, Mrs. Hopeton—Emily!" Philip cried. "We may not meet again—thus—for years. I will not needlessly recall the past. I only mean to speak of my offence,—to acknowledge it, and exonerate you from any share in the misunderstanding which—made us what we are. You cannot feel the burden of an unpardoned fault; but will you not allow me to lighten mine?"

A softer change came over her stately form. Her arm relaxed, and the wild-flowers fell upon the ground.

"I was wrong, first," Philip went on, "in not frankly confiding to you the knowledge of a boyish illusion and disappointment. I had been heartlessly treated: it was a silly affair, not worth the telling now; but the leaven of mistrust it left behind was not fully worked out of my nature. Then, too, I had private troubles, which my pride—sore, just then, from many a trifling prick, at which I should now laugh—led me to conceal. I need not go over the appearances which provoked me into a display of temper as unjust as it was unmanly,—it is enough to say that all circumstances combined to make me impatient, suspicious, fiercely jealous. I never paused to reflect that you could not know the series of aggravations which preceded our misunderstanding. I did not guess how far I was giving expression to *them*, and unconsciously transferring to you the offences of others. Nay, I exacted a completer surrender of your woman's pride, because a woman had already chosen to make a plaything of my green boy-love. There is no use in speaking of any of the particulars of our quarrel; for I confess to you that I was recklessly, miserably wrong. But the time has come when you can afford to be generous, when you can allow yourself to speak my forgiveness. Not for the sake of anything I might have been to you, but as a true woman, dealing with her brother-man, I ask your pardon!"

Mrs. Hopeton could not banish the memory of the old tenderness which pleaded for Philip in her heart. He had spoken no word which could offend or alarm her: they were safely divided by a gulf which might never be bridged, and perhaps it was well that a purely human reconciliation should now clarify what was turbid in the past, and reunite them by a bond pure, though eternally sad. She came slowly towards him, and gave him her hand.

"All is not only pardoned, Philip," she said, "but it is now doubly my duty to forget it. Do not suppose, however, that I have had no other than reproachful memories. My pride was as unyielding as yours, for it led me to the defiance which you could not then endure. I, too, was haughty and imperious. I recall every word I uttered, and I know that you have not forgotten them. But let there be equal and final justice between us: forget my words, if you can, and forgive me!"

Philip took her hand, and held it softly in his own. No power on earth could have prevented their eyes from meeting. Out of the far-off distance of all dead joys, over all abysses of fate, the sole power which time and will are powerless to tame, took swift possession of their natures. Philip's eyes were darkened and softened by a film of gathering tears: he cried in a broken voice:—

"Yes, pardon!—but I thought pardon might be peace. Forget? Yes, it would be easy to forget the past, if,—O Emily, we have never been parted until now!"

She had withdrawn her hand, and covered her face. He saw, by the convulsive tremor of her frame, that she was fiercely suppressing her emotion. In another moment she looked up, pale, cold, and almost defiant.

"Why should you say more?" she asked. "Mutual forgiveness is our duty, and there the duty ends. Leave me now!"

Philip knew that he had betrayed himself. Not daring to speak another word he bowed and walked rapidly away. Mrs. Hopeton stood, with her hand pressed upon her bosom, until he had disappeared among the farther trees: then she sat down, and let her withheld tears flow freely.

Presently the merry whoops and calls of children met her ear. She gathered together the fallen flowers, rose and took her way across the meadows towards a little stone schoolhouse, at the foot of the nearest hill. Lucy Henderson already advanced to meet her. There was still an hour or two of sunshine, but the mellow, languid heat of the day was over, and the breeze winnowing down the valley brought with it the smell of the blossoming vernal grass.

The two women felt themselves drawn towards each other, though neither had as yet divined the source of their affectionate instinct. Now, looking upon Lucy's pure, gently firm, and reliant face, Mrs. Hopeton, for the second or third time in her life, yielded to a sudden, powerful impulse, and said: "Lucy, I foresee that I shall need the love and the trust of a true woman: where shall I find it if not in you?"

"If mine will content you," said Lucy.

"O my dear!" Mrs. Hopeton cried; "none of us can stand alone. God has singular trials for us, sometimes, and the use and the conquest of a trouble may both become clear in the telling of it. The heart can wear itself out with its own bitterness. You see, I force my confidence upon you, but I know you are strong to receive it."

"At least," Lucy answered, gravely, "I have no claim to strength unless I am willing to have it tested."

"Then let me make the severest test at once: I shall have less courage if I delay. Can you comprehend the nature of a woman's trial, when her heart resists her duty? "

A deep blush overspread Lucy's face, but she forced herself to meet Mrs. Hopeton's gaze. The two women were silent a moment; then the latter threw her arms around Lucy's neck and kissed her.

"Let us walk!" she said. "We shall both find the words we need."

They moved away over the fragrant, shining meadows. Down the valley, at the foot of the blue cape which wooed their eyes, and perhaps suggested to their hearts that mysterious sense of hope which lies in landscape distances, Elwood Withers was directing his gang of workmen. Over the eastern hill, Joseph Asten stood among his fields, hardly recognizing their joyous growth. The smoke of Philip's forge rose above the trees to the northward. So many disappointed hearts, so many thwarted lives! What strand shall be twisted out of the broken threads of these destinies, thus drawn so near to each other? What new forces—fatal or beneficent—shall be developed from these elements?

Mr. Hopeton, riding homewards along the highway, said to himself: "It's a pleasant country, but what slow, humdrum lives the people lead!"

16. WHITMAN, STOKER, AND WILDE

Justin Martin in *Rebel Souls: Walt Whitman and America's First Bohemians* tells us, "During the years in Camden, Whitman played host to a steady stream of distinguished visitors. Oscar Wilde, Bram Stoker, and an ancient Longfellow crossed the Delaware to see him."[33] The visits from Wilde and Stoker are of particular note, because though they knew one another to the point of being rivals over the same (female) sweetheart, they arrived in Camden by completely different means. This is from David J. Skal's *Something in the Blood: The Untold Story of Bram Stoker, the Man Who Wrote Dracula*:

> Both Dubliners, Wilde and Stoker were familiar if not completely friendly acquaintances from the 1870s until Oscar's trial and imprisonment in 1895. As I wrote nearly a quarter century ago, "Wilde and Stoker present a fascinating set of Victorian bookends, shadow-mirrors in uneasy reciprocal orbits." [...] Both were deeply influenced by intelligent and assertive mothers (of diametrically opposed temperaments); both attended Trinity College; both were drawn to the theatre, were fascinated by folklore and fairy tales, admired Walt Whitman and Henry Irving, and gravitated romantically to a beautiful Dublin girl, Florence Balcombe. Oscar, perhaps, courted his "Florrie" out of an aesthetic ardor; Stoker actually married her, though their marriage would be called passionless. Both men wrote masterpieces of macabre fiction about Victorian monsters that drain and destroy. And both expressed an enduring fascination with the conundrums of sex and gender—Bram in his writings, and Oscar, far more messily, in his life. It is also fascinating that Stoker was drawn to Wilde's parents as flamboyant surrogates to his own conventional, straitlaced family. While one of *Dracula's* most famous lines— "Children of the night—what music they make!"—immediately brings to mind the vocal stylings of Bela Lugosi, it was the flamboyantly theatrical mother of Oscar Wilde who provided the original inspiration. Lady Wilde's son, like a character from a classic Gothic novel, was a hovering doppelganger throughout Stoker's life, both creatively and psychosexually—in the same way *The Picture of Dorian Gray* shadows and illuminates *Dracula*. It is no

coincidence that Wilde was persecuted as a sexual threat to Victorian London at the same cultural moment Stoker created the greatest sex monster of all time.[43]

According to Kaya Genç, it was Lady Wilde who was the means by which Bram Stoker and Oscar Wilde met:

> Stoker and Wilde were probably first introduced to each other during one of the famous evening matinees of Jane Wilde, Oscar's flamboyant mother. A fiercely nationalistic poet with a passion for writing, Lady Wilde loved society and hosted a literary salon which was held every Saturday in Wilde's family house on Merrion Square, Dublin. Having befriended Oscar's older brother Willie, who was his classmate at Trinity, Stoker admired the intellectual boldness of the Wilde family and was a fan of the storytelling gifts of Sir William Wilde. During his wife's matinees, Sir William would take refuge in his study where he was followed by a group of curious attendees, among them the young Stoker. There he would recount many interesting stories; the *Journal* features an entry that transcribes a tale of robbery "told by Sir W. Wilde."[18]

Not only did she first introduce her son to Stoker, according to Schmidgall, "Oscar Wilde's mother, Lady Wilde (known also as Speranza), buying one of the earliest copies of *Leaves of Grass*, [recited] from it to her son."[40] He notes that Stoker too found Whitman's poems, and admired them:

> There are those "strangers" who would read the steamy Calamus poems and happily recognize a kindred sexual spirit. We will see later that Bram Stoker, the author of that homoerotic extravaganza *Dracula*, was such a reader. In 1872, at the age of twenty-four, he wrote Whitman a wonderfully effusive letter thanking him for "many happy hours" spent reading his poems "with my door locked late at night."[40]

For Stoker's full letters to Whitman, see [A.15]. Genç explains the significance:

> Th[e] admiration for Whitman is a telltale sign of writerly Victorian homosexuality, and was not the least of Stoker's shared interests with Oscar Wilde. At first sight, it seems as if no writer of his generation could have been more different from Stoker than the flamboyant figure of Wilde. Seven years his junior, Wilde was nothing if not unhidden in his sexual preferences. On the contrary, Wilde's life was a concerted effort to remove boundaries between one's private and public selves. He favored revealing secrets (those of his own and of others), instead of keeping them. But Stoker and Wilde met

at an early age and remained life-long acquaintances. By the time of Wilde's death in 1900, though, Stoker wasn't among his two dozen mourners. In 1912, the year of his own death, Stoker was so fiercely homophobic that he went so far as to demand imprisonment of all homosexual authors in Britain—a group to which he, inevitably, belonged.[18]

That these two men each found their way to visiting Walt Whitman is remarkable. As stated by Talia Schaffer in "'A Wilde Desire Took Me': The Homoerotic History of Dracula," "According to [Eve] Sedwick, photographs and books of Whitman and admiring references to Whitman, 'functioned as badges of homosexual recognition' in the England of the fin-de-siècle."[38] Wilde managed to follow after his idol to the point of outpacing him: "After Wilde's trial, 'the desire of Oscar Wilde' became a euphemism for homosexuality"[38] (for more on Wilde's name as watch-word, see Chapter 19: Calamus as Cruising Apparatus), something that Bram Stoker took great pains to distance himself from, regardless of what he shared privately with Wilde or with Whitman. After Wilde's conviction and prison sentence, Stoker wrote several articles that talked carefully around Wilde, never once using his name, but still clearly condemning him. Schaffer explains:

> [After Wilde's conviction] Stoker identifies with the national anti-Wilde homophobia, partly to disguise his own vulnerability as a gay man, partly because it justifies his belief in the value of the closet, and partly from horror at the monstrous image of Wilde produced by the media, which would haunt men of 'his kind.' [He wrote], "[I]t is the coarseness and unscrupulousness of certain writers of fiction which has brought the evil; on their heads be it." The article argues that these authors are criminal because they teach their otherwise 'normal' readers to experience homosexual desire.[38]

Like Bayard Taylor, what Stoker would confess to understanding personally before Walt Whitman, he would later disavow and distance himself from in public. Wilde once put the phenomenon nicely in his essay "The Critic as Artist," saying, "Man is least himself when he talks in his own person. Give him a mask, and he will tell you the truth."[59]

See the next section, Chapter 17: Whitman and Stoker for more details on their correspondence and meeting. Continue to the section after that, Chapter 18: Whitman and Wilde for details on Wilde's visit to Camden.

XVII

A STORM

"I have a plan," said Julia, a week or two later. "Can you guess it? No, I think not; yet you *might*! O, how lovely the light falls on your hair: it is perfect satin!"

She had one hand on his shoulder, and ran the fingers of the other lightly through his brown locks. Her face, sparkling all over with a witching fondness, was lifted towards his. It was the climax of an amiable mood which had lasted three days.

What young man can resist a playful, appealing face, a soft, caressing touch? Joseph smiled as he asked,—

"Is it that I shall wear my hair upon my shoulders, or that we shall sow plaster on the clover-field, as old Bishop advised you the other day?"

"Now you are making fun of my interest in farming; but wait another year! I am trying earnestly to understand it, but only so that ornament—beauty—what was the word in those lines you read last night?—may grow out of use. That's it—Beauty out of Use! I know I've bored you a little sometimes—just a little, now, confess it!—with all my questions; but this is something different. Can't you think of anything that would make our home, O *so* much more beautiful?"

"A grove of palm-trees at the top of the garden? Or a lake in front, with marble steps leading down to the water?"

"You perverse Joseph! No: something possible, something practicable, something handsome, something profitable! Or, are you so old-fashioned that you think we must drudge for thirty years, and only take our pleasure after we grow rheumatic?"

Joseph looked at her with a puzzled, yet cheerful face.

"You don't understand me yet!" she exclaimed. "And indeed, indeed, I dread to tell you, for one reason: you have such a tender regard for old associations,—not that I'd have it otherwise, if I could. I like it: I trust I have the same feeling; yet a little sentiment sometimes interferes practically with the improvement of our lives."

Joseph's curiosity was aroused. "What do you mean, Julia?" he asked.

"No!" she cried; "I will not tell you until I have read part of pa's letter, which came this afternoon. Take the arm-chair, and don't interrupt me."

She seated herself on the window-sill and opened the letter. "I saw," she said, "how uneasy you felt when the call came for the fourth instalment of ten per cent on the Amaranth shares, especially after I had so much difficulty in persuading you not to sell the half. It surprised me, although I knew that, where pa is concerned, there's a good reason for everything. So I wrote to him the other day, and this is what he says,—you remember, Kanuck is the company's agent on the spot:—

"'Tell Joseph that in matters of finance there's often a wheel within a wheel. Blenkinsop, of the Chowder Company, managed to get a good grab of our shares through a third party, of whom we had not the slightest suspicion. I name no name at present, from motives of prudence. We only discovered the circumstance after the third party left for Europe. Looking upon the Chowder as a rival, it is our desire, of course, to extract this entering wedge before it has been thrust into our vitals, and we can only accomplish the end by still keeping secret the discovery of the torpedoes (an additional expense, I might remark), and calling for fresh instalments from *all* the stockholders. Blenkinsop, not being within the inside ring,—and no possibility of *his* getting in!—will naturally see only the blue of disappointment where we see the rose of realized expectations. Already, so Kanuck writes to me, negotiations are on foot which will relieve our Amaranth of this parasitic growth, and a few weeks—days—hours, in fact, may enable us to explode and triumph! I was offered, yesterday, by one of our shrewdest operators, who has been silently watching us, ten shares of the Sinnemahoning Hematite for eight of ours. Think of that,—the Sinnemahoning Hematite! No better stock in the market, if you remember the quotations! Explain the significance of the figures to your husband, and let him see that he has—but no, I will restrain myself and make no estimate. I will only mention, under the seal of the profoundest secrecy, that the number of shafts now sinking (or being sunk) will give an enormous flowing capacity when the electric spark fires the mine, and I should not wonder if our shares then soared high over the pinnacles of all previous speculation!'

"No, nor I!" Julia exclaimed as she refolded the letter; "it is certain,—positively certain! I have never known the Sinnemahoning Hematite to be less than 147. What do you say, Joseph?"

"I hope it may be true," he answered. "I can't feel so certain, while an accident—the discovery of the torpedo-plan, for instance—might change the prospects of the Amaranth. It will be a great relief when the time comes to 'realize,' as your father says."

"You only feel so because it is your first experience; but for your sake I will consent that it shall be the last. We shall scarcely need any more than this will bring us; for, as pa says, a mere competence in the city is a splendid fortune in the country. You need leisure for books and travel and society, and you shall have it. Now, let us make a place for both!"

Thereupon she showed him how the parlor and rear bedroom might be thrown into one; where there were alcoves for bookcases and space for a piano; how a new veranda might be added to the western end of the house; how the plastering might be renewed, a showy cornice supplied, and an air of elegant luxury given to the new apartment. Joseph saw and listened, conscious at once of a pang at changing the ancient order of things, and a temptation to behold a more refined comfort in its place. He only asked to postpone the work; but Julia pressed him so closely, with such a multitude of unanswerable reasons, that he finally consented to let a mechanic look at the house, and make an estimate of the expense.

In such cases, the man who deliberates is lost.

His consent once reluctantly exacted, Julia insisting that she would take the whole charge of directing the work, a beginning was made without delay, and in a few days the ruin was so complete that the restoration became a matter of necessity.

Julia kept her word only too faithfully. With a lively, playful manner in the presence of the workmen, but with a cold, inflexible obstinacy when they were alone, she departed from the original plan, adding showy and expensive features, every one of which, Joseph presently saw, was devised to surpass the changes made by the Hopetons in their new residence. His remonstrances produced no effect, and he was precluded from a practical interference by the fear of the workmen guessing his domestic trouble. Thus the days dragged on, and the breach widened without an effort on either side to heal it.

The secret of her temporary fondness gave him a sense of positive disgust when it arose in his memory. He now suspected a selfish purpose in her caresses, and sought to give her no chance of repeating them, but in the company of others he was forced to endure a tenderness which, he was surprised to find, still half deceived him, as it wholly deceived his neighbors. He saw, too,—and felt himself powerless to change the impression,—that Julia's popularity increased with her knowledge of the people, while their manner towards him was a shade less frank and cordial than formerly. He knew that the changes in his home were so much needless extravagance, to them; and that Julia's oft-repeated phrase (always accompanied with a loving look), "Joseph is making the old place so beautiful for me!" increased their mistrust, while seeming to exalt him as a devoted husband.

It is not likely that she specially intended this result; while, on the other hand, he somewhat exaggerated its character. Her object was simply to retain her growing ascendency: within the limits where her peculiar faculties had been exercised she was nearly perfect; but she was indifferent to tracing the consequences of her actions beyond those limits. When she ascertained Mr. Chaffinch's want of faith in Joseph's entire piety, she became more regular in her attendance at his church, not so much to prejudice her husband by the contrast, as to avoid the suspicion which he had incurred. To Joseph, however, in the bitterness of his deception, these actions seemed either hostile or heartless; he was repelled from the clearer knowledge of a nature so foreign to his own. So utterly foreign: yet how near beyond all others it had once seemed!

It was not a jealousy of the authority she assumed which turned his heart from her: it was the revelation of a shallowness and selfishness not at all rare in the class from which she came, but which his pure, guarded youth had never permitted him to suspect in any human being. A man familiar with men and women, if he had been caught in such toils, would have soon discovered some manner of controlling her nature, for the very shrewdest and falsest have their vulnerable side. It gave Joseph, however, so much keen spiritual pain to encounter her in her true character, that such a course was simply impossible.

Meanwhile the days went by; the expense of labor and material had already doubled the estimates made by the mechanics; bills were presented for payment, and nothing was heard from the Amaranth. Money was a necessity, and there was no alternative but to obtain a temporary loan at a county town, the centre of transactions for all the debtors and creditors of the neighboring country. It was a new and disagreeable experience for Joseph to appear in the character of a borrower, and he adopted it most reluctantly; yet the reality was a greater trial than he had suspected. He found that the most preposterous stories of his extravagance were afloat. He was transforming his house into a castle: he had made, lost, and made again a large fortune in petroleum; he had married a wealthy wife and squandered her money; he drove out in a carriage with six white horses; he was becoming irregular in his habits and heretical in his religious views; in short, such marvellous powers of invention had been exercised that the Arab story-tellers were surpassed by the members of that quiet, sluggish community.

It required all his self-control to meet the suspicions of the money-agents, and convince them of the true state of his circumstances. The loan was obtained, but after such a wear and tear of flesh and spirit as made it seem a double burden.

When he reached home, in the afternoon, Julia instantly saw, by his face, that all had not gone right. A slight effort, however, enabled her to say carelessly and cheerfully,—

"Have you brought me my supplies, dear?"

"Yes," he answered curtly.

"Here is a letter from pa," she then said. "I opened it, because I knew what the subject must be. But if you're tired, pray don't read it now, for then you may be impatient. There's a little more delay."

"Then I'll not delay to know it," he said, taking the letter from her hand. A printed slip, calling upon the stockholders of the Amaranth to pay a *fifth* instalment, fell out of the envelope. Accompanying it there was a hasty note from B. Blessing: "Don't be alarmed my dear son-in-law! Probably a mere form. Blenkinsop still holds on, but we think this will bring him at once. If it don't, we shall very likely have to go on *with* him, even if it obliges us to unite the Amaranth and the Chowder. In any case, we shall ford or bridge this little Rubicon within a fortnight. Have the money ready, if convenient, but do not forward unless I give the word. We hear, through third parties, that Clementina (who is now at Long Branch) receives much attention from Mr. Spelter, a man of immense wealth, but, I regret to say, no refinement."

Joseph smiled grimly when he finished the note. "Is there never to be an end of humbug?" he exclaimed.

"There, now!" cried Julia; "I knew you'd be impatient. You are so unaccustomed to great operations. Why, the Muchacho Land Grant—I remember it, because pa sold out just at the wrong time—hung on for seven years!"

"D— curse the Muchacho Land Grant, and the Amaranth too!"

"Aren't you ashamed!" exclaimed Julia, taking on a playful air of offence; "but you're tired and hungry, poor fellow!" Therewith she put her hands on his shoulders, and raised herself on tiptoe to kiss him.

Joseph, unable to control his sudden instinct, swiftly turned away his head.

"O you wicked husband, you deserve to be punished! she cried, giving him what was meant to be a light tap on the cheek.

It was a light tap, certainly; but perhaps a little of the annoyance which she banished from her face had lodged, unconsciously, in her fingers. They left just sting enough to rouse Joseph's heated blood. He started back a step, and looked at her with flaming eyes.

"No more of that, Julia! I know, *now*, how much your arts are worth. I am getting a vile name in the neighborhood,—losing my property,—losing my own self-respect,— because I have allowed you to lead me! Will you be content with what you have done, or must you go on until my ruin is complete?"

Before he had finished speaking she had taken rapid counsel with herself, and decided. "Oh, oh! such words to me!" she groaned, hiding her face between her hands. I never thought *you* could be so cruel! I had *such* pleasure in seeing you rich and free, in trying to make your home beautiful; and now this little delay, which no business man would think anything of, seems to change your very nature! But I will not think it's your true self: something has worried you to-day,—you have heard some foolish story—"

"It is not the worry of to-day," he interrupted, in haste to state his whole grievance, before his weak heart had time to soften again,—"it is the worry of months past! It is because I thought you true and kind-hearted, and I find you selfish and hypocritical! It is very well to lead me into serious expenses, while so much is at stake, and now likely to be lost,—it is very well to make my home beautiful, especially when you can outshine Mrs. Hopeton! It is easy to adapt yourself to the neighbors, and keep on the right side of them, no matter how much your husband's character may suffer in the process!"

"That will do!" said Julia, suddenly becoming rigid. She lifted her head, and apparently wiped the tears from her eyes. "A little more and it would be too much for even *me*! What do I care for 'the neighbors'? persons whose ideas and tastes and habits of life are so different from mine? I have endeavored to be friendly with them for *your* sake: I have taken special pains to accommodate myself to their notions, just because I intended they should justify *you* in choosing me! I believed—for you told me so—that there was no calculation in love, that money was dross in comparison; and how could I imagine that you would so soon put up a balance and begin to weigh the two? Am I your wife or your slave? Have I an equal share in what is yours, or am I here merely to increase it? If there is to be a question of dollars and cents between us, pray have my allowance fixed, so that I may not overstep it, and may save myself from such reproaches! I knew you would be disappointed in pa's letter: I have been anxious and uneasy since it came, through my sympathy with you, and was ready to make any sacrifice that might relieve your mind; and now you seem to be full of unkindness and injustice! What shall I do, O what shall I do?"

She threw herself upon a sofa, weeping hysterically.

"Julia!" he cried, both shocked and startled by her words, "you purposely misunderstand me. Think how constantly I have yielded to you, against my own better judgment! When have you considered my wishes?"

"When?" she repeated: then, addressing the cushion with a hopeless, melancholy air, "he asks, when! How could I misunderstand you? your words were as plain as daggers. If you were not aware how sharp they were, call them back to your mind when these mad, unjust suspicions have left you! I trusted you so perfectly, I was looking forward to such a happy future, and now—now, all seems so dark! It is like a flash of lightning: I am weak and giddy: leave me,—I can bear no more!"

She covered her face, and sobbed wretchedly.

"I am satisfied that you are not as ignorant as you profess to be," was all Joseph could say, as he obeyed her command, and left the room. He was vanquished, he knew, and a little confused by his wife's unexpected way of taking his charges in flank instead of meeting them in front, as a man would have done. *Could* she be sincere? he asked himself. Was she really so ignorant of herself, as to believe all that she had uttered? There seemed to be not the shadow of hypocrisy in her grief and indignation. Her tears were real: then why not her smiles and caresses? Either she was horribly, incredibly false,—worse than he dared dream her to be,—or so fatally unconscious of her nature that nothing short of a miracle could ever enlighten her. One thing only was certain: there was now no confidence between them; and there might never be again.

He walked slowly forth from the house, seeing nothing, and unconscious whither his feet were leading him.

17. WHITMAN AND STOKER

Like Charles Warren Stoddard, Schmidgall points out that Bram Stoker was another "detected person" upon reading *Leaves of Grass*:

> [Stoker] was moved in 1872, at the age of twenty-four, to write the author. The gushing letter he first composed, however, lay in a drawer for four years before the odor of *Calamus aromaticus* finally overwhelmed him and he mailed it. In his cover letter of 1876, Stoker says, "I write this openly because I feel with you one must be open." (When Horace Traubel reread the letter to Whitman in 1889, Whitman said this sentence had "hit me hard" and added, "That's it: that's me, as I hope I am: it's *Leaves of Grass* if *Leaves of Grass* is anything.")[40]

From Stoker's writings to Whitman: "sometimes a word or a phrase of yours takes me away from the world around me and places me in an ideal land. . . ." It sounds not unlike the "great valley" talked about in *Joseph and His Friend*. See [A.15] for both of Stoker's introductory letters to Whitman, and Whitman's response. Traubel recorded further thoughts on those communications from Whitman:

> After hearing the draft read aloud, Whitman said, "Horace, I call that an extraordinary occurrence: that he should have let himself go in that style. . . . It all sounds easy and informal to me—not verbally stiff in the joints anywhere."[39]

Whitman had more to say of Stoker, and eventually the two met in person. The following is from Meredith Hindley's feature for *Humanities* magazine, "When Bram Met Walt," Volume 33:

> Whitman shared the exchange of letters with his friend Horace Traubel, who recorded their conversation in *With Walt Whitman in Camden*. "He was

a sassy youngster," Whitman said of Stoker. "[A]s to burning the epistle up or not—it never occurred to me to do anything at all: what the hell did I care whether he was pertinent or impertinent? he was fresh, breezy, Irish: that was the price paid for admission—and enough: he was welcome!" Whitman had also noticed that Stoker had written more to himself than to the poet. "I could not but warmly respond to that which is actually personal: I do it with my whole heart."

[...]

In March 1884, the Lyceum tour stopped in Philadelphia, making it possible for Stoker finally to meet his literary idol. Stoker envisioned slipping away to call on his hero, but when [Henry] Irving found out about his plan he asked to come along. Irving was a casual fan at best, but he couldn't pass up the chance to meet the famous Walt Whitman. On the afternoon of March 20, they called at the house of Thomas Donaldson, one of Whitman's friends and benefactors. Like many in the poet's circle, Donaldson wrote a memoir of their friendship, *Walt Whitman: The Man* (1896), which gives us another account of the meeting.

They found the poet sitting in Donaldson's parlor. "On the opposite side of the room sat an old man of leonine appearance," wrote Stoker. "He was burly, with a large head and high forehead slightly bald. Great shaggy masses of grey-white hair fell over his collar. His moustache was large and thick and fell over his mouth so as to mingle with the top of the mass of the bushy flowing beard." Donaldson introduced Irving first, then Stoker. Whitman leaned forward in his chair and held out his hand. "Bram Stoker— Abraham Stoker is it?" Stoker said yes and they shook hands as two old friends. Stoker would have to wait to speak to Whitman, as the honor of one-on-one conversation fell first to Irving. The poet and actor talked for "a good while and seemed to take to each other mightily." Irving ventured that Whitman reminded him of Tennyson, a comparison the poet heartily embraced. For his part, Whitman was struck by Irving's demeanor—"his gentle and unaffected manners and his evident intellectual power and heart."

When Stoker finally got his chance, Whitman did not disappoint. "I found him all that I had ever dreamed of, or wished for in him: large-minded, broad-viewed, tolerant to the last degree; incarnate sympathy; understanding with an insight that seemed more than human." They spoke as old friends and traded gossip about mutual acquaintances in Dublin. "Before we parted he asked me to come see him at his home in Camden whenever I could manage it. Need I say that I promised." Whitman found much to like about Stoker too, calling him "an adroit lad." "He's like a breath of good, healthy, breezy sea air," he told Donaldson.

Two years passed before Stoker could make the trip to Camden. In the fall of 1886, he traveled to New York to make arrangements for the Lyceum's forthcoming tour of Faust. On November 2, he took the train down to Philadelphia and met up with Donaldson, who accompanied him on the visit. Whitman's house at 328 Mickle Street was "a small ordinary one in a row, built of the usual fine red brick which marks Philadelphia and gives it an appearance so peculiarly Dutch." They arrived to find Whitman sitting in a big rocking chair that had been a gift from Donaldson's children. "He seemed feebler, and when he rose from his chair or moved about the room did so with difficulty. I could notice his eyes better now. They were not so quick and searching as before."

Whitman's mind remained sharp, and their conversation roamed from London literary gossip to Irving's latest stage triumphs to Abraham Lincoln. When Stoker confessed his admiration for Lincoln, Whitman declared, "No one will ever know the real Abraham Lincoln or his place in history!" Stoker asked Whitman about his "startlingly vivid" account of Lincoln's assassination at the hands of John Wilkes Booth. The essay had been published in *Specimen Days*, the poet's autobiography. Whitman said that while he hadn't been present when the president was shot, he had "spent the better part of the night interviewing many of those who were present." [See Chapter 22: Whitman's Peter for more on those first-hand accounts.] Whitman's account was pure fiction—he had been in New York at the time of the assassination. But Stoker was captivated. "The memory of that room will never leave me," he wrote.

Stoker's conversation with Whitman ended up playing a starring role in a lecture he had started writing and would deliver at the London Institution. Stoker incorporated Whitman's proclamation—significantly embellished—into the lecture: "Not long since Walt Whitman said to me: 'No man knows—no one in the future can ever know Abraham Lincoln. He was much greater—so much vaster even than his surroundings—what is not known of him is so much more than what is, that the true man can never be known on earth.'"

Stoker had one last meeting with Whitman in December 1887, when the Lyceum Theatre ventured to the United States for another tour. Once again, he met up with Donaldson to make the pilgrimage to Mickle Street, where he found Whitman "hale and well." "His hair was more snowy white than ever and more picturesque. He looked like King Lear in Ford Madox Brown's picture," wrote Stoker.

After the old friends exchanged affectionate greetings, Stoker broached with Whitman a subject of some delicacy: editing some of his poems. Stoker had been discussing the idea with their mutual friend Talcott Williams, editor of the Philadelphia Press. If Whitman would let them cut about one hundred lines his books could go into every house in America. "Is that not worth the sacrifice?" asked Stoker. Whitman gave a swift retort, according to Stoker:

"It would not be any sacrifice. So far as I am concerned they might cut a thousand. It is not that—it is quite another matter:"—here both face and voice grew rather solemn—"when I wrote as I did I thought I was doing right and right makes for good. I think so still. I think that all that God made is for good—that the work of His hands is clean in all ways if used as He intended! If I was wrong I have done harm. And for that I deserve to be punished by being forgotten! It has been and cannot not-be. No, I shall never cut a line so long as I live!"

Despite the tense discussion, Whitman and Stoker parted friends. Whitman even sent Stoker off with a keepsake: an autographed 1872 edition of *Leaves of Grass* and a photograph of himself.

"That was the last time that I ever saw the man who for nearly twenty years had held my heart as a dear friend," wrote Stoker. Whitman passed away in March of 1892, his body finally giving out after a bout of pneumonia. When Stoker passed through Philadelphia in 1894, he was shocked to learn that Whitman had left something for him in Donaldson's care: the original notes from the lecture Whitman gave about Lincoln at the Chestnut Street Opera House on April 15, 1886.

"This was my Message from the Dead," wrote Stoker.[27]

XVIII

ON THE RAILROAD TRACK

STILL WALKING, WITH bent head, and a brain which vainly strove to work its way to clearness through the perplexities of his heart, Joseph went on. When, wearied at last, though not consciously calmer, he paused and looked about him, it was like waking from a dream. Some instinct had guided him on the way to Philip's forge: the old road had been moved to accommodate the new branch railway, and a rapid ring of hammers came up from the embankment below. It was near the point of the hill where Lucy's schoolhouse stood, and even as he looked she came, accompanied by her scholars, to watch the operation of laying the track. Elwood Withers, hale, sunburnt, full of lusty life, walked along the sleepers directing the workmen.

"He was right,—only too right!" muttered Joseph to himself. "Why could I not see with his eyes? 'It's the bringing up,' he would say; but that is not all. I have been an innocent, confiding boy, and thought that years and acres had made me a man. O, *she* understood me—she understands me now; but in spite of her, God helping me, I shall yet be a man."

Elwood ran down the steep side of the embankment, greeted Lucy, and helped her to the top, the children following with whoops and cries.

"Would it have been different," Joseph further soliloquized, "if Lucy and I had loved and married? It is hardly treating Elwood fairly to suppose such a thing, yet—a year ago—I might have loved her. It is better as it is: I should have stepped upon a true man's heart. Have they drawn nearer? and if so, does he, with his sturdier nature, his surer knowledge, find no flaw in her perfections?"

A morbid curiosity to watch the two suddenly came upon him. He clambered over the fence, crossed the narrow strip of meadow, and mounted the embankment. Elwood's back was towards him, and he was just saying: "It all comes of taking an interest in what you're doing. The practical part is easy enough, when you once have the principles. I can manage the theodolite already, but I need a little showing when I come to the calculations.

Somehow, I never cared much about study before, but here it's all applied as soon as you've learned it, and that fixes it, like, in your head."

Lucy was listening with an earnest, friendly interest on her face. She scarcely saw Joseph until he stood before her. After the first slight surprise, her manner towards him was quiet and composed: Elwood's eyes were bright, and there was a fresh intelligence in his appearance. The habit of command had already given him a certain dignity.

"How can *I* get knowledge which may be applied as soon as learned?" Joseph asked, endeavoring to assume the manner furthest from his feelings. "I'm still at the foot of the class, Lucy," he added, turning to her.

"How?" Elwood replied. "I should say by going around the world alone. That would be about the same for you as what these ten miles I'm overseeing are to me. A little goes a great way with me, for I can only pick up one thing at a time."

"What kind of knowledge are you looking for, Joseph?" Lucy gravely asked.

"Of myself," said he, and his face grew dark.

"That's a true word!" Elwood involuntarily exclaimed. He then caught Lucy's eye, and awkwardly added: "It's about what we all want, I take it."

Joseph recovered himself in a moment, and proposed looking over the work. They walked slowly along the embankment, listening to Elwood's account of what had been done and what was yet to do, when the Hopeton carriage came up the highway, near at hand. Mrs. Hopeton sat in it alone.

"I was looking for you, Lucy," she called. "If you are going towards the cutting, I will join you there."

She sent the coachman home with the carriage, and walked with them on the track. Joseph felt her presence as a relief, but Elwood confessed to himself that he was a little disturbed by the steady glance of her dark eyes. He had already overcome his regret at the interruption of his rare and welcome chance of talking with Lucy, but then Joseph knew his heart, while this stately lady looked as if she were capable of detecting what she had no right to know. Nevertheless, she was Lucy's friend, and that fact had great weight with Elwood.

"It's rather a pity to cut into the hills and bank up the meadows in this way, isn't it?" he asked.

"And to disturb my school with so much hammering," Lucy rejoined; "when the trains come I must retreat."

"None too soon," said Mrs. Hopeton. "You are not strong, Lucy, and the care of a school is too much for you."

Elwood thanked her with a look, before he knew what he was about.

"After all," said Joseph, "why shouldn't nature be cut up? I suppose everything was given up to us to use, and the more profit the better the use, seems to be the rule of the world. 'Beauty grows out of Use,' you know."

His tone was sharp and cynical, and grated unpleasantly on Lucy's sensitive ear.

"I believe it is a rule in art," said Mrs. Hopeton, "that mere ornament, for ornament's sake, is not allowed. It must always seem to answer some purpose, to have a necessity for its existence. But, on the other hand, what is necessary should be beautiful, if possible."

"A loaf of bread, for instance," suggested Elwood.

They all laughed at this illustration, and the conversation took a lighter turn. By this time they had entered the narrower part of the valley, and on passing around a sharp curve of the track found themselves face to face with Philip and Madeline Held.

If Mrs. Hopeton's heart beat more rapidly at the unexpected meeting, she preserved her cold, composed bearing. Madeline, bright and joyous, was the unconscious agent of unconstraint, in whose presence each of the others felt immediately free.

"Two inspecting committees at once!" cried Philip. "It is well for you, Withers, that you didn't locate the line. My sister and I have already found several unnecessary curves and culverts."

"And *we* have found a great deal of use and no beauty," Lucy answered.

"Beauty!" exclaimed Madeline. "What is more beautiful than to see one's groceries delivered at one's very door? Or to have the opera and the picture-gallery brought within two hours' distance? How far are we from a lemon, Philip?"

"You were a lemon, Mad, in your vegetable, pre-human state; and you are still acid and agreeable."

"Sweets to the sweet!" she gayly cried. "And what, pray, was Miss Henderson?"

"Don't spare me, Mr. Held," said Lucy, as he looked at her with a little hesitation.

"An apple."

"And Mrs. Hopeton?"

"A date-palm," said Philip, fixing his eyes upon her face. She did not look up, but an expression which he could not interpret just touched her lips and faded.

"Now, it's your turn, Miss Held," Elwood remarked: "what were we men?"

"O, Philip a prickly pear, of course; and you, well, some kind of a nut; and Mr. Asten—"

"A cabbage," said Joseph.

"What vanity! Do you imagine that you are all head,—or that your heart is in your head? Or that you keep the morning dew longer than the rest of us?

"It might well be," Joseph answered; and Madeline felt her arm gently pinched by Philip, from behind. She had tact enough not to lower her pitch of gayety too suddenly, but her manner towards Joseph became grave and gentle. Mrs. Hopeton said but little: she looked upon the circling hills, as if studying their summer beauty, while the one desire in her heart was to be away from the spot,—away from Philip's haunting eyes.

After a little while, Philip seemed to be conscious of her feeling. He left his place on the opposite side of the track, took Joseph's arm and led him a little aside from the group.

"Philip, I want you!" Joseph whispered; "but no, not quite yet. There is no need of coming to you in a state of confusion. In a day or two more I shall have settled a little."

"You are right," said Philip: "there is no opiate like time, be there never so little of it. I felt the fever of your head in your hand. Don't come to me, until you feel that it is the one thing which must be done I think you know why I say so."

"I do!" Joseph exclaimed. "I am just now more of an ostrich than anything else; I should like to stick my head in the sand, and imagine myself invisible. But—Philip—here are six of us together. One other, I know, has a secret wound, perhaps two others: is it always so in life? I think I am selfish enough to be glad to know that I am not specially picked out for punishment."

Philip could not help smiling. "Upon my soul," he said, "I believe Madeline is the only one of the six who is not busy with other thoughts than those we all seem to utter. Specially picked out? There is no such thing as special picking out, in this world! Joseph, it may seem hard and schoolmaster-like in me again to say 'wait!' yet that is the only word I can say."

"Good evening, all!" cried Elwood. "I must go down to my men; but I'd be glad of such an inspection as this, a good deal oftener."

"I'll go that far with you," said Joseph.

Mrs. Hopeton took Lucy's arm with a sudden, nervous movement. "If you are not too tired, let us walk over the hill," she said; "I want to find the right point of view for sketching our house."

The company dissolved. Philip, as he walked up the track with his sister, said to himself: "Surely she was afraid of me. And what does her fear indicate? What, if not that the love she once bore for me still lives in her heart, in spite of time and separated fates? I should not, *dare* not think of her; I shall never again speak a word to her which her husband might not hear; but I cannot tear from me the dream of what she might be, the knowledge of what she is, false, hopeless, fatal, as it all may be!"

"Elwood," said Joseph, when they had walked a little distance in silence, "do you remember the night you spent with me, a year ago?"

"I'm not likely to forget it."

"Let me ask you one question, then. Have you come nearer to Lucy Henderson?"

"If no further off means nearer, and it almost seems so in my case,—yes!"

"And you see no difference in her,—no new features of character, which you did not guess, at first?"

"Indeed, I do!" Elwood emphatically answered. "To me she grows less and less like any other woman,—so right, so straightforward, so honest in all her ways and thoughts! If I am ever tempted to do anything—well, not exactly mean, you know, but such as a man might as well leave undone, I have only to say to myself: 'If you're not thoroughly good, my boy, you'll lose her!' and that does the business, right away. Why, Joseph, I'm proud of myself, that I mean to deserve her!"

"Ah!" A sigh, almost a groan, came from Joseph's lips. "What will you think of me?" he said. "I was about to repeat your own words,—to warn you to be cautious, and take time, and test your feelings, and not to be too sure of *her* perfection! What can a young man know about women? He can only discover the truth after marriage, and then—they are indifferent how it affects him—*their* fortunes are made!"

"I know," answered Elwood, turning his head away slightly; "but there's a difference between the women you seek, and work to get, and the women who seek, and work to get you."

"I understand you."

"Forgive me for saying it!" Elwood cried, instantly repenting his words. "I couldn't help seeing and feeling what you know now. But what man—leastways, what friend—could ha' said it to you with any chance of being believed? You were like a man alone in a boat above a waterfall; only *you* could bring yourself to shore. If I stood on the bank and called, and you didn't believe me, what then? The Lord knows, I'd give this right arm, strong as it is, to put you back where you were a year ago."

"I've been longing for frankness, and I ought to bear it better," said Joseph. "Put the whole subject out of your thoughts, and come and see me as of old. It is quite time I should learn to manage my own life."

He grasped Elwood's hand convulsively, sprang down the embankment, and took to the highway. Elwood looked after him a minute, then slowly shook his head and walked onward towards the men.

Meanwhile, Mrs. Hopeton and Lucy had climbed the hill, and found themselves on the brow of a rolling upland, which fell on the other side towards the old Calvert place. The day was hot. Mrs. Hopeton's knees trembled under her, and she sank on the soft grass at the foot of a tree. Lucy took a seat beside her.

"You know so much of my trouble," said the former, when the coolness and rest had soothed her, "and I trust you so perfectly, that I can tell you all, Lucy. Can you guess the man whom I loved, but must never love again?"

"I have sometimes thought—" but here Lucy hesitated.

"Speak the name in your mind, or, let me say 'Philip Held' for you! Lucy, what am I to do? he loves me still: he told me so, just now, where we were all together below there!"

Lucy turned with a start, and gazed wonderingly upon her friend's face.

"Why does he continue telling me what I must not hear? with his eyes, Lucy! in the tones of his voice, in common words which I am forced to interpret by *his* meaning! I had learned to bear my inevitable fate, for it is not an unhappy one; I can bear even his presence, if he were generous enough to close his heart as I do,—either that, or to avoid me; for I now dread to meet him again."

"Is it not," Lucy asked, "because the trial is new, and takes you by surprise and unprepared? May you not be fearing more than Mr. Held has expressed or, at least, intended?"

"The speech that kills, or makes alive, needs no words. What I mean is, there is no *resistance* in his face. I blush for myself, I am indignant at my own pitiful weakness, but something in his look to-day made me forget everything that has passed since we were parted. While it lasted, I was under a spell,—a spell which it humiliates me to remember. Your voices sounded faint and far off; all that I have, and hold, seemed to be slipping from me. It was only for a moment, but, Lucy, it frightened me. My will is strong, and I think I can depend upon it; yet what if some influence beyond my control were to paralyze it?"

"Then you must try to win the help of a higher will; our souls always win something of that which they wrestle and struggle to reach. Dear Mrs. Hopeton, have you never thought that we are still as children who cannot have all they cry for? Now that you know, what you fear, do not dread to hold it before your mind and examine what it is: at least,

I think that would be my instinct,—to face a danger at once when I found I could not escape it."

"I have no doubt you are right, Lucy," said Mrs. Hopeton; but her tone was sad, as if she acquiesced without clearly believing.

"It seems very hard," Lucy continued, "when we cannot have the one love of all others that we need, harder still when we must put it forcibly from our hearts. But I have always felt that, when we can bring ourselves to renounce cheerfully, a blessing will follow. I do not know how, but I must believe it. Might it not come at last through the love that we have, though it now seems imperfect?"

Mrs. Hopeton lifted her head from her knees, and sat erect. "Lucy," she said, "I do not believe you are a woman who would ask another to bear what is beyond your own strength. Shall I put you to the test?"

Lucy, though her face became visibly paler, replied: "I did not mean to compare my burden with yours; but weigh me, if you wish. If I am found wanting, you will show me wherein."

"Your one love above all others is lost to you. Have you conquered the desire for it?"

"I think I have. If some soreness remains, I try to believe that it is the want of the love which I know to be possible, not that of the—the person."

"Then could you be happy with what you call an imperfect love?"

Lucy blushed a little, in spite of herself. "I am still free," she answered, "and not obliged to accept it. If I were bound, I hope I should not neglect my duty."

"What if another's happiness depended on your accepting it? Lucy, my eyes have been made keen by what I have felt. I saw to-day that a man's heart follows you, and I guess that you know it. Here is no imperfect love on his part: were you his wife, could you learn to give him so much that your life might become peaceful and satisfied?"

"You do, indeed, test me!" Lucy murmured. "How can I know? What answer can I make? I have shrunk from thinking of that, and I cannot feel that my duty lies there. Yet, if it were so, if I were already bound, irrevocably, surely all my present faith must be false if happiness in some form did not come at last!"

"I believe it would, to you!" cried Mrs. Hopeton. "Why not to me? Do you think I have ever looked for *love* in my husband? It seems, now, that I have been content to know that he was proud of me. If I seek, perhaps I may find more than I have dreamed of; and if I find,—if indeed and truly I find,—I shall never more lack self-possession and will!"

She rose to her full height, and a flush came over the pallor of her cheeks. "Yes," she continued, "rather than feel again the humiliation of to-day, I will trample all my nature down to the level of an imperfect love!"

"Better," said Lucy, rising also,—"better to bend only for a while to the imperfect, that you may warm and purify and elevate it, until it shall take the place of the perfect in your heart."

The two women kissed each other, and there were tears on the cheeks of both.

18. WHITMAN AND WILDE

Oscar Wilde visited Walt Whitman in Camden as well:

The Philadelphia publisher J. M. Stoddart was responsible for the famous meeting of Oscar Wilde and Whitman at Mickle Street on January 18, 1882. Whitman greatly admired Stoddart, who later became the first to publish Wilde's novel *The Picture of Dorian Gray* (in *Lippincott's Magazine* in 1890), and reminisced about him and the meeting thus: "There is no airisfines about him—no *hauteur*. Years back he came over with Oscar Wilde, when Wilde was here in America and the noise over him was at its height. They came in great style—with a flunky and all that. And what struck me then, instantly, in Stoddart, was his eminent tact. He said to me, 'If you are willing—will excuse me—I will go off for an hour or so—come back again—leaving you together,' etc. I told him, 'We would be glad to have you stay—but do not feel to come back in an hour. Don't come for two or three.' And he did not—I think did not come till nightfall. And all I have had to do with him since is equally to his credit."[39]

According to Stoddart, "In free conversation with intimate friends, the poet did not trouble to conceal his liking for handsome youths." Stoddart's told-to version of the private audience with Whitman described how, "after embracing, greeting each other as 'Oscar' and 'Walt,' the two talked of nothing but pretty boys, of how insipid was the love of women, and of what other poets, Swinburne in particular, had to say about these tastes." Wilde had no doubts about the tastes of Walt Whitman, and later suggestively told another friend, George Ives, that "I still have the kiss of Walt Whitman on my lips."[43]

It is, in fact, a remarkable irony that Stoddart was Wilde's companion for the excursions to Camden. Several years later, he would be instrumental in the writing of two Wilde fictions [...]. In 1889, while in London looking for new material for *Lippincott's Magazine*, Stoddart dined with Arthur Conan Doyle and Wilde and came away with promises from both to write for him. Doyle produced the second of his Holmes novels, *The Sign of Four*, and Wilde eventually responded with "The Fisherman and His Soul," by far the longest, most ambitious and fascinating of his children's tales. Stoddart, however, apparently found the tale inappropriate for his readers and rejected it. Wilde's second submission, several months later, turned out to be *The Picture of Dorian Gray*. It occupied the first hundred pages of the July 1890 issue of *Lippincott's* and a year later, much revised and lengthened, appeared in book form.[40]

It is interesting to note that, based on this meeting with Wilde and one more later interaction where Wilde told Doyle he should go see his new play ("Ah, you must go. It is wonderful. It is genius!"), Doyle recorded in his autobiographical work *Memories and Adventures* what he thought regarding Wilde's 'ruin': "I thought at the time, and still think, that the monstrous development which ruined him was pathological, and that a hospital rather than a police court was the place for its consideration."[8] It's one of the more merciful opinions of the time, certainly kinder than Bram Stoker's reactions (see <u>Chapter 16: Whitman, Stoker, and Wilde</u>).

It is further interesting to point out that the *Lippincott's Magazine* version of *The Picture of Dorian Gray* is shorter than the later version of the novel, published on its own in 1891, a version which also contains small attempts to censor or at least soften the original homosexual content of the story. Specificities like 'romance' and 'devoted' and 'something in his nature that was purely feminine in its tenderness' are removed, and several instances of touch between men (placing a hand on someone's shoulder or walking "arm in arm") are taken out as well. The murder of Basil Hallward is changed from Dorian's 32nd birthday to his 38th to hide the secret about Wilde's own 32nd year, which is when he first had sexual contact with another man (Robert Ross, his life-long devoted friend), and this particularly telling bit of dialogue from Basil to Dorian is cut completely: "It is quite true that I have worshipped you with far more romance of feeling than a man usually gives to a friend. Somehow, I had never loved a woman."[60]

Wilde visited Walt Whitman in Camden, where the poet was then living with his brother and sister-in-law. Wilde told Whitman that his mother had purchased a copy of *Leaves of Grass* when it was first published, that Lady Wilde had read the poems to her son, and that later, at Oxford, he and his friends carried *Leaves* to read on their walks.[14]

Being so familiar with Whitman via his mother, Wilde said, "I have come to you as one with whom I have been acquainted almost from the cradle."[40]

Flattered, Whitman offered Wilde, whom he later described as "a fine large handsome youngster," some of his sister-in-law's homemade elderberry wine, and they conversed for two hours. Asked later by a friend how he managed to get the elderberry wine down, Wilde replied: "If it had been vinegar I would have drunk it all the same, for I have an admiration for that man which I can hardly express." In a letter to Whitman postmarked 1 March, Wilde writes: "Before I leave America I must see you again. There is no one in this wide great world of America whom I love and honour so much." Wilde was true to his word, making a second visit to Whitman the following May.[14]

Later, both men have occasion to remember their meetings and their impressions of one another:

> Seven years after visiting him, Wilde said of Whitman: "The chief value of his work is in its prophecy, not in its performance. He has begun a prelude to larger themes. He is the herald of a new era. As a man he is the precursor of a fresh type."[40]

Whitman would agree with that assessment, and in fact wrote it down as his intention at about the same time:

> On a scrap of paper Walt jotted what he was after at this time of his life (seven years after Oscar's Camden visit): "A poem which more familiarly addresses those who will, in future ages under me, (Because I write with reference to being far better understood then than I can possibly be now.)" This desire might have generated in his "Poets to Come" (1860) the line "I myself but write one or two indicative words for the future."[40]

There are a lot of occasions where Whitman and Wilde are of the same mind:

> Oscar Wilde enjoyed his cozy visit with Whitman at Mickle Street [...], more than a dozen years before the premiere of his play *An Ideal Husband*. One flippant line in that play, however, perfectly captures Whitman's habitual attitude toward advice, whether from enemies or friends: "I always pass on good advice. It is the only thing to do with it. It is never any use to oneself."[39]

Specifically, Whitman's words to Traubel on a few occasions were:

> "Take my word for it—don't take advice!" Four days later: "'And you, Horace: listen to this: Take one more piece of advice and then stop.' What piece? 'Never take advice!' W. laughed heartily."[39]

Another eerily similar instance of quotation, first Whitman:

"I admire a good many of my enemies more than I admire some of my friends."[39]

And Wilde:

"I choose my friends for their good looks, my acquaintances for their good characters, and my enemies for their good intellects. A man cannot be too careful in the choice of his enemies. I have not got one who is a fool."[60]

More assessments of Wilde from Whitman were recorded by Traubel:

"I never completely make Wilde out—for good or bad. He writes exquisitely—is as lucid as a star on a clear night—but there seems to be a little substance lacking at the root—something—what is it? I have no sympathy with the crowd of scorners who want to crowd him off the earth."[39]

"Wilde may have been some of him fraud at the time but was not all fraud. My letter from him [see below] seems wholly sincere. He has extraordinary brilliancy of genius with perhaps rather too little root in eternal soils."[39]

Shortly after his visit to Mickle Street in 1882, Wilde wrote Whitman an effusive letter from New York that ends, "there is no one in this wide great world of America whom I love and honor so much." Before giving this letter up to Traubel, Whitman commented, "There is no parade in this note: it wears the simplest clothes—has no sunflower in its button hole—has in fact a cast of virgin simplicity, sincerity." After Traubel read the letter, Whitman added, "It all rings sound and true to me there. Everybody's been so in the habit of looking at Wilde cross-eyed, sort of, that they have charged a defect of their vision up against Wilde as a weakness in his character."[39]

"Wilde was very friendly to me—was and is, I think—both Oscar and his mother—Lady Wilde—and thanks be most to the mother, that greater, more important individual. Oscar was here—came to see me—and he impressed me as a strong, able fellow, too."[39]

Wilde on Whitman:

Oscar Wilde's one published review of Whitman appeared in the Pall Mall Gazette (January 25, 1889); it seems that a copy made its way to Mickle Street, but since it was unsigned Whitman does not acknowledge Wilde as its author. In the review, Wilde writes that Whitman "is the herald to a new era. As a man he is the precursor of a fresh type. He is a factor in the heroic and spiritual evolution of the human being."[39]

To read Wilde's *Pall Mall Gazette* review, "The Gospel According to Walt Whitman," see [A.17]. For the full letters between Wilde and Whitman, see [A.16]. Whitman's one real criticism of Wilde's tact has in it another bit of prophesy:

> After Oscar Wilde visited Whitman at Mickle Street in 1882, Walt told a reporter for the *Press* of Philadelphia that he permitted himself but one criticism of the visiting apostle of art for art's sake: "Why, Oscar, it always seems to me that the fellow who makes a dead set at beauty by itself is in a bad way."[39]

He said at another time to Traubel:

> "Think of it—art for art's sake. Let a man really accept that—let that really be his ruling thought—and he is lost."[39]

For Whitman's curious connection to the true instrument of Wilde's downfall—his meeting Lord Alfred Douglas—see <u>Chapter 19: Calamus as Cruising Apparatus</u>.

XIX

THE "WHARF-RAT"

On his way hone Joseph reviewed the quarrel with a little more calmness, and, while admitting his own rashness and want of tact, felt relieved that it had occurred. Julia now knew, at least, how sorely he had been grieved by her selfishness, and she had thus an opportunity, if she really loved him, of showing whether her nature were capable of change. He determined to make no further reference to the dissension, and to avoid what might lead to a new one. He did not guess, as he approached the house, that his wife had long been watching at the front window, in an anxious, excited state, and that she only slipped back to the sofa and covered her head just before he reached the door.

For a day or two she was silent, and perhaps a little sullen; but the payment of the most pressing bills, the progress of the new embellishments, and the necessity of retaining her affectionate playfulness in the presence of the workmen, brought back her customary manner. Now and then a sharp, indirect allusion showed that she had not forgotten, and had not Joseph closed his teeth firmly upon his tongue, the household atmosphere might have been again disturbed.

Not many days elapsed before a very brief note from Mr. Blessing announced that the fifth instalment would be needed. He wrote in great haste, he said, and would explain everything by a later mail.

Joseph was hardly surprised now. He showed the note to Julia, merely saying: "I have not the money, and if I had he could scarcely expect me to pay it without knowing the necessity. My best plan will be to go to the city at once."

"I think so, too," she answered. "You will be far better satisfied when you have seen pa, and he can also help you to raise the money temporarily, if it is really inevitable. He knows all the capitalists."

"I shall do another thing, Julia. I shall sell enough of the stock to pay the instalment; nay, I shall sell it all, if I can do so without loss."

"Are you—" she began fiercely, but, checking herself, merely added, "see pa first, that's all I stipulate."

Mr. Blessing had not returned from the Custom-House when Joseph reached the city. He had no mind to sit in the dark parlor and wait; so he plunged boldly into the labyrinth of clerks, porters, inspectors, and tide-waiters. Everybody knew Blessing, but nobody could tell where he was to be found. Finally someone, more obliging than the rest, said: "Try the Wharf-Rat!"

The Wharf-Rat proved to be a "saloon" in a narrow alley behind the Custom-House. On opening the door, a Venetian screen prevented the persons at the bar from being immediately seen, but Joseph recognized his father-in-law's voice, saying, "Straight, if you please!" Mr. Blessing was leaning against one end of the bar, with a glass in his hand, engaged with an individual of not very prepossessing appearance. He remarked to the latter, almost in a whisper (though the words reached Joseph's ears), "You understand, the collector can't be seen every day; it takes time, and—more or less capital. The doorkeeper and others expect to be feed."

As Joseph approached, he turned towards him with an angry, suspicious look, which was not changed into one of welcome so soon that a flash of uncomfortable surprise did not intervene. But the welcome once there, it deepened and mellowed, and became so warm and rich that only a cold, contracted nature could have refused to bathe in its effulgence.

"Why!" he cried, with extended hands, "I should as soon have expected to see daisies growing in this sawdust, or to find these spittoons smelling like hyacinths! Mr. Tweed, one of our rising politicians, Mr. Asten, my son-in-law! Asten, of Asten Hall, I might almost say, for I hear that your mansion is assuming quite a palatial aspect. Another glass, if you please: your throat must be full of dust, Joseph,—*pulvis faucibus hæsit*, if I might be allowed to change the classic phrase."

Joseph tried to decline, but was forced to compromise on a moderate glass of ale; while Mr. Blessing, whose glass was empty, poured something into it from a black bottle, nodded to Mr. Tweed, and saying, "Always straight!" drank it off.

"You would not suppose," he then said to Joseph, "that this little room, dark as it is, and not agreeably fragrant, has often witnessed the arrangement of political manœuvres which have decided the City, and through the City the State. I have seen together at that table at midnight, Senator Slocum, and the Honorables Whitstone, Hacks, and Larruper. Why, the First Auditor of the Treasury was here no later than last week! I frequently transact some of the confidential business of the Custom-House within these precincts, as at present."

"Shall I wait for you outside?" Joseph asked.

"I think it will not be necessary. I have stated the facts, Mr. Tweed, and if you accept them, the figures can be arranged between us at any time. It is a simple case of algebra: by taking *x*, you work out the unknown quantity."

With a hearty laugh at his own smartness, he shook the "rising politician's" hand and left the Wharf-Rat with Joseph.

"We can talk here as well as in the woods," he said. "Nobody ever hears anything in this crowd. But perhaps we had better not mention the Amaranth by name, as the operation has been kept so very close. Shall we say 'Paraguay' instead, or—still better— 'Reading,' which is a very common stock? Well, then, I guess you have come to see me in relation to the Reading?"

Joseph, as briefly as possible, stated the embarrassment he suffered, on account of the continued calls for payment, the difficulty of raising money for the fifth instalment, and bluntly expressed his doubts of the success of the speculation. Mr. Blessing heard him patiently to the end, and then, having collected himself, answered:—

"I understand, most perfectly, your feeling in the matter. Further, I do not deny that in respect to the time of realizing from the Am—Reading, I should say—I have also been disappointed. It has cost me no little trouble to keep my own shares intact, and my stake is so much greater than yours, for it is my *all*! I am ready to unite with the Chowder, at once: indeed, as one of the directors, I mentioned it at our last meeting, but the proposition, I regret to say, was not favorably entertained. We are dependent, in a great measure, on Kanuck, who is on the spot superintending the Reading; he has been telegraphed to come on, and promises to do so as soon as the funds now called for are forthcoming. My faith, I hardly need intimate, is firm."

"My only resource, then," said Joseph, "will be to sell a portion of my stock, I suppose?"

"There is one drawback to that course, and I am afraid you may not quite understand my explanation. The—Reading has not been introduced in the market, and its *real* value could not be demonstrated without betraying the secret lever by which we intend hoisting it to a fancy height. We could only dispose of a portion of it to capitalists whom we choose to take into our confidence. The same reason would be valid against hypothecation."

"Have *you* paid this last instalment?" Joseph suddenly asked.

"N—no; not wholly; but I anticipate a temporary accommodation. If Mr. Spelter deprives me of Clementina, as I hear (through third parties) is daily becoming more probable, my family expenses will be so diminished that I shall have an ample margin; indeed, I shall feel like a large paper copy, with my leaves uncut!"

He rubbed his hands gleefully; but Joseph was too much disheartened to reply.

"*This* might be done," Mr. Blessing continued. "It is not certain that all the stockholders have yet paid. I will look over the books, and if such be the case, your delay would not be a sporadic delinquency if otherwise, I will endeavor to gain the consent of my fellow-directors to the introduction of a new capitalist, to whom a small portion of your interest may be transferred. I trust you perceive the relevancy of this caution. We do not mean that our flower shall always blush unseen, and waste its sweetness on the oleaginous air; we only wish to guard against its being 'untimely ripped' (as Shakespeare says) from its parent stalk. I can well imagine, how incomprehensible all this may appear to you. In all probability much of *your* conversation at home, relative to crops and the like; would be to me an unknown dialect. But I should not, therefore, doubt your intelligence and judgment in such matters."

Joseph began to grow impatient. "Do I understand you to say, Mr. Blessing," be asked, "that the call for the fifth instalment *can* be met by the sale of a part of my stock?"

"In an ordinary case it might not—under the peculiar circumstances of our operation—be possible. But I trust I do not exaggerate my own influence when I say that it is within *my* power to arrange it. If you will confide it to my hands, you understand, of course, that a slight formality is necessary,—a power of attorney?"

Joseph, in his haste and excitement, had not considered this, or any other legal point: Mr. Blessing was right.

"Then, supposing the shares to be worth only their par value," he said, "the power need not apply to more than one-tenth of my stock?"

Mr. Blessing came into collision with a gentleman passing him. Mutual wrath was, aroused, followed by mutual apologies. "Let us turn into the other street," he said to Joseph; "really, our lives are hardly safe in this crowd; it is nearly three o'clock, and the banks will soon be closed."

"It would be prudent to allow a margin," he resumed, after their course had been changed: "the money market is very tight, and if a *necessity* were suspected, most capitalists are unprincipled enough to exact according to the urgency of the need. I do not say—nor do I at all anticipate—that it would be so in your case; still, the future is a sort of dissolving view, and my suggestion is that of the merest prudence. I have no doubt that double the amount—say one-fifth of your stock—would guard us against all contingencies. If you prefer not to intrust the matter to my hands, I will introduce you to Honeyspoon Brothers, the bankers,—the elder Honeyspoon being a director,—who will be very ready to execute your commission."

What could Joseph do? It was impossible to say to Mr. Blessing's face that he mistrusted him: yet he certainly did not trust! He was weary of plausible phrases, the import of which he was powerless to dispute, yet which were so at variance with what seemed to be the facts of the case. He felt that he was lifted aloft into a dazzling, secure atmosphere, but as often as he turned to look at the wings which upheld him, their plumage shriveled into dust, and he fell an immense distance before his feet touched a bit of reality.

The power of attorney was given. Joseph declined Mr. Blessing's invitation to dine with him at the Universal Hotel, the Blessing table being "possibly a little lean to one accustomed to the bountiful profusion of the country," on the plea that he must return by the evening train; but such a weariness and disgust came over him that he halted at the Farmers' Tavern, and took a room for the night. He slept until long into the morning, and then, cheered in spirit through the fresh vigor of all his physical functions, started homewards.

19. CALAMUS AS CRUISING APPARATUS

Considering the stories that come out of Whitman's "avowal" letters (see Chapter 15: Avowals to Walt Whitman, it's clear that *Leaves of Grass* and the "Calamus" poems especially had a significant impact on gay men of the time. Not only did it put expression to their own feelings and reveal those feelings to themselves, not only did it cause some of them to reveal themselves to Whitman (no matter how closeted they remained in their own lives), it also helped to reveal their 'friends.' Serving as a kind of Rorschach test, if another man sees what you see in the Calamus plant's phallic spadix, then he is a man of your own kind and free to engage with. Not every introduction to a fellow member of the club (see Chapter 20: Contemporary Camerados for actual 'gay clubs' of the 19th century) came with the perfect look of recognition on display in *Joseph and His Friend* (or experienced by Walt Whitman on more than one occasion; see Chapter 21: Whitman's Boys and Chapter 22: Whitman's Peter); for those murkier meetings, *Leaves of Grass* became an indicator, a test, as was previously mentioned in Chapter 16: Whitman, Stoker, and Wilde. As to Whitman's intentions in writing the book, here are his own words:

> The image Whitman offered to the Englishman Edward Carpenter during a visit in 1884 about the writing of *Leaves* was, "There is something in my nature furtive like an old hen! You see a hen wandering up and down a hedgerow, looking apparently quite unconcerned, but presently she finds a concealed spot, and furtively lays an egg, and comes away as though nothing had happened! That is how I felt in writing *Leaves of Grass*."[40]

One particularly pointed example of the love of Whitman connecting the dots has to do with Oscar Wilde:

> That the writings of Whitman and Wilde attracted very similar "avowal" letters (as Whitman called them) from heartened young gay men is charmingly demonstrated by Lionel Johnson, an undergraduate at New College, Oxford. As an eighteen-year-old, he wrote to Whitman on 20 October 1885 to say

that "in all constant thoughts and acts of my last few years, your words have been my guides and true oracles. . . . I should feel shame for myself, were I not to show the reality of my gratitude to you, even through the weakness of words—you, whom I thankfully acknowledge for my veritable master and dear brother." Johnson says that he received *Leaves of Grass* "from the hands of a most dear friend" and assures Whitman that "the help and exaltation I have won from it have been won by many another boy and young man." Whitman's response on hearing this letter reread by Traubel: "That sounds very ripe for a boy of eighteen—ripe enough already to shed fruit. . . . Keep a weather eye open for that boy: he will appear again." Johnson apparently did not do so, but five years later (and still at New College) he did appear on Wilde's horizon. On 18 February 1890 Johnson wrote to a friend: "On Saturday at mid-day . . . I was roused by a pathetic and unexpected note from Oscar: he plaintively besought me to get up and see him. Which I did. . . . He discoursed, with infinite flippancy, of everyone: lauded the *Dial*: laughed at Pater: and consumed all my cigarettes. I am in love with him." Johnson, it might be said, was to prove the unwitting sealer of Wilde's fate, for it was he who lent his copy of *The Picture of Dorian Gray* to Alfred Douglas. Douglas became "passionately absorbed" in it—read it nine times over, he said—and succeeded in getting Johnson to introduce him to Wilde. The rest was to be sad history.[40]

For Johnson's full letter to Walt Whitman, see [A.18]. As stated previously in Chapter 16: Whitman, Stoker, and Wilde, Wilde soon took on the mantle of Whitman by being so conspicuously in favor of affection between men:

Wilde received many such idolatrous letters as those Stoddard [and] Johnson [...] wrote to Whitman. Almost none survive, though several gracious responses by Wilde suggest the flavor of them. One letter that did survive was from Clyde Fitch, a gay man who later became the first hugely successful American playwright. He appears already to have been to bed with Wilde when he wrote a similar adulatory letter after reading "The Portrait of Mr. W. H." [A story about an attempt to uncover the identity of Mr. W. H., the dedicatee of Shakespeare's *Sonnets*, based on a theory that the sonnets were addressed to one Willie Hughes, portrayed in the story as a boy actor who specialized in playing women in Shakespeare's company.] "*I* believe in Willie Hughes," he says, calling the story "great—and *fine*," and the letter ends with this astonishing salutation: "Invent me a language of love. *You* could do it, Bewilderdly, All yours Clyde." Over the decades, *Leaves of Grass* succeeded in evoking from those readers who sensed some kind of special affinity numerous letters and not a few personal visits to Camden. Many were doubtless lost in the clutter of Mickle Street, and Whitman may have destroyed the more extravagantly explicit ones (like Fitch's to Wilde), but some of them survived long enough to get into Traubel's hands and be recorded. They give us a flavor of how successful that elaborate long-distance cruising apparatus called *Leaves of Grass* was.[40]

See <u>Chapter 15: Avowals to Walt Whitman</u> for more. Such use of *Leaves of Grass* stretches into even further generations:

Gore Vidal in *Palimpsest*, calculated that by the age of twenty-five he had managed more than a thousand sexual experiences, and yet all his life he has considered his Great Love to be a prep-school classmate who died on Iwo Jima. Decades later Vidal learned that the boy had written from Guam, shortly before a Japanese grenade killed him, to request from his mother a copy of *Leaves of Grass*. "This set off a tremor," Vidal writes. "He and I certainly lived out the *Calamus* idyll."[40]

In Wilde's essay "The Decay of Lying," he puts forth that "Life imitates art far more than art imitates Life."[59] There are examples in fiction where the mention of *Leaves of Grass* or Walt Whitman's name act as a clue for what kind of man a character is:

In his 1913 story "Out of the Sun," Edward Irenaeus Prime-Stevenson describes a very particular library: "Ah, his books! The library of almost every man of like making-up whose life has been largely solitary . . . is companioned from youth up by innermost literary sympathies of his type. Dayneford stood now before his bookcase, reading over mechanically the titles of a special group of volumes—mostly small ones. They were crowded into a few lower shelves, as if they sought to avoid other literary society, to keep themselves to themselves, to shun all unsympathetic observation. Tibullus, Propertius and the Greek Antologists [*sic*] pressed against Al Nafsewah and Cakani and Hafiz. A little further along stood Shakespeare's Sonnets, and those by Buonarrotti; along with Tennyson's "In Memoriam," Woodberry's "The North-Shore Watch," and Walt Whitman. Back of Platen's bulky "Tagebuch" lay his poems. Next to them cam Wilbrandt's "Fridolins Heimliche Infamen," Emil Vacano's "Humbug," and a group of psychologic works by Krafft-Ebbing and Ellis and Moll. There was a thin book in which were bound together, in a richly-decorated arabesque cover, some six or seven stories from Mardrus' French translation of "The Thousand Nights and a Night"—remorsely [*sic*] separated from their original companions. On a lower shelf, rested David Christie Murray's "Val Strange" and one or two other old novels; along with Dickens' "David Copperfield," the anonymous "Tim," and Vachell's "The Hill," companioned by Mayne's "Intersexes," "Imre" and "Sebastian au Plus Bel Age."[30]

One might like to remind Prime-Stevenson that modesty forbids name-dropping his own books under his pseudonym Xavier Mayne [see Introduction: America's First Gay Novel? for more on Prime-Stevenson], but Whitman the self-reviewer (see [A.12]) and poet of "Song of Myself" certainly wouldn't.

Likewise, "Gil" Gilchrist in Russell Thatcher's *The Captain* reads *Leaves of Grass* as a hint to what he is, a possible homosexual.[1] In the same way, Wilde's name too came to mean what he was infamously proven to be in court, a man who did sexual things with other men. Wilde's name becomes the word for "the love that dare not speak its name," a phrase coined in a poem by Wilde's dubious lover, Lord Alfred Douglas. It's used so in E.M. Forster's *Maurice* (written in 1913-1914, published after Forster's death in 1971), when the main character confesses to his doctor by saying, "I am an unspeakable of the Oscar Wilde sort."[15] Schmidgall points out an instance of Forster comparing himself to Whitman as well:

> E. M. Forster wrote in a 1915 letter about the just-finished manuscript of his daringly gay novel *Maurice*: "Whitman nearly anticipated me but he doesn't really know what he was after, or only half knew—shirked, even to himself, the statement." Monumental crust, these condescension about shirking the bold statement coming from Forster, one might well think. Whitman, after all, waited only until his late thirties to publish his gay personality. Forster, on the other hand, kept the *Maurice* ms. in his desk until he died at the age of ninety-one. (To be sure, homosexuality was a punishable offense in England until 1967.) The author safely dead, the novel finally appeared in 1971, a perfectly timed literary aubade to greet the post-Stonewall era.[40]

Forster's book, as late as it appeared in publication, was not the only one to use Oscar Wilde's name as shorthand. In that way, Meyer Levin's *Compulsion* (1956) pre-dates its use of Wilde's name for homosexuality, while fictionalizing the relationship between real-life murderers (and lovers) Leopold and Loeb. The characters of the boys, Judd Steiner and Artie Strauss, invoke Dorian Gray's name to speak of manly love as well:

> It was one of those moments when Artie looked so golden, so perfect, stretched in his powder-blue pullover, that Judd had an urge in front of all of them to call him Dorian.

> *

> The steam hissed softly, and Artie, relaxed in his Morris chair, his face in a desk-light glow, the petulant lips full-blown in his anger at the frat—in that moment Artie was Dorian Gray.

> *

What his Dorian was revealing to him might be interpreted by the superficial as a mild kleptomania.

*

Artie turned his face to him, this time, and there was the Dorian smile. "You want to make that a deal?"

*

"I don't mean there's anything wrong with him; it's just he's such a conceited intellectual. He thinks women are inferior. [...] You know what he sometimes called Artie? Dorian." Myra sucked her lip again. We looked at each other.

*

"What exactly is a pervert, Sid? I guess I'm supposed to know, but I don't." I explained, trying not to reveal that my own knowledge was limited. I said it was like Oscar Wilde.[32]

In this case it was accurate, for Nathan Leopold did have homosexual feelings for Richard Loeb, and would exchange participation in criminal activity (including the murder they committed) for sexual favors. During their defense, Attorney Clarence Darrow quoted the poetry of a man mentioned previously, A.E. Housman (*A Shropshire Lad*, 1896), whose brother Laurence Housman was also homosexual, and once visited Oscar Wilde in his Parisian exile after Wilde's 1897 release from prison. Laurence Housman recorded the episode in his essay, "Echo de Paris; A Study from Life" (1923).

XX

A CRISIS

JOSEPH HAD MADE half the distance between Oakland Station and his farm, walking leisurely, when a buggy, drawn by an aged and irreproachable gray horse, came towards him. The driver was the Reverend Mr. Chaffinch. He stopped as they met.

"Will you turn back, as far as that tree?" said the clergyman, after greetings had been exchanged. "I have a message to deliver."

"Now," he continued, reining up his horse in the shade, "we can talk without interruption. I will ask you to listen to me with the spiritual, not the carnal ear. I must not be false to my high calling, and the voice of my own conscience calls me to awaken yours."

Joseph said nothing, but the flush upon his face was that of anger, not of confusion, as Mr. Chaffinch innocently supposed.

"It is hard for a young man, especially one wise in his own conceit, to see how the snares of the Adversary are closing around him. We cannot plead ignorance, however, when the Light is there, and we willfully turn our eyes from it. You are walking on a road, Joseph Asten, it may seem smooth and fair to you, but do you know where it leads? I will tell you: to Death and Hell!"

Still Joseph was silent.

"It is not too late! Your fault, I fear, is that you attach merit to works, as if works could save you! You look to a cold, barren morality for support, and imagine that to do what is called 'right' is enough for God! You shut your eyes to the blackness of your own sinful heart, and are too proud to acknowledge the vileness and depravity of man's nature; but without this acknowledgment your morality (as you call it) is corrupt, your good works (as you suppose them to be) will avail you naught. You are outside the pale of Grace, and while you continue there, knowing the door to be open, there is no Mercy for you!"

The flush on Joseph's face faded, and he became very pale, but he still waited. "I hope," Mr. Chaffinch continued, after a pause, "that your silence is the beginning of conviction. It only needs an awakening, an opening of the eyes in them that sleep. Do you not recognize your guilt, your miserable condition of sin?"

"No!"

Mr. Chaffinch started, and an ugly, menacing expression came into his face.

"Before you speak again," said Joseph, "tell me one thing! Am I indebted for this Catechism to the order—perhaps I should say the request—of my wife?"

"I do not deny that she has expressed a Christian concern for your state; but I do not wait for a request when I see a soul in peril. If I care for the sheep that willingly obey the shepherd, how much more am I commanded to look after them which stray, and which the wolves and bears are greedy to devour!"

"Have you ever considered, Mr. Chaffinch," Joseph rejoined, lifting his head and speaking with measured clearness, "that an intelligent man may possibly be aware that he has an immortal soul,—that the health and purity and growth of that soul may possibly be his first concern in life,—that no other man can know, as he does, its imperfections, its needs, its aspirations which rise directly towards God; and that the attempt of a stranger to examine and criticize, and perhaps blacken, this most sacred part of his nature, may possibly be a pious impertinence?"

"Ah, the natural depravity of the heart!" Mr. Chaffinch groaned.

"It is not the depravity, it is the only pure quality which the hucksters of doctrine, the money-changers in God's temple of Man, cannot touch! Shall I render a reckoning to *you* on the day when souls are judged? Are *you* the infallible agent of the Divine Mercy? What blasphemy!"

Mr. Chaffinch shuddered. "I wash my hands of you!" he cried. "I have had to deal with many sinners in my day, but I have found no sin which came so directly from the Devil as the pride of the mind. If you were rotten in all your members from the sins of the flesh, I might have a little hope. Verily, it shall go easier with the murderer and the adulterer on that day than with such as ye!"

He gave the horse a more than saintly stroke, and the vehicle rattled away. Joseph could not see the predominance of routine in all that Mr. Chaffinch had said. He was too excited to remember that certain phrases are transmitted, and used without a thought of their tremendous character; he applied every word personally, and felt it as an outrage in all the sensitive fibres of his soul. And who had invoked the outrage? His wife: Mr. Chaffinch had confessed it. What representations had she made?—he could only measure them by the character of the clergyman's charges. He sat down on the bank, sick at heart; it was impossible to go home and meet her in his present frame of mind.

Presently he started up, crying aloud: "I will go to Philip! He cannot help me, I know, but I must have a word of love from a friend, or I shall go mad!"

He retraced his steps, took the road up the valley, and walked rapidly towards the Forge. The tumult in his blood gradually expended its force, but it had carried him along more swiftly than he was aware. When he reached the point where, looking across the valley, now narrowed to a glen, he could see the smoke of the Forge near at hand, and even catch a glimpse of the cottage on the knoll, he stopped. Up to this moment he had felt, not reflected; and a secret instinct told him that he should not submit his trouble to Philip's riper manhood until it was made clear and coherent in his own mind. He must keep Philip's love, at all hazards; and to keep it he must not seem simply a creature of moods and sentiments, whom his friend might pity, but could not respect.

He left the road, crossed a sloping field on the left, and presently found himself on a bank overhanging the stream. Under the wood of oaks and hemlocks the laurel grew in rich, shining clumps; the current, at this point deep, full, and silent, glimmered through the leaves, twenty feet below; the opposite shore was level, and green with an herbage which no summer could wither. He leaned against a hemlock bole, and tried to think, but it was not easy to review the past while his future life overhung him like a descending burden which he had not the strength to lift. Love betrayed, trust violated, aspiration misinterpreted, were the spiritual aspects; a divided household, entangling obligations, a probability of serious loss, were the material evils which accompanied them. He was so unprepared for the change that he could only rebel, not measure, analyze, and cast about for ways of relief.

It was a miserable strait in which he found himself; and the more he thought—or, rather, seemed to think—the less was he able to foresee any other than an unfortunate solution. What were his better impulses, if men persisted in finding them evil? What was life, yoked to such treachery and selfishness? Life had been to him a hope, an inspiration, a sound, enduring joy; now it might never be so again! Then what a release were death!

He walked forward to the edge of the rock. A few pebbles, dislodged by his feet, slid from the brink, and plunged with a bubble and a musical tinkle into the dark, sliding waters. One more step, and the release which seemed so fair might be attained. He felt a morbid sense of delight in playing with the thought. Gathering a handful of broken stones, he let them fall one by one, thinking, "So I hold my fate in my hand." He leaned over and saw a shifting, quivering image of himself projected against the reflected sky, and a fancy, almost as clear as a voice, said: "This is your present self: what will you do with it beyond the gulf, where only the soul superior to circumstances here receives a nobler destiny?"

He was still gazing down at the flickering figure, when a step came upon the dead leaves. He turned and saw Philip, moving stealthily towards him, pale, with outstretched hand. They looked at each other for a moment without speaking.

"I guess your thought, Philip," Joseph then said. "But the things easiest to do are sometimes the most impossible."

"The bravest man may allow a fancy to pass through his mind, Joseph, which only the coward will carry into effect."

"I am not a coward!" Joseph exclaimed.

Philip took his hand, drew him nearer, and flinging his arms around him, held him to his heart.

Then they sat down, side by side.

"I was up the stream, on the other side, trolling for trout," said Philip, "when I saw you in the road. I was welcoming your coming, in my heart: then you stopped, stood still, and at last turned away. Something in your movements gave me a sudden, terrible feeling of anxiety: I threw down my rod, came around by the bridge at the Forge, and followed you here. Do not blame me for my foolish dread."

"Dear, dear friend," Joseph cried, "I did not mean to come to you until I seemed stronger and more rational in my own eyes. If that were a vanity, it is gone now: I confess my weakness and ignorance. Tell me, if you can, why this has come upon me? Tell me why nothing that I have been taught, why no atom of the faith which I still must cling to, explains, consoles, or remedies any wrong of my life!"

"Faiths, I suspect," Philip answered, "are, like laws, adapted to the average character of the human race. You, in the confiding purity of your nature, are not an average man: you are very much above the class, and if virtue were its own reward, you would be most exceptionally happy. Then the puzzle is, what's the particular use of virtue?"

"I don't know, Philip, but I don't like to hear you ask the question. I find myself so often on the point of doubting all that was my Truth a little while ago; and yet, why should my misfortunes, as an individual, make the truth a lie? I am only one man among millions who *must* have faith in the efficacy of virtue. Philip, if I believed the faith to be false, I think I should still say, 'Let it be preached!'"

Joseph related to Philip the whole of his miserable story, not sparing himself, nor concealing the weakness which allowed him to be entangled to such an extent. Philip's brow grew dark as he listened, but at the close of the recital his face was calm, though stern.

"Now," said he,—"now put this aside for a little while, and give your ear (and your heart too, Joseph) to *my* story. Do not compare my fortune with yours, but let us apply to both the laws which seem to govern life, and see whether justice is possible."

Joseph had dismissed his wife's suspicion, after the dinner at Hopeton's, so immediately from his memory, that he had really forgotten it; and he was not only startled, but also a little shocked, by Philip's confession. Still, he saw that it was only the reverse form of his own experience, not more strange, perhaps not more to be condemned, yet equally inevitable.

"Is there no way out of this labyrinth of wrong?" Philip exclaimed. "Two natures, as far apart as Truth and Falsehood, monstrously held together in the most intimate, the holiest of bonds,—two natures destined for each other monstrously kept apart by the same bonds! Is life to be so sacrificed to habit and prejudice? I said that Faith, like Law, was fashioned for the average man: then there must be a loftier faith, a juster law, for the men—and the women—who cannot shape themselves according to the common-place pattern of society,—who were born with instincts, needs, knowledge, and rights—ay, *rights!*—of their own!"

"But, Philip," said Joseph, "we were both to blame: you through too little trust, I through too much. We have both been rash and impatient: I cannot forget that; and how are we to know that the punishment, terrible as it seems, is disproportioned to the offence?"

"We know this, Joseph,—and who can know it and be patient?—that the power which controls our lives is pitiless, unrelenting! There is the same punishment for an innocent mistake as for a conscious crime. A certain Nemesis follows ignorance, regardless how good and pure may be the individual nature. Had you even guessed your wife's true character just before marriage; your very integrity, your conscience, and the conscience of the world, would have compelled the union, and Nature would not have mitigated her selfishness to reward you with a tolerable life. O no! You would still have suffered as now. Shall a man with a heart feel this horrible injustice, and not rebel? Grant that I am rightly punished for my impatience, my pride, my jealousy, how have *you* been rewarded for your stainless youth, your innocent trust, your almost miraculous goodness? Had you known the world better, even though a part of your knowledge might have been evil, you would have escaped this fatal marriage. Nothing can be more certain; and will you simply groan and bear? What compensating fortune have you, or can you ever expect to find?"

Joseph was silent at first; but Philip could see, from the trembling of his hands, and his quick breathing, that he was profoundly agitated. "There is something within me," he said, at last, "which accepts everything you say; and yet, it alarms me. I feel a mighty temptation in your words: they could lead me to snap my chains, break violently away from my past and present life, and surrender myself to will and appetite. O Philip, if we could make our lives wholly our own! If we could find a spot—"

"I know such a spot!" Philip cried, interrupting him,—"a great valley, bounded by a hundred miles of snowy peaks; lakes in its bed; enormous hillsides, dotted with groves of ilex and pine; orchards of orange and olive; a perfect climate, where it is bliss enough just to breathe, and freedom from the distorted laws of men, for none are near enough to enforce them! If there is no legal way of escape for you, here, at least, there is no force which can drag you back, once you are there: I will go with you, and perhaps—perhaps—"

Philip's face glowed, and the vague alarm in Joseph's heart took a definite form. He guessed what words had been left unspoken.

"If we could be sure!" he said.

"Sure of what? Have I exaggerated the wrong in your case? Say we should be outlaws there, in our freedom!—here we are fettered outlaws."

"I have been trying, Philip, to discover a law superior to that under which we suffer, and I think I have found it. If it be true that ignorance is equally punished with guilt; if causes and consequences, in which there is neither pity nor justice, govern our lives,— then what keeps our souls from despair but the infinite pity and perfect justice of God? Yes, here is the difference between human and divine law! This makes obedience safer than rebellion. If you and I, Philip, stand above the level of common natures, feeling higher needs and claiming other rights, let us shape them according to the law which is above, not that which is below us!"

Philip grew pale. "Then you mean to endure in patience, and expect me to do the same?" he asked.

"If I can. The old foundations upon which my life rested are broken up, and I am too bewildered to venture on a random path. Give me time; nay, let us both strive to wait a little. I see nothing clearly but this: there is a Divine government, on which I lean now as never before. Yes, I say again, the very wrong that has come upon us makes God necessary!"

It was Philip's turn to be agitated. There was a simple, solemn conviction in Joseph's voice which struck to his heart. He had spoken from the heat of his passion, it is true, but he had the courage to disregard the judgment of men, and make his protest a reality. Both natures shared the desire, and were enticed by the daring of his dream; but out of Joseph's deeper conscience came a whisper, against which the cry of passion was powerless.

"Yes, we will wait," said Philip, after a long pause. "You came to me, Joseph, as you said, in weakness and confusion: I have been talking of your innocence and ignorance. Let us not measure ourselves in this way. It is not experience alone which creates manhood. What will become of us I cannot tell, but I will not, I dare not, say you are wrong!"

They took each other's hands. The day was fading, the landscape was silent, and only the twitter of nesting birds was heard in the boughs above them. Each gave way to the impulse of his manly love, rarer, alas! but as tender and true as the love of woman, and they drew nearer and kissed each other. As they walked back and parted on the highway, each felt that life was not wholly unkind, and that happiness was not yet impossible.

20. CONTEMPORARY CAMERADOS

There are more men of letters and note who were living with the same desires, some men like Whitman and Wilde, and others more like Stoker and Taylor. Of the closeted variety, we have Herman Melville and his unrequited feelings for Nathanial Hawthorne, author of *The Scarlet Letter* (for an examples of these letters to Hawthorne, the responses to which have not survived, see [A.19]):

> In 1850, Melville wrote that Hawthorne had "dropped germanous seeds into my soul" and had "shot his strong New England roots into the hot soil of my soul." Was his review expressing genteel love or did he just want to get plowed? Did he even know himself? Similarly, Halleck chose to clothe his sentiments for Drake in sexually charged metaphors as well as modified marriage (same-sex holy union). Melville's scatological figurativeness has more in common with the homosexual pattern of an earlier American period than his own.[22]

His writing in *Moby Dick; Or, The Whale* is phallic enough, with this passage of sailors squeezing the lumps out of whale spermaceti that is startlingly reminiscent of what Whitman calls "amorous wet." From Chapter 94, "A Squeeze of the Hand," we have:

> Squeeze! squeeze! squeeze! all the morning long; I squeezed that sperm till I myself almost melted into it; I squeezed that sperm till a strange sort of insanity came over me; and I found myself unwittingly squeezing my co-laborers' hands in it, mistaking their hands for the gentle globules. Such an abounding, affectionate, friendly, loving feeling did this avocation beget; that at last I was continually squeezing their hands, and looking up into their eyes sentimentally; as much as to say,—Oh! my dear fellow beings, why should we longer cherish any social acerbities, or know the slightest ill-humor or envy! Come; let us squeeze hands all round; nay, let us all squeeze ourselves

into each other; let us squeeze ourselves universally into the very milk and sperm of kindness.[26]

Along with *Moby Dick*, his short novel *Billy Budd* has both a captain and a rival of the titular character being drawn maddeningly to Billy's "smooth face, all but feminine in purity of natural complexion." His stories of sea-faring, including *Typee: A Peep at Polynesian Life*, like Charles Warren Stoddard's tales of the South Sea islands, explore the homoeroticism on display in foreign lands. From *Playing the Game*:

> With the recent publication of Edwin Haviland Miller's *Melville* (1975), the foundation seems to be laid for Herman Melville to emerge as the nineteenth-century godfather of homosexual fiction in this country. Miller carries Richard Chase's 1949 observation that Melville loved men better than women to the specific conclusion that in the 1850s Melville had a profoundly traumatic, unrequited love for Nathaniel Hawthorne. Although Miller's biography is based on a Fruedian rather than an unabashedly gay framework, its well-documented thesis reveals how homoeroticism serves as a key not only to *Billy Budd* but to everything from *Typee* to *Clarel*.[1]

Ultimately, however, Melville believed (as Stoker did) in the closet:

> Melville's "I and My Chimney" is the source of "the closet"—and of its integrity. The wife of "I" supposes the chimney to contain a secret closet, and badgers her husband to open it. In the end, however, "I" prevails: "Besides, even if there were a secret closet, secret it should remain, and secret it shall. Yes, wife, here for once I must say my say. Infinite sad mischief has resulted from the profane bursting open of secret recesses."[30]

Speaking of Charles Warren Stoddard, he was more of the Whitman and Wilde sort, freer for knowing himself through "Calamus" and his travels, and a lot more open about it:

> [In 1863] Charles Warren Stoddard had just turned twenty and had recently moved to San Francisco from New York City. As an aspiring poet, he was profoundly influenced by the third edition of *Leaves of Grass*. For Stoddard, the work suggested dazzling new possibilities of subject and form. The young poet was experimenting with free verse and publishing his efforts in the *Golden Era* under the pseudonym "Pip Pepperpod." Stoddard was especially affected by Whitman's "Calamus" poems, which he would always credit with helping him to realize his sexual orientation. In the years ahead, Stoddard would publish poetry, fiction, and memoirs, assembling a body of work distinguished for its time by an unusually relaxed and open attitude toward homosexuality. "I am what I was when I was born," he once said. Among Stoddard's works

are *South-Sea Idyls* (an erotically charged travelogue published in 1873) and *For the Pleasure of His Company* (a 1903 novel).[33]

See Introduction: America's First Gay Novel? and Chapter 3: Twin Love for more on Stoddard's life and works. See Chapter 15: Avowals to Walt Whitman and [A.14] for more of Stoddard's communications with Walt Whitman.

Another who relished the knowledge brought to him by Whitman and the "Calamus" poems is John Addington Symonds:

> Symonds's memoirs, published nearly a century after his 1893 death, reveal the cause of his persistence: he was convinced *Leaves of Grass*, and the Calamus poems in particular, played a crucial role in coming to terms with his homosexuality. Symonds tells of beginning in the late 1860s to write for his own eyes—as a "kind of mental masturbation"—a cycle of poems "illustrating the love of man for man in all periods of civilization." Then he explains, "very early after the commencement of this cycle, I came across W. Whitman's *Leaves of Grass*. I was sitting with F. M. Myers in his rooms at Trinity, Cambridge, when he stood up, seized a book and shouted out in his nasal intonation with those brazen lungs of his, 'Long I thought that knowledge alone would content me' [Calamus #8, 1860 ed.]. This fine poem, omitted from later editions of *Leaves of Grass*, formed part of Calamus. The book became for me a sort of Bible. Inspired by Calamus, I adopted another method of palliative treatment, and tried to invigorate the emotion I could not shake off by absorbing Whitman's conception of comradeship. The process was not without its bracing benefit. My desires grew manlier, more defined, more direct, more daring by contact with Calamus. . . . I can now declare with sincerity that my abnormal inclinations, modified by Whitman's idealism and penetrated with his democratic enthusiasm, have brought me into close and profitable sympathy with human beings even while I sinned against law and conventional morality."
>
> [...]
>
> Symonds wrote numerous letters to Whitman, which Whitman summed up as "warm (not too warm), a bit inquisitive, ingratiating." The first one, dated October 7, 1871, carries this introduction—"I am an Englishman, married, with three children, and am aged thirty"—and includes a poem, Symonds says, "in which you may perchance detect some echo, faint and feeble, of your Calamus." He also asserts that "since the time when I first took up *Leaves of Grass* in a friend's room at Trinity College Cambridge six years ago till now, your poems have been my constant companions." Whitman greatly admired Symonds. He said to Horace that Symonds "is the quintessence of culture: he is the culture of culture of culture—the essence of an essence." This was in spite of Symonds being decidedly of the literary

aristocracy: "Symonds, of the literati a distinguished member—among the most distinguished . . . a man of books about whom it cannot be said, 'he don't know what he's talking about.'" The admiration was mutual. In Symonds's memoirs [...] he wrote that Whitman's "concrete passionate faith in the world, combined with the man's multiform experience, his human sympathy, his thrill of love and comradeship, sent a current of vitalizing magnetism through my speculations." Symonds makes clear that, in spite of the poet's reticence, reading *Leaves of Grass* significantly helped him find "contentment in love—not the human kindly friendly love which I had given liberally to my beloved wife and children, my father and my sister and my companions, but in the passionate sexual love of comrades." Later, as Whitman remarked, Symonds's letters became "more intimate, more personal, more throbbing." The last Symonds letter was written from Davos, Switzerland, "in the deep night" and is dated February 27/28, 1892, just one month before Whitman died. In this letter (written to Traubel), certainly one of the most moving of all the avowals, Symonds asserts that "I might have been a mere English gentleman, had I not read *Leaves of Grass* in time." Alluding to his own homosexual activities, the married father of three children also lauds Whitman for making him "love my brethren, & seek them out with more perhaps of passion than he would himself approve." Whitman reacted emotionally to the reading of this letter, as Traubel records: "Several times he cried out, 'Loving Symonds! Dear Symonds!' and several times he had me reread passages. [Horace asks,] 'Do you hear it all?' 'Every word, every word—I am attentive to every word,' which was very evident—the tears gushing out of his eyes, and his whole body and brain evidently stirred by the words of the letters." Though Walt had deep affection for Symonds the man, he could still be harsh on Symonds the critic. Of an essay, "Democratic Art, with special reference to Walt Whitman," the poet snidely commented, "I doubt whether he has gripp'd 'democratic art' by the nuts, or *L of G.* either." He also spoke of the "ponderosity" of Symonds's books and of their being "deep, heavy, bookish, [they] infer not things or thoughts at first hand but at third or fourth hand, & after the college point of view—the essays are valuable, but appear to me to be elderly chestnuts mainly."[39]

Being honest while being safe from prosecution and ruin at the same time was a difficult line to walk:

Even deeply sympathetic readers could end up in such a rhetorical quandary, as Symonds did in the candid appreciation he published the year after Whitman died (and on the day of his own death). Symonds found "a distinctly sensuous side to his conception of adhesiveness," but elaborately avoided the *acts* that might result from this sensuality with the usual verbiage of noble asexuality: "Whitman possessed a specially keen sense of the fine restraint and continence, the cleanliness and chastity, that are inseparable from the perfectly virile and physically complete nature of healthy manhood."[39]

Symonds was a longtime correspondent with Whitman, and in 1890 he famously wrote Whitman to ask him about the homosexual imagery of Whitman's Calamus poems, wherein Whitman flatly denied Symonds's analysis and claimed, as proof of his heterosexuality, to have fathered six illegitimate children, "a fantastic if long-lived claim frequently invoked in discussions of Whitman's sexual identity."[2] See Chapter 22: Whitman's Peter for more of Symonds's writing on Whitman.

Whitman had ways of talking near to and around the subject of masculine love, had in fact "looser lips"[22] than the likes of Fitz-Greene Halleck or Bram Stoker, but far tighter lips than Symonds or Wilde:

In the quirky language of phrenology, "adhesiveness" was the capacity for intense and meaningful same-sex friendship. Its symbol was two women embracing. By contrast, "amativeness" referred to romantic love between a man and a woman. Whitman, who took great pride in his phrenological reading, received one of his highest scores for adhesiveness. (He rated a 6.) Whitman loved to twist words and phrases, appropriating them, lending them new meaning. In his poetry, he employed a number of coded terms for passionate attachments among men such as "comrades" and "adhesiveness."[33]

Not only did Whitman adopt words for his own meanings, he also coined the unique term "camerado" for his particular use. The Calamus plant, known also as "sweet flag" (see Chapter 29: Leaves and Fruits for more detail on the plant) helps suggest the kind of signaling that needed to be done, a sort of flag code able to be read only by those in the know (which later becomes quite literal with the handkerchief cruising codes of the 1970s and 80s). This is all done in order to pass under the notice of those whom Bayard Taylor grimly acknowledges in his dedication of *Joseph and His Friend*, people who simply will not read such books, because they do not understand them.

Besides using coded works of writing for communication and exchange, there were also gentlemen's clubs one could join if one understood their true purpose, clubs through which Whitman, Taylor, and Halleck made each other's acquaintances:

The Ugly Club was exclusive to the point of secrecy, and Halleck's private solicitation for Abraham S. Fowler to join, on the condition that his looks had not altered since Halleck had last seen him, demonstrates the typical camp of correspondence between members. Fowler was also congratulated on his qualifying "deformities" by the club's secretary whose whimsical letter speaks for all members who "anticipate the pleasure of feasting their eyes on your ugliness." Though the club threw all-male balls (a feature of molly-like clubs in nineteenth-century American cities), there is no evidence it was an exclusively homosexual body. Clubs that did cater to homosexual clientele were the Artistic Club, the Black Rabbit, the Golden Rule Pleasure Club, the Little Bucks, the Palm, Manilla Hall, and Paresis Hall. [...] Halleck was elected the Ugly Club's poet laureate in October 1814.

[...]

Taylor [...] served as a link between Halleck and Walt Whitman at another liberal establishment. Robert K. Martin believes that Halleck and Whitman met through Taylor as regular clients of Charles Pfaff, whose restaurant bar catered to a homosexual clientele. Pfaff's was patronized by "writers, whores, queens and street-car drivers" as well as by editor Henry Clapp, Whitman's "friend and companion in the Pfaff's restaurant coterie." Whitman frequented Pfaff's bohemian bar between 1857 and 1861, where he doted over his "'darlings and gossips,' who gathered at Pfaff's Restaurant on Broadway near Bleeker Street in Greenwich Village." Whitman supposedly read "Beat! Beat! Drums!" to an audience at Pfaff's, and his uncollected poem "The Two Vaults" was based on the underground establishment. The poem reflects the "bright eyes of beautiful young men!" strutting the bar in an unreal "pageant"; the hungry narrator longs to "arrest" one of them "as they flit along" in the literal and figurative underground bar. Pfaff's joins the list of New York sites (bathhouses, wharves, and parks) where homosexuals met and returned to boarding houses for sex or patronized male prostitutes throughout the 1840s and 1850s.[22]

However, even being among the right society, in the company of like-minded friends, not everyone can make it. What follows are the circumstances surrounding the suicide of a mutual friend of Fitz-Greene Halleck and Joseph Rodman Drake:

On December 12, 1817, Drake informed "My Dear Fitz" that their close friend, Walter Franklin, had committed suicide. Hardly "capable of writing," Drake wanted to give Halleck the news himself and added that Franklin's reason for shooting himself were "obscure": "No writing, no paper, tending to throw any light on it, has been found." Franklin had spent his last full day alive entirely with Drake, who noticed "no agitation in his manner, no depression of spirits, to lead to any suspicion of the state of his mind." "From ten in the morning until late at night," Drake had found Franklin's demeanor "more placidly cheerful than ever" and observed "a gentleness in [Franklin's] mirth which was unusual with him, but I attributed it to our reconciliation. It was on Monday that he called on me first, and from that time he was with me almost constantly until the fatal morning. Many circumstances have occurred to prove that the deed was long premeditated. A number of expressions which he made use of in conversation with me, at the time obscure, are now elucidated; but they were used in a pleasant conversation, and uttered in too gay a tone to make any impression on me at the time." Drake was stunned by Franklin's plan to lie on his sister's bed, place a mirror between his knees, and aim a gun at his forehead. Drake depicts the dead man as in a state of near ecstasy on the day preceding his death, having made up with him after some unspecified falling out. The above letter was signed "Faithfully yours, J. R. Drake" and implied that Halleck was already familiar with the conflict that had existed between Drake and Franklin.

In sharp contrast, Halleck had anticipated Franklin's suicide. What Drake had only realized in retrospect, Halleck had foreseen, as he conveyed in a letter to his sister three days after Drake had written him. Having just returned to New York, Halleck wrote, "One of my most intimate friends shot himself." He tells Maria that he had met Franklin, a nineteen-year-old clerk for the United State Bank, through Drake two years earlier and that "we have since been bosom friends." He describes the boy as an "extraordinary character in every respect," whose intellect was "strong, and powerful, and energetic far beyond his years; an enthusiast in poetry, in music, in every thing."

Franklin had had much in common with Halleck who was sensitive to Franklin's "continual gloom which, even in his most cheerful hours, and in the midst of the maddest mirth, was always perceivable. He was the handsomest being I ever saw. He was six feet high, perfectly proportioned, and had as fine a face as nature ever formed." Rescinding the most handsome award from Drake, Halleck describes his dead friend as physically irresistible. The homoerotic eulogy to Franklin is followed by clues that Franklin was self-destructive and Halleck knew "he intended to shoot himself. . . . we had often conversed on suicide, and I joined him in the opinion that the world contained nothing worth living for." Halleck and Franklin's private discussions were apparently kept from Drake.

Halleck's graphic picture of the suicide included additional details. He adds that the pistol's "ball passed through [Franklin's] temple and lodged in the wall. His death must have been instantaneous, and without a pang, for his countenance was perfectly calm and unruffled, not a muscle distorted, nor even a curl of the lip to denote agony. I need not paint the anguish of a father's, mother's, brother's, and sister's feelings, or of a young lady to whom he was betrothed." The reconstruction of Franklin's death scene cannot possibly have been an eye-witness account because Halleck arrived back in New York days after the corpse was discovered. Surely, the picture Halleck imagined satisfied his own need to believe that his troubled friend had found peace.[22]

XXI

UNDER THE WATER

JOSEPH SAID NOTHING that evening concerning the result of his trip to the city, and Julia, who instantly detected the signs which a powerful excitement had left upon his face, thought it prudent to ask no immediate questions. She was purposely demonstrative in little arrangements for his comfort, but spared him her caresses; she did not intend to be again mistaken in choosing the time and occasion of bestowing them.

The next morning, when he felt that he could speak calmly, Joseph told her what he had done, carefully avoiding any word that might seem to express disappointment, or even doubt.

"I hope you are satisfied that pa will make it easy for you?" she ventured to say.

"He thinks so." Then Joseph could not help adding: "He depends, I imagine, upon your sister Clementina marrying a Mr. Spelter,—'a man of immense wealth, but, I regret to say, no refinement.'"

Julia bit her lip, and her eyes assumed that hard, flinty look which her husband knew so well. "If Clementina marries immense wealth," she exclaimed, with a half-concealed sneer, "she will become simply insufferable! But what difference can that make in pa's business affairs?"

The answer tingled on Joseph's tongue: "Probably he expects Mr. Spelter to indorse a promissory note"; but he held it back. "What *I* have resolved to do is this," he said. "In a day or two—as soon as I can arrange to leave—I shall make a journey to the oil region, and satisfy myself where and what the Amaranth is. Your own practical instincts will tell you, Julia, that this intention of mine must be kept secret, even from your father."

She leaned her head upon her hand, and appeared to reflect. When she looked up her face had a cheerful, confiding expression.

"I think you are right," she then said. "If—if things should not happen to be *quite* as they are represented, you can secure yourself against any risk—and pa, too—before the others know of it. You will have the inside track; that is, if there is one. On the other hand, if all is right, pa can easily manage, if some of the others are shaky in their faith, to get their stock at a bargain. I am sure he would have gone out there himself, if his official services were not so important to the government."

It was a hard task for Joseph to keep his feelings to himself.

"And now," she continued,—"now I know you will agree to a plan of mine, which I was going to propose. Lucy Henderson's school closes this week, and Mrs. Hopeton tells me she is a little overworked and ailing. It would hardly help her much to go home, where she could not properly rest, as her father is a hard, avaricious man, who can't endure idleness, except, I suppose, in a corpse (so these people seem to me). I want to ask Lucy to come here. I think you always liked her" (here Julia shot a swift, stealthy glance at Joseph), "and so she will be an agreeable guest for both of us. She shall just rest and grow strong. While you are absent, I shall not seem quite so lonely. You may be gone a week or more, and I shall find the separation very hard to bear, even with her company."

"Why has Mrs. Hopeton not invited her?" Joseph asked.

"The Hopetons are going to the sea-shore in a few days. She would take Lucy as a guest but there is one difficulty in the way. She thinks Lucy would accept the trip and the stay there as an act of hospitality, but that she cannot (or thinks she cannot) afford the dresses that would enable her to appear in Mrs. Hopeton's circle. But it is just as well: I am sure Lucy would feel more at home *here*."

"Then by all means ask her!" said Joseph. "Lucy Henderson is a noble girl, for she has forced a true-hearted man to love her, without return."

"Ind-e-e-d!"

Julia's drawl denoted surprise and curiosity, but Joseph felt that once more he had spoken too quickly. He endeavored to cover his mistake by a hearty acquiescence in the plan, which was speedily arranged between them, in all its details, Lucy's consent being taken for granted.

It required, however, the extreme of Julia's powers of disguise, aided by Joseph's frank and hearty words and Mrs. Hopeton's influence, to induce Lucy to accept the invitation. Unable to explain wholly to herself, much less mention to any other, the instinct which held her back, she found herself, finally, placed in a false position, and then resolved to blindly trust that she was doing right, inasmuch as she could not make it clear that she was doing wrong. Her decision once taken, she forcibly banished all misgivings, and determined to find nothing but a cheerful and restful holiday before her.

And, indeed, the first day or two of her residence at the farm, before Joseph's departure, brought her a more agreeable experience than she had imagined. Both host and hostess were busy, the latter in the household and the former in the fields, and when they met at meals or in the evening, her presence was an element which compelled an appearance of harmony. She was surprised to find so quiet and ordered a life in two persons whom she had imagined to be miserably unfitted for each other, and began to suspect that she had been seriously mistaken.

After Joseph left, the two women were much together. Julia insisted that she should do nothing, and amiably protested at first against Lucy giving her so much of her society; but, little by little, the companionship was extended and became more frank and intimate. Lucy was in a charitable mood, and found it very easy to fancy that Julia's character had been favorably affected by the graver duties which had come with her marriage. Indeed, Julia found many indirect ways of hinting as much: she feared she had seemed flighty (perhaps a little shallow); looking back upon her past life she could see that such a charge would not be unjust. Her education had been so superficial; all city education of young women was false; they were taught to consider external appearances, and if they felt a void in their nature which these would not fill, whither could they turn for counsel or knowledge?

Her face was sad and thoughtful while she so spoke; but when, shaking her dark curls with a pretty impatience, she would lift her head and ask, with a smile: "But it is not too late, in my case, is it? I'm really an older child, you know,"—Lucy could only answer: "Since you know what you need, it can never be too late. The very fact that you *do* know, proves that it will be easy for you."

Then Julia would shake her head again, and say, "O, you are too kind, Lucy; you judge my nature by your own."

When the friendly relation between them had developed a little further, Julia became—though still with a modest reticence—more confiding in relation to Joseph.

"He is so good, so very, very true and good," she said; one day, "that it grieves me, more than I can tell, to be the cause of a little present anxiety of his. As it is only a business matter, some exaggerated report of which you have probably heard (for I know there have been foolish stories afloat in the neighborhood), I have no hesitation about confiding it to you. Perhaps you can advise me how to atone for my error; for, if it was an error, I fear it cannot be remedied now; if not, it will be a relief to me to confess it."

Thereupon she gave a minute history of the Amaranth speculation, omitting the energy of her persuasion with Joseph, and presenting very strongly her father's views of a sure and splendid success soon to follow. "It was for Joseph's sake," she concluded, "rather than my own, that I advised the investment; though, knowing his perfect unselfishness, I fear he complied only for mine. He had guessed already, it seems to me now, that we women like beauty as well as comfort about our lives; otherwise, he would hardly have undertaken these expensive improvements of our home. But, Lucy, it terrifies me to think that pa and Joseph and I may have been deceived! The more I shut my mind against the idea the more it returns to torment me. I, who brought so little to him, to be the instrument of such a loss! O, if you were not here, how could I endure the anxiety and the absence?"

She buried her face in her handkerchief, and sobbed.

"I know Joseph to be good and true," said Lucy, "and I believe that he will bear the loss cheerfully, if it should come. But it is never good to 'borrow trouble,' as we say in the country. Neither the worst nor the best things which we imagine ever come upon us."

"You are wrong!" cried Julia, starting up and laughing gleefully; "I *have* the best thing, in my husband! And yet, you are right, too: no worst thing can come to me, while I keep him!"

Lucy wished to visit the Hopetons before their departure for the sea-shore, and Julia was quite ready to accompany her. Only, with the willfulness common to all selfish natures, she determined to arrange the matter in her own way. She drove away alone the next morning to the post-office, with a letter for Joseph, but never drew rein until she had reached Coventry Forge. Philip being absent, she confided to Madeline Held her wish (and Lucy's) that they should all spend an afternoon together, on the banks of the stream,—a free society in the open air instead of a formal one within doors. Madeline entered into the plan with joyous readiness, accepting both for herself and for Philip. They all met together too rarely, she said: a lunch or a tea under the trees would be delightful: there was a little skiff which might be borrowed, and they might even catch and cook their own fish, as the most respectable people did in the Adirondacks.

Julia then drove to the Hopetons in high spirits. Mr. Hopeton found the proposed party very pleasant, and said at once to his wife: "We have still three days, my dear: we can easily spare to-morrow?"

"Mrs. Asten is very kind," she replied; "and her proposition is tempting: but I should not like to go without you, and I thought your business might—"

"O there is nothing pressing," he interrupted. "I shall enjoy it exceedingly, especially the boat, and the chance of landing a few trout."

So it was settled. Lucy, it is true, felt a dissatisfaction which she could scarcely conceal, and possibly did not, to Julia's eyes; but it was not for her own sake. She must seem grateful for a courtesy meant to favor both herself and her friend, and a little reflection reconciled her to the plan. Mrs. Hopeton dared not avoid Philip Held and it might be well if she carried away with her to the sea-shore a later and less alarming memory of him. Lucy's own desire for a quiet talk with the woman in whom she felt such a loving interest was of no consequence, if this was the result.

They met in the afternoon, on the eastern side of the stream, just below the Forge, where a little bay of level shore, shaded by superb trees, was left between the rocky bluffs. Stumps and a long-fallen trunk furnished them with rough tables and seats; there was a natural fireplace among some huge tumbled stones; a spring of icy crystal gushed out from the foot of the bluff; and the shimmering, murmuring water in front, with the meadows beyond burning like emerald flame in the sunshine, offered a constant delight to the senses.

All were enchanted with the spot, which Philip and Madeline claimed as their discovery. The gypsy spirit awoke in them, and while they scattered here and there, possessed with the influences of the place, and constantly stumbling upon some new charm or convenience, Lucy felt her heart grow light for her friend, and the trouble of her own life subside. For a time no one seemed to think of anything but the material arrangements. Mr. Hopeton's wine-flasks were laid in the spring to cool; Philip improvised a rustic table upon two neighboring stumps; rough seats were made comfortable, dry sticks collected for fire-wood, stores unpacked and placed in readiness, and every little preliminary of labor, insufferable in a kitchen, took on its usual fascination in that sylvan nook.

Then they rested from their work. Mr. Hopeton and Philip lighted cigars and sat to leeward, while the four ladies kept their fingers busy with bunches of maiden-hair and faint wildwood blossoms, as they talked. It really seemed as if a peace and joy from beyond their lives had fallen upon them. Madeline believed so, and Lucy hoped so: let us hope so, too, and not lift at once the veil which was folded so closely over two restless hearts!

Mr. Hopeton threw away the stump of his cigar, adjusted his fishing-tackle, and said: "If we are to have a trout supper, I must begin to troll at once."

"May I go with you?" his wife asked.

"Yes," he answered, smiling, "if you will not be nervous. But I hardly need to make that stipulation with you, Emily."

Philip assisted her into the unsteady little craft, which was fastened to a tree. Mr. Hopeton seated himself carefully, took the two light, short oars, and held himself from the shore, while Philip loosened the rope.

"I shall row up stream," he said, "and then float back to you, trolling as I come. When I see you again, I hope I can ask you to have the coals ready."

Slowly, and not very skillfully, he worked his way against the current, and passed out of sight around a bend in the stream. Philip watched Mrs. Hopeton's slender figure as she sat in the stern, listlessly trailing one hand in the water. "Does she feel that my eyes, my thoughts, are following her?" he asked; but she did not once turn her head.

"Philip!" cried Madeline, "here are three forlorn maidens, and you the only Sir Isumbras, or whoever is the proper knight! Are you looking into the stream, expecting the 'damp woman' to arise? She only rises for fishermen: she will come up and drag Mr. Hopeton down. Let me invoke the real nymph of this stream!" She sang:—

> "'Sabrina fair,
>   Listen where thou art sitting
> Under the glassy, cool, translucent wave,
>   In twisted braids of lilies knitting
> The loose train of thy amber-dropping hair;
>   Listen for dear honor's sake,
> Goddess of the silver lake,
>   Listen and save!'"

Madeline did not know what she was doing. She could not remark Philip's paleness in the dim green light where they sat, but she was struck by the startled expression of his eyes.

"One would think you really expected Sabrina to come," she laughed. "Miss Henderson, too, looks as if I had frightened her. You and I, Mrs. Asten, are the only cool, unimaginative brains in the party. But: perhaps it was all owing to my poor voice? Come now, confess it! I don't expect you to say,—

> "'Can any mortal mixture of earth's mould
> Breathe such divine, enchanting ravishment?'"

"I was trying to place the song," said Lucy; "I read it once."

"If anyone could evoke a spirit, Madeline," Philip replied, "it would be you. But the spirit would be no nymph; it would have little horns and hoofs, and you would be glad to get rid of it again."

They all laughed at this, and presently, at Julia's suggestion, arranged the wood they had collected, and kindled a fire. It required a little time and patience to secure a strong blaze, and in the great interest which the task called forth the Hopetons were forgotten.

At last Philip stepped back, heated and half stifled, for a breath of fresher air, and, turning, saw the boat between the trees gliding down the stream. "There they are!" he cried; "now, to know our luck!"

The boat was in midstream, not far from a stony strip which rose above the water. Mrs. Hopeton sat musing with her hands in her lap, while her husband, resting on his knees and one hand, leaned over the bow, watching the fly which trailed at the end of his line. He seemed to be quite unconscious that an oar, which had slowly loosened itself from the lock, was floating away behind the boat.

"You are losing your oars!" Philip cried.

Mr. Hopeton started, as from a dream of trout, dropped his line and stretched forward suddenly to grasp the oar. The skiff was too light and unbalanced to support the motion. It rocked threateningly; Mrs. Hopeton, quite forgetting herself, started to her feet, and, instantly losing her equilibrium, was thrown headlong into the deeper water. The skiff whirled back, turned over, and before Mr. Hopeton was aware of what had happened, he plunged full length, face downwards, into the shallower current.

It was all over before Madeline and Lucy reached the bank, and Philip was already in the stream. A few strokes brought him to Mrs. Hopeton, who struggled with the current as she rose to the surface, but made no outcry. No sooner had she touched Philip than she seized and locked him in her arms, and he was dragged down again with her. It was only the physical clinging to life: if some feeble recognition at that moment told her whose was the form she held and made powerless, it could not have abated an atom of her frantic instinctive force.

Philip felt that they had drifted into water beyond his depth. With great exertion he freed his right arm and sustained himself and her a moment at the surface. Mrs. Hopeton's head was on his shoulder; her hair drifted against his face, and even the desperation of the struggle could not make him insensible to the warmth of her breast upon his own. A wild thought flashed upon and stung his brain: she was his at last—his in death, if not in life!

His arm slackened, and they sank slowly together. Heart and brain were illuminated with blinding light, and the swift succession of his thoughts compressed an age into the fragment of a second. Yes, she was his now: clasping him as he clasped, their hearts beating against each other; with ever slower pulsations, until they should freeze into one. The world, with its wrongs and prejudices, lay behind them; the past was past, and only a short and painless atonement intervened between the immortal possession of souls! Better that it should end thus: he had not sought this solution, but he would not thrust it from him.

But, even as his mind accepted it, and with a sense of perfect peace, he heard Joseph's voice, saying, "We must shape our lives according to the law which is above, not that which is below us." Through the air and the water, on the very rock which now overhung his head, he again saw Joseph bending, and himself creeping towards him with outstretched hand. Ha! who was the coward now? And again Joseph spake, and his words were: "The very wrong that has come upon us makes God necessary." God? Then how would God in his wisdom fashion their future life? Must they sweep eternally, locked in an unsevering embrace, like Paolo and Francesca, around some dreary circle of Hell? Or must the manner of entering that life together be the act to separate them eternally? Only the inevitable act dare ask for pardon; but here, if not will or purpose, was at least submission without resistance! Then it seemed to him that Madeline's voice came again to him, ringing like a trumpet through the waters, as she sang:—

"Listen for dear honor's sake,
Goddess of the silver lake,
Listen and save!"

He pressed his lips to Mrs. Hopeton's unconscious brow, his heart saying, "Never, never again!" released himself by a sudden, powerful effort, seized her safely, as a practiced swimmer, shot into light and air, and made for the shallower side of the stream. The upturned skiff was now within reach, and all danger was over.

Who could guess that the crisis of a soul had been reached and passed in that breath of time under the surface? Julia's long, shrill scream had scarcely come to an end; Mr. Hopeton, bewildered by his fall, was trying to run towards them through water up to his waist, and Lucy and Madeline looked on, holding their breath in an agony of suspense. In another moment Philip touched bottom, and raising Mrs. Hopeton in his arms, carried her to the opposite bank.

She was faint and stunned, but not unconscious. She passively allowed Philip to support her until Mr. Hopeton, struggling through the shallows; drew near with an expression of intense terror and concern on his broad face. Then, breaking from Philip, she half fell, half flung herself into his arms, laid her head upon his shoulder, and burst into a fit of hysterical weeping.

Tears began to run down the honest man's cheeks, and Philip, turning away, busied himself with righting the boat and recovering the oars.

"O my darling!" said Mr. Hopeton, "what should I do if I had lost you?"

"Hold me, keep me, love me!" she cried. "I must not leave you!"

He held her in his arms, he kissed her, he soothed her with endearing words. She grew calm, lifted her head, and looked in his eyes with a light which he had never yet seen in them. The man's nature was moved and stirred: his lips trembled, and the tears still slowly trickled from his eyes.

"Let me set you over!" Philip called from the stream. "The boat is wet, but then neither of us is dry. We have, fortunately, a good fire until the carriage can be brought for Mrs. Hopeton, and your wine will be needed at once."

They had no trout, nor indeed any refreshment, except the wine. Philip tried to rally the spirits of the party, but Julia was the only one who at all seconded his efforts; the others had been too profoundly agitated. Mr. and Mrs. Hopeton were grave; it seemed scarcely possible for them to speak, and yet, as Lucy remarked with amazement, the faces of both were bright and serene.

"I shall never invoke another water-nymph," said Madeline, as they were leaving the spot.

"Yes!" Philip cried, "always invoke Sabrina, and the daughter of Locrine will arise for you, as she arose to-day."

"That is, not at all?"

"No," said Philip, "she arose."

21. WHITMAN'S BOYS

Speaking of Whitman's "darlings and gossips" in <u>Chapter 20: Contemporary Camerados</u>, more detail is provided here:

> When Whitman first started going to Pfaff's (pronounced *fafs*, an underground saloon in every sense of the word; during the 1850s, it was dim, gaslit, and packed with artists, the meeting place of America's first Bohemians), he was in a serious relationship with a man named Fred Vaughan. Often, he and Vaughan would sit together at a table in Pfaff's and it appears the two men even lived together for a time on Classon Avenue in Brooklyn. Vaughan ended up getting married and settled into a rather conventional life. He worked a series of jobs such as insurance salesman and elevator operator and with his wife raised four sons. He also became a terrible alcoholic. In the early 1870s, after roughly a decade of silence, Vaughan reconnected with Whitman, writing him several letters, one of which includes the following heart-rending passage: "I never stole, robbed, cheated, nor defrauded any person out of anything, and yet I feel that I have not been honest to myself—my family nor my friends." In the letters, Vaughan never spells out the source of his anguish. Perhaps it was the result of living in a state that felt unnatural to him. One letter includes, "My love my Walt is with you always."
>
> [...]
>
> Whitman described [the young men at Pfaff's] as "beautiful" and credited this circle with providing the "quiet lambent electricity of real friendship." He addressed them as "my darlings and gossips" and "my darling, dearest boys."[33]

Whitman, as friendly as he was and as much as he celebrated life and his love for manly "camerados" in his poems, seems at times like he might have been the most popular camerado east of the Mississippi:

Whitman's notebooks are filled with brief descriptions of the men he encountered:

- Tom Egbert, conductor Myrtle av. open neck, sailor looking
- Mark Gaynor, young, 5 ft. 7 in, black mustache, plumber
- Saturday night Mike Ellis—wandering at the cor of Lexington av. & st.—took him home to 150 37th street,—4th story back room—bitter cold night—works in Stevenson's Carriage factory.
- Dan'l Spencer . . . somewhat feminine—5th av (44) (May 29)—told me he had never been in a fight and did not drink at all . . . slept with me Sept 3d.
- *Thos Gray* good looking young Scotchman elegantly dress'd,—does the tricks, cutting hs finger &c—at Pfaff's . . .
- John McNelly night Oct 7 young man, drunk, walk'd up Fulton & High st. home works in Brooklyn flour mills had been with some friends return'd from the war
- *David Wilson*—night of Oct. 11, '62, walking up from Middagh—slept with me—works in blacksmith shop in Navy Yard—lives in Hampden st.— walks together Sunday afternoon & night—is about 19[33]

XXII

KANUCK

When he set forth upon his journey, Joseph had enough of natural shrewdness to perceive that his own personal interest in the speculation were better kept secret. The position of the Amaranth property, inserted like a wedge between the Fluke and Chowder Companies, was all the geography he needed; and he determined to assume the character of a curious traveller,—at least for a day or two,—to keep his eyes and ears open, and learn as much as might be possible to one outside the concentric "rings" of oil operations.

He reached Corry without adventure, and took passage in the train to Oil City, intending to make the latter place the starting-point of his investigations. The car was crowded, and his companion on the seat was a keen, witty, red-faced man, with an astonishing diamond pin and a gold watch-chain heavy enough to lift an anchor. He was too restless, too full of "operative" energy, to travel in silence, as is the universal and most dismal American habit; and before they passed three stations he had extracted from Joseph the facts that he was a stranger, that he intended visiting the principal wells, and that he might possibly (Joseph allowing the latter point to be inferred) be tempted to invest something, if the aspects were propitious.

"You must be sure to take a look at *my* wells," said the stranger; "not that any of our stock is in the market,—it is never offered to the public, unless accidentally,—but they will give you an illustration of the magnitude of the business. All wells, you know, sink after a while to what some people call the normal flowing capacity (we oilers call it 'the everidge run'), and so it was reported of ourn. But since we've begun to torpedo them, it's almost equal to the first tapping, though I don't suppose it'll hold out so long."

"Are the torpedoes generally used?" Joseph asked, in some surprise.

"They're generally *tried*, anyhow. The cute fellow who first hit upon the idea meant to keep it dark, but the oilers, you'll find, have got their teeth skinned, and what they can't find out isn't worth finding out! Lord! I torpedoed my wells at midnight, and it wasn't a week before the Fluke was at it, bustin' and bustin' all their dry auger-holes!"

"The *what!*" Joseph exclaimed.

"Fluke. Queer name, isn't it? But that's nothing: we have the Crinoline, the Pipsissaway, the Mud-Lark, and the Sunburst, between us and Tideoute."

"What is the name of your company, if I may ask?"

"About as queer as any of 'em,—the Chowder."

Joseph started, in spite of himself. "It seems to me I have heard of that company," he managed to say.

"O no doubt," replied the stranger. "'T isn't often quoted in the papers, but it's *known.* I'm rather proud of it, for I got it up. I was boring—boss, though—at three dollars a day, two years ago, and now I have my forty thousand a year, 'free of income tax,' as the Insurance Companies say. But then, where one is lucky like the Chowder, a hundred busts."

Joseph rapidly collected himself while the man was speaking. "I should very much like to see your wells," he said. "Will you be there a day or two from now? My name is Asten,—not that you have ever heard of it before."

"Shall be glad to hear it again, though, and to see you," said the man. "My name is Blenkinsop."

Again it was all that Joseph could do to restrain his astonishment.

"I suppose you are the President of the Chowder?" he ventured to say.

"Yes," Mr. Blenkinsop answered, "since it's a company. It was all mine at the start, but I wanted capital, and I had to work 'em."

"What other important companies are there near you?"

"None of any account, except the Fluke and the Depravity. *They* flow tolerable now, after torpedoing. To be sure, there are kites and catches with all sorts o' names,—the Pennyroyal, the Ruby, the Wallholler (whatever *that* is), and the Amaranth,—ha, ha!"

"I think I have heard of the Amaranth," Joseph mildly remarked.

"Lord! are you *bit* already?" Mr. Blenkinsop exclaimed, fixing his small, sharp eyes on Joseph's face.

"I—I really don't know what you mean."

"No offence: I thought it likely, that's all. The Amaranth is Kanuck's last dodge. He keeps mighty close, but if he don't feather his nest in a hurry, at somebody's expense, *I* ain't no judge o' men!"

Joseph did not dare to mention the Amaranth again. He parted with Mr. Blenkinsop at Tarr Farm, and went on to Oil City where he spent a day in unprofitable wanderings, and then set out up the river, first to seek the Chowder wells, and afterwards to ascertain whether there was any perennial beauty in the Amaranth.

The first thing which he remarked was the peculiar topography of the region. The Chowder property was a sloping bottom, gradually rising from the river to a range of high hills a quarter of a mile in the rear. Just above this point the river made a sharp horseshoe bend, washing the foot of the hills for a considerable distance, and then curving back again, with a second tract of bottom-land beyond. On the latter, he was informed, the Fluke wells were located. The inference was therefore irresistible that the Amaranth Company must be the happy possessor of the lofty section of hills dividing the two.

"Do they get oil up there?" he asked of Blenkinsop's foreman, pointing to the ragged, barren heights.

They may get skunk oil, or rattle-snake oil," the man answered. Them'll do to peddle, but you can't fill tanks with 'em. I hear they've got a company for that place,—th' Amaranth, they call it,—but any place'll do for derned fools. Why, look'ee here! We've got seven hundred feet to bore: now, jest put twelve hundred more atop o' that, and guess whether they can even pump oil, with the Chowder and Fluke both sides of 'em! But it does for green 'uns, as well as any other place."

Joseph laughed,—a most feeble, unnatural, ridiculous laugh.

"I'll walk over that way to the Fluke," he said. "I should like to see how such things are managed."

"Then be a little on your guard with Kanuck, if you meet him," the man good-naturedly advised. "Don't ask him too many questions."

It was a hot, wearisome climb to the timber-skeletons on the summit (more like gibbets than anything else), which denoted shafts to the initiated as well as the ignorant eye. There were a dozen or more, but all were deserted.

Joseph wandered from one to the other, asking himself, as he inspected each, "Is this the splendid speculation?" What was there in that miserable shabby, stony region, a hundred acres of which would hardly pasture a cow, whence wealth should come? Verily, as stony and as barren were the natures of the men, who on this wretched basis built their cheating schemes!

A little farther on he came to a deep ravine, cleaving the hills in twain. There was another skeleton in its bed, but several shabby individuals were gathered about it,—the first sign of life or business he had yet discovered.

He hastened down the steep declivity, the warning of the Chowder foreman recurring to his mind, yet it seemed so difficult to fix his policy in advance that he decided to leave everything to chance. As he approached he saw that the men were laborers, with the exception of a tall, lean individual, who looked like an unfortunate clergyman. He had a sallow face, lighted by small, restless, fiery eyes, which reminded Joseph, when they turned upon him, of those of a black snake. His greeting was cold and constrained, and his manner said plainly, "The sooner you leave the better I shall be satisfied."

"This is a rough country for walking," said Joseph; "how much farther is it to the Fluke wells?"

"Just a bit," said one of the workmen.

Joseph took a seat on a stone, with the air of one who needed rest. "This well, I suppose," he remarked, "belongs to the Amaranth?"

"Who told you so?" asked the lean, dark man.

"They said below, at the Chowder, that the Amaranth was up here."

"Did Blenkinsop send you this way?" the man asked again.

"Nobody sent me," Joseph replied. "I am a stranger, taking a look at the oil country. I have never before been in this part of the State."

"May I ask your name?"

"Asten," said Joseph, unthinkingly.

"Asten! I think I know where that name belongs. Let me see."

The man, pulled out a large dirty envelope from his breast-pocket, ran over, several papers, unfolded one, and presently asked,—

"Joseph Asten?"

"Yes." (Joseph set his teeth, and silently cursed his want of forethought.)

"Proprietor of ten thousand dollars' worth of stock in the Amaranth! Who sent you here?"

His tone, though meant to be calm, was fierce and menacing. Joseph rose; scanned the faces of the Workmen, who listened with a malicious curiosity, and finally answered, with a candor which seemed to impress, while it evidently disappointed the questioner:—

"No one sent me, and no one, beyond my own family, knows that I am here. I am a farmer, not a speculator. I was induced to take the stock from representations which have not been fulfilled, and which, I am now convinced, never will be fulfilled. My habit is, when I cannot get the truth from others, to ascertain it for myself. I presume you are Mr. Kanuck?"

The man did not answer immediately, but the quick, intelligent glance of one of the workmen showed Joseph that his surmise was correct. Mr. Kanuck conversed apart with the men, apparently giving private orders, and then said, with a constrained civility:—

"If you are bound for the Fluke, Mr. Asten, I will join you. I am also going in that direction, and we can talk on the way."

They toiled up the opposite side of the ravine in silence. When they had reached the top and taken breath, Mr. Kanuck commenced:—

"I must infer that you have little faith in anything being realized from the Amaranth. Any man, ignorant of the technicalities of boring, might be discouraged by the external appearance of things; and I shall therefore not endeavor to explain to you my grounds of hope, unless you will agree to join me for a month or two and become practically acquainted with the locality and the modes of labor."

"That is unnecessary," Joseph replied.

"You being a farmer, of course I could not expect it. On the other hand, I think I can appreciate your,—disappointment, if we must call it so, and I should be willing, under certain conditions, to save you, not from positive loss, because I do not admit the possibility of that, but from what, at present, may seem loss to you. Do I make my meaning clear?"

"Entirely," Joseph replied, "except as to the conditions."

"We are dealing on the square, I take it?"

"Of course."

"Then," said Mr. Kanuck, "I need only intimate to you how important it is that I should develop our prospects. To do this, the faith of the principal stockholders must not be disturbed, otherwise the funds without which the prospects cannot be developed may fail me at the critical moment. Your hasty and unintelligent impressions, if expressed in a reckless manner, might do much to bring about such a catastrophe. I must therefore stipulate that you keep such impressions to yourself. Let me speak to you as man to man, and ask you if your expressions, not being founded on knowledge, would be honest? So far from it, you will be bound in all fairness, in consideration of my releasing you and restoring you what you have ventured, to adopt and disseminate the views of an expert,—namely, mine."

"Let me put it into fewer words," said Joseph. "You will buy my stock, repaying me what I have disbursed, if, on my return, I say nothing of what I have seen, and express my perfect faith (adopting your views) in the success of the Amaranth?"

"You have stated the conditions a little barely, perhaps, but not incorrectly. I only ask for perfect fairness, as between man and man."

"One question first, Mr. Kanuck. Does Mr. Blessing know the *real* prospects of the Amaranth?"

"No man more thoroughly, I assure you, Mr. Asten. Indeed, without Mr. Blessing's enthusiastic concurrence in the enterprise, I doubt whether we could have carried the work so far towards success. His own stock, I may say to you,—since we understand each other,—was earned by his efforts. If you know him intimately, you know also that he has no visible means of support. But he has what is much more important to us,—a thorough knowledge of men and their means."

He rubbed his hands, and laughed softly. They had been walking rapidly during the conversation, and now came suddenly upon the farthest crest of the hills, where the ridge fell away to the bottom occupied by the Fluke wells. Both paused at this point.

"On the square, then!" said Mr. Kanuck, offering his hand. "Tell me where you will be to-morrow morning, and our business can be settled in five minutes. You will carry out your part of the bargain, as man to man, when you find that I carry out mine."

"Do you take me for an infernal scoundrel?" cried Joseph, boiling over with disgust and rage.

Mr. Kanuck stepped back a pace or two. His sallow face became livid, and there was murder in his eyes. He put his hand into his breast, and Joseph, facing him, involuntarily did the same. Not until long afterwards, when other experiences had taught him the significance of the movement, did he remember what it then meant.

"So! that's your game, is it?" his antagonist said, hissing the words through his teeth. "A spy, after all! Or a detective, perhaps? I was a fool to trust a milk-and-water face: but one thing I tell you,—you may get away, but come back again if you dare!"

Joseph said nothing, but gazed steadily in the man's eyes, and did not move from his position so long as he was within sight. Then, breathing deeply, as if relieved from the dread of an unknown danger, he swiftly descended the hill.

That evening, as he sat in the bar-room of a horrible shanty (called a hotel), farther up the river, he noticed a pair of eyes fixed intently upon him: they belonged to one of the workmen in the Amaranth ravine. The man made an almost imperceptible signal, and left the room. Joseph followed him.

"Hush!" whispered the former. "Don't come back to the hill; and get away from here to-morrow morning, if you can!" With these words he darted off and disappeared in the darkness.

The counsel was unnecessary. Joseph, with all his inexperience of the world, saw plainly that his only alternatives were loss—or connivance. Nothing was to be gained by following the vile business any further. He took the earliest possible train, and by the afternoon of the following day found himself again in the city.

He was conscious of no desire to meet Mr. Blessing, yet the pressure of his recent experience seemed to drive him irresistibly in that direction. When he rang the bell, it was with the hope that he should find nobody at home. Mr. Blessing, however, answered the summons, and after the first expression of surprise, ushered him into the parlor.

"I am quite alone," he said; "Mrs. Blessing is passing the evening with her sister, Mrs. Woollish, and Clementina is still at Long Branch. I believe it is as good as settled that we are to lose her; at least she has written to inquire the extent of my available funds, which, in her case, is tantamount to—very much more."

Joseph determined to avoid all digressions, and insist on the Amaranth speculation, once for all, being clearly discussed. He saw that his father-in-law became more uneasy and excited as he advanced in the story of his journey, and, when it was concluded, did not seem immediately prepared to reply. His suspicions, already aroused by Mr. Kanuck's expressions, were confirmed, and a hard, relentless feeling of hostility took possession of his heart.

"I—I really must look into this," Mr. Blessing stammered, at last. "It seems incredible: pardon me, but I would doubt the statements, did they come from other lips than yours. It is as if I had nursed a dove in my bosom, and unexpectedly found it to be a—a basilisk!"

"It can be no serious loss to you," said Joseph, "since you received your stock in return for services."

"That is true: I was not thinking of myself. The real sting of the cockatrice is, that I have innocently misled you."

"Yet I understood you to say you had ventured your all?"

"My all of hope—my all of expectation!" Mr. Blessing cried. "I dreamed I had overtaken the rainbow at last; but this—this is senna—quassia—aloes!" My nature is so confiding that I accept the possibilities of the future as present realities, and build upon them as if they were Quincy granite. And yet, with all my experience, my acknowledged sagacity, my acquaintance with the hidden labyrinths of finance, it seems impossible that I can be so deceived! There must be some hideous misunderstanding: I have calculated all the elements, prognosticated all the planetary aspects, so to speak, and have not found a whisper of failure!"

"You omitted one very important element," Joseph said.

"What is that? I might have employed a detective, it is true—"

"No!" Joseph replied. "Honesty!"

Mr. Blessing fell back in his chair, weeping bitterly.

"I deserve this!" he exclaimed. "I will not resent it. I forgive you in advance of the time when you shall recognize my sincere, my heartfelt wish to serve you! Go, go: let me not recriminate! I meant to be, and still mean to be, your friend: but spare my too confiding child!"

Without a word of good-by, Joseph took his hat and hastened from the house. At every step the abyss of dishonesty seemed to open deeper before his feet. Spare the too confiding child! Father and daughter were alike: both mean, both treacherous, both unpardonably false to him.

With such feelings he left the city, next morning, and made his way homewards.

22. WHITMAN'S PETER

The clear outlier of the young men in Whitman's life was a Rebel-soldier-turned-omnibus-conductor. They met nearly as miraculously as Joseph meets his friend Philip in Bayard Taylor's story:

> His name was Peter Doyle. He worked as a conductor on one of the large horse-drawn omnibuses—with seats enough to accommodate roughly twenty people—that traversed the capital streets. The two first met, during an evening downpour, when Whitman boarded Doyle's car at a stop along Pennsylvania Avenue.[33]

> [Doyle's recollection:] "You ask where I first met him? It is a curious story. We felt to each other at once. I was a conductor. The night was very stormy,—he had been over to see Burroughs before he came down to take the car—the storm was awful. Walt had his blanket—it was thrown round his shoulders—he seemed like an old sea-captain. He was the only passenger, it was a lonely night, so I thought I would go in and talk with him. Something in me made me do it and something in him drew me that way. He used to say there was something in me had the same effect on him. Anyway, I went into the car. We were familiar at once—I put my hand on his knee—we understood. He did not get out at the end of the trip—in fact went all the way back with me. I think the year of this was 1866. From that time on we were the biggest sort of friends."[40]

Whitman remained on the omnibus that first night, traveling past his stop, staying in that empty car with Doyle all the way to the end of the line. The poet's description is concise: "Love, love, love!"

Doyle was twenty-one years old and handsome, with blue eyes, wavy light-brown hair, and a mustache. At five-foot-eight, he was shorter than Whitman and slimmer. He had an easy smile and was quick to laughter, but his expressions were never entirely free of a certain sad aspect.[33]

They spent time together just as they first met, with hardly a single word needed to communicate:

> Whitman and Doyle went long stretches without exchanging a solitary word. "It was the most taciturn mutual admiration society I ever attended," a stranger who saw them together would recall. But they had the kind of relationship in which they savored small moments, little shared intimacies. One time, the two men bought a watermelon at a market and sat down in front to eat it. Whitman took out a pocketknife and cut it in half. Some people walking past snickered at the sight of two grown men gorging on watermelon. "They can have the laugh—we have the melon," Whitman told Doyle. Years later, both men would vividly remember this tiny episode.[33]

After Whitman's death and with Peter Doyle's consent, Richard Bucke published Whitman's letters to Doyle. Here is what John Addington Symonds (see: Chapter 15: Avowals to Walt Whitman, Chapter 20: Contemporary Camerados) says of the letters and the light they shed upon Whitman's "Calamus" poems; his thoughts are included in the introductory material of Dr. Bucke's *Calamus: A Series of Letters Written During the Years 1868-1880 by Walt Whitman to a Young Friend (Peter Doyle)*:

> I have been privileged to read a series of letters addressed by Whitman to a young man, whom I will call P., and who was tenderly beloved by him. They throw a flood of light upon "Calamus," and are superior to any commentary. It is greatly to be hoped that they may be published. Whitman, it seems, met P. at Washington not long before the year 1869 when the lad was about eighteen years of age. They soon became attached, Whitman's friendship being returned with at least equal warmth by P. The letters breathe a purity and simplicity of affection, a naïveté and reasonableness, which are very remarkable considering the unmistakable intensity of the emotion. Throughout them, Whitman shows the tenderest and wisest care for his young friend's welfare, helps him in material ways, and bestows upon him the best advice, the heartiest encouragement, without betraying any sign of patronage or preaching. Illness soon attacked Walt. He retired to Camden, and P., who was employed as "baggage-master on the freight trains" of a railway, was for long unable to visit him. There is something very wistful in the words addressed from a distance by the aging poet to this "son of responding kisses." I regret that we do not possess P.'s answers. Yet, probably, to most readers, they would not appear highly interesting; for it is clear he was only an artless and uncultured workman. – John Addington Symonds in *Walt Whitman—A Study*[3]

Dr. Bucke was careful to tiptoe around the exact nature of the relationship Whitman and Doyle shared in his introduction to *Calamus: A Series of Letters*, writing:

> That the friendship existing between Walt Whitman and Peter Doyle was, as compared with the average sentiment that passes under that name, exceptional and remarkable there can be no doubt, but it does not seem at all clear that there was anything about it which was out of the regular and ordinary course when considered as a fact in the life of Whitman.[3]

A passage from one of Whitman's letters to Doyle:

> About the "tiresome" all I have to say is—to say nothing—only a good smacking kiss, and many of them—and taking in return many, many, many, from my dear son—good loving ones too—which will do more credit to his lips than growling and complaining at his father.[3]

Peter Doyle drifted from Whitman after Whitman suffered a partial paralysis and moved in with his brother and sister-in-law in Camden.

> Whitman, for his part, remembered Doyle fondly [...]. "Pete was never a scholar: we had no scholar affinities," he told Traubel, "but he was a big rounded everyday working man full to the brim of the real substance of God." On another occasion Walt called Pete "a great big hearty full-blooded everyday divinely generous working man."[40]

> "It was at that time, in Washington, that I got to know Peter Doyle—a Rebel, a car-driver, a soldier. . . . Ah yes! we would walk together for miles and miles, never sated. Often we would go on for some time without a word, then talk. . . . Washington was then the grandest of all the cities for such strolls. . . . Oh! the long, long walks, way into the nights!—in the after hours—sometimes lasting till two or three in the morning! The air, the stars, the moon, the water—what a fulness of inspiration they imparted!—what exhilaration! . . . I remember one place in Maryland in particular to which we would go. How splendid, above all, was the moon—the full moon, the half moon: and then the wonder, the delight, of the silences. . . . It was a great, a precious, a memorable, experience. To get the ensemble of *Leaves of Grass* you have got to include such things as these—the walks, Pete's friendship: yes, such things: they are absolutely necessary to the completion of the story."[39]

Doyle remembered Whitman just as fondly when Dr. Bucke and Horace Traubel interviewed him after Whitman's death:

"I have Walt's raglan here [*goes to closet—puts it on*], I now and then put it on, lay down, think I am in the old times. Then he is with me again. It's the only thing I kept amongst many old things. When I get it on and stretched out on the old sofa I am very well contented. It is like Aladdin's lamp. I do not ever for a minute lose the old man. He is always near by. When I am in trouble—in a crisis—I ask myself, 'What would Walt have done under these circumstances?' and whatever I decide Walt would have done that I do."[3]

Traubel records that Doyle made an appearance at Whitman's funeral:

Whole row of reporters in hallway, ranged up the stairs. People curious to see Walt's room, but we soon cleared them all out and locked the doors. . . . Someone was sure Peter Doyle was seen somewhere in the crowd, but I saw nothing of him till we had got to Harleigh, when he was pointed out to me (by Burroughs) up the hill, twirling a switch in his hand, his tall figure and big soft hat impressively set against the white-blue sky. (Returning, we stopped our carriage, seeing him on the road, leisurely walking, and Burroughs called him, he running up, shaking hands all around and calmly talking some to us, as to himself and Walt. Is on a Providence line of railroad. . . . Seemed immobile, not greatly moved by the occasion, yet was sincere and simple and expressed in his demeanor the powers by which he must have attracted Walt.)[39]

It seems that Whitman, for a time, had found what he was looking for just as the protagonist in *Joseph and His Friend* does. From one of his notebooks, Whitman describes a scene reminiscent of the moment when Philip, concerned that Joseph is contemplating suicide at the water's edge, kisses and comforts him, to remind him what life is worth living for:

Fatigued by their journey they sat down on Nature's divan whence they regarded the sky. Pressing one another's hands, shoulder to shoulder, neither knowing why, both became oppressed, their mouths opened, without uttering a word they kissed one another. Near them the hyacinth and the violet marrying their perfume, on raising their heads they both saw God who smiled at them from his azure balcony: Love one another[,] said he[,] it is for that I have clothed your path in velvet; kiss one another, I am not looking. Love one another, love one another and if you are happy, instead of a prayer to thank me, kiss again.[40]

XXIII

JULIA'S EXPERIMENT

IN THE MEANTIME the Hopetons had left for the sea-shore, and the two women, after a drive to Magnolia, remained quietly on the farm. Julia employed the days in studying Lucy with a soft, stealthy, unremitting watchfulness which the latter could not suspect, since, in the first place, it was a faculty quite unknown to her, and, secondly, it would have seemed absurd because inexplicable. Neither could she guess with what care Julia's manner and conversation were adapted to her own. She was only surprised to find so much earnest desire to correct faults, such artless transparency of nature. Thus an interest quite friendly took the place of her former repulsion of feeling, of which she began to be sincerely ashamed.

Moreover, Julia's continual demonstration of her love for Joseph, from which Lucy at first shrank with a delicate tremor of the heart, soon ceased to affect her. Nay, it rather seemed to interpose a protecting barrier between her present and the painful memory of her past self. She began to suspect that all regret was now conquered, and rejoiced in the sense of strength which could only thus be made clear to her mind. Her feeling towards Joseph became that of a sister or a dear woman friend; there could be no harm in cherishing it; she found a comfort in speaking to Julia of his upright, unselfish character, his guilelessness and kindness of heart.

The work upon the house was nearly finished, but new and more alarming bills began to come in; and worse was in store. There was a chimney-piece, "the loveliest ivory veins through the green marble," Julia said, which she had ordered from the city; there were boxes and packages of furniture already on hand, purchased without Joseph's knowledge and with entire faith in the virtues of the Amaranth. Although she still clung to that faith with a desperate grip, the sight of the boxes did not give her the same delight as she had felt in ordering them. She saw the necessity of being prepared, in advance, for either alternative. It was not in her nature to dread any scene or circumstance of life (although she had found the *appearance* of timidity very available, and could assume it admirably); the question which perplexed her was, how to retain and strengthen her ascendency over Joseph?

It is needless to say that the presence of Lucy Henderson was a part of her plan, although she held a more important service in reserve. Lucy's warm, frank expressions of friendship for Joseph gave her great satisfaction, and she was exhaustless in inventing ways to call them forth.

"You look quite like another person, Lucy," she would say; "I really think the rest has done you good."

"I am sure of it," Lucy answered.

"Then you must be in no hurry to leave. We must build you up, as the doctors say; and, besides, if—if this speculation *should* be unfortunate —O, I don't dare to think of it!—there will be such a comfort to me, and I am sure to Joseph also, in having you here until we have learned to bear it. We should not allow our minds to dwell on it so much, you know; we should make an exertion to hide our disappointment in your presence, and that would be *such* a help! Now you will say I am borrowing trouble, but do, pray, make allowances for me, Lucy! Think how everything has been kept from me that I ought to have known!"

"Of course, I will stay a little while for your sake," Lucy answered; "but Joseph is a man, and most men bear bad luck easily. He would hardly thank me for condoling with him."

"O, no, no!" Julia cried; "he thinks *everything* of you! He was *so* anxious for you to come here! he said to me, 'Lucy Henderson is a noble, true-hearted girl, and you will love her at once,' as I did, Lucy, when I first saw you, but without knowing why, as I now do."

A warm color came into Lucy's face, but she only shook her head and said nothing.

The two women had just risen from the breakfast-table the next morning, when a shadow fell into the room through the front window, and a heavy step was heard on the stone pavement of the veranda. Julia gave a little start and shriek, and seized Lucy's arm. The door opened and Joseph was there. He had risen before daybreak and taken the earliest train from the city. He had scarcely slept for two nights; his face was stern and haggard, and the fatigue, instead of exhausting, had only added to his excitement.

Julia sprang forward, threw her arms around him, and kissed him repeatedly. He stood still and passively endured the caress, without returning it; then, stepping forward, he gave his hand to Lucy. She felt that it was cold and moist, and she did not attempt to repress the quick sympathy which came into her face and voice.

Julia guessed something of the truth instantly, and nothing but the powerful necessity of continuing to play her part enabled her to conceal the bitter anger which the contrast between Joseph's greeting to her and to Lucy aroused in her heart. She stood for a moment as if paralyzed, but in reality to collect herself; then, approaching her husband, she stammered forth: "O, Joseph—I'm afraid—I don't dare to ask you what—what news you bring. You didn't write—I've been so uneasy—and now I see from your face—that something is wrong."

He did not answer.

"Don't tell me all at once, if it's very bad!" she then cried: "but, no! it's my duty to hear it, my duty to bear it,—Lucy has taught me that,—tell me all, tell me *all*, this moment!"

"You and your father have ruined me: that is all."

"Joseph!" The word sounded like the essence of tender protest, of heart-breaking reproach. Lucy rose quietly and moved towards the door.

"Don't leave me, Lucy!" was Julia's appeal.

"It is better that I should go," Lucy answered, in a faint voice, and left the room.

"But, Joseph," Julia resumed, with a wild, distracted air, "why do you say such terrible things? I really do not know what you mean. What have you learned? what have you seen?"

"I have seen the Amaranth!"

"Well! Is there no oil?"

"O yes, plenty of oil!" he laughed; "skunk oil and rattlesnake oil! It is one of the vilest cheats that the Devil ever put into the minds of bad men."

"O, poor pa!" Julia cried; "what a terrible blow to him!"

"'Poor pa!' Yes, my discovery of the cheat is a terrible blow to 'poor pa,'—he did not calculate on its being found out so soon. When I learned from Kanuck that all the stock he holds was given to him for services,—that is, for getting the money out of the pockets of innocents like myself,—you may judge how much pity I feel for poor pa! I told him the fact to his face, last night, and he admitted it."

"Then," said Julia, "if the others know nothing, he may be able to sell his stock to-day,—his and yours; and we may not lose much after all."

"I should have sent you to the oil region, instead of going myself," Joseph answered, with a sneer. "You and Kanuck would soon have come to terms. He offered to take my stock off my hands, provided I would go back to the city and make such a report of the speculation as he would dictate."

"*And you didn't do it?*" Julia's voice rose almost to a scream, as the words burst involuntarily from her lips.

The expression on Joseph's face showed her that she had been rash; but the words were said, and she could only advance, not recede.

"It is *perfectly* legitimate in business," she continued. "Every investment in the Amaranth was a venture,—every stockholder knew that he risked losing his money! There is not one that would not save himself in that way, if he had the chance. But you pride yourself on being so much better than other men! Mr. Chaffinch is right; you have what he calls a 'moral pride'! You—"

"Stop!" Joseph interrupted. "Who was it that professed such concern about my faith? Who sent Mr. Chaffinch to insult me?"

"Faith and business are two different things: all the churches know that. There was Mr. Sanctus, in the city: he subscribed ten thousand dollars to the Church of the Acceptance: he couldn't pay it, and they levied on his property, and sold him out of house and home! Really, you are as ignorant of the world as a baby!"

"God keep me so, then!" he exclaimed.

"However," she resumed, after a pause, "since you insist on our bearing the loss, I shall expect of your moral pride that you bear it patiently, if not cheerfully. It is far from being ruin to us. The rise in property will very likely balance it, and you will still be worth what you were."

"That is not all," he said. "I will not mention my greatest loss, for you are incapable of understanding it; but how much else have you saddled me with? Let me have a look at it!"

He crossed the hall and entered the new apartment, Julia following. Joseph inspected the ceiling, the elaborate and overladen cornices, the marble chimney-piece, and finally peered into the boxes and packages, not trusting himself to speak while the extent of the absurd splendor to which she had committed him grew upon his mind. Finally he said, striving to make his voice calm, although it trembled in his throat: "Since you were so free to make all these purchases, perhaps you will tell me how they are to be paid for?"

"Let me manage it, then," she answered. "There is no hurry. These country mechanics are always impatient,—I should call them impertinent, and I should like to teach them a lesson. Sellers are under obligations to the buyers, and they are bound to be accommodating. They have so many bills which are never paid, that an extension of time is the least they can do. Why, they will always wait a year, two years, three years, rather than lose."

"I suppose so."

"Then," said Julia, deceived by Joseph's quiet tone, "their profits are so enormous, that it would only be fair to reduce the bills. I am sure, that if I were to mention that you were embarrassed by heavy losses, and press them hard, they would compromise with me on a moderate amount. You know they allow what is called a margin for losses,—pa told me, but I forget how much,—they always expect to lose a certain percentage; and, of course, it can make no difference by whom they lose it. You understand, don't you?"

"Yes: it is very plain."

"Pa could help me to get both a reduction and an extension of time. The bills have not all been sent, and it will be better to wait two or three months after they have come in. If the dealers are a little uneasy in advance, they will be all the readier to compromise afterwards."

Joseph walked up and down the hollow room, with his hands clasped behind his back and his eyes fixed upon the floor. Suddenly he stopped before her and said: "There is another way."

"Not a better one, I am certain."

"The furniture has not yet been unpacked, and can be returned to them uninjured. Then the bills need not be paid at all."

"And we should be the laughing-stock of the neighborhood!" she cried, her eyes flashing. "I *never* heard of anything so ridiculous! If the worst comes to the worst, you can sell Bishop those fifty acres over the hill, which he stands ready to take, any day. But you'd rather have a dilapidated house —no parlor,—guests received in the dining-room and the kitchen,—the Hopetons and your friends, the Helds, sneering at us behind our backs! And what would your credit be worth? We shall not even get trusted for groceries at the village store, if you leave things as they are!"

Joseph groaned, speaking to himself rather than answering her: "Is there no way out of this? What is done is done; shall I submit to it, and try to begin anew? or—"

He did not finish the sentence. Julia turned her head, so that only the chimney-piece and the furniture could see the sparkle of triumph in her eyes. She felt that she had maintained her position; and, what was far more, she now clearly saw the course by which she could secure it.

She left the room, drawing a full breath of relief as the door closed behind her. The first shock of the evil news was over, and it had not fallen quite so heavily as she had feared. There were plenty of devices in store whereby all that was lost might be recovered. Had not her life at home been an unbroken succession of devices? Was she not seasoned to all manner of ups and downs, and wherefore should this first failure disconcert her? The loss of the money was, in reality, much less important to her than the loss of her power over Joseph. Weak as she had supposed him to be, he had shown a fierce and unexpected resistance, which must be suppressed now, or it might crush her whole plan of life. It seemed to her that he was beginning to waver: should she hasten a scheme by which she meant to entrap him into submission,—a subtle and dangerous scheme, which must either wholly succeed, or, wholly failing, involve her in its failure?

Rapidly turning over the question in her mind, she entered her bed-room. Locking the door, she walked directly to the looking-glass; the curtain was drawn from the window, and a strong light fell upon her face.

"This will never do!" she said to herself. "The anxiety and excitement have made me thin again and I seem to have no color." She unfastened her dress, bared her neck, and pushed the ringlets behind her ears. "I look pinched; a little more, and I shall look old. If I were a perfect brunette or a perfect blonde, there would be less difficulty; but I have the most provoking, unmanageable complexion! I must bring on the crisis at once, and then see if I can't fill out these hollows."

She heard the front door opening, and presently saw Joseph on the lawn. He looked about for a moment, with a heavy, bewildered air, and then slowly turned towards the garden. She withdrew from the window, hesitated a moment, murmured to herself, "I will try, there cannot be a better time!" and then, burying her face in her hands and sobbing, rushed to Lucy's room.

"O Lucy!" she cried, "help me, or I am lost! How can I tell you? it is harder than I ever dreamed!"

"Is the loss so very serious,—so much more than you feared?" Lucy asked.

"Not that—O, if that were all! But Joseph—" Here Julia's sobs became almost hysterical. "He is so cruel; I *did* advise him, as I told you, for *his* sake, and now he says that pa and I have combined to cheat him! I don't think he knows how dreadful his words are. I would sooner die than hear any more of them! Go to him, Lucy; he is in the garden; perhaps he will listen to you. I am afraid, and I never thought I should be afraid of *him!*"

"It is very, very sad," said Lucy. "But if he is in such an excited condition he will surely resent my coming. What can I say?"

"Say only what you heard me speak! Tell him of my anxiety, my self-reproach! Tell him that even if he *will* believe that pa meant to deceive him, he must not believe it of me! You know, Lucy, how he wrongs me in his thoughts; if you knew how hard it is to be wronged by a husband, you would pity me!"

"I do pity you, Julia, from my very heart; and the proof of it is, that I will try to do what you ask, against my own sense of its prudence. If Joseph repels my interference, I shall not blame him."

"Heaven bless you, Lucy! He will not repel you, he cannot!" Julia sobbed. "I will lie down and try to grow calm." She rose from the bed, upon which she had flung herself, and tottered through the door. When she had reached her own room, she again looked at her image in the glass, nodded and smiled.

Lucy walked slowly along, the garden paths, plucking a flower or two, and irresolute how to approach Joseph. At last, descending the avenue of box, she found him seated in the semicircular enclosure, gazing steadfastly down the valley, but (she was sure) not seeing the landscape. As he turned his head at her approach, she noticed that his eyelids were reddened and his lips compressed with an expression of intense pain.

"Sit down, Lucy: I am a grim host, to-day," he said, with a melancholy attempt at a smile.

Lucy had come to him with a little womanly indignation, for Julia's sake, in her heart; but it vanished utterly, and the tears started into her eyes. For a moment she found it impossible to speak.

"I shall not talk of my ignorance any more, as I once did," Joseph continued. "If there is a class in the school of the world, graded according to experience of human meanness and treachery and falsehood, I ought to stand at the head."

Lucy stretched out her hand in protest. "Do not speak so bitterly, Joseph; it pains me to hear you."

"How would you have me speak?"

"As a man who will not see ruin before him because a part of his property happens to slip from him,—nay, if all were lost! I always took you to be liberal, Joseph, never careful of money for money's sake, and I cannot understand how your nature should be changed now, even though you have been the victim of some dishonesty."

"'Some dishonesty'! You are thinking only of money: what term would you give to the betrayal of a heart, the ruin of a life?"

"Surely, Joseph, you do not, you cannot mean—"

"My wife, of course. It needed no guessing."

"Joseph!" Lucy cried, seizing the opportunity, "indeed you do her wrong! I know what anxiety she has suffered during your absence. She blamed herself for having advised you to risk so much in an uncertain speculation, dreaded your disappointment, resolved to atone for it, if she could! She may have been rash and thoughtless, but she never meant to deceive you. If you are disappointed in some qualities, you should not shut your eyes and refuse to see others. I know, now, that I have myself not been fair in my judgment of Julia. A nearer acquaintance has led me to conceive what disadvantages of education, for which she is not responsible, she is obliged to overcome: she sees, she admits them, and she *will* overcome them. You, as her husband, are bound to show her a patient kindness—"

"Enough!" Joseph interrupted; "I see that you have touched pitch, also. Lucy, your first instinct was right. The woman whom I am bound to look upon as my wife is false and selfish in every fibre of her nature; how false and selfish I only can know, for to *me* she takes off her mask!"

"Do you believe *me*, then?" Lucy's words were slightly defiant. She had not quite understood the allusion to touching pitch, and Joseph's indifference to her advocacy seemed to her unfeeling.

"I begin to fear that Philip was right," said Joseph, not heeding her question. "Life is relentless: ignorance or crime, it is all the same. And if God cares less about our individual wrongs than we flatter ourselves He does, what do we gain by further endurance? Here is Lucy Henderson, satisfied that my wife is a suffering angel; thinks *my* nature is changed, that *I* am cold-hearted and cruel, while I know Lucy to be true and noble, and deceived by the very goodness of her own heart!"

He lifted his head, looked in her face a moment, and then went on: —

"I am sick of masks; we all wear them. Do you want to know the truth, Lucy? When I look back I can see it very clearly, now. A little more than a year ago the one girl who began to live in my thoughts was *you!* Don't interrupt me: I am only speaking of what *was*. When I went to Warriner's, it was in the hope of meeting you, not Julia Blessing. It was not yet love that I felt, but I think it would have grown to that, if I had not been led away by the cunningest arts ever a woman devised. I will not speculate on what might have been: if I had loved you, perhaps there would have been no return: had there been, I should have darkened the life of a friend. But this I say; I honor and esteem you, Lucy, and the loss of your friendship, if I now lose it, is another evil service which my wife has done me."

Joseph little suspected how he was torturing Lucy. She must have been more than woman, had not a pang of wild regret for the lost fortune, and a sting of bitter resentment against the woman who had stolen it, wrung her heart. She became deadly pale, and felt that her whole body was trembling.

"Joseph," she said, "you should not, must not, speak so to me."

"I suppose not," he answered, letting his head sink wearily; "it is certainly not conventional; but it is true, for all that! I could tell you the whole story, for I can read it backwards, from now to the beginning, without misunderstanding a word. It would make no difference; she is simple, natural, artless, amiable, for all the rest of the world, while to me—"

There was such despondency in his voice and posture, that Lucy, now longing more than ever to cheer him, and yet discouraged by the failure of her first attempt, felt sorely troubled.

"You mistake me, Joseph," she said, at last, "if you think you have lost my friendship, my sincerest sympathy. I can see that your disappointment is a bitter one, and my prayer is that you will not make it bitterer by thrusting from you the hopeful and cheerful spirit you once showed. We all have our sore trials."

Lucy found her own words very, mechanical, but they were the only ones that came to her lips. Joseph did not answer; he still sat, stooping, with his elbows on his knees, and his forehead resting on his palms.

"If I am deceived in Julia," she began again, "it is better to judge too kindly than too harshly. I know you cannot change your sentence against her now, nor, perhaps, very soon. But you are bound to her for life, and you must labor—it is your sacred duty—to make that life smoother and brighter for both. I do not know how, and I have no right to condemn you if you fail. But, Joseph, make the attempt now, when the most unfortunate experience that is likely to come to you is over; make it, and it may chance that, little by little, the old confidence will return, and you will love her again."

Joseph started to his feet. "Love her!" he exclaimed, with suppressed passion,—"love her! I hate her!"

There was a hissing, rattling sound, like that of some fierce animal at bay. The thick foliage of two of the tall box-trees was violently parted. The branches snapped and gave way: Julia burst through, and stood before them.

24. SIGNS OF THE TIME

Among the men who sought and reached for their friends, it is important to remember the context and difficulty of even making the effort, to remember why some men (like Stoker and Melville) did not try too hard lest they end up committing a suicide of some sort (like Walter Franklin, the friend of Drake and Halleck [see <u>Chapter 20: Contemporary Camerados</u>], and Oscar Wilde effectively did by being so bold).

Had Halleck been born in an earlier generation, he would have witnessed a sodomy trial resulting in the execution of Guilford's own founding father. [...] In 1646, William Plaine (or Plane), who seven years earlier had founded the town, was executed. Plaine, "being a married man, had committed sodomy with two persons in England" prior to having "corrupted a great part of the youth of Guilford by masturbation . . . above a hundred times." Plaine did not appear to have been coercive, and the tone of resistance in his testimony showed no remorse for challenging either sexual propriety or theological authority. John Winthrop, himself an author of homoerotic correspondence in the Jonathan and David vein, accused Plaine of implanting young men with "the seeds of atheism," not to mention his biological seed. While sexual accusations against Plaine appear sound, "the term *sodomites* was used to condemn those who held unorthodox theological beliefs" as well. Even those not charged with sodomy who objected to the political inducement of colonial sodomy trials faced dire consequences by 1624. In contradictory terms, the married Plaine was also guilty of "frustrating the ordinance of marriage and hindering the generation of mankind." [...] Two years before Halleck's birth, George Washington reported the discharge of a lieutenant who had attempted sodomy on another soldier and was to be "drummed out of Camp . . . by all the Drummers and Fifers in the Army never to return; The Drummers and Fifers to attend on the Grand Parade." [...] Connecticut state law officially condoned killing homosexuals until Halleck was in his thirties.[22]

Even with all secrecy and attempts at discretion, that is the world in which these stories and poems were written. Wilde took part in an anonymous work too, *Teleny*, anonymous because it was more explicit than anyone could dare to produce publicly:

In 1889, Charles Hirsch (later to become a publisher in Paris) was running the Librairie Parisienne on Coventry Street in London. Among his regular clients was Oscar Wilde, who purchased from him not only books in French (among them novels by Zola and Maupassant), but what Hirsch calls works of a "Socratic" nature. Nor did Wilde usually come alone to the bookstore; often he was accompanied by "distinguished young men" of a literary or artistic appearance who showed him "a familiar deference."

One afternoon Wilde arrived at the bookstore with a small, carefully sealed package, which he asked Hirsch to hold for a friend who would show him Wilde's card. Hirsch agreed, and in due course one of the young men Hirsch had met in Wilde's company came by for the package. Several days later the same young man brought it back, leaving it to be picked up by another young man. Altogether three exchanges of this kind took place, and the last young man, "less discreet" than the other two, brought back the package in a rather "poorly wrapped" condition. When Hirsch opened it, he discovered the manuscript of a novel transcribed in several different handwritings, and full of marginal additions and erasures. He misread the title as *Feleny*. "It was evident," he wrote, "that several writers of unequal merit had collaborated on this anonymous but profoundly interesting work."

One wonders, in this post-Freudian age, at Hirsch's misreading. After all, wouldn't publishing *Teleny*—as Hirsch would later do in a French translation—be to risk, in England, conviction on a *felony* charge? (Curiously, the English edition sets the story in Paris; the French one in London.)[30]

XXIV

FATE

THE FACE THAT so suddenly glared upon them was that of a Gorgon. The ringlets were still pushed behind her ears and the narrowness of the brow was entirely revealed; her eyes were full of cold, steely light; the nostrils were violently drawn in, and the lips contracted, as if in a spasm, so that the teeth were laid bare. Her hands were clenched, and there was a movement in her throat as of imprisoned words or cries; but for a moment no words came.

Lucy, who had started to her feet at the first sound, felt the blood turn chill in her veins, and fell, rather than sank, upon the seat again.

Joseph was hardly surprised, and wholly reckless. This eavesdropping was nothing worse than he already knew; indeed, there was rather a comfort in perceiving that he had not overestimated her capacity for treachery. There was now no limit; anything was possible.

"There is *one* just law, after all," he said, "the law that punishes listeners. You have heard the truth, for once. You have snared and trapped me, but I don't take to my captor more kindly than any other animal. From this moment I choose my own path, and if you still wish to appear as my wife, you must adapt your life to mine!"

"You mean to brazen it out, do you!" Julia cried, in a strange, hoarse, unnatural voice. "That's not so easy! I have not listened to no purpose: I have a hold upon your precious 'moral pride' at last!"

Joseph laughed scornfully.

"Yes, laugh, but it is in my hands to make or break you! There is enough decent sentiment in this neighborhood to crush a married man who dares to make love to an unmarried girl! As to the girl who sits still and listens to it, I say nothing; her reputation is no concern of mine!"

Lucy uttered a faint cry of horror.

"If you choose to be so despicable," said Joseph, "you will force me to set my truth against your falsehood. Wherever you tell your story, I shall follow with mine. It will be a wretched, a degrading business; but for the sake of Lucy's good name, I have no alternative. I have borne suspicion, misrepresentation, loss of credit,—brought upon me by you,—patiently, because they affected only myself; but since I am partly responsible in bringing to this house a guest for your arts to play upon and entrap, I am doubly bound to protect her against you. But I tell you, Julia, beware! I am desperate; and it is ill meddling with a desperate man! You may sneer at my moral pride, but you dare not forget that I have another quality,—manly self-respect,—which it will be dangerous to offend."

If Julia did not recognize, in that moment, that her subject had become her master, it was because the real, unassumed rage which convulsed her did not allow her to perceive anything clearly. Her first impulse was to scream and shriek, that servant and farm-hand might hear her, and then to repeat her accusation before them; but Joseph's last words, and the threatening sternness of his voice withheld her.

"So?" she said, at last; "*this* is the man who was all truth, and trust, and honor! With you the proverb seems to be reversed; it's off with the new love and on with the old. You can insult and threaten me in *her* presence! Well—go on: play out your little love-scene: I shall not interrupt you. I have heard enough to darken my life from this day!"

She walked away from them, up the avenue. Her dress was torn, her arms scratched and bleeding. She had played her stake and failed,—miserably, hopelessly failed. Her knees threatened to give way under her at every step, but she forced herself to walk erect, and thus reached the house without once looking back.

Joseph and Lucy mechanically followed her with their eyes. Then they turned and gazed at each other a moment without speaking. Lucy was very pale, and the expression of horror had not yet left her face.

"She told me to come to you," she stammered. She begged me, with tears, to try and soften your anger against her; and then—oh, it is monstrous!"

"Now I see the plan!" Joseph exclaimed; "and I, in my selfish recklessness, saying what there was no need to utter, have almost done as she calculated,—have exposed you to this outrage! Why should I have recalled the past at all? I was not taking off a mask, I was only showing a scar—no, not even a scar, but a bruise!—which I ought to have forgotten. Forget it, too, Lucy, and, if you can, forgive me!"

"It is easy to forgive—everything but my own blindness," Lucy answered. "But there is one thing which I must do immediately: I must leave this house!"

"I see that," said Joseph, sadly. Then, as if speaking to himself, he murmured: "Who knows what friends will come to it in the future? Well, I will bear what can be borne; and afterwards,—there is Philip's valley. A free outlaw is better than a fettered outlaw!"

Lucy feared that his mind was wandering. He straightened himself to his full height, drew a deep breath, and exclaimed: "Action is a sedative in such cases, isn't it? Dennis has gone to the mill; I will get the other horse from the field and drive you home. Or, stay! will you not go to Philip Held's cottage for a day or two? I think his sister asked you to come."

"No, no!" cried Lucy; "you must not go! I will wait for Dennis."

"No one must suspect what has happened here this morning, unless Julia compels me to make it known, and I don't think she will. It is, therefore, better that I should take you. It will put me, I hope, in a more rational frame of mind. Go quietly to your room and make your preparations. I will see Julia, and if there is no further scene now, there will be none of the kind henceforth. She is cunning when she is calm."

On reaching the house Joseph went directly to his wife's bed-room. The necessity of an immediate interview could not be avoided, since Lucy was to leave. When he opened the door, Julia, who was bending over an open drawer of her bureau, started up with a little cry of alarm. She closed the drawer hastily, and began to arrange her hair at the mirror. Her face in the glass was flushed, but its expression was sullen and defiant.

"Julia," he said, as coolly as possible, "I am going to take Lucy home. Of course you understand that she cannot stay here an hour longer. You overheard my words to her, and you know just how much they were worth. I expect now, that—for *your* sake as much as hers or mine—you will behave towards her at parting in such a way that the servants may find no suggestions of gossip or slander."

"And if I don't choose to obey you?"

"I am not commanding. I propose a course which your own mind must find sensible. You have 'a deuced sharp intellect,' as your father said, on our wedding-day."

Joseph bit his tongue: he felt that he might have omitted this sting. But he was so little accustomed to victory, that he did not guess how thoroughly he had already conquered.

"Pa loved me, nevertheless," she said, and burst into tears.

Her emotion seemed real, but he mistrusted it.

"What can I do?" she sobbed: "I will try. I thought I was your wife, but I am not much more than your slave."

The foolish pity again stole into Joseph's heart, although he set his teeth and clenched his hands against it. "I am going for the horse," he said, in a kinder tone. "When I come back from this drive, this afternoon, I hope I shall find you willing to discuss our situation dispassionately, as I mean to do. We have not known each other fairly before to-day, and our plan of life must be rearranged."

It was a relief to walk forth, across the silent, sunny fields; and Joseph had learned to accept a slight relief as a substitute for happiness. The feeling that the inevitable crisis was over, gave him, for the first time in months, a sense of liberation. There was still a dreary and painful task before him, and he hardly knew why he should be so cheerful; but the bright, sweet currents of his blood were again in motion, and the weight upon his heart was lifted by some impatient, joyous energy.

The tempting vision of Philip's valley, which had haunted him from time to time, faded away. The angry tumult through which he had passed appeared to him like a fever, and he rejoiced consciously in the beginning of his spiritual convalescence. If he could simply suspend Julia's active interference in his life, he might learn to endure his remaining duties. He was yet young; and how much strength and knowledge had come to him—through sharpest pain, it was true—in a single year! Would he willingly return to his boyish innocence of the world, if that year could be erased from his life? He was not quite sure. Yet his nature had not lost the basis of that innocent time, and he felt that he must still build his future years upon it.

Thus meditating, he caught the obedient horse, led him to the barn, and harnessed him to the light carriage which Julia was accustomed to use. His anxiety concerning her probable demeanor returned as he entered the house. The two servant-women were both engaged, in the hall, in some sweeping or scouring operation, and might prove to be very inconvenient witnesses. The workmen in the new parlor—fortunately, he thought—were absent that day.

Lucy Henderson, dressed for the journey, sat in the dining-room. "I think I will go to Madeline Held for a day or two," she said; "I made a half-promise to visit her after your return."

"Where is Julia?"

"In her bed-room. I have not seen her. I knocked at the door, but there was no answer."

Joseph's trouble returned. "I will see her myself," he said, sternly; "she forgets what is due to a guest."

"No, I will go again," Lucy urged, rising hastily; "perhaps she did not hear me."

She followed him into the hall. Scarcely had he set his foot upon the first step of the staircase, when the bed-room door above suddenly burst open, and Julia, with a shriek of mortal terror, tottered down to the landing. Her face was ashy, and the dark-blue rings around her sunken eyes made them seem almost like the large sockets of a skull. She leaned against the railing, breathing short and hard.

Joseph sprang up the steps, but as he approached her she put out her right hand, and pushed against his breast with all her force, crying out: "Go away! You have killed me!"

The next moment she fell senseless upon the landing.

Joseph knelt and tried to lift her. "Good God! she is dead!" he exclaimed.

"No," said Lucy, after taking Julia's wrist, "it is only a fainting fit. Bring some water, Susan."

The frightened woman, who had followed them, rushed down the stairs.

"But she must be ill, very ill," Lucy continued. "This is not an ordinary swoon. Perhaps the violent excitement has brought about some internal injury. You must send for a physician as soon as possible."

"And Dennis not here! I ought not to leave her; what shall I do?"

"Go yourself, and instantly! The carriage is ready. I will stay and do all that can be done during your absence."

Joseph delayed until, under the influence of air and water, Julia began to recover consciousness. Then he understood Lucy's glance,—the women were present and she dared not speak,—that he should withdraw before Julia could recognize him.

He did not spare the horse, but the hilly road tried his patience. It was between two and three miles to the house of the nearest physician, and he only arrived, anxious and breathless, to find that the gentleman had been called away to attend another patient. Joseph was obliged to retrace part of his road, and drive some distance in the opposite direction, in order to summon a second. Here, however, he was more fortunate. The physician was just sitting down to an early dinner, which he persisted in finishing, assuring

Joseph, after ascertaining such symptoms of the case as the latter was able to describe, that it was probably a nervous attack, "a modified form of hysteria." Notwithstanding he violated his own theory of digestion by eating rapidly, the minutes seemed intolerably long. Then his own horse must be harnessed to his own sulky, during which time he prepared a few doses of valerian, belladonna, and other palliatives, which he supposed might be needed.

Meanwhile, Lucy and the woman had placed Julia in her own bed, and applied such domestic restoratives as they could procure, but without any encouraging effect. Julia appeared to be conscious, but she shook her head when they spoke to her, and even, so Lucy imagined, attempted to turn it away. She refused the tea, the lavender and ginger they brought, and only drank water in long, greedy draughts. In a little while she started up, with clutchings and incoherent cries, and then slowly sank back again, insensible.

The second period of unconsciousness was longer and more difficult to overcome. Lucy began to be seriously alarmed as an hour, two hours, passed by, and Joseph did not return. Dennis was despatched in search of him, carrying also a hastily penciled note to Madeline Held, and then Lucy, finding that she could do nothing more, took her seat by the window and watched the lane, counting the seconds, one by one, as they were ticked off by the clock, in the hall.

Finally a horse's head appeared above the hedge, where it curved around the shoulder of the hill: then the top of a carriage,—Joseph at last! The physician's sulky was only a short distance in the rear. Lucy hurried down and met Joseph at the gate.

"No better,—worse, I fear," she said, answering his look.

"Dr. Hartman," he replied,—"Worrall was away from home,—thinks it is probably a nervous attack. In that case it can soon be relieved."

"I hope so, but I fancy there is danger."

The doctor now arrived, and after hearing Lucy's report, shook his head. "It is not an ordinary case of hysteria," he remarked; "let me see her at once."

When they entered the room Julia opened her eyes languidly, fixed them on Joseph, and slowly lifted her hand to her head. "What has happened to me?" she murmured, in a hardly audible whisper.

"You had a fainting fit," he answered, "and I have brought the doctor. This is Dr. Hartman; you do not know him, but he will help you: tell him how you feel, Julia!"

"Cold!" she said, "cold! Sinking down somewhere! *Will* he lift me up?"

The physician made a close examination, but seemed to become more perplexed as he advanced. He administered only a slight stimulant, and then withdrew from the bedside. Lucy and the servant left the room, at his request, to prepare some applications.

"There is something unusual here," he whispered, drawing Joseph aside. "She has been sinking rapidly since the first attack. The vital force is very low: it is in conflict with some secret enemy, and it cannot resist much longer, unless we discover that enemy at once. I will do my best to save her, but I do not yet see how."

He was interrupted by a noise from the bed. Julia was vainly trying to rise: her eyes were wide and glaring. "No, no!" came from her lips, "I will not die! I heard you. Joseph, I will try—to be different—but—I must live—for that!"

Then her utterance became faint and indistinct, and she relapsed into unconsciousness. The physician re-examined her with a grave, troubled face. "She need not be conscious," he said, "for the next thing I shall do. I will not interrupt this syncope at once; it may, at least, prolong the struggle. What have they been giving her?"

He picked up, one by one, the few bottles of the household pharmacy which stood upon the bureau. Last of all, he found an empty glass shoved behind one of the supports of the mirror. He looked into it, held it against the light, and was about to set it down again, when he fancied that there was a misty appearance on the bottom, as if from some delicate sediment. Stepping to the window, he saw that he had not been mistaken. He collected a few of the minute granulations on the tip of his forefinger, touched them to his tongue, and, turning quickly to Joseph, whispered:—

"She is poisoned!"

"Impossible!" Joseph exclaimed; "she could not have been so mad!"

"It is as I tell you! This form of the operation of arsenic is very unusual, and I did not suspect it; but now I remember that it is noted in the books. Repeated syncopes, utter nervous prostration, absence of the ordinary burning and vomiting, and signs of rapid dissolution; it fits the case exactly! If I had some oxy-hydrate of iron, there might still be a possibility, but I greatly fear—"

"Do all you can!" Joseph interrupted. "She must have been insane! Do not tell me that you have *no* antidote!"

"We must try an emetic, though it will now be very dangerous. Then oil, white of egg,"—and the doctor hastened down to the kitchen.

Joseph walked up and down the room, wringing his hands. Here was a horror beyond anything he had imagined. His only thought was to save the life which she, in the madness of passion, must have resolved to take; she must not, *must not*, die now; and yet she seemed to be already in some region on the very verge of darkness, some region where it was scarcely possible to reach and pull her back. What could be done? Human science was baffled; and would God, who had allowed him to be afflicted through her, now answer his prayer to continue that affliction? But, indeed, the word "affliction" was not formed in his mind; the only word which he consciously grasped was "Life! life!"

He paused by the bedside and gazed upon her livid skin, her sunken features: she seemed already dead. Then, sinking on his knees, he tried to pray, if that was prayer which was the single intense appeal of all his confused feelings. Presently he heard a faint sigh; she slightly moved; consciousness was evidently returning.

She looked at him with half-opened eyes, striving to fix upon something which evaded her mind. Then she said, in the faintest broken whisper: "I did love you—I *did*—and *do*—love you! But—you—you hate me!"

A pang sharper than a knife went through Joseph's heart. He cried, through his tears: "I did not know what I said! Give me your forgiveness, Julia! Pardon me, not because I ask it, but freely, from your heart, and I will bless you!"

She did not speak, but her eyes softened, and a phantom smile hovered upon her lips. It was no mask this time: she was sacredly frank and true. Joseph bent over her and kissed her.

"O Julia!" he said, "why did you do it? Why did you not wait until I could speak with you? Did you think you would take a burden off yourself or me?"

Her lips moved, but no voice came. He lifted her head, supported her, and bent his ear to her mouth. It was like the dream of a voice:—

"I—did—not—mean—"

There it stopped. The doctor entered the room, followed by Lucy.

"First the emetic," said the former.

"For God's sake, be silent!" Joseph cried, with his ear still at Julia's lips. The doctor stepped up softly and looked at her. Then, seating himself on the bed beside Joseph, he laid his hand upon her heart. For several minutes there was silence in the room.

Then the doctor removed his hand, took Julia's head out of Joseph's arms, and laid it softly upon the pillow.

She was dead.

24. THE GOOD GRAY POET

Discretion mattered quite a bit. Whitman, for putting his name proudly on his *Leaves of Grass*, often suffered consequences for it. On one occasion his book even got him fired from a position (not as horrifying as having his work brought against him as evidence in court, as Wilde's *The Picture of Dorian Gray* was, but not so far down the ladder from it). The fallout of the dismissal also occasioned his being name The Good Gray Poet in the press (see [A.21]. Here are the initial details from Dr. Bucke:

> Some time before the close of the war, [Walt] was appointed to a clerkship in the Department of the Interior; but was shortly afterwards discharged by a new Secretary, Hon. James Harlan, "because he was the author of *an indecent book.*" He was immediately given an equally good place (secured through the good offices of W. D. O'Connor and J. Hubley Ashton) in the office of Attourney-General James Speed. That dismissal brought out the pamphlet (to be given presently) called "The Good Gray Poet," which was adjudged at the time by Henry J. Raymond to be the most brilliant monogram in American literature. It is worth while to put on record here a brief memorandum of this dismissal. Walt Whitman at the period was dividing all his spare time between visits to the wounded and sick still left in several army hospitals at Washington, and composing the poem "When Lilacs Last in the Dooryard Bloom'd." The morning after he was dismissed, his friend, Mr. Ashton, (who had himself sat in the President's Cabinet, and who occupied a national legal position), drove down to the Patent Office and had a long interview with Secretary Harlan on the subject of the dismissal. [...] Mr. A. asked why Whitman was dismissed, whether he had been found inattentive to his duties or incompetent for them. Mr. Harlan said No, there was no complaint on those points; as far as he knew, W. was a competent and faithful clerk. Mr. A. said, "Whitman is the author of *Leaves of Grass.*" Mr. A. said, "Is *that* the reason?" The Secretary said, "Yes, it is"—and then

made a statement essentially to the following purport: He was exploring the Department after office hours, and in one of the rooms he found *Leaves of Grass*. He took it up and thought it so odd, that he carried it to his own office awhile, and examined it. There were marks by or upon the pieces all through the book. He found in some of these marked passages matter so outrageous that he determined to discharge the writer, etc. Mr. A. responded by a brief statement of the theory of *Leaves of Grass*—that any bad construction put upon the passage alluded to was not warranted either by the actual principle of the poems or the intentions of the author. Mr. Harlan said he couldn't help that—the author of *Leaves of Grass* was a free lover, etc. Mr. A. said, "Mr. Harlan, I *know* Walt Whitman personally and well, and if you will listen to me, I will tell you what his life has been and is." He then went on with quite a long narrative. Mr. Harlan finally said, "You have changed my opinion of Mr. Whitman's personal character; but I shall adhere to my decision dismissing him." Mr. A. commenced some further remarks, when Mr. Harlan summarily said, "It's no use, Mr. A., I will not have the man who wrote *Leaves of Grass* in this Department, if the President himself were to order his reinstatement. I would resign myself sooner than put him back." Mr. Harlan then broke into a long and vehement tirade against the book and its writer, to which Mr. A. made no reply, but bowed and took his leave.[4]

Whitman himself explained the situation to Horace Traubel:

Secretary Harlan . . . abstracted the book [*Leaves of Grass*] from my desk drawer at night after I had gone, put it back again, and discharged me next day. . . . The more or less anonymous young writers and journalists of Washington were greatly incensed—made my cause their own—wrote almost violently about it: but the papers generally as well as literary people either ignored the incident altogether or made light of it. This was the hour for O'Connor: O'Connor was the man for this hour: and from that time on the "good gray," William's other name for me, has stuck.

   Note: Whitman's dismissal took place on June 30, 1865; the offending book was the 1860 edition [for specifics on that edition, see Chapter 11: Leaves of Grass]. [William] O'Connor, then a minor government clerk, published his rousing pamphlet defending Whitman, "The Good Gray Poet," in New York in 1866. Just after making the preceding remarks, Whitman added, "Long after Harlan acknowledged to one of the newspapers in St. Louis: 'The removal of Whitman was the mistake of my life.'"[39]

Whitman himself did not hold a grudge against Mr. Harlan:

Don't ever assail Harlan as if he was a scoundrel: he wasn't: he was only a fool: there was only a dim light in his noddle: he had to steer by that light: what else could he do? Then, Horace, remember this too—that he was afterwards sorry for it: I have been told so by newspaper men . . . he told them he thought it was a mistake: he was a bigot—that was all: yet he had the courage of his conviction . . . his heart said "throw Walt Whitman out": so out I went: I have always had a latent sneaking admiration for his cowardly despicable act. After all, the meanest feature of it all was not his dismissal of me but his rooting in my desk in the dead of the night looking for evidence against me. What instinct ever drove him to my desk? He must have had some intimation from some one that I was what I was. [39]

For that rousing pamphlet in its entirety, see [A.21]. For a later letter revisiting the topic, written by O'Connor for the occasion of inclusion of "The Good Gray Poet" in Dr. Bucke's biography, *Walt Whitman*, see [A.20].

XXV

THE MOURNERS

"It cannot be!" cried Joseph, looking at the doctor with an agonized face; "it is too dreadful!"

"There is no room for doubt in relation to the cause. I suspect that her nervous system has been subjected to a steady and severe tension, probably for years past. This may have induced a condition, or at least a temporary paroxysm, during which she was—you understand me—not wholly responsible for her actions. You must have noticed whether such a condition preceded this catastrophe."

Lucy looked from one to the other, and back to the livid face on the pillow, unable to ask a question, and not yet comprehending that the end had come. Joseph arose at the doctor's words.

"That is my guilt," he said. "I was excited and angry, for I had been bitterly deceived. I warned her that her life must henceforth conform to mine: my words were harsh and violent. I told her that we had at last ascertained each other's true natures, and proposed a serious discussion for the purpose of arranging our common future, this afternoon. Can she have misunderstood my meaning? It was not separation, not divorce: I only meant to avoid the miserable strife of the last few weeks. Who could imagine that this would follow?"

Even as he spoke the words Joseph remembered the tempting fancy which had passed through his own mind,—and the fear of Philip,—as he stood on the brink of the rock, above the dark, sliding water. He covered his face with his hands and sat down. What right had he to condemn her, to pronounce her mad? Grant that she had been blinded by her own unbalanced, excitable nature rather than consciously false; grant that she had really loved him, that the love survived under all her vain and masterful ambition,—and how could he doubt it after the dying words and looks?—it was then easy to guess how sorely she had been wounded, how despair should follow her fierce excitement! Her words, "Go away! *you* have killed me!" were now explained. He groaned in the bitterness of his self-accusation. What were all the trials he had endured to this? How light seemed the burden from which he was now free! how gladly would he bear it, if the day's words and deeds could be unsaid and undone!

The doctor, meanwhile, had explained the manner of Julia's death to Lucy Henderson. She, almost overcome with this last horror, could only agree with his conjecture, for her own evidence confirmed it. Joseph had forborne to mention her presence in the garden, and she saw no need of repeating his words to her; but she described Julia's convulsive excitement, and her refusal to admit her to her room, half an hour before the first attack of the poison. The case seemed entirely clear to both.

"For the present," said the doctor, "let us say nothing about the suicide. There is no necessity for a *post-mortem* examination: the symptoms, and the presence of arsenic in the glass; are quite sufficient to establish the cause of death. You know what a foolish idea of disgrace is attached to families here in the country when such a thing happens, and Mr. Asten is not now in a state to bear much more. At least, we must save him from painful questions until after the funeral is over. Say as little as possible to him: he is not in a condition to listen to reason: he believes himself guilty of her death."

"What shall I do?" cried Lucy: "will you not stay until the man Dennis returns? Mr. Asten's aunt must be fetched immediately."

It was not a quarter of an hour before Dennis arrived, followed by Philip and Madeline Held.

Lucy, who had already despatched Dennis, with a fresh horse, to Magnolia, took Philip and Madeline into the dining-room, and hurriedly communicated to them the intelligence of Julia's death. Philip's heart gave a single leap of joy; then he compelled himself to think of Joseph and the exigencies of the situation.

"You cannot stay here alone," he said. "Madeline must keep you company. I will go up and take care of Joseph: we must think of both the living and the dead."

No face could have been half so comforting in the chamber of death as Philip's. The physician had, in the meantime, repeated to Joseph the words he had spoken to Lucy, and now Joseph said, pointing to Philip, "Tell *him* everything!"

Philip, startled as he was, at once comprehended the situation. He begged Dr. Hartman to leave all further arrangements to him, and to summon Mrs. Bishop, the wife of one of Joseph's near neighbors, on his way home. Then, taking Joseph by the arm, he said:—

"Now come with me. We will leave this room awhile to Lucy and Madeline; but neither must you be alone. If I am anything to you, Joseph, now is the time when my presence should be some slight comfort. We need not speak, but we will keep together."

Joseph clung the closer to his friend's arm, without speaking, and they passed out of the house. Philip led him, mechanically, towards the garden, but as they drew near the avenue of box-trees Joseph started back, crying out:—

"Not there!—O, not there!"

Philip turned in silence, conducted him past the barn into the grass-field, and mounted the hill towards the pin-oak on its summit. From this point the house was scarcely visible behind the fir-trees and the huge weeping-willow, but the fair hills around seemed happy under the tender sky, and the melting, vapory distance, seen through the southern opening of the valley, hinted of still happier landscapes beyond. As Joseph contemplated the scene, the long strain upon his nerves relaxed: he leaned upon Philip's shoulder, as they sat side by side, and wept passionately.

"If she had not died!" he murmured, at last.

Philip was hardly prepared for this exclamation, and he did not immediately answer.

"Perhaps it is better for me to talk," Joseph continued. "You do not know the whole truth, Philip. You have heard of her madness, but not of my guilt. What was it I said when we last met? I cannot recall it now; but I know that I feared to call my punishment unjust. Since then I have deserved it all, and more. If I am a child why should I dare to handle fire? If I do not understand life, why should I dare to set death in motion?

He began, and related everything that had passed since they parted on the banks of the stream. He repeated the words that had been spoken in the house and in the garden, and the last broken sentences that came from Julia's lips. Philip listened with breathless surprise and attention. The greater part of the narrative made itself clear to his mind; his instinctive knowledge of Julia's nature enabled him to read much further than was then possible to Joseph; but there was a mystery connected with the suicide which he could not fathom. Her rage he could easily understand; her apparent submission to Joseph's request, however,—her manifest desire to live, on overhearing the physician's fears,—her last incomplete sentence, "I—did—not—mean—" indicated no such fatal intention, but the reverse. Moreover, she was too inherently selfish, even in the fiercest paroxysm of disappointment, to take her own life, he believed. All the evidence justified him in this view of her nature, yet at the same time rendered her death more inexplicable.

It was no time to mention these doubts to Joseph. His only duty was to console and encourage.

"There is no guilt in accident" he said. "It was a crisis which must have come and you took the only course possible to a man. If she felt that she was defeated, and her mad act was the consequence, think of your fate had she felt herself victorious!"

"It could have been no worse than it was," Joseph answered. "And she might have changed: I did not give her time. I have accused my own mistaken education, but I had no charity, no pity for hers!"

When they descended the hill Mrs. Bishop had arrived, and the startled household was reduced to a kind of dreary order. Dennis, who had driven with speed, brought Rachel Miller at dusk and Philip and Madeline then departed, taking Lucy Henderson with them. Rachel was tearful, but composed; she said little to her nephew, but there was a quiet, considerate tenderness in her manner which soothed him more than any words.

The reaction from so much fatigue and excitement almost prostrated him. When he went to bed in his own guestrooms feeling like a stranger in a strange house, he lay for a long time between sleep and waking, haunted by all the scenes and personages of his past life. His mother's face, so faded in memory, came clear and fresh from the shadows; a boy whom he had loved in his school-days floated with fair, pale features just before his closed eyes; and around and between them there was woven a web of twilights and moonlights, and sweet sunny days, each linked to some grief or pleasure of the buried years. It was a keen, bitter joy, a fascinating torment, from which he could not escape. He was caught and helplessly ensnared by the phantoms, until, late in the night, the strong claim of nature drove them away and left him in a dead, motionless, dreamless slumber.

Philip returned in the morning, and devoted the day not less to the arrangements which must necessarily be made for the funeral than to standing between Joseph and the awkward and inquisitive sympathy of the neighbors. Joseph's continued weariness favored Philip's exertions, while at the same time it blunted the edge of his own feelings, and helped him over that cold, bewildering, dismal period, during which a corpse is lord of the mansion and controls the life of its inmates.

Towards evening Mr. and Mrs. Blessing, who had been summoned by telegraph, made their appearance. Clementina did not accompany them. They were both dressed in mourning: Mrs. Blessing was grave and rigid, Mr. Blessing flushed and lachrymose. Philip conducted them first to the chamber of the dead and then to Joseph.

"It is so sudden, so shocking!" Mrs. Blessing sobbed; "and Julia always seemed so healthy! What have you done to her, Mr. Asten, that she should be cut off in the bloom of her youth?"

"Eliza!" exclaimed her husband, with his handkerchief to his eyes; "do not say anything which might sound like a reproach to our heart-broken son! There are many foes in the citadel of life: they may be undermining our—our foundations at this very moment!"

"No, said Joseph; "you, her father and mother, must hear the truth. I would give all I have in the world if I were not obliged to tell it."

It was, at the best, a painful task; but it was made doubly so by exclamations, questions, intimations, which he was forced to hear. Finally, Mrs. Blessing asked, in a tone of alarm:—

"How many persons know of this?"

"Only the physician and three of my friends," Joseph answered.

"They must be silent! It might ruin Clementina's prospects if it were generally known. To lose one daughter and to have the life of another blasted would be too much."

"Eliza," said her husband, "we must try to accept whatever is inevitable. It seems to me that I no more recognize Julia's usually admirable intellect in her—yes, I must steel myself to say the word!—her suicide, than I recognized her features just now! unless Decay's effacing fingers have already swept the lines where beauty lingers. I warned her of the experiment, for such I felt it to be; yet in this last trying experience I do not complain of Joseph's disappointment, and his temporary—trust it is only temporary—suspicion. We must not forget that he has lost more than we have."

"Where is—" Joseph began, endeavoring to turn the conversation from this point.

"Clementina? I knew you would find her absence unaccountable. We instantly forwarded a telegram to Long Branch: the answer said, 'My grief is great, but it is quite impossible to come.' Why impossible she did not particularize, and we can only conjecture.

When I consider her age and lost opportunities, and the importance which a single day, even a fortunate situation, may possess for her at present, it seems to remove some of the sharpness of the serpent's tooth. Neither she nor we are responsible for Julia's rash taking off; yet it is always felt as a cloud which lowers upon the family. There was a similar case among the De Belsains, during the Huguenot times, but we never mention it. For your sake silence is rigidly imposed upon us; since the preliminary—what shall I call it?—disharmony of views?—would probably become a part of the narrative."

"Pray do not speak of that now!" Joseph groaned.

"Pardon me; I will not do so again. Our minds naturally become discursive under the pressure of grief. It is easier for me to talk at such times than to be silent and think. My power of recuperation seems to be spiritual as well as physical; it is congenital, and therefore exposes me to misconceptions. But we can close over the great abyss of our sorrow, and hide it from view in the depth of our natures, without dancing on the platform which covers it."

Philip turned away to hide a smile, and even Mrs. Blessing exclaimed: "Really, Benjamin, you are talking heartlessly!"

"I do not mean it so," he said, melting into tears, "but so much has come upon me all at once! If I lose my buoyancy, I shall go to the bottom like a foundered ship! I was never cut out for the tragic parts of life; but there are characters who smile on the stage and weep behind the scenes. And, you know, the Lord loveth a cheerful giver."

He was so touched by the last words he spoke, that he leaned his head upon his arms and wept bitterly.

Then Mrs. Blessing, weeping also, exclaimed: "O, don't take on so, Benjamin!"

Philip put an end to the scene, which was fast becoming a torment to Joseph. But, later in the evening, Mr. Blessing again sought the latter, softly apologizing for the intrusion, but declaring that he was compelled, then and there, to make a slight explanation.

"When you called the other evening," he said, "I was worn out, and not competent to grapple with such an unexpected revelation of villany. I had been as ignorant of Kanuck's real character as you were. All our experience of the world is sometimes at fault; but where the Reverend Dr. Lellifant was first deceived, my own case does not seem so flagrant. Your early information, however, enabled me (through third parties) to secure a partial sale of the stock held by yourself and me,—at something of a sacrifice it is true; but I prefer not to dissociate myself entirely from the enterprise. I do not pretend to be more than the merest tyro in geology; nevertheless, as I lay awake last night,—being, of course, unable to sleep after the shock of the telegram,—I sought relief in random scientific fancies. It occurred to me that since the main Chowder wells are 'spouting,' their source or reservoir must be considerably higher than the surface. Why might not that source be found under the hills of the Amaranth? If so, the Chowder would be tapped at the fountain-head and the flow of Pactolean grease would be ours! When I return to the city I shall need instantly—after the fearful revelations of to-day—some violently absorbing occupation; and what could be more appropriate? If anything could give repose to Julia's unhappy shade, it would be the knowledge that her faith in the Amaranth was at last justified! I do not presume to awaken your confidence: it has been too deeply shaken; all I ask is, that I may have the charge of your shares, in order—without calling upon you for the expenditure of another cent, you understand—to rig a jury-mast on the wreck, and, D. V., float safely into port!"

"Why should I refuse to trust you with what is already worthless?" said Joseph.

"I will admit even *that*, if you desire. 'Exitus acta probat,' was Washington's motto; but I don't consider that we have yet reached the *exitus*! Thank you, Joseph! Your question has hardly the air of returning confidence, but I will force myself to consider it as such, and my labor will be to deserve it."

He wrung Joseph's hand, shed a few more tears, and betook himself to his wife's chamber. "Eliza, let us be calm: we never know our strength until it has been tried," he said to her, as he opened his portmanteau and took from it the wicker-covered flask.

Then came the weariest and dreariest day of all,—when the house must be thrown open to the world; when in one room the corpse must be displayed for solemn stares and whispered comments, while in another the preparation of the funeral meats absorbs all the interest of half a dozen busy women; when the nearest relatives of the dead sit together in a room up-stairs, hungering only for the consolations of loneliness and silence; when all talk under their voices, and uncomfortably fulfil what they believe to be their solemn duty; and when even Nature is changed to all eyes, and the mysterious gloom of an eclipse seems to fall from the most unclouded sun.

There was a general gathering of the neighbors from far and near. The impression seemed to be—and Philip was ready to substantiate it—that Julia had died in consequence of a violent convulsive spasm, which some attributed to one cause and some to another.

The Rev. Mr. Chaffinch made his way, as by right, to the chamber of the mourners. Rachel Miller was comforted in seeing him, Mr. and Mrs. Blessing sadly courteous, and Joseph strengthened himself to endure with patience what might follow. After a few introductory words, and a long prayer, the clergyman addressed himself to each, in turn, with questions or remarks which indicated a fierce necessity of resignation.

"I feel for you, brother," he said, as he reached Joseph and, bent over his chair. "It is an inscrutable visitation, but I trust you submit, in all obedience?"

Joseph bowed silently.

"He has many ways of searching the heart," Mr. Chaffinch continued. "Your one precious comfort must be that *she* believed, and that she is now in glory. O, if you would but resolve to follow in her footsteps! He shows His love, in that He chastens you: it is a stretching out of His hand, a visible offer of acceptance, this on one side, and the lesson of our perishing mortality on the other! Do you not feel your heart awfully and tenderly moved to approach Him?"

Joseph sat, with bowed head, listening to the smooth, unctuous, dismal voice at his ear, until the tension of his nerves became a positive physical pain. He longed to cry aloud, to spring up and rush away; his heart was moved, but not awfully and tenderly. It had been yearning towards the pure Divine Light in which all confusions of the soul are disentangled; but now some opaque foreign substance intervened, and drove him back upon himself. How long the torture lasted he did not know. He spake no word, and made no further sign.

Then Philip took him and Rachel Miller down, for the last conventional look at the stony, sunken face. He was seated here and led there; he was dimly conscious of a crowd, of murmurs and steadfast faces; he heard someone whisper, "How dreadfully pale he looks!" and wondered whether the words could possibly refer to him. Then there was the welcome air and the sunshine, and Dennis driving them slowly down the lane, following a gloomy vehicle, in which *something*—not surely the Julia whom he knew—was carried.

He recalled but one other such stupor of the senses: it was during the performance of the marriage ceremony.

But the longest day wears out at last; and when night came only Philip was beside him. The Blessings had been sent to Oakland Station for the evening train to the city, and Joseph's shares in the Amaranth Company were in their portmanteau.

25. THE CIVIL WAR

ONE OF THE topics incensing William O'Connor in his defense of Whitman, "The Good Gray Poet," is some criticism that was brought against Whitman by a Mr. Thomas Wentworth Higginson (friend of Emily Dickenson, see <u>Chapter 13: Perceptions of Whitman</u>), who wrote a series of pieces from 1881 to 1898 belittling Whitman, including an essay called "Unmanly Manhood" published in the *Women's Journal*, arguing against Whitman deserving a pension for his hospital work during the war because he *chose* to be a nurse instead of a soldier:

> There is, it is true, a class of men whose claims are intermediate between those of the soldiers and those of the women. There were many men who, being rejected from enlistment for physical defects, sought honorably to serve their country as hospital nurses or agents of the Sanitary Commission. A beginning has been made in the way of pensioning these men in the case of the proposed pension for Mr. Whitman, the poet; although he . . . deliberately preferred service in the hospital rather than in the field.[14]

O'Connor railed against this opinion in his pamphlet on Whitman published after Whitman's dismissal from a clerk job for being the author of *Leaves of Grass* (which Higginson disliked as much as he despised Whitman himself):

> Mr. Higginson avers that Walt Whitman ought to become the focal point of million-fingered scorn for having served in the hospitals! It appears that the old poet performed a pathetic, a sublime, an immortal service—he tended the wounded and dying soldiers throughout the whole war, and for years afterward, until the last hospital disappeared. O, but this was infamous! Shame on such "unmanly manhood," yells the Rev. Mr. Higginson! He should have personally "followed the drum," declares this soldier of the army of the Lord, himself a volunteer colonel. In bald words, instead of volunteering for the ghastly, the mournful, the perilous labors of those swarming infernos, the

hospitals, Walt Whitman should have enlisted in the rank and file. From all which, I gather that Mr. Higginson would have cast a stone at Jean Valjean for going down without a musket into the barricades.[4]

During the war, Whitman traveled to the front line in search of his brother, George:

As 1862 staggered along, Whitman became increasingly anxious. He and his family in Brooklyn were worried about George. They were able to follow the progress of his regiment through newspaper accounts. What they could glean was alarming. The 51ˢᵗ seemed to be involved in far more than its fair share of combat. Throughout the year, George's regiment saw action in a dizzying succession of major battles: Roanoke Island, New Bern, Cedar Mountain, Chantilly, and South Mountain. George was also at Antietam, where 3,654 men were killed during a few hours of close-range fighting in a Maryland cornfield. That battle remains the single deadliest day in American combat history.[33]

To find his brother (who ended up being alive and well and promoted to Captain when Whitman located his regiment), Whitman traveled to Falmouth, Virginia, where he stayed on with his brother for over a week, keeping his customary notebooks all the while, and jotting down overheard slang, such as noting that a "healthy beat" was a reliable soldier, while a "dead beat" was someone full of excuses.[33] After Whitman "learned that two soldiers from Brooklyn were laid up at a hospital in the capital,"[33] he made his way to Washington, D.C. to become a hospital helper, or as he referred to himself, a Soldiers' Missionary:

Whitman fell into the habit of distributing various items to the soldiers. His notebooks are filled with their modest requests:

+ David S. Giles, co. F. 28ᵗʰ N.J.V.bed 52 W. 6— . . . wants an apple
+ Hiram Scholis—bed 3—Ward E.—26ᵗʰ N. York—wants some pickles—a bottle of pickles
+ Henry D. Boardman co. B 27ᵗʰ Conn Vol. . . . Bed 25 . . . wants a *rice pudding* milky & not very sweet.

Whenever Whitman set out for the hospitals, he would bring a leather haversack, slung over his shoulder, stuffed with items. [...] Nearly half of his pay [from a government job in the paymaster's office] was devoted to goods for the wounded soldiers. [...] A few months into his hospital service, Whitman bought a cheap wine-colored suit. He wore it every day, the trousers tucked into heavy leather boots. He hadn't shaved since leaving Brooklyn. The total effect—reddish suit, bushy beard, the haversack—was like a Bohemian Santa Claus. [...] Colonel Richard Hinton recalled, "Walt Whitman didn't bring any tracts or Bibles; he didn't ask if you loved the Lord, and didn't seem to care whether you did or not." Instead, at Hinton's request, "this old heathen came and gave me a pipe and tobacco . . . about the most joyous moment of my life."[33]

Whitman wrote of his hospital work in his letters:

Washington, October 11th, 1863: I am continually moving around the hospitals. One I got to oftenest these last three months is "Armory Square," as it is large, generally full of the worst wounds and sickness, and is among the least visited. To this or some other I never miss a day or evening. Above all, the poor boys welcome simple kindness, loving affection (some are so fervent, so hungering for this)—poor fellows, how young they are, lying there with their pale faces, and that mute look in the eyes. Oh, how one gets to love them, often, particular cases, so suffering, so good, so manly and yet simple. Abby, you would all smile to see me among them—many of them like children. Ceremony is quite discarded—they suffer and get exhausted and so weary—not a few are on their dying beds—lots of them have grown to expect, as I leave at night, that we should kiss each other, sometimes quite a number; I have to go round. There is little petting in a soldier's life in the field, but, Abby, I know what is in their hearts, always waiting, though they may be unconscious of it themselves.[4]

Another first-hand account of Whitman's hospital activity (and its aftermath on Whitman's health) exists in a letter by John Swinton:

I knew him in his splendid prime, when his familiar figure was daily seen on Broadway, and when he was brooding over those extraordinary poems which have since been put into half a dozen languages, and commanded the homage of many of the greatest minds in modern literature. From then to the time of his paralysis I know of his life and deeds. Rich in good works and in saddening trials, he has remained the same genuine man, in whom the well-springs of poetry give perpetual freshness to the passing years. His paralysis was the result of his exhausting labors among our sick and wounded soldiers in the hospitals near Washington during the war. I saw something of these labors when I was visiting the hospitals. I can testify, as countless others can, that for at least three years the "Good Gray Poet" spent a large portion of his time, day and night, in the hospitals, as nurse and comforter of those who had been maimed or otherwise prostrated in the service of their country. I first heard of him among the sufferers on the Peninsula after a battle there. Subsequently I saw him, time and again, in the Washington hospitals, or wending his way there with basket or haversack on his arm, and the strength of beneficence suffusing his face. His devotion surpassed the devotion of woman. It would take a volume to tell of his kindness, tenderness, and thoughtfulness.

Never shall I forget one night when I accompanied him on his rounds through a hospital, filled with those wounded young Americans whose heroism he has sung in deathless numbers. There were three rows of cots, and each cot bore its man. When he appeared, in passing along, there was a smile of affection and welcome on every face, however wan, and his presence seemed to light up the place as it might be lit by the presence of the Son of Love. From cot to cot they called him, often in tremulous tones or in whispers; they embraced him, they touched his hand, they gazed at him. To one he gave a few words of cheer, for another he wrote a letter home, to others he gave an orange, a few comfits, a cigar, a pipe and tobacco, a sheet of paper or a postage stamp, all of which and many other things were in his capacious haversack. From another he would receive a dying message for mother, wife, or sweetheart; for another he would promise to go an errand; to another, some special friend, very low, he would give a manly farewell kiss. He did the things for them which no nurse or doctor could do, and he seemed to leave a benediction at every cot as he passed along. The lights had gleamed for hours in the hospital that night before he left it, and as he took his way towards the door, you could hear the voice of many a stricken hero calling, "Walt, Walt, Walt, come again! come again!"[4]

Those calls and kisses from the soldiers led to a couple notable attachments for Whitman:

When a soldier named Tom Sawyer rejoined the 11th Massachusetts Volunteers, Whitman pursued him with a series of mooning letters. "If you should come safe out of this war," the poet wrote, "we should come together again in some place where we could make our living, and be true comrades and never be separated while life lasts." […] Whitman wondered whether the intensity of his feelings had left the soldier bewildered: "I suppose my letters sound strange & unusual to you as it is, but I am only expressing the truth in them, I do not trouble myself on that account." As time went on, Whitman despaired of ever hearing back from Sawyer: "I do not know why you do not write to me. Do you wish to shake me off?"

Sawyer, evidently, was spooked by this onslaught of needy epistles. He wasn't exactly a wordsmith, either, being—per Whitman's usual preferences— something of a raw, uneducated young man. After many months, Sawyer wrote Whitman a brief note: "I hardly know what to say to you in this letter for it is my first one to you. . . . I hope you will forgive me and in the future I will do better and I hope we may meet again in this world."

Granted, Sawyer held out the possibility of seeing one another again. But what comes through most clearly is his hesitancy. Whitman knew enough about matters of the heart to recognize that this wasn't going to work out.[33]

Another "youngster" Whitman remembered later to Traubel:

Some of my best friends in the hospitals were probably Southern boys. I remember one in particular, right off—a Kentucky youngster (a mere youngster), illiterate, extremely: I wrote several letters for him to his parents, friends: fine, honest, ardent, chivalrous. I found myself loving him like a son: he used to kiss me good night—kiss me. He got well, he passed out with the crowd, went home, the war was over. We never met again. Oh! I could tell you a hundred such tales . . . there's a lot of that stuff I never put down anywhere—some of the best of it.[39]

Though Whitman attributed the loss of his pre-war perfect health and his later paralysis to a case of "hospital malaria,"[2] Whitman did not regret having done the work:

I was always between two loves at that time: I wanted to be in New York, I had to be in Washington: I was never in the one place but I was restless for the other: my heart was distracted: yet it never occurred to me for a minute that there were two things to do—that I had any right or call to abandon my work: it was a religion with me. A religion? Well—every man has a religion: has something in heaven or earth which he will give up everything else for— something which absorbs him, possesses itself of him, makes him over into its image: something: it may be something regarded by others as very paltry, inadequate, useless: yet it is his dream, it is his lodestar, it is his master. That, whatever it is, seized upon me, made me its servant, slave: induced me to set aside the other ambitions: a trail of glory in the heavens, which I followed, followed, with a full heart. When once I am convinced I never let go. . . . I had to give up health for it—my body—the vitality of my physical self. . . . I never weighed what I gave for what I got but I am satisfied with what I got. What did I get? Well—I got the boys, for one thing: the boys: thousands of them: they were, they are, they will be mine. I gave myself for them: myself: I got the boys: then I got *Leaves of Grass*: but for this I would never have had *Leaves of Grass*—the consummated book (the last confirming word): I got that: the boys, the *Leaves*: I got them.[39]

Whitman's poems about the Civil War (see Chapter 11: Leaves of Grass for examples) came from the unique point of view of an observer not only of the frontline camps, but of the hospital aftermath. Whitman was also privy to a first-hand account of Lincoln's assassination from Peter Doyle (see: Chapter 22: Whitman's Peter and Chapter 28:

Lincoln and Whitman for further information), who happened to be in Ford's Theater on the night of the president's death. According to Doyle:

> "Walt was not at the theater the night Lincoln was shot. It was me he got all that from in the book—they are almost my words. I heard that the President and his wife would be present and made up my mind to go. There was a great crowd in the building. I got into the second gallery. There was nothing extraordinary in the performance. I saw everything on the stage and was in a good position to see the President's box. I heard the pistol shot. I had no idea what it was, what it meant—it was sort of muffled. I really knew nothing of what had occurred until Mrs. Lincoln leaned out of the box and cried, 'The President is shot!' I needn't tell you what I felt then, or saw. It is all put down in Walt's piece—that piece is exactly right. I saw Booth on the cushion of the box, saw him jump over, saw him catch his foot, which turned, saw him fall on the stage. He got up on his feet, cried out something which I could not hear for the hub-hub and disappeared. I suppose I lingered almost the last person. A soldier came into the gallery, saw me still there, called to me: 'Get out of here! we're going to burn this damned building down!' I said: 'If that is so I'll get out!'"[3]

Doyle too had a unique double-vantage of the war itself, pledged at different times to both sides:

> Two weeks into the Civil War, Doyle enlisted as a Confederate soldier, drawn by the promise of a steady pay. He joined the Richmond Fayette Light Artillery and was involved in a number of major engagements before being wounded at Antietam. George Whitman also fought at Antietam, though he was across the battle lines from Doyle, on the Union side of that blood-sotted Maryland cornfield.
>
> Doyle was laid up in a Richmond hospital for several months. During that time, he petitioned to be discharged from military service. This was granted on the condition that Doyle promise not to give aid to the enemy. Not a problem: he didn't have any stake in this conflict. Union, Confederate—they were mere abstractions to him.
>
> In a statement, sworn and notarized, Doyle indicated that he was going to return to Ireland. But then he decided instead to move to Washington, DC, planning to reconnect with some family who now lived there. While heading north, as Doyle attempted to cross Federal lines, he was detained by Union troops. For three weeks, he was confined to the Old Capitol Prison. On agreeing to pledge loyalty to the Union—once again, no problem—he was released on May 11, 1863.[33]

Meanwhile, Fitz-Greene Halleck would not touch the subject of the war with his poetics, nor even align himself whole-heartedly with either side:

> Halleck [...] refused requests for poems on the Civil War. Not even Abraham Lincoln's praise moved Halleck to write on that subject. In 1860, Lincoln wrote a mutual friend: "I am greatly obliged for the volume of your friend, Fitz-Greene Halleck's poems," adding, "Many a month has passed since I have met with anything more admirable than his beautiful lines." Halleck could not support either side of the Civil War and wrote Mrs. John Rush on November 21, 1861, that both sides were at fault. [...] In his last conversation with Joel Benton, Halleck expressed relief that "'the crime of Slavery'" had been "cured" by the war.[22]

XXVI

THE ACCUSATION

FOR A FEW days it almost seemed to Joseph that the old order of his existence had been suddenly restored, and the year of his betrothal and marriage had somehow been intercalated into his life simply as a test and trial. Rachel Miller was back again, in her old capacity, and he did not yet see—what would have been plain to any other eyes—that her manner towards him was far more respectful and considerate than formerly. But, in fact, she made a wide distinction between the "boy" that he had been and the man and widower which he had come to be. At first, she had refused to see the dividing line: having crossed it, her new course soon became as natural and fixed as the old. She was the very type of a mechanically developed old maid,—inflexibly stern towards male youth, devotedly obedient to male maturity.

Joseph had been too profoundly moved to lose at once the sense of horror which the manner of Julia's death had left in his heart. He could not forgive himself for having, though never so ignorantly, driven her to madness. He was troubled, restless, unhappy; and the mention of his loss was so painful that he made every effort to avoid hearing it. Some of his neighbors, he imagined, were improperly curious in their inquiries. He felt bound, since the doctor had suggested it, since Philip and Lucy had acquiesced, and Mrs. Blessing had expressed so much alarm lest it might become known, to keep the suicide a secret; but he was driven so closely by questions and remarks that his task became more and more difficult.

Had the people taken offence at his reticence? It seemed so; for their manner towards him was certainly changed. Something in the look and voice; an indefinable uneasiness at meeting him; an awkward haste and lame excuses for it,—all these things forced themselves upon his mind. Elwood Withers, alone, met him as of old, with even a tenderer though a more delicately veiled affection; yet in Elwood's face he detected the signs of a grave trouble. It could not be possible, he thought, that Elwood had heard some surmise, or distorted echo, of his words to Lucy in the garden,—that there had been another listener besides Julia!

There were times, again, when he doubted all these signs, when he ascribed them to his own disturbed mind, and decided to banish them from his memory. He would stay quietly at home, he resolved, and grow into a healthier mood: he would avoid the society of men, until he should cease to wrong them by his suspicions.

First, however, he would see Philip; but on reaching the Forge he found Philip absent. Madeline received him with a subdued kindness in which he felt her sympathy; but it was also deeper, he acknowledged to himself, than he had any right to claim.

"You do not see much of your neighbors, I think, Mr. Asten?" she asked. The tone of her voice indicated a slight embarrassment.

"No," he answered; "I have no wish to see any but my friends."

"Lucy Henderson has just left us. Philip took her to her father's, and was intending to call at your place on his way home. I hope you will not miss him. That is," she added, while a sudden flush of color spread over her face, "I want you to see him to-day. I beg you won't take my words as intended for a dismissal."

"Not now, certainly," said Joseph. But he rose from his seat as he spoke.

Madeline looked both confused and pained. "I know that I spoke awkwardly," she said, "but indeed I was very anxious. It was also Lucy's wish. We have been talking about you this morning."

"You are very kind. And yet—I ought to wish you a more cheerful subject."

What was it in Madeline's face that haunted Joseph on his way home? The lightsome spirit was gone from her eyes, and they were troubled as if by the pressure of tears, held back by a strong effort. Her assumed calmness at parting seemed to cover a secret anxiety; he had never before seen her bright, free nature so clouded.

Philip, meanwhile, had reached the farm, where he was received by Rachel Miller.

"I am glad to find that Joseph is not at home," he said; "there are some things which I need to discuss with you, before I see him. Can you guess what they are? Have you heard nothing,—no stories?"

Rachel's face grew pale, yet there was a strong fire of indignation in her eyes. "Dennis told me an outrageous report he had heard in the village," she said: "if you mean the same thing, you did well to see me first. You can help me to keep this insult from Joseph's knowledge."

"If I could I would, Miss Rachel. I share your feeling about it; but suppose the report were now so extended—and of course in a more exaggerated form the farther it goes— that we cannot avoid its probable consequences? This is not like a mere slander, which can be suffered to die of itself. It is equivalent to a criminal charge, and must be faced."

She clasped her hands, and stared at him in terror.

"But why," she faltered—"why does anyone *dare* to make such a charge? And against the best, the most innocent—"

"The fact of the poisoning cannot be concealed," said Philip. "It appears, moreover, that one of the women who was in the house on the day of Julia's death heard her cry out to Joseph: 'Go away,—you have killed me!' I need not take up the reports any further; there is enough in these two circumstances to excite the suspicions of those who do not know Joseph as we do. It is better, therefore, to meet those suspicions before they come to us in a legal form."

"What can we do?" cried Rachel; "it is terrible!'

"One course is clear, if it is possible. We must try to discover not only the cause of Julia's suicide, but the place where she procured the poison, and her design in procuring it. She must have had it already in the house."

"I never thought of that. And her ways were so quiet and sly! How shall we ever find it out? O, to think that, dead and gone as she is, she can yet bring all this upon Joseph!"

"Try to be calm, Miss Rachel," said Philip. "I want your help, and you must have all your wits about you. First, you must make a very careful examination of her clothing and effects, even to the merest scrap of paper. A man's good name—a man's life, sometimes— hangs upon a thread, in the most literal sense. There is no doubt that Julia meant to keep a secret, and she must have had a strong reason; but we have a stronger one, now, to discover it. First, as to the poison; was there any arsenic in the house when Julia came?"

"Not a speck! I never kept it, even for rats."

"Then we shall begin with ascertaining where she bought it. Let us make our investigations secretly, and as speedily as possible. Joseph need not know, at present, what we have undertaken, but he must know the charge that hangs over him. Unless I tell him, he may learn it in a more violent way. I sent Elwood Withers to Magnolia yesterday, and his report leaves me no choice of action."

Rachel Miller felt, from the stern gravity of Philip's manner, that he had not exaggerated Joseph's danger. She consented to be guided by him in all things; and this point being settled, they arranged a plan of action and communication, which was tolerably complete by the time Joseph returned.

As gently as possible Philip broke the unwelcome news; but, lightly as he pretended to consider it, Joseph's instinct saw at once what might be the consequences. The circumstances were all burned upon his consciousness, and it needed no reflection to show him how completely he was entangled in them.

"There is no alternative," he said, at last. "It was a mistake to conceal the cause of her death from the public: it is easy to misunderstand her exclamation, and make my crime out of her madness. I see the whole connection! This suspicion will not stop where it is. It will go further; and therefore I must anticipate it. I must demand a legal inquiry before the law forces one upon me. If it is not my only method of defense, it is certainly my best!"

"You are right!" Philip exclaimed. "I knew this would be your decision; I said so to Madeline this morning."

Now Madeline's confused manner became intelligible to Joseph. Yet a doubt still lingered in his mind. "Did she, did Madeline question it?" he asked.

"Neither she nor Lucy Henderson. If you do this, I cannot see how it will terminate without a trial. Lucy may then happen to be an important witness."

Joseph started. "*Must* that be!" he cried. "Has not Lucy been already forced to endure enough for my sake? Advise me, Philip! Is there any other way than that I have proposed?"

"I see no other. But your necessity is far greater than that for Lucy's endurance. She is a friend, and there can be no sacrifice in so serving you. What are we all good for, if not to serve you in such a strait?"

"I would like to spare her, nevertheless," said Joseph, gloomily. "I meant so well towards all my friends, and my friendship seems to bring only disgrace and sorrow."

"Joseph!" Philip exclaimed, "you have saved one friend from more than disgrace and sorrow! I do not know what might have come, but you called me back from the brink of an awful, doubtful eternity! You have given me an infinite loss and an infinite gain! I only ask you, in return, to obey your first true, proud instinct of innocence, and let me, and Lucy, and Elwood be glad to take its consequences, for your sake!"

"I cannot help myself," Joseph answered. "My rash impatience and injustice will come to light, and that may be the atonement I owe. If Lucy will spare herself, and report me truly, as I must have appeared to her, she will serve me best."

"Leave that, now! The first step is what most concerns us. When will you be ready to demand a legal investigation?

"At once!—to-morrow!"

"Then we will go together to Magnolia. I fear we cannot change the ordinary forms of procedure, and there must be bail for your appearance at the proper time."

"Already on the footing of a criminal?" Joseph murmured, with a sinking of the heart. He had hardly comprehended, up to this moment, what his position would be.

The next day they drove to the county town. The step had not been taken a moment too soon, for such representations had been made that a warrant for Joseph's arrest was in the hands of the constable, and would have been served in a few hours. Philip and Mr. Hopeton, who also happened to be in the town by a fortunate chance (though Philip knew how the chance came), offered to accept whatever amount of bail might be demanded. The matter was arranged as privately as possible, but it leaked out in some way, and Philip was seriously concerned lest the curiosity—perhaps, even, the ill-will—of a few persons might be manifested towards Joseph. He visited the offices of the county papers, and took care that the voluntary act should be stated in such a manner as to set its character properly before the people. Everything, he felt, depended on securing a fair and unprejudiced judgment of the case.

This, indeed, was far more important than even he suspected. In a country where the press is so entirely free, and where, owing to the lazy, indifferent habit of thought—or, rather, habit of *no* thought—of the people, the editorial views are accepted without scrutiny, a man's good name or life may depend on the coloring given to his acts by a few individual minds, it is especially necessary to keep the balance even, to offset one statement by another, and prevent a partial presentation of the case from turning the scales in advance. The same phenomena were as likely to present themselves here, before a small public, as in the large cities, where the whole population of the country become a more or less interested public. The result might hinge, not upon Joseph's personal character as his friends knew it, but upon the political party with which he was affiliated, the church to which he belonged,—nay, even upon the accordance of his personal sentiments with the public sentiment of the community in which he lived. If he had dared to defy the latter, asserting the sacred right of his own mind to the largest liberty, he was already a marked man. Philip did not understand the extent and power of the external influences which control what we complacently call "justice," but he knew something of the world, and acted in reality more prudently than he supposed.

He was calm and cheerful for Joseph's sake; yet, now that the matter was irrevocably committed to the decision of a new, uninterested tribunal, he began to feel the gravity of his friend's position.

"I almost wish," Joseph said, as they drove homewards, "that no bail had been granted. Since the court meets in October, a few weeks of seclusion would do me no harm; whereas now I am a suspected person to nearly all whom I may meet."

"It is not agreeable," Philip answered, "but the discipline may be useful. The bail terminates when the trial commences, you understand, and you will have a few nights alone, as it is,—quite enough, I imagine, to make you satisfied with liberty under suspicion. However I have one demand to make, Joseph! I have thought over all possible lines of defense; I have secured legal assistance for you, and we are agreed as to the course to be adopted. I do not think you can help us at all. If we find that you can, we will call upon you; in the meantime, wait and hope!"

"Why should I not?" Joseph asked. "I have nothing to fear, Philip."

"No!" But Philip's emphatic answer was intended to deceive. He was purposely false, knew himself to be so, and yet his conscience never troubled him less!

When they reached the farm, Philip saw by Rachel Miller's face that she had a communication to make. It required a little management to secure an interview with her without Joseph's knowledge; but some necessity for his presence at the barn favored his friend. No sooner were they alone than Rachel approached Philip hastily and said, in a hurried whisper:—

"Here! I have found something, at last! It took a mighty search: I thought I never *should* come upon the least bits that we could make anything of: but this was in the upper part of a box where she kept her rings and chains, and such likes! Take it,—it makes me uncomfortable to hold it in my fingers!"

She thrust a small paper into his hand.

It was folded very neatly, and there was an apothecary's label on the back. Philip read: "Ziba Linthicum's Drug store, No. 77 Main St., Magnolia." Under this printed address was written in large letters the word "Arsenic." On unfolding the paper he saw that a little white dust remained in the creases: quite enough to identify the character of the drug.

"I shall go back to-morrow!" he said. "Thank Heaven, we have got one clew to the mystery! Joseph must know nothing of this until all is explained; but while I am gone make another and more thorough search! Leave no corner unexplored: I am sure we shall find something more."

"I'd rip up her dresses!" was Rachel's emphatic reply. "That is, if it would do any good. But perhaps feeling of the lining and the hems might be enough. I'll take every drawer out, and move the furniture! But I must wait for daylight: I'm not generally afeared, but there is some things, you know, which a body would as lief not do by night, with cracks and creaks all around you, which you don't seem to hear at other times."

26. LINCOLN AND HALLECK

On President Lincoln's opinions on Halleck's poetry, here is a bulletin from the Lincoln National Life Foundation in Fort Wayne, Indiana:

Lincoln Lore
Bulletin of the Lincoln National Life Foundation

Dr. Louis A. Warren, Editor.
Published each week by The Lincoln National Life Insurance Company,
Fort Wayne, Indiana. Number 421, May 3, 1937.

LINCOLN'S ADMIRATION FOR HALLECK'S POEMS

Lincoln's love for the poets is well known and his ability to quote from many of them is a matter of record. It is interesting to note that before public opinion had placed a very high value on the work of Fitz-Greene Halleck, Lincoln had expressed his admiration for several of Halleck's lines. Less than three weeks before Lincoln's death, he was visited by James Grant Wilson and some friends. Mr. Wilson made this memorandum in his diary at that time: "The President at the White House read to three intimate friends with much power and pathos, Halleck's "Alnwick Castle" and "Marco Bozzaris."

James Grant Wilson was traveling abroad in the summer of 1856 and spent a day with Robert Burns' youngest sister, Isabella, who is said to have resembled the poet more than any other member of the family. She was over eighty years old and the last survivor of the Burnses. In talking about her brother she expressed the opinion that nothing had been written about him which was equal to the lines the poet Halleck had contributed.

In the month of April, 1860, Mr. Wilson was located in Chicago where he was publishing a literary journal called The Record. His office was in the Portland Block on Dearborn Street where Leonard Volk also had his studio on the sixth floor. One day Lincoln, who was then giving Volk some sittings, was met on the stairway by Wilson and invited to visit his office on his return from the studio.

Lincoln was very much interested in the busts of Shakespeare and Burns, which adorned Mr. Wilson's office and which he had brought from Stratford and Ayr. Mr. Lincoln was led to comment, "They are my two favorite authors, and I must manage to see their birthplaces some day, if I can contrive to cross the Atlantic." Shortly after this visit Mr. Wilson presented Abraham Lincoln with a copy of Halleck's poems and in the letter which accompanied the book, Wilson mentioned the fact that he had met Robert Burns' sister. Lincoln acknowledged the receipt of the book with the following letter:

Springfield, May 2, 1860

Mr. James G. Wilson.

My Dear Friend: I am greatly obliged for the volume of your friend Fitz-Greene Halleck's poems. Many a month has passed since I have met with anything more admirable than his beautiful lines on Burns. With Alnwick Castle, Marco Bozzaris, and Red Jacket, I am also much pleased.

It is wonderful that you should have seen and known a sister of Robert Burns. You must tell me something about her when we meet again.

Yours very truly,
A. Lincoln.

Lincoln, always a great admirer of Burns, thought Halleck's long tribute to him which contained thirty-eight stanzas a very beautiful poem. These two verses must have especially impressed him; and how much more they impress those who have stood at Lincoln's birthplace and the Lincoln National Memorial.

I've stood beside the cottage bed
 Where the Bard-peasant first drew breath;
A straw-thatched roof above his head,
A straw-wrought couch beneath.

*

And I have stood beside the pile,
 His monument—that tells to Heaven
The homage of earth's proudest isle
 To that Bard-peasant given!

From "Alnwick Castle" the opening lines must have impressed Lincoln. His own people had always been a migratory family, living on the very frontiers of western civilization. Not so the royal family of Alnwick Castle:

> Home of the Percy's high-born race,
> Home of their beautiful and brave,
> Alike their birth and burial place,
> Their cradle and their grave!

"Red Jacket," a poem eulogizing an Indian chief, "also a Monarch born," is far removed from the atmosphere of Alnwick Castle but was quite familiar to Lincoln. A single stanza in which the chief's eloquence is praised, may have indirectly influenced the writing of the Gettysburg Address when he told a friend that it was to be "short, short, short."

> Is eloquence?—Her spell is thine that reaches
> The heart, and makes the wisest head its sport;
> And there's one rare, strange virtue in thy speeches,
> The secret of their mastery—they are short.

The closing lines of "Marco Bozzaris" must have impressed Lincoln deeply and they were prophetic of his own place in history.

> And even she who gave thee birth.
> Will, by their pilgrim-circled hearth,
> Talk of thy doom without a sigh:
> For thou art Freedom's now, and Fame's;
> One of the few, the immortal names.
> That were not born to die.[21]

For more thoughts on these poems, see Edgar Allan Poe's criticisms on Halleck, [A.7].

XXVII

THE LABELS

THE WORK AT Coventry Forge was now so well organized that Philip could easily give the most of his time to Joseph's vindication. He had secured the services of an excellent country lawyer, but he also relied much upon the assistance of two persons,—his sister Madeline and Elwood Withers: Madeline, from her rapid, clear insight, her shrewd interpretation of circumstances; and Elwood as an active, untiring practical agent.

The latter, according to agreement, had ridden up from his section of the railway, and was awaiting Philip when he returned home.

Philip gave them the history of the day,—this time frankly, with all the signs and indications which he had so carefully kept from Joseph's knowledge. Both looked aghast; and Elwood bent an ivory paper-cutter so suddenly in his hands that it snapped in twain. He colored like a girl.

"It serves me right," he said. "Whenever my hands are idle, Satan finds mischief for 'em,—as the spelling-book says. But just so the people bend and twist Joseph Asten's character, and just so unexpectedly his life may snap in their hands!"

"May the omen be averted!" Madeline cried. "Put down the pieces, Mr. Withers! You frighten me."

"No, it is reversed!" said Philip. "Just so Joseph's friends will snap this chain of circumstances. If you begin to be superstitious, I must look out for other aids. The tracing of the poison is a more fortunate step than I hoped, at the start. I cannot at all guess to what it may lead, but there is a point beyond which even the most malignant fate has no further power over an innocent man. Thus far we have met nothing but hostile circumstances: there seems to be more than Chance in the game, and I have an idea that the finding of this paper will break the evil spell. Come now, Madeline, and you, Withers, give me your guesses as to what my discovery shall be to-morrow!"

After a pause, Madeline answered: "It must have been purchased—perhaps even by

Mr. Asten—for rats or mice; and she may have swallowed the drug in a fit of passion."

"*I* think," said Elwood, "that she bought it for the purpose of poisoning Joseph! Then, may be, the glasses were, changed, as I've heard tell of a man whose wife changed his coffee-cup because there was a fly in it, giving him hers, and thereby innocently killed him when *he* meant to ha' killed her."

"Ha!" Philip cried; "the most incredible things, apparently, are sometimes the most natural! I had not thought of this explanation."

"O Philip!" said Madeline, "that would be a new horror! Pray, let us not think of it: indeed, indeed, we must not guess anymore."

Philip strove to put the idea from his mind: he feared lest it might warp his judgment and mislead him in investigations which it required a cool, sharp intellect to prosecute. But the idea would not stay away: it haunted him precisely on account of its enormity, and he rode again to Magnolia the next day with a foreboding sense of some tragic secret about to be revealed.

But he never could have anticipated the actual revelation.

There was no difficulty in finding Ziba Linthicum's drugstore. The proprietor was a lank, thin-faced man, with projecting, near-sighted eyes, and an exceedingly prim, pursed mouth. His words, uttered in the close, wiry twang peculiar to Southern Pennsylvania, seemed to give him a positive relish: one could fancy that his mouth watered slightly as he spoke. His long, lean lips had a settled smirk at the corner, and the skin was drawn so tightly over his broad, concave chin-bone that it shone, as if polished around the edges.

He was waiting upon a little girl when Philip entered; but he looked up from his scales, bowed, smiled, and said: "In a moment, if you please."

Philip leaned upon the glass case, apparently absorbed in the contemplation of the various soaps and perfumes under his eyes, but thinking only of the paper in his pocket-book.

"Something in this line, perhaps? Mr. Linthicum, with a still broader smile, began to enumerate: "These are from the Society Hygiennick—"

"No," said Philip, "my business is especially private. I take it for granted that you have many little confidential matters entrusted to you."

"Oh, undoubtedly, sir! Quite as much so as a physician."

"You are aware also that mistakes sometimes occur in making up prescriptions, or in using them afterwards?"

"Not by *me*, I should hope. I keep a record of every dangerous ingredient which goes out of my hands."

"Ah!" Philip exclaimed. Then he paused, uncertain how much to confide to Mr. Linthicum's discretion. But, on mentioning his name and residence, he found that both himself and Mr. Hopeton were known—and favorably, it seemed—to the apothecary. He knew the class of men to which the latter belonged,—prim, fussy, harmlessly vain persons, yet who take as good care of their consciences as of their cravats and shirt-bosoms. He produced the paper without further delay.

"That was bought here, certainly," said Mr. Linthicum. "The word 'Arsenic' is written in my hand. The date when, and the person by whom it was purchased, must be in my register. Will you go over it with me?"

He took a volume from a drawer, and beginning at the last entry, they went slowly backward over the names, the apothecary saying: "This is confidential: I rely upon your seeing without remembering."

They had not gone back more than two or three weeks before Philip came upon a name that made his heart stand still. There was a record in a single line:—

"*Miss Henderson. Arsenic.*"

He waited a few seconds, until he felt sure of his voice. Then he asked: "Do you happen to know Miss Henderson?"

"Not at all! A perfect stranger."

"Call you, perhaps, remember her appearance?"

"Let me see," said Mr. Linthicum, biting the end of his forefinger; "that must have been the veiled lady. The date corresponds. Yes, I feel sure of it, as all the other poison customers are known to me."

"Pray describe her then!" Philip exclaimed.

"Really, I fear that I cannot. Dressed in black, I think; but I will not be positive. A soft, agreeable voice, I am sure."

"Was she alone? Or was anyone else present?"

"Now I *do* recall one thing," the apothecary answered. "There was an agent of a wholesale city firm—a travelling agent, you understand—trying to persuade me into an order on his house. He stepped on one side as she came to the counter, and he perhaps saw her face more distinctly, for he laughed as she left, and said something about a handsome girl putting her lovers out of their misery."

But Mr. Linthicum could remember neither the name of the agent nor that of the firm which he represented. All Philip's questioning elicited no further particulars, and he was obliged to be satisfied with the record of the day and probable hour of the purchase, and with the apothecary's promise of the strictest secrecy.

He rode immediately home, and after a hasty consultation with Madeline, remounted his horse and set out to find Lucy Henderson. He was fortunate enough to meet her on the highway, on her way to call upon a neighbor. Springing from his horse he walked beside her, and announced his discovery at once.

Lucy remembered the day when she had accompanied Julia to Magnolia, during Joseph's absence from home. The time of the day, also, corresponded to that given by the apothecary.

"Did you visit the drug-store?" Philip asked.

"No," she answered, "and I did not know that Julia had. I paid two or three visits to acquaintances, while she did her shopping, as she told me."

"Then try and remember, not only the order of those visits, but the time occupied by each," said Philip. "Write to your friends, and ask them to refresh their memories. It has become an important point, for—the poison was purchased in your name!"

"Impossible!" Lucy cried. She gazed at Philip with such amazement that her innocence was then fixed in his mind, if it had not been so before.

"Yes, I say 'impossible!' too," he answered. "There is only one explanation. Julia Asten gave your name instead of her own when she purchased it."

"Oh!" Lucy's voice sounded like a hopeless personal protest against the collective falsehood and wickedness of the world.

"I have another chance to reach the truth," said Philip. "I shall find the stranger,—the travelling agent,—if it obliges me to summon every such agent of every wholesale drughouse in the city! It is at least a positive fortune that we have made this discovery now."

He looked at his watch. "I have just time to catch the evening train," he said, hurriedly, "but I should like to send a message to Elwood Withers. If you pass through that wood on the right, you will see the track just below you. It is not more than half a mile from here; and you are almost sure to find him at or near the unfinished tunnel. Tell him to see Rachel Miller, and if anything further has been found, to inform my sister Madeline at once. That is all. I make no apology for imposing the service on you: good-by, and keep up your faith, Lucy!"

He pressed her hand, sprang into the saddle, and cantered briskly away.

Lucy, infected by his haste, crossed the field, struggled through the under-growth of the wild belt of wood, and descended to the railway track, without giving herself time to think. She met a workman near the mouth of the tunnel, and not daring to venture in, sent by him a summons to Elwood. It was not many minutes before he appeared.

"Something has happened, Lucy?" he exclaimed.

"Philip thinks he has made a discovery," she answered, "and I come to you as his messenger." She then repeated Philip's words.

"Is that all?" Elwood asked, scanning her face anxiously. "You do not seem quite like your real self, Lucy."

She sat down upon the bank. "I am out of breath," she said; "I must have walked faster than I thought."

"Wait a minute!" said he. He ran up the track, to where a little side-glen crossed it, sprang down among the bushes, and presently reappeared with a tin cup full of cold, pure spring water.

The draught seemed to revive her at once. "It is not all, Elwood," she said. "Joseph is not the only one, now, who is implicated by the same circumstances."

"Who else?—not Philip Held!"

"No," she answered, very quietly, "it is a woman. Her name is Lucy Henderson."

Before Elwood could speak, she told him all that she had heard from Philip. He could scarcely bring his mind to accept its truth.

"Oh, the—" he began; "but, no! I will keep the words to myself. There is something deeper in this than any of us has yet looked for! Depend upon it, Lucy, she had a plan in getting you there!"

Lucy was silent. She fancied she knew Julia's plan already.

"Did she mean to poison Joseph herself, and throw the suspicion on you? And now by her own death, after all, she accomplishes her chief end! It is a hellish tangle, whichever way I look; but they say that the truth will sooner or later put down any amount of lies, and so it must be, here. We must get at the truth, the whole truth, and nothing but the truth! Do you not say so, Lucy?"

"Yes!" she answered firmly, looking him in the face.

"Ay, though *all* should come to light! We can't tell what it may be necessary to say. They may go to work and unravel Joseph's life, and yours, and mine, and hold up the stuff for everybody to look at. Well, let 'em! say I. If there are dark streaks in mine, I guess they'll look tolerably fair beside that one black heart. We're here alone, Lucy; there may not be a chance to say it soon again, so I'll say now, that if need comes to publish what I said to you one night a year ago, —to publish it for Joseph's sake, or your sake,—don't keep back a single word! The worst would be, some men or women might think me conceited."

"No, Elwood!" she exclaimed: "that reproach would fall on me! You once offered me your help, and I—I fear I spurned it; but I will take it now. Nay, I beg you to offer it to me again, and I will accept it with gratitude!"

She rose, and stretched out her hand.

Elwood clasped it tenderly, held it a moment, and seemed about to speak. But although his lips parted, and there was a movement of the muscles of his throat, he did not utter a word. In another moment he turned, walked a few yards up the track, and then came back to her.

"No one could mistake you for Julia Asten," he said. "You are at least half a head taller than she was. Your voice is not at all the same: the apothecary will surely notice the difference! Then an *alibi*, as they call it, can be proved."

"So Philip Held thought. But if my friends should not remember the exact time,— what should I then do?"

"Lucy, don't ask yourself the question now! It seems to me that the case stands this way: one evil woman has made a trap, fallen into it herself, and taken the secret of its make away with her. There is nothing more to be invented, and so we hold all that we gain. While we are mining, where's the counter-mining to come from? Who is to lie us out of our truth? There isn't much to stand on yet, I grant; but another step—the least little thing—may give us all the ground we want!"

He spoke so firmly and cheerily that Lucy's despondent feeling was charmed away. Besides, nothing could have touched her more than Elwood's heroic self-control. After the miserable revelation which Philip had made, it was unspeakably refreshing to be brought into contact with a nature so sound and sweet and strong. When he had led her by an easier path up the hill, and they had parted at the end of the lane leading to her father's house, she felt, as never before, the comfort of relying so wholly on a faithful man friend.

Elwood took his horse and rode to the Asten farm. Joseph's face brightened at his appearance, and they talked as of old, avoiding the dark year that lay between their past intimacy and its revival. As in Philip's case, it was difficult to communicate secretly with Rachel Miller; but Elwood, with great patience, succeeded in looking his wish to speak with her, and uniting her efforts with his own. She adroitly turned the conversation upon a geological work which Joseph had been reading.

"I've been looking into the subject myself," Elwood said. "Would you let me see the book: it may be the thing I want."

"It is on the book-shelf in your bedroom, Joseph," Rachel remarked.

There was time enough for Elwood to declare his business, and for Rachel to answer: "Mr. Held said every scrap, and it is but a scrap, with half a name on it. I found it behind and mostly under the lower drawer in the same box. I'll get it before you leave, and give it to you when we shake hands. Be careful, for he may make something out of it, after all. Tell him there isn't a stitch in a dress but I've examined, and a mortal work it was!"

It was late before Elwood could leave; nevertheless, he rode to Coventry Forge. The scrap of paper had been successfully transferred, and his pressing duty was to deliver it into the hands of Madeline Held. He found her anxiously waiting, in accordance with Philip's instructions.

When they looked at the paper, it seemed, truly, to be a worthless fragment. It had the character, also, of an apothecary's label, but the only letters remaining were those forming the end of the name, apparently —ers, and a short distance under them —Sts.

"Behind and mostly under the lower drawer of her jewel-case," said Madeline, musingly. "I think I might guess how it came there. She had seen the label, which had probably been forgotten, and then, as she supposed, had snatched it away and destroyed it, without noticing that this piece, caught behind the drawer, had been torn off. But there is no evidence—and perhaps none can be had—that the paper contained poison."

"Can you make anything out of the letters?" Elwood asked.

"The 'Sts' certainly means 'Streets' —now, I see! It is a corner house! This makes the place a little more easy to be identified. If Philip cannot find it, I am sure a detective can. I will write to him at once."

"Then I'll wait and ride to the office with the letter," said Elwood.

Madeline rose, and commenced walking up and down the room: she appeared to be suddenly and unusually excited.

"I have a new suspicion," she said, at last. "Perhaps I am in too much of a hurry to make conjectures, because Philip thinks I have a talent for it,—and yet, this grows upon me every minute! I hope—oh, I hope I am right!"

She spoke with so much energy that Elwood began to share her excitement without knowing its cause. She noticed the eager, waiting expression of his face.

"You must really pardon me, Mr. Withers. I believe I was talking to myself rather than to you; I will not mention my fancy until Philip decides whether it is worth acting upon. There will be no harm if each of us finds a different clew, and follows it. Philip will hardly leave the city tomorrow. I shall not write, but go down with the first train in the morning!"

Elwood took his leave, feeling hopeful and yet very restless.

It was a long while before Madeline encountered Philip. He was busily employed in carrying out his plan of tracing the travelling agent,—not yet successful, but sanguine of success. He examined the scrap of paper which Madeline brought, listened to her reasons for the new suspicion which had crossed her mind, and compared them with the little evidence already collected.

"Do not let us depend too seriously on this," he then said; "there is about an even chance that you are right. We will keep it as an additional and independent test, but we dare not lose sight of the fact that the law will assume Joseph's guilt, and we must establish his innocence, first of all. Nay, if we can simply prove that Julia, and not Lucy, purchased the poison, we shall save both! But, at the same time, I will try to find this —ers, who lives in a corner-house, and I will have a talk with old Blessing this very evening."

"Why not go now?"

"Patience, you impetuous girl! I mean to take no step without working out every possible result in advance. If I were not here in the city, I would consult with Mr. Pinkerton before proceeding further. Now I shall take you to the train: you must return to Coventry, and watch and wait there."

When Philip called at the Blessing mansion, in the evening, he found only Mrs. Blessing at home. She was rigid and dreary in her mourning, and her reception of him was almost repellant in its stiff formality.

"Mr. Blessing is absent," she explained, inviting Philip to a seat by a wave of her hand. "His own interests rendered a trip to the Oil Regions imperative; it is a mental distraction which I do not grudge him. This is a cheerless household, sir,—one daughter gone forever, and another about to leave us. How does Mr. Asten bear his loss?"

Philip thereupon, as briefly and forcibly as possible, related all that had occurred. "I wish to consult Mr. Blessing," he concluded, "in relation to the possibility of his being able to furnish any testimony on his son-in-law's side. Perhaps you, also—"

"No!" she interrupted. "I know nothing whatever! If the trial (which I think most unnecessary and shocking) gets into the city papers, it will be a terrible scandal for us. When will it come on, did you say?"

"In two or three weeks."

"There will be barely time!" she cried.

"For that reason," said he, "I wish to secure the evidence at once. All the preparations for the defense must be completed within that time."

"Clementina," Mrs. Blessing continued, without heeding his words, "will be married about the first of October. Mr. Spelter has been desirous of making a bridal tour in Europe. She did not favor the plan; but it seems to me like an interposition of Heaven!"

Philip rose, too disgusted to speak. He bowed in silence, and left the house.

27. LINCOLN AND BUCHANAN

The question of America's first gay president sits interestingly between the 15th and 16th: James Buchanan and Abraham Lincoln.

During the latter part of the 1850s, James Buchanan was president. He was an even less capable executive, if that's possible, than his predecessor, Pierce. Buchanan was a so-called doughface, a Northerner sympathetic to the interests of Southern slaveholders. The term suggests a highly changeable person, capable of molding his features to curry the favor of varied constituencies. Duality ran deep in Buchanan's nature. Before becoming president, he had been a wealthy lawyer who owned a sprawling estate in Lancaster, Pennsylvania, called Wheatland, modeled after a Southern plantation. Predictably, he pleased no one during his presidency.

By the late 1850s, there didn't exist a single official US institution that wasn't in crisis: Congress, an actual battleground; territorial governments, a farce; the Supreme Court, utterly suspect following the *Dred Scott* decision. Scott was a slave who sued for freedom on the grounds that his master had moved with him to Wisconsin, a free territory. But the Court ruled that a black person had no right to sue. Further, the Court handed down a ruling so broad as to make it difficult to arrest the spread of slavery into the Northern territories. Buchanan worked secretly behind the scenes, obtaining his desired outcome for the case by pressuring a couple of justices, an egregious violation of the separation of powers. In this way, Buchanan, arguably the worst president in US history, played a role in *Dred Scott*, often considered the nadir of the US Supreme Court. The ruling led to rampant uncertainty about the nation's future. That uncertainty, in turn, was a major factor in sparking the Panic of 1857. On top of everything else, the economy was in shambles.[33]

There is a lot of evidence that James Buchanan, one of America's most inauspicious presidents, was homosexual:

[Jim] Loewen at the *History News Network* is one of several historians who believe that James Buchanan, who served from 1857 to 1861, was in fact our first gay president. He is the only president to have remained a bachelor throughout his life. (His niece, Harriet Lane, handled the duties of First Lady during his term in office.) He shared a home with William Rufus King, an Alabama Senator and Vice President under Buchanan's predecessor, Franklin Pierce. Their relationship was reportedly so close that Andrew Jackson and other contemporaries referred to them as "Miss Nancy" and "Aunt Fancy" [among other nicknames, such as "Mr. and Mrs. Buchanan," his "better half" "rigged out in her best clothes," and "the Siamese twins" according to Loewen].

In one letter to a confidante dated May 13, 1844, Buchanan wrote about his life after King moved to Paris to become the American ambassador to France: "I am now 'solitary and alone,' having no companion in the house with me. I have gone a wooing to several gentlemen, but have not succeeded with any one of them. I feel that it is not good for man to be alone; and should not be astonished to find myself married to some old maid who can nurse me when I am sick, provide good dinners for me when I am well, and not expect from me any very ardent or romantic affection."[5]

James Buchanan ("despised by Walt Whitman"[39]) won the election in 1856, and Lincoln (whom Whitman contributed to the immortalization of in his poems "When Lilacs Last in the Dooryard Bloom'd" and "O Captain! My Captain!"—see Chapter 11: Leaves of Grass) took on the immense challenge of a dividing nation in 1861. Here is Whitman's take on America's presidents, as spoken to Traubel:

"I never knew a president to totally fail. ["Even Johnson?" Traubel asks.] Even Andy Johnson. In all the line of Presidents I do not think we have had one absolute failure—I think every President so far has made more or less honest use of the office. If they had all of them except Lincoln been inadequate, impossible, he would have redeemed, justified, the tribe. But there have been other forcible goodsized men: there was Jackson: he was a great character: true gold: not a line false or for effect—unmined, ungorged, unanything, in fact—anything wholly done, completed—just the genuine ore in the rough. Jackson had something of [Thomas] Carlyle in him: a touch of irascibility: quarrelsome, testy, threatening humors: still was always finally honest, like Carlyle: Jackson was virile and instant. Look at some of the other Presidents: take Andy Johnson and Frank Pierce, who were the worst of the lot: they tried every way they knew how to steady up—to redeem themselves from their weaknesses. Take Buchanan: he was perhaps the weakest of the President tribe—the very unablest: he was a gentleman—meant to do well—was almost basely inert in the one crisis of his career."[39]

As far as the men in President Lincoln's life, they start with Joshua Fry Speed:

Detractors of Lincoln's possible homosexuality, such as historian David Herbert Donald, often say there is no new evidence on Lincoln. Yet historians continue to draw fresh conclusions from Lincoln's letters. Those who attempt to refute Lincoln's possible "homosexuality" usually focus on one particular incident—of the many—that supports the theory: his relationship with Speed.

[...]

In 1837, Lincoln moved to Springfield, Ill., to practice law and enter politics. That's where he met [...] Joshua Fry Speed, [who] became his bed partner for a while. Beyond the revelation that Lincoln and Speed had an intimate friendship, little has been written about how diligently Speed worked for Lincoln's legal and political career. Speed's name popped up in many of Lincoln's legal filings and on the Illinois Whig Party's central committee. The two were almost inseparable. Most Lincoln historians agree this relationship was the strongest and most intimate of the president's life. What they don't agree on is why they slept in the same bed together for four years when they had the space and means to sleep separately, as was expected of men their age. They were no longer young and poor. And this was a house with ample room, unlike the hotels that accommodated Lincoln and his team on the road; then, it was common to sleep two or more in a bed.

By 1840, both Lincoln and Speed—now 31 and 26—were considered well past the marrying age. Both bachelors reportedly were hesitant to tie the knot, but it was a de-facto requirement to have a wife if you wanted to move in political circles—or at least create the perception of interest in marriage. Both Speed and Lincoln dreaded this "requirement," as evidenced by Lincoln's letters. Speed takes the marriage plunge first and moves back to Kentucky, leaving Lincoln. At this precise time, Lincoln suffered a mental breakdown. Historians have been all over the map as to what caused the breakdown, but it was so intense that friends, including Herndon, worried he would take his own life. Lincoln only recovered after Speed invited him to visit him and his new wife in Kentucky.

Lincoln's most emotional and intimate writings were contained in his letters to Speed. From the time they lived together until shortly after Speed married and moved to Kentucky, Lincoln always signed his letters "forever yours" or "yours forever."

Lincoln wrote to Speed shortly before the latter's Feb. 15, 1842 wedding: "When this shall reach you, you will have been Fanny's husband several days. You know my desire to befriend you is everlasting—that I will never cease, while I know how to do any thing. But you will always hereafter, be on ground that I have never occupied, and consequently, if advice were needed,

I might advise wrong.

"I am now fully convinced, that you love her as ardently as you are capable of loving … If you went through the ceremony calmly, or even with sufficient composure not to excite alarm in any present, you are safe, beyond question, and in two or three months, to say the most, will be the happiest of men.

"I hope with tolerable confidence, that this letter is a plaster for a place that is no longer sore. God grant it may be so.

"I would desire you to give my particular respects to Fanny, but perhaps you will not wish her to know you have received this, lest she should desire to see it. Make her write me an answer to my last letter to her at any rate. I would set great value upon another letter from her.

"P.S. I have not been quite a man ever since you left."[41]

Even after Lincoln married Mary Todd on Nov. 4, 1842, and even after the Civil War broke out (with Speed living in a border state, Kentucky), their correspondence continued unabated, and Speed came to spend a night with Lincoln in the president's cottage at the Soldier's Home (just north of the White House).

After Speed's marriage, Lincoln's close male friendships also included a "schoolboy crush" on the first Union soldier killed in the war, Elmer Ellsworth:

After hearing of the tragedy, Lincoln wept openly and went with Mrs. Lincoln to view the soldier's body. Lincoln arranged for Ellsworth to lay in state in the White House, followed by a funeral. The president was inconsolable for days.[41]

Another companion was David Derickson, a military Captain who served as his bodyguard and also slept in his bed:

Lincoln and his bodyguard became close, and historians Tripp and David Herbert Donald noted two recorded mentions that Lincoln and Derickson slept in the same bed: Derickson's superior, Lt. Col. Thomas Chamberlain, and Tish Fox, the wife of Assistant Navy Secretary Gustavus Fox, both wrote about it. Tish wrote in her diary that Derickson was devoted to Lincoln and "when Mrs. Lincoln was away, they slept together."

[T]here were more than just two eyewitnesses to this relationship. After the war, Chamberlain published an account of the regiment called "History of the 150th Regiment of Pennsylvania Volunteers, Second Regiment, Bucktail Brigade." Before it was published, many members of the company reviewed the manuscript and no one objected to the following:

"[Lincoln] was not long in placing the officers in his two companies at their ease in his presence, and Capts. Derickson and Crozier were shortly on a footing of such marked friendship with him that they were often summoned to dinner or breakfast at the presidential board. Capt. Derickson, in particular, advanced so far in the president's confidence and esteem that in Mrs. Lincoln's absence he frequently spent the night at his cottage, sleeping in the same bed with him, and—it is said—making use of his excellency's nightshirt! Thus began an intimacy which continued unbroken until the following spring ..." The Bucktails witnessed the relationship between the president and his bodyguard, which was public enough that they knew Derickson kept him company when Mrs. Lincoln traveled, and wore his nightshirt. Historical interpretations aside, why would the president, then in his 50s, sleep with his bodyguard?

[...]

Taken individually, accounts of Lincoln with other men may not offer enough proof that he was gay. But the pattern reveals a man who, in his sexual prime, slept exclusively with another man for four years [...]; who wrote a poem about a boy marrying a boy [see (A.22)]; and who, as president, slept with his bodyguard. From historical records, one can conclude that Lincoln enjoyed sleeping with men. He did so when it was acceptable in youth and poverty, and also when he was older and successful. While it is documented that Lincoln slept with several men, there is only one confirmed woman who shared his bed—Todd.[41]

XXVIII

THE TRIAL

As the day of trial drew nigh, the anxiety and activity of Joseph's friends increased, so that even the quiet atmosphere wherein he lived was disturbed by it. He could not help knowing that they were engaged in collecting evidence, but in as much as Philip always said, "You can do nothing!" he forced himself to wait with such patience as was possible. Rachel Miller, who had partly taken the hired man, Dennis, into her confidence, hermetically sealed the house to the gossip of the neighborhood; but her greatest triumph was in concealing her alarm, as the days rolled by and the mystery was not yet unravelled.

There was not much division of opinion in the neighborhood, however. The growing discord between husband and wife had not been generally remarked: they were looked upon as a loving and satisfied couple. Joseph's integrity of character was acknowledged, and, even had it been doubted, the people saw no motive for crime. His action in demanding a legal investigation also operated favorably upon public opinion.

The quiet and seclusion were beneficial to him. His mind became calmer and clearer; he was able to survey the past without passion, and to contemplate his own faults with a sense of wholesome bitterness rather than pain. The approaching trial was not a pleasant thing to anticipate, but the worst which he foresaw was the probability of so much of his private life being laid bare to the world. Here, again, his own words returned to condemn him. Had he not said to Lucy, on the morning of that fatal day, "I am sick of masks!" Had he not threatened to follow Julia with his own miserable story? The system of checks which restrain impulse, and the whirl of currents and counter-currents which govern a man's movement through life, began to arrange themselves in his mind. True wisdom, he now felt, lay in understanding these, and so employing them as to reach individual liberty of action through law, and not outside of it. He had been shallow and reckless, even in his good impulses; it was now time to endure quietly for a season what their effect had been.

The day previous to the trial Philip had a long consultation with Mr. Pinkerton. He had been so far successful that the name and whereabouts of the travelling agent had been discovered: the latter had been summoned, but he could not possibly arrive before the next day. Philip had also seen Mr. Blessing, who entered with great readiness into his plans, promised his assistance in ascertaining the truth of Madeline's suspicion, and would give his testimony as soon as he could return from New York, whither he had gone to say farewell to Mrs. Clementina Spelter, before her departure for Paris on a bridal journey. These were the two principal witnesses for the defense, and it was yet uncertain what kind of testimony they would be able to give.

"We must finish the other witnesses," Mr. Pinkerton said, "(who, in spite of all we can do, will strengthen the prosecution), by the time you reach here. If Spenham gives us trouble, as I am inclined to suspect, we cannot well spare you the first day, but I suppose it cannot be helped."

"I will send a telegram to Blessing, in New York, to make sure," Philip answered. "Byle and Glanders answer for their agent, and I can try him with the photograph on the way out. If that succeeds, Blessing's failure will be of less consequence."

"If only they do not reach Linthicum in the meantime! I will prolong the impaneling of the jury, and use every other liberty of delay allowed me; yet I have to be cautious. This is Spenham's first important case, and he is ambitious to make capital."

Mr. Spenham was the prosecuting attorney, who had just been elected to his first term of service in that capacity. He had some shrewdness as a criminal lawyer, and a great deal of experience of the subterranean channels of party politics. This latter acquirement, in fact, was the secret of his election, for he was known to be coarse, unscrupulous, and offensive. Mr. Pinkerton was able to foresee his probable line of attack, and was especially anxious, for that reason, to introduce testimony which would shorten the trial.

When the hour came, and Joseph found that Philip was inevitably absent, the strength he had summoned to his heart seemed to waver for an instant. All his other friends were present, however: Lucy Henderson and Madeline came with the Hopetons, and Elwood Withers stood by his side so boldly and proudly that he soon recovered his composure.

The court-room was crowded, not only by the idlers of the town, but also many neighbors from the country. They were grave and silent, and Joseph's appearance in the place allotted to the accused seemed to impress them painfully. The preliminaries occupied some time, and it was nearly noon before the first witness was called.

This was the physician. He stated, in a clear, business-like manner, the condition in which he found Julia, his discovery of the poison, and the unusual character of its operation, adding his opinion that the latter was owing to a long-continued nervous tension, culminating in hysterical excitement. Mr. Spenham questioned him very closely as to Joseph's demeanor, and his expressions before and after the death. The point of attack which he selected was Julia's exclamation: "Joseph, I will try to be different, but I must live for that!"

"These words," he said, "indicate a previous threat on the part of the accused. His helpless victim—"

Mr. Pinkerton protested against the epithet. But his antagonist found numberless ways of seeming to take Joseph's guilt for granted, and thus gradually to mould the pliant minds of a not very intelligent jury. The physician was subjected to a rigid cross-examination, in the course of which he was led to state that he, himself, had first advised that the fact of the poisoning should not be mentioned until after the funeral. The onus of the secrecy was thus removed from Joseph, and this was a point gained.

The next witness was the servant-woman, who had been present in the hall when Julia fell upon the landing of the staircase. She had heard the words, "Go away! you have killed me!" spoken in a shrill, excited voice. She had already guessed that something was wrong between the two. Mr. Asten came home looking quite wild and strange; he didn't seem to speak in his usual voice; he walked about in a restless way, and then went into the garden. Miss Lucy followed him, and then Mrs. Asten; but in a little while *she* came back, with her dress torn and her arms scratched; she, the witness, noticed this as Mrs. Asten passed through the hall, tottering as she went and with her fists shut tight. Then Mr. Asten went upstairs to her bedroom; heard them speaking, but not the words; said to Sally, who was in the kitchen, "It's a real tiff and no mistake," and Sally remarked, "They're not used to each other yet, as they will be in a year or two."

The witness was with difficulty kept to a direct narrative. She had told the tale so often that every particular had its fixed phrases of description, and all the questioning on both sides called forth only repetitions. Joseph listened with a calm, patient air; nothing had yet occurred for which he was not prepared. The spectators, however, began to be deeply interested, and a sharp observer might have noticed that they were already taking sides.

Mr. Pinkerton soon detected that, although the woman's statements told against Joseph, she possessed no friendly feeling for Julia. He endeavored to make the most of this; but it was not much.

When Lucy Henderson's name was called, there was a stir of curiosity in the audience. They knew that the conference in the garden, from which Julia had returned in such an excited condition, must now be described. Mr. Spenham pricked up his red ears, ran his hand through his stubby hair, and prepared himself for battle; while Mr. Pinkerton, already in possession of all the facts, felt concerned only regarding the manner in which Lucy might give them. This was a case where so much depended on the impression produced by the individual!

By the time Lucy was sworn she appeared to be entirely composed; her face was slightly pale, but calm, and her voice steady. Mrs. Hopeton and Madeline Held sat near her, and Elwood Withers, leaning against a high railing, was nearly opposite.

There was profound silence as she began, and the interest increased as she approached the time of Joseph's return, She described his appearance, repeated the words she had heard, reproduced the scene in her own chamber, and so came, step by step, to the interview in the garden. The trying nature of her task now became evident. She spoke slowly, and with longer pauses; but whichever way she turned in her thought, the inexorable necessity of the whole truth stared her in the face.

"Must I repeat everything?" she asked. "I am not sure of recollecting the words precisely as they were spoken."

"You can certainly give the substance," said Mr. Spenham. "And be careful that you omit nothing: you are on your oath, and you ought to know what that means."

His words were loud and harsh. Lucy looked at the impassive face of the judge, at Elwood's earnest features, at the attentive jurymen, and went on.

When she came to Joseph's expression of the love that might have been possible, she gave also his words: "Had there been, I should have darkened the life of a friend."

"Ha!" exclaimed Mr. Spenham, "we are coming upon the motive of the murder."

Again Mr. Pinkerton protested, and was sustained by the court.

"Tell the jury," said Mr. Spenham, "whether there had been any interchange of such expressions between you and the accused previous to his marriage!"

This question was objected to, but the objection was overruled.

"None whatever!" was the answer.

Julia's sudden appearance, the accusation she made, and the manner in which Joseph met it, seemed to turn the current of sympathy the other way. Lucy's recollection of this scene was very clear and complete: had she wished it, she could not have forgotten a word or a look. In spite of Mr. Spenham's angry objections, she was allowed to go on and relate the conversation between Joseph and herself after Julia's return to the house. Mr. Pinkerton made the best use of this portion of the evidence, and it seemed that his side was strengthened, in spite of all unfavorable appearances.

"This is not all!" exclaimed the prosecuting attorney. "A married man does not make a declaration of love—"

"Of a past *possible* love," Mr. Pinkerton interrupted.

"A very fine hair-splitting indeed! A 'possible' love and a 'possible' return, followed by a 'possible' murder and a 'possible' remarriage! Our duty is to remove possibilities and establish facts. The question is, Was there no previous affection between the witness and the accused? This is necessary to prove a motive. I ask, then, the woman—I beg pardon, the lady—what were her sentiments towards the husband of the poisoned before his marriage, at the time of the conversation in the garden, and now?"

Lucy started, and could not answer. Mr. Pinkerton came to her aid. He protested strongly against such a question, though he felt that there was equal danger in answering it or leaving it unanswered. A portion of the spectators, sympathizing with Lucy, felt indignant at Mr. Spenham's demand; another portion, hungry for the most private and intimate knowledge of all the parties concerned, eagerly hoped that it would be acceded to.

Lucy half turned, so that she caught a glimpse of Joseph. He was calm, but his eyes expressed a sympathetic trouble. Then she felt her gaze drawn to Elwood, who had become a shade paler, and who met her eyes with a deep, inscrutable expression. Was he thinking of his recent words to her,—"If need comes to publish what I said to you, don't keep back a single word!" She felt sure of it, for all that he said was in her mind. Her decision was made: for truth's sake, and under the eye of God, she would speak. Having so resolved, she shut her mind to all else, for she needed the greatest strength of either woman or man.

The judge had decided that she was not obliged to answer the question. There was a murmur, here and there, among the spectators.

"Then I will use my freedom of choice," said Lucy, in a firm voice, "and answer it."

She kept her eyes on Elwood as she spoke, and compelled him to face her. She seemed to forget judge, jury, and the curious public, and to speak only to his ear.

"I am here to tell the whole truth, God helping me," she said. "I do not know how what I am required to say can touch the question of Joseph Asten's guilt or innocence; but I cannot pause to consider that. It is not easy for a woman to lay bare her secret heart to the world; I would like to think that every man who hears me has a wife, a sister, or a beloved girl of his choice, and that he will try to understand my heart through his knowledge of hers. I *did* cherish a tenderness which might have been love—I cannot tell—for Joseph Asten before his betrothal. I admit that his marriage was a grief to me at the time, for, while I had not suffered myself to feel any hope, I could not keep the feeling of disappointment out of my heart. It was both my blame and shame: I wrestled with it, and with God's help I overcame it."

There was a simple pathos in Lucy's voice, which pierced directly to the hearts of her hearers. She stood before them as pure as Godiva in her helpful nakedness. She saw on Elwood's cheek the blush which did not visit hers, and the sparkle of an unconscious tear. Joseph had hidden his face in his hands for a moment, but now looked up with a sadness which no man there could misinterpret.

Lucy had paused, as if waiting to be questioned, but the effect of her words had been so powerful and unexpected that Mr. Spenham was not quite ready. She went on:—

"When I say that I overcame it, I think I have answered everything. I went to him in the garden against my own wish, because his wife begged me with tears and sobs to intercede for her: I could not guess that he had ever thought of me otherwise than as a friend. I attributed his expressions to his disappointment in marriage, and pardoned him when he asked me to forget them—"

"O, no doubt!" Mr. Spenham interrupted, looking at the jury; "after all we have heard, they could not have been very disagreeable!"

Elwood made a rapid step forward; then, recollecting himself, resumed his position against the railing. Very few persons noticed the movement.

"They were very unwelcome," Lucy replied: "under any other circumstances, it would not have been easy to forgive them."

"And this former—'tenderness,' I think you called it," Mr. Spenham persisted, "—do you mean to say that you feel nothing of it at present?"

There was a murmur of indignation all over the room. If there is anything utterly incomprehensible to a vulgar nature, it is the natural delicacy of feeling towards women, which is rarely wanting even to the roughest and most ignorant men. The prosecution had damaged itself, and now the popular sympathy was wholly and strongly with Lucy.

"I have already answered that question," she said. "For the holy sake of truth, and of my own free-will, I have opened my heart. I did it, believing that a woman's first affection is pure, and would be respected; I did it, hoping that it might serve the cause of an innocent man; but now, since it has brought upon me doubt and insult, I shall avail myself of the liberty granted to me by the judge, and speak no word more!"

The spectators broke into applause, which the judge did not immediately check. Lucy's strength suddenly left her; she dropped into her seat and burst into tears.

"I have no further question to ask the witness," said Mr. Pinkerton.

Mr. Spenham inwardly cursed himself for his blunder,—not for his vulgarity, for of that he was sublimely unconscious,—and was only too ready to be relieved from Lucy's presence.

She rose to leave the court, Mrs. Hopeton accompanying her; but Elwood Withers was already at her side, and she leaned upon his arm as they passed through the crowd. The people fell back to make a way, and not a few whispered some honest word of encouragement. Elwood breathed heavily, and the veins on his forehead were swollen.

Not a word was spoken until they reached the hotel. Then Lucy, taking Elwood's hand, said: "Thank you, true, dear friend! I can say no more now. Go back, for Joseph's sake, and when the day is over come here and tell me, if you can, that I have not injured him in trying to help him."

When Elwood returned to the court-room, Rachel Miller was on the witness stand. Her testimony confirmed the interpretation of Julia's character which had been suggested by Lucy Henderson's. The sweet, amiable, suffering wife began to recede into the background, and the cold, false, selfish wife to take her place.

All Mr. Spenham's cross-examination failed to give the prosecution any support until he asked the question:—

"Have you discovered nothing whatever, since your return to the house, which will throw any light upon Mrs. Asten's death?"

Mr. Pinkerton, Elwood, and Madeline all felt that the critical moment had come. Philip's absence threatened to be a serious misfortune.

"Yes," Rachel Miller answered.

"Ah!" exclaimed the prosecuting attorney, rubbing his hair; "what was it?"

"The paper in which the arsenic was put up."

"Will you produce that paper?" he eagerly asked.

"I cannot now," said Rachel; "I gave it to Mr. Philip Held, so that he might find out something more."

Joseph listened with a keen, undisguised interest. After the first feeling of surprise that such an important event had been kept from his knowledge, his confidence in Philip's judgment reassured him.

"Has Mr. Philip Held destroyed that paper?" Mr. Spenham asked.

"He retains it, and will produce it before this court tomorrow," Mr. Pinkerton replied.

"Was there any mark, or label, upon it, which indicated the place where the poison had been procured?"

"Yes," said Rachel Miller.

"State what it was."

"Ziba Linthicum's drug-store, No. 77 Main Street, Magnolia," she replied, as if the label were before her eyes.

"Let Ziba Linthicum be summoned at once!" Mr. Spenham cried.

Mr. Pinkerton, however, arose and stated that the apothecary's testimony required that of another person who was present when the poison was purchased. This other person had been absent in a distant part of the country, but had been summoned, and would arrive, in company with Mr. Philip Held, on the following morning. He begged that Mr. Linthicum's evidence might be postponed until then, when he believed that the mystery attending the poisoning would be wholly explained.

Mr. Spenham violently objected, but he again made the mistake of speaking for nearly half an hour on the subject,—an indiscretion into which he was led by his confirmed political habits. By the time the question was decided, and in favor of the defense, the afternoon was well advanced, and the court adjourned until the next day.

28. LINCOLN AND WHITMAN

As stated in the previous section (<u>Chapter 27: Lincoln and Buchanan</u>), Walt Whitman had a deep affinity for President Lincoln:

> [While living in D.C.] Whitman saw Lincoln so often that he began to notice variations in his appearance and demeanor. "I had a good view of the president last evening," Whitman wrote to his mother, "—he looks more careworn even than usual—his face with deep cut lines, seams, & his *complexion* gray, through very dark skin, a curious looking man, very sad." Whitman saw Lincoln so often that it must have seemed almost real when he pronounced, "I love the President personally."[33]

President Lincoln once noticed Walt Whitman too:

> An eye-witness and participator relates, in a letter to a friend, the following anecdote of Abraham Lincoln: It was in the winter-time, I think in '64, I went up to the White House with a friend of mine, an M. C., who had some business with the President. He had gone out, so we didn't stop; but coming down stairs, quite near the door, we met the President coming in, and we stept back into the East Room, and stood near the front windows, where my friend had a confab with him. It didn't last more than three or four minutes; but there was something about a letter my friend had handed the President, and Mr. Lincoln had read it, and was holding it in his hand thinking it over, and looking out of the window, when Walt Whitman went by, on the White House walk in front, quite slow, with his hands in the breast-pockets of his overcoat, and a sizeable felt hat on, and his head pretty well up, just as I have often seen him on Broadway. Mr. Lincoln asked who that was, or something of the kind. I spoke up, mentioning the name, Walt Whitman, and said he was the author of *Leaves of Grass*. Mr. Lincoln didn't say anything, but took a good look, till Whitman was quite gone by. Then he says—(I can't give you his way of saying it, but it was quite emphatic and odd)—"Well," he says, "*he*

looks like a MAN." He said it pretty loud, but in a sort of absent way, and with the emphasis on the words I have underscored. He didn't say any more, but began to talk again about the letter; and in a minute or so we went off.[4]

Apparently that is not unusual for Walt Whitman, who had a remarkably attractive look and demeanor:

No description can give any idea of the extraordinary physical attractiveness of the man. I do not speak now of the affection of friends and those who are much with him, but of the magnetism exercised by him upon people who merely see him for a few minutes or pass him on the street. An intimate friend of the author's, after knowing Walt Whitman a few days, said in a letter: "As for myself, it seems to me now that I have always known him and loved him." And in another letter, written from a town where the poet had been staying for a few days, the same person says: "Do you know, every one who met him here seems to love him."

The following is the experience of a person well known to the present writer. He called on Walt Whitman and spent an hour at his home in Camden, in the autumn of 1877. He had never seen the poet before, but he had been profoundly reading his works for some years. He said that Walt Whitman only spoke to him about a hundred words altogether, and these quite ordinary and commonplace; that he did not realize anything peculiar while with him, but shortly after leaving a state of mental exaltation set in, which he could only describe by comparing to slight intoxication by champagne, or to falling in love! [...] He tells me that at first he used often to speak to friends and acquaintances of his feeling for Walt Whitman and the *Leaves*, but after a time he found that he could not make himself understood, and that some even thought his mental balance impaired. He gradually learned to keep silence upon the subject, but the feeling did not abate, nor its influence upon his life grow less.[4]

In fact, Whitman was so recognizable it caused him to be rumored about, and in knowing that, he thought of Lincoln's legends as well:

"I meet new Walt Whitmans every day. There are a dozen of me afloat." This comment on the public's tendency to multiply—and falsify—perceptions of celebrities caused Whitman immediately to think of Lincoln: "Now, there's Abraham Lincoln: people get to know his traits, his habits of life, some of his characteristics set off in the most positive relief: soon all sorts of stories are fathered on him—some of them true, some of them apocryphal—volumes of stories (stories decent and indecent) fathered on him: legitimate stories, illegitimate: and so Lincoln comes to us more or less falsified."[39]

Whitman's own poem about Lincoln's death brought with it more fame than pleased Whitman, however, since its formal style was not the one he preferred:

> Traubel brings Whitman a newspaper squib that suggests "the world would be better off today" if the poet had written a volume of "My Captains" instead of filling "a scrap-basket with waste and calling it a book." Whitman lets fly: "I'm honest when I say, damn 'My Captain' and all the 'My Captains' in my book! This is not the first time I have been irritated into saying I'm almost sorry I ever wrote the poem. . . . I say that if I'd written a whole volume of 'My Captains' I'd deserve to be spanked and sent to bed with the world's compliments. [...] The thing that tantalizes me most is not its rhythmic imperfection or its imperfection as a ballad or rhymed poem (it is damned bad in all that, I do believe) but the fact that my enemies and some of my friends who half doubt me, look upon it as a concession made to the philistines—that makes me mad." A typical philistine of the day was Thomas Wentworth Higginson (Emily Dickinson's dismal confidant [see Chapter 13: Perceptions of Whitman and Chapter 25: The Civil War for more of Higginson's criticisms of Whitman]), whom Whitman despised ("poor water enough"). In an article titled "Literary High-Water Marks" that came to Walt's attention in November 1890, Higginson utters the sort of comment on "Captain" that turned the poet against it: "In some cases, as in Whitman's 'O Captain, My Captain,' the high-water mark may have been attained precisely at the moment when the poet departed from his theory and confined himself most nearly to the laws he was wont to spurn."[39]

See [A.13] and Chapter 11: Leaves of Grass for selected Whitman poems, including "O Captain! My Captain!" Also note that Whitman was aware of Lincoln's estimation of him, as documented by Traubel:

> Whitman rejoiced greatly when one particular letter, long lost among his papers, finally appeared. It was a letter written from New York by A. Van Rensellaer and dated July 30, 1865. It seemed to verify a story that had long circulated about Lincoln making an approving remark about the poet on a day in the winter of 1864 when the president looked out a window and saw Whitman walking by the White House. Rensellaer, who was present, relates in his letter [the above story]. [Traubel] looked up after reading this letter aloud and saw that Whitman "looked extra pleased." Whitman then preened a bit: "I have sometimes thought you had an idea we were romancing a bit in telling that story about Lincoln: now you can see for yourself that we've kept strictly, literally prosaically to the figures—have added nothing to them."[39]

XXIX

NEW EVIDENCE

ELWOOD ACCOMPANIED JOSEPH to the prison where he was obliged to spend the night, and was allowed to remain with him until Mr. Pinkerton (who was endeavoring to reach Philip by telegraph) should arrive.

Owing to Rachel Miller's forethought, the bare room was sufficiently furnished. There was a clean bed, a chair or two, and a table, upon which stood a basket of provisions.

"I suppose I must eat," said Joseph, "as a matter of duty. If you will sit down and join me, Elwood, I will try."

"If I could have that fellow Spenham by the throat for a minute," Elwood growled, "it would give me a good appetite. But I will take my share, as it is: I never can think rightly when I'm hungry. Why, there is enough for a picnic! sandwiches, cold chicken, pickles, cakes, cheese, and two bottles of coffee, as I live! Just think that we're in a hotel, Joseph! It's all in one's notion, leastways for a single night; for you can go where you like to-morrow!"

"I hope so," said Joseph, as he took his seat. Elwood set the provisions before him, but he did not touch them. After a moment of hesitation he stretched out his hand and laid it on Elwood's shoulder.

"Now, old boy!" Elwood cried: "I know it. What you mean is unnecessary, and I won't have it."

"Let me speak!"

"I don't see why I should, Joseph. It's no more than I guessed. She didn't love me: you were tolerably near together once, and if you should now come nearer—"

But he could not finish the sentence; the words stuck in his throat.

"Great Heaven!" Joseph exclaimed, starting to his feet; "what are you thinking of? Don't you see that Lucy Henderson and I are parted forever by what has happened to-day? Didn't you hear her say that she overcame the tenderness which might have become love, as I overcame mine for her? Neither of us can recall that first feeling, any more than we can set our lives again in the past. I shall worship her as one of the purest and noblest souls that breathe; but love her? make her my wife? It could never, never be! No, Elwood! I was wondering whether you could pardon me the rashness which has exposed her to to-day's trial."

Elwood began to laugh strangely. "You are foolish, Joseph," he said. "Pshaw! I can't hold my knife. These sudden downs and then ups are too much for a fellow! Pardon you? Yes, on one condition—that you empty your plate before you speak another word to me!"

They were both cheerful after this, and the narrow little room seemed freer and brighter to their eyes. It was late before Mr. Pinkerton arrived: he had waited in vain for an answer from Philip. Elwood's presence was a relief to him, for he did not wish to excite Joseph by a statement of what he expected to prove unless the two witnesses had been really secured. He adroitly managed, however, to say very little while seeming to say a great deal, and Joseph was then left to such rest as his busy memory might allow him.

Next morning there was an even greater crowd in the court-room. All Joseph's friends were there, with the exception of Lucy Henderson, who, by Mr. Pinkerton's advice, remained at the hotel. Philip had not arrived, but had sent a message saying that all was well, and he would come in the morning train.

Mr. Spenham, the evening before, had ascertained the nature of Mr. Linthicum's evidence. The apothecary, however, was only able to inform him of Philip's desire to discover the travelling agent, without knowing his purpose. In the name recorded as that of the purchaser of the poison Mr. Spenham saw a weapon which would enable him to repay Lucy for his discomfiture, and to indicate, if not prove, a complicity of crime, in which Philip Held also, he suspected, might be concerned.

The court opened at nine o'clock, and Philip could not be on hand before ten. Mr. Pinkerton endeavored to procure the examination of Dennis, and another subordinate witness, before the apothecary; but he only succeeded in gaining fifteen minutes' time by the discussion. Mr. Ziba Linthicum was then called and sworn. He carried a volume under his arm.

As Philip possessed the label, Mr. Linthicum could only testify to the fact that a veiled lady had purchased so many grains of arsenic of him on a certain day; that he kept a record of all sales of dangerous drugs; and that the lady's name was recorded in the book which he had brought with him. He then read the entry:—

"*Miss Henderson. Arsenic.*"

Although Mr. Pinkerton had whispered to Joseph, "Do not be startled when he reads the name!" it was all the latter could do to suppress an exclamation. There was a murmur and movement through the whole court.

"We have now both the motive and the co-agent of the crime," said Mr. Spenham, rising triumphantly. "After the evidence which was elicited yesterday, it will not be difficult to connect the two. If the case deepens in enormity as it advances, we may be shocked, but we have no reason to be surprised. The growth of free-love sentiments, among those who tear themselves loose from the guidance of religious influences, naturally leads to crime; and the extent to which this evil has been secretly developed is not suspected by the public.

Testimony can be adduced to show that the accused, Joseph Asten, has openly expressed his infidelity; that he repelled with threats and defiance a worthy minister of the Gospel, whom his own pious murdered wife had commissioned to lead him into the true path. The very expression which the woman Lucy Henderson testified to his having used in the garden,—'I am sick of masks,'—what does it mean? What but unrestrained freedom of the passions,—the very foundation upon which the free-lovers build up their pernicious theories? The accused cannot complain if the law lifts the mask from his countenance, and shows his nature in all its hideous deformity. But another mask, also, must be raised: I demand the arrest of the woman Lucy Henderson!"

Mr. Pinkerton sprang to his feet. In a measured, solemn voice, which contrasted strongly with the loud, sharp tones of the prosecuting attorney, he stated that Mr. Linthicum's evidence was already known to him; that it required an explanation which would now be given in a few minutes, and which would completely exonerate Miss Henderson from the suspicion of having purchased the poison, or even having any knowledge of its purchase. He demanded that no conclusion should be drawn from evidence which would mislead the minds of the jury: he charged the prosecuting attorney with most unjustly assailing the characters of both Joseph Asten and Lucy Henderson, and invoked, in the name of impartial justice, the protection of the court.

He spoke both eloquently and earnestly; but the spectators noticed that he looked at his watch from minute to minute. Mr. Spenham interrupted him, but he continued to repeat his statements, until there came a sudden movement in the crowd, near the outer door of the hall. Then he sat down.

Philip led the way, pressing the crowd to right and left in his eagerness. He was followed by a tall young man, with a dark moustache and an abundance of jewelry, while Mr. Benjamin Blessing, flushed and perspiring, brought up the rear. The spectators were almost breathless in their hushed, excited interest. Philip seized Joseph's hand, and, bending nearer, whispered, "You are free!" His eyes sparkled and his face glowed.

Room was made for the three witnesses, and after a brief whispered consultation between Philip and Mr. Pinkerton, Elwood was despatched to bring Lucy Henderson to the court.

"May it please the Court," said Mr. Pinkerton, "I am now able to fulfil that promise which I this moment made. The evidence which was necessary to set forth the manner of Mrs. Asten's death, and which will release the court from any further consideration of the present case, is in my hands. I therefore ask leave to introduce this evidence without any further delay."

After a little discussion the permission was granted, and Philip Held was placed upon the stand.

He first described Joseph's genuine sorrow at his wife's death, and his self-accusation of having hastened it by his harsh words to her in the morning. He related the interview at which Joseph, on learning of the reports concerning him, had immediately decided to ask for a legal investigation, and in a simple, straightforward way, narrated all that had been done up to the time of consulting Ziba Linthicum's poison record.

"As I knew it to be quite impossible that Miss Lucy Henderson could have been the purchaser," he began—

Mr. Spenham instantly objected, and the expression was ruled out by the Court.

"Then," Philip resumed, "I determined to ascertain who had purchased the arsenic. Mr. Linthicum's description of the lady was too vague to be recognized. It was necessary to identify the travelling agent who was present; for this purpose I went to the city, ascertained the names and addresses of all the travelling agents of all the wholesale drug firms, and after much time and correspondence discovered the man,—Mr. Case, who is here present. He was in Persepolis, Iowa, when the summons reached him, and would have been here yesterday but for an accident on the Erie Railway.

"In the mean time I had received the small fragment of another label, and by the clew which the few letters gave me I finally identified the place as the drug-store of Wallis and Erkers, at the corner of Fifth and Persimmon Streets. There was nothing left by which the nature of the drug could be ascertained, and therefore this movement led to nothing which could be offered as evidence in this court,—that is, by the druggists themselves, and they have not been summoned. It happened, however, by a coincidence which only came to light this morning, that—"

Here Philip was again interrupted. His further testimony was of less consequence. He was sharply cross-examined by Mr. Spenham as to his relations with Joseph, and his object in devoting so much time to procuring evidence for the defense; but he took occasion, in replying, to express his appreciation of Joseph's character so emphatically, that the prosecution lost rather than gained. Then the plan of attack was changed. He was asked whether he believed in the Bible, in future rewards and punishments, in the views of the so-called free-lovers, in facile divorce and polygamy. He was too shrewd, however, to lay himself open to the least misrepresentation, and the moral and mental torture which our jurisprudence has substituted for the rack, thumb-screws, and Spanish boots of the Middle Ages finally came to an end.

Then the tall young man, conscious of his own elegance, took his place. He gave his name and occupation as Augustus Fitzwilliam Case, commercial traveler for the house of Byle and Glanders, wholesale druggists.

"State whether you were in the drug-store of Ziba Linthicum, No. 77 Main Street, in this town, on the day of the entry in Mr. Linthicum's book."

"I was."

"Did you notice the person who called for arsenic?"

"I did."

"What led you specially to notice her?"

"It is my habit," said the witness. "I am impressible to beauty, and I saw at once that the lady had what I call—style. I recollect thinking, 'More style than could be expected in these little places.'"

"Keep your thoughts to yourself!" cried Mr. Spenham.

"Describe the lady as correctly as you can," said Mr. Pinkerton.

"Something under the medium size; a little thin, but not bad lines,—what I should call jimp, natty, or 'lissome,' in the Scotch dialect. A well-trained voice; no uncertainty about it,—altogether about as keen and wide-awake a woman as you'll find in a day's travel."

"You guessed all this from her figure?" Mr. Spenham asked, with a sneer.

"Not entirely. I saw her face. I suppose something in my appearance or attitude attracted her attention. While Mr. Linthicum was weighing the arsenic she leaned over the counter, let her veil fall forward slightly, and gave me a quick side-look. I bent a little at the same time, as if to examine the soaps, and I saw her face in a three-quarter position, as the photographers say."

"Can you remember her features distinctly?"

"Quite so. In fact, it is difficult for me to forget a female face. Hers was just verging on the sharp, but still tolerably handsome. Hair quite dark, and worn in ringlets; eyebrows clean and straight; mouth a little too thin for my fancy; and eyes—well, I couldn't undertake to say exactly what color they were, for she seemed to have the trick—common in the city—of letting the lids droop over them."

"Were you able to judge of her age?"

"Tolerably, I should say. There is a certain air of preservation which enables a practiced eye to distinguish an old girl from a young one. She was certainly not to be called young,—somewhere between twenty-eight and thirty-five."

"You heard the name she gave Mr. Linthicum?"

"Distinctly. Mr. Linthicum politely stated that it was his custom to register the names of all those to whom he furnished either poisons or prescriptions requiring care in being administered. She said, 'You are *very* particular, sir;' and, a moment afterward, 'Pardon me, perhaps it is necessary.'—'What name, then?' he asked. I thought she hesitated a moment, but this I will not say positively; whether or not, the answer was, 'Miss Henderson.' She went out of the store with a light, brisk step."

"You are sure you would be able to recognize the lady?" Mr. Pinkerton asked.

"Quite sure." And Mr. Augustus Fitzwilliam Case smiled patronizingly, as if the question were superfluous.

Mr. Pinkerton made a sign to Lucy, and she arose.

"Look upon this lady!" he said to the witness.

The latter made a slight, graceful inclination of his head, as much as to say, "Pardon me, I am compelled to stare." Lucy quietly endured his gaze.

"Consider her well," said the lawyer, "and then tell the jury whether she is the person."

"No considerment is necessary. This lady has not the slightest resemblance to Miss Henderson. She is younger, taller, and modelled upon a wholly different style."

"Will you now look at this photograph?"

"Ah!" the witness exclaimed; "you can yourself judge of the correctness of my memory! Here is Miss Henderson herself, and in three-quarter face, as I saw her!"

"That," said Mr. Pinkerton, addressing the judge and jury, "that is the photograph of Mrs. Julia Asten."

The spectators were astounded, and Mr. Spenham taken completely aback by this revelation. Joseph and Elwood both felt that a great weight had been lifted from their hearts. The testimony established Julia's falsehood at the same time, and there was such an instant and complete revulsion of opinion that many persons present at once suspected her of a design to poison Joseph.

"Before calling upon Mr. Benjamin Blessing, the father of the late Mrs. Asten, for his testimony," said Mr. Pinkerton,—"and I believe he will be the last witness necessary,—I wish to show that, although Miss Lucy Henderson accompanied Mrs. Asten to Magnolia, she could not have visited Mr. Linthicum's drug-store at the time indicated; nor, indeed, at any time during that day. She made several calls upon friends, each of whom is now in attendance, and their joint evidence will account for every minute of her stay in the place. The base attempt to blacken her fair name imperatively imposes this duty upon me."

No objection was made, and the witnesses were briefly examined in succession. Their testimony was complete.

"One mystery still remains to be cleared up," the lawyer continued; "the purpose of Mrs. Asten in purchasing the poison, and the probable explanation of her death. I say 'probable,' because absolute certainty is impossible. But I will not anticipate the evidence. Mr. Benjamin Blessing, step forward, if you please!"

29. LEAVES AND FRUITS

Here is background information on the Calamus plant that leant its name to Walt Whitman's *Leaves of Grass*:

> [Referencing William Wood*ville's Medical* Botany of 1832:] Woodville observed that this species "usually grows in stagnant waters, and the sides of rivers, producing its flowers in May and June" and is "the only true aromatic plant indigenous to northern climates." It was also called *Calamus aromaticus* or *odoratus*, sea-sedge, myrtle sedge, and sweet sedge. Thoreau knew it as sweet flag or critchicrotches and noted its aroma: "How agreeable and surprising the peculiar fragrance of the sweet flag when it is bruised." William Salmon, in his *Botanologia* of 1710, reported that the spirit derived from *Calamus* made "a Noble and Generous Cordial, chears the Heart, revives the Spirits, and strengthens Universal Nature." He also recommended it as a cataplasm— applied "to the Testicles, it wonderfully abates their Swelling." Whitman saw a stand of the plant on a Delaware River excursion late in life and rhapsodized, "*Leaves of Grass!* The largest leaves of grass known! Calamus! Yes, that is calamus! Profuse, rich, noble, upright, emotional!"[40]

Halleck too worked with nature's bounty to describe his manly love:

> Halleck's favorite metaphor to describe his love for Drake was the plant, tree, or flower. A leaf or leaves dominate much of his poetry, as does his favorite color green and the combination of green and grass. The use of green as a central symbol of homosexuality throughout the nineteenth century has been well documented. From Halleck's own green umbrella (an "inseparable companion") to Wilde's trademark green carnation, the color was associated with plant life that can exist without heterosexual birth. As natural symbols of self-creation, plants inverted the view of homosexuality as unnatural and also suggested self-determination. Lavender flowers accompanied the allusion.[22]

Herman Melville, in his letters to Nathaniel Hawthorne, can't help but bring up the flower of the same name: "Well, the Hawthorne is a sweet flower; may it flourish in every hedge."[11] For the rest of that sweet letter, see [A.19].

In support of the eventual ripening of "slow fruit":

Whitman's "youth" and his coming-out as a poet and homosexual were somewhat delayed, as sometimes happens in gay lives (Oscar Wilde also achieved true flamboyance only in his mid-thirties). In fact, Whitman, perhaps thinking of himself, suggested one day with a fine unintended pun that "slow fruit" is the best. Traubel read aloud an idolizing letter from a young Englishman—who, incidentally, later became a member of Wilde's gay coterie [Lionel Johnson, see Chapter 15: Avowals to Walt Whitman and Chapter 19: Calamus as Cruising Apparatus]—and Walt observed, "That sounds very ripe for a boy of eighteen.... It is singular how soon some natures come to a head and how long it takes others to ripen, though I believe, as a rule, the slow fruit is the best," Leaves of Grass was slow fruit indeed, but it was written by a still essentially youthful Whitman albeit not to the eye (he had gone quite gray by thirty). This, by the way, is perhaps the place to note that each of the first three truly epochal fictions of homosexual liberation was written by a slow fruit who was thirty-five years old at the time: Leaves of Grass, The Picture of Dorian Gray, and Thomas Mann's Death in Venice.[40]

XXX

MR. BLESSING'S TESTIMONY

ON ENTERING THE court-room Mr. Blessing had gone to Joseph, given his hand a long, significant grasp, and looked in his face with an expression of triumph, almost of exultation. The action was not lost upon the spectators or the jury, and even Joseph felt that it was intended to express the strongest faith in his innocence.

When the name was called there was a movement in the crowd, and a temporary crush in some quarters, as the people thrust forward their heads to see and listen. Mr. Blessing, bland, dignified, serene, feeling that he was the central point of interest, waited until quiet had been restored, slightly turning his head to either side, as if to summon special attention to what he should say.

After being sworn, and stating his name, he thus described his occupation:—

"I hold a position under government; nominally, it is a Deputy Inspectorship in the Custom-House, yet it possesses a confidential—I might say, if modesty did not prevent, an advisory—character."

"In other words, a Ward Politician!" said Mr. Spenham.

"I must ask the prosecuting attorney," Mr. Blessing blandly suggested, "not to define my place according to his own political experiences."

There was a general smile at these words; and a very audible chuckle from spectators belonging to the opposite party.

"You are the father of the late Mrs. Julia Asten?"

"I am—her unhappy father, whom nothing but the imperious commands of justice, and the knowledge of her husband's innocence of the crime with which he stands charged, could have compelled to appear here, and reveal the painful secrets of a family, which—"

Here Mr. Spenham interrupted him.

"I merely wish to observe," Mr. Blessing continued, with a stately wave of his hand towards the judge and jury, "that the De Belsains and their descendants may have been frequently unfortunate, but were never dishonorable. I act in their spirit when I hold duty to the innocent living higher than consideration for the unfortunate dead."

Here he drew forth a handkerchief, and held it for a moment to his eyes.

"Did you know of any domestic discords between your daughter and her husband?"

"I foresaw that such might be, and took occasion to warn my daughter, on her wedding-day, not to be too sure of her influence. There was too much disparity of age, character, and experience. It could not be called crabbed age and rosy youth, but there was difference enough to justify Shakespeare's doubts. I am aware that the court requires ocular—or auricular—evidence. The only such I have to offer is my son-in-law's own account of the discord which preceded my daughter's death."

"Did this discord sufficiently explain to you the cause and manner of her death?"

"My daughter's nature—I do not mean to digress, but am accustomed to state my views clearly—my daughter's nature was impulsive. She inherited my own intellect, but modified by the peculiar character of the feminine nervous system. Hence she might succumb to a depression which I should resist. She appeared to be sure of her control over my son-in-law's nature, and of success in an enterprise, in which—I regret to say— my son-in-law lost confidence. I assumed, at the time, that her usually capable mind was unbalanced by the double disappointment, and that she had rushed, unaneled, to her last account. This, I say, was the conclusion forced upon me; yet I cannot admit that it was satisfactory. It seemed to disparage my daughter's intellectual power: it was not the act which I should have anticipated in any possible emergency."

"Had you no suspicion that her husband might have been instrumental?" Mr. Spenham asked.

"He? he is simply incapable of that, or *any* crime!"

"We don't want assertions," said Mr. Spenham, sternly.

"I beg pardon of the court," remarked Mr. Blessing; "it was a spontaneous expression. The touch of nature cannot always be avoided."

"Go on, sir!"

"I need not describe the shock and sorrow following my daughter's death," Mr. Blessing continued, again applying his handkerchief. "In order to dissipate it, I obtained a leave of absence from my post,—the exigencies of the government fortunately admitting of it,—and made a journey to the Oil Regions, in the interest of myself and my son-in-law. While there I received a letter from Mr. Philip Held, the contents of which—"

"Will you produce the letter?" Mr. Spenham exclaimed.

"It can be produced, if necessary. I will state nothing further, since I perceive that this would not be admissible evidence. It is enough to say that I returned to the city without delay, in order to meet Mr. Philip Held. The requirements of justice were more potent with me than the suggestions of personal interest. Mr. Held had already, as you will have noticed from his testimony, identified the fragment of paper as having emanated from the drug-store of Wallis and Erkers, corner of Fifth and Persimmon Streets. I accompanied him to that drug-store, heard the statements of the proprietors, in answer to Mr. Held's questions,—statements which, I confess, surprised me immeasurably (but

I could not reject the natural deductions to be drawn from them), and was compelled, although it overwhelmed me with a sense of unmerited shame, to acknowledge that there was plausibility in Mr. Held's conjectures. Since they pointed to my elder daughter, Clementina, now Mrs. Spelter, and at this moment tossing upon the ocean-wave, I saw that Mr. Held might possess a discernment superior to my own. But for a lamentable cataclysm, he might have been my son-in-law, and I need not say that I prefer that refinement of character which comes of good blood to the possession of millions—"

Here Mr. Blessing was again interrupted, and ordered to confine himself to the simple statement of the necessary facts.

"I acknowledge the justice of the rebuke," he said. "But the sentiment of the *mens conscia recti* will sometimes obtrude through the rigid formula of Themis. In short, Mr. Philip Held's representations—"

"State those representations at once, and be done with them!" Mr. Spenham cried.

"I am coming to them presently. The Honorable Court understands, I am convinced, that a coherent narrative, although moderately prolix, is preferable to a disjointed narrative, even if the latter were terse as Tacitus. Mr. Held's representations, I repeat, satisfied me that an interview with my daughter Clementina was imperative. There was no time to be lost, for the passage of the nuptial pair had already been taken in the *Ville de Paris*. I started at once, sending a telegram in advance, and in the same evening arrived at their palatial residence in Fifth Avenue. Clementina's nature, I must explain to the Honorable Court, is very different from that of her sister,—the reappearance, I suspect, of some lateral strain of blood. She is reticent, undemonstrative,—in short, frequently inscrutable. I suspected that a direct question might defeat my object; therefore, when I was alone with her the next morning,—my son-in-law, Mr. Spelter, being called to a meeting of Erie of which he is one of the directors,—I said to her:'My child, you are perfectly blooming! Your complexion was always admirable, but now it seems to me incomparable!'"

"This is irrelevant!" cried Mr. Spenham.

"By no means! It is the very *corpus delicti*,—the foot of Hercules,—the milk (powder would be more appropriate) in the cocoa-nut!" Clementina smiled in her serene way, and made no reply. 'How do you keep it up now?' I asked, tapping her cheek;'you must be careful, here: all persons are not so discreet as Wallis and Erkers.' She was astounded, stupefied, I might say, but I saw that I had reached the core of truth.'Did you suppose I was ignorant of it?' I said, still very friendly and playfully.'Then it was Julia who told you!' she exclaimed.'And if she did,' I answered, 'what was the harm? I have no doubt that Julia did the same thing.' 'She was always foolish,' Clementina then said; 'she envied me my complexion, and she watched me until she found out. I told her that it would not do for any except blondes, like myself, and *her* complexion was neither one thing nor the other. And I couldn't see that it improved much, afterwards.'"

Mr. Pinkerton saw that the jurymen were puzzled, and requested Mr. Blessing to explain the conversation to them.

"It is my painful duty to obey; yet a father's feelings may be pardoned if he shrinks from presenting the facts at once in their naked—unpleasantness. However, since the use of arsenic as a cosmetic is so general in our city, especially among blondes, as Wallis and Erkers assure me, my own family is not an isolated case. Julia commenced using the drug, so Clementina informed me, after her engagement with Mr. Asten, and only a short time before her marriage. To what extent she used it, after that event, I have no means of knowing; but, I suspect, less frequently, unless she feared that the disparity of age between her and her husband was becoming more apparent. I cannot excuse her duplicity in giving Miss Henderson's name instead of her own at Mr. Linthicum's drug store, since the result might have been so fearfully fatal; yet I entreat you to believe that there may have been no inimical *animus* in the act. I attribute her death entirely to an over-dose of the drug, voluntarily taken, but taken in a moment of strong excitement."

The feeling of relief from suspense, not only among Joseph's friends, but throughout the crowded court-room, was clearly manifested: all present seemed to breathe a lighter and fresher atmosphere.

Mr. Blessing wiped his forehead and his fat cheeks, and looked benignly around. "There are a hundred little additional details," he said, "which will substantiate my evidence; but I have surely said sufficient for the ends of justice. The heavens will not fall because I have been forced to carve the emblems of criminal vanity upon the sepulchre of an unfortunate child,—but the judgment of an earthly tribunal may well be satisfied. However, I am ready," he added, turning towards Mr. Spenham; "apply all the engines of technical procedure, and I shall not wince."

The manner of the prosecuting attorney was completely changed. He answered respectfully and courteously, and his brief cross-examination was calculated rather to confirm the evidence for the defense than to invalidate it.

Mr. Pinkerton then rose and stated that he should call no other witnesses. The fact had been established that Mrs. Asten had been in the habit of taking arsenic to improve her complexion; also that she had purchased much more than enough of the drug to cause death, at the store of Mr. Ziba Linthicum, only a few days before her demise, and under circumstances which indicated a desire to conceal the purchase. There were two ways in which the manner of her death might be explained: either she had ignorantly taken an over-dose, or, having mixed the usual quantity before descending to the garden to overhear the conversation between Mr. Asten and Lucy Henderson, had forgotten the fact in the great excitement which followed, and thoughtlessly added as much more of the poison. Her last words to her husband, which could not be introduced as evidence, but might now be repeated, showed that her death was the result of accident, and not of design. She was thus absolved of the guilt of suicide, even as her husband of the charge of murder.

Mr. Spenham, somewhat to the surprise of those who were unacquainted with his true character, also stated that he should call no further witness for the prosecution. The testimonies of Mr. Augustus Fitzwilliam Case and Mr. Benjamin Blessing—although the latter was unnecessarily ostentatious and discursive—were sufficient to convince him that the prosecution could not make out a case. He had no doubt whatever of Mr. Joseph Asten's innocence. Lest the expressions which he had been compelled to use, in the performance of his duty, might be misunderstood, he wished to say that he had the highest respect for the characters of Mr. Asten and also of Miss Lucy Henderson. He believed the latter to be a refined and virtuous lady, an ornament to the community in which she resided. His language towards her had been professional,—by no means personal. It was in accordance with the usage of the most eminent lights of the bar; the ends of justice required the most searching examination, and the more a character was criminated the more brightly it would shine forth to the world after the test had been successfully endured. He was simply the agent of the law, and all respect of persons was prohibited to him while in the exercise of his functions.

The judge informed the jurymen that he did not find it necessary to give them any instructions. If they were already agreed upon their verdict, even the formality of retiring might be dispensed with.

There was a minute's whispering back and forth among the men, and the foreman then rose and stated that they were agreed.

The words "Not Guilty!" spoken loudly and emphatically, were the signal for a stormy burst of applause from the audience. In vain the court-crier, aided by the constables, endeavored to preserve order. Joseph's friends gathered around him with their congratulations; while Mr. Blessing, feeling that some recognition of the popular sentiment was required, rose and bowed repeatedly to the crowd. Philip led the way to the open air, and the others followed, but few words were spoken until they found themselves in the large parlor of the hotel.

Mr. Blessing had exchanged some mysterious whispers with the clerk, on arriving; and presently two negro waiters entered the room, bearing wine, ice, and other refreshments. When the glasses had been filled, Mr. Blessing lifted his with an air which imposed silence on the company, and thus spake: "'Out of the abundance of the heart the mouth speaketh.' There may be occasions when silence is golden, but to-day we are content with the baser metal. A man in whom we all confide, whom we all love, has been rescued from the labyrinth of circumstances; he comes to us as a new Theseus, saved from the Minotaur of the Law! Although Mr. Held, with the assistance of his fair sister, was the Ariadne who found the clew, it has been my happy lot to assist in unrolling it; and now we all stand together, like our classic models on the free soil of Crete, to chant a pæan of deliverance. While I propose the health and happiness and good-fortune of Joseph Asten, I beg him to believe that my words come *ab imo pectore*,—from my inmost heart: if any veil of mistrust, engendered by circumstances which I will not now recall, still hangs between him and myself, I entreat him to rend that veil, even as David rent his garments, and believe in my sincerity, if he cannot in my discretion!"

Philip was the only one, besides Joseph, who understood the last allusion. He caught hold of Mr. Blessing's hand and exclaimed: "Spoken like a man!"

Joseph stepped instantly forward. "I have again been unjust," he said, "and I thank you for making me feel it. You have done me an infinite service, sacrificing your own feelings, bearing no malice against me for my hasty and unpardonable words, and showing a confidence in my character which—after what has passed between us—puts me to shame. I am both penitent and grateful: henceforth I shall know you and esteem you!"

Mr. Blessing took the offered hand, held it a moment, and then stammered, while the tears started from his eyes: "Enough! Bury the past a thousand fathoms deep! I can still say: *foi de Belsain!*"

"One more toast!" cried Philip. "Happiness and worldly fortune to the man whom misfortunes have bent but cannot break,—who has been often deceived, but who never purposely deceived in turn,—whose sentiment of honor has been to-day so nobly manifested,—Benjamin Blessing!"

While the happy company were pouring out but not exhausting their feelings, Lucy Henderson stole forth upon the upper balcony of the hotel. There was a secret trouble in her heart, which grew from minute to minute. She leaned upon the railing, and looked down the dusty street, passing in review the events of the two pregnant days, and striving to guess in what manner they would affect her coming life. She felt that she had done her simple duty: she had spoken no word which she was not ready to repeat; yet in her words there seemed to be the seeds of change.

After a while the hostler brought a light carriage from the stable, and Elwood Withers stepped into the street below her. He was about to take the reins, when he looked up, saw her, and remained standing. She noticed the intensely wistful expression of his face.

"Are you going, Elwood,—and alone?" she asked.

"Yes," he said eagerly; and waited.

"Then I will go with you,—that is, if you will take me." She tried to speak lightly and playfully.

In a few minutes they were out of town, passing between the tawny fields and under the russet woods. A sweet west wind fanned them with nutty and spicy odors, and made a crisp, cheerful music among the fallen leaves.

"What a delicious change!" said Lucy, "after that stifling, dreadful room."

"Ay, Lucy—and think how Joseph will feel it! And how near, by the chance of a hair, we came of missing the truth!"

"Elwood!" she exclaimed, "while I was giving my testimony, and I found your eyes fixed on me, were you thinking of the counsel you gave me, three weeks ago, when we met at the tunnel?"

"I was!"

"I knew it, and I obeyed. Do you now say that I did right?"

"Not for that reason," he answered. "It was your own heart that told you what to do. I did not mean to bend or influence you in any way: I have no right."

"You have the right of a friend," she whispered.

"Yes," said he, "I sometimes take more upon myself than I ought. But it's hard, in my case, to hit a very fine line."

"O, you are now unjust to yourself, Elwood. You are both strong and generous."

"I am not strong! I am this minute spoiling my good luck. It *was* a luck from Heaven to me, Lucy, when you offered to ride home with me, and it *is*, now—if I could only swallow the words that are rising into my mouth!"

She whispered again: "Why should you swallow them?"

"You are cruel! when you have forbidden me to speak, and I have promised to obey!"

"After all you have heard?" she asked.

"All the more for what I have heard."

She took his hand, and cried, in a trembling voice: "I have been cruel, in remaining blind to your nature. I resisted what would have been—what will be, if you do not turn away—my one happiness in this life! Do not speak—let *me* break the prohibition! Elwood, dear, true, noble heart,—Elwood, I love you!"

"Lucy!"

And she lay upon his bosom.

30. ARSENIC AND FACE

For context and explanation on what causes the death of Julia Blessing in *Joseph and His Friend*, here is an excerpt from "The Poisonous Beauty Advice Columns of Victorian England" by Natalie Zarrelli:

> In Victorian England, these were some of the ways women began their daily beauty routines. Unfortunately, cosmetics of the era were plagued by caustic chemicals that could also cause bodily addiction. And, similar to today, the advice on how, if, and when to use these treatments came from the era's most popular beauty columns.
>
> One such column, from *Harper's Bazaar*, was called "The Ugly Girl Papers: Or, Hints for the Toilet." It was written by a Mrs. S.D. Powers, a beauty expert of the time, and became so popular that it was re-published in 1874 as an anthology. The "Ugly Girl Papers" has the tone of a wise aunt with endless advice on how to solve your beauty woes. […]
>
> According to Powers, women's beauty was an elaborate, skilled, and semi-secret performance. "Everybody knows they are inventions, and accepts them as such, like paste brilliants at a theatre," she wrote.
>
> Victorian beauty ideals were unsurprisingly obsessed with pallor: upper class white women chased even whiter skin, a symbol that their privilege never left them working in the sun. "It was all about how to make your skin more translucent," says Alexis Karl, a perfumer and lecturer who has researched Victorian cosmetics extensively.
>
> There were two dominant makeup styles in the 1800s: "natural" and "painted." The ideals of "natural" skin care conjured images of the "English Rose"; a wholesomely beautiful woman with good morals, but Karl notes "it was understood that there was a lot of artifice going on." The "painted" beauty regime was seen as a bit risqué; these women were not hiding their artifice nor their desire to be beautiful.

Similar to the "no-makeup makeup" trend that exists today, the natural look was often achieved through unnatural preparations, many of them homemade. Modern beauty practices belie the roots of current ideals: a chemical called Taraxacum is suggested as a sort of 1800s chemical peel by Powers, who says "the compress acts like a mild but imperceptible blister, and leaves a new skin, soft as an infant's."

To keep the face fresh, she advises coating the face with opium overnight, followed by a brisk wash of ammonia in the morning. For the woman with sparse eyebrows and eyelashes, mercury was often recommended as a nightly eye treatment, eradicating the need to use heavy makeup. "The look of the consumptive was very desirable: the woman with the watery eyes and pale skin, which of course was from the cadaver in the throes of death," says Karl.

To get this near-death look, women would squeeze a few drops citrus juice or perfume into their eyes, or reach for some belladonna drops, which lasted longer, but also caused blindness. Pale skin was encouraged with veils, gloves and parasols, but could also be bought: Sears & Roebuck sold a popular product called Dr. Rose's Arsenic Complexion Wafers, which were just that—little white chalk wafers filled with arsenic for delicate nibbling. They were specifically advertised as "perfectly harmless."

Arsenic, a natural metalloid found in the earth's crust, is an extremely toxic compound that can be tolerated for a time when eaten in small amounts (and has occasionally been used in medicine). Long-term exposure, however, is extremely unpleasant: nervous system and kidney damage, hair loss, conjunctivitis and growths called arsenical keratoses plague the body along with, yes, vitiligo, which causes pigment loss in the skin. Arsenic, which became addictive as a person's tolerance built, was used in as many forms as possible.

Lola Montez, a Victorian actress and traveling beauty writer, wrote in her book *The Arts of Beauty* about how women in Bohemia (now a part of the Czech Republic) regularly bathed in arsenic springs, "which gave their skins a transparent whiteness." She also warned of the price: "once they habituate themselves to the practice, they are obliged to keep it up the rest of their days, or death would speedily follow."

Though beauty-related deaths were not always reported as arsenic poisoning, it wasn't that Victorian women didn't know arsenic was toxic or addictive. It was not uncommon for it to be used as a poison by murderesses of the era, and by the late 1800s arsenic was known to be a dangerous ingredient when used in dyes and wallpaper. The use of arsenic in small quantities for skin lightening was considered so effective that it continued for decades.[64]

XXXI

BEGINNING ANOTHER LIFE

IT WAS HARD for the company of rejoicing friends, at the hotel in Magnolia, to part from each other. Mr. Blessing had tact enough to decline Joseph's invitation, but he was sorely tempted by Philip's, in which Madeline heartily joined. Nevertheless, he only wavered for a moment; a mysterious resolution strengthened him, and taking Philip to one side, he whispered:—

"Will you allow me to postpone, not relinquish, the pleasure? Thanks! A grave duty beckons,—a task, in short, without which the triumph of to-day would be dramatically incomplete. I must speak in riddles, because this is a case in which a whisper might start the overhanging avalanche; but I am sure you will trust me."

"Of course I will!" Philip cried, offering his hand.

"*Foi de Belsain!*" was Mr. Blessing's proud answer, as he hurried away to reach the train for the city.

Joseph looked at Philip, as the horses were brought from the stable, and then at Rachel Miller, who, wrapped in her great crape shawl, was quietly waiting for him.

"We must not separate all at once," said Philip, stepping forward. "Miss Miller, will you invite my sister and myself to take tea with you this evening?"

Philip had become one of Rachel's heroes; she was sure that Mr. Blessing's testimony and Joseph's triumphant acquittal were owing to his exertions. The Asten farm could produce nothing good enough for his entertainment,—that was her only trouble.

"Do tell me the time o' day," she said to Joseph, as he drove out of town, closely followed by Philip's light carriage. "It's three days in one to me, and a deal more like day after to-morrow morning than this afternoon. Now, a telegraph would be a convenience; I could send word and have chickens killed and picked, against we got there."

Joseph answered her by driving as rapidly as the rough country roads permitted, without endangering horse and vehicle. It was impossible for him to think coherently, impossible to thrust back the single overwhelming prospect of relief and release which had burst upon his life. He dared to admit the fortune which had come to him through death, now that his own innocence of any indirect incitement thereto had been established. The future was again clear before him; and even the miserable discord of the past year began to recede and form only an indistinct background to the infinite pity of the death-scene. Mr. Blessing's testimony enabled him to look back and truly interpret the last appealing looks, the last broken words; his heart banished the remembrance of its accusations, and retained only—so long as it should beat among living men—a deep and tender commiseration. As for the danger he had escaped, the slander which had been heaped upon him, his thoughts were above the level of life which they touched. He was nearer than he suspected to that only true independence of soul which releases a man from the yoke of circumstances.

Rachel Miller humored his silence as long as she thought proper, and then suddenly and awkwardly interrupted it. "Yes," she exclaimed; "there's a little of the old currant wine is the cellar-closet! Town's-folks generally like it, and we used to think it good to stay a body's stomach for a late meal,—as it'll be apt to be. But I've not asked you how you relished the supper, though Elwood, to be sure, allowed that all was tolerable nice. And I see the Lord's hand in it, as I hope you do, Joseph; for the righteous is never forsaken. We can't help rejoice, where we ought to be humbly returning thanks, and owning our unworthiness; but Philip Held is a friend, if there ever was one; and the white hen's brood, though they are new-fashioned fowls, are plump enough by this time. I disremember whether I asked Elwood to stop—"

"There he is!" Joseph interrupted; "turning the corner of the wood before us! Lucy is with him,—and they must both come!"

He drove on rapidly, and soon overtook Elwood's lagging team. The horse, indeed, had had his own way, and the sound of approaching wheels awoke Elwood from a trance of incredible happiness. Before answering Joseph, he whispered to Lucy:—

"What shall we say? It'll be the heaviest favor I've ever been called upon to do a friend."

"Do it, then!" she said: "the day is too blessed to be kept for ourselves alone."

How fair the valley shone, as they came into it out of the long glen between the hills! What cheer there was, even in the fading leaves; what happy promise in the mellow autumn sky! The gate to the lane stood open; Dennis, with a glowing face, waited for the horse. He wanted to say something, but not knowing how, shook hands with Joseph, and then pretended to be concerned with the harness. Rachel, on entering the kitchen, found her neighbor, Mrs. Bishop, embarked on a full tide of preparation. Two plump fowls, scalded and plucked, lay upon the table!

This was too much for Rachel Miller. She had borne up bravely through the trying days, concealing her anxiety lest it might be misinterpreted, hiding even her grateful emotion, to make her faith in Joseph's innocence seem the stronger; and now Mrs. Bishop's thoughtfulness was the slight touch under which she gave way. She sat down and cried.

Mrs. Bishop, with a stew-pan in one hand, while she wiped her sympathetic eyes with the other, explained that her husband had come home an hour before, with the news; and that she just guessed help would be wanted, or leastways company, and so she had made bold to begin; for, though the truth had been made manifest, and the right had been proved, as anybody might know it would be, still it was a trial, and people needed to eat more and better under trials than at any other time. "You may not feel inclined for victuals; but there's the danger! A body's body must be supported, whether or no."

Meanwhile, Joseph and his guests sat on the veranda, in the still, mild air. He drew his chair near to Philip's, their hands closed upon each other, and they were entirely happy in the tender and perfect manly love which united them. Madeline sat in front, with a nimbus of sunshine around her hair, feeling also the embarrassment of speech at such a moment, yet bravely endeavoring to gossip with Lucy on other matters. But Elwood's face, so bright that it became almost beautiful, caught her eye: she glanced at Philip, who answered with a smile; then at Lucy, whose cheek bloomed with the loveliest color; and, rising without a word, she went to the latter and embraced her.

Then, stretching her hand to Elwood, she said: "Forgive me, both of you, for showing how glad I am!"

"Philip!" Joseph cried, as the truth flashed upon him; "life is not always unjust! It is we who are impatient."

They both arose and gave hands of congratulation; and Elwood, though so deeply moved that he scarcely trusted himself to speak, was so frankly proud and happy,—so purely and honestly *man* in such a sacred moment,—that Lucy's heart swelled with an equally proud recognition of his feeling. Their eyes met, and no memory of a mistaken Past could ever again come like a cloud across the light of their mutual faith.

"The day was blessed already," said Philip; "but this makes it perfect."

No one knew how the time went by, or could afterwards recall much that was said. Rachel Miller, with many apologies, summoned them to a sumptuous meal; and when the moon hung chill and clear above the creeping mists of the valley, they parted.

The next evening, Joseph went to Philip at the Forge. It was well that he should breathe another atmosphere, and dwell, for a little while, within walls where no ghosts of his former life wandered. Madeline, the most hospitably observant of hostesses, seemed to have planned the arrangements solely for his and Philip's intercourse. The short evening of the country was not half over, before she sent them to Philip's room, where a genial wood-fire prattled and flickered on the hearth, with two easy-chairs before it.

Philip lighted a pipe and they sat down. "Now, Joseph," said he, "I'll answer 'Yes!' to the question in your mind."

"You have been talking with Bishop, Philip?"

"No; but I won't mystify you. As I rode up the valley, I saw you two standing on the hill, and could easily guess the rest. A large estate in this country is only an imaginary fortune. You are not so much of a farmer, Joseph, that it will cut you to the heart and make you dream of ruin to part with a few fields; if you were, I should say get that weakness out of you at once! A man should *possess* his property, not be possessed by it."

"You are right," Joseph answered; "I have been fighting against an inherited feeling."

"The only question is, will the sale of those fifty acres relieve you of all present embarrassments?"

"So far, Philip, that a new mortgage of about half the amount will cover what remains."

"Bravo!" cried Philip. "This is better than I thought. Mr. Hopeton is looking for sure, steady investments, and will furnish whatever you need. So there is no danger of foreclosure."

"Things seem to shape themselves almost too easily now," Joseph answered. I see the old, mechanical routine of my life coming back: it should be enough for me, but it is not; can you tell me why, Philip?"

"Yes: it never was enough. The most of our neighbors are cases of arrested development. Their intellectual nature only takes so many marks, like a horse's teeth; there is a point early in their lives, where its form becomes fixed. There is neither the external influence, nor the inward necessity, to drive them a step further. They find the Sphinx dangerous, and keep out of her way. Of course, as soon as they passively begin to accept *what is*, all that was fluent or plastic in them soon hardens into the old moulds. Now, I am not very wise, but this appears to me to be truth; that life is a grand centrifugal force, forever growing from a wider circle towards one that is still wider. Your stationary men may be necessary, and even serviceable; but to me—and to you, Joseph—there is neither joy nor peace except in some kind of growth."

"If we could be always sure of the direction!" Joseph sighed.

"That's the point!" Philip eagerly continued. "If we stop to consider danger in advance, we should never venture a step. A movement is always clear after it has been made, not often before. It is enough to test one's intention; unless we are tolerably bad, something guides us, and adjusts the consequences of our acts. Why, we are like spiders, in the midst of a million gossamer threads, which we are all the time spinning without knowing it! Who are to measure our lives for us? Not other men with other necessities! and so we come back to the same point again, where I started. Looking back now, can you see no gain in your mistake?"

"Yes, a gain I can never lose. I begin to think that haste and weakness also are vices, and deserve to be punished. It was a dainty, effeminate soul you found, Philip,—a moral and spiritual Sybarite, I should say now. I must have expected to lie on rose-leaves, and it was right that I should find thorns."

"I think," said Philip, "the world needs a new code of ethics. We must cure the unfortunate tendencies of some qualities that seem good, and extract the good from others that seem evil. But it would need more than a Luther for such a Reformation. I confess I am puzzled, when I attempt to study moral causes and consequences in men's lives. It is nothing but a tangle, when I take them collectively. What if each of us were, as I half suspect, as independent as a planet, yet all held together in one immense system? Then the central force must be our close dependence on God, as I have learned to feel it through you."

"Through me!" Joseph exclaimed.

"Do you suppose we can be so near each other without giving and taking? Let us not try to get upon a common ground of faith or action: it is a thousand times more delightful to discover that we now and then reach the same point by different paths. This reminds me, Joseph, that our paths ought to separate now, for a while. It is you who should leave,—but only to come back again, 'in the fullness of time.' Heaven knows, I am merciless to myself in recommending it."

"You are right to try me. It is time that I should know something of the world. But to leave, now—so immediately—"

"It will make no difference," said Philip. "Whether you go or stay, there will be stories afloat. The bolder plan is the better."

The subject was renewed the next morning at breakfast. Madeline heartily seconded Philip's counsel, and took a lively part in the discussion.

"We were in Europe as children," she said to Joseph, "and I have very clear and delightful memories of the travel."

"I was not thinking especially of Europe," he answered. "I am hardly prepared for such a journey. What I should wish is, not to look idly at sights and shows, but to have some active interest or employment, which would bring me into contact with men. Philip knows my purpose."

"Then," said Madeline, "why not hunt on Philip's trail? I have no doubt you can track him from Texas to the Pacific by the traditions of his wild pranks and adventures! How I should enjoy getting hold of a few chapters of his history!"

"Madeline, you are a genius!" Philip cried. "How could I have forgotten Wilder's letter, a fortnight ago, you remember? One need not be a practical geologist to make the business report he wants; but Joseph has read enough to take hold, with the aid of the books I can give him! If it is not too late!"

"I was not thinking of that, Philip," Madeline answered. "Did you not say that the place was—"

She hesitated. "Dangerous?" said Philip. "Yes. But if Joseph goes there, he will come back to us again."

"O, don't invoke misfortune in that way!"

"Neither do I," he gravely replied; "but I can see the shadow of Joseph's life thrown ahead, as I can see my own."

"I think I should like to be *sent* into danger," said Joseph.

Philip smiled: "As if you had not just escaped the greatest! Well,—it was Madeline's guess which most helped to avert it, and now it is her chance word which will probably send you into another one."

Joseph looked up in astonishment. "I don't understand you, Philip," he said.

"O Philip!" cried Madeline.

"I had really forgotten," he answered, "that you knew nothing of the course by which we reached your defense. Madeline first suggested to me that the poison was sometimes used as a cosmetic, and on this hint, with Mr. Blessing's help, the truth was discovered."

"And I did not know how much I owe to you!" Joseph exclaimed, turning towards her.

"Do not thank me," she said, "for Philip thinks the fortunate guess may be balanced by an evil one."

"No, no!" Joseph protested, noticing the slight tremble in her voice; "I will take it as a good omen. Now I know that danger will pass me by, if it comes!"

"If your experience should be anything like mine," said Philip, "you will only recognize the danger when you can turn and look back at it. But, come! Madeline has less superstition in her nature than she would have us believe. Wilder's offer is just the thing; I have his letter on file, and will write to him at once. Let us go down to my office at the Forge!"

The letter was from a capitalist who had an interest in several mines in Arizona and Nevada. He was not satisfied with the returns, and wished to send a private, confidential agent to those regions, to examine the prospects and operations of the companies and report thereupon. With the aid of a map the probable course of travel was marked out, and Joseph rejoiced at the broad field of activity and adventure which it opened to him.

He stayed with Philip a day or two longer, and every evening the fire made a cheery accompaniment to the deepest and sweetest confidences of their hearts, now pausing as if to listen, now rapidly murmuring some happy, inarticulate secret of its own. As each gradually acquired full possession of the other's past, the circles of their lives, as Philip said, were reciprocally widened; but as the horizon spread, it seemed to meet a clearer sky. Their eyes were no longer fixed on the single point of time wherein they breathed. Whatever pain remained, melted before them and behind them into atmospheres of resignation and wiser patience. One gave his courage and experience, the other his pure instinct, his faith and aspiration; and a new harmony came from the closer interfusion of sweetness and strength.

When Joseph returned home, he at once set about putting his affairs in order, and making arrangements for an absence of a year or more. It was necessary that he should come in contact with most of his neighbors, and he was made aware of their good will without knowing that it was, in many cases, a reaction from suspicion and slanderous gossip. Mr. Chaffinch had even preached a sermon, in which no name was mentioned, but everybody understood the allusion. This was considered to be perfectly right, so long as the prejudices of the people were with him, and Julia was supposed to be the pious and innocent victim of a crime. When, however, the truth had been established, many who had kept silent now denounced the sermon, and another on the deceitfulness of appearances, which Mr. Chaffinch gave on the following Sabbath, was accepted as the nearest approach to an apology consistent with his clerical dignity.

Joseph was really ignorant of these proceedings, and the quiet, self-possessed, neighborly way in which he met the people gave them a new impression of his character. Moreover, he spoke of his circumstances, when it was necessary, with a frankness unusual among them; and the natural result was that his credit was soon established on as sound a basis as ever. When, through Philip's persistence, the mission to the Pacific coast was secured, but little further time was needed to complete the arrangements. By the sacrifice of one-fourth of his land, the rest was saved, and entrusted to good hands during his absence. Philip, in the meantime, had fortified him with as many hints and instructions as possible, and he was ready, with a light heart and a full head, to set out upon the long and uncertain journey.

31. THE SOCIETY OF FRIENDS

The Society of Friends (also called the Friends Church or the Quakers) is a Christian group that arose in mid-17th-century England, dedicated to living in accordance with the "Inward Light," or direct inward apprehension of God, without creeds, clergy, or other ecclesiastical forms.[13] Bayard Taylor, Fitz-Greene Halleck, and Walt Whitman each had family backgrounds that involved the Friends Church to various extents; some details of their Quaker histories and later-in-life opinions regarding the Society of Friends are collected below:

Bayard Taylor
Taylor's family were Quakers up until his grandfather marrying a Mennonite and being expelled from the Society:

> His father, Joseph Taylor, was a direct descendant in the sixth generation of Robert Taylor of the Little Leigh, Cheshire, who came over with William Penn, and settled near the Brandywine Creek. The family lived obedient to Quaker principles until Bayard's grandfather, John Taylor, married Ann Bucher, daughter of Christian Bucher, a Swiss Mennonite of Lancaster County, and granddaughter of Melchior Breneman, a Mennonite minister whose grandfather came from Switzerland in the Mennonite emigration of 1709, and took up a large tract of land south of the present city of Lancaster. For refusing to say that he was sorry for his runaway love match, John Taylor was expelled from meeting. [...] Although Joseph Taylor was not a member of the Society of Friends, his children were instructed in Quaker manners and beliefs, and upon Quaker principles the steadfast faith and simple morals of Bayard Taylor rested. [However, there is still] his future rebellion against the "pious Quaker repression" of which he speaks in "Home Pastorals."

> > "Weary am I with all this preaching the force of example,
> > Painful duty to self, and painfuller still to one's neighbor,

> Moral shibboleths, dinned in one's ears with slavering unction,
> Till, for the sake of a change, profanity loses its terrors."[45]

He spoke of the Society of Friends in his letters and writings as an adult, and about his last attempt to win the good regard of his Quaker neighbors:

Dec. 30, 1872. Three months ago I was moved to begin a narrative poem, the conception of which had been haunting my mind for five or six years. Once begun, I could not leave the subject; I dropped all other work, and by the beginning of November had finished an idyllic narrative poem of more than 2,100 lines, in blank verse. The title is "Lars," and the scene is laid partly in Norway and partly on the banks of the Delaware. I have brought Quaker peace and Berserker rage into conflict, and given the triumph to the former.
    [...]
March 29, 1873. You will have seen before this what I wrote last fall. I do not know how it will be received by the public, but the few friends who have read the poem are satisfied with it. The plan has been in my head for five or six years, and as it is probably the last poem I shall write embodying home (that is, Pennsylvania or Quaker) elements, I tried to do my best. The story is entirely my own invention. I must say that if the Quakers are not satisfied with my presentation of them and their peaceful creed, they do not deserve a place in our literature. My experiences, however, have taught me not to hope for much immediate recognition either of this work or of any other I may write. But I am quite content with the appreciation of the few best minds.[24]

Fitz-Greene Halleck
Halleck's family had the reverse of Taylor's bad luck with the Friends, his ancestor being disinherited for marrying *into* the Society rather than expelled for marrying outside of it:

Halleck's ancestry was [...] dating to the Pilgrim era when Peter Hallock, one of the thirteen Puritan leaders who left England in 1638, landed at Hallock's Neck, Southold, Long Island, in 1640. [...] The Puritan legacy was quickly challenged by Hallock's eldest son, [John, who was] disinherited for marrying a Quaker.[22]

[Peter] gives his property to his wife Margaret, his four sons, John, Thomas, Peter, and William, and his five daughters. The will implies deep sorrow that his eldest son, John, had married into and joined the proscribed Society of Friends, who in that age were regarded by civil enactments almost as outlaws, and, accordingly, sadly persecuted; and has the proviso that, if any one of his sons "shall apostatize from the Protestant doctrine and faith," or "wilfully and of set purpose contemn and neglect the public worship of God suitable thereto," what is here willed to him shall pass over to "the next lawful heir that shall steadfastly profess and own the said doctrine and faith." He, however, relents sufficiently to add the following clause; "also, my will is that my son, John Hollyoake, whom, as an obstinate apostate, I do reject and deprive of all other estate, yet I do hereby give unto him, his heirs and assigns forever, my second lot at Wading Creek, with the appurtenances thereunto belonging, which is all "that he is ever to have of my estate."[62]

Fitz-Greene Halleck "retained a diluted sense of this prejudice against the Society of Friends"[22] throughout his life, as is displayed below:

> It is a curious circumstance, worthy of mention, that one of John's descendants inserted in his will a bar to his children's leaving, as his ancestor William did to his joining, the Society of Friends. Of the poet's opinion of business Quakers we have the testimony of William Cullen Bryant, who said, at a public dinner in 1868: "I remember what a witty acquaintance of mine said, some twenty years since, of certain persons engaged in trade, who were of the denomination of Quakers and none the worse for that, I hope. He said: 'They are the most dangerous of dishonest men. They will never cheat you, not they; but, by the help of plain, friendly, and apparently sincere manners, they will manage so that you will cheat yourself.' The person who said this was the poet Halleck."[62]

Walt Whitman

Whitman's own parents were Quakers, but of a dissident group that was guided by the circuit-rider Elias Hicks.[2] His thoughts on the Society of Friends were recorded by Traubel, with all of Whitman's multitudes at play:

> "My father was not, properly speaking, a Quaker: he was a friend, I might almost say a follower, of [the Quaker orator and reformer] Elias Hicks: my mother came partly of Quaker stock: all her leanings were that way—her sympathies: her fundamental emotional tendencies."[39]

*

> "Too much is often said—perhaps even by me—about my Quaker lineage. There was some of it there, but back, altogether among the women, with my own dear mother and grandmother and her mother again. It is lucky for me if I take after the women in my ancestry, as I hope I do: they were so superior, so truly the more pregnant forces in our family history."[39]

*

"I think the world has never paid enough deference to that principle of Quakers, which, in their meetings, prevents a mere majority from deciding policies, actions. One vote or several not being sufficient to make a rule operative. Always suggesting to me a silent sweet deference to minorities, to the spirit: not doing all out of awe of numbers. I am sure it is a rebuking contrast to all that is accepted in the methods of legislation. Let us keep it in mind."[39]

*

Whitman spoke of his "conviction that a thing is because it is, being what it is because it must be just that—as a tree is a tree, a river a river, the sky the sky. A curious affinity exists right there between me and the Quakers, who always say, this is so or so because of some inner justifying fact—because it could not be otherwise. I remember a beautiful old Quakeress saying to me once: 'Walt—I feel thee is right—I could not tell why but I feel thee is right!'—and that seemed to me to be more significant than much that passes for reason in the world."[39]

*

One day Whitman recalled a time early in life when he considered becoming a Quaker. In the end, he said, "I put it aside as impossible: I was never made to live inside a fence." Traubel then asked whether Whitman thought *Leaves* could have been written if he had "turned Quaker," and he replied, "It is more than likely not—quite probably not—almost certainly not."[39]

*

"The Quakers are very clannish, though I am not that way myself. I am like the cabbage in the fable which forgot it was a cabbage: a very varied experience has washed me clean of that fault."[39]

XXXII

LETTERS

I. JOSEPH TO PHILIP

CAMP —, *ARIZONA, October 19, 1868.*
Since I wrote to you from Prescott, dear Philip, three months have passed, and I have had no certain means of sending you another letter. There was, first, Mr. Wilder's interest at —, the place hard to reach, and the business difficult to investigate. It was not so easy, even with the help of your notes, to connect the geology of books with the geology of nature; these rough hills don't at all resemble the clean drawings of strata. However, I have learned all the more rapidly by not assuming to know much, and the report I sent contained a great deal more than my own personal experience. The duty was irksome enough, at times; I have been tempted by the evil spirits of ignorance, indolence, and weariness, and I verily believe that the fear of failing to make good your guaranty for my capacity was the spur which kept me from giving way. Now, habit is beginning to help me, and, moreover, my own ambition has something to stand on.

I had scarcely finished and forwarded my first superficial account of the business as it appeared to me, when a chance suddenly offered of joining a party of prospectors, some of whom I had already met: as you know, we get acquainted in little time, and with no introductions in these parts. They were bound, first, for some little-known regions in Eastern Nevada, and then, passing a point which Mr. Wilder wished me to visit (and which I could not have reached so directly from any other quarter), they meant to finish the journey at Austin. It was an opportunity I could not let go, though I will admit to you, Philip, that I also hoped to overtake the adventures, which had seemed to recede from me, rainbow-fashion, as I went on.

Some of the party were old Rocky Mountain men, as wary as courageous; yet we passed through one or two straits which tested all their endurance and invention. I won't say how I stood the test; perhaps I ought to be satisfied that I came through to the end, and am now alive and cheerful. To be sure, there are many other ways of measuring our strength. This experience wouldn't help me the least in a discussion of principles, or in organizing any of the machinery of society. It is rather like going back to the first ages of mankind, and being tried in the struggle for existence. To me, that is a great deal. I feel as if I had been taken out of civilization and set back towards the beginning, in order to work my way up again.

But what is the practical result of this journey? you will ask. I can hardly tell, at present: if I were to state that I have been acting on your system of life rather than my own,—that is, making ventures without any certainty of the consequences,—I think you would shake your head. Nevertheless, in these ten months of absence I have come out of my old skin and am a livelier snake than you ever knew me to be. No, I am wrong; it is hardly a venture after all, and my self-glorification is out of place. I have the prospect of winning a great deal where a very little has been staked, and the most timid man in the world might readily go that far. Again you will shake your head; you remember "The Amaranth." How I should like to hear what has become of that fearful and wonderful speculation!

Pray give me news of Mr. Blessing. All those matters seem to lie so far behind me, that they look differently to my eyes. Somehow, I can't keep the old impressions; I even begin to forget them. You said, Philip, that he was not intentionally dishonest, and something tells me you are right. We learn men's characters rapidly in this rough school, because we cannot get away from the close, rough, naked contact. What surprises me is that the knowledge is not only good for present and future use, but that I can take it with me into my past life. One weakness is left, and you will understand it. I blush to myself,—I am ashamed of my early innocence and ignorance. This is wrong; yet, Philip, I seem to have been so unmanly,—at least so unmasculine! I looked for love, and fidelity, and all the virtues, on the surface of life; believed that a gentle tongue was the sign of a tender heart; felt a wound when some strong and positive, yet differently moulded being approached me! Now, here are fellows prickly as a cactus, with something at the core as true and tender as you will find in a woman's heart. They would stake their lives for me sooner than some persons (whom we know) would lend me a hundred dollars, without security! Even your speculator, whom I have met in every form, is by no means the purely mercenary and dangerous man I had supposed.

In short, Philip, I am on very good terms with human nature; the other nature does not suit me so well. It is a grand thing to look down into the canton of the Colorado, or to see a range of perfectly clear and shining snow-peaks across the dry sage-plains; but oh, for one acre of our green meadows! I dreamed of them, and the clover-fields, and the woods and running streams, through the terrific heat of the Nevada deserts, until the tears came. It is nearly a year since I left home: I should think it fifty years!

With this mail goes another report to Mr. Wilder. In three or four months my task will be at an end, and I shall then be free to return. Will you welcome the brown-faced, full-bearded man, broad in cheeks and shoulders, as you would the—but how did I use to look, Philip? It was a younger brother you knew; but he has bequeathed all of his love, and more, to the older.

II. PHILIP TO JOSEPH

COVENTRY FORGE, Christmas Day.
When Madeline hung a wreath of holly around your photograph this morning, I said to it as I say now: "A merry Christmas, Joseph, wherever you are!" It is a calm sunny day, and my view, as you know, reaches much further through the leafless trees; but only the meadow on the right is green. You, on the contrary, are enjoying something as near to Paradise in color, and atmosphere, and temperature (if you are, as I guess, in Southern California), as you will ever be likely to see.

Yes, I will welcome the new man, although I shall see more of the old one in him than you perhaps think,—nor would I have it otherwise. We don't change the bases of our lives, after all: the forces are differently combined, otherwise developed, but they hang, I fancy, to the same roots. Nay, I'll leave preaching until I have you again at the old fireside. You want news from home, and no miserable little particular is unimportant. I've been there, and know what kind of letters are welcome.

The Neighborhood (I like to hover around a while, before alighting) is still a land where all things always seem the same. The trains run up and down our valley, carrying a little of the world boxed up in shabby cars, but leaving no mark behind. In another year the people will begin to visit the city more frequently; in still another, the city people will find their way to us; in five years, population will increase and property will rise in value. This is my estimate, based on a plentiful experience.

Last week, Madeline and I attended the wedding of Elwood Withers. It was at the Hopeton's, and had been postponed a week or two, on account of the birth of a son to our good old business-friend. There are two events for you! Elwood, who has developed, as I knew he would, into an excellent director of men and material undertakings, has an important contract on the new road to the coal regions. He showed me the plans and figures the other day, and I see the beginning of wealth in them. Lucy, who is a born lady, will save him socially and intellectually. I have never seen a more justifiable marriage. He was pale and happy, she sweetly serene and confident; and the few words he said at the breakfast, in answer to the health which Hopeton gave in his choice Vin d'Aï, made the unmarried ladies envy the bride. Really and sincerely, I came away from the house more of a Christian than I went.

You know all, dearest friend: was it not a test of my heart to see that *she* was intimately, fondly happy? It was hardly any more the face I once knew. I felt the change in the touch of her hand. I heard it in the first word she spoke. I did not dare to look into my heart to see if something there were really dead, for the look would have called the dead to life. I made one heroic effort, heaved a stone over the place, and sealed it down forever. Then I felt your arm on my shoulder, your hand on my breast. I was strong and joyous; Lucy, I imagined, looked at me from time to time, but with a bright face, as if she divined what I had done. Can she have ever suspected the truth?

Time is a specific administered to us for all spiritual shocks; but change of habit is better. Why may I not change in quiet as you in action? It seems to me, sometimes, as I sit alone before the fire, with the pipe-stem between my teeth, that each of us is going backward through the other's experience. You will thus prove my results as I prove yours. Then, parted as we are, I see our souls lie open to each other in equal light and warmth, and feel that the way to God lies through the love of man.

Two years ago, how all our lives were tangled! Now, with so little agency of our own, how they are flowing into smoothness and grace! Yours and mine are not yet complete, but they are no longer distorted. One disturbing, yet most pitiable, nature has been removed; Elwood, Lucy, the Hopetons, are happy; you and I are healed of our impatience. Yes, there is something outside of our own wills that works for or against us, as we may decide. If I once forgot this, it is all the clearer now.

I have forgotten one other,—Mr. Blessing. The other day I visited him in the city. I found him five blocks nearer the fashionable quarter, in a larger house. He was elegantly dressed, and wore a diamond on his bosom. He came to meet me with an open letter in his hand.

"From Mrs. Spelter, my daughter," he said, waving it with a grand air,— "an account of her presentation to the Emperor Napoleon. The dress was— let me see—blue moiré and Chantilly lace; Eugénie was quite struck with her figure and complexion."

"The world seems to treat you well," I suggested.

"Another turn of the wheel. However, it showed me what I am capable of achieving, when a strong spur is applied. In this case the spur was, as you probably guess, Mr. Held,—honor. Sir, I prevented a cataclysm! You of course know the present quotations of the Amaranth stock, but you can hardly be aware of my agency in the matter. When I went to the Oil Region with the available remnant of funds, Kanuck had fled. Although the merest tyro in geology, I selected a spot back of the river-bluffs, in a hollow of the undulating table-land, sunk a shaft, and—succeeded! It was what somebody calls an inspired guess. I telegraphed instantly to a friend, and succeeded in purchasing a moderate portion of the stock—not so much as I desired —before its value was known. As for the result, *si monumentum quæris, circumspice!*"

I wish I could give you an idea of the air with which he said this, standing before me with his feet in position, and his arms thrown out in the attitude of Ajax defying the lightning.

I ventured to inquire after your interest. "The shares are here, sir, and safe," he said, "worth not a cent less than twenty-five thousand dollars."

I urged him to sell them and deposit the money to your credit, but this he refused to do without your authority. There was no possibility of depreciation, he said: very well, if so, this is your time to sell. Now, as I write, it occurs to me that the telegraph may reach you. I close this, therefore, at once, and post over to the office at Oakland.

Madeline says: "A merry Christmas from me!" It is fixed in her head that you are still exposed to some mysterious danger. Come back, shame her superstition, and make happy your

PHILIP.

III. JOSEPH TO PHILIP.

SAN FRANCISCO, June 3, 1869.

Philip, Philip, I have found your valley!

After my trip to Oregon, in March, I went southward, along the western base of the Sierra Nevada, intending at first to cross the range; but falling in with an old friend of yours, a man of the mountains and the sea, of books and men, I kept company with him, on and on, until the great wedges of snow lay behind us, and only a long, low, winding pass divided us from the sands of the Colorado Desert. From the mouth of this pass I looked on a hundred miles of mountains; there were lakes glimmering below; there were groves of ilex on the hillsides, an orchard of oranges, olives, and vines in the hollow, millions of flowers hiding the earth, pure winds, fresh waters, and remoteness from all conventional society. I have never seen a landscape so broad, so bright, so beautiful!

Yes, but we will only go there on one of these idle epicurean journeys of which we dream, and then to enjoy the wit and wisdom of our generous friend, not to seek a refuge from the perversions of the world! For I have learned another thing, Philip: the freedom we craved is not a thing to be found in this or that place. Unless we bring it with us, we shall not find it.

The news of the decline of the Amaranth stock, in your last, does not surprise me. How fortunate that my telegraphic order arrived in season! It was in Mr. Blessing's nature to hold on; but he will surely have something left. I mean to invest half of the sum in his wife's name, in any case; for the "prospecting" of which I wrote you, last fall, was a piece of more than ordinary luck. You must have heard of White Pine, by this time. We were the discoverers, and reaped a portion of the first harvest, which is never equal to the second; but this way of getting wealth is so incredible to me, even after I have it, that I almost fear the gold will turn into leaves or pebbles, as in the fairy tales. I shall not tell you what my share is: let me keep one secret,—nay, two,—to carry home!

More incredible than anything else is now the circumstance that we are within a week of each other. This letter, I hope, will only precede me by a fortnight. I have one or two last arrangements to make, and then the locomotive will cross the continent too slowly for my eager haste. Why should I deny it? I am homesick, body and soul. Verily, if I were to meet Mr. Chaffinch in Montgomery Street, I should fling myself upon his neck, before coming to my sober senses. Even he is no longer an antipathy: I was absurd to make one of him. I have but one left; and Eugénie's admiration of her figure and complexion does not soften it in the least.

How happy Madeline's letter made me! After I wrote to her, I would have recalled mine, at any price; for I had obeyed an impulse, and I feared foolishly. What you said of her "superstition" might have been just, I thought. But I believe that a true-hearted woman always values impulses, because she is never at a loss to understand them. So now I obey another, in sending the enclosed. Do you know that her face is as clear in my memory as yours? and as—but why should I write, when I shall so soon be with you?

32. ON WOMEN, AND
A MARRIAGE BELOW ZERO

These men of masculine affection in the 1800s, being that they were in a prescriptive society, did not always hold the best opinions on women, whether they were sacrificed "on the alter of Hymen"[22] (as Halleck phrased it) or not.

Fitz-Greene Halleck
Halleck's opinion of Sarah Eckford Drake, the wife of his own Joseph Rodman Drake, never wavered from dislike and disrespect.

> In 1930, Percy Hutchison portrayed Halleck as "always 'bachelor-minded'" and noted that when Drake became engaged "Fitz-Greene was not a little irritated." "Bachelor" was a euphemism for homosexual by the time of Hutchison's portrait, and the code word was even applied to lesbians.[22]

In fact, another phrase that appears a lot in homosexual love-talk of this time is the expression "in kind," which is found explained in a lesbian love letter from actress Adah Isaacs Menken (a fellow attendee to Pfaff's Bohemian vault, see Chapter 20: Contemporary Camerados for more on the bar restaurant's clientele) trying to woo another woman into her embrace:

> Do you believe in the deepest and tenderest love between women? Do you believe that women often love each other with as much fervor and excitement as they do men? . . . We find the rarest and most perfect beauty in the affections of one woman for another. . . . The electricity of the one flashes and gleams through the other, to be returned not only in *degree* as between man and women, but in *kind* as between precisely similar organizations.[33]

The phrase "in kind" means a giving of something similar to what is received, and echoes what T.E. Lawrence seemed to long for when he wrote of desire in *Seven Pillars of Wisdom* (see Chapter 15: Avowals to Walt Whitman). Meanwhile, Halleck's assumption about what was exchanged between men and women amounted to an accusation that his friend Drake only married Sarah Eckford for the comfort of her money, which was not a widely held opinion:

> Drake's biographer, Frank Lester Pleadwell, challenged Halleck's statement that the doctor had sold himself and came close to naming the cause of Halleck's crass remarks. Pleadwell claimed that Halleck was "almost a misogynist, certainly a complete disbeliever in married happiness.[22]

It's hard to forget while reading *Joseph and His Friend* that the story is, at its center (despite the title pointing out Joseph's 'Friend'), mostly about a bad marriage. True to life, the character of Julia Blessing is given the role of liar, manipulator, and obstacle to happiness, which is how Halleck viewed women:

> Halleck's misogyny may have stemmed from a sublimated homosexuality, but his verse reveals "a clearly defined distinction between the love of men, pure, holy, and virtuous, and the love of women, impure and destructive."[22]

Sarah didn't return his hostility at all, and in fact seemed to believe that he might be her comfort after the death of Drake:

> Sarah Eckford Drake demonstrated one-sided romantic interest in Halleck after her husband's death. Joseph Drake's biographer states that Drake's widow "could have changed her name to Halleck. But Halleck was a confirmed bachelor."[22]

This did not soften his opinion on Sarah, as hadn't Drake's naming of their daughter Janet Halleck Drake (nicknamed 'Joe' for her father)[22]:

> Halleck never regretted the attack on Drake's wife [that Drake married her only for money] although her descendants were offended for generations to come. [22]

Just before meeting Drake, Halleck was flippant about the pursuit from women, "knew that women were fascinated with him, but he was still searching for an unmarried man of his own."[22] (For a poem by Halleck lamenting the unwedded state from the point of view of a girl, see [A.4].) Writing to his sister Maria, he was practically catty about it:

> New York, Feb'y 2d, 1813. "There appears to be quite a marrying fashion in your town at present. Three or four, I think, I have been informed of lately. Hold up your heads, girls. Hope is still at the bottom of the box."[62]

And after meeting Drake, he was all the more amused by female efforts:

1816-1817. "The women, particularly, seemed much pleased with us, and 'tis a truth that a stranger always finds a more welcome reception from the women than the men, particularly if he happens to be young and good-looking, begging your sex's pardon."[62]

After the death of Drake, though the women remained the same, Halleck would have considered himself a widower, and no longer held out any hope for anyone. Halleck remained an 'eligible' bachelor for the rest of his life, eventually moving back with his sister until the end of his days.

Walt Whitman

Not as prickly as Halleck, Walt Whitman had better sympathies for women, or at least certain types of them:

> David Reynolds [*Walt Whitman's America: A Cultural Biography*, 1995] quotes the remark about *Leaves* being "a woman's book" and approves: "It was so, in the most far-ranging sense." But then, he also quotes with approval Whitman's description of the Real Woman as "strong and arrogant," "well-muscled," and capable of "brawny embraces"—not seeming to see in this the arrant "why can't a woman be more like a man" misogyny of Bernard Shaw's Henry Higgins. Whitman proved himself a perfect Higgins, in fact, talking one day about the much admired wife of his friend Joe Gilder: "Jeannette Gilder—Jennie—was here today, with some beautiful girls. She is large, splendid, frank, *manly*—yes, she should have been a man."[40]

Incidentally, Sherlock Holmes has the same strange regard for women. (Holmes, though fictional, was also a bachelor with Wildean eccentricities that may have arisen from Arthur Conan Doyle's meeting Oscar Wilde on the occasion of the character's second installment, see Chapter 18: Whitman and Wilde for more of that meeting.) The only woman Holmes held any special regard for was Irene Adler, with "the face of the most beautiful of women and the mind of the most resolute of men."[9] He respects her best for her ability to be more like a man, so much so that she often passes as one in the street, and beyond that manages to outsmart Holmes like a true equal (in fact she bests him more thoroughly than "the Napoleon of crime," Moriarty). Before the appearance of Irene, Holmes illustrated the divide between the sexes as by saying, "the most winning woman I ever knew was hanged for poisoning three little children for their insurance-money, and the most repellant man of my acquaintance is a philanthropist who has spent nearly a quarter of a million upon the London poor."[9] That opinion is put forth in *The Sign of Four*, the story commissioned alongside Wilde's for *Lippincott's Magazine*.

Horace Traubel once went out of his way to ask Walt Whitman why he never married. Whitman's answer is not unlike the one he gave for why he never became a Quaker (see Chapter 31: The Society of Friends), essentially because he didn't want to be encumbered:

On the evening of the 1ˢᵗ of August, 1880, as we were sitting together on the veranda of the "Hub House," among the Thousand Islands of the St. Lawrence, I said to Walt Whitman, "It seems to me surprising that you never married. Did you remain single of set purpose?" He said, "No, I have hardly done anything in my life of set purpose, in the way you mean." After a minute, he added, "I suppose the chief reason why I never married must have been an overmastering passion for entire freedom, unconstraint; I had an instinct against forming ties that would bind me." I said, "Yes, it was the instinct of self-preservation. Had you married at the usual age, *Leaves of Grass* would never have been written."[4]

Again, the same conclusion is reached: with religion there would have been no *Leaves*, and with a wife there would have been no *Leaves*, and without *Leaves* would there have truly been a Walt Whitman? Probably not. According to Peter Doyle (see: Chapter 22: Whitman's Peter), women were a non-issue for Whitman:

"I never knew a case of Walt's being bothered by a woman. In fact, he had nothing special to do with any women except Mrs. O'Connor and Mrs. Burroughs. His disposition was different. Women in that sense never came into his head."[3]

To put it as Whitman might have put it, there's this exchange of phrase between him and Horace Traubel:

When Traubel happened to use the idiomatic phrase, "he's not built that way," Whitman recalled: "Years ago in New York there was an expression similar...." He paused a moment, "but it was indelicate. The phrase was, 'He does not hang that way.' You see its import."[39]

His 'disposition,' or his hanging position, did not keep him entirely from having opinions on women, as here is his Halleck-like opinion of Ralph Waldo Emerson's (see Chapter 12: Whitman and Emerson) wife and daughter:

"I, of course knew nothing of Emerson's first wife, but the second I knew— met—and to me she was a hideous unlikely woman. How Emerson could ever have got spliced to her beats my explanation." When Walt called Emerson's daughter, Ellen, "the old hag," Horace demurred. Walt reiterated: "She is a nasty old hag—a Puritan gone to seed." When Horace remarks on her reputation as Emerson's "right hand helper," Walt shook his head, "Not so: interferer." "Ellen hates me like the devil—always did." The next day Whitman elaborated on the reason for such uncharacteristic ferocity: "Ellen? Oh! that hag! She is a hag! That guardian, watcher—afraid the great old man would make a mistake, commit some error! She is repulsive to me beyond utterance. . . . [N]either of them—neither mother nor daughter—was our woman at all. [...] Think of Emerson—the great, the free, the pure—united in marriage to a conventional woman: yes, a conventional woman and worse, a fanatically conventional woman."[39]

The women who 'interfere' with the otherwise 'great, free, and pure' men in his life are vile to him. He's not the only one to feel that way.

A Marriage Below Zero

There is another book close in the running for an early gay novel, but it's not of the types described in the introduction. All of those books, including *Joseph and His Friend*, are about men who find joy, comfort, and love in other men, with women as either nonentities outside of being convenient means of conversation, or as obstacles in need of being sorted out (a Madeline Held or a Julia Blessing). There is a book from 1889 where the other side of the story in *Joseph and His Friend* is told, from the point of view of the wife. Roger Austen describes the plot in *Playing the Game*:

> Perhaps the first novel published in America which sketches homosexuality in the darker colors of evil was *A Marriage Below Zero* by "Alan Dale," published by Dillingham in New York in 1889. Very little is known of the author's life, but it appears that he was really Alfred J. Cohen, a music and drama critic for the New York *Evening World* from 1887 to 1895. It seems unlikely that "Dale" was gay; whatever the case, he certainly wrote a melodramatically anti-gay novel.
>
> The first part of this drawing-room tale is set in England, where Elsie Bouverie meets and marries the "pretty" twenty-five-year-old Arthur Ravener, whose best friend is Captain Jack Dillingham. The two men are known in society as Damon and Pythias, since they are so often together, but it is difficult to imagine what Arthur sees in Jack, who is an unpleasant, ugly man ten years older than he, with a puffy face and beady black eyes. He is, in short, the homosexual as villain.

It's interesting to note here that Halleck and Drake were indeed known as "the Damon and Pythias of American poets"[22], Damon and Pythias being a celebrated pair of friends in Greek legend who came to signify the willingness to sacrifice oneself for the sake of a friend. When one of the two friends is condemned to death by Dionysius I, tyrant of Syracuse, he asks to be granted time to put his affairs in order. Dionysius refuses until the other of the two offers to die in his stead if he doesn't return at the appointed time. When the condemned man returns at the appointed time, Dionysius is so moved by their friendship that he releases both.[13] Austen's analysis goes on:

Even though there is a hint that the marriage is Arthur's way of "borrowing a cloak of respectability," Elsie continues to believe in her kindly husband during the first months of their marriage. Eventually the fact that it is never consummated begins to prey on her mind, and her more worldly mother suggests hiring a private detective to investigate the possibility of another woman. In a melodramatic scene, Elsie journeys to London one night to call at Arthur's townhouse, where she discovers her husband, pale and trembling, in the company of Captain Jack.

The setting shifts to New York, where Arthur has been advised to take a rest cure to recover from the emotional collapse occasioned by his wife's discovery. While in New York, Elsie and Arthur go to hear a famed preacher, whose sermon deals with Sodom and Gomorrah, and Arthur's face becomes white "as death." Arthur deserts his wife and travels incognito to Paris with Jack. When Elsie reads Arthur's note breaking off their marriage, she swoons, but then determines to chase after him in "one more effort to save my husband from a fate which I did not understand." She arrives in Paris as the newspapers are publishing the exposé of a homosexual scandal "that was agitating the never very placid surface of Parisian society," and finally in a hotel room she finds her husband dead from an overdose of laudanum. Staring down at her is a picture frame that contains two portraits, one of her husband and the other of Captain Jack. This is the overwrought conclusion of the novel: "My grief gave place to a violent, overpowering sense of anger. Tearing the frame from the wall, I threw it roughly to the floor. The glass broke with a crisp, short noise; but with my feet I crushed it into atoms. Then stooping down, I picked up the photographs, and tore them into smallest pieces. In the same frenzied manner, I went to the window, opened it, and gathering up the bits of glass— regardless of the fact that they cut my hands until the blood flowed freely—I flung them with the torn photographs from the window, and looked from it until I saw them scatter in all directions. Then turning away, and without another look at the dead form in the chair, I left the room and the hotel."[1]

One man's melodrama, however, is another woman's tragedy. The book is put into a fairer context in *Pages Passed from Hand to Hand*:

A Marriage Below Zero attracted the attention of Edward Irenaeus Prime-Stevenson [author of *Imre*, see <u>Introduction: America's First Gay Novel?</u>], who wrote of it in *The Intersexes*: "The story, not one of any artistic development, narrates (in the person of a neglected wife) her marriage with an uranian, apparently a passivist [the sexual submissive], who cannot shake off his sexual bondage to an older and coarser man, an officer. The story ends in the young husband's suicide in Paris, after an homosexual scandal has ostracised him." Other critical responses were frighteningly banal considering the novel's content: the *New York Graphic*, having first identified the author as "that well-known man about town and flâneur, who writes under the name of Alan Dale," went on to describe the book as "extremely moral in its teachings," while the *Cincinnati Enquirer* called *A Marriage Below Zero* "very bright and pleasing . . . the writer has a delightful way of telling his story."

The few contemporary readers of *A Marriage Below Zero* have tended to see it as merely homophobic. Noel I. Garde, writing in the July 1958 issue of *The Mattachine Review* (the magazine of the homophilic Mattachine Society), observed that the novel's unhappy ending established "the accepted standard for homosexual novels in the years to follow." (Forster echoed the same sentiment in the "terminal note" of *Maurice*: "Happiness is its keynote— which by the way . . . has made the book more difficult to publish." [See more of Forster and *Maurice* in Chapter 19: Calamus as Cruising Apparatus.] More recently Roger Austen, in *Playing the Game: The Homosexual Novel in America* (1977), identified *A Marriage Below Zero* as perhaps the first novel to sketch "homosexuality in the darker colors of evil" and concluded that Dale "certainly wrote a melodramatically anti-gay novel." Such a criticism is misguided, however, because it equates the author's viewpoint with that of his heroine, whose perspective counts; how often have the Constance Wildes of the world had the chance to tell their stories? (Apropos Wilde, it is worth noting that the homosexual scandal at the end of *A Marriage Below Zero* does not echo, but instead anticipates, the one that brought down the playwright six years later.)

A Marriage Below Zero is a cruel book, yet its cruelty is the cruelty of truth.[30]

For a book like *Joseph and His Friend*, where the villain is a wife who manages to kill herself by her own scheming, thankfully removing her presence (the problem) from everyone else's life (but not before managing to harass them from beyond the grave first), it is worth noting just how little trouble most of these wives ever caused their husbands, especially when compared to the harm done to them. For the Constance Wildes, for women who turned down the advances of Wildes only to end up married to severely closeted Stokers (like Florence Balcombe), for the Sarah Eckford Drakes left without their husbands *nor* the help of his 'loving friends,' it should be noted that *A Marriage Below Zero* begins with a quote from Lord Byron (who himself left behind an ill-treated wife, and was so dearly beloved by Halleck and Taylor—see Chapter 8: Halleck and the Death of Byron—that they wept on hearing the news of his death). For all the talk we've heard of *Leaves*, seeds, and fruits (see: Chapter 11: Leaves of Grass, Chapter 29: Leaves and Fruits), there's this to keep in mind:

I seek no sympathies, nor need;
The thorns which I have reap'd are of the tree
I planted,—they have torn me,—and I bleed:
I should have known what fruit would spring from such a seed.
                                                           Byron.[7]

XXXIII

ALL ARE HAPPY

THREE WEEKS AFTER the date of Joseph's last letter Philip met him at the railroad station in the city. Brown, bearded, fresh, and full of joyous life after his seven days' journey across the continent, he sprang down from the platform to be caught in his friend's arms.

The next morning they went together to Mr. Blessing's residence. That gentleman still wore a crimson velvet dressing-gown, and the odor of the cigar, which he puffed in a rear room, called the library (the books were mostly Patent Office and Agricultural Reports, with Faublas and the Decamerone), breathed plainly of the Vuelte Abajo.

"My dear boy!" he cried, jumping up and extending his arms, "Asten of Asten Hall! After all your moving accidents by flood and field, back again! This is—is—what shall I say? compensation for many a blow of fate! And my brave Knight with the Iron Hand, sit down, though it be in Carthage, and let me refresh my eyes with your faces!"

"Not Carthage yet, I hope," said Joseph.

"Not quite, if I adhere strictly to facts," Mr. Blessing replied; "although it threatens to be my Third Punic War. There is even a slight upward tendency in the Amaranth shares, and if the company were in my hands, we should soon float upon the topmost wave. But what can I do? The Honorable Whaley and the Reverend Dr. Lellifant were retained on account of their names; Whaley made president, and I—being absent at the time developing the enterprise, not only *pars magna* but *totus teres atque rotundus*, ha! ha!—I was put off with a director's place. Now I must stand by, and see the work of my hands overthrown. But 'tis ever thus!"

He heaved a deep sigh. Philip, most heroically repressing a tendency to shriek with laughter, drew him on to state the particulars, and soon discovered, as he had already suspected, that Mr. Blessing's sanguine temperament was the real difficulty; it was still possible for him to withdraw, and secure a moderate success.

When this had been made clear, Joseph interposed.

"Mr. Blessing," said he, "I cannot forget how recklessly, in my disappointment, I charged you with dishonesty. I know also that you have not forgotten it. Will you give me an opportunity of atoning for my injustice?—not that *you* require it, but that I may, henceforth, have less cause for self-reproach."

"Your words are enough!" Mr. Blessing exclaimed. "I excused you long ago. You, in your pastoral seclusion—"

"But I have not been secluded for eighteen months past," said Joseph, smiling. "It is the better knowledge of men which has opened my eyes. Besides, you have no right to refuse me; it is Mrs. Blessing whom I shall have to consult."

He laid the papers on the table, explaining that half the amount realized from his shares of the Amaranth had been invested, on trust, for the benefit of Mrs. Eliza Blessing.

"You have conquered—*vincisti!*" cried Mr. Blessing, shedding tears. "What can I do? Generosity is so rare a virtue in the world, that it would be a crime to suppress it!"

Philip took advantage of the milder mood, and plied his arguments so skillfully that at last the exuberant pride of the De Belsain blood gave way.

"What shall I do, without an object,—a hope, a faith in possibilities?" Mr. Blessing cried. "The amount you have estimated, with Joseph's princely provision, is a competence for my old days; but how shall I fill out those days? The sword that is never drawn from the scabbard rusts."

"But," said Philip, gravely, "you forget the field for which you were destined by nature. These operations in stocks require only a low order of intellect; you were meant to lead and control multitudes of men. With your fluency of speech, your happy faculty of illustration, your power of presenting facts and probabilities, you should confine yourself exclusively to the higher arena of politics. Begin as an Alderman; then, a Member of the Assembly; then, the State Senate; then—"

"Member of Congress!" cried Mr. Blessing, rising, with flushed face and flashing eyes. "You are right! I have allowed the necessity of the moment to pull me down from my proper destiny! You are doubly right! My creature comforts once secured, I can give my time, my abilities, my power of swaying the minds of men,—come, let us withdraw, realize, consolidate, invest, at once!"

They took him at his word, and before night a future, free from want, was secured to him. While Philip and Joseph were on their way to the country by a late train, Mr. Blessing was making a speech of an hour and a half at one of the primary political meetings.

There was welcome through the valley when Joseph's arrival was known. For two or three days the neighbors flocked to the farm to see the man whose adventures, in a very marvelous form, had been circulating among them for a year past. Even Mr. Chaffinch called, and was so conciliated by his friendly reception, that he, thenceforth, placed Joseph in the ranks of those "impracticable" men, who *might* be nearer the truth than they seemed: it was not for us to judge.

Every evening, however, Joseph took his saddle-horse and rode up the valley to Philip's Forge. It was not only the inexpressible charm of the verdure to which he had so long been a stranger,—not only the richness of the sunset on the hills, the exquisite fragrance of the meadow-grasses in the cool air,—nay, not entirely the dear companionship of Philip which drew him thither. A sentiment so deep and powerful that it was yet unrecognized,—a hope so faint that it had not yet taken form,—was already in his heart. Philip saw, and was silent.

But, one night, when the moon hung over the landscape, edging with sparkling silver the summits of the trees below them, when the air was still and sweet and warm, and filled with the diffused murmurs of the stream, and Joseph and Madeline stood side by side, on the curving shoulder of the knoll, Philip, watching them from the open window, said to himself: "They are swiftly coming to the knowledge of each other; will it take Joseph further from my heart, or bring him nearer? It ought to fill me with perfect joy, yet there is a little sting of pain somewhere. My life had settled down so peacefully into what seemed a permanent form; with Madeline to make a home and brighten it for me, and Joseph to give me the precious intimacy of a man's love, so different from woman's, yet so pure and perfect! They have destroyed my life, although they do not guess it. Well, I must be vicariously happy, warmed in my lonely sphere by the far radiation of their nuptial bliss, seeing a faint reflection of some parts of myself in their children, nay, claiming and making them *mine* as well, if it is meant that my own blood should not beat in other hearts. But will this be sufficient? No! either sex is incomplete alone, and a man's full life shall be mine! Ah, you unconscious lovers, you simple-souled children, that know not what you are doing, I shall be even with you in the end! The world is a failure, God's wonderful system is imperfect, if there is not now living a noble woman to bless me with her love, strengthen me with her self-sacrifice, purify me with her sweeter and clearer faith! I will wait: but I shall find her!"

THE END

33. IN CONCLUSION

The composition of this volume evolved over a year-long reading and research process, to become the sort of stories-behind-the-story book that you are holding now. *Joseph and His Friend* is remarkable, not for its simple plot or for the writing itself, but for what it was aiming to do in America in 1870, and for what it managed to say without getting banned from publication or bringing ruin on the author's life.

As far as interest to be found beyond the book itself, one peep under the surface of Bayard Taylor's life led to what was easy to think of as a daisy-chain, one link to another, with petals for playing 'he loves me, he loves me not.' But the connections all spiral out, double back, and loop together too intricately: from Taylor to Walt Whitman, from Whitman across the ocean, to Stoker, to Wilde, to the Calamus Cognoscenti all over the world, to the sailors who shared their wonder at places where men were free to touch one another, to the landscape of nineteenth-century America, to the brother-against-brother Civil War, and to the assassination of a President who may well have been a fellow 'camerado.'

For all the talk of leaves and seeds, the metaphor seems to be more perfectly suited to mushrooms: fruiting bodies attached through an underground network, with spores capable of asexual reproduction, often growing in what's called 'fairy rings,' each body sometimes standing far apart from the others, but clearly in a connected circle. To borrow a phrase from a reviewer, the information included behind each chapter of *Joseph and His Friend* is meant to conduct the reader on a tour through a familiar city's secret history; you know these names, you've heard of these books, but now the connections between them all should be even clearer, and perhaps more further-reaching than you knew before.

In that sense, America's 'first gay novel' is part of a fairy ring, perhaps the first body to appear above the surface, but with a web of foundation underneath it, and with ever more bodies emerging on the edges, expanding out.

BIOGRAPHICAL REFERENCE

ASTOR, JOHN JACOB – (born July 17, 1763, Waldorf, Germany—died March 29, 1848, New York, New York, United States), fur magnate and founder of a renowned family of Anglo-American capitalists, business leaders, and philanthropists. His American Fur Company is considered the first American business monopoly. Employer and benefactor of Fitz-Greene Halleck.[13]

BIERCE, AMBROSE – (born June 24, 1842, Meigs county, Ohio, United States—died 1914, Mexico?), American newspaperman, wit, satirist, and author of sardonic short stories based on themes of death and horror, including "An Occurrence at Owl Creek Bridge" and *The Devil's Dictionary*. His life ended in an unsolved mystery after traveling to Mexico during the revolution led by Pancho Villa. His last known communication, written from Chihuahua City on December 26, 1913, ended with, "As to me, I leave here tomorrow for an unknown destination."[28][13]

BOKER, GEORGE HENRY – (born October 6, 1823, Philadelphia, Pennsylvania, United States—died January 2, 1890, Philadelphia, Pennsylvania), a poet, playwright, and diplomat, Boker's collections of poems include *Poems of the War* (1864), *Konigsmark* (1869), and *The Book of the Dead* (1882). His historical dramas and verse-plays include *Calynos* (1848), *Leonore de Guzman* (1853), and *Francesca da Rimini* (1855), generally considered his best work. Though little read now, Boker was a well-known playwright during the mid-nineteenth century, and his plays were staged in London, New York, and Philadelphia. Boker was a lifetime close friend of Bayard Taylor and Richard Henry Stoddard.[19]

BUCHANAN, JAMES – (born April 23, 1791, near Mercersburg, Pennsylvania,United States—died June 1, 1868, near Lancaster, Pennsylvania), 15th president of the United States (1857–61), a moderate Democrat whose efforts to find a compromise in the conflict between the North and the South failed to avert the Civil War (1861–65). A bachelor president, he appointed his niece Harriet Lane as hostess in the White House.[13]

BUCKE, RICHARD MAURICE – (born March 18, 1837 in Methwold, England—died February 19, 1902 in London, Ontario, Canada), Bucke was a Canadian physician and student of the human mind who became one of Walt Whitman's most devoted friends and supporters in the poet's later years. The seventh of ten children of the Reverend Horatio

Walpole Bucke and Clarissa Andrews, he married Jessie Maria Gurd in Mooretown, Upper Canada on 7 Sept. 1865, they had five sons and three daughters. He produced (among other works) *Walt Whitman* (1883), *The Wound Dresser: A Series of Letters Written from the Hospitals of Washington* (1898), his letters can be found in *Medical Mystic: Letters of Dr. Bucke to Walt Whitman and His Friends (1977)*, and he compiled *Calamus: A Series of Letters Written During the Years 1868-1880 by Walt Whitman to a Young Friend (Peter Doyle)* (1897).[14][42]

BUFLEB, AUGUST – (born 1807–died 1874), a German businessman and landowner who formed an intense and admiring friendship with Bayard Taylor during their travels in Egypt in 1851, on a steamer ship from Smyrna to Alexandria. Taylor later married Bufleb's wife's niece, Maria Hansen (daughter of Peter Hansen, the German astronomer) in October, 1857. Bufleb built a house for Taylor and his bride in the garden of his own home at Gotha.[35][23][12]

BURROUGHS, JOHN – (born April 3, 1837, Roxbury, New York, United States—died March 29, 1921 on a train near Kingsville, Ohio), an American naturalist and nature essayist, active in the United States conservation movement. Friend of Walt Whitman's and frequenter of Pfaff's beer cellar.[58]

BYRON, LORD GEORGE GORDON – (born January 22, 1788, London, England—died April 19, 1824, Missolonghi, Greece), 6th Baron Byron, British Romantic poet, and satirist whose poetry and personality captured the imagination of Europe. Renowned as the "gloomy egoist" of his autobiographical poem *Childe Harold's Pilgrimage* (1812–18) in the 19th century, he is now more generally esteemed for the satiric realism of *Don Juan* (1819–24).[13]

CARPENTER, EDWARD – (born August 29, 1844, Brighton, Sussex, England—died June 28, 1929, Guildford, Surrey), English writer identified with social and sexual reform, and the late 19th-century anti-industrial Arts and Crafts Movement.[13]

DALE, ALAN – pseudonym for Alfred J. Cohen (born May 14, 1861, Birmingham, England—died May 21, 1928, on train en route from Plymouth to Birmingham), an influential British theatre critic, playwright, and book author of the late Victorian and early 20th Century eras, author of *A Marriage Below Zero* (1889).[58]

DEKAY, JAMES ELLSWORTH – (born October 12, 1792, Lisbon, Portugal – died November 21, 1851, Oyster Bay, New York, United States), an American doctor who devoted himself to natural history, and, in the State Survey of New York, the Department of Zoology was assigned to him. It was through Dr. DeKay that Halleck and Drake became acquainted in the summer 1815, and in 1833 his brother, George Coleman DeKay, married the only daughter of Joseph Rodman Drake.[21]

Douglas, Lord Alfred Bruce – nicknamed Bosie (born October 22, 1870, Powick, England—died March 20, 1945, Lancing), a British author, poet, translator, and political commentator, better known as the friend and lover of Oscar Wilde, whose father the Marquess of Queensberry brought the original criminal charge against Wilde that eventually led to his conviction for gross indecency.[58]

Doyle, Peter George – (born June 3, 1843 [?], Limerick City, Ireland – died April 19, 1907, Philadelphia, Pennsylvania, United States), his importance in the emotional life of Walt Whitman is well established. The romantic friendship that sprang up in 1865 between the streetcar conductor and the poet spanned the years of Whitman's residence in Washington, D.C., and continued nearly up through Whitman's death in Camden, in 1892.[2]

Drake, Joseph Rodman – (born August 7, 1795, New York City, United States—died September 21, 1820, New York City), Romantic poet who contributed to the beginnings of a U.S. national literature by a few memorable lyrics before his early death, close friend of Fitz-Greene Halleck and fellow contributor to the satirical "Croaker Papers."[13]

Emerson, Ralph Waldo – (born May 25, 1803, Boston, Massachusetts, United States—died April 27, 1882, Concord, Massachusetts), American lecturer, poet, and essayist, the leading exponent of New England Transcendentalism. [13]

Franklin, Walter – (died 1817), a mutual friend of Fitz-Greene Halleck and Joseph Rodman Drake who committed suicide by shooting himself in 1817 after spending his final day with Drake.[62]

Halleck, Fitz-Greene – (born July 8, 1790, Guilford, Connecticut, United States—died November 19, 1867, Guilford, Connecticut), the inspiration for *Joseph and His Friend* for his friendship with Joseph Rodman Drake. American poet, leading member of the Knickerbocker group, and known for both his satirical and romantic verse. An employee in various New York City banks, and assistant to John Jacob Astor, Halleck wrote only as an avocation. In collaboration with Drake he contributed to the satirical "Croaker Papers" for the *New York Evening Post* in 1819, and on the death of Drake he wrote the moving tribute beginning "Green be the turf above thee."[13]

Hawthorne, Nathaniel – (born July 4, 1804, Salem, Massachusetts, United States—died May 19, 1864, Plymouth, New Hampshire), American novelist and short-story writer who was a master of the allegorical and symbolic tale. One of the greatest fiction writers in American literature, he is best known for *The Scarlet Letter* (1850) and *The House of the Seven Gables* (1851).[13]

Housman, A. E. – in full Alfred Edward Housman (born March 26, 1859, Fockbury, Worcestershire, England—died April 30, 1936, Cambridge), English scholar and celebrated poet whose lyrics express a Romantic pessimism in a spare, simple style, best know for his poetry collection, *A Shropshire Lad* (1896). Housman spent his life in unreciprocated love for his best friend, Moses Jackson.[13]

Housman, Laurence – (born July 18, 1865, Bromsgrove, Worcestershire, England—died February 20, 1959, Glastonbury, Somerset), English artist and writer who reached his widest public with a series of plays about the Victorian era, of which the most successful was *Victoria Regina* (1934). He was a younger brother of the poet A.E. Housman.[13]

Jackson, Andrew – byname Old Hickory (born March 15, 1767, Waxhaws region, South Carolina, United States—died June 8, 1845, the Hermitage, near Nashville, Tennessee), military hero and 7th president of the United States (1829–37). He was the first U.S. president to come from the area west of the Appalachians, and the first to gain office by a direct appeal to the mass of voters. His political movement has since been known as Jacksonian Democracy.[13]

Lawrence, T. E. – in full Thomas Edward Lawrence, byname Lawrence of Arabia, also called (from 1927) T.E. Shaw (born August 16, 1888, Tremadoc, Caernarvonshire, Wales—died May 19, 1935, Clouds Hill, Dorset, England), British archaeological scholar, military strategist, and author, best known for his legendary war activities in the Middle East during World War I, and for his account of those activities in *Seven Pillars of Wisdom* (1926).[13]

Lincoln, Abraham – byname Honest Abe, the Rail-Splitter, or the Great Emancipator (born February 12, 1809, near Hodgenville, Kentucky, United States—died April 15, 1865, Washington, D.C.), 16th president of the United States (1861–65), who preserved the Union during the American Civil War and brought about the emancipation of the slaves.[13]

Melville, Herman – (born August 1, 1819, New York City, United States—died September 28, 1891, New York City), American novelist, short-story writer, and poet, best known for his novels of the sea, including his masterpiece, *Moby Dick* (1851).[13]

O'Connor, William – (born 1832—died 1889) a journalist who wrote a vindication of Whitman in "The Good Gray Poet" (published in 1866), which aroused sympathy for the victim of injustice after Whitman was dismissed from employment for being the author of *Leaves of Grass*.[14]

Poe, Edgar Allan – (born January 19, 1809, Boston, Massachusetts, United States—died October 7, 1849, Baltimore, Maryland), American short-story writer, poet, critic, and editor who is famous for his cultivation of mystery and the macabre. His tale "The

Murders in the Rue Morgue" (1841) initiated the modern detective story, and the atmosphere in his tales of horror is unrivaled in American fiction. His "The Raven" (1845) numbers among the best-known poems in the national literature.[13]

PRIME-STEVENSON, EDWARD IRENAEUS – byname Xavier Mayne (born January 29, 1858, Madison, New Jersey, United States—died July 23, 1942, Lausanne, Switzerland), American author of *The Intersexes* (1908), a defense of homosexuality from a scientific, legal, historical, and personal perspective, and *Imre: A Memorandum* (1906), styled as "a little psychological romance" by its author, which recounts the developing love between a thirty-something British aristocrat and a twenty-five-year-old Magyar military officer. The story's ending is unprecedented—the first in gay literature where homosexuals are united and happy as the tale closes.[20]

STODDARD, CHARLES WARREN – (born August 7, 1843, Rochester, New York, United States—died April 23, 1909, Monterey, California), an American author and editor, and homosexual contemporary of Robert Louis Stevenson, Herman Melville, and Walt Whitman. He was a journalist, a lecturer at the Catholic University of America from 1889 to 1902, and for a brief period Mark Twain's secretary. Stoddard was the author of *For the Pleasure of His Company* (1903), which is called the first overtly homosexual American novel. Inspired to sexual self-awareness by reading Whitman's "Calamus" poems, Stoddard gained his first homosexual experiences with the natives of Hawaii and Tahiti, about whom he wrote his best stories, those collected in *South-Sea Idyls* (1874, 1892) and *The Island of Tranquil Delights* (1904). The subtle eroticism of Stoddard's tropical tales was evidently lost on his audience—except for "Xavier Mayne" (Edward Prime-Stevenson), who noted their significance in *The Intersexes* (1908).[6][17][14]

STODDARD, RICHARD HENRY – (born July 2, 1825, Hingham, Massachusetts, United States—died May 12, 1903, New York), American poet, critic, and editor, more important as a figure in New York literary circles in the late 19th century than for his own verse. He was a lifetime friend of Bayard Taylor and George Boker.[13]

STODDART, JOSEPH M. – (born 1845 – died 1921), managing editor of *Lippincott's Magazine* (published in Philadelphia from 1868 to 1915), which commissioned a story from Arthur Conan Doyle and Oscar Wilde in the same meeting (the second appearance of Sherlock Holmes in *The Sign of Four*, and what would eventually be *The Picture of Dorian Gray*). Stoddart is also the man who brought Oscar Wilde to Walt Whitman's house on Mickle Street in Camden in 1882.[37]

SYMONDS, JOHN ADDINGTON – (born October 5, 1840, Bristol, Gloucestershire, England—died April 19, 1893, Rome, Italy), English essayist, poet, and biographer best known for his cultural history of the Italian Renaissance. Symonds' own poetry was published in the volumes *Many Moods* (1878), *New and Old* (1880), *Animi Figura*

(1882), and *Vagabunduli Libellus* (1884), his powerful love sonnets discreetly obscuring the homosexual nature of the erotic experience described. His *A Problem in Greek Ethics* (written 1871; privately printed 1883) and *A Problem in Modern Ethics* (privately printed 1891) were two of the first serious works on the subject of homosexuality.[13]

STOKER, BRAM – byname of Abraham Stoker (born November 8, 1847, Clontarf, County Dublin, Ireland—died April 20, 1912, London, England), Irish writer best known as the author of the Gothic horror tale *Dracula*.[13]

TAYLOR, BAYARD – in full James Bayard Taylor (born January 11, 1825, Kennett Square, Pennsylvania, United States—died Dec. 19, 1878, Berlin, Germany), American author known primarily for his lively travel narratives and for his translation of J.W. von Goethe's *Faust*, author of *Joseph and His Friend*.[13]

TRAUBEL, HORACE – (born December 19, 1858, Camden, New Jersey, United States—died September 3, 1919, Bon Echo, Ontario, Canada), Traubel is best known as the author of a nine-volume biography of Whitman's final four years, *With Walt Whitman in Camden*. He visited the poet virtually daily from the mid-1880s until Whitman's death in 1892, and he began taking copious notes of their conversations in March of 1888. Every night he transcribed his notes and published three large volumes of them (1906, 1908, 1914) before his death, leaving behind manuscripts for six more. His original goal had been to bring out one volume a year until all were in print, but the final two volumes did not appear until 1996, over a century after they were written.[14]

WHITMAN, WALT – in full Walter Whitman (born May 31, 1819, West Hills, Long Island, New York, United States—died March 26, 1892, Camden, New Jersey), American poet, journalist, and essayist whose verse collection *Leaves of Grass* is a landmark in the history of American literature.[13]

WILDE, OSCAR – in full Oscar Fingal O'Flahertie Wills Wilde (born October 16, 1854, Dublin, Ireland—died November 30, 1900, Paris, France), Irish wit, poet, and dramatist whose reputation rests on his only novel, *The Picture of Dorian Gray* (1891), and on his comic masterpieces *Lady Windermere's Fan* (1892) and *The Importance of Being Earnest* (1895). He was a spokesman for the late 19th century Aesthetic movement in England, which advocated art for art's sake, and he was the object of civil and criminal suits involving homosexuality, which resulted in his imprisonment and exile (1895–97).[13]

WORKS CITED
AND CONSULTED

[1]Austen, Roger. *Playing the Game: The Homosexual Novel in America*. Indianapolis: Bobbs-Merrill, 1977.

[2]Bloom, Harold and Temple Cone. *Walt Whitman (Bloom's Classic Critical Views)*. Blooms Literary Criticism, October 1, 2007.

[3]Bucke, Richard Maurice, M.D. *Calamus: A Series of Letters Written During the Years 1868-1880 by Walt Whitman to a Young Friend (Peter Doyle)*. Boston: Laurens Maynard, 1897.

[4]Bucke, Richard Maurice, M.D. *Walt Whitman*. Philadelphia, David McKay, 1883.

[5]Cooney, Katherine. "Who Was Our First Gay President?" *Time Inc.* May 17, 2012. http://newsfeed.time.com/2012/05/17/who-was-our-first-gay-president/. Accessed February 26, 2017.

[6]Crowley, John W. "Stoddard, Charles Warren." *glbtq: An Encyclopedia of Gay, Lesbian, Bisexual, Transgender, and Queer Culture*. Chicago: May 15, 2002, http://www.glbtq.com/literature/stoddard_cw.html. Accessed February 7, 2015.

[7]Dale, Alan. *A Marriage Below Zero: A Novel*. G.W. Dillingham, 1889.

[8]Doyle, Arthur Conan. *Memories and Adventures*. Cambridge University Press, Feb 16, 2012.

[9]Doyle, Arthur Conan. *Sherlock Holmes: The Complete Stories*. Wordsworth Editions, 1989.

[10]Ellmann, Richard. *Oscar Wilde*. Knopf Doubleday Publishing Group, Sep 4, 2013.

[11]Emerson, Warren. "Melville to Hawthorne: 'Well, the Hawthorne is a sweet flower; may it flourish in every hedge.'" *The Literary Table*. March 13, 2012. https://literarytable.com/2012/03/13/melville-to-hawthorne-well-the-hawthorne-is-a-sweet-flower-may-it-flourish-in-every-hedge/. Accessed February 26, 1988.

[12] *Encyclopedia Britannica: a dictionary of arts, sciences, literature and general information.* Cambridge: U Press, 1911, http://encyclopedia.jrank.org/. Accessed 26 Feb. 2017.

[13] *Encyclopædia Britannica.* Encyclopædia Britannica, Inc., n.d., https://www.britannica.com/. Accessed 26 Feb. 2017.

[14] Folsom, Ed and Kenneth M. Price, editors. *The Walt Whitman Archive.* University of Nebraska–Lincoln, 2017, http://whitmanarchive.org/. Accessed 26 February, 2017.

[15] Forster, E.M. *Maurice.* W. W. Norton & Company, December 17, 2005.

[16] Gale, Robert L. *An Ambrose Bierce Companion.* Greenwood Publishing Group, 2001.

[17] Garland, Peter. "Celebrating Charles Warren Stoddard." *The Bay Area Reporter.* August 7, 2014, http://www.ebar.com/arts/art_article.php?sec=books&article=863. Accessed February 1, 2017.

[18] Genç, Kaya. "Coming Out of the Coffin." *The New Inquiry.* https://thenewinquiry.com/essays/coming-out-of-the-coffin/. Accessed 26 Feb. 2017.

[19] "George Henry Boker." *Poetry Foundation.* Chicago: Poetry Foundation, 2017, https://www.poetryfoundation.org/poems-and-poets/poets/detail/george-henry-boker. Accessed February 26, 2017.

[20] Gifford, James J. "Stevenson, Edward Irenaeus Prime-." *glbtq: An Encyclopedia of Gay, Lesbian, Bisexual, Transgender, and Queer Culture.* Chicago: February 28, 2004, http://www.glbtq.com/literature/stevenson_eip.html. Accessed March 10, 2007.

[21] Halleck, Fitz-Greene, and Joseph Rodman Drake. *The Poetical Works of Fitz-Greene Halleck: With Extracts from Those of Joseph Rodman Drake.* New York: D. Appleton and Company, 1869.

[22] Hallock, John W. M. *The American Byron: Homosexuality and the Fall of Fitz-Greene Halleck.* Madison: University of Wisconsin Press, 2000.

[23] Hansen-Taylor, Marie and Horace E. Scudder. *Life and Letters of Bayard Taylor, Volume 1.* Houghton, Mifflin and Company, 1895 (Fifth Edition).

[24] Hansen-Taylor, Marie and Horace E. Scudder. *Life and Letters of Bayard Taylor, Volume 2.* Houghton, Mifflin and Company, 1895 (Fifth Edition).

[25]Housman, Laurence. *My Brother, A. E. Housman: Personal Recollections Together with Thirty Hitherto Unpublished Poems.* Kennikat Press, 1969.

[26]Melville, Herman. *Delphi Complete Works of Herman Melville (Illustrated).* Delphi Classics, Nov 17, 2013.

[27]Hindley, Meredith. "When Bram Met Walt." *Humanities,* Volume 33, Number 6. November/December 2012, https://www.neh.gov/humanities/2012/novemberdecember/feature/when-bram-met-walt. Accessed February 26, 2017.

[28]Joshi, S.T. and David E. Schultz. *A Much Misunderstood Man: Selected Letters of Ambrose Bierce.* Columbus: The Ohio State University Press, 2003.

[29]Lawrence, T.E. *Seven Pillars of Wisdom: A Triumph.* Anchor Books, 1991.

[30]Leavitt, David and Mark Mitchell. *Pages Passed from Hand to Hand: The Hidden Tradition of Homosexual Literature in English from 1748 to 1914.* Boston: Houghton Mifflin, 1997.

[31]LeMaster, J.R. and Donald D. Kummings, eds., *The Routledge Encyclopedia Walt Whitman.* New York: Garland Publishing, 1998.

[32]Levin, Meyer. *Compulsion.* Fig Tree Books, LLC, 2015.

[33]Martin, Justin. *Rebel Souls: Walt Whitman and America's First Bohemians.* Boston, MA: Da Capo Press, a member of the Perseus Books Group, 2014.

[34]"New name: Kennett Public Library." *The Unionville Times,* 13 Feb. 2015, http://www.unionvilletimes.com/?p=24735. Accessed February 26, 2017.

[35]Nissen, Axel. *Manly Love: Romantic Friendship in American Fiction.* The University of Chicago Press, 2009.

[36]Poe, Edgar Allan. "Critical Notices." *Southern Literary Messenger,* Vol. II, No. 3, April 1836.

[37]Redmond, Christopher. *Lives Beyond Baker Street: A Biographical Dictionary of Sherlock Holmes's Contemporaries.* Andrews UK Limited, Dec 19, 2016.

[38]Schaffer, Talia. "'A Wilde Desire Took Me': The Homoerotic History of Dracula." *ELH,* vol. 61, no. 2, 1994, pp. 381–425., www.jstor.org/stable/2873274. Accessed February 26, 2017

[39] Schmidgall, Gary and Horace Traubel. *Intimate with Walt, Selections from Whitman's Conversations with Horace Traubel, 1888-1892*. University of Iowa, 2001.

[40] Schmidgall, Gary. *Walt Whitman, A Gay Life*. New York: Dutton, 1997.

[41] Segal, Mark. "The men behind the man: Abraham Lincoln's gay lovers." *Bilerico Report*, February 15, 2016. http://www.lgbtqnation.com/2016/02/the-men-behind-the-man-abraham-lincolns-gay-lovers/. Accessed February 26, 2017.

[42] Shortt, S.E.D. "Bucke, Richard Maurice," *Dictionary of Canadian Biography*, vol. 13. University of Toronto/Université Laval, 1994, http://www.biographi.ca/en/bio/bucke_richard_maurice_13E.html. Accessed February 1, 2017.

[43] Skal, David J. *Something in the Blood: The Untold Story of Bram Stoker, the Man Who Wrote Dracula*. W. W. Norton & Company, 2016.

[44] Slater, Joseph. "The Case of Drake and Halleck." *Early American Literature*, Vol. 8, No. 3 (Winter, 1974), pp. 285-297.

[45] Smyth, Albert Henry. *Bayard Taylor*. Boston: Houghton, Mifflin, 1896.

[46] Stoddard, Charles Warren. *South-Sea Idyls*. Charles Scribner's Sons, 1895.

[47] Taylor, Bayard. "Diversions of the Echo Club." *The Atlantic Monthly*, Vol. 30. Boston: James R. Osgood and Company, July 1872. pp. 83.

[48] Taylor, Bayard. "Fitz-Greene Halleck." *The Library of the World's Best Literature. An Anthology in Thirty Volumes*, 1917. http://www.bartleby.com/library/prose/5151.html. Accessed February 26, 2017.

[49] Taylor, Bayard. *The Echo club, And Other Literary Diversions*. Boston, J. R. Osgood and Company, 1876.

[50] Taylor, Bayard. "Fitz-Greene Halleck." *The North American Review*, Vol. 125, No. 257 (Jul. - Aug., 1877), pp. 60-67.

[51] Taylor, Bayard. *Joseph and his Friend: A Story of Pennsylvania*. New York: G.P. Putnam & Sons, 1870.

[52] Taylor, Bayard. *The Poetical Works of Bayard Taylor*. Houghton, Mifflin and Company, 1907.

[53] Taylor, Bayard. "Twin-Love." *The Atlantic Monthly*, Vol. 28, No. 167. September, 1871. pp. 257-266.

[54] Weldon, Glen. "Grad Student Discovers A Lost Novel Written By Walt Whitman." *National Public Radio*. February 21, 2017. www.npr.org/sections/thetwo-way/2017/02/21/516442353/grad-student-discovers-a-lost-novel-written-by-walt-whitman. Accessed February 26, 2017.

[55] Wermuth, Paul Charles. *Bayard Taylor*. New York: Twayne Publishers, 1973.

[56] Whitman, Walt. *Leaves of Grass*. Brooklyn: Fowler & Wells, 1856. 2nd Edition

[57] Whitman, Walt. *Leaves of Grass*. Philadelphia: David McKay, 1891–92. 9th Edition

[58] Wikipedia. *Wikipedia, The Free Encyclopedia*. Wikipedia, The Free Encyclopedia. https://www.wikipedia.org/. Accessed February 26, 2017.

[59] Wilde, Oscar. *The Complete Works of Oscar Wilde: Stories, Plays, Poems & Essays*. Imprint: Harper Perennial, 2008.

[60] Wilde, Oscar. *The Picture of Dorian Gray (The Lippincott's Edition)*. Creation Books, 2000.

[61] Williams, Andrew. *The Toxic Morsel: T.E. Lawrence and the Mint*. Peter Lang, 2008.

[62] Wilson, James Grant. *Life and Letters of Fitz-Greene Halleck*. New York: D. Appleton and Company, 1869.

[63] Wolfe, Daniel. *Lives of Notable Gay Men and Lesbians: T. E. Lawrence*. Chelsea House Publishers, 1995.

[64] Zarrelli, Natalie. "The Poisonous Beauty Advice Columns of Victorian England." *Atlas Obscura*. December 17, 2015. http://www.atlasobscura.com/articles/the-poisonous-beauty-advice-columns-of-victorian-england. Accessed February 26, 2017.

APPENDICES

A1

[A.1]

Asia Minor: Smyrna
TO A PERSIAN BOY.

In the Bazaar at Smyrna

The gorgeous blossoms of that magic tree
Beneath whose shade I sat a thousand nights
Breathed from their opening petals all delights
Embalmed in spice of Orient Poesy,
When first, young Persian, I beheld thine eyes,
And felt the wonder of thy beauty grow
Within my brain, as some fair planet's glow
Deepens, and fills the summer evening skies.
From under thy dark lashes shone on me
The rich, voluptuous soul of Eastern land,
Impassioned, tender, calm, serenely sad,—
Such as immortal Hafiz felt when he
Sang by the fountain-streams of Rocnabad,
Or in the bowers of blissful Samarcand.

BAYARD TAYLOR, 1851

[52] Taylor, Bayard. *The Poetical Works of Bayard Taylor*. Houghton, Mifflin and Company, 1907.

A2

[A.2]
ON THE HEADLAND.

I sit on the lonely headland,
Where the sea-gulls come and go:
The sky is gray above me,
And the sea is gray below.

There is no fisherman's pinnace
Homeward or outward bound;

I see no living creature
In the world's deserted round.

I pine for something human,
Man, woman, young or old,—
Something to meet and welcome,
Something to clasp and hold.

I have a mouth for kisses,
But there's no one to give or take,
I have a heart in my bosom
Beating for nobody's sake.

O warmth of love that is wasted!
Is there no one to stretch a hand?
No other heart that hungers
In all the living land?

I could fondle the fisherman's baby,
And rock it into rest;
I could take the sunburnt sailor,
Like a brother, to my breast.

I could clasp the hand of any
Outcast of land or sea,
If the guilty palm but answered
The tenderness in me!

The sea might rise and drown me,—
Cliffs fall and crush my head,—
Were there one to love me, living,
Or weep to see me dead!

BAYARD TAYLOR, 1855

[52] Taylor, Bayard. *The Poetical Works of Bayard Taylor*. Houghton, Mifflin and Company, 1907.

[A.3]

TWIN-LOVE.

When John Vincent, after waiting twelve years, married Phebe Etheridge, the whole neighborhood experienced that sense of relief and satisfaction which follows the triumph of the right. Not that the fact of a true love is ever generally recognized and respected when it is first discovered; for there is a perverse quality in American human nature which will not accept the existence of any fine, unselfish passion, until it has been tested and established beyond peradventure. There were two views of the case when John Vincent's love for Phebe, and old Reuben Etheridge's hard prohibition of the match, first became known to the community. The girls and boys, and some of the matrons, ranged themselves at once on the side of the lovers, but a large majority of the older men and a few of the younger supported the tyrannical father.

Reuben Etheridge was rich, and, in addition to what his daughter would naturally inherit from him, she already possessed more than her lover, at the time of their betrothal. This in the eyes of one class was a sufficient reason for the father's hostility. When low natures live (as they almost invariably do) wholly in the present, they neither take tenderness from the past nor warning from the possibilities of the future. It is the exceptional men and women who remember their youth. So, these lovers received a nearly equal amount of sympathy and condemnation; and only slowly, partly through their quiet fidelity and patience, and partly through the improvement in John Vincent's worldly circumstances, was the balance changed. Old Reuben remained an unflinching despot to the last: if any relenting softness touched his heart, he sternly concealed it; and such inference as could be drawn from the fact that he, certainly knowing what would follow his death, bequeathed his daughter her proper share of his goods, was all that could be taken for consent.

They were married: John, a grave man in middle age, weather-beaten and worn by years of hard work and self-denial, yet not beyond the restoration of a milder second youth; and Phebe a sad, weary woman, whose warmth of longing had been exhausted, from whom youth and its uncalculating surrenders of hope and feeling had gone forever. They began their wedded life under the shadow of the death out of which it grew; and when, after a ceremony in which neither bridesmaid nor groomsman stood by their side, they united their divided homes, it seemed to their neighbors that a separated husband and wife had come together again, not that the relation was new to either.

John Vincent loved his wife with the tenderness of an innocent man, but all his tenderness could not avail to lift the weight of settled melancholy which had gathered upon her. Disappointment, waiting, yearning, indulgence in long lament and self-pity, the morbid cultivation of unhappy fancies—all this had wrought its work upon her, and it was too late to effect a cure. In the night she awoke to weep at his side, because of the years when she had awakened to weep alone; by day she kept up her old habit of foreboding, although the evening steadily refuted the morning; and there were times when, without any apparent cause, she would fall into a dark, despairing mood which her husband's greatest care and cunning could only slowly dispel.

Two or three years passed, and new life came to the Vincent farm. One day, between midnight and dawn, the family pair was doubled; the cry of twin sons was heard in the hushed house. The father restrained his happy wonder in his concern for the imperilled life of the mother; he guessed that she had anticipated death, and she now hung by a thread so slight that her simple will might snap it. But her will, fortunately, was as faint as her consciousness; she gradually drifted out of danger, taking her returning strength with a passive acquiescence rather than with joy. She was hardly paler than her wont, but the lurking shadow seemed to have vanished from her eyes, and John Vincent felt that her features had assumed a new expression, the faintly perceptible stamp of some spiritual change.

It was a happy day for him when, propped against his breast and gently held by his warm, strong arm, the twin boys were first brought to be laid upon her lap. Two staring, dark-faced creatures, with restless fists and feet, they were alike in every least feature of their grotesque animality. Phebe placed a hand under the head of each, and looked at them for a long time in silence.

"Why is this?" she said, at last, taking hold of a narrow pink ribbon, which was tied around the wrist of one.

"He's the oldest, sure," the nurse answered. "Only by fifteen minutes or so, but it generally makes a difference when twins come to be named; and you may see with your own eyes that there's no telling of 'em apart otherways."

"Take off the ribbon, then," said Phebe quietly; "*I* know them."

"Why, ma'am, it's always done, where they're so like! And I'll never be able to tell which is which; for they sleep and wake and feed by the same clock. And you might mistake, after all, in giving 'em names—"

"There is no oldest or youngest, John; they are two and yet one: this is mine, and this is yours."

"I see no difference at all, Phebe," said John; "and how can we divide them?"

"We will not divide," she answered; "I only meant it as a sign."

She smiled, for the first time in many days. He was glad of heart, but did not understand her. "What shall we call them?" he asked. "Elias and Reuben, after our fathers?"

"No, John; their names must be David and Jonathan."

And so they were called. And they grew, not less, but more alike, in passing through the stages of babyhood. The ribbon of the older one had been removed, and the nurse would have been distracted, but for Phebe's almost miraculous instinct. The former comforted herself with the hope that teething would bring a variation to the two identical mouths; but no! they teethed as one child. John, after desperate attempts, which always failed in spite of the headaches they gave him, postponed the idea of distinguishing one from the other, until they should be old enough to develop some dissimilarity of speech, or gait, or habit. All trouble might have been avoided, had Phebe consented to the least variation in their dresses; but herein she was mildly immovable.

"Not yet," was her set reply to her husband; and one day, when he manifested a little annoyance at her persistence, she turned to him, holding a child on each knee, and said with a gravity which silenced him thenceforth: "John, can you not see that our burden has passed into them? Is there no meaning in this—that two children who are one in body and face and nature, should be given to us at our time of life, after such long disappointment

and trouble? Our lives were held apart; theirs were united before they were born, and I dare not turn them in different directions. Perhaps I do not know all that the Lord intended to say to us, in sending them; but His hand is here!"

"I was only thinking of their good," John meekly answered. "If they are spared to grow up, there must be some way of knowing one from the other."

"*They* will not need it, and I, too, think only of them. They have taken the cross from my heart, and I will lay none on theirs. I am reconciled to my life through them, John; you have been very patient and good with me, and I will yield to you in all things but in this. I do not think I shall live to see them as men grown; yet, while we are together, I feel clearly what it is right to do. Can you not, just once, have a little faith without knowledge, John?"

"I'll try, Phebe," he said. "Any way, I'll grant that the boys belong to you more than to me."

Phebe Vincent's character had verily changed. Her attacks of semi-hysterical despondency never returned; her gloomy prophecies ceased. She was still grave, and the trouble of so many years never wholly vanished from her face; but she performed every duty of her life with at least a quiet willingness, and her home became the abode of peace; for passive content wears longer than demonstrative happiness.

David and Jonathan grew as one boy: the taste and temper of one was repeated in the other, even as the voice and features. Sleeping or waking, grieved or joyous, well or ill, they lived a single life, and it seemed so natural for one to answer to the other's name, that they probably would have themselves confused their own identities, but for their mother's unerring knowledge. Perhaps unconsciously guided by her, perhaps through the voluntary action of their own natures, each quietly took the other's place when called upon, even to the sharing of praise or blame at school, the friendships and quarrels of the playground. They were healthy and happy lads, and John Vincent was accustomed to say to his neighbors, "They're no more trouble than one would be; and yet they're four hands instead of two."

Phebe died when they were fourteen, saying to them, with almost her latest breath, "Be one, always!" Before her husband could decide whether to change her plan of domestic education, they were passing out of boyhood, changing in voice, stature, and character with a continued likeness which bewildered and almost terrified him. He procured garments of different colors, but they were accustomed to wear each article in common, and the result was only a mixture of tints for both. They were sent to different schools, to be returned the next day, equally pale, suffering, and incapable of study. Whatever device was employed, they evaded it by a mutual instinct which rendered all external measures unavailing. To John Vincent's mind their resemblance was an accidental misfortune, which had been confirmed through their mother's fancy. He felt that they were bound by some deep, mysterious tie, which, inasmuch as it might interfere with all practical aspects of life, ought to be gradually weakened. Two bodies, to him, implied two distinct men, and it was wrong to permit a mutual dependence which prevented either from exercising his own separate will and judgment.

But, while he was planning and pondering, the boys became young men, and he was an old man. Old, and prematurely broken; for he had worked much, borne much, and his large frame held only a moderate measure of vital force. A great weariness fell upon him, and his powers began to give way, at first slowly, but then with accelerated failure. He saw the end coming, long before his sons suspected it; his doubt, for their sakes, was the only thing which made it unwelcome. It was "upon his mind" (as his Quaker neighbors would say) to speak to them of the future, and at last the proper moment came.

It was a stormy November evening. Wind and rain whirled and drove among the trees outside, but the sitting-room of the old farm-house was bright and warm. David and Jonathan, at the table, with their arms over each other's backs and their brown locks mixed together, read from the same book: their father sat in the ancient rocking-chair before the fire, with his feet upon a stool. The housekeeper and hired man had gone to bed, and all was still in the house.

John waited until he heard the volume closed, and then spoke.

"Boys," he said, "let me have a bit of talk with you. I don't seem to get over my ailments rightly,— never will, maybe. A man must think of things while there's time, and say them when they *have* to be said. I don't know as there's any particular hurry in my case; only, we never can tell, from one day to

another. When I die, every thing will belong to you two, share and share alike, either to buy another farm with the money out, or divide this: I won't tie you up in any way. But two of you will need two farms for two families; for you won't have to wait twelve years, like your mother and me."

"We don't want another farm, father!" said David and Jonathan together.

"I know you don't think so, now. A wife seemed far enough off from me when I was your age. You've always been satisfied to be with each other, but that can't last. It was partly your mother's notion; I remember her saying that our burden had passed into you. I never quite understood what she meant, but I suppose it must rather be the opposite of what *we* had to bear."

The twins listened with breathless attention while their father, suddenly stirred by the past, told them the story of his long betrothal.

"And now," he exclaimed, in conclusion, "it may be putting wild ideas into your two heads, but I must say it! *That* was where I did wrong—wrong to her and to me,—in waiting! I had no right to spoil the best of our lives; I ought to have gone boldly, in broad day, to her father's house, taken her by the hand, and led her forth to be my wife. Boys, if either of you comes to love a woman truly, and she to love you, and there is no reason why God (I don't say man) should put you asunder, do as I ought to have done, not as I did! And, maybe, this advice is the best legacy I can leave you."

"But, father," said David, speaking for both, "we have never thought of marrying."

"Likely enough," their father answered; "we hardly ever think of what surely comes. But to me, looking back, it's plain. And this is the reason why I want you to make me a promise, and as solemn as if I was on my death-bed. Maybe I shall be, soon."

Tears gathered in the eyes of the twins. "What is it, father?" they both said.

"Nothing at all to any other two boys, but I don't know how *you'll* take it. What if I was to ask you to live apart for a while?"

"O father!" both cried. They leaned together, cheek pressing cheek, and hand clasping hand, growing white and trembling. John Vincent, gazing into the fire, did not see their faces, or his purpose might have been shaken.

"I don't say *now*," he went on. "After a while,

when—well, when I'm dead. And I only mean a beginning, to help you toward what *has* to be. Only a month; I don't want to seem hard to you; but that's little, in all conscience. Give me your word: say, 'For mother's sake!'"

There was a long pause. Then David and Jonathan said, in low, faltering voices, "For mother's sake, I promise."

"Remember that you were only boys to her. She might have made all this seem easier, for women have reasons for things no man can answer. Mind, within a year after I'm gone!"

He rose and tottered out of the room.

The twins looked at each other: David said, "Must we?" and Jonathan, "How can we?" Then they both thought, "It may be a long while yet." Here was a present comfort, and each seemed to hold it firmly in holding the hand of the other, as they fell asleep side by side.

The trial was nearer than they imagined. Their father died before the winter was over; the farm and other property was theirs, and they might have allowed life to solve its mysteries as it rolled onwards, but for their promise to the dead. This must be fulfilled, and then—one thing was certain; they would never again separate.

"The sooner the better," said David. "It shall be the visit to our uncle and cousins in Indiana. You will come with me as far as Harrisburg; it may be easier to part there than here. And our new neighbors, the Bradleys, will want your help for a day or two, after getting home."

"It is less than death," Jonathan answered, "and why should it seem to be more? We must think of father and mother, and all those twelve years; now I know what the burden was."

"And we have never really borne any part of it! Father must have been right in forcing us to promise."

Every day the discussion was resumed, and always with the same termination. Familiarity with the inevitable step gave them increase of courage; yet, when the moment had come and gone, when, speeding on opposite trains, the hills and valleys multiplied between them with terrible velocity, a pang like death cut to the heart of each, and the divided life became a chill, oppressive dream.

During the separation no letters passed between them. When the neighbors asked Jonathan for news of his brother, he always replied, "He is well," and avoided further speech with such evidence of pain that they spared him. An hour before the month drew to an end, he walked forth alone, taking the road to the nearest railway station. A stranger who passed him at the entrance of a thick wood, three miles from home, was thunderstruck on meeting the same person shortly after, entering the wood from the other side; but the farmers in the near fields saw two figures issuing from the shade, hand in hand.

Each knew the other's month, before they slept, and the last thing Jonathan said, with his head on David's shoulder, was, "You must know our neighbors, the Bradleys, and especially Ruth." In the morning, as they dressed, taking each other's garments at random, as of old, Jonathan again said, "I have never seen a girl that I like so well as Ruth Bradley. Do you remember what father said about loving and marrying? It comes into my mind whenever I see Ruth; but she has no sister."

"But we need not both marry," David replied, "that might part us, and this will not. It is for always now."

"For always, David."

Two or three days later Jonathan said, as he started on an errand to the village: "I shall stop at the Bradleys this evening, so you must walk across and meet me there."

When David approached the house, a slender, girlish figure, with her back towards him, was stooping over a bush of great crimson roses, cautiously clipping a blossom here and there. At the click of the gate-latch she started and turned towards him. Her light gingham bonnet, falling back, disclosed a long oval face, fair and delicate, sweet brown eyes, and brown hair laid smoothly over the temples. A soft flush rose suddenly to her cheeks, and he felt that his own were burning.

"O Jonathan!" she exclaimed, transferring the roses to her left hand, and extending her right, as she came forward.

He was too accustomed to the name to recognize her mistake at once, and the word "Ruth!" came naturally to his lips.

"I should know your brother David has come," she then said; "even if I had not heard so. You look so bright. How glad I am!"

"Is he not here?" David asked.

"No; but there he is now, surely!" She turned towards the lane, where Jonathan was dismounting. "Why, it is yourself over again, Jonathan!"

As they approached, a glance passed between the twins, and a secret transfer of the riding-whip to David set their identity right with Ruth, whose manner toward the latter innocently became shy with all its friendliness, while her frank, familiar speech was given to Jonathan, as was fitting. But David also took the latter to himself, and when they left, Ruth had apparently forgotten that there was any difference in the length of their acquaintance.

On their way homewards David said: "Father was right. We must marry, like others, and Ruth is the wife for us,—I mean for you, Jonathan. Yes, we must learn to say *mine* and *yours*, after all, when we speak of her."

"Even she cannot separate us, it seems," Jonathan answered. "We must give her some sign, and that will also be a sign for others. It will seem strange to divide ourselves; we can never learn it properly; rather let us not think of marriage."

"We cannot help thinking of it; she stands in mother's place now, as we in father's."

Then both became silent and thoughtful. They felt that something threatened to disturb what seemed to be the only possible life for them, yet were unable to distinguish its features, and therefore powerless to resist it. The same instinct which had been born of their wonderful spiritual likeness told them that Ruth Bradley already loved Jonathan: the duty was established, and they must conform their lives to it. There was, however, this slight difference between their natures—that David was generally the first to utter the thought which came to the minds of both. So when he said, "We shall learn what to do when the need comes," it was a postponement of all foreboding. They drifted contentedly towards the coming change.

The days went by, and their visits to Ruth Bradley were continued. Sometimes Jonathan went alone, but they were usually together, and the tie which united the three became dearer and sweeter as it was more closely drawn. Ruth learned to distinguish between the two when they were before her: at least she said so, and they were willing to believe it. But she was hardly aware how nearly alike was the happy warmth in her bosom produced by either pair of dark gray eyes and the soft half-smile which played around either mouth. To them she seemed to be drawn within the mystic circle which separated them from others—she, alone; and they no longer imagined a life in which she should not share.

Then the inevitable step was taken. Jonathan declared his love, and was answered. Alas! he almost forgot David that late summer evening, as they sat in the moonlight, and over and over again assured each other how dear they had grown. He felt the trouble in David's heart when they met.

"Ruth is ours, and I bring her kiss to you," he said, pressing his lips to David's; but the arms flung around him trembled, and David whispered, "Now the change begins."

"O, this cannot be our burden!" Jonathan cried, with all the rapture still warm in his heart.

"If it is, it will be light, or heavy, or none at all, as we shall bear it," David answered, with a smile of infinite tenderness.

For several days he allowed Jonathan to visit the Bradley farm alone, saying that it must be so on Ruth's account. Her love, he declared, must give her the fine instinct which only their mother had ever possessed, and he must allow it time to be confirmed. Jonathan, however, insisted that Ruth already possessed it; that she was beginning to wonder at his absence, and to fear that she would not be entirely welcome to the home which must always be equally his.

David yielded at once.

"You must go alone," said Jonathan, "to satisfy yourself that she knows us at last."

Ruth came forth from the house as he drew near. Her face beamed; she laid her hands upon his shoulders and kissed him. "Now you cannot doubt me, Ruth!" he said, gently.

"Doubt you, Jonathan!" she exclaimed with a fond reproach in her eyes. "But you look troubled; is any thing the matter?"

"I was thinking of my brother," said David, in a low tone.

"Tell me what it is," she said, drawing him into the little arbor of woodbine near the gate. They took seats side by side on the rustic bench. "He thinks I may come between you: is it not that?" she asked. Only one thing was clear to David's mind—that she would surely speak more frankly and freely of him to the supposed Jonathan than to his real self. This once he would permit the illusion.

"Not more than must be," he answered. "He knew all from the very beginning. But we have been like one person in two bodies, and any change seems to divide us."

"I feel as you do," said Ruth. "I would never consent to be your wife, if I could really divide you. I love you both too well for that."

"Do you love me?" he asked, entirely forgetting his representative part.

Again the reproachful look, which faded away as she met his eyes. She fell upon his breast, and gave him kisses which were answered with equal tenderness. Suddenly he covered his face with his hands, and burst into a passion of tears.

"Jonathan! O Jonathan!" she cried, weeping with alarm and sympathetic pain.

It was long before he could speak; but at last, turning away his head, he faltered, "I am David!"

There was a long silence.

When he looked up she was sitting with her hands rigidly clasped in her lap: her face was very pale.

"There it is, Ruth," he said; "we are one heart and one soul. Could he love, and not I? You cannot decide between us, for one is the other. If I had known you first, Jonathan would be now in my place. What follows, then?"

"No marriage," she whispered.

"No!" he answered; "we brothers must learn to be two men instead of one. You will partly take my place with Jonathan; I must live with half my life, unless I can find, somewhere in the world, your other half."

"I cannot part you, David!"

"Something stronger than you or me parts us, Ruth. If it were death, we should bow to God's will: well, it can no more be got away from than death or judgment. Say no more: the pattern of all this was drawn long before we were born, and we cannot do any thing but work it out."

He rose and stood before her. "Remember this, Ruth," he said; "it is no blame in us to love each other. Jonathan will see the truth in my face when we meet, and I speak for him also. You will not see me again until your wedding-day, and then no more afterwards—but, yes! *Once*, in some far-off time, when you shall know me to be David, and still give me the kiss you gave to-day."

"Ah, after death!" she thought: "I have parted them forever." She was about to rise, but fell upon the seat again, fainting. At the same moment Jonathan appeared at David's side.

No word was said. They bore her forth and supported her between them until the fresh breeze had restored her to consciousness. Her first glance rested on the brother's hands, clasping; then, looking from one to the other, she saw that the cheeks of both were wet.

"Now, leave me," she said, "but come to-morrow, Jonathan!" Even then she turned from one to the other, with a painful, touching uncertainty, and stretched out both hands to them in farewell.

How that poor twin heart struggled with itself is only known to God. All human voices, and as they believed, also the Divine Voice, commanded the division of their interwoven life. Submission would have seemed easier, could they have taken up equal and similar burdens; but David was unable to deny that his pack was overweighted. For the first time, their thoughts began to diverge.

At last David said: "For mother's sake, Jonathan, as we promised. She always called you *her* child. And for Ruth's sake, and father's last advice: they all tell me what I must do."

It was like the struggle between will and desire, in the same nature, and none the less fierce or prolonged because the softer quality foresaw its ultimate surrender. Long after he felt the step to be inevitable, Jonathan sought to postpone it, but he was borne by all combined influences nearer and nearer to the time.

And now the wedding-day came. David was to leave home the same evening, after the family dinner under his father's roof. In the morning he said to Jonathan: "I shall not write until I feel that I have become other than now, but I shall always be here, in you, as you will be in me, everywhere. Whenever you want me, I shall know it; and I think I shall know when to return."

The hearts of all the people went out towards them as they stood together in the little village church. Both were calm, but very pale and abstracted in their expression, yet their marvellous likeness was still unchanged. Ruth's eyes were cast down so they could not be seen; she trembled visibly, and her voice was scarcely audible when she spoke the vow. It was only known in the neighborhood that David was going to make another journey. The truth could hardly have been guessed by persons whose ideas follow the narrow round of their own experiences; had it been, there would probably have been more condemnation than sympathy. But in a vague way the presence of some deeper element was felt—the falling of a shadow, although the outstretched wing was unseen. Far above them, and above the shadow, watched the Infinite Pity, which was not denied to three hearts that day.

It was a long time, more than a year, and Ruth was lulling her first child on her bosom, before a letter came from David. He had wandered westwards, purchased some lands on the outer line of settlement, and appeared to be leading a wild and lonely life. "I know now," he wrote, "just how much there is to bear, and how to bear it. Strange men come between us, but you are not far off when I am alone on these plains. There is a place where I can always meet you, and I know that you have found it,—under the big ash-tree by the barn. I think I am nearly always there about sundown, and on moonshiny nights, because we are then nearest together; and I never sleep without leaving you half my blanket. When I first begin to wake I always feel your breath, so we are never really parted for long. I do not know that I can change much; it is not easy; it is like making up your mind to have different colored eyes and hair, and I can only get sunburnt and wear a full beard. But we are hardly as unhappy as we feared to be; mother came the other night, in a dream, and took us on her knees. O, come to me, Jonathan, but for one day! No, you will not find me; I am going across the Plains!"

And Jonathan and Ruth? They loved each other tenderly; no external trouble visited them; their home was peaceful and pure; and yet, every room and stairway and chair was haunted by a sorrowful ghost. As a neighbor said after visiting them, "There seemed to be something lost." Ruth saw how constantly and how unconsciously Jonathan turned to see his own every feeling reflected in the missing eyes; how his hand sought another, even while its fellow pressed hers; how half-spoken words, day and night, died upon his lips, because they could not reach the twin-ear. She knew not how it came, but her own nature took upon itself the same habit. She felt that she received a less measure of love than she gave—not from Jonathan, in whose whole, warm, transparent heart

no other woman had ever looked, but something of her own passed beyond him and never returned. To both their life was like one of those conjurer's cups, seemingly filled with red wine, which is held from the lips by the false crystal hollow.

Neither spoke of this: neither dared to speak. The years dragged out their slow length, with rare and brief messages from David. Three children were in the house, and still peace and plenty laid their signs upon its lintels. But at last Ruth, who had been growing thinner and paler ever since the birth of her first boy, became seriously ill. Consumption was hers by inheritance, and it now manifested itself in a form which too surely foretold the result. After the physician had gone, leaving his fatal verdict behind him, she called to Jonathan, who, bewildered by his grief, sank down on his knees at her bedside and sobbed upon her breast.

"Don't grieve," she said; "this is my share of the burden. If I have taken too much from you and David, now comes the atonement. Many things have grown clear to me. David was right when he said that there was no blame. But my time is even less than the doctor thinks: where is David? Can you not bid him come?"

"I can only call him with my heart," he answered. "And will he hear me now, after nearly seven years?"

"Call, then!" she eagerly cried. "Call with all the strength of your love for him and for me, and I believe he will hear you!"

The sun was just setting. Jonathan went to the great ash-tree, behind the barn, fell upon his knees, and covered his face, and the sense of an exceeding bitter cry filled his heart. All the suppressed and baffled longing, the want, the hunger, the unremitting pain of years, came upon him and were crowded into the single prayer, "Come, David, or I die!" Before the twilight faded, while he was still kneeling, an arm came upon his shoulder, and the faint touch of another cheek upon his own. It was hardly for the space of a thought, but he knew the sign.

"David will come!" he said to Ruth.

From that day all was changed. The cloud of coming death which hung over the house was transmuted into fleecy gold. All the lost life came back to Jonathan's face, all the unrestful sweetness of Ruth's brightened into a serene beatitude. Months had passed since David had been heard from; they knew not how to reach him without many delays; yet neither dreamed of doubting his coming.

Two weeks passed, three, and there was neither word nor sign. Jonathan and Ruth thought, "He is near," and one day a singular unrest fell upon the former. Ruth saw it, but said nothing until night came, when she sent Jonathan from her bedside with the words, "Go and meet him?"

An hour afterwards she heard double steps on the stone walk in front of the house. They came slowly to the door; it opened; she heard them along the hall and ascending the stairs; then the chamber-lamp showed her the two faces, bright with a single, unutterable joy.

One brother paused at the foot of the bed; the other drew near and bent over her. She clasped her thin hands around his neck, kissed him fondly, and cried, "Dear, dear David!"

"Dear Ruth," he said, "I came as soon as I could. I was far away, among wild mountains, when I felt that Jonathan was calling me. I knew that I must return, never to leave you more, and there was still a little work to finish. Now we shall all live again!"

"Yes," said Jonathan, coming to her other side, "try to live, Ruth!"

Her voice came clear, strong, and full of authority. "I *do* live, as never before. I shall take all my life with me when I go to wait for one soul, as I shall find it there! Our love unites, not divides, from this hour!"

The few weeks still left to her were a season of almost superhuman peace. She faded slowly and painlessly, taking the equal love of the twin-hearts, and giving an equal tenderness and gratitude. Then first she saw the mysterious need which united them, the fulness and joy wherewith each completed himself in the other. All the imperfect past was enlightened, and the end, even that now so near, was very good.

Every afternoon they carried her down to a cushioned chair on the veranda, where she could enjoy the quiet of the sunny landscape, the presence of the brothers seated at her feet, and the sports of her children on the grass. Thus, one day, while David and Jonathan held her hands and waited for her to wake from a happy sleep, she went before them, and, ere they guessed the truth, she was waiting for their one soul in the undiscovered land.

And Jonathan's children, now growing into manhood and girlhood, also call David "father." The marks left by their divided lives have long since vanished from their faces; the middle-aged men, whose hairs are turning gray, still walk hand in hand, still sleep upon the same pillow, still have their common wardrobe, as when they were boys. They talk of "our Ruth" with no sadness, for they believe that death will make them one, when, at the same moment, he summons both. And we who know them, to whom they have confided the touching mystery of their nature, believe so too.

[53] Taylor, Bayard. "Twin-Love." *The Atlantic Monthly*, Vol. 28, No. 167. September, 1871. pp. 257-266.

[A.4]

SONG.
By Miss **

Air: "To ladies' eyes a round, boy."
——Moore

The winds of March are humming
    Their parting song, their parting song,
And summer skies are coming,
    And days grow long, and days grow long.
I watch, but not in gladness,
    Our garden-tree, our garden-tree;
It buds, in sober sadness.
    Too soon for me, too soon for me.
      My second winter's over,
        Alas! and I, alas! and I
      Have no accepted lover:
        Don't ask me why, don't ask me why.

Tis not asleep or idle
    That Love has been, that Love has been,
For many a happy bridal
    The year has seen, the year has seen;
I've done a bridemaid's duty.
    At three or four, at three or four;
My best bouquet had beauty.
    Its donor more, its donor more.
      My second winter's over,
        Alas! and I, alas! and I
      Have no accepted lover:
        Don't ask me why, don't ask me why.

His flowers my bosom shaded
 One sunny day, one sunny day;
The next they fled and faded,
 Beau and bouquet, beau and bouquet.
In vain, at balls and parties,
 I've thrown my net, I've thrown my net;
This waltzing, watching heart is
 Unchosen yet, unchosen yet.
  My second winter's over,
   Alas! and I, alas! and I
  Have no accepted lover:
   Don't ask me why, don't ask me why.

They tell me there's no hurry
 For Hymen's ring, for Hymen's ring;
And I'm too young to marry:
 'Tis no such thing,'tis no such thing.
The next spring-tides will dash on
 My eighteenth year, my eighteenth year;
It puts me in a passion.
  Oh, dear, oh dear! oh dear, oh dear!
  My second winter's over,
   Alas! and I, alas! and I
  Have no accepted lover:
   Don't ask me why, don't ask me why.

Fitz-Greene Halleck

[62]Wilson, James Grant. *Life and Letters of Fitz-Greene Halleck*. New York: D. Appleton and Company, 1869.

Tears fell, when thou wert dying,
 From eyes unused to weep,
And long where thou art lying,
 Will tears the cold turf steep.

When hearts, whose truth was proven,
 Like thine, are laid in earth,
There should a wreath be woven
 To tell the world their worth;

And I, who woke each morrow
 To clasp thy hand in mine,
Who shared thy joy and sorrow,
 Whose weal and woe were thine:

It should be mine to braid it
 Around thy faded brow,
But I've in vain essayed it,
 And feel I can not now.

While memory bids me weep thee,
 Nor thoughts nor words are free,
The grief is fixed too deeply
 That mourns a man like thee.

Fitz-Greene Halleck

[21]Halleck, Fitz-Greene, and Joseph Rodman Drake. *The Poetical Works of Fitz-Greene Halleck: With Extracts from Those of Joseph Rodman Drake*. New York: D. Appleton and Company, 1869.

[A.5]

ON THE DEATH OF JOSEPH RODMAN DRAKE, OF NEW YORK, SEPT., 1820.

 "The good die first,
 And they, whose hearts are dry as summer dust,
 Burn to the socket."
   —Wordsworth

Green be the turf above thee,
 Friend of my better days!
None knew thee but to love thee,
 Nor named thee but to praise.

[A.6]

FITZ-GREENE HALLECK.
Bayard Taylor

Address at the dedication of the Halleck
Monument
Guilford, Connecticut, July 8th, 1869.

We have been eighty years an organized nation, ninety-three years an independent people, more than two hundred years an American race; and to-day, for the first time in our history, we meet to dedicate publicly, with appropriate honors, a monument to an American poet. The occasion is thus lifted above the circle of personal memories which inspired it, and takes its place as the beginning of a new epoch in the story of our culture. It carries our thoughts back of the commencement of this individual life, into the elements from which our literature grew; and forward, far beyond the closing of the tomb before us, into the possible growth and glory of the future.

The rhythmical expression of emotion, or passion, or thought, is a need of the human race coeval with speech, universal as religion, the prophetic forerunner as well as the last-begotten offspring of civilization. Poetry belongs equally to the impressible childhood of a people and to the refined ease of their maturity. It is both the instinctive effort of nature and the loftiest ideal of art; receding to farther and farther spheres of spiritual beauty as men rise to the capacity for its enjoyment. But our race was transferred, half-grown, from the songs of its early ages and the inspiring associations of its past, and set here face to face with stern tasks which left no space for the lighter play of the mind. The early generations of English bards gradually become foreign to us; for their songs, however sweet, were not those of our home. We profess to claim an equal share in Chaucer and Spenser and Shakespeare, but it is a hollow pretense. They belong to our language, but we cannot truly feel that they belong to us as a people. The destiny that placed us on this soil robbed us of the magic of tradition, the wealth of romance, the suggestions of history, the sentiment of inherited homes and customs, and left us, shorn of our lisping childhood, to create a poetic literature for ourselves.

It is not singular, therefore, that this continent should have waited long for its first-born poet. The intellect, the energy of character, the moral force,—even the occasional taste and refinement,—which were shipped hither from the older shores, found the hard work of history already portioned out for them; and the Muses discovered no nook of guarded leisure, no haunt of sweet contemplation, which might tempt them to settle among us. Labor may be prayer, but it is not poetry. Liberty of conscience and worship, practical democracy, the union of civil order and personal independence, are ideas which may warm the hearts and brains of men; but the soil in which they strike root is too full of fresh, unsoftened forces to produce the delicate wine of song. The highest product of ripened intellect cannot be expected in the

nonage of a nation. The poetry of our colonial and revolutionary periods is mostly a spiritless imitation of inferior models in the parent country. If here and there some timid, uncertain voice seems to guess the true language, we only hear it once or twice; like those colonized nightingales which for one brief summer gave their new song to the Virginian moonlights, and then disappeared. These early fragments of our poetry are chanted in the midst of such profound silence and loneliness that they sound spectrally to our ears. Philip Freneau is almost as much a shade to us as are his own hunter and deer.

In the same year in which the Constitution of the United States was completed and adopted, the first poet was born,—Richard Henry Dana. Less than three years after him Fitz-Greene Halleck came into the world,—the lyrical genius following the grave and contemplative Muse of his elder brother. In Halleck, therefore, we mourn our first loss out of the first generation of American bards; and a deeper significance is thus given to the personal honors which we lovingly pay to his memory. Let us be glad, not only that these honors have been so nobly deserved, but also that we find in him a fitting representative of his age! Let us forget our sorrow for the true man, the steadfast friend, and rejoice that the earliest child of song whom we return to the soil that bore him for us, was the brave, bright, and beautiful growth of a healthy, masculine race! No morbid impatience with the restrictions of life, no fruitless lament over an unattainable ideal, no inherited gloom of temperament, such as finds delight in what it chooses to call despair, ever muffled the clear notes of his verse, or touched the sunny cheerfulness of his history. The cries and protests, the utterances of "world-pain," with which so many of his contemporaries in Europe filled the world, awoke no echo in his sound and sturdy nature. His life offers no enigmas for our solution. No romantic mystery floats around his name, to win for him the interest of a shallow sentimentalism. Clear, frank, simple, and consistent, his song and his life were woven into one smooth and even thread. We would willingly pardon in him some expression of dissatisfaction with a worldly fate which in certain respects seemed inadequate to his genius; but we find that he never uttered it. The basis of his nature was a knightly bravery, of such firm and enduring temper that it kept from him even the ordinary sensitiveness of the poetic character. From the time of his studies as a boy, in the propitious kitchen which heard his first callow numbers, to the last days of a life which had seen no liberal popular recognition of his deserts, he accepted his fortune with the perfect dignity of a man who cannot stoop to discontent. During his later visits to New York, the simplest, the most unobtrusive, yet the cheerfulest man to be seen among the throngs of Broadway, was Fitz-Greene Halleck. Yet with all his simplicity, his bearing was strikingly gallant and fearless; the carriage of his head suggested the wearing of a helmet. The genial frankness and grace of his manner in his intercourse with men has suggested to others the epithet "courtly"; but I prefer to call it *manly*, as the expression of a rarer and finer quality than is usually found in the atmosphere of courts.

Halleck was loyal to himself as a man, and he was also loyal to his art as a poet. His genius was essentially lyrical, and he seems to have felt instinctively its natural limitations. He quietly and gratefully accepted the fame which followed his best productions, but he never courted public applause. Even the swift popularity of the Croaker series could not seduce him to take advantage of the tide, which then promised a speedy flood. At periods in his history when anything from his pen would have been welcomed by a class of readers whose growing taste found so little sustenance at home, he remained silent because he felt no immediate personal necessity of poetic utterance. The German poet Uhland said to me: "I cannot now say whether I shall write any more, because I only write when I feel the positive need; and this is independent of my will, or the wish of others." Such was also the law of Halleck's mind, and of the mind of every poet who reveres his divine gift. God cannot accept a mechanical prayer; and I do not compare sacred things with profane when I say that a poem cannot be accepted which does not compel its own inspired utterance. He is the true priest of the human heart and the human soul who rhythmically expresses the emotions and the aspirations of his own.

It has been said of Halleck as of Campbell, that "he was afraid of the shadow which his own fame cast before him." I protest against the use of a clever epigrammatic sentence to misinterpret the poetic nature to men. The inference is that poets write merely for that popular recognition which is called fame; and having attained a certain degree, fear to lose it by later productions which may not prove so acceptable. A writer influenced by such a consideration never deserved the name of poet. It is an unworthy estimate of his character which thus explains the honest and honorable silence of Fitz-Greene Halleck. The quality of genius is not to be measured by its productive activity. The brain which gave us 'Alnwick Castle,' 'Marco Bozzaris,' 'Burns,' and 'Red Jacket,' was not exhausted; it was certainly capable of other and equally admirable achievements: but the fortunate visits of the Muse are not to be compelled by the poet's will; and Halleck endured her absence without complaint, as he had enjoyed her favors without ostentation. The very fact that he wrote so little, proclaims the sincerity of his genius, and harmonizes with the entire character of his life. It was enough for him that he first let loose the Theban eagle in our songless American air. He was glad and satisfied to know that his lyrics have entered into and become a part of the national life; that

"Sweet tears dim the eyes unshed,
And wild vows falter on the tongue,"

when his lines, keen and flexible as fire, burn in the ears of the young who shall hereafter sing, and fight, and labor, and love, for "God and their native land!"

It is not necessary that we should attempt to determine his relative place among American poets. It is sufficient that he has his assured place, and that his name is a permanent part of our literary history. It is sufficient that he deserves every honor which we can render to his memory, not only as one of the very first representatives of American song, but from his intrinsic quality as a poet. Let us rather be thankful for every star set in our heaven, than seek to ascertain how they differ from one another in glory. If any critic would diminish the loving enthusiasm of those whose lives have been brightened by the poet's personal sunshine, let him remember that the sternest criticism will set the lyrics of Halleck higher than their author's unambitious estimate. They will in time fix their own just place in our poetic annals. Halleck is still too near our orbit for the computation of an exact parallax; but we may safely leave his measure of fame to the decision of impartial Time. A poem which bears within itself its own right to existence, will not die. Its rhythm is freshly fed from the eternal pulses of beauty, whence flows the sweetest life of the human race. Age cannot quench its original fire, or repetition make dull its immortal music. It forever haunts that purer atmosphere which overlies the dust and smoke of our petty cares and our material interests—often indeed calling to us like a distant clarion, to keep awake the senses of intellectual delight which would else perish from our lives. The poetic literature of a land is the finer and purer ether above its material growth and the vicissitudes of its history. Where it was vacant and barren for us, except perchance a feeble lark-note here and there, Dana, Halleck, and Bryant rose together on steadier wings, and gave voices to the solitude: Dana with a broad, grave undertone, like that of the sea; Bryant with a sound as of the wind in summer woods, and the fall of waters in mountain dells; and Halleck with strains blown from a silver trumpet, breathing manly fire and courage. Many voices have followed them; the ether rings with new melodies, and yet others come to lure all the aspirations of our hearts, and echo all the yearnings of our separated destiny: but we shall not forget the forerunners who rose in advance of their welcome, and created their own audience by their songs.

Thus it is that in dedicating a monument to Fitz-Greene Halleck to-day, we symbolize the intellectual growth of the American people. They have at last taken that departure which represents the higher development of a nation,—the capacity to value the genius which cannot work with material instruments; which is unmoved by Atlantic Cables, Pacific Railroads, and any show of marvelous statistical tables; which grandly dispenses with the popular measures of success; which simply expresses itself, without *consciously* working for the delight of others; yet which, once recognized, stands thenceforth as a part of the glory of the whole people. It is a token that we have relaxed the rough work of two and a half centuries, and are beginning to enjoy that rest and leisure out of which the grace and beauty of civilization grow. The pillars of our political fabric have been slowly and massively raised, like the drums of Doric columns; but they still need the crowning capitals and the sculptured entablature. Law, and Right, and Physical Development build well, but they are cold, mathematical architects: the Poet and the Artist make beautiful the temple. Our natural tendency, as

a people, is to worship positive material achievement in whatever form it is displayed; even the poet must be a partisan before the government will recognize his existence. So much of our intellectual energy has been led into the new paths which our national growth has opened, so exacting are the demands upon working brains, that taste and refinement of mind, and warm appreciation of the creative spirit of beauty, are only beginning to bloom here and there among us, like tender exotic flowers. "The light that never was on sea or land" shines all around us, but few are the eyes whose vision it clarifies. Yet the faculty is here, and the earnest need. The delight in art, of which poetry is the highest manifestation, has ceased to be the privilege of a fortunate few, and will soon become, let us hope, the common heritage of the people. If any true song has heretofore been sung to unheeding ears, let us behold, in this dedication, the sign that our reproach is taken away,—that henceforth every new melody of the land shall spread in still expanding vibrations, until all shall learn to listen!

The life of the poet who sleeps here represents the long period of transition between the appearance of American poetry and the creation of an appreciative and sympathetic audience for it. We must honor him all the more that in the beginning he was content with the few who heard him; that the agitations of national life through which he passed could not ruffle the clear flow of his song; and that, with a serene equanimity of temper which is the rarest American virtue, he saw, during his whole life, wealth and personal distinction constantly passing into less deserving hands, without temptation and without envy. All popular superstitions concerning the misanthropy or the irritable temper of genius were disproved in him: I have never known a man so independent of the moods and passions of his generation. We cannot regret that he should have been chosen to assist in the hard pioneer work of our literature, because he seemed to be so unconscious of its privations. Yet he and his co-mates have walked a rough, and for the most part a lonely track, leaving a smoother way broken for their followers. They have blazed their trails through the wilderness, and carved their sounding names on the silent mountain peaks; teaching the scenery of our homes a language, and giving it a rarer and tenderer charm than even the atmosphere of great historic deeds.

Fitz-Greene Halleck has set his seal upon the gray rock of Connecticut, on the heights of Weehawken, on the fair valley of Wyoming, and the Field of the Grounded Arms. He has done his manly share in forcing this half-subdued nature in which we live, to accept a human harmony, and cover its soulless beauty with the mantle of his verse.

However our field of poetic literature may bloom, whatever products of riper culture may rise to overshadow its present growths, the memory of Halleck is perennially rooted at its entrance. Recognizing the purity of his genius, the nobility of his character, we gratefully and affectionately dedicate to him this monument. There is no cypress in the wreath which we lay upon his grave. We do not meet to chant a dirge over unfulfilled promises or an insufficient destiny. We have no willful defiance of the world to excuse, no sensitive protest to justify. Our hymn of consecration is cheerful, though solemn. Looking forward from this hallowed ground, we can only behold a future for our poetry, sunnier than its past. We see the love of beauty born from the servitude to use; the recognition of an immortal ideal element gradually evolved from the strength of natures which have conquered material forces; the growth of all fine and gracious attributes of imagination and fancy, to warm and sweeten and expand the stately coldness of intellect. We dream of days when the highest and deepest utterances of rhythmical thought shall be met with grateful welcome, not with dull amazement or mean suspicion. We wait for voices which shall no more say to the poet, "Stay here, at the level of our delight in you!"—but which shall say to him, "Higher, still higher! though we may not reach you, yet in following we shall rise!" And as our last prophetic hope, we look for that fortunate age when the circle of sympathy, now so limited, shall be coextensive with the nation, and when, even as the poet loves his land, his land shall love her poet!

[48] Taylor, Bayard. "Fitz-Greene Halleck." *The Library of the World's Best Literature. An Anthology in Thirty Volumes*, 1917. http://www.bartleby.com/library/prose/5151.html. Accessed February 26, 2017.

[A.7]

JOSEPH RODMAN DRAKE— FITZ-GREENE HALLECK.
—Edgar Allan Poe

The Culprit Fay, and other Poems by Joseph Rodman Drake. New York: George Dearborn.

Alnwick Castle, with other Poems, by Fitz-Greene Halleck. New York: George Dearborn.

Before entering upon the detailed notice which we propose of the volumes before us, we wish to speak a few words in regard to the present state of American criticism.

It must be visible to all who meddle with literary matters, that of late years a thorough revolution has been effected in the censorship of our press. That this revolution is infinitely for the worse we believe. There was a time, it is true, when we cringed to foreign opinion—let us even say when we paid most servile deference to British critical dicta. That an American book could, by any possibility, be worthy perusal, was an idea by no means extensively prevalent in the land; and if we were induced to read at all the productions of our native writers, it was only after repeated assurances from England that such productions were not altogether contemptible. But there was, at all events, a shadow of excuse, and a slight basis of reason for a subserviency so grotesque. Even now, perhaps, it would not be far wrong to assert that such basis of reason may still exist. Let us grant that in many of the abstract sciences—that even in Theology, in Medicine, in Law, in Oratory, in the Mechanical Arts, we have no competitors whatever, still nothing but the most egregious national vanity would assign us a place, in the matter of Polite Literature, upon a level with the elder and riper climes of Europe, the earliest steps of whose children are among the groves of magnificently endowed Academies, and whose innumerable men of leisure, and of consequent learning, drink daily from those august fountains of inspiration which burst around them everywhere from out the tombs of their immortal dead, and from out their hoary and trophied monuments of chivalry and song. In paying then, as a nation, a respectful and not undue deference to a supremacy rarely questioned but by prejudice or ignorance, we should, of course, be doing nothing more than acting in a rational manner. The *excess* of our subserviency was blamable—but, as we have before said, this very excess might have found a shadow of excuse in the strict justice, if properly regulated, of the principle from which it issued. Not so, however, with our present follies. We are becoming boisterous and arrogant in the pride of a too speedily assumed literary freedom. We throw off, with the most presumptuous and unmeaning hauteur, *all* deference whatever to foreign opinion—we forget, in the puerile inflation of vanity, that *the world* is the true theatre of the biblical histrio—we get up a hue and cry about the necessity of encouraging native writers of merit—we blindly fancy that we can accomplish this by indiscriminate puffing of good, bad, and indifferent, without taking the trouble to consider that what we choose to denominate encouragement is thus, by its general application, rendered precisely the reverse. In a word, so far from being ashamed of the many disgraceful literary failures to which our own inordinate vanities and misapplied patriotism have lately given birth, and so far from deeply lamenting that these daily puerilities are of home manufacture, we adhere pertinaciously to our original blindly conceived idea, and thus often find ourselves involved in the gross paradox of liking a stupid book the better, because, sure enough, its stupidity is American.

Deeply lamenting this unjustifiable state of public feeling, it has been our constant endeavor, since assuming the Editorial duties of this Journal, to stem, with what little abilities we possess, a current so disastrously undermining the health and prosperity of our literature. We have seen our efforts applauded by men whose applauses we value. From all quarters we have received abundant private as well as public testimonials in favor of our *Critical Notices*, and, until very lately, have heard from no respectable source one word impugning their integrity or candor. In looking over, however, a number of the New York Commercial Advertiser, we meet with the following paragraph.

"The last number of the Southern Literary Messenger is very readable and respectable. The contributions to the Messenger are much better than the original matter. The critical department of this work—much as it would seem to boast itself of impartiality and discernment,—is in our opinion decidedly *quacky*. There is in it a great assumption of acumen, which is completely unsustained. Many a work has been slashingly condemned therein, of which the critic himself could not write a page, were he to die for it. This affectation of eccentric sternness in criticism, without the power to back one's suit withal, so far from deserving praise, as some suppose, merits the strongest reprehension."
—[*Philadelphia Gazette.*]

"We are entirely of opinion with the Philadelphia Gazette in relation to the Southern Literary Messenger, and take this occasion to express our total dissent from the numerous and lavish encomiums we have seen bestowed upon its critical notices. Some few of them have been judicious, fair and candid; bestowing praise and censure with judgement and impartiality; but by far the greater number of those we have read, have been flippant, unjust, untenable and uncritical. The duty of the critic is to act as judge, not as enemy, of the writer whom he reviews; a distinction of which the Zoilus of the Messenger seems not to be aware. It is possible to review a book sincerely, without bestowing opprobrious epithets upon the writer, to condemn with courtesy, if not with kindness. The critic of the Messenger has been eulogized for his scorching and scarifying abilities, and he thinks it incumbent upon him to keep up his reputation in that line, by sneers, sarcasm and downright abuse; by straining his vision with microscopic intensity in search of faults, and shutting his eyes, with all his might to beauties. Moreover, we have detected him, more than once, in blunders quite as gross as those on which it was his pleasure to descant."

In the paragraph from the Philadelphia Gazette, (which is edited by Mr. Willis Gaylord Clark, one of the editors of the Knickerbocker) we find nothing at which we have any desire to take exception. Mr. C. has a right to think us quacky if he pleases, and we do not remember having assumed for a moment that we could write a single line of the works we have reviewed. But there is something equivocal, to say the least, in the remarks of Col. Stone. He acknowledges that "*some* of our notices have been judicious, fair, and candid bestowing praise and censure with judgment and impartiality." This being the case, how can he reconcile his *total* dissent from the public verdict in our favor, with the dictates of justice? We are accused too of bestowing "opprobrious epithets" upon writers whom we review and in the paragraphs so accusing us are called nothing less than "flippant, unjust and uncritical."

But there is another point of which we disapprove. While in our reviews we have at all times been particularly careful not to deal in generalities, and have never, if we remember aright, advanced in any single instance an unsupported assertion, our accuser has forgotten to give us any better evidence of our flippancy, injustice, personality, and gross blundering, than the solitary *dictum* of Col. Stone. We call upon the Colonel for assistance in this dilemma. We wish to be shown our blunders that we may correct them—to be made aware of our flippancy that we may avoid it hereafter—and above all to have our personalities pointed out that we may proceed forthwith with a repentant spirit, to make the *amende honorable*. In default of this aid from the Editor of the Commercial we shall take it for granted that we are neither blunderers, flippant, personal, nor unjust.

————

Who will deny that in regard to individual poems no definitive opinions can exist, so long as to Poetry in the abstract we attach no definitive idea? Yet it is a common thing to hear our critics, day after day, pronounce, with a positive air, laudatory or condemnatory sentences, *en masse*, upon material works of whose merits or demerits they have, in the first place, virtually confessed an utter ignorance, in confessing it ignorance of all determinate principles by which to regulate a decision. Poetry has never been defined to the satisfaction of all parties. Perhaps, in the present condition of language it never will be. Words cannot hem it in. Its intangible and purely spiritual nature refuses to be bound down within the widest horizon of mere sounds. But it is not, therefore, misunderstood—at least, not by all men is it misunderstood. Very far from it, if indeed, there be any one circle of thought distinctly and palpably marked out from amid the jarring and tumultuous chaos of human intelligence, it is that evergreen and radiant Paradise which the true poet knows, and knows alone, as the limited realm of his authority—as the circumscribed Eden of his dreams. But a definition is a thing of

words—a conception of ideas. And thus while we readily believe that Poesy, the term, it will be troublesome, if not impossible to define—still, with its image vividly existing in the world, we apprehend no difficulty in so describing Poesy, the Sentiment, as to imbue even the most obtuse intellect with a comprehension of it sufficiently distinct for all the purposes of practical analysis.

To look upwards from any existence, material or immaterial to its *design*, is, perhaps, the most direct, and the most unerring method of attaining a just notion of the nature of the existence itself. Nor is the principle at fault when we turn our eyes from Nature even to Natures God. We find certain faculties, implanted within us, and arrive at a more plausible conception of the character and attributes of those faculties, by considering, with what finite judgment we possess, the *intention* of the Deity in so implanting them within us, than by any actual investigation of their powers, or any speculative deductions from their visible and material effects. Thus, for example, we discover in all men a disposition to look with reverence upon superiority, whether real or supposititious. In some, this disposition is to be recognized with difficulty, and, in very peculiar cases, we are occasionally even led to doubt its existence altogether, until circumstances beyond the common routine bring it accidentally into development. In others again it forms a prominent and distinctive feature of character, and is rendered palpably evident in its excesses. But in all human beings it is, in a greater or less degree, finally perceptible. It has been, therefore, justly considered a primitive sentiment. Phrenologists call it Veneration. It is, indeed, the instinct given to man by God as security for his own worship. And although, preserving its nature, it becomes perverted from its principal purpose, and although swerving from that purpose, it serves to modify the relations of human society—the relations of father and child, of master and slave, of the ruler and the ruled—its primitive essence is nevertheless the same, and by a reference to primal causes, may at any moment be determined.

Very nearly akin to this feeling, and liable to the same analysis, is the Faculty of Ideality—which is the sentiment of Poesy. This sentiment is the sense of the beautiful, of the sublime, and of the mystical. Thence spring immediately admiration of the fair flowers, the fairer forests, the bright valleys and rivers and mountains of the Earth—and love of the gleaming stars and other burning glories of Heaven—and, mingled up inextricably with this love and this admiration of Heaven and of Earth, the unconquerable desire—to know. Poesy is the sentiment of Intellectual Happiness here, and the Hope of a higher Intellectual Happiness hereafter.

Imagination is its soul. With the *passions* of mankind—although it may modify them greatly—although it may exalt, or inflame, or purify, or control them—it would require little ingenuity to prove that it has no inevitable, and indeed no necessary co-existence. We have hitherto spoken of poetry in the abstract: we come now to speak of it in its everyday acceptation—that is to say, of the practical result arising from the sentiment we have considered.

And now it appears evident, that since Poetry, in this new sense, *is* the practical result, expressed in language, of this Poetic Sentiment in certain individuals, the only proper method of testing the merits of a poem is by measuring its capabilities of exciting the Poetic Sentiments in others.

And to this end we have many aids—in observation, in experience, in ethical analysis, and in the dictates of common sense. Hence the *Poeta nascitur*, which is indisputably true if we consider the Poetic Sentiment, becomes the merest of absurdities when we regard it in reference to the practical result. We do not hesitate to say that a man highly endowed with the powers of Causality—that is to say, a man of metaphysical acumen—will, even with a very deficient share of Ideality, compose a finer poem (if we test it, as we should, by its measure of exciting the Poetic Sentiment) than one who, without such metaphysical acumen, shall be gifted, in the most extraordinary degree, with the faculty of Ideality. For a poem is not the Poetic faculty, but the *means* of exciting it in mankind. Now these means the metaphysician may discover by analysis of their effects in other cases than his own, without even conceiving the nature of these effects—thus arriving at a result which the unaided Ideality of his competitor would be utterly unable, except by accident, to attain. It is more than possible that the man who, of all writers, living or dead, has been most successful in writing the purest of all poems—that is to say, poems which excite more purely, most

exclusively, and most powerfully the imaginative faculties in men—owed his extraordinary and almost magical preeminence rather to metaphysical than poetical powers. We allude to the author of Christabel, of the Rime of the Ancient Mariner, and of Love—to Coleridge—whose head, if we mistake not its character, gave no great phrenological tokens of Ideality, while the organs of Causality and Comparison were most singularly developed.

Perhaps at this particular moment there are no American poems held in so high estimation by our countrymen, as the poems of Drake, and of Halleck. The exertions of Mr. George Dearborn have no doubt a far greater share in creating this feeling than the lovers of literature for its own sake and spiritual uses would be willing to admit. We have indeed seldom seen more beautiful volumes than the volumes now before us. But an adventitious interest of a loftier nature—the interest of the living in the memory of the beloved dead—attaches itself to the few literary remains of Drake. The poems which are now given to us with his name are nineteen in number; and whether all, or whether even the best of his writings, it is our present purpose to speak of these alone, since upon this edition his poetical reputation to all time will most probably depend.

It is only lately that we have read *The Culprit Fay*. This is a poem of six hundred and forty irregular lines, generally iambic, and divided into thirty-six stanzas, of unequal length. The scene of the narrative, as we ascertain from the single line,

The moon looks down on old *Cronest*,

is principally in the vicinity of West Point on the Hudson. The plot is as follows. An Ouphe, one of the race of Fairies, has "broken his vestal vow,"

He has loved an earthly maid
And left for her his woodland shade;
He has lain upon her lip of dew,
And sunned him in her eye of blue,
Fann'd her cheek with his wing of air,
Play'd with the ringlets of her hair,
And, nestling on her snowy breast,
Forgot the lily-kings behest—

in short, he has broken Fairy-law in becoming enamored of a mortal. The result of this misdemeanor we could not express so well as the poet, and will therefore make use of the language put into the mouth of the Fairy-King who reprimands the criminal.

> Fairy! Fairy! list and mark,
>   Thou hast broke thine elfin chain,
> Thy flame-wood lamp is quench'd and dark
>   And thy wings are dyed with a deadly stain.

The Ouphe being in this predicament, it has become necessary that his case and crime should be investigated by a jury of his fellows, and to this end the "shadowy tribes of air" are summoned by the "sentry elve" who has been awakened by the "wood-tick"—are summoned we say to the "elfin-court" at midnight to hear the doom of the *Culprit Fay.* "Had a stain been found on the earthly fair," whose blandishments so bewildered the little Ouphe, his punishment would have been severe indeed. In such case he would have been (as we learn from the Fairy judge's exposition of the criminal code,)

> Tied to the hornet's shardy wings;
> Tossed on the pricks of nettles' stings;
> Or seven long ages doomed to dwell
> With the lazy worm in the walnut shell;
> Or every night to writhe and bleed
> Beneath the tread of the centipede;
> Or bound in a cobweb dungeon dim
> His jailer a spider huge and grim,
> Amid the carrion bodies to lie
> Of the worm and the bug and the murdered fly—

Fortunately, however, for the Culprit, his mistress is proved to be of "sinless mind" and under such redeeming circumstances the sentence is, mildly, as follows—

> Thou shalt seek the beach of sand
> Where the water bounds the elfin land,
> Thou shalt watch the oozy brine
> Till the sturgeon leaps in the bright moonshine,
> Then dart the glistening arch below,
> * * * * * *
> And catch a drop from his silver bow.
>   If the spray-bead be won
> The stain of thy wing is washed away,
> But another errand must be done
>   Ere thy crime be lost for aye;

> Thy flame-wood lamp is quenched and dark,
> Thou must re-illume its spark.
> Mount thy steed and spur him high
> To the heaven's blue canopy;
> And when thou seest a shooting star
> Follow it fast and follow it far—
> The last faint spark of its burning train
> Shall light the elfin lamp again.

Upon this sin, and upon this sentence, depends the web of the narrative, which is now occupied with the elfin difficulties overcome by the Ouphe in washing away the stain of his wing, and re-illuming his flame-wood lamp. His soiled pinion having lost its power, he is under the necessity of wending his way on foot from the Elfin court upon Cronest to the river beach at its base. His path is encumbered at every step with "bog and briar," with "brook and mire," with "beds of tangled fern," with "groves of night-shade," and with the minor evils of ant and snake. Happily, however, a spotted toad coming in sight, our adventurer jumps upon her back, and "bridling her mouth with a silk-weed twist" bounds merrily along

> Till the mountain's magic verge is past
> And the beach of sand is reached at last.

Alighting now from his "courser-toad" the Ouphe folds his wings around his bosom, springs on a rock, breathes a prayer, throws his arms above his head,

> Then tosses a tiny curve in air
> And plunges in the waters blue.

Here, however, a host of difficulties await him by far too multitudinous to enumerate. We will content ourselves with simply stating the names of his most respectable assailants. These are the "spirits of the wave" dressed in "snail-plate armor" and aided by the "mailed shrimp," the "prickly prong," the "blood-red leech," the "stony star-fish," the "jellied quarl," the "soldier-crab," and the "lancing squab." But the hopes of our hero are high, and his limbs are strong, so

> He spreads his arms like the swallow's wing,
> And throws his feet with a frog-like fling.

All however, is to no purpose.

On his thigh the leech has fixed his hold,
The quarl's long arms are round him roll'd,
The prickly prong has pierced his skin,
And the squab has thrown his javelin,
The gritty star has rubb'd him raw,
And the crab has struck with his giant claw;
He bawls with rage, and he shrieks with pain
He strikes around but his blows are vain—

So then,

He turns him round and flies amain
With hurry and dash to the beach again.

Arrived safely on land our Fairy friend now gathers the dew from the "sorrel-leaf and henbane-bud" and bathing therewith his wounds, finally ties them up with cobweb. Thus recruited, he

—treads the fatal shore
As fresh and vigorous as before.

At length espying a "purple-muscle shell" upon the beach, he determines to use it as a boat and thus evade the animosity of the water spirits whose powers extend not above the wave. Making a "sculler's notch" in the stern, and providing himself with an oar of the bootle-blade, the Ouphe a second time ventures upon the deep. His perils are now diminished, but still great. The imps of the river heave the billows up before the prow of the boat, dash the surges against her side, and strike against her keel. The quarl uprears "his island-back" in her path, and the scallop, floating in the rear of the vessel, spatters it all over with water. Our adventurer, however, bails it out with the colen bell (which he has luckily provided for the purpose of catching the drop from the silver bow of the sturgeon,) and keeping his little bark warily trimmed, holds on his course undiscomfited.

The object of his first adventure is at length discovered in a "brownbacked sturgeon," who

Like the heaven-shot javelin
Springs above the waters blue,
And, instant as the star-fall light
Plunges him in the deep again,
But leaves an arch of silver bright,
The rainbow of the moony main.

From this rainbow our Ouphe succeeds in catching, by means of his colen bell cup, a "droplet of the sparkling dew." One half of his task is accordingly done—

His wings are pure, for the gem is won.

On his return to land, the ripples divide before him, while the water-spirits, so rancorous before, are obsequiously attentive to his comfort. Having tarried a moment on the beach to breathe a prayer, he "spreads his wings of gilded blue" and takes his way to the elfin court—there resting until the cricket, at two in the morning, rouses him up for the second portion of his penance. His equipments are now an "acorn-helmet," a "thistle-down plume," a corslet of the "wild-bee's" skin, a cloak of the "wings of butterflies," a shield of the "shell of the lady-bug," for lance "the sting of a wasp," for sword a "blade of grass," for horse "a fire-fly," and for spurs a couple of "cockle seed." Thus accoutred,

Away like a glance of thought he flies
To skim the heavens and follow far
The fiery trail of the rocket-star.

In the Heavens he has new dangers to encounter. The "shapes of air" have begun their work—a "drizzly mist" is cast around him—"storm, darkness, sleet and shade" assail him—"shadowy hands" twitch at his bridle-rein—"flame-shot tongues" play around him—"fiendish eyes" glare upon him—and

Yells of rage and shrieks of fear
Come screaming on his startled ear.

Still our adventurer is nothing daunted.

He thrusts before, and he strikes behind,
Till he pierces the cloudy bodies through
And gashes the shadowy limbs of wind.

and the Elfin makes no stop, until he reaches the "bank of the milky way." He there checks his courser, and watches "for the glimpse of the planet shoot." While thus engaged, however, an unexpected adventure befalls him. He is approached by a company of the "sylphs of Heaven attired in sunset's crimson pall." They dance around him, and "skip before him on the plain." One receiving his "wasp-sting lance," and another taking his bridle-rein,

> With warblings wild they lead him on,
> To where, through clouds of amber seen,
> Studded with stars resplendent shone
> The palace of the sylphid queen.

A glowing description of the queen's beauty follows: and as the form of an earthly Fay had never been seen before in the bowers of light, she is represented as falling desperately in love at first sight with our adventurous Ouphe. He returns the compliment in some measure, of course; but, although "his heart bent fitfully," the "earthly form imprinted there" was a security against a too vivid impression. He declines, consequently, the invitation of the queen to remain with her and amuse himself by "lying within the fleecy drift," "hanging upon the rainbow's rim," having his "brow adorned with all the jewels of the sky," "sitting within the Pleiad ring," "resting upon Orion's belt" "riding upon the lightning's gleam," "dancing upon the orbed moon," and "swimming within the milky way."

> Lady, he cries, I have sworn to-night
> On the word of a fairy knight
> To do my sentence task aright

The queen, therefore, contents herself with bidding the Fay an affectionate farewell—having first directed him carefully to that particular portion of the sky where a star is about to fall. He reaches this point in safety, and in despite of the "fiends of the cloud," who "bellow very loud," succeeds finally in catching a "glimmering spark" with which he returns triumphantly to Fairy-land. The poem closes with an Io Paean chaunted by the elves in honor of these glorious adventures.

It is more than probable that from ten readers of the *Culprit Fay*, nine would immediately pronounce it a poem betokening the most extraordinary powers of imagination, and of these nine, perhaps five or six, poets themselves, and fully impressed with the truth of what we have already assumed, that Ideality is indeed the soul of the Poetic Sentiment, would feel embarrassed between a half-consciousness that they *ought* to admire the

production, and a wonder that they *do not*. This embarrassment would then arise from an indistinct conception of the results in which Ideality is rendered manifest. Of these results some few are seen in the *Culprit Fay*, but the greater part of it is utterly destitute of any evidence of imagination whatever. The general character of the poem will, we think, be sufficiently understood by any one who may have taken the trouble to read our foregoing compendium of the narrative. It will be there seen that what is so frequently termed the imaginative power of this story, lies especially—we should have rather said is thought to lie—in the passages we have quoted, or in others of a precisely similar nature. These passages embody, principally, mere specifications of qualities, of habiliments, of punishments, of occupations, of circumstances, &c., which the poet has believed in unison with the size, firstly, and secondly with the nature of his Fairies. To all which may be added specifications of other animal existences (such as the toad, the beetle, the lance-fly, the fire-fly and the like) supposed also to be in accordance. An example will best illustrate our meaning upon this point—

> He put his acorn helmet on;
> It was plumed of the silk of the thistle down:
> The corslet plate that guarded his breast
> Was once the wild bee's golden vest;
> His cloak of a thousand mingled dyes,
> Was formed of the wings of butterflies;
> His shield was the shell of a lady-bug queen,
> Studs of gold on a ground of green;
> And the quivering lance which he brandished bright
> Was the sting of a wasp he had slain in fight.

We shall now be understood. Were any of the admirers of the *Culprit Fay* asked their opinion of these lines, they would most probably speak in high terms of the *imagination* they display. Yet let the most stolid and the most confessedly unpoetical of these admirers only try the experiment, and he will find, possibly to his extreme surprise, that he himself will have no difficulty whatever in substituting for the equipments of the Fairy, as assigned by the poet, other equipments equally comfortable, no doubt, and equally in unison with the preconceived size, character, and other qualities of the equipped. Why we could accoutre him as well ourselves—let us see.

His blue-bell helmet, we have heard
Was plumed with the down of the
       hummingbird,
The corslet on his bosom bold
Was once the locust's coat of gold,
His cloak, of a thousand mingled hues,
Was the velvet violet, wet with dews,
His target was, the crescent shell
Of the small sea Sidrophel,
And a glittering beam from a maiden's eye
Was the lance which he proudly wav'd on high.

The truth is, that the only requisite for writing verses of this nature, *ad libitum*, is a tolerable acquaintance with the qualities of the objects to be detailed, and a very moderate endowment of the faculty of Comparison—which is the chief constituent of *Fancy* or the powers of combination. A thousand such lines may be composed without exercising in the least degree the Poetic Sentiment, which is Ideality, Imagination, or the creative ability. And, as we have before said, the greater portion of the *Culprit Fay* is occupied with these, or similiar things, and upon such, depends very nearly, if not altogether, its reputation. We select another example—

But oh! how fair the shape that lay
       Beneath a rainbow bending bright,
She seem'd to the entranced Fay
       The loveliest of the forms of light;
Her mantle was the purple rolled
       At twilight in the west afar;
'T was tied with threads of dawning gold,
       And button'd with a sparkling star.
Her face was like the lily roon
       That veils the vestal planet's hue;
Her eyes, two beamlets from the moon
       Set floating in the welkin blue.
Her hair is like the sunny beam,
And the diamond gems which round it gleam
Are the pure drops of dewy even,
That ne'er have left their native heaven.

Here again the faculty of Comparison is alone exercised, and no mind possessing the faculty in any ordinary degree would find a difficulty in substituting for the materials employed by the poet other materials equally as good. But viewed as

mere efforts of the Fancy and without reference to Ideality, the lines just quoted are much worse than those which were taken earlier. A congruity was observable in the accoutrements of the Ouphe, and we had no trouble in forming a distinct conception of his appearance when so accoutred. But the most vivid powers of Comparison can attach no definitive idea to even "the loveliest form of light," when habited in a mantle of "rolled purple tied with threads of dawn and buttoned with a star," and sitting at the same time under a rainbow with "beamlet" eyes and a visage of "lily roon."

But if these things evince no Ideality in their author, do they not excite it in others?—if so, we must conclude, that without being himself imbued with the Poetic Sentiment, he has still succeeded in writing a fine poem—a supposition as we have before endeavored to show, not altogether paradoxical. Most assuredly we think not. In the case of a great majority of readers the only sentiment aroused by compositions of this order is a species of vague wonder at the writer's *ingenuity*, and it is this indeterminate sense of wonder which passes but too frequently current for the proper influence of the Poetic power. For our own part we plead guilty to a predominant sense of the ludicrous while occupied in the perusal of the poem before us—a sense whose promptings we sincerely and honestly endeavored to quell, perhaps not altogether successfully, while penning our compend of the narrative. That a feeling of this nature is utterly at war with the Poetic Sentiment will not be disputed by those who comprehend the character of the sentiment itself. This character is finely shadowed out in that popular although vague idea so prevalent throughout all time, that a species of melancholy is inseparably connected with the higher manifestations of the beautiful. But with the numerous and seriously-adduced incongruities of the *Culprit Fay*, we find it generally impossible to connect other ideas than those of the ridiculous. We are bidden, in the first place, and in a tone of sentiment and language adapted to the loftiest breathings of the Muse, to imagine a race of Fairies in the vicinity of West Point. We are told, with a grave air, of their camp, of their king, and especially of their sentry, who is a wood-tick. We are informed that an Ouphe of about an inch in height has committed a deadly sin in falling in love with a mortal maiden, who may, very possibly, be six feet in her stockings. The consequence to the Ouphe is—what? Why, that he has "dyed his wings," "broken his elfin chain," and "quenched his flame-wood lamp." And he is therefore sentenced to what? To catch a spark from the tail of a falling star, and a drop of water from the belly of a sturgeon. What are his equipments for the first adventure? An acorn-helmet, a thistle-down plume, a butterfly cloak, a lady-bug shield, cockle-seed spurs, and a fire-fly horse. How does he ride to the second? On the back of a bullfrog. What are his opponents in the one? "Drizzle-mists," "sulphur and smoke," "shadowy hands and flame-shot tongues." What in the other? "Mailed shrimps," "prickly prongs," "blood-red leeches," "jellied quarls," "stony star fishes," "lancing squabs" and "soldier crabs." Is that all? No—Although only an inch high he is in imminent danger of seduction from a "sylphid queen," dressed in a mantle of "rolled purple," "tied with threads of dawning gold," "buttoned with a sparkling star," and sitting under a rainbow with "beamlet eyes" and a countenance of "lily roon." In our account of all this matter we have had reference to the book—and to the book alone. It will be difficult to prove us guilty in any degree of distortion or exaggeration. Yet such are the puerilities we daily find ourselves called upon to admire, as among the loftiest efforts of the human mind, and which not to assign a rank with the proud trophies of the matured and vigorous genius of England, is to prove ourselves at once a fool; a maligner, and no patriot.

As an instance of what may be termed the sublimely ridiculous we quote the following lines—

> With sweeping tail and quivering fin,
>   Through the wave the sturgeon flew,
> And like the heaven-shot javelin,
>   He sprung above the waters blue.

> Instant as the star-fall light,
>   He plunged into the deep again,
> But left an arch of silver bright
>   The rainbow of the moony main.

> *It was a strange and lovely sight*
>   *To see the puny goblin there;*
> *He seemed an angel form of light*
>   *With azure wing and sunny hair,*
>   *Throned on a cloud of purple fair*

> *Circled with blue and edged with white*
>   *And sitting at the fall of even*
>   *Beneath the bow of summer heaven.*

The verses here italicized, if considered without their context, have a certain air of dignity, elegance, and chastity of thought. If however we apply the context, we are immediately overwhelmed with the grotesque. It is impossible to read without laughing, such expressions as "It was a strange and lovely sight"—"He seemed an angel form of light"—"And sitting at the fall of even, beneath the bow of summer heaven" to a Fairy—a goblin—an Ouphe—half an inch high, dressed in an acorn helmet and butterfly-cloak, and sitting on the water in a muscleshell, with a "brown-backed sturgeon" turning somersets over his head. In a world where evil is a mere consequence of good, and good a mere consequence of evil—in short where all of which we have any conception is good or bad only by comparison—we have never yet been fully able to appreciate the validity of that decision which would debar the critic from enforcing upon his readers the merits or demerits of a work by placing it in juxta-position with another. It seems to us that an adage has had more to do with this popular feeling than any just reason founded upon common sense. Thinking thus, we shall have no scruple in illustrating our opinion in regard to what *is not* Ideality or the Poetic Power, by an example of what is.

We have already given the description of the Sylphid Queen in the *Culprit Fay*. In the *Queen Mab* of Shelley a Fairy is thus introduced—

> Those who had looked upon the sight
>   Passing all human glory,
> Saw not the yellow moon,
> Saw not the mortal scene,
> Heard not the night wind's rush,
> Heard not an earthly sound,
> Saw but the fairy pageant,
> Heard but the heavenly strains
> That filled the lonely dwelling—

and thus described—

> The Fairy's frame was slight, yon fibrous cloud
> That catches but the faintest tinge of even,
> And which the straining eye can hardly seize

When melting into eastern twilight's shadow,
Were scarce so thin, so slight; but the fair star
That gems the glittering coronet of morn,
Sheds not a light so mild, so powerful,
As that which, bursting from the Fairy's form,
Spread a purpureal halo round the scene,
Yet with an undulating motion,
Swayed to her outline gracefully.

In these exquisite lines the Faculty of mere Comparison is but little exercised—that of Ideality in a wonderful degree. It is probable that in a similar case the poet we are now reviewing would have formed the face of the Fairy of the "fibrous cloud," her arms of the "pale tinge of even," her eyes of the "fair stars," and her body of the "twilight shadow." Having so done, his admirers would have congratulated him upon his *imagination*, not, taking the trouble to think that they themselves could at any moment *imagine* a Fairy of materials equally as good, and conveying an equally distinct idea. Their mistake would be precisely analogous to that of many a schoolboy who admires the imagination displayed in *Jack the Giant-Killer*, and is finally rejoiced at; discovering his own imagination to surpass that of the author, since the monsters destroyed by Jack are only about forty feet in height, and he himself has no trouble in imagining some of one hundred and forty. It will, be seen that the Fairy of Shelley is not a mere compound of incongruous natural objects, inartificially put together, and unaccompanied by any *moral* sentiment—but a being, in the illustration of whose nature some physical elements are used collaterally as adjuncts, while the main conception springs immediately *or thus apparently springs*, from the brain of the poet, enveloped in the moral sentiments of grace, of color, of motion—of the beautiful, of the mystical, of the august—in short of *the ideal*.

It is by no means our intention to deny that in the *Culprit Fay* are passages of a different order from those to which we have objected—passages evincing a degree of imagination not to be discovered in the plot, conception, or general execution of the poem. The opening stanza will afford us a tolerable example.

'Tis the middle watch of a summer's night—
The earth is dark but the heavens are bright
Naught is seen in the vault on high

But the moon, and the stars, and the cloudless sky,
And the flood which rolls its milky hue
A river of light on the welkin blue.
The moon looks down on old Cronest,
She mellows the shades of his shaggy breast,
And seems his huge gray form to throw
In a silver cone on the wave below;
His sides are broken by spots of shade,
By the walnut bow and the cedar made,
And through their clustering branches dark
Glimmers and dies the fire-fly's spark—
Like starry twinkles that momently break
Through the rifts of the gathering tempest rack.

There is Ideality in these lines—but except in the case of the words italicized—it is Ideality *not of a high order*. We have, it is true, a collection of natural objects, each individually of great beauty, and, if actually seen as in nature, capable of exciting in any mind, through the means of the Poetic Sentiment more or less inherent in all, a certain sense of the beautiful. But to view such natural objects as they exist, and to behold them through the medium of words, are different things. Let us pursue the idea that such a collection as we have here will produce, of necessity, the Poetic Sentiment, and we may as well make up our minds to believe that a catalogue of such expressions as moon, sky, trees, rivers, mountains, &c., shall be capable of exciting it,—it is merely an extension of the principle. But in the line "the earth is dark, but the heavens are bright" besides the simple mention of the "dark earth" "and the bright heaven," we have, directly, the moral sentiment of the brightness of the sky compensating for the darkness of the earth—and thus, indirectly, of the happiness of a future state compensating for the miseries of the present. All this is effected by the simple introduction of the word *but* between the "dark earth" and the "bright heaven"—this introduction, however, was prompted by the Poetic Sentiment, and by the Poetic Sentiment alone. The case is analogous in the expression "glimmers and dies," where the imagination is exalted by the moral sentiment of beauty heightened in dissolution.

In one or two shorter passages of the *Culprit Fay* the poet will recognize the purely ideal, and be able at a glance to distinguish it from that baser alloy upon which we have descanted. We give them without farther comment.

The winds *are whist*, and the owl is still,
The bat in the shelvy rock *is hid*
And naught is heard on the *lonely* hill
But the cricket's chirp and the answer *shrill*
Of the gauze-winged katy-did;
And the plaint of the *wailing* whippoorwill
Who mourns *unseen*, and ceaseless sings
Ever a note of wail and wo—

Up to the vaulted firmament
His path the fire-fly courser bent,
And at every gallop on the wind
He flung a glittering spark behind.

He blessed the force of the charmed line
And he banned the water-goblins' spite,
For he saw around in the *sweet moonshine,*
Their little wee faces above the brine,
Griggling and laughing with all their might
At the piteous hap of the Fairy wight.

The poem "To a Friend" consists of fourteen Spenserian stanzas. They are fine spirited verses, and probably were not supposed by their author to be more. Stanza the fourth, although beginning nobly, concludes with that very common exemplification of the bathos, the illustrating natural objects of beauty or grandeur by references to the tinsel of artificiality.

Oh! for a seat on Appalachia's brow,
That I might scan the glorious prospects round,
Wild waving woods, and rolling floods below,
Smooth level glades and fields with grain
    embrowned,
High heaving hills, with tufted forests crowned,
Rearing their tall tops to the heaven's blue
    dome,
And emerald isles, *like banners green un-wound,*
Floating along the take, while round them roam
Bright helms of billowy blue, and plumes of dancing
    foam.

In the *Extracts from Leon* are passages not often surpassed in vigor of passionate thought and expression—and which induce us to believe not only that their author would have succeeded better in prose romance than in poetry, but that his attention would have naturally fallen into the former direction, had the Destroyer only spared him a little longer.

This poem contains also lines of far greater poetic power than any to be found in the *Culprit Fay*. For example—

The stars have lit in heaven their lamps of gold,
The *viewless* dew falls lightly on the world;
The gentle air *that softly sweeps the leaves*
A strain of faint unearthly music weaves:
As when the harp of heaven remotely plays,
Or cygnets wail—or song of *sorrowing* fays
That *float amid the moonshine glimmerings pale,*
On wings of woven air in some enchanted vale.

Niagara is objectionable in many respects, and in none more so than in its frequent inversions of language, and the artificial character of its versification. The invocation,

Roar, raging torrent! and thou, mighty river,
Pour thy white foam on the valley below!
Frown ye dark mountains,

is ludicrous—and nothing more. In general, all such invocations have an air of the burlesque. In the present instance we may fancy the majestic Niagara replying, "Most assuredly I will roar, whether, worm! thou tellest me or not."

The American Flag commences with a collection of those bald conceits, which we have already shown to have no dependence whatever upon the Poetic Power—springing altogether from Comparison.

When Freedom from her mountain height
    Unfurled her standard to the air,
She tore the azure robe of night
    And set the stars of glory there.
She mingled with its gorgeous dyes
The milky baldric of the skies,
And striped its pure celestrial white
With streakings of the morning light;
Then from his mansion in the sun
She called her eagle bearer down
And gave into his mighty hand
    The symbol of her chosen land.

Let us reduce all this to plain English, and we have—what? Why, a flag, consisting of the "azure robe of night," "set with stars of glory," interspersed with "streaks of morning light," relieved with a few pieces of "milky way," and the whole carried by an "eagle bearer," that is to say, an eagle ensign, who bears aloft this "symbol of our chosen land" in his "mighty hand," by which we are to understand his claw. In the second stanza, "the thunder-drum of Heaven" is bathetic and grotesque in the highest degree—a commingling of the most sublime music of Heaven with the most utterly contemptible and common-place of Earth. The two concluding verses are in a better spirit, and might almost be supposed to be from a different hand. The images contained in the lines

> When Death careering on the gale
> Sweeps darkly round the bellied sail,
> And frighted waves rush wildly back,
> Before the broadsides reeling rack,

are of the highest order of Ideality. The deficiencies of the whole poem may be best estimated by reading it in connection with "Scots wha hae," with the "Mariners of England," or with "Hohenlinden." It is indebted for its high and most undeserved reputation to our patriotism—not to our judgment.

The remaining poems in Mr. Dearborn's edition of Drake, are three Songs; Lines in an Album; Lines to a Lady; Lines on leaving New Rochelle; Hope; A Fragment; To—; To Eva; To a Lady; To Sarah; and Bronx. These are all poems of little compass, and with the exception of Bronx and a portion of the Fragment, they have no character distinctive from the mass of our current poetical literature. Bronx, however, is in our opinion, not only the best of the writings of Drake, but altogether a lofty and beautiful poem, upon which his admirers would do better to found a hope of the writer's ultimate reputation than upon the *niaiseries* of the *Culprit Fay*. In the *Fragment* is to be found the finest individual passage in the volume before us, and we quote it as a proper finale to our review.

> Yes! thou art lovelier now than ever;
>   How sweet't would be *when all the air*
> *In moonlight swims,* along thy river
>   To couch upon the grass, and hear
> Niagra's everlasting voice
>   Far in the deep blue west away;
> That dreamy and poetic noise
>   We mark not in the glare of day,

> Oh! how unlike its torrent-cry,
>   When o'er the brink the tide is driven,
> As if the vast and sheeted sky
>   In thunder fell from Heaven.

Halleck's poetical powers appear to us essentially inferior, upon the whole, to those of his friend Drake. He has written nothing at all comparable to *Bronx*. By the hackneyed phrase, *sportive elegance*, we might possibly designate at once the general character of his writings and the very loftiest praise to which he is justly entitled.

Alnwick Castle is an irregular poem of one hundred and twenty-eight lines—was written, as we are informed, in October 1822—and is descriptive of a seat of the Duke of Northumberland, in Northumberlandshire, England. The effect of the first stanza is materially impaired by a defect in its grammatical arrangement. The fine lines,

> Home of the Percy's high-born race,
>   Home of their beautiful and brave,
> Alike their birth and burial place,
>   Their cradle and their grave!

are of the nature of an invocation, and thus require a continuation of the address to the "Home, &c." We are consequently disappointed when the stanza proceeds with—

> Still sternly o'er the castle gate
> *Their* house's Lion stands in state
>   As in *his* proud departed hours;
> And warriors frown in stone on high,
> And feudal banners "flout the sky"
>   Above *his* princely towers.

The objects of allusion here vary, in an awkward manner, from the castle to the Lion, and from the Lion to the towers. By writing the verses thus the difficulty would be remedied.

> Still sternly o'er the castle gate
> *Thy* house's Lion stands in state,
>   As in his proud departed hours;
> And warriors frown in stone on high,
> And feudal banners "flout the sky"
>   Above *thy* princely towers.

The second stanza, without evincing in any measure the loftier powers of a poet, has that quiet air of grace, both in thought and expression, which seems to be the prevailing feature of the Muse of Halleck.

> A gentle hill its side inclines,
>   Lovely in England's fadeless green,
> To meet the quiet stream which winds
>   Through this romantic scene
> As silently and sweetly still,
> As when, at evening, on that hill,
>   While summer's wind blew soft and low,
> Seated by gallant Hotspur's side
> His Katherine was a happy bride
>   A thousand years ago.

There are one or two brief passages in the poem evincing a degree of rich imagination not elsewhere perceptible throughout the book. For example—

> Gaze on the Abbey's ruined pile:
>   Does not the succoring Ivy keeping,
> Her watch around it seem to smile
>   As o'er a lov'd one sleeping?

and,

> One solitary turret gray
>   Still tells in melancholy glory
> The legend of the Cheviot day.

The commencement of the fourth stanza is of the highest order of Poetry, and partakes, in a happy manner, of that quaintness of expression so effective an adjunct to Ideality, when employed by the Shelleys, the Coleridges and the Tennysons, but so frequently debased, and rendered ridiculous, by the herd of brainless imitators.

> Wild roses by the abbey towers
>   Are gay in their young bud and bloom:
> *They were born of a race of funeral flowers,*
> That garlanded in long-gone hours,
>   A Templar's knightly tomb.

The tone employed in the concluding portions of Alnwick Castle, is, we sincerely think, reprehensible, and unworthy of Halleck. No true poet can unite in any manner the low burlesque with the ideal, and not be conscious of incongruity and of a profanation. Such verses as

> Men in the coal and cattle line
>   From Tevoit's bard and hero land,
>   From royal Berwick's beach of sand,
>   From Wooler, Morpeth, Hexham, and
>   Newcastle upon Tyne.

may lay claim to oddity—but no more. These things are the defects and not the beauties of *Don Juan.* They are totally out of keeping with the graceful and delicate manner of the initial portions of *Alnwick Castle,* and serve no better purpose than to deprive the entire poem of all unity of effect. If a poet must be farcical, let him be just that, and nothing else. To be drolly sentimental is bad enough, as we have just seen in certain passages of the *Culprit Fay,* but to be sentimentally droll is a thing intolerable to men, and Gods, and columns.

Marco Bozzaris appears to have much lyrical without any high order of *ideal* beauty. *Force* is its prevailing character—a force, however, consisting more in a well ordered and sonorous arrangement of this metre, and a judicious disposal of what may be called the circumstances of the poem, than in the true *material* of lyric vigor. We are introduced, first, to the Turk who dreams, at midnight, in his guarded tent,

> of the hour
> When Greece her knee in suppliance bent,
>   Should tremble at his power—

He is represented as revelling in the visions of ambition.

> In dreams through camp and court he bore
> The trophies of a conqueror;
> In dreams his song of triumph heard;
> Then wore his monarch's signet ring;
> Then pressed that monarch's throne—a king;
> As wild his thoughts and gay of wing
>   As Eden's garden bird.

In direct contrast to this we have Bozzaris watchful in the forest, and ranging his band of Suliotes on the ground, and amid the memories of Plataea. An hour elapses, and the Turk awakes from his visions of false glory—to die. But Bozzaris dies—to awake. He dies in the flush of victory to awake, in death, to an ultimate certainty of Freedom. Then follows an invocation to death. His terrors under ordinary circumstances are contrasted with the glories of the dissolution of Bozzaris, in which the approach of the Destroyer is

>   welcome as the cry
> That told the Indian isles were nigh
>   To the world-seeking Genoese,
> When the land-wind from woods of palm,
> And orange groves and fields of balm,
>   Blew o'er the Haytian seas.

The poem closes with the poetical apotheosis of Marco Bozzaris as

> One of the few, the immortal names
>   That are not born to die.

It will be seen that these arrangements of the subject are skillfully contrived—perhaps they are a little too evident, and we are enabled too readily by the perusal of one passage, to anticipate the succeeding. The rhythm is highly artificial. The stanzas are well adapted for vigorous expression— the fifth will afford a just specimen of the versification of the whole poem.

> Come to the bridal Chamber, Death!
> Come to the mother's when she feels
> For the first time her first born's breath;
>   Come when the blessed seals
> That close the pestilence are broke,
> And crowded cities wail its stroke;
> Come in consumption's ghastly form,
> The earthquake shock, the ocean storm;
> Come when the heart beats high and warm,
>   With banquet song and dance, and wine;
> And thou art terrible—the tear,
> The groan, the knell, the pall, the bier;
> And all we know, or dream, or fear
>   Of agony, are thine.

Granting, however, to *Marco Bozzaris*, the minor excellences we have pointed out we should be doing our conscience great wrong in calling it, upon the whole, any more than a very ordinary matter. It is surpassed, even as a lyric, by a multitude of foreign and by many American compositions of a similar character. To Ideality it has few pretensions, and the finest portion of the poem is probably to be found in the verses we have quoted elsewhere—

> Thy grasp is welcome as the hand
> Of brother in a foreign land;
> Thy summons welcome as the cry
> That told the Indian isles were nigh
>   To the world-seeking Genoese,
> When the land-wind from woods of palm
> And orange groves, and fields of balm
> Blew o'er the Haytian seas.

The verses entitled *Burns* consist of thirty-eight quatrains—the three first lines of each quatrain being of four feet, the fourth of three. This poem has many of the traits of *Alnwick Castle*, and bears also a strong resemblance to some of the writings of Wordsworth. Its chief merits, and indeed the chief merit, so we think, of all the poems of Halleck is the merit of *expression*. In the brief extracts from *Burns* which follow, our readers will recognize the peculiar character of which we speak.

> Wild Rose of Alloway! my thanks:
>   Thou mind'st me of *that autumn noon*
> *When first we met upon "the banks*
>   *And braes o'bonny Doon"*—
> —
> Like thine, beneath the thorn-tree's bough,
>   My sunny hour was glad and brief—
> We've crossed the winter sea, *and thou*
>   *Art withered—flower and leaf,*
> —
> *There have been loftier themes than his,*
>   *And longer scrolls and louder lyres*
> *And lays lit up with Poesy's*
>   *Purer and holier fires.*
> —
> *And when he breathes his master-lay*
>   *Of Alloways witch-haunted wall*
> All passions in our frames of clay
>   Come thronging at his call.
> —
> Such graves as his are pilgrim-shrines,
>   Shrines to no code or creed confined—
> *The Delphian vales, the Palastines,*
>   *The Meccas of the mind.*
> —

They linger by the Doon's low trees,
    And pastoral Nith, and wooded Ayr,
And round thy Sepulchres, Dumfries!
    The Poet's tomb is there.

Wyoming is composed of nine Spenserian stanzas. With some unusual excellences, it has some of the worst faults of Halleck. The lines which follow are of great beauty.

I then but dreamed: thou art before me now,
    In life—a vision of the brain no more,
I've stood upon the wooded mountain's brow,
    That beetles high thy love! valley o'er;
And now, *where winds thy river's greenest shore,*
    Within a bower of sycamores am laid;
And winds as soft and sweet as ever bore
    The fragrance of wild flowers through sun and
        shade
Are singing in the trees, whose low boughs press
        my head.

The poem, however, is disfigured with the mere burlesque of some portions of Alnwick Castle—with such things as

            he would look *particularly droll*
    In his Iberian boot and Spanish plume;

and

            A girl of sweet sixteen
    Love-darting eyes and tresses like the morn
    Without a shoe or stocking—hoeing corn,

mingled up in a pitiable manner with images of real beauty.

The Field of the Grounded Arms contains twenty-four quatrains, without rhyme, and, we think, of a disagreeable versification. In this poem are to be observed some of the finest passages of Halleck. For example—

    "Strangers! your eyes are on that valley fixed
    Intently, as we gaze on vacancy,
        When the mind's wings o'erspread
        The spirit world of dreams.

and again—

O'er sleepless seas of grass whose waves are flowers.

Red-Jacket has much power of expression with little evidence of poetical ability. Its humor is very fine, and does not interfere, in any great degree, with the general tone of the poem.

A Sketch should have been omitted from the edition as altogether unworthy of its author.

The remaining pieces in the volume are *Twilight, Psalm cxxxvii; To * * * *; Love; Domestic Happiness; Magdalen; From the Italian; Woman; Connecticut; Music; On the Death of Lieut. William Howard Allen; A Poet's Daughter;* and *On the Death of Joseph Rodman Drake.* Of the majority of these we deem it unnecessary to say more than that they partake, in a more or less degree, of the general character observable in the poems of Halleck. The *Poet's Daughter* appears to us a particularly happy specimen of that general character, and we doubt whether it be not the favorite of its author. We are glad to see the vulgarity of

    I'm busy in the cotton trade
        And sugar line,

omitted in the present edition. The eleventh stanza is certainly not English as it stands—and besides it is altogether unintelligible. What is the meaning of this?

    But her who asks, though first among
    The good, the beautiful, the young,
    The birthright of a spell more strong
        Than these have brought her.

The *Lines on the Death of Joseph Rodman Drake,* we prefer to any of the writings of Halleck. It has that rare merit in composition of this kind—the union of tender sentiment and simplicity. This poem consists merely of six quatrains, and we quote them in full.

    Green be the turf above thee,
        Friend of my better days!
    None knew thee but to love thee,
        Nor named thee but to praise.

    Tears fell when thou wert dying
        From eyes unused to weep,
    And long, where thou art lying,
        Will tears the cold turf steep.

When hearts whose truth was proven,
    Like thine are laid in earth,
There should a wreath be woven
    To tell the world their worth.

And I, who woke each morrow
    To clasp thy hand in mine,
Who shared thy joy and sorrow,
    Whose weal and woe were thine —

It should be mine to braid it
    Around thy faded brow,
But I've in vain essayed it,
    And feel I cannot now.

While memory bids me weep thee,
    Nor thoughts nor words are free,
The grief is fixed too deeply,
    That mourns a man like thee.

If we are to judge from the subject of these verses, they are a work of some care and reflection. Yet they abound in faults. In the line,

Tears fell when thou wert dying;

wert is not English.

Will tears the cold turf steep,

is an exceedingly rough verse. The metonymy involved in

There should a wreath be woven
    To *tell* the world their worth,

is unjust. The quatrain beginning,

And I who woke each morrow,

is ungrammatical in its construction when viewed in connection with the quatrain which immediately follows. "Weep thee" and "deeply" are inaccurate rhymes—and the whole of the first quatrain,

Green be the turf, &c.

although beautiful, bears too close a resemblance to the still more beautiful lines of William Wordsworth,

She dwelt among the untrodden ways
    Beside the springs of Dove,
A maid whom there were none to praise
    And very few to love.

As a versifier Halleck is by no means equal to his friend, all of whose poems evince an ear finely attuned to the delicacies of melody. We seldom meet with more inharmonious lines than those, generally, of the author of *Alnwick Castle*. At every step such verses occur as,

And *the* monk's hymn and minstrel's song—
True *as* the steel of *their* tried blades—
For him the joy of *her* young years—
Where *the* Bard-peasant first drew breath—
And withered *my* life's leaf like thine—

in which the proper course of the rhythm would demand an accent upon syllables too unimportant to sustain it. Not infrequently, too, we meet with lines such as this,

Like torn branch from death's leafless tree,

in which the multiplicity of consonants renders the pronunciation of the words at all, a matter of no inconsiderable difficulty.

But we must bring our notice to a close. It will be seen that while we are willing to admire in many respects the poems before us, we feel obliged to dissent materially from that public opinion (perhaps not fairly ascertained) which would assign them a very brilliant rank in the empire of Poesy. That we have among us poets of the loftiest order we believe—but we do not believe that these poets are Drake and Halleck.

[36] Poe, Edgar Allan. "Critical Notices." *Southern Literary Messenger*, Vol. II, No. 3, April 1836.

[A.8]

CORRESPONDENCE: TAYLOR AND WHITMAN.

Kennett Square, Penna.
Nov. 12, 1866

My dear Sir:

I send to you by the same mail which takes this note, a copy of my last poem "The Picture of St. John." I do not know whether the subject of the poem (the growth and development of the artist-nature, and its relation to life) will much interest you, but I hope you will here and there find something drawn immediately from nature. I am, at least, not aware that anything in the book is simulated or forced: whether successful or not, it is an honest conscientious effort.

I value, above all things, *sincerity* in literature; hence I am not one of those who overlook your remarkable powers of expression, your broad, vital reverence for humanity, because some things you have said repel them. The age is over-squeamish, and, for my part, I prefer the honest nude to the suggestive half-draped. I think the proper question to be asked is: does a certain thing *need* to be said? If so, let it be said! The worst form of immorality, I have found, veils itself in decent words.

There is one quality I recognize in you, which warmly and constantly attracts me. That is, your deep and tender reverence for Man—your unwearied, affectionate, practical fraternity. There is too little of this quality in the world, and the race will be better and happier in proportion as it is manifested.

I shall be in Washington on the 27th of December, to lecture, and hope that I shall then be able to meet you personally. If you can spare me an hour or two after the lecture, you will greatly oblige
Your friend,
Bayard Taylor

"Bayard Taylor to Walt Whitman, 12 November 1866." *The Walt Whitman Archive.* Gen. ed. Ed Folsom and Kenneth M. Price. Accessed 16 November 2016. <http://www.whitmanarchive.org>.

*

A8

ATTORNEY GENERAL'S
OFFICE, *Washington,*
Nov. 18, *1866.*

My dear Mr. Taylor,

I have received your letter of the 12th. The friendly pages thereof have given me pleasure, & I wish to proffer you my friendship in response. Should I not see you at the lecture, I hope you will do me the honor to call upon me at the Attorney General's office here, in the Treasury Building, where I am employed.

Your book also came safely. I accept it, as a kind & valuable gift—& heartily thank you.

Permit me to send you, in return, a copy of the new edition of Leaves of Grass. I send it herewith by same mail. Truly hoping to see you—for the present, Farewell.
Walt Whitman.

"Walt Whitman to Bayard Taylor, 18 November 1866." *The Walt Whitman Archive.* Gen. ed. Ed Folsom and Kenneth M. Price. Accessed 16 November 2016. <http://www.whitmanarchive.org>.

*

Kennett Square, Penna.
Dec. 2, 1866

My dear Whitman:

I find your book and cordial letter, on returning home from a lecturing tour in New York, and heartily thank you for both. I have had the first edition of your "Leaves of Grass" among my books, since its first appearance, and have read it many times. I may say, frankly, that there are two things in it which I find nowhere else in literature, though I find them in my own nature. I mean the awe and wonder and reverence and beauty of Life, as expressed in the human body, with the physical attraction and delight of mere contact which it inspires, and that tender and noble love of man for man which once certainly existed, but now almost seems to have gone out of the experience of the race. I think there is nothing in your volume which I do not fully comprehend in the sense in which you wrote; I always try to judge an author from his own standpoint rather than mine, but in this case the two nearly coincide. We should differ rather in regard to form than substance, I suspect. There is not one word of your large and beautiful sympathy for men, which I cannot take into my own heart, nor one of those subtle and wonderful physical affinities you describe which I cannot comprehend. I say these things, not in the way of praise, but because I know from my own experience that correct appreciation of an author is less frequent than it should be. It is welcome to me, and may be so to you.

I did not mean to write so much when I commenced, and will only say that I will be in Washington on the 27th—only for that night— and would be very glad if we can come together for awhile after my lecture is over. I am afraid I shall not arrive in time to call at the Dep't before the lecture, but if I can I will. If not, will you either come to Willard's or tell me where to find you, and oblige

Your friend,
Bayard Taylor

"Bayard Taylor to Walt Whitman, 2 December 1866." *The Walt Whitman Archive*. Gen. ed. Ed Folsom and Kenneth M. Price. Accessed 16 November 2016. <http://www.whitmanarchive.org>.

[A.9]

TAYLOR: TRIBUNE PARODY.

The *New-York Tribune* printed a devastating parody by Bayard Taylor in 1871 (reprinted in his *Echo Club* [2nd ed., 1876], 169–170).[14] The poem follows:

WALT WHITMAN.

Who was it sang of the procreant urge, recounted
    sextillions of subjects?
Who by myself, the Kosmos, yawping abroad,
    concerned not at all about either the
    effect or the answer;
Straddling the Continent, gathering into my hairy
    bosom the growths, whatever they were,
    and nothing slighted, nothing forgotten?
Allez! I am the One, the only One, and this is my
    Chant Democratique.
Where is he that heard not, and she that heard
    not, and they that heard not, before and
    during and after?

All is wholesome and clean, and all is the effluent
    strain, impeccable, sweet, of the clasper
    of comrades.
If there were anything else, I would sing it;
But there is nothing, no jot or tittle, or least little
    scraping of subject or matter:
No, there is nothing at all, and all of you know it.

[49] Taylor, Bayard. *The Echo club, And Other Literary Diversions*. Boston, J. R. Osgood and Company, 1876.

[A.10]

TAYLOR: ECHO CLUB PARODY.

An excerpt from Bayard Taylor's "Diversions of the Echo Club" published in *The Atlantic Monthly* in 1872, a parody that includes this review of Walt Whitman:

THE GANNET. But the changes of popular taste in the two countries are very similar. This is evident in the cases of Bret Harte and Hay; but Walt Whitman seems to have a large circle of enthusiastic admirers in England, and only some half-dozen disciples among us. Do you suppose that the passages of his "Leaves of Grass," which are prose catalogues to us, or the phrases which are our slang, have a kind of poetical charm there, because they are not understood?

ZOILUS. As Tartar or Mongolian "Leaves of Grass" might have to us? Very likely. There are splendid lines and brief passages in Walt Whitman: there is a modern, half-Bowery-boy, half-Emersonian apprehension of the old Greek idea of physical life, which many take to be wholly new on account of the singular form in which it is presented. I will even admit that the elements of a fine poet exist in him, in a state of chaos. It is curious that while he proclaims his human sympathies to be without bounds, his intellectual sympathies should be so narrow. There never was a man at once so arrogant, and so tender towards his fellow-men.

THE ANCIENT. You have very correctly described him. The same art which he despises would have increased his power and influence. He forgets that the poet must not only have somewhat to say, but must strenuously acquire the power of saying it most purely and completely. A truer sense of art would have prevented that fault which has been called immorality, but is only a coarse, offensive frankness.

[49] Taylor, Bayard. *The Echo club, And Other Literary Diversions*. Boston, J. R. Osgood and Company, 1876.

[A.11]

EMERSON'S LETTER.

Ralph Waldo Emerson's Letter to Walt Whitman, as reprinted in *Leaves of Grass*, without permission from Emerson:

CONCORD. MASSACHUSETTS, 21 July, 1855.

DEAR SIR—

I am not blind to the worth of the wonderful gift of "LEAVES OF GRASS." I find it the most extraordinary piece of wit and wisdom that America has yet contributed. I am very happy in reading it, as great power makes us happy. It meets the demand I am always making of what seemed the sterile and stingy nature, as if too much handiwork, or too much lymph in the temperament, were making our western wits fat and mean.

I give you joy of your free and brave thought. I have great joy in it. I find incomparable things said incomparably well, as they must be. I find the courage of treatment which so delights us, and which large perception only can inspire.

I greet you at the beginning of a great career, which yet must have had a long foreground somewhere, for such a start. I rubbed my eyes a little, to see if this sunbeam were no illusion; but the solid sense of the book is a sober certainty. It has the best merits, namely, of fortifying and encouraging. I did not know until I last night saw the book advertised in a newspaper that I could trust the name as real and available for a post-office. I wish to see my benefactor, and have felt much like striking my tasks and visiting New York to pay you my respects.

R. W. EMERSON.

[14] Folsom, Ed and Kenneth M. Price, editors. *The Walt Whitman Archive*. University of Nebraska–Lincoln, 2017, http://whitmanarchive.org/. Accessed 26 February, 2017.

[A.12]

WALT WHITMAN AND HIS POEMS.

Walt Whitman [unsigned in original]
United States Review,
September 1855, p. 205-12.

AN American bard at last! One of the roughs, large, proud, affectionate, eating, drinking, and breeding, his costume manly and free, his face sunburnt and bearded, his posture strong and erect, his voice bringing hope and prophecy to the generous races of young and old. We shall cease shamming and be what we really are. We shall start an athletic and defiant literature. We realize now how it is, and what was most lacking. The interior American republic shall also be declared free and independent.

For all our intellectual people, followed by their books, poems, novels, essays, editorials, lectures, tuitions, and criticism, dress by London and Paris modes, receive what is received there, obey the authorities, settle disputes by the old tests, keep out of rain and sun, retreat to the shelter of houses and schools, trim their hair, shave, touch not the earth barefoot, and enter not the sea except in a complete bathing-dress. One sees unmistakably genteel persons, travelled, college-learned, used to be served by servants, conversing without heat or vulgarity, supported on chairs, or walking through handsomely-carpeted parlors, or along shelves bearing well-bound volumes, and walls adorned with curtained and collared portraits, and china things, and nick-nacks. But where in American literature is the first show of America? Where are the gristle and beards, and broad breasts, and space and ruggedness and nonchalance that the souls of the people love? Where is the tremendous outdoors of these States? Where is the majesty of the federal mother, seated with more than antique grace, calm, just, indulgent to her brood of children, calling them around her regarding the little and the large and the younger and the older with perfect impartiality? Where is the vehement growth of our cities? Where is the spirit of the strong rich life of the American mechanic, farmer, sailor, hunter, and miner? Where is the huge composite of all other nations, cast in a fresher and brawnier matrix, passing adolescence, and needed this day, live and arrogant, to lead the marches of the world?

Self-reliant, with haughty eyes, assuming to himself all the attributes of his country, steps Walt Whitman into literature, talking like a man unaware that there was ever hitherto such a production as a book, or such a being as a writer. Every move of him has the free play of the muscle of one who never knew what it was to feel that he stood in the presence of a superior. Every word that falls from his mouth shows silent disdain and defiance of the old theories and forms. Every phrase announces new laws; not once do his lips unclose except in conformity with them. With light and rapid touch he first indicates in prose the principles of the foundation of a race of poets so deeply to spring from the American people, and become ingrained through them, that their Presidents shall not be the common referees so much as that great race of poets shall. He proceeds himself to exemplify this new school, and set models for their expression and range of subjects. He makes audacious and native use of his own body and soul. He must re-create poetry with the elements always at hand. He must imbue it with himself as he is, disorderly, fleshy, and sensual, a lover of things, yet a lover of men and women above the whole of the other objects of the universe. His work is to be achieved by unusual methods. Neither classic or romantic is he, nor a materialist any more than a spiritualist. Not a whisper comes out of him of the old stock talk and rhyme of poetry—not the first recognition of gods or goddesses, or Greece or Rome. No breath of Europe, or her monarchies, or priestly conventions, or her notions of gentlemen and ladies founded on the idea of caste, seems ever to have fanned his face or been inhaled into his lungs. But in their stead pour vast and fluid the fresh mentality of this mighty age, and the realities of this mighty continent, and the sciences and inventions and discoveries of the present world. Not geology, nor mathematics, nor chemistry, nor navigation, nor astronomy, nor anatomy, nor physiology, nor engineering, is more true to itself than Walt Whitman is true to them. They and the other sciences underlie his whole superstructure. In the beauty of the work of the poet, he affirms, are the tuft and final applause of science.

Affairs then are this man's poems. He will still inject nature through civilization. The movement of his verses is the sweeping movement of great currents of living people, with a general government, and state and municipal governments, courts, commerce, manufactures, arsenals, steamships, railroads, telegraphs, cities with paved streets, and aqueducts, and police and gas—myriads of travellers arriving and departing—newspapers, music, elections and all the features and processes of the nineteenth century in the wholesomest race and the only stable form of politics at present upon the earth. Along his words spread the broad impartialities of the United States. No innovations must be permitted on the stern severities of our liberty and equality. Undecked also is this poet with sentimentalism, or jingle, or nice conceits or flowery similes. He appears in his poems surrounded by women and children, and by young men, and by common objects and qualities. He gives to each just what belongs to it, neither more or less. The person nearest him, that person he ushers hand in hand with himself. Duly take places in his flowing procession, and step to the sounds of the newer and larger music, the essences of American things, and past and present events—the enormous diversity of temperature and agriculture and mines—the tribes of red aborigines—the weather-beaten vessels entering new ports, or making landings on rocky coasts—the first settlements north and south—the rapid stature and impatience of outside control—the sturdy defiance of '76, and the war and peace, and the leadership of Washington, and the formation of the Constitution—the Union always calm and impregnable—the perpetual coming of immigrants—the wharf-hemmed cities and superior marine—the unsurveyed interior— the log-house, and clearings, and wild animals, and hunters, and trappers—the fisheries, and whaling, and gold-digging—the endless gestation of new states—the convening of Congress every December, the members coming up from all climates, and from the utter-most parts—the noble character of the free American workman and workwoman—the fierceness of the people when well-roused—the ardor of their friendships—the large amativeness— the Yankee swap—the New York fireman, and the target excursion—the southern plantation life—the character of the north-east, and of the north-west and south-west—and the character of America and the American people everywhere. For these the old usages of poets afford Walt Whitman no means sufficiently fit and free, and he rejects the old usages. The style of the bard that is waited for is to be transcendent and new. It is to be indirect and not direct or descriptive or epic. Its quality is to go through these to much more. Let the age and wars (he says) of other nations be chanted, and their eras and characters be illustrated, and that finish the verse. Not so (he continues) the great psalm of the republic. Here the theme is creative and has vista. Here comes one among the well-beloved stonecutters, and announces himself, and plans with decision and science, and sees the solid and beautiful forms of the future where there are now no solid forms.

The style of these poems, therefore, is simply their own style, new-born and red. Nature may have given the hint to the author of the "Leaves of Grass", but there exists no book or fragment of a book, which can have given the hint to them. All beauty, he says, comes from beautiful blood and a beautiful brain. His rhythm and uniformity he will conceal in the roots of his verses, not to be seen of themselves, but to break forth loosely as lilies on a bush, and take shapes compact as the shapes of melons, or chestnuts, or pears.

The poems of the "Leaves of Grass" are twelve in number. Walt Whitman at first proceeds to put his own body and soul into the new versification:

"I celebrate myself,
And what I assume you shall assume,
For every atom belonging to me, as good
        belongs to you."

He leaves houses and their shuttered rooms, for the open air. He drops disguise and ceremony, and walks forth with the confidence and gayety of a child. For the old decorums of writing he substitutes new decorums. The first glance out of his eyes electrifies him with love and delight. He will have the earth receive and return his affection; he will stay with it as the bride-groom stays with the bride. The cool-breathed ground, the slumbering and liquid trees, the just-gone sunset, the vitreous pour of the full moon, the tender and growing night, he salutes and touches, and they touch him. The sea supports him, and hurries him off with its powerful and crooked fingers. Dash me with amorous wet! then he says, I can repay you.

By this writer the rules of polite circles are dismissed with scorn. Your stale modesties, he says, are filthy to such a man as I.

"I believe in the flesh and the appetites,
Seeing, hearing, and feeling are miracles, and
        each part and tag of me is a miracle.
I do not press my finger across my mouth,
I keep as delicate around the bowels as around
        the head and heart."

No sniveller, or tea-drinking poet, no puny clawback or prude, is Walt Whitman. He will bring poems fit to fill the days and nights—fit for men and women with the attributes of throbbing blood and flesh. The body, he teaches, is beautiful. Sex is also beautiful. Are you to be put down, he seems to ask, to that shallow level of literature and conversation that stops a man's recognizing the delicious pleasure of his sex, or a woman hers? Nature he proclaims inherently pure. Sex will not be put aside; it is a great ordination of the universe. He works the muscle of the male and the teeming fibre of the female throughout his writings, as wholesome realities, impure only by deliberate intention and effort. To men and women he says: You can have healthy and powerful breeds of children on no less terms than these of mine. Follow me and there shall be taller and nobler crops of humanity on the earth.

In the "Leaves of Grass" are the facts of eternity and immortality, largely treated. Happiness is no dream, and perfection is no dream. Amelioration is my lesson, he says with calm voice, and progress is my lesson and the lesson of all things. Then his persuasion becomes a taunt, and his love bitter and compulsory. With strong and steady call he addresses men. Come, he seems to say, from the midst of all that you have been your whole life surrounding yourself with. Leave all the preaching and teaching of others, and mind only these words of mine.

"Long enough have you dreamed contemptible
        dreams,
Now I wash the gum from your eyes,
You must habit yourself to the dazzle of the
        light and of every moment of your life.

Long have you timidly waded, holding a plank
    by the shore,
Now I will you to be a bold swimmer,
To jump off in the midst of the sea, and rise
    again and nod to me and shout, and
    laughingly dash with your hair.
I am the teacher of athletes,
He that by me spreads a wider breast than my
    own proves the width of my own,
He most honors my style who learns under it
    to destroy the teacher.
The boy I love, the same becomes a man not
    through derived power but in his own
    right,
Wicked, rather than virtuous out of
    conformity or fear,
Fond of his sweetheart, relishing well his
    steak,
Unrequited love or a slight cutting him worse
    than a wound cuts,
First rate to ride, to fight, to hit the bull's eye,
    to sail a skiff; to sing or play on the banjo,
Preferring scars and faces pitted with small-
    pox over all latherers and those that keep
    out of the sun.

I teach straying from me, yet who can stray
    from me?
I follow you whoever you are from the
    present hour;
My words itch at your ears till you
    understand them.
I do not say these things for a dollar, or to fill
    up the time while I wait for a boat;
It is you talking just as much as myself—I act
    as the tongue of you.
It was tied in your mouth—in mine it begins
    to be loosened.

I swear I will never mention love or death
    inside a house,
And I swear I never will translate myself at
    all, only to him or her who privately stays
    with me in the open air."

The eleven other poems have each distinct purposes, curiously veiled. Theirs is no writer to be gone through with in a day or a month. Rather it is his pleasure to elude you and provoke you for deliberate purposes of his own.

Doubtless in the scheme this man has built for himself the writing of poems is but a proportionate part of the whole. It is plain that public and private performance, politics, love, friendship, behavior, the art of conversation, science, society, the American people, the reception of the great novelties of city and country, all have their equal call upon him and receive equal attention. In politics he could enter with the freedom and reality he shows in poetry. His scope of life is the amplest of any yet in philosophy. He is the true spiritualist. He recognizes no annihilation, or death, or loss of identity. He is the largest lover and sympathizer that has appeared in literature. He loves the earth and sun, and the animals. He does not separate the learned from the unlearned, the Northerner from the Southerner, the white from the black, or the native from the immigrant just landed at the wharf. Every one, he seems to say, appears excellent to me, every employment is adorned, and every male and female glorious.

    "The press of my foot to the earth springs
        a hundred affections,
    They scorn the best I can do to relate them.

    I am enamored of growing out-doors,
    Of men that live among cattle or taste of the
        ocean or woods,
    Of the builders and steerers of ships, of the
        wielders of axes and mauls, of the drivers
        of horses,
    I can eat and sleep with them, week in and
        week out.

    What is commonest and cheapest and
        nearest and easiest is Me,
    Me going in for my chances, spending for vast
        returns,
    Adorning myself to bestow myself on the
        first that will take me,
    Not asking the sky to come down to my good
        will,
    Scattering it freely for ever."

If health were not his distinguishing attribute, this poet would be the very harlot of persons. Right and left he flings his arms, drawing men and women with undeniable love to his close embrace, loving the clasp of their hands, the touch of their necks and breasts, and the sound of their voice. All else seems to burn up under his fierce affection for persons. Politics, religion, institutions, art, quickly fall aside before them. In the whole universe, he says, I see nothing more divine than human souls.

"When the psalm sings instead of singer,
When the script preaches instead of the
    preacher,
When the pulpit descends and goes instead
    of the carver that carved the supporting
    desk,
When the sacred vessels or the bits of
    the eucharist, or the lath and plast,
    procreate as effectually as the young
    silversmiths or bakers, or the masons in
    their overalls,
When a university course convinces like a
    slumbering woman and child convince,
When the minted gold in the vault smiles like
    the night-watchman's daughter,
When warrantee deeds loafe in chairs
    opposite, and are my friendly companions,
I intend to reach them my hand and make
    as much of them as I make of men and
    Women."

Who then is that insolent unknown? Who is it, praising himself as if others were not fit to do it, and coming rough and unbidden among writers to unsettle what was settled, and to revolutionize, in fact, our modern civilization? Walt Whitman was born on Long-Island, on the hills about thirty miles from the greatest American city, on the last day of May, 1819, and has grown up in Brooklyn and New York to be thirty-six years old, to enjoy perfect health, and to understand his country and its spirit.

Interrogations more than this, and that will not be put off unanswered, spring continually through the perusal of these Leaves of Grass:

If there were to be selected, out of the incalculable volumes of printed matter in existence, any single work to stand for America and her times, should this be the work?

Must not the true American poet indeed absorb all others, and present a new and far more ample and vigorous type?

Has not the time arrived for a school of live writing and tuition consistent with the principles of these poems? consistent with the free spirit of this age, and with the American truths of politics? consistent with geology, and astronomy, and all science and human physiology? consistent with the sublimity of immortality and the directness of common-sense?

If in this poem the United States have found their poetic voice, and taken measure and form, is it any more than a beginning? Walt Whitman himself disclaims singularity in his work, and announces the coming after him of great successions of poets, and that he but lifts his finger to give the signal.

Was he not needed? Has not literature been bred in and in long enough? Has it not become unbearably artificial?

Shall a man of faith and practice in the simplicity of real things be called eccentric, while the disciple of the fictitious school writes without question?

Shall it still be the amazement of the light and dark that freshness of expression is the rarest quality of all?

You have come in good time, Walt Whitman! In opinions, in manners, in costumes, in books, in the aims and occupancy of life, in associates, in poems, conformity to all unnatural and tainted customs passes without remark, while perfect naturalness, health, faith, self-reliance, and all primal expressions of the manliest love and friendship, subject one to the stare and controversy of the world.

[14]Folsom, Ed and Kenneth M. Price, editors. The Walt Whitman Archive. University of Nebraska–Lincoln, 2017, http://whitmanarchive.org/. Accessed 26 February, 2017.

[A.13]

A13

1—POEM OF WALT WHITMAN, AN AMERICAN.

I celebrate myself,
And what I assume you shall assume,
For every atom belonging to me, as good belongs to
    you.

I loafe and invite my soul,
I lean and loafe at my ease, observing a spear of
    summer grass.

Houses and rooms are full of perfumes—the shelves
    are crowded with perfumes,
I breathe the fragrance myself, and know it and like it,
The distillation would intoxicate me also, but I shall
    not let it.

The atmosphere is not a perfume, it has no taste of
    the distillation, it is odorless,
It is for my mouth forever, I am in love with it,
I will go to the bank by the wood, and become
    undisguised and naked,
I am mad for it to be in contact with me.

The smoke of my own breath,
Echoes, ripples, buzzed whispers, love-root, silk-
    thread, crotch, vine,
My respiration and inspiration, the beating of my
    heart, the passing of blood and air
    through my lungs,
The sniff of green leaves and dry leaves, and of the
    shore and dark-colored sea-rocks, and of
    hay in the barn,
The sound of the belched words of my voice, words
    loosed to the eddies of the wind,
A few light kisses, a few embraces, a reaching around
    of arms,
The play of shine and shade on the trees as the supple
    boughs wag,
The delight alone, or in the rush of the streets, or
    along the fields and hill-sides,
The feeling of health, the full-noon trill, the song of
    me rising from bed and meeting the sun.

Have you reckoned a thousand acres much? have you
    reckoned the earth much?
Have you practiced so long to learn to read?
Have you felt so proud to get at the meaning of poems?

Stop this day and night with me, and you shall
    possess the origin of all poems,
You shall possess the good of the earth and sun—
    there are millions of suns left,
You shall no longer take things at second or third
    hand, nor look through the eyes of the
    dead, nor feed on the spectres in books,

You shall not look through my eyes either, nor take
    things from me,
You shall listen to all sides, and filter them from
    yourself.

I have heard what the talkers were talking, the talk of
    the beginning and the end,
But I do not talk of the beginning or the end.

There was never any more inception than there is
    now,
Nor any more youth or age than there is now,
And will never be any more perfection than there is now,
Nor any more heaven or hell than there is now.

Urge, and urge, and urge,
Always the procreant urge of the world.

Out of the dimness opposite equals advance—always
    substance and increase, always sex,
Always a knit of identity, always distinction, always a
    breed of life.
To elaborate is no avail—learned and unlearned feel
    that it is so.

Sure as the most certain sure, plumb in the uprights,
    well entretied, braced in the beams,
Stout as a horse, affectionate, haughty, electrical,
I and this mystery here we stand.

Clear and sweet is my soul, and clear and sweet is all
    that is not my soul.

Lack one lacks both, and the unseen is proved by the
    seen,
Till that becomes unseen, and receives proof in its
    turn.

Showing the best and dividing it from the worst, age
    vexes age,
Knowing the perfect fitness and equanimity of things,
    while they discuss I am silent, and go
    bathe and admire myself.

Welcome is every organ and attribute of me, and of
    any man hearty and clean,
Not an inch nor a particle of an inch is vile, and none
    shall be less familiar than the rest.

I am satisfied—I see, dance, laugh, sing;
As the hugging and loving Bed-fellow sleeps at my
    side through the night, and withdraws at
    the peep of the day,
And leaves for me baskets covered with white towels,
    swelling the house with their plenty,
Shall I postpone my acceptation and realization, and
    scream at my eyes,
That they turn from gazing after and down the road,
And forthwith cipher and show me to a cent,
Exactly the contents of one, and exactly the contents
    of two, and which is ahead?

Trippers and askers surround me,
People I meet—the effect upon me of my early life, of
    the ward and city I live in, of the nation,
The latest news, discoveries, inventions, societies,
    authors old and new,
My dinner, dress, associates, looks, work,
    compliments, dues,
The real or fancied indifference of some man or
    woman I love,
The sickness of one of my folks, or of myself, or
    ill-doing, or loss or lack of money, or
    depressions or exaltations,
They come to me days and nights and go from me
    again,
But they are not the Me myself.

Apart from the pulling and hauling stands what I am,
Stands amused, complacent, compassionating, idle,
    unitary,
Looks down, is erect, bends an arm on an impalpable
    certain rest,
Looks with its side-curved head, curious what will
    come next,
Both in and out of the game, and watching and
    wondering at it.

Backward I see in my own days where I sweated
    through fog with linguists and
    contenders,
I have no mockings or arguments—I witness and
    wait.

I believe in you, my soul—the other I am must not
    abase itself to you,
And you must not be abased to the other.

Loafe with me on the grass, loose the stop from your
    throat,
Not words, not music or rhyme I want—not custom
    or lecture, not even the best,
Only the lull I like, the hum of your valved voice.

I mind how we lay in June, such a transparent
    summer morning,
You settled your head athwart my hips, and gently
    turned over upon me,
And parted the shirt from my bosom-bone, and
    plunged your tongue to my bare-stript
    heart,
And reached till you felt my beard, and reached till
    you held my feet.

Swiftly arose and spread around me the peace and joy
    and knowledge that pass all the art and
    argument of the earth,
And I know that the hand of God is the promise of
    my own,
And I know that the spirit of God is the brother of
    my own,
And that all the men ever born are also my brothers,
    and the women my sisters and lovers,
And that a kelson of the creation is love,
And limitless are leaves, stiff or drooping in the fields,
And brown ants in the little wells beneath them,
And mossy scabs of the worm-fence, heaped stones,
    elder, mullen, pokeweed.

A child said, What is the grass? fetching it to me with
    full hands;
How could I answer the child? I do not know what it
    is any more than he.

I guess it must be the flag of my disposition, out of
    hopeful green stuff woven.

Or I guess it is the handkerchief of the Lord,
A scented gift and remembrancer, designedly
    dropped,
Bearing the owner's name someway in the corners,
    that we may see and remark, and say
    Whose?

Or I guess the grass is itself a child, the produced babe
    of the vegetation.

Or I guess it is a uniform hieroglyphic,
And it means, Sprouting alike in broad zones and
    narrow zones,
Growing among black folks as among white,
Kanuck, Tuckahoe, Congressman, Cuff, I give them
    the same, I receive them the same.

And now it seems to me the beautiful uncut hair of graves.

Tenderly will I use you, curling grass,
It may be you transpire from the breasts of young
    men,
It may be if I had known them I would have loved
    them,

It may be you are from old people, and from women,
    and from offspring taken soon out of
    their mothers' laps,
And here you are the mothers' laps.

This grass is very dark to be from the white heads of
    old mothers,
Darker than the colorless beards of old men,
Dark to come from under the faint red roofs of
    mouths.

O I perceive after all so many uttering tongues!
And I perceive they do not come from the roofs of
    mouths for nothing.

I wish I could translate the hints about the dead
    young men and women,
And the hints about old men and mothers, and the
    offspring taken soon out of their laps.

What do you think has become of the young and
    old men?
And what do you think has become of the women
    and children?

They are alive and well somewhere,
The smallest sprout shows there is really no death,
And if ever there was, it led forward life, and does not
    wait at the end to arrest it,
And ceased the moment life appeared.

All goes onward and outward—nothing collapses,
And to die is different from what any one supposed,
    and luckier.

Has any one supposed it lucky to be born?
I hasten to inform him or her, it is just as lucky to die,
    and I know it.

I pass death with the dying, and birth with the
    new-washed babe, and am not contained
    between my hat and boots,
And peruse manifold objects, no two alike, and every
    one good,
The earth good, and the stars good, and their adjuncts
    all good.

I am not an earth nor an adjunct of an earth,
I am the mate and companion of people, all just as
    immortal and fathomless as myself;
They do not know how immortal, but I know.

Every kind for itself and its own—for me mine, male
    and female,
For me those that have been boys and that love
    women,
For me the man that is proud, and feels how it stings
    to be slighted,
For me the sweetheart and the old maid—for me
    mothers and the mothers of mothers,
For me lips that have smiled, eyes that have shed
    tears,
For me children and the begetters of children.
Who need be afraid of the merge?
Undrape! you are not guilty to me, nor stale, nor
    discarded,
I see through the broadcloth and gingham, whether
    or no,
And am around, tenacious, acquisitive, tireless, and
    can never be shaken away.

The little one sleeps in its cradle,
I lift the gauze and look a long time, and silently brush
    away flies with my hand.

The youngster and the red-faced girl turn aside up the
    bushy hill,
I peeringly view them from the top.

The suicide sprawls on the bloody floor of the
    bedroom,
It is so—I witnessed the corpse—there the pistol had
    fallen.

The blab of the pave, the tires of carts, sluff of boot-
    soles, talk of the promenaders,
The heavy omnibus, the driver with his interrogat-ing
    thumb, the clank of the shod horses on
    the granite floor,
The snow-sleighs, the clinking, shouted jokes, pelts of
    snow-balls,
The hurrahs for popular favorites, the fury of roused
    mobs,
The flap of the curtained litter, the sick man in-side,
    borne to the hospital,
The meeting of enemies, the sudden oath, the blows
    and fall,
The excited crowd, the policeman with his star,
    quickly working his passage to the centre
    of the crowd,
The impassive stones that receive and return so many
    echoes,
The souls moving along—are they invisible, while the
    least of the stones is visible?
What groans of over-fed or half-starved who fall sun-
    struck, or in fits,
What exclamations of women taken suddenly, who
    hurry home and give birth to babes,
What living and buried speech is always vibrating
    here, what howls restrained by decorum,
Arrests of criminals, slights, adulterous offers made,
    acceptances, rejections with convex lips,
I mind them or the resonance of them—I come and
    I depart.

The big doors of the country-barn stand open and
    ready,
The dried grass of the harvest-time loads the slow-
    drawn wagon,
The clear light plays on the brown gray and green
    intertinged,
The armfuls are packed to the sagging mow;
I am there, I help, I came stretched atop of the load,
I felt its soft jolts, one leg reclined on the other;
I jump from the cross-beams and seize the clover and
    timothy,
And roll head over heels, and tangle my hair full of
    wisps.

Alone, far in the wilds and mountains, I hunt,
Wandering, amazed at my own lightness and glee,
In the late afternoon choosing a safe spot to pass the
    night,

Kindling a fire and broiling the fresh-killed game,
Soundly falling asleep on the gathered leaves, my dog
    and gun by my side.

The Yankee clipper is under her three sky-sails, she
    cuts the sparkle and scud,
My eyes settle the land—I bend at her prow or shout
    joyously from the deck.

The boatmen and clam-diggers arose early and
    stopped for me,
I tucked my trowser-ends in my boots and went and
    had a good time,
You should have been with us that day round the
    chowder-kettle.

I saw the marriage of the trapper in the open air
    in the far-west—the bride was a red girl,
    Her father and his friends sat near, cross-
    legged and dumbly smoking—they had
    moccasins to their feet and large thick
    blankets hanging from their shoulders,
On a bank lounged the trapper, he was dressed mostly
    in skins, his luxuriant beard and curls
    protected his neck,
One hand rested on his rifle, the other hand held
    firmly the wrist of the red girl,
She had long eyelashes, her head was bare, her
    coarse straight locks descended upon her
    voluptuous limbs and reached to her feet.

The runaway slave came to my house and stopped
    outside,
I heard his motions crackling the twigs of the wood-
    pile,
Through the swung half-door of the kitchen I saw
    him limpsy and weak,
And went where he sat on a log, and led him in and
    assured him,
And brought water and filled a tub for his sweated
    body and bruised feet,
And gave him a room that entered from my own, and
    gave him some coarse clean clothes,
And remember perfectly well his revolving eyes and
    his awkwardness,
And remember putting plasters on the galls of his
    neck and ankles;
He staid with me a week before he was recuperated
    and passed north,

I had him sit next me at table—my fire-lock leaned in
    the corner.

Twenty-eight young men bathe by the shore,
Twenty-eight young men, and all so friendly,
Twenty-eight years of womanly life, and all so lonesome.

She owns the fine house by the rise of the bank,
She hides, handsome and richly drest, aft the blinds of
    the window.

Which of the young men does she like the best?
Ah, the homeliest of them is beautiful to her.

Where are you off to, lady? for I see you,
You splash in the water there, yet stay stock still in
    your room.

Dancing and laughing along the beach came the
    twenty-ninth bather,
The rest did not see her, but she saw them and loved
    them.

The beards of the young men glistened with wet, it
    ran from their long hair,
Little streams passed all over their bodies.

An unseen hand also passed over their bodies,
It descended tremblingly from their temples and ribs.

The young men float on their backs, their white bellies
    bulge to the sun, they do not ask who
    seizes fast to them,
They do not know who puffs and declines with
    pendant and bending arch,
They do not think whom they souse with spray.

The butcher-boy puts off his killing-clothes, or
    sharpens his knife at the stall in the
    market,
I loiter, enjoying his repartee and his shuffle and
    break-down.

Blacksmiths with grimed and hairy chests environ the
    anvil,
Each has his main-sledge—they are all out—there is
    a great heat in the fire.

From the cinder-strewed threshold I follow their
    movements,
The lithe sheer of their waists plays even with their
    massive arms,
Overhand the hammers roll, overhand so slow,
    overhand so sure,
They do not hasten, each man hits in his place.

The negro holds firmly the reins of his four horses,
    the block swags underneath on its tied-
    over chain,

The negro that drives the huge dray of the stone-yard,
    steady and tall he stands poised on one
    leg on the string-piece,
His blue shirt exposes his ample neck and breast, and
    loosens over his hip-band,
His glance is calm and commanding, he tosses the
    slouch of his hat away from his forehead,
The sun falls on his crispy hair and moustache, falls on
    the black of his polish'd and perfect limbs.

I behold the picturesque giant and love him, and I do
    not stop there,
I go with the team also.

In me the caresser of life wherever moving, backward
    as well as forward slueing,
To niches aside and junior bending.

Oxen that rattle the yoke or halt in the shade! what is
    that you express in your eyes?
It seems to me more than all the print I have read in
    my life.

My tread scares the wood-drake and wood-duck, on
    my distant and day-long ramble,
They rise together, they slowly circle around;
I believe in those winged purposes,
And acknowledge, red, yellow, white, playing within
    me,
And consider green and violet, and the tufted crown,
    intentional,
And do not call the tortoise unworthy because she is
    not something else,
And the mocking-bird in the swamp never studied
    the gamut, yet trills pretty well to me,
And the look of the bay mare shames silliness out of me.

The wild gander leads his flock through the cool
night,
Ya-honk! he says, and sounds it down to me like an
invitation;
The pert may suppose it meaningless, but I listen
close,
I find its purpose and place up there toward the
November sky.

The sharp-hoofed moose of the north, the cat on the
house-sill, the chickadee, the prairie-dog,
The litter of the grunting sow as they tug at her teats,
The brood of the turkey-hen, and she with her half-
spread wings,
I see in them and myself the same old law.

The press of my foot to the earth springs a hun-dred
affections,
They scorn the best I can do to relate them.

I am enamoured of growing outdoors,
Of men that live among cattle, or taste of the ocean or
woods,
Of the builders and steerers of ships, of the wielders
of axes and mauls, of the drivers of horses,
I can eat and sleep with them week in and week out.

What is commonest, cheapest, nearest, easiest, is Me,
Me going in for my chances, spending for vast returns,
Adorning myself to bestow myself on the first that
will take me,
Not asking the sky to come down to my good-will,
Scattering it freely forever.

The pure contralto sings in the organ-loft,
The carpenter dresses his plank, the tongue of his
foreplane whistles its wild ascending lisp,
The married and unmarried children ride home to
their thanksgiving dinner,
The pilot seizes the king-pin, he heaves down with a
strong arm,
The mate stands braced in the whale-boat, lance and
harpoon are ready,
The duck-shooter walks by silent and cautious
stretches,
The deacons are ordained with crossed hands at the altar,
The spinning-girl retreats and advances to the hum of
the big wheel,

The farmer stops by the bars of a Sunday and looks at
the oats and rye,
The lunatic is carried at last to the asylum, a
confirmed case,
He will never sleep any more as he did in the cot in
his mother's bedroom;
The jour printer with gray head and gaunt jaws works
at his case,

He turns his quid of tobacco, his eyes get blurred with
the manuscript;
The malformed limbs are tied to the anatomist's table,
What is removed drops horribly in a pail;
The quadroon girl is sold at the stand—the drunkard
nods by the bar-room stove,
The machinist rolls up his sleeves—the policeman
travels his beat—the gate-keeper marks
who pass,
The young fellow drives the express-wagon—I love
him though I do not know him,
The half-breed straps on his light boots to compete in
the race,
The western turkey-shooting draws old and young—
some lean on their rifles, some sit on logs,
Out from the crowd steps the marksman, takes his
position, levels his piece;
The groups of newly-come immigrants cover the
wharf or levee,
The woolly-pates hoe in the sugar-field, the overseer
views them from his saddle,
The bugle calls in the ball-room, the gentlemen run
for their partners, the dancers bow to each
other,
The youth lies awake in the cedar-roofed garret, and
harks to the musical rain,
The Wolverine sets traps on the creek that helps fill
the Huron,
The reformer ascends the platform, he spouts with his
mouth and nose,
The company returns from its excursion, the darkey
brings up the rear and bears the well-
riddled target,
The squaw, wrapt in her yellow-hemmed cloth, is
offering moccasins and bead-bags for sale,
The connoisseur peers along the exhibition-gallery
with half-shut eyes bent side-ways,
The deck-hands make fast the steamboat, the plank is
thrown for the shore-going passengers,
The young sister holds out the skein, the elder sister

winds it off in a ball, and stops now and
then for the knots,

The one-year wife is recovering and happy, a week ago
she bore her first child,

The clean-haired Yankee girl works with her sewing-
machine, or in the factory or mill,

The nine months' gone is in the parturition chamber,
her faintness and pains are advancing,

The paving-man leans on his two-handed rammer—
the reporter's lead flies swiftly over the
note-book—the sign-painter is lettering
with red and gold,

The canal-boy trots on the tow-path—the book-
keeper counts at his desk—the
shoemaker waxes his thread,

The conductor beats time for the band, and all the
performers follow him,

The child is baptised—the convert is making the first
professions,

The regatta is spread on the bay—how the white sails
sparkle!

The drover watches his drove, he sings out to them
that would stray,

The pedlar sweats with his pack on his back, the
purchaser higgles about the odd cent,

The camera and plate are prepared, the lady must sit
for her daguerreotype,

The bride unrumples her white dress, the minute-
hand of the clock moves slowly,

The opium-eater reclines with rigid head and just-
opened lips,

The prostitute draggles her shawl, her bonnet bobs on
her tipsy and pimpled neck,

The crowd laugh at her blackguard oaths, the men
jeer and wink to each other,

(Miserable! I do not laugh at your oaths, nor jeer you;)

The President holds a cabinet council, he is
surrounded by the Great Secretaries,

On the piazza walk five friendly matrons with twined
arms,

The crew of the fish-smack pack repeated layers of
halibut in the hold,

The Missourian crosses the plains, toting his wares
and his cattle,

The fare-collector goes through the train, he gives
notice by the jingling of loose change,

The floor-men are laying the floor—the tinners are
tinning the roof—the masons are calling
for mortar,

In single file, each shouldering his hod, pass onward
the laborers,

Seasons pursuing each other, the indescribable crowd
is gathered—it is the Fourth of July—
what salutes of cannon and small arms!

Seasons pursuing each other, the plougher ploughs,
the mower mows, and the winter-grain
falls in the ground,

Off on the lakes the pike-fisher watches and waits by
the hole in the frozen surface,

The stumps stand thick round the clearing, the
squatter strikes deep with his axe,

Flatboatmen make fast toward dusk near the cotton-
wood or pekan-trees,

Coon-seekers go through the regions of the Red
river, or through those drained by the
Tennessee, or through those of the
Arkansaw,

Torches shine in the dark that hangs on the
Chattahoochee or Altamahaw,

Patriarchs sit at supper with sons and grandsons and
great-grandsons around them,

In walls of adobe, in canvass tents, rest hunters and
trappers after their day's sport,

The city sleeps and the country sleeps,

The living sleep for their time, the dead sleep for their
time,

The old husband sleeps by his wife, and the young
husband sleeps by his wife;

And these one and all tend inward to me, and I tend
outward to them,

And such as it is to be of these, more or less, I am.

I am of old and young, of the foolish as much as the
wise,

Regardless of others, ever regardful of others,

Maternal as well as paternal, a child as well as a man,

Stuffed with the stuff that is coarse, and stuffed with
the stuff that is fine,

One of the great nation, the nation of many nations,
the smallest the same, the largest the
same,

A southerner soon as a northerner, a planter
nonchalant and hospitable,

A Yankee bound my own way, ready for trade, my
joints the limberest joints on earth and
the sternest joints on earth,

A Kentuckian walking the vale of the Elkhorn in my
deer-skin leggings,

A boatman over lakes or bays, or along coasts—a
 Hoosier, Badger, Buckeye,
A Louisianian or Georgian, a Poke-easy from sand-
 hills and pines,
At home on Canadian snow-shoes, or up in the bush,
 or with fishermen off Newfoundland,
At home in the fleet of ice-boats, sailing with the rest,
 and tacking,
At home on the hills of Vermont, or in the woods of
 Maine, or the Texan ranch,
Comrade of Californians, comrade of free north-
 westerners, loving their big proportions.
Comrade of raftsmen and coalmen, comrade of all
 who shake hands and welcome to drink
 and meat,
A learner with the simplest, a teacher of the
 thoughtfulest,
A novice beginning, experient of myriads of sea-sons,
Of every hue, trade, rank, of every caste and religion,
Not merely of the New World, but of Africa, Europe,
 Asia—a wandering savage,
A farmer, mechanic, artist, gentleman, sailor, lover, quaker,
A prisoner, fancy-man, rowdy, lawyer, physician, priest.

I resist anything better than my own diversity,
And breathe the air, and leave plenty after me,
And am not stuck up, and am in my place.

The moth and the fish-eggs are in their place,
The suns I see, and the suns I cannot see, are in their
 place,
The palpable is in its place, and the impalpable is in
 its place.

These are the thoughts of all men in all ages and
 lands, they are not original with me,
If they are not yours as much as mine, they are
 nothing, or next to nothing,
If they do not enclose everything, they are next to
 nothing,
If they are not the riddle and the untying of the riddle,
 they are nothing,
If they are not just as close as they are distant, they are
 nothing.

This is the grass that grows wherever the land is and
 the water is,
This is the common air that bathes the globe.

This is the breath of laws, songs, behaviour,
This is the tasteless water of souls, this is the true
 sustenance,
It is for the illiterate, it is for the judges of the supreme
 court, it is for the federal capitol and the
 state capitols,
It is for the admirable communes of literats,
 composers, singers, lecturers, engineers,
 savans,
It is for the endless races of work-people, farmers,
 seamen.

These are trills of thousands of clear cornets, screams
 of octave flutes, strike of triangles.

I play not a march for victors only, I play great
 marches for conquered and slain persons.

Have you heard that it was good to gain the day?
I also say it is good to fall—battles are lost in the same
 spirit in which they are won.

I beat triumphal drums for the dead, I blow through
 my embouchures my loudest and gayest
 music to them.
Vivas to those who have failed! and to those whose
 war-vessels sank in the sea! and those
 themselves who sank in the sea!
And to all generals that lost engagements! and all
 overcome heroes! and the numberless
 unknown heroes, equal to the greatest
 heroes known!

This is the meal pleasantly set, this is the meat and
 drink for natural hunger,
It is for the wicked just the same as the righteous—I
 make appointments with all,
I will not have a single person slighted or left away,
The kept-woman, sponger, thief, are hereby invited—
 the heavy-lipped slave is invited, the
 venerealee is invited,
There shall be no difference between them and the rest.

This is the press of a bashful hand, this is the float and
 odor of hair,
This is the touch of my lips to yours, this is the
 murmur of yearning,
This is the far-off depth and height reflecting my own
 face,

This is the thoughtful merge of myself, and the outlet
again.

Do you guess I have some intricate purpose?
Well, I have—for the April rain has, and the mica on
the side of a rock has.

Do you take it I would astonish?
Does the daylight astonish? Does the early red-start,
twittering through the woods?
Do I astonish more than they?

This hour I tell things in confidence,
I might not tell everybody, but I will tell you.

Who goes there! hankering, gross, mystical, nude?
How is it I extract strength from the beef I eat?

What is a man anyhow? What am I? What are you?

All I mark as my own, you shall offset it with your
own,
Else it were time lost listening to me.

I do not snivel that snivel the world over,
That months are vacuums, and the ground but
wallow and filth,
That life is a suck and a sell, and nothing remains at
the end but threadbare crape and tears.

Whimpering and truckling fold with powders for
invalids, conformity goes to the fourth-
removed,
I cock my hat as I please, indoors or out.

Shall I pray? Shall I venerate and be ceremonious?
I have pried through the strata, analyzed to a hair,
Counselled with doctors, calculated close, found no
sweeter fat than sticks to my own bones.

In all people I see myself—none more, not one a
barleycorn less,
And the good or bad I say of myself I say of them.

And I know I am solid and sound,
To me the converging objects of the universe
perpetually flow,
All are written to me, and I must get what the writing
means.

I know I am deathless,
I know this orbit of mine cannot be swept by a
carpenter's compass,
I know I shall not pass like a child's carlacue cut with a
burnt stick at night.

I know I am august,
I do not trouble my spirit to vindicate itself or be
understood,
I see that the elementary laws never apologize,
I reckon I behave no prouder than the level I plant my
house by, after all.

I exist as I am, that is enough,
If no other in the world be aware, I sit content,
And if each and all be aware, I sit content.

One world is aware, and by far the largest to me, and
that is myself,
And whether I come to my own today, or in ten
thousand or ten million years,
I can cheerfully take it now, or with equal cheerfulness
I can wait.

My foothold is tenoned and mortised in granite,
I laugh at what you call dissolution,
And I know the amplitude of time.

I am the poet of the body,
And I am the poet of the soul.

The pleasures of heaven are with me, and the pains of
hell are with me,
The first I graft and increase upon myself, the latter I
translate into a new tongue.

I am the poet of the woman the same as the man,
And I say it is as great to be a woman as to be a man,
And I say there is nothing greater than the mother of
men.

I chant the chant of dilation or pride,
We have had ducking and deprecating about enough,
I show that size is only development.

Have you outstript the rest? are you the President?
It is a trifle—they will more than arrive there every
one, and still pass on.

I am he that walks with the tender and growing night,
I call to the earth and sea, half-held by the night.

Press close, bare-bosomed night! press close,
       magnetic, nourishing night!
Night of south winds! night of the large few stars!
Still, nodding night! mad, naked, summer night!

Smile, O voluptuous, cool-breathed earth!
Earth of the slumbering and liquid trees!
Earth of departed sunset! earth of the mountains,
       misty-topt!
Earth of the vitreous pour of the full moon, just
       tinged with blue!
Earth of shine and dark, mottling the tide of the river!
Earth of the limpid gray of clouds, brighter and
       clearer for my sake!
Far-swooping elbowed earth! rich, apple-blossomed
       earth!
Smile, for your lover comes!

Prodigal, you have given me love! therefore I to you
       give love!
O unspeakable passionate love!

Thruster holding me tight, and that I hold tight!
We hurt each other as the bridegroom and the bride
       hurt each other.

You sea! I resign myself to you also, I guess what you
       mean,
I behold from the beach your crooked inviting fingers,
I believe you refuse to go back without feeling of me,
We must have a turn together—I undress—hurry me
       out of sight of the land,
Cushion me soft, rock me in billowy drowse,
Dash me with amorous wet, I can repay you.

Sea of stretched ground-swells!
Sea breathing broad and convulsive breaths!
Sea of the brine of life! sea of unshovelled and always-
       ready graves!
Howler and scooper of storms! capricious and dainty
       sea!
I am integral with you—I too am of one phase, and of
       all phases.

Partaker of influx and efflux, extoller of hate and
       conciliation,

Extoller of amies, and those that sleep in each others'
       arms.

I am he attesting sympathy,
Shall I make my list of things in the house, and skip
       the house that supports them?

I am the poet of commonsense, and of the
       demonstrable, and of immortality,
And am not the poet of goodness only—I do not
       decline to be the poet of wickedness also.

Washes and razors for foofoos—for me freckles and a
       bristling beard.

What blurt is this about virtue and about vice?
Evil propels me, and reform of evil propels me—
       I stand indifferent,
My gait is no fault-finder's or rejecter's gait,
I moisten the roots of all that has grown.

Did you fear some scrofula out of the unflagging
       pregnancy?
Did you guess the celestial laws are yet to be worked
       over and rectified?

I step up to say that what we do is right, and what we
       affirm is right, and some is only the ore
       of right,
Witnesses of us, one side a balance, and the antipodal
       side a balance,
Soft doctrine as steady help as stable doctrine,
Thoughts and deeds of the present, our rouse and
       early start.

This minute that comes to me over the past decillions,
There is no better than it and now.

What behaved well in the past, or behaves well today,
       is not such a wonder,
The wonder is always and always how can there be a
       mean man or an infidel.

Endless unfolding of words of ages!
And mine a word of the modern—a word en-masse,
A word of the faith that never balks,
One time as good as another time—here or
       henceforward it is all the same to me,
A word of reality, materialism first and last imbueing.

Hurrah for positive science! long live exact
     demonstration!
Fetch stonecrop, mix it with cedar and branches of
     lilac,
This is the lexicographer, this the chemist, this made a
     grammar of the old cartouches,
These mariners put the ship through dangerous
     unknown seas,
This is the geologist, this works with the scalpel, and
     this is a mathematician.

Gentlemen, I receive you and attach and clasp hands
     with you,
The facts are useful and real—they are not my
     dwelling—I enter by them to an area of
     the dwelling.

I am less the reminder of property or qualities, and
     more the reminder of life,
And go on the square for my own sake and for others'
     sakes,
And make short account of neuters and geldings, and
     favor men and women fully equipped,
And beat the gong of revolt, and stop with fugitives
     and them that plot and conspire.
Walt Whitman, an American, one of the roughs, a
     kosmos,
Disorderly, fleshy, sensual, eating, drinking, breeding,
No sentimentalist, no stander above men and women,
     or apart from them—no more modest
     than immodest.

Unscrew the locks from the doors!
Unscrew the doors themselves from their jambs!

Whoever degrades another degrades me, and whatever
     is done or said returns at last to me,
And whatever I do or say, I also return.

Through me the afflatus surging and surging—
     through me the current and index.

I speak the pass-word primeval, I give the sign of
     democracy,
By God! I will accept nothing which all cannot have
     their counterpart of on the same terms.

Through me many long dumb voices,
Voices of the interminable generations of slaves,

Voices of prostitutes, and of deformed persons,
Voices of the diseased and despairing, and of thieves
     and dwarfs,
Voices of cycles of preparation and accretion,
And of the threads that connect the stars, and of
     wombs, and of the fatherstuff,
And of the rights of them the others are down upon,
Of the trivial, flat, foolish, despised,
Fog in the air, beetles rolling balls of dung.

Through me forbidden voices,
Voices of sexes and lusts—voices veiled, and I remove
     the veil,
Voices indecent, by me clarified and transfigured.

I do not press my finger across my mouth,
I keep as delicate around the bowels as around the
     head and heart,
Copulation is no more rank to me than death is.

I believe in the flesh and the appetites,
Seeing, hearing, feeling, are miracles, and each part
     and tag of me is a miracle.

Divine am I inside and out, and I make holy whatever
     I touch or am touched from,
The scent of these arm-pits is aroma finer than prayer,
This head is more than churches, bibles, creeds.

If I worship any particular thing, it shall be some of
     the spread of my own body,
Translucent mould of me, it shall be you!
Shaded ledges and rests, firm masculine coulter, it
     shall be you!
Whatever goes to the tilth of me, it shall be you!
You my rich blood! your milky stream, pale strippings
     of my life!
Breast that presses against other breasts, it shall be
     you!
My brain, it shall be your occult convolutions!
Root of washed sweet-flag, timorous pond-snipe, nest
     of guarded duplicate eggs, it shall be you!
Mixed tussled hay of head, beard, brawn, it shall be
     you!
Trickling sap of maple, fibre of manly wheat, it shall
     be you!
Sun so generous, it shall be you!
Vapors lighting and shading my face, it shall be you!
You sweaty brooks and dews, it shall be you!

Winds whose soft-tickling genitals rub against me, it
    shall be you!
Broad muscular fields, branches of live-oak, loving
    lounger in my winding paths, it shall be you!
Hands I have taken, face I have kissed, mortal I have
    ever touched, it shall be you!

I dote on myself, there is that lot of me, and all so
    luscious,
Each moment, and whatever happens, thrills me with
    joy.

I cannot tell how my ankles bend, nor whence the
    cause of my faintest wish,
Nor the cause of the friendship I emit, nor the cause
    of the friendship I take again.

To walk up my stoop is unaccountable, I pause to
    consider if it really be,
That I eat and drink is spectacle enough for the great
    authors and schools,
A morning-glory at my window satisfies me more
    than the metaphysics of books.

To behold the day-break!
The little light fades the immense and diaphanous
    shadows,
The air tastes good to my palate.

Hefts of the moving world at innocent gambols,
    silently rising, freshly exuding,
Scooting obliquely high and low.

Something I cannot see puts upward libidinous
    prongs,
Seas of bright juice suffuse heaven.

The earth by the sky staid with, the daily close of their
    junction,
The heaved challenge from the east that moment over
    my head,
The mocking taunt, See then whether you shall be
    master!

Dazzling and tremendous, how quick the sun-rise
    would kill me,
If I could not now and always send sun-rise out of me.

We also ascend dazzling and tremendous as the sun,

We found our own, my soul, in the calm and cool of
    the day-break.

My voice goes after what my eyes cannot reach,
With the twirl of my tongue I encompass worlds, and
    volumes of worlds.

Speech is the twin of my vision, it is unequal to
    measure itself.

It provokes me forever,
It says sarcastically, Walt, you understand enough,
    why don't you let it out then?

Come now, I will not be tantalized, you conceive too
    much of articulation.
Do you not know how the buds beneath are folded?
Waiting in gloom, protected by frost,
The dirt receding before my prophetical screams,
I underlying causes, to balance them at last,
My knowledge my live parts, it keeping tally with the
    meaning of things,
Happiness, which, whoever hears me, let him or her
    set out in search of this day.

My final merit I refuse you—I refuse putting from me
    the best I am.

Encompass worlds, but never try to encompass me,
I crowd your noisiest talk by looking toward you.

Writing and talk do not prove me,
I carry the plenum of proof, and every thing else, in
    my face,
With the hush of my lips I confound the topmost
    skeptic.

I think I will do nothing for a long time but listen,
To accrue what I hear into myself, to let sounds
    contribute toward me.

I hear bravuras of birds, bustle of growing wheat,
    gossip of flames, clack of sticks cooking
    my meals.
I hear the sound I love, the sound of the human voice,

I hear all sounds as they are tuned to their uses,
    sounds of the city and sounds out of the
    city, sounds of the day and night,

Talkative young ones to those that like them, the
       recitative of fish-pedlars and fruit-pedlars,
      the loud laugh of work-people at their
      meals,
The angry base of disjointed friendship, the faint
      tones of the sick,
The judge with hands tight to the desk, his shaky lips
      pronouncing a death-sentence,
The heave'e'yo of stevedores unlading ships by the
      wharves, the refrain of the anchor-lifters,
The ring of alarm-bells, the cry of fire, the whirr of
      swift-streaking engines and hose-carts, with
      premonitory tinkles and colored lights,
The steam-whistle, the solid roll of the train of
      approaching cars,
The slow-march played at night at the head of the
      association,
They go to guard some corpse, the flag-tops are
      draped with black muslin.

I hear the violincello or man's heart's complaint,
I hear the keyed cornet, it glides quickly in through
      my ears, it shakes mad-sweet pangs
      through my belly and breast.
I hear the chorus, it is a grand-opera—this indeed is
      music!

A tenor large and fresh as the creation fills me,
The orbic flex of his mouth is pouring and filling me
      full.

I hear the trained soprano, she convulses me like the
      climax of my love-grip,
The orchestra wrenches such ardors from me, I did
      not know I possessed them,
It throbs me to gulps of the farthest down horror,
It sails me, I dab with bare feet, they are licked by the
      indolent waves,
I am exposed, cut by bitter and poisoned hail,
Steeped amid honeyed morphine, my windpipe
      squeezed in the fakes of death,
Let up again to feel the puzzle of puzzles,
And that we call Being.

To be in any form, what is that?
If nothing lay more developed, the quahaug in its
      callous shell were enough.

Mine is no callous shell,
I have instant conductors all over me, whether I pass
      or stop,
They seize every object and lead it harmlessly through
      me.
I merely stir, press, feel with my fingers, and am happy,
To touch my person to some one else's is about as
      much as I can stand.

Is this then a touch? quivering me to a new identity,
Flames and ether making a rush for my veins,
Treacherous tip of me reaching and crowding to help
      them,
My flesh and blood playing out lightning to strike
      what is hardly different from myself,
On all sides prurient provokers stiffening my limbs,
Straining the udder of my heart for its withheld drip,
Behaving licentious toward me, taking no denial,
Depriving me of my best, as for a purpose,
Unbuttoning my clothes, holding me by the bare
      waist,
Deluding my confusion with the calm of the sun-light
      and pasture-fields,
Immodestly sliding the fellow-senses away,
They bribed to swap off with touch, and go and graze
      at the edges of me,
No consideration, no regard for my draining strength
      or my anger,
Fetching the rest of the herd around to enjoy them
      awhile,
Then all uniting to stand on a head-land and worry
      me.

The sentries desert every other part of me,
They have left me helpless to a red marauder,
They all come to the head-land, to witness and assist
      against me.

I am given up by traitors!
I talk wildly, I have lost my wits, I and nobody else am
      the greatest traitor,
I went myself first to the head-land, my own hands
      carried me there.

You villain touch! what are you doing? my breath is
      tight in its throat,
Unclench your floodgates! you are too much for me.

Blind, loving, wrestling touch! sheathed, hooded,
    sharp-toothed touch!
Did it make you ache so, leaving me?

Parting, tracked by arriving—perpetual payment of
    the perpetual loan,
Rich showering rain, and recompense richer
    afterward.

Sprouts take and accumulate—stand by the curb
    prolific and vital,
Landscapes, projected, masculine, full-sized, golden.
All truths wait in all things,
They neither hasten their own delivery, nor resist it,
They do not need the obstetric forceps of the surgeon,
The insignificant is as big to me as any,
What is less or more than a touch?

Logic and sermons never convince,
The damp of the night drives deeper into my soul.

Only what proves itself to every man and woman is
    so,
Only what nobody denies is so.

A minute and a drop of me settle my brain,
I believe the soggy clods shall become lovers and
    lamps,
And a compend of compends is the meat of a man or
    woman,
And a summit and flower there is the feeling they
    have for each other,
And they are to branch boundlessly out of that lesson
    until it becomes omnific,
And until every one shall delight us, and we them.

I believe a leaf of grass is no less than the journey-
    work of the stars,
And the pismire is equally perfect, and a grain of sand,
    and the egg of the wren,
And the tree-toad is a chef-d'ouvre for the highest,
And the running blackberry would adorn the parlors
    of heaven,
And the narrowest hinge in my hand puts to scorn all
    machinery,
And the cow crunching with depressed head sur-
    passes any statue,
And a mouse is miracle enough to stagger sextillions
    of infidels,

And I could come every afternoon of my life to look at
    the farmer's girl boiling her iron teakettle
    and baking short-cake.

I find I incorporate gneiss, coal, long-threaded moss,
    fruits, grains, esculent roots,
And am stucco'd with quadrupeds and birds all over,
And have distanced what is behind me for good
    reasons,
And call any thing close again, when I desire it.

In vain the speeding or shyness,
In vain the plutonic rocks send their old heat against
    my approach,
In vain the mastadon retreats beneath its own
    powdered bones,
In vain objects stand leagues off, and assume manifold
    shapes,
In vain the ocean settling in hollows, and the great
    monsters lying low,
In vain the buzzard houses herself with the sky,
In vain the snake slides through the creepers and logs,
In vain the elk takes to the inner passes of the woods,
In vain the razor-billed auk sails far north to
    Labrador,
I follow quickly, I ascend to the nest in the fissure of
    the cliff.

I think I could turn and live with animals, they are so
    placid and self-contained,
I stand and look at them sometimes half the day long.

They do not sweat and whine about their condition,
They do not lie awake in the dark and weep for their
    sins,
They do not make me sick discussing their duty to
    God,
No one is dissatisfied, not one is demented with the
    mania of owning things,
Not one kneels to another, nor to his kind that lived
    thousands of years ago,
Not one is respectable or industrious over the whole
    earth.
So they show their relations to me, and I accept them,

They bring me tokens of myself, they evince them
    plainly in their possession.

I do not know where they got those tokens,
I may have passed that way untold times ago and
    negligently dropt them,
Myself moving forward then and now and forever,
Gathering and showing more always and with
    velocity,
Infinite and omnigenous, and the like of these among
    them,
Not too exclusive toward the reachers of my
    remembrancers,
Picking out here one that I love, choosing to go with
    him on brotherly terms.

A gigantic beauty of a stallion, fresh and responsive to
    my caresses,
Head high in the forehead, wide between the ears,
Limbs glossy and supple, tail dusting the ground,
Eyes well apart, full of sparkling wickedness, ears
    finely cut, flexibly moving.

His nostrils dilate, my heels embrace him, his well-
    built limbs tremble with pleasure, we
    speed around and return.

I but use you a moment, then I resign you stallion, do
    not need your paces, out-gallop them,
Myself, as I stand or sit, passing faster than you.

Swift wind! space! my soul! now I know it is true,
    what I guessed at,
What I guessed when I loafed on the grass,
What I guessed while I lay alone in my bed, and again
    as I walked the beach under the paling
    stars of the morning.

My ties and ballasts leave me—I travel, I sail, my
    elbows rest in the sea-gaps,
I skirt the sierras, my palms cover continents,
I am afoot with my vision.

By the city's quadrangular houses, in log-huts,
    camping with lumber-men,
Along the ruts of the turnpike, along the dry gulch
    and rivulet bed,

Weeding my onion-patch, hoeing rows of carrots and
    parsnips, crossing savannas, trailing in
    forests,

Prospecting, gold-digging, girdling the trees of a new
    purchase,
Scorched ankle-deep by the hot sand, hauling my
    boat down the shallow river,
Where the panther walks to and fro on a limb
    overhead, where the buck turns furiously
    at the hunter,
Where the rattle-snake suns his flabby length on a
    rock, where the otter is feeding on fish,
Where the alligator in his tough pimples sleeps by the
    bayou,
Where the black bear is searching for roots or honey,
    where the beaver pats the mud with his
    paddle-tail,
Over the growing sugar, over the cotton-plant, over
    the rice in its low moist field,
Over the sharp-peaked farm-house, with its scalloped
    scum and slender shoots from the gutters,
Over the western persimmon, over the long-leaved
    corn, over the delicate blue-flowered flax,
Over the white and brown buckwheat, a hummer and
    buzzer there with the rest,
Over the dusky green of the rye as it ripples and
    shades in the breeze,
Scaling mountains, pulling myself cautiously up,
    holding on by low scragged limbs,
Walking the path worn in the grass and beat through
    the leaves of the brush,
Where the quail is whistling betwixt the woods and
    the wheat-lot,
Where the bat flies in the July eve, where the great
    gold-bug drops through the dark,
Where the flails keep time on the barn floor,
Where the brook puts out of the roots of the old tree
    and flows to the meadow,
Where cattle stand and shake away flies with the
    tremulous shuddering of their hides,
Where the cheese-cloth hangs in the kitchen, where
    andirons straddle the hearth-slab, where
    cob-
    webs fall in festoons from the rafters,
Where trip-hammers crash, where the press is
    whirling its cylinders,
Wherever the human heart beats with terrible throes
    out of its ribs,

Where the pear-shaped balloon is floating aloft,
    floating in it myself and looking
    composedly down,

Where the life-car is drawn on the slip-noose, where
    the heat hatches pale-green eggs in the
    dented sand,

Where the she-whale swims with her calves and never
    forsakes them,

Where the steam-ship trails hind-ways its long
    pennant of smoke,

Where the ground-shark's fin cuts like a black chip
    out of the water,

Where the half-burned brig is riding on unknown
    currents,

Where shells grow to her slimy deck, where the dead
    are corrupting below,

Where the striped and starred flag is borne at the
    head of the regiments,

Approaching Manhattan, up by the long-stretching
    island,

Under Niagara, the cataract falling like a veil over my
    countenance,

Upon a door-step, upon the horse-block of hard
    wood outside,

Upon the race-course, or enjoying picnics or jigs, or a
    good game of base-ball,

At he-festivals, with blackguard jibes, ironical license,
    bull-dances, drinking, laughter,

At the cider-mill, tasting the sweet of the brown
    sqush, sucking the juice through a straw,

At apple-peelings, wanting kisses for all the red fruit
    I find,

At musters, beach-parties, friendly bees, huskings,
    house-raisings;

Where the mocking-bird sounds his delicious gurgles,
    cackles, screams, weeps,

Where the hay-rick stands in the barn-yard, where
    the dry-stalks are scattered, where the
    brood cow waits in the hovel,

Where the bull advances to do his masculine work,
    where the stud to the mare, where the
    cock is treading the hen,

Where heifers browse, where geese nip their food
    with short jerks,

Where sun-down shadows lengthen over the limit-
    less and lonesome prairie,

Where herds of buffalo make a crawling spread of the
    square miles far and near,

Where the humming-bird shimmers, where the neck
    of the long-lived swan is curving and
    winding,

Where the laughing-gull scoots by the shore, where

she laughs her near-human laugh,

Where bee-hives range on a gray bench in the garden,
    half-hid by the high weeds,

Where band-necked partridges roost in a ring on the
    ground with their heads out,

Where burial coaches enter the arched gates of a
    cemetery,

Where winter wolves bark amid wastes of snow and
    icicled trees,

Where the yellow-crowned heron comes to the edge
    of the marsh at night and feeds upon
    small crabs,

Where the splash of swimmers and divers cool the
    warm noon,

Where the katy-did works her chromatic reed on the
    walnut-tree over the well,

Through patches of citrons and cucumbers with
    silver-wired leaves,

Through the salt-lick or orange glade, under conical
    firs,

Through the gymnasium, through the curtained
    saloon, through the office or public hall,

Pleased with the native, pleased with the foreign,
    pleased with the new and old,

Pleased with women, the homely as well as the
    handsome,

Pleased with the quakeress as she puts off her bonnet
    and talks melodiously,

Pleased with the tunes of the choir of the white-
    washed church,

Pleased with the earnest words of the sweating
    Methodist preacher, or any preacher—
    looking seriously at the camp-meeting,

Looking in at the shop-windows in Broadway the
    whole forenoon, pressing the flesh of my
    nose to the thick plate-glass,

Wandering the same afternoon with my face turned
    up to the clouds,

My right and left arms round the sides of two friends,
    and I in the middle;

Coming home with the bearded and dark-cheeked
    bush-boy, riding behind him at the drape
    of the day,

Far from the settlements, studying the print of
    animals' feet, or the moccasin print,

By the cot in the hospital reaching lemonade to a
    feverish patient,

By the coffined corpse when all is still examining with
    a candle,

Voyaging to every port to dicker and adventure,
Hurrying with the modern crowd, as eager and fickle
      as any,
Hot toward one I hate ready in my madness to knife
      him,
Solitary at midnight in my back yard, my thoughts
      gone from me a long while,
Walking the old hills of Judea, with the beautiful
      gentle god by my side,
Speeding through space, speeding through heaven
      and the stars,
Speeding amid the seven satellites, and the broad ring,
      and the diameter of eighty thousand
      miles,
Speeding with tailed meteors, throwing fire-balls like
      the rest,
Carrying the crescent child that carries its own full
      mother in its belly,
Storming, enjoying, planning, loving, cautioning,
Backing and filling, appearing and disappearing,
I tread day and night such roads.

I visit the orchards of spheres and look at the product,
And look at quintillions ripened, and look at
      quintillions green.

I fly the flight of the fluid and swallowing soul,
My course runs below the soundings of plummets.

I help myself to material and immaterial,
No guard can shut me off, no law can prevent me.
I anchor my ship for a little while only,
My messengers continually cruise away, or bring their
      returns to me.

I go hunting polar furs and the seal, leaping chasms
      with a pike-pointed staff, clinging to
      topples of brittle and blue.

I ascend to the fore-truck, I take my place late at night
      in the crow's-nest, we sail through the
      arctic sea, it is plenty light enough,
Through the clear atmosphere I stretch around on the
      wonderful beauty,

The enormous masses of ice pass me and I pass them,
      the scenery is plain in all directions,
The white-topped mountains show in the distance, I
      fling out my fancies toward them,

We are approaching some great battle-field in which
      we are soon to be engaged,
We pass the colossal out-posts of the encampments,
      we pass with still feet and caution,
Or we are entering by the suburbs some vast
      and ruined city, the blocks and fallen
      architecture more than all the living cities
      of the globe.

I am a free companion, I bivouac by invading
      watchfires.
I turn the bridegroom out of bed and stay with the
      bride myself,
I tighten her all night to my thighs and lips.

My voice is the wife's voice, the screech by the rail of
      the stairs,
They fetch my man's body up, dripping and drowned.

I understand the large hearts of heroes,
The courage of present times and all times,
How the skipper saw the crowded and rudderless
      wreck of the steam-ship, and death
      chasing it up and down the storm,
How he knuckled tight, and gave not back one inch,
      and was faithful of days and faithful of
      nights,
And chalked in large letters, Be of good cheer,
      We will not desert you,
How he saved the drifting company at last,
How the lank loose-gowned women looked when
      boated from the side of their prepared
      graves,
How the silent old-faced infants, and the lifted sick,
      and the sharp-lipped unshaved men,
All this I swallow, it tastes good, I like it well, it
      becomes mine,
I am the man, I suffered, I was there.

The disdain and calmness of martyrs,
The mother, condemned for a witch, burnt with dry
      wood, her children gazing on,
The hounded slave that flags in the race, leans by the
      fence, blowing, covered with sweat,

The twinges that sting like needles his legs and neck,
      the murderous buck-shot and the bullets,
All these I feel or am.

I am the hounded slave, I wince at the bite of the dogs,
Hell and despair are upon me, crack and again crack
      the marksmen,
I clutch the rails of the fence, my gore dribs, thinned
      with the ooze of my skin,
I fall on the weeds and stones,
The riders spur their unwilling horses, haul close,
Taunt my dizzy ears, beat me violently over the head
      with whip-stocks.

Agonies are one of my changes of garments,
I do not ask the wounded person how he feels, I
      myself become the wounded person,
My hurt turns livid upon me as I lean on a cane and
      observe.

I am the mashed fireman with breastbone broken,
      tumbling walls buried me in their debris,
Heat and smoke I inspired, I heard the yelling shouts
      of my comrades,
I heard the distant click of their picks and shovels,
They have cleared the beams away, they tenderly life
      me forth.

I lie in the night air in my red shirt, the pervading
      hush is for my sake.
Painless after all I lie, exhausted but not so unhappy,
White and beautiful are the faces around me, the
      heads are bared of their fire-caps,
The kneeling crowd fades with the light of the torches.

Distant and dead resuscitate,
They show as the dial or move as the hands of me—I
      am the clock myself.

I am an old artillerist, I tell of my fort's bombardment,
      I am there again.

Again the reveille of drummers, again the attacking
      cannon, mortars, howitzers,
Again the attacked send cannon responsive;
I take part, I see and hear the whole,
The cries, curses, roar, the plaudits for well-aimed
      shots,
The ambulanza slowly passing, trailing its red drip,
Workmen searching after damages, making
      indispensable repairs,
The fall of grenades through the rent roof, the fan-
      shaped explosion,

The whizz of limbs, heads, stone, wood, iron, high in
      the air.

Again gurgles the mouth of my dying general, he
      furiously waves with his hand,
He gasps through the clot, Mind not me—mind—
      the entrenchments.

I tell not the fall of Alamo, not one escaped to tell the
      fall of Alamo,
The hundred and fifty are dumb yet at Alamo.

Hear now the tale of a jet-black sunrise,
Hear of the murder in cold-blood of four hundred
      and twelve young men.

Retreating, they had formed in a hollow square, with
      their baggage for breast-works,
Nine hundred lives out of the surrounding enemy's,
      nine times their number, was the price
      they took in advance,
Their colonel was wounded and their ammunition
      gone,
They treated for an honorable capitulation, received
      writing and seal, gave up their arms,
      marched back prisoners of war.
They were the glory of the race of rangers,
Matchless with horse, rifle, song, supper, courtship,
Large, turbulent, brave, handsome, generous, proud,
      affectionate,
Bearded, sunburnt, dressed in the free costume of
      hunters,
Not a single one over thirty years of age.

The second Sunday morning they were brought
      out in squads and massacred—it was
      beautiful early summer,
The work commenced about five o'clock and was over
      by eight.

None obeyed the command to kneel,
Some made a mad and helpless rush, some stood
      stark and straight,

A few fell at once, shot in the temple or heart, the
      living and dead lay together,
The maimed and mangled dug in the dirt, the new-
      comers saw them there,
Some, half-killed, attempted to crawl away,

These were dispatched with bayonets, or battered
     with the blunts of muskets,
A youth not seventeen years old seized his assassin,
     till two more came to release him,
The three were all torn, and covered with the boy's
     blood.
At eleven o'clock began the burning of the bodies;
That is the tale of the murder of the four hundred and
     twelve young men,
And that was a jet-black sunrise.

Did you read in the sea-books of the old-fashioned
     frigate-fight?
Did you learn who won by the light of the moon and stars?

Our foe was no skulk in his ship, I tell you,
His was the English pluck, and there is no tougher or
     truer, and never was, and never will be,
Along the lowered eve he came, horribly raking us.

We closed with him, the yards entangled, the cannon
     touched,
My captain lashed fast with his own hands.

We had received some eighteen-pound shots under
     the water,
On our lower-gun-deck two large pieces had burst
     at the first fire, killing all around and
     blowing up overhead.

Ten o'clock at night and the full moon shining, and
     the leaks on the gain, and five feet of
     water reported,
The master-at-arms loosing the prisoners confined in
     the after-hold, to give them a chance for
     themselves.

The transit to and from the magazine was now
     stopped by the sentinels,
They saw so many strange faces that they did not
     know whom to trust.

Our frigate was afire, the other asked if we demanded
     quarter? if our colors were struck and the
     fighting done?

I laughed content when I heard the voice of my little
     captain,

We have not struck, he composedly cried, We have
     just begun our part of the fighting.

Only three guns were in use,
One was directed by the captain himself against the
     enemy's main-mast,
Two, well served with grape and canister, silenced his
     musketry and cleared his decks.

The tops alone seconded the fire of this little battery,
     especially the main-top,
They all held out bravely during the whole of the
     action.

Not a moment's cease,
The leaks gained fast on the pumps, the fire eat
     toward the powder-magazine,
One of the pumps was shot away, it was generally
     thought we were sinking.

Serene stood the little captain,
He was not hurried, his voice was neither high nor
     low,
His eyes gave more light to us than our battle-
     lanterns.

Toward twelve at night, there in the beams of the
     moon they surrendered to us.

Stretched and still lay the midnight,
Two great hulls motionless on the breast of the
     darkness,
Our vessel riddled and slowly sinking, preparations to
     pass to the one we had conquered,
The captain on the quarter-deck coldly giving his
     orders through a countenance white as a
     sheet,
Near by, the corpse of the child that served in the
     cabin,
The dead face of an old salt with long white hair and
     carefully curled whiskers,
The flames, spite of all that could be done, flickering
     aloft and below,
The husky voices of the two or three officers yet fit
     for duty,
Formless stacks of bodies, bodies by themselves, dabs
     of flesh upon the masts and spars,
Cut of cordage, dangle of rigging, slight shock of the
     soothe of waves,

Black and impassive guns, litter of powder-parcels,
    strong scent,
Delicate sniffs of sea-breeze, smells of sedgy grass and
    fields by the shore, death-messages given
    in change to survivors,
The hiss of the surgeon's knife, the gnawing teeth of
    his saw,
Wheeze, cluck, swash of falling blood, short wild
    scream, long dull tapering groan,
These so, these irretrievable.

O Christ! My fit is mastering me!
What the rebel said, gaily adjusting his throat to the
    rope-noose,
What the savage at the stump, his eye-sockets empty,
    his mouth spirting whoops and defiance,
What stills the traveler come to the vault at Mount Vernon,
What sobers the Brooklyn boy as he looks down the
    shores of the Wallabout and remembers
    the prison ships,
What burnt the gums of the red-coat at Saratoga
    when he surrendered his brigades,
These become mine and me every one, and they are
    but little,
I become as much more as I like.

I become any presence or truth of humanity here,
And see myself in prison shaped like another man,
And feel the dull unintermitted pain.

For me the keepers of convicts shoulder their carbines
    and keep watch,
It is I let out in the morning and barred at night.

Not a mutineer walks hand-cuffed to the jail, but I am
    hand-cuffed to him and walk by his side,
I am less the jolly one there, and more the silent one,
    with sweat on my twitching lips.

Not a youngster is taken for larceny, but I go up too,
    and am tried and sentenced.

Not a cholera patient lies at the last gasp, but I also lie
    at the last gasp,
My face is ash-colored, my sinews gnarl, away from
    me people retreat.

Askers embody themselves in me, and I am em-
    bodied in them,

I project my hat, sit shame-faced, beg.
I rise extatic through all, sweep with the true
    gravitation,
The whirling and whirling is elemental within me.

Somehow I have been stunned. Stand back!
Give me a little time beyond my cuffed head,
    slumbers, dreams, gaping,
I discover myself on the verge of a usual mistake.

That I could forget the mockers and insults!
That I could forget the trickling tears, and the blows
    of the bludgeons and hammers!
That I could look with a separate look on my own
    crucifixion and bloody crowning!

I remember, I resume the overstaid fraction,
The grave of rock multiplies what has been confided
    to it, or to any graves,
The corpses rise, the gashes heal, the fastenings roll
    away.

I troop forth replenished with supreme power, one of
    an average unending procession,
We walk the roads of Ohio, Massachusetts, Virginia,
    Wisconsin, Manhattan Island, New
    Orleans, Texas, Montreal, San Francisco,
    Charleston, Havana, Mexico,
Inland and by the sea-coast and boundary lines, and
    we pass all boundary lines.
Our swift ordinances are on their way over the whole
    earth,
The blossoms we wear in our hats are the growth of
    two thousand years.

Eleves, I salute you!
I see the approach of your numberless gangs, I see you
    understand yourselves and me,
And know that they who have eyes are divine, and the
    blind and lame are equally divine,
And that my steps drag behind yours, yet go before
    them,
And are aware how I am with you no more than I am
    with everybody.

The friendly and flowing savage, Who is he?
Is he waiting for civilization, or past it and mastering
    it?

Is he some south-westerner, raised out-doors? Is he
       Canadian?
Is he from the Mississippi country? from Iowa,
       Oregon, California? from the mountains?
       Prairie-life, bush-life? from the sea?
Wherever he goes men and women accept and desire
       him;
They desire he should like them, touch them speak to
       them, stay with them.
Behaviour lawless as snow-flakes, words simple as
       grass, uncombed head, laughter, naivete,
Slow-stepping feet, common features, common
       modes and emanations,
They descend in new forms from the tips of his
       fingers,
They are wafted with the odor of his body or breath,
       they fly out of the glance of his eyes.

Flaunt of the sun-shine, I need not your bask, lie over!
You light surfaces only, I force surfaces and depths
       also.

Earth! you seem to look for something at my hands,
Say old top-knot! what do you want?

Man or woman! I might tell how I like you, but
       cannot,
And might tell what it is in me, and what it is in you,
       but cannot,
And might tell the pinings I have, the pulse of my
       nights and days.

Behold I do not give lectures or a little charity,
What I give I give out of myself.

You there, impotent, loose in the knees, open your
       scarfed chops till I blow grit within you,
Spread your palms, and lift the flaps of your pockets,
I am not to be denied, I compel, I have stores plenty
       and to spare,
And any thing I have I bestow;
I do not ask who you are, that is not important to me,
You can do nothing, and be nothing, but what I will
       infold you.

To a drudge of the cotton-fields or cleaner of privies I
       lean—on his right cheek I put the family kiss,
And in my soul I swear, I never will deny him.

On women fit for conception I start bigger and
       nimbler babes,
This day I am jetting the stuff of far more arrogant
       republics.

To any one dying, thither I speed and twist the knob
       of the door,
Turn the bed-clothes toward the foot of the bed,
Let the physician and the priest go home.

I seize the descending man, I raise him with resistless
       will.

O despairer, here is my neck,
By God! you shall not go down! hang your whole
       weight upon me.

I dilate you with tremendous breath, I buoy you up,
Every room of the house do I fill with an armed force,
       lovers of me, bafflers of graves,
Sleep! I and they keep guard all night,
Not doubt, not decease shall dare to lay finger upon
       you,
I have embraced you, and henceforth possess you to
       myself,
And when you rise in the morning you will find what
       I tell you is so.

I am he bringing help for the sick as they pant on their
       backs,
And for strong upright men I bring yet more needed
       help.

I heard what was said of the universe,
Heard it and heard it of several thousand years;
It is middling well as far as it goes, but is that all?

Magnifying and applying come I,
Outbidding at the start the old cautious hucksters,
The most they offer for mankind and eternity less
       than a spirt of my own seminal wet,
Taking myself the exact dimensions of Jehovah—
       lithographing Kronos, Zeus his son,
       Hercules his grandson—buying drafts of
       Osiris, Isis, Belus, Brahma, Buddha—in
       my portfolio placing Manito loose, Allah
       on a leaf, the crucifix engraved—with
       Odin, and the hideous-faced Mexitli, and
       every idol and image,

Taking them all for what they are worth, and not a
        cent more,
Admitting they were alive and did the work of their day,
Admitting they bore mites, as for unfledged birds,
        who have now to rise and fly and sing for
        themselves,
Accepting the rough deific sketches to fill out better in
        myself—bestowing them freely on each
        man and woman I see,
Discovering as much, or more, in a framer framing a
        house,
Putting higher claims for him there with his rolled-up
        sleeves, driving the mallet and chisel,
Not objecting to special revelations, considering a
        curl of smoke or a hair on the back of my
        hand just as curious as any revelation,
Those ahold of fire-engines and hook-and-ladder
        ropes no less to me than the gods of the
        antique wars,
Minding their voices peal through the crash of
        destruction,
Their brawny limbs passing safe over charred laths,
        their white foreheads whole and unhurt
        out of the flames,
By the mechanic's wife with her babe at her nipple
        interceding for every person born,
Three scythes at harvest whizzing in a row from three
        lusty angels with shirts bagged out at
        their waists,
The snag-toothed hostler with red hair redeeming
        sins past and to come,
Selling all he possesses, travelling on foot to fee
        lawyers for his brother, and sit by him
        while he is tried for forgery;
What was strewn in the amplest strewing the square
        rod about me, and not filling the square
        rod then,
The bull and the bug never worshipped half enough,
Dung and dirt more admirable than was dreamed,
The supernatural of no account—myself waiting my
        time to be one of the supremes,
The day getting ready for me when I shall do as much
        good as the best, and be as prodigious,
Guessing when I am it will not tickle me much to
        receive puffs out of pulpit or print;
By my life-lumps! becoming already a creator!
Putting myself here and now to the ambushed womb
        of the shadows!

A call in the midst of the crowd,
My own voice, orotund, sweeping, final.

Come my children,
Come my boys and girls, my women, household,
        intimates,
Now the performer launches his nerve, he has passed
        his prelude on the reeds within.

Easily written, loose-fingered chords! I feel the thrum
        of their climax and close.

My head slues round on my neck,
Music rolls, but not from the organ—folks are around
        me, but they are no household of mine.

Ever the hard unsunk ground,
Ever the eaters and drinkers, ever the upward and
        downward sun, ever the air and the
        ceaseless tides,
Ever myself and my neighbors, refreshing, wicked, real,
Ever the old inexplicable query, ever that thorned
        thumb, that breath of itches and thirsts,
Ever the vexer's hoot! hoot! till we find where the sly
        one hides, and bring him forth;
Ever love, ever the sobbing liquid of life,
Ever the bandage under the chin, ever the tressels of
        death.

Here and there with dimes on the eyes walking,
To feed the greed of the belly the brains liberally
        spooning,
Tickets buying, taking, selling, but in to the feast never
        once going,
Many sweating, ploughing, thrashing, and then the
        chaff for payment receiving,
A few idly owning, and they the wheat continually
        claiming.

This is the city, and I am one of the citizens,
Whatever interests the rest interests me—politics,
        markets, newspapers, schools, benevolent
        societies, improvements, banks, tariffs,
        steamships, factories, stocks, stores, real
        estate, personal estate.

They who piddle and patter here in collars and tailed
        coats, I am aware who they are—they are
        not worms or fleas,

I acknowledge the duplicates of myself—the weakest
    and shallowest is deathless with me,
What I do and say, the same waits for them;
Every thought that flounders in me, the same
    flounders in them.
I know perfectly well my own egotism,
I know my omnivorous words, and cannot say any less,
And would fetch you, whoever you are, flush with
    myself.

My words are words of a questioning, and to indicate
    reality;
This printed and bound book—but the printer, and
    the printing-office boy?
The marriage estate and settlement—but the body
    and mind of the bridegroom? also those
    of the bride?
The panorama of the sea—but the sea itself?
The well-taken photographs—but your wife or friend
    close and solid in your arms?
The fleet of ships of the line, and all the modern
    improvements—but the craft and pluck
    of the admiral?
The dishes and fare and furniture—but the host and
    hostess, and the look out of their eyes?
The sky up there—yet here, or next door, or across
    the way?
The saints and sages in history—but you your-self?
Sermons, creeds, theology—but the human brain,
    and what is called reason, and what is
    called love, and what is called life?
I do not despise you, priests,
My faith is the greatest of faiths, and the least of
    faiths,
Enclosing all worship ancient and modern, and all
    between ancient and modern,
Believing I shall come again upon the earth after five
    thousand years,
Waiting responses from oracles, honoring the gods,
    saluting the sun,
Making a fetish of the first rock or stump, powow-ing
    with sticks in the circle of obis,
Helping the lama or brahmin as he trims the lamps of
    the idols,
Dancing yet through the streets in a phallic
    procession—rapt and austere in the
    woods, a gymnosophist,
Drinking mead from the skull-cup, to shastas and
    vedas admirant, minding the koran,

Walking the teokallis, spotted with gore from the
    stone and knife, beating the serpent-skin
    drum,
Accepting the gospels, accepting him that was
    crucified, knowing assuredly that he is
    divine,
To the mass kneeling, to the puritan's prayer rising,
    sitting patiently in a pew,
Ranting and frothing in my insane crisis, waiting
    dead-like till my spirit arouses me,
Looking forth on pavement and land, and outside of
    pavement and land,
Belonging to the winders of the circuit of circuits.

One of that centripetal and centrifugal gang, I turn
    and talk like a man leaving charges be-
    fore a journey.

Down-hearted doubters, dull and excluded,
Frivolous, sullen, moping, angry, affected, dis-
    heartened, atheistical,
I know every one of you, I know the unspoken
    interrogatories,
By experience I know them.

How the flukes splash!
How they contort, rapid as lightning, with spasms
    and spouts of blood!

Be at peace, bloody flukes of doubters and sullen
    mopers,
I take my place among you as much as among any,
The past is the push of you, me, all, precisely the same,
Day and night are for you, me, all,
And what is yet untried and afterward is for you, me,
    all, precisely the same.

I do not know what is untried and afterward,
But I know it is sure, alive, sufficient.

Each who passes is considered, each who stops is
    considered, not a single one can it fail.

It cannot fail the young man who died and was buried,
Nor the young woman who died and was put by his
    side,
Nor the little child that peeped in at the door, and
    then drew back and was never seen again,

Nor the old man who has lived without purpose, and
    feels it with bitterness worse than gall,
Nor him in the poor-house tubercled by rum and the
    bad disorder,
Nor the numberless slaughtered and wrecked, nor
    the brutish koboo called the ordure of
    humanity,
Nor the sacs merely floating with open mouths for
    food to slip in,
Nor any thing in the earth, or down in the oldest
    graves of the earth,
Nor any thing in the myriads of spheres, nor one of
    the myriads of myriads that inhabit them,
Nor the present, nor the least wisp that is known.

It is time to explain myself—let us stand up.

What is known I strip away, I launch all men and women
    forward with me into the unknown.

The clock indicates the moment, but what does
    eternity indicate?

Eternity lies in bottomless reservoirs, its buckets are
    rising forever and ever,
They pour, they pour, and exhale away.

We have thus far exhausted trillions of winters and
    summers,
There are trillions ahead, and trillions ahead of them.

Births have brought us richness and variety,
And other births will bring us richness and variety.

I do not call one greater and one smaller,
That which fills its period and place is equal to any.

Were mankind murderous or jealous upon you, my
    brother, my sister?
I am sorry for you, they are not murderous or jealous
    upon me,
All has been gentle with me, I keep no account with
    lamentation;
What have I to do with lamentation?

I am an acme of things accomplished, and I an
    encloser of things to be.

My feet strike an apex of the apices of the stairs,
On every step bunches of ages, and larger bunches
    between the steps,
All below duly traveled, and still I mount and mount.

Rise after rise bow the phantoms behind me,
Afar down I see the huge first Nothing, I know I was
    even there,
I waited unseen and always, and slept through the
    lethargic mist,
And took my time, and took no hurt from the fœtid
    carbon.

Long I was hugged close—long and long.

Immense have been the preparations for me,
Faithful and friendly the arms that have helped me.

Cycles ferried my cradle rowing and rowing like
    cheerful boatmen,
For room to me stars kept aside in their own rings,
They sent influences to look after what was to hold
    me.

Before I was born out of my mother generations
    guided me,
My embryo has never been torpid, nothing could
    overlay it,
For it the nebula cohered to an orb, the long slow
    strata piled to rest it on, vast vegetables
    gave it sustenance,
Monstrous sauroids transported it in their mouths,
    and deposited it with care.

All forces have been steadily employed to complete
    and delight me,
Now I stand on this spot with my soul.

Span of youth! ever-pushed elasticity! manhood,
    balanced, florid, full!

My lovers suffocate me!
Crowding my lips, thick in the pores of my skin,
Jostling me through streets and public halls, coming
    naked to me at night,
Crying by day Ahoy! from the rocks of the river,
    swinging and chirping over my head,
Calling my name from flower-beds, vines, tangled
    under-brush,

Or while I swim in the bath, or drink from the pump
        at the corner, or the curtain is down at the
        opera, or I glimpse at a woman's face in
        the rail-road car,
Lighting on every moment of my life,
Bussing my body with soft balsamic busses,
Noiselessly passing handfuls out of their hearts and
        giving them to be mine.
Old age superbly rising! Ineffable grace of dying days!

Every condition promulges not only itself, it
        promulges what grows after and out of
        itself,
And the dark hush promulges as much as any.

I open my scuttle at night and see the far-sprinkled
        systems,
And all I see, multiplied as high as I can cipher, edge
        but the rim of the farther systems.

Wider and wider they spread, expanding, always
        expanding,
Outward, outward, forever outward.

My sun has his sun, and round him obediently
        wheels,
He joins with his partners a group of superior circuit,
And greater sets follow, making specks of the greatest
        inside them.

There is no stoppage, and never can be stoppage,
If I, you, the worlds, all beneath or upon their
        surfaces, and all the palpable life, were this
        moment reduced back to a pallid float, it
        would not avail in the long run,
We should surely bring up again where we now stand,
And as surely go as much farther, and then farther
        and farther.
A few quadrillions of eras, a few octillions of cubic
        leagues, do not hazard the span, or make
        it impatient,
They are but parts, any thing is but a part.

See ever so far, there is limitless space outside of that,
Count ever so much, there is limitless time around that.

My rendezvous is appointed,
The Lord will be there and wait till I come on perfect
        terms.

I know I have the best of time and space, and was
        never measured, and never will be
        measured.

I tramp a perpetual journey,
My signs are a rain-proof coat, good shoes, and a staff
        cut from the woods,
No friend of mine takes his ease in my chair,
I have no chair, no church, no philosophy,
I lead no man to a dinner-table, library, exchange,
But each man and each woman of you I lead upon a
        knoll,
My left hand hooks you round the waist,
My right hand points to landscapes of continents, and
        a plain public road.

Not I, not any one else, can travel that road for you,
You must travel it for yourself.

It is not far, it is within reach,
Perhaps you have been on it since you were born, and
        did not know,
Perhaps it is every where on water and on land.

Shoulder your duds, I will mine, let us hasten forth,
Wonderful cities and free nations we shall fetch as
        we go.

If you tire, give me both burdens and rest the chuff of
        your hand on my hip,
And in due time you shall repay the same service to
        me,
For after we start we never lie by again.

This day before dawn I ascended a hill and looked at
        the crowded heaven,
And I said to my spirit, When we become the
        enfolders of those orbs, and the pleasure
        and knowledge of every thing in them,
        shall we be filled and satisfied then?
And my spirit said No, we level that lift to pass and
        continue beyond.

You are also asking me questions, and I hear you,
I answer that I cannot answer, you must find out for
        yourself.

Sit awhile wayfarer,
Here are biscuits to eat, here is milk to drink,

But as soon as you sleep and renew yourself in sweet
    clothes, I will certainly kiss you with my
    good-bye kiss, and open the gate for your
    egress hence.

Long enough have you dreamed contemptible dreams,
Now I wash the gum from your eyes,
You must habit yourself to the dazzle of the light, and
    of every moment of your life.

Long have you timidly waded holding a plank by the
    shore,
Now I will you to be a bold swimmer,
To jump off in the midst of the sea, rise again, nod to
    me, shout, laughingly dash with your hair.

I am the teacher of athletes,
He that by me spreads a wider breast than my own
    proves the width of my own,
He most honors my style who learns under it to
    destroy the teacher.

The boy I love, the same becomes a man, not through
    derived power, but in his own right,
Wicked, rather than virtuous out of conformity of
    fear,
Fond of his sweetheart, relishing well his steak,
Unrequited love, or a slight, cutting him worse than a
    wound cuts,
First rate to ride, to fight, to hit the bull's eye, to sail a
    skiff, to sing a song, or play on the banjo,
Preferring scars, and faces pitted with small-pox, over
    all latherers and those that keep out of
    the sun.

I teach straying from me, yet who can stray from me?
I follow you, whoever you are, from the present hour,
My words itch at your ears till you understand them.

I do not say these things for a dollar, or to fill up the
    time while I wait for a boat,
It is you talking just as much as myself, I act as the
    tongue of you,
It was tied in your mouth, in mine it begins to be
    loosened.

I swear I will never mention love or death inside a
    house,

And I swear I never will translate myself at all, only to
    him or her who privately stays with me in
    the open air.

If you would understand me, go to the heights or
    water-shore,
The nearest gnat is an explanation, and a drop or
    motion of waves a key,
The maul, the oar, the hand-saw, second my words.

No shuttered room or school can commune with me,
But roughs and little children better than they.

The young mechanic is closest to me, he knows me
    pretty well,
The wood-man that takes his axe and jug with him,
    shall take me with him all day,
The farm-boy ploughing in the field feels good at the
    sound of my voice,
In vessels that sail my words sail—I go with
    fishermen and seamen, and love them,
My face rubs to the hunter's face when he lies down
    alone in his blanket,
The driver thinking of me does not mind the jolt of
    his wagon,
The young mother and old mother comprehend me,
The girl and the wife rest the needle a moment, and
    forget where they are,
They and all would resume what I have told them.

I have said that the soul is not more than the body,
And I have said that the body is not more than the
    soul,
And nothing, not God, is greater to one than one's-
    self is,

And whoever walks a furlong without sympathy, walks
    to his own funeral, dressed in his shroud,
And I or you, pocketless of a dime, may purchase the
    pick of the earth,
And to glance with an eye, or show a bean in its pod,
    confounds the learning of all times,
And there is no trade or employment but the young
    man following it may become a hero,
And there is no object so soft but it makes a hub for
    the wheeled universe,
And any man or woman shall stand cool and
    supercilious before a million universes.

And I call to mankind, Be not curious about God,
For I, who am curious about each, am not curious
about God,
No array of terms can say how much I am at peace
about God, and about death.

I hear and behold God in every object, yet I
understand God not in the least,
Nor do I understand who there can be more
wonderful than myself.

Why should I wish to see God better than this day?
I see something of God each hour of the twenty-four,
and each moment then,
In the faces of men and women I see God, and in my
own face in the glass,
I find letters from God dropped in the street, and
every one is signed by God's name,
And I leave them where they are, for I know that others
will punctually come forever and ever.

And as to you death, and you bitter hug of mortality,
it is idle to try to alarm me.

To his work without flinching the accoucheur comes,
I see the elder-hand, pressing, receiving, supporting,
I recline by the sills of the exquisite flexible doors, mark
the outlet, mark the relief and escape.

And as to you corpse, I think you are good manure,
but that does not offend me,
I smell the white roses sweet-scented and growing,
I reach to the leafy lips, I reach to the polished breasts
of melons.
And as to you life, I reckon you are the leavings of
many deaths,
No doubt I have died myself ten thousand times before.

I hear you whispering there, O stars of heaven,
O suns, O grass of graves, O perpetual transfers and
promotions, if you do not say any-thing,
how can I say anything?

Of the turbid pool that lies in the autumn forest,
Of the moon that descends the steeps of the soughing
twilight,
Toss, sparkles of day and dusk! Toss on the black
stems that decay in the muck!
Toss to the moaning gibberish of the dry limbs!

I ascend from the moon, I ascend from the night,
And perceive of the ghastly glimmer the sunbeams
reflected,
And debouch to the steady and central from the
offspring great or small.

There is that in me—I do not know what it is—but I
know it is in me.

Wrenched and sweaty, calm and cool then my body
becomes,
I sleep—I sleep long.

I do not know it—it is without name—it is a word unsaid,
It is not in any dictionary, utterance, symbol.

Something it swings on more than the earth I swing on,
To it the creation is the friend whose embracing
awakes me.

Perhaps I might tell more. Outlines! I plead for my
brothers and sisters.

Do you see, O my brothers and sisters?
It is not chaos or death—it is form, union, plan—it is
eternal life—it is happiness.

The past and present wilt—I have filled them,
emptied them,
And proceed to fill my next fold of the future.
Listener up there! here you! what have you to confide
to me?
Look in my face while I snuff the sidle of evening,
Talk honestly, no one else hears you, and I stay only a
minute longer.

Do I contradict myself?
Very well then, I contradict myself,
I am large, I contain multitudes.

I concentrate toward them that are nigh, I wait on the
door-slab.

Who has done his day's work? who will soonest be
through with his supper?
Who wishes to walk with me?

Will you speak before I am gone? will you prove
already too late?

The spotted hawk swoops by and accuses me —he
    complains of my gab and my loitering.

I too am not a bit tamed—I too am untranslatable,
I sound my barbaric yawp over the roofs of the world.

The last scud of day holds back for me,
It flings my likeness, after the rest, and true as any, on
    the shadowed wilds,
It coaxes me to the vapor and the dusk.

I depart as air, I shake my white locks at the run-away
    sun,
I effuse my flash in eddies, and drift it in lacy jags.

I bequeath myself to the dirt, to grow from the grass
    I love,
If you want me again, look for me under your boot-
    soles.

You will hardly know who I am, or what I mean,
But I shall be good health to you nevertheless,
And filter and fibre your blood.

Failing to fetch me at first, keep encouraged,
Missing me one place, search another,
I stop some where waiting for you.

          (*Leaves of Grass*, 1856; 2nd Edition)
          http://whitmanarchive.org/published/
                    LG/1856/poems/1

[A.14]

CORRESPONDENCE: STODDARD AND WHITMAN.

Date: February 8, 1867

To Walt Whitman. Poet..

My very dear Sir
    If you will reply to this I shall be satisfied; and
where one is so easily made happy—will you grudge
a little inconvenience?
    I should be very proud of your autograph,
and because I know it to be a healthful pleasure I
anticipate my hearo-worship is pardonable.
    You are well known here and much talked
of—and we are looking for a fresh edition of your
poems. How long must we wait?
    I am approaching my twenty-fourth
birthday—and stand upon the order of printing a
small selection of my own rhymes—being assisted
in this (perhaps unwise move) by my friends. May I
send you a copy of my book in June?—when it will
be safely out. D. V.
    Please answer me—if possible, and be
sure—if you so far honor me—I shall thank your
indulgence, rather than mistrust that my verses have
afforded you any pleasure.
    I am, dear Sir—
    Yours faithfully

                  Chas. W. Stoddard..
      San Francisco—Cal. 8th Feb—1867.

                        *

MY FRIEND

I have a friend who is so true to me,
We may not parted be.

Though I strayed, on to the uttermost,
Yet is his voice not lost.

If I am madly-deaf for having erred,
Still may I hear his word.

If sin hath slain mine honor, straight appears,
The river of his tears,

Wherein I find redemption: tenderly
He woos my fear away,

And searches out some star of hope, above,
So boundless in his love.

When from the loathed grave I shall arise,
He'll hail me from the skies.

Who else would seek me in corruption's dress
With a so kind caress?

Though I am weak, there is a hope of power;
He is my mighty tower;

Like as a flame to fright the gloom away;
He is my perfect day.

A14

I am the homely bulb that tops the reed—
He is the precious seed.

I am the rudest shell the vext-waves whirl—
He is the priceless pearl.

Thou art indeed my friend while ages roll,
O! thou my deathless soul.

C. W. S.

*

AT ANCHOR.

A sailor by the green home-shore,
While seas are ebbing from his view,
Doth all his earthly joys renew:
He sings the songs he sang of yore;

He spies his little cot, he smiles
With a full joy ne'er felt before—
He holds that one bare prospect more
Than all the summer of the isles.

The quiet home is his; the trees
Sprang from the seeds his grandsires laid,
Among the mould; within the glade
The myrtles rustle in the breeze.

Above a treasured little grave,
His earthly lost, his first deep woe!
Not any land that he may know
Beyond the purple of the wave

Hath such a jewel in its breast.
He loves each rock and stream and dell;
'Tis only here he cares to dwell,
'Tis ever here he longs to rest.

This is his home of joy and ease:
And better is the myrtle tomb
Than all the heavy dusks that gloom
The groves of spice beyond the seas.

C. W. S.

*

AT THE SPRING.

I knew a cumbrous hill,
From whose green breast did daintily distill
A throbbing rill.

This is the artery,
And further on the crystal heart must be,
Thought said to me.

All other I forsook,
To follow every twist and curious crook
Of this wild brook.

Among deep mosses set,
I found the glimmering fount that did beget
The rivulet.

No other eye had known
Its secret, nor ear heard—for it made moan
Always alone.

I quaffed its water clear;
Its limpid music babbled to mine ear
With voice sincere.

Then such a silence fell
Upon me, mantling me, as where a spell
Is wont to dwell.

Yet fled I from the place
At a rude rustling; and fear gave me chase
In my disgrace.

'Twas a slim water-snake
Slipt like an arrow through the shivering brake.
And left no wake.

But cleft the placid spring
And waved its flaming sword, its forked sting,
In a charmed ring.

*   *   *   *   *   *   *

So was the fountain spoiled
Within its lucid walls a devil coiled—
My trust was foiled.

Chas. Warren Stoddard.
San Francisco, Cal.

*

THE SECRET WELL
I know a well so deep and cool
And hid, the crystal-hearted pool
Hath never thrilled a swallow's throat
Or sweetened a lark's note.

No fainting stag, though perishing,
Hath ventured to disturb this spring;
No leopard with its fiery breast
This fountain dares molest.

No cunning silver-cased trout
The sheltered source can e'er search out—
No tongue but mine may ever tell
The secret of this well.

I build about its guarded rim
With added stones: I know the dim
Still twilight of its mossy cell,
Where the sweet waters dwell.

For spirits go between us two
With flasks; they brim with softest dew.
I drink and am refreshed and seem
As living in a dream.

This well, that is alone for me,
Is all a fount of memory;
And every year that I have known
Is as an added stone.

My willing thoughts, as spirits, haste
To draw the draught I love to taste.
There is an ever full supply
Yet who may drink but I?

C. W. S.

*

A RHYME OF LIFE.
If life be as a flame that death doth kill:
Burn little candle lit for me.
With a pure spark, that I may rightly see
To word my song and utterly
God's plan fulfill.

If life be as a flower that blooms and dies:
Forbid the cunning frost that slays
With Judas-kiss, and trusting love betrays:
Forever may my song of praise
Untainted rise

If life be as a voyage, or foul, or fair:
Oh! bid me not my banners furl
For adverse gale, or wave in angry whirl,
Till I have found the gates of pearl
And anchored there.

C. W. S.

*

CHERRIES AND GRAPES.
Not the cherries' nerveless flesh,
However fair, however fresh,
May ever hope my love to win
For Ethiope blood and satin skin.

Their lustre rich, and deep their dye,
Yet under all their splendors lie—
To what I cannot tribute grant—
Their hateful hearts of adamant.

I love the amber globes that hold
That dead-delicious wine of gold;
A thousand torrid suns distill
Such liquors as those flagons fill.

Yet tropic gales with souls of musk
Should steep my grapes in steams of dusk;
An orient Eden nothing lacks
To spice their purple silken sacks.

C. W. S.

*

MADRIGAL.
A maid is sitting by a brook,
The sweetest of sweet creatures:
I pass that way with my good book
Yet cannot read, nor cease to look
Upon her winsome features.

Amongst the blushes on her cheek
Her small, white hand reposes:
I am a shepherd, for I seek
That wilful lamb, with fleece so sleek,
Feeding among the roses!

C. W. S.

*

Date: March 2, 1869
1869
Honolulu. Hawaiian Islands.
2nd March.

To Walt Whitman.

May I quote you a couplet from your "Leaves of Grass"? "Stranger! If you, passing, meet me, "and desire to speak to me, why "should you not speak to me?" And why should I not speak to you?"

—I am the stranger who, passing, desires to speak to you. Once before I have done so, offering you a few feeble verses. I do not wonder you did not reply to them. Now my voice is stronger, I ask, why will you not speak to me?

So fortunate as to be traveling in these very interesting islands I have done wonders in my intercourse with these natives. For the first time I act as my nature prompts me. It would not answer in America, as a general principle, not even in California where men are tolerably bold. This is my mode of life:—At dusk I reach some village, a few grass huts by the sea or in some valley. The native villagers gather about me, for strangers are not common in these parts. I observe them closely. Superb looking, many of them. Fine heads. Glorious eyes that question, observe and then trust or distrust with an infallible instinct. Proud, defiant lips, a matchless physique, grace and freedom in every motion. I mark one, a lad of eighteen or twenty years who is regarding me. I call him to me, ask his name giving mine in return. He speaks it over and over, manipulating my body unconsciously, as it were, with bountiful and unconstrained love. I go to his grass-house, eat with him his simple food, sleep with him upon his mats, and at night sometimes waken to find him watching me with earnest, patient looks, his arm over my breast and around me. In the morning he hates to have me go. I hate as much to leave him. Over and over I think

of him as I travel: he doubtless recalls me some times, perhaps wishes me back with him. We were known to one another, perhaps twelve hours. Yet I cannot forget him. Any thing that pertains to him now interests me.

You will easily imagine, my dear sir, how delightful I find this life. I read your Poems with a new spirit, to understand them as few may be able to. And I wish more than ever that I might possess a few lines from your pen. I want your personal magnetism to quicken mine, how else shall I have it? Do write me a few lines for they will be of immense value to me.

I wish it were possible to get your photograph. The small Lithograph I have of you is not wholly satisfactory. But I would not ask so much of you. Only a page with your name & mine as you write it—Is this too much?

My address is San Francisco, Cal Box 1005. P. O. I shall immediately return there.

In all places I am the same to you. Chas. Warren Stoddard..[14]

*

Washington,
June 12, 1869
Charles W. Stoddard,

Dear Sir:

Your letters have reached me. I cordially accept your appreciation, & reciprocate your friendship. I do not write many letters, but like to meet people. Those tender & primitive personal relations away off there in the Pacific Islands, as described by you, touched me deeply.[3]

In answer to your request, I send you my picture—it was taken three months since. I also send a newspaper.

Farewell, my friend. I sincerely thank you, & hope some day to meet you.

Walt Whitman

*

1870
2nd April
St Francisco Cal

To Walt Whitman.

In the name of Calamus listen to me! Before me hangs your beautiful photograph, twice precious, since it is your gift to me. Near at hand lies your beloved vol. and with it the Notes of Mr. Burrough.

May I not thank you for your picture and your letter? May I not tell you over and over that where I go your go with me, in poem and picture and the little vol of notes also, for I read and reread trying to see you in the flesh as I so long to see you!

I wrote you last from the Sandwich Islands. I shall before long be even farther from you than ever for I think of sailing towards Tahiti in about five weeks.

I know there is but one hope for me. I must get amongst people who are not afraid of instincts and who scorn hypocracy. I am numbed with the frigid manners of the Christians; barbarism has given me the fullest joy of my life and I long to return to it and be satisfied. May I not send you a proze idyl where in I confess how dear it is to me?

There is much truth in it and I am praying that you may like it a little. If I could only know that it has pleased you I should bless my stars fervantly.

I have been in vain trying to buy from our Library a copy of your "Leaves" Edt. of 1855—I think it your first & I have somewhere read that you set the type for it yourself—Is it true? Do you think I could obtain a copy of it by addressing some Eastern publisher or book seller?

You say you "don't write many letters". O, if you would only reply to this within the month! I could then go into the South Seas feeling sure of your friendship and I should try to life the real life there for your sake as well as for my own.

Forgive me if I have wearied you: I will be silent and thoughtful in future, but in any case know, dear friend that I am grateful for your indulgence.

Affectionately yours
Chas. Warren Stoddard..
Box 1005. P. O.
San Francisco Cal.
(my address *always*)

[14]Folsom, Ed and Kenneth M. Price, editors. *The Walt Whitman Archive*. University of Nebraska–Lincoln, 2017, http://whitmanarchive.org/. Accessed 26 February, 2017.

CORRESPONDENCE: STOKER AND WHITMAN.

Dublin, Feb. 14, 1876.

My dear Mr. Whitman.

I hope you will not consider this letter from an utter stranger a liberty. Indeed, I hardly feel a stranger to you, nor is this the first letter that I have written to you. My friend Edward Dowden has told me often that you like new acquaintances or I should rather say friends. And as an old friend I send you an enclosure which may interest you. Four years ago I wrote the enclosed draft of a letter which I intended to copy out and send to you—it has lain in my desk since then—when I heard that you were addressed as Mr. Whitman. It speaks for itself and needs no comment. It is as truly what I wanted to say as that light is light. The four years which have elapsed have made me love your work fourfold, and I can truly say that I have ever spoken as your friend. You know what hostile criticism your work sometimes evokes here, and I wage a perpetual war with many friends on your behalf. But I am glad to say that I have been the means of making your work known to many who were scoffers at first. The years which have passed have not been uneventful to me, and I have felt and thought and suffered much in them, and I can truly say that from you I have had much pleasure and much consolation—and I do believe that your open earnest speech has not been thrown away on me or that my life and thought fail to be marked with its impress. I write this openly because I feel that with you one must be open. We have just had tonight a hot debate on your genius at the Fortnightly Club in which I had the privilege of putting forward my views—I think with success. Do not think me cheeky for writing this. I only hope we may sometime meet and I shall be able perhaps to say what I cannot write. Dowden promised to get me a copy of your new edition and I hope that for any other work which you may have you will let me always be an early subscriber. I am sorry that you're not strong. Many of us are hoping to see you in Ireland. We had arranged to have a meeting for you. I do not know if you like getting letters. If you do I shall only be too happy to send you news of how thought goes among the men I know. With truest wishes for your health and happiness believe me,

Your friend

Bram Stoker

*

Dublin, Ireland, Feb. 18, 1872.

If you are the man I take you to be you will like to get this letter. If you are not I don't care whether you like it or not and only ask that you put it into the fire without reading any farther. But I believe you will like it. I don't think there is a man living, even you who are above the prejudices of the class of small-minded men, who wouldn't like to get a letter from a younger man, a stranger, across the world—a man living in an atmosphere prejudiced to the truths you sing and your manner of singing them. The idea that arises in my mind is whether there is a man living who would have the pluck to burn a letter in which he felt the smallest atom of interest without reading it. I believe you would and that you believe you would yourself. You can burn this now and test yourself, and all I will ask for my trouble of writing this letter, which for all I can tell you may light your pipe with or apply to some more ignoble purpose—is that you will in some manner let me know that my words have tested your impatience. Put it in the fire if you like—but if you do you will miss the pleasure of the next sentence which ought to be that you have conquered an unworthy impulse. A man who is certain of his own strength might try to encourage himself a piece of bravo, but a man who can write, as you have written, the most candid words that ever fell from the lips of a mortal man—a man to whose candor Rousseau's *Confessions* is reticence—can have no fear for his own strength. If you have gone this far you may read the letter and I feel in writing now that I am talking to you. If I were before your face I would like to shake hands with you, for I feel that I would like you. I would like to call YOU Comrade and to talk to you as men who are not poets do not often talk. I think that at first a man would be ashamed, for a man cannot in a moment break the habit of comparative reticence that has become second nature to him; but I know I would not long be ashamed to be natural before you. You are a true man, and I would like to be one myself, and so I would be towards you as a brother and as a pupil to his master. In this age no man becomes worthy of

the name without an effort. You have shaken off the shackles and your wings are free. I have the shackles on my shoulders still—but I have no wings. If you are going to read this letter any further I should tell you that I am not prepared to "give up all else" so far as words go. The only thing I am prepared to give up is prejudice, and before I knew you I had begun to throw overboard my cargo, but it is not all gone yet. I do not know how you will take this letter. I have not addressed you in any form as I hear that you dislike to a certain degree the conventional forms in letters. I am writing to you because you are different from other men. If you were the same as the mass I would not write at all. As it is I must either call you Walt Whitman or not call you at all—and I have chosen the latter course. I do not know whether it is unusual for you to get letters from utter strangers who have not even the claim of literary brotherhood to write you. If it is you must be frightfully tormented with letters and I am sorry to have written this. I have, however, the claim of liking you—for your words are your own soul and even if you do not read my letter it is no less a pleasure to me to write it. Shelley wrote to William Godwin and they became friends. I am not Shelley and you are not Godwin and so I will only hope that sometime I may meet you face to face and perhaps shake hands with you. If I ever do it will be one of the greatest pleasures of my life … The way I came to you was this. A notice of your poems appeared some two years ago or more in *Temple Bar* magazine. I glanced at it and took its dictum as final, and laughed at you among friends. *I say it to my own shame but not to regret for it has taught me a lesson to last my life out—without ever having seen your poems.* More than a year after I heard two men in College talking of you. One of them had your book (Rossetti's edition) and was reading aloud some passages at which both laughed. They chose only those passages which are most foreign to British ears and made fun of them. Something struck me that I had judged you hastily. I took home the volume and read far into the night. Since then I have to thank you for many happy hours, for I have read your poems with my door locked late at night and I have read them on the seashore where I could look all round me and see no more sign of human life than the ships out at sea: and here I often found myself waking up from a reverie with the book open before me. I love all poetry, and high generous thoughts make the tears rush to my eyes, but sometimes a word or a phrase of yours takes me away from the world around me and places me in an ideal land surrounded by realities more than any poem I ever read. Last year I was sitting on the beach on a summer's day reading your preface to the *Leaves of Grass* as printed in Rossetti's edition … One thought struck me and I pondered over it for several hours—"the weather-beaten vessels entering new ports," you who wrote the words know them better than I do: and to you who sing of your land of progress the words have a meaning that I can only imagine. But be assured of this Walt Whitman—that a man of less than half your own age, reared a conservative in a conservative country, and who has always heard your name cried down by the great mass of people who mention it, here felt his heart leap towards you across the Atlantic and his soul swelling at the words or rather the thoughts. It is vain for me to quote an instances of what thoughts of yours I like best—for I like them all and you must feel you are reading the true words of one who feels with you. You see, I have called you by your name. I have been more candid with you—have said more about myself to you than I have said to anyone before. You will not be angry with me if you have read so far. You will not laugh at me for writing this to you. It was no small effort that I began to write and I feel reluctant to stop, but I must not tire you any more. If you would ever care to have more you can imagine, for you have a great heart, how much pleasure it would be to me to write more to you. How sweet a thing it is for a strong healthy man with a woman's eye and a child's wishes to feel that he can speak to a man who can be if he wishes father, and brother and wife to his soul. I don't think you will laugh, Walt Whitman, nor despise me, but at all events I thank you for all the love and sympathy you have given me in common with my kind.

—Bram Stoker

*

41 STEVENS ST. CAMBDEN,
1. JERSEY, COR. WEST.
U.S. AMERICA,

March 6, '76

Bram Stoker,—My dear young man,—Your letters have been most welcome to me—welcome to me as a Person and then as Author—I don't know which most. You did so well to write to me so unconventionally, so fresh, so manly, and affectionately too. I, too, hope (though it is not probable) that we will some day personally meet each other. Meantime, I send my friendship and thanks.

Edward Dowden's letter containing among others your subscription for a copy of my new edition has just been recd. I shall send the book very soon by express in a package to his address. I have just written to E.D.

My physique is entirely shatter'd—doubtless permanently—from paralysis and other ailments. But I am up and dress'd, and get out every day a little, live here quite lonesome, but hearty, and good spirits.—Write to me again.

—Walt Whitman

[14]Folsom, Ed and Kenneth M. Price, editors. *The Walt Whitman Archive.* University of Nebraska–Lincoln, 2017, http://whitmanarchive.org/. Accessed 26 February, 2017.

[A.16]

A16

CORRESPONDENCE: WILDE AND WHITMAN.

1267 Broadway, New York

My Dear Dear Walt—

Swinburne has just written to me to say as follows.

"I am sincerely interested and gratified by your account of Walt Whitman and the assurance of his kindly and friendly feeling towards me: and I thank you, no less sincerely, for your kindness in sending me word of it. As sincerely can I say, what I shall be freshly obliged to you if you will assure him of in my name, that I have by no manner of means relaxed my admiration of his noblest works—such parts, above all, of his writings, as treat of the noblest subjects, material and spiritual, with which poetry can deal—I have always thought it, and I believe it will be hereafter generally thought his highest and surely most enviable distinction that he never speaks so well as when he speaks of great matters—Liberty, for instance, and Death.

This of course does not imply that I do, or rather it implies that I do not agree with all his theories, or admire all his work in anything like equal measure—a form of admiration which I should by no means desire for myself and am as little prepared to bestow on another—considering it a form of scarcely indirect insult"

There! You see how you remain in our hearts—and how simply and grandly Swinburne speaks of you knowing you to be simple and grand yourself.

Will you in return send me for Swinburne a copy of your Essay on Poetry—the pamphlet—with your name and his on it—it would please him so much. Before I leave America I must see you again—there is no one in this wide great world of America whom I love and honor so much.

With warm affection, and honorable admiration,

Oscar Wilde

[14]Folsom, Ed and Kenneth M. Price, editors. *The Walt Whitman Archive*. University of Nebraska–Lincoln, 2017, http://whitmanarchive.org/. Accessed 26 February, 2017.

A17 [A.17]

THE GOSPEL ACCORDING TO WALT WHITMAN.
Oscar Wilde

January 25, 1889
The Pall Mall Gazette 25 January 1889: 3.

"No one will get at my verses who insists upon viewing them as a literary performance, or as aiming mainly towards art and æstheticism. *Leaves of Grass* has been chiefly the outcropping of my own emotional and other personal nature—an attempt from first to last to put a *Person*, a human being (myself, in the latter half of the nineteenth century, in America) freely, fully and truly on record. I could not find any similar personal record in current literature that satisfied me." In these words Walt Whitman gives us the true attitude we should adopt towards his work, having indeed a much saner view of the value and meaning of that work than either his eloquent admirers or noisy detractors can boast of possessing. His last book, *November Boughs* as he calls it, published in the winter of the old man's life, reveals to us, not indeed a soul's tragedy, for its last note is one of joy and hope and noble and unshaken faith in all that is fine and worthy of such faith, but certainly the drama of a human soul, and puts on record with a simplicity that has in it both sweetness and strength the record of his spiritual development and of the aim and motive both of the manner and the matter of his work. His strange mode of expression is shown in these pages to have been the result of deliberate and self-conscious choice. The "barbaric yawp," which he sent over "the roofs of the world" so many years ago, and which wrung from Mr. Swinburne's lips such lofty panegyric in song and such loud clamorous censure in prose, appears here in what will be to many an entirely new light. For in his very rejection of art Walt Whitman is an artist. He tried to produce a certain effect by certain means and he succeeded. There is much method in what many have termed his madness, too much method indeed some may be tempted to fancy.

In the story of his life, as he tells it to us, we find him at the age of sixteen beginning a definite and philosophical study of literature:—

Summers and falls, I used to go off, sometimes for a week at a stretch, down in the country, or to Long Island's seashores—there in the presence of outdoor influences, I went over thoroughly the Old and New Testaments, and absorb'd (probably to better advantage for me than in any library or indoor room—it makes such difference *where* you read) Shakspere, Ossian, the best translated versions I could get of Homer, Æschylus, Sophokles, the old German Nibelungen,[1] the ancient Hindoo poems, and one or two other masterpieces, Dante's among them. As it happen'd I read the latter mostly in an old wood. The Iliad I read first thoroughly on the peninsula of Orient, north-east end of Long Island, in a sheltered hollow of rocks and sand, with the sea on each side. (I have wondered since why I was not overwhelmed by those mighty masters. Likely because I read them, as described, in the full presence of Nature, under the sun, with the far-spreading landscapes and vistas, or the sea rolling in.)

Edgar Allan Poe's amusing bit of dogmatism that, for our occasions and for our day, there can be no such thing as a long poem, fascinated him: "The same thought had been haunting my mind before," he says, "but Poe's argument, though short, work'd the sum out and proved it to me:" and the English translation of the Bible seems to have suggested to him the possibility of a poetic form which while retaining the spirit of poetry would still be free from the trammels of rhyme and of a definite metrical system. Having thus to a certain degree settled upon what one might call the *technique* of Whitmanism, he began to brood upon the nature of that spirit that was to give life to the strange form. The central point of the poetry of the future seemed to him to be necessarily "an identical body and soul," a personality in fact, which personality he tells us frankly, "after many considerations and ponderings I deliberately settled should be myself." However for the true creation and revealing of this personality, at first only dimly felt, a new stimulus was needed. This came from the Civil War. After describing the many dreams and passions of his boyhood and early manhood he goes on to say:—

These, however, and much more might have gone on and come to naught (almost positively would have come to naught) if a sudden, vast, terrible, direct and indirect stimulus for new and national declamatory expression had not been given to me. It is certain, I say, that, although I had made a start before, only from the occurrence of the Secession War, and what it showed me as by flashes of lightning, with the emotional depths it sounded and arous'd (of course, I don't mean in my own heart only, I saw it just as plainly in others, in millions) that only from the strong flare and provocation of that war's sights and scenes the final reasons-for-being of an autochthonic and passionate song definitely came forth. I went down to the war-fields of Virginia, lived thenceforward in camp, saw great battles and the days and nights afterwards—partook of all the fluctuations, gloom, despair, hopes again aroused, courage evoked—death readily risked— the *cause* too—along and filling those agonistic and lurid following years, the real parturition years of the henceforth homogeneous Union. Without those three or four years and the experiences they gave, "Leaves of Grass" would not now be existing.

Having thus obtained the necessary stimulus for the quickening and awakening of the personal self, some day to be endowed with universality, he sought to find new notes of song, and passing beyond the mere passion for expression—he aimed at "Suggestiveness" first. "I round and finish little, if anything; and could not, consistently with my scheme. The reader will have his or her part to do, just as much as I have had mine. I seek less to state or display any theme of thought, and more to bring you, reader, into the atmosphere of the theme or thought—there to pursue your own flight." Another "impetus word" is Comradeship, and other "word-signs" are Good Cheer, Content, and Hope. Individuality, especially, he sought for:—

I have allowed the stress of my poems from beginning to end to bear upon American individuality and assist it—not only because that is a great lesson in Nature, amid all her generalizing laws, but as a counterpoise to the levelling tendencies of Democracy—and for other reasons. Defiant of ostensible literary and other conventions, I avowedly chant "the great pride of a man in himself," and permit it to be more or less a *motif* of nearly all my verse. I think this pride indispensable to an American. I think it not inconsistent with obedience, humility, deference, and self-questioning.

*

A new theme also was to be found in the relation of the sexes, conceived in a natural, simple, and healthy form, and he protests against poor Mr. William Rossetti's attempt to Bowdlerize and expurgate his song.

From another point of view "Leaves of Grass" is avowedly the song of Sex, and Amativeness, and even Animality—though meanings that do not usually go with these words are behind all, and will duly emerge; and all are sought to be lifted into a different light and atmosphere. Of this feature intentionally palpable in a few lines, I shall only say the espousing principle of those lines so gives breath to my whole scheme that the bulk of the pieces might as well have been left unwritten were those lines omitted…Universal as are certain facts and symptoms of communities there is nothing so rare in modern conventions and poetry as their normal recognizance. Literature is always calling in the doctor for consultation and confession, and always giving evasions and swathing suppressions in place of that "heroic nudity" on which only a genuine diagnosis can be built. And in respect to editions of "Leaves of Grass" in time to come (if there should be such) I take occasion now to confirm those lines with the settled convictions and deliberate renewals of thirty years, and to hereby prohibit, as far as mine can do so, any elision of them.

*

But beyond all these notes and moods and motives is the lofty spirit of a grand and free acceptance of

A18

all things that are worthy of existence. "I desired," he says, "to formulate a poem whose every thought or fact should indirectly or directly be or connive at an implicit belief in the wisdom, health, mystery, or beauty of every process, every concrete object, every human or other existence, not only consider'd from the point of view of all, but of each." His two final utterances are that really great poetry is always the result of a national spirit, and not the privilege of a polished and select few; and that the sweetest and strongest songs yet remain to be sung.

Such are the views contained in the opening essay, "A Backward Glance o'er Travel'd Roads," as he calls it: but there are many other essays in this fascinating volume, some on poets such as Burns and Lord Tennyson, for whom Walt Whitman has a profound admiration: some on old actors and singers, the elder Booth, Forrest, Alboni, and Mario being his special favourites: others on the native Indians, on the Spanish element in American nationality, on Western slang, on the poetry of the Bible, and on Abraham Lincoln. But Walt Whitman is at his best when he is analyzing his own work, and making schemes for the poetry of the future. Literature to him has a distinctly social aim. He seeks to build up the masses by "building up grand individuals." And yet literature itself must be preceded by noble forms of life. "The best literature is always the result of something far greater than itself—not the hero but the portrait of the hero. Before there can be recorded history or poem there must be the transaction." Certainly in Walt Whitman's views there is a largeness of vision, a healthy sanity, and a fine ethical purpose. He is not to be placed with the professional littérateurs of his country, Boston novelists, New York poets, and the like. He stands apart, and the chief value of his work is in its prophecy not in its performance. He has begun a prelude to larger themes. He is the herald to a new era. As a man he is the precursor of a fresh type. He is a factor in the heroic and spiritual evolution of the human being. If Poetry has passed him by, Philosophy will take note of him.

[14]Folsom, Ed and Kenneth M. Price, editors. *The Walt Whitman Archive*. University of Nebraska–Lincoln, 2017, http://whitmanarchive.org/. Accessed 26 February, 2017.

[A.18]

CORRESPONDENCE: JOHNSON AND WHITMAN.

The College
Winchester
Hampshire
England.

Dear Walt Whitman:

I write to you, though personally unknown, as writing to a dear friend: because, though happy to call many about me by the name of friends, I have no truer friend than yourself: if friendship means the receiving of light and delight and strength from the spirit of a brother man. I have lived as yet but eighteen years: yet in all the constant thoughts and acts of my last few years, your words have been my guides and true oracles. I cannot hope to see you face to face, and tell you this: but you will at least believe it and feel that I am not writing from an unworthy spirit of self-assertion: but that I should feel shame for myself, were I not to show the reality of my gratitude to you, even through the weakness of words—you, whom I thankfully acknowledge for my veritable master and dear brother.

You, in your age and glorious approach to the sure future of death—you will know that I am speaking neither empty adulation nor shallow shams.

I am proud of belonging to the oldest school of any in England—to the great foundation of the strong priest and ruler, William of Wykeham: and it was under the shadows of the ancient walls of his college, still flourishing through the influence of his powerful personality, that I first received "Leaves of Grass" from the hands of a most dear friend. And the help and exaltation that I won from it have been won by many another boy and young man, of those in whose hands rests the immediate history of the coming years—to make it splendid with strong actions and strong asserted truths. It is in your works, as in the great powers of earth and sea, that the inspiring force of no school is to be found: certain to dare all things by the strength of body and soul inseparable.

Whether I am right or not in writing to you, I neither know nor care: I do know that I cannot keep silence.

I am, in love and reverence,
Lionel Johnson

[14] Folsom, Ed and Kenneth M. Price, editors. *The Walt Whitman Archive*. University of Nebraska–Lincoln, 2017, http://whitmanarchive.org/. Accessed 26 February, 2017.

[A.19]

CORRESPONDENCE: MELVILLE AND HAWTHORNE.

Pittsfield, July 17th, [1852?]

My Dear Hawthorne:—This name of "Hawthorne" seems to be ubiquitous. I have been on something of a tour lately, and it has saluted me vocally & typographically in all sorts of places & in all sorts of ways.—I was at the solitary Crusoeish island of Naushon (one of the Elisabeth group) and there, on a stately piazza, I saw it gilded on the back of a very new book, and in the hands of a clergyman.—I went to visit a gentleman in Brooklyne, and as we were sitting at our wine, in came the lady of the house, holding a beaming volume in her hand, from the city—"My Dear," to her husband, "I have brought you Hawthorne's new book." I entered the cars at Boston for this place. In came a lively boy "Hawthorne's new book!"—In good time I arrived home. Said my lady-wife "there is Mr Hawthorne's new book, come by mail" And this morning, lo! on my table a little note, subscribed Hawthorne again.—Well, the Hawthorne is a sweet flower; may it flourish in every hedge.

I am sorry, but I can not at present come to see you at Concord as you propose.—I am but just returned from a two weeks' absence; and for the last three months & more I have been an utter idler and a savage—out of doors all the time. So, the hour has come for me to sit down again.

Do send me a specimen of your sand-hill, and a sunbeam from the countenance of Mrs. Hawthorne, and a vine from the curly arbor of Master Julian.

As I am only just home, I have not yet got far into the book but enough to see that you have most admirably employed materials which are richer than I had fancied them. Especially at this day, the volume is welcome, as an antidote to the mooniness of some dreamers—who are merely dreamers——Yet who the deviant a dreamer?

H Melville

My remembrances to Miss Una & Master Julian—& the "compliments" & perfumes of the season to the "Rose-bud."

[11] Emerson, Warren. "Melville to Hawthorne: 'Well, the Hawthorne is a sweet flower; may it flourish in every hedge.'" *The Literary Table*. March 13, 2012. https://literarytable.com/2012/03/13/melville-to-hawthorne-well-the-hawthorne-is-a-sweet-flower-may-it-flourish-in-every-hedge/. Accessed February 26, 1988.

A19

A20

[A.20]

MR. O CONNOR'S LETTER, 1883.

WASHINGTON, D. C., U. S. A.,
February 22d, 1883;
DR. R. M. BUCKE, LONDON,
ONTARIO, CANADA.

DEAR SIR:

It is nearly eighteen years since I published the impassioned protest against the mean and monstrous wrong done by the Hon. James Harlan to Walt Whitman, which you ask leave to reprint in your Appendix. The warmest friend of that old outburst might think of it as one might of the ring of flame he had seen Cotopaxi send with a blast into the tropic azure—a burning meteor thrown up to circle and shimmer for a moment in the upper air—then vanish. That it is to reappear and remain I shall owe to you. I thank you gratefully, but less for the kind personal honor your request does me, than for the opportunity you offer to make my otherwise ephemeral work a sharer in the enduring life assured to your volume. A pamphlet like mine,—crude, extemporaneous, fragmentary, the birth of an exigency, the utterance evoked by outrage, the voice of an indignant heart,—is, no matter what its cause or purpose, the accident of an hour, and can ordinarily have but the hour's existence. This is sternly true of far better compositions of this class than mine. Who reads now the masterly "Labienus" of Rogeard? Who remembers those arrows of lightnings, the bright, barbed feuilletons of Paul

Louis Courier? Even the shafts of the great sagittary, Rochefort, are already regathered into the black quiver of yesterday. But a book, with its long fore ground of premeditation,—especially a book with such a subject, such an aim as yours, and written from your vantage-ground of science, and with your ardent intelligence and power,—can lay great bases for eternity. For my brochure to be linked to such a one is, therefore, a pledge of its perpetuity, and in this I feel cause for satisfaction. Not because of any merit I attach to pages of whose faults and deficiencies I am only too well aware, and which I wish I had had time and ability to make better, but because those pages hold the record of the one action of my life which I could wish might never be forgotten, even though it had brought upon me, and was still to bring, every misfortune and every dishonor. Long as I had revered Walt Whitman, and deeply as I had valued his book, I had never, up to the date of his expulsion from office, written a single line in his interest, considering, as I still consider, both him and his works subjects far beyond my powers. Even the twelve years of shameful persecution, ostracism, and insult, which followed the publication of his second edition, the exclusion of any specimen of his poetry from the anthologies of American song, the closing of the doors of all periodicals to his contributions, the insolent rejections of his work by the peddlers who call themselves publishers, the infamous calumnies invented and set in circulation by persons of repute respecting his personal conduct and character, the affectation of shuddering aversion practised in certain quarters at the sight of his face or the mention of his name, the showered misrepresentation and abuse of his poems by the reviewers and journalists,—even all this I witnessed and endured with as much composure as is compatible with scorn, knowing, in the noble words of Ellery Channing, that "who writes by fate the critics shall not kill, nor all the assassins of the great review," certain that, in the trumpet phrase of Leibnitz, "Another time shall come, worthier than ours, in which, hatreds being subdued, truth shall triumph," and that then Walt Whitman and his mighty volume would fail not of their meed of veneration. But when I saw the poetaster and the plagiary, the hypocrite and the prude, the eunuch and the fop, the poisoner and the blackguard, the snake and the hog, the gnat and the midge, all the

creatures of the marsh and the copse, all the vermin of the kennel and the sewer, every monkey that mops and mows in the curule chair of Longinus fancying himself a critic, every chinch that poses on the triclinium of Horace imagining himself an author—when I saw the whole paltry and venomous swarm condense, as in some tale of enchantment, into a demon in the garb of an inquisitor;— when the Harlanunculi became resolved into the Harlan, and to moral animosity succeeded material consequences;—when I saw a man deprived of his employment, publicly degraded, and an official stigma set upon his name, simply and only because he had once, years before, published an honest book—and noted that among all our scholars and literati not one voice—not a single one—was raised even in the faintest deprecation of this dastardly outrage, welcomed instead with the silence that gives consent, and with gibes and guffaws of approval— then I felt that even for a writer so inexperienced and obscure as I, the hour of duty had arrived, and in the pages you reprint I did my best, as I have said in another place, to secure for the infamy of Mr. Harlan's action undying remembrance. It is because I did this—it is because, as Dr. Johnson says, I did what nobody else thought worth doing—that I am glad to have the record perpetuated in your volume. Let shame or credit follow, I care not which, nor have I ever cared. The man who tried to make an author suffer for his book I tried to brand! This is all the claim I make for my pamphlet, and that pamphlet is my act. I vaunt it and I stand by

I have spoken, you will remember, of the hour of Mr. Marian's explorations in the Department, and I regret now that in the haste of the composition I did not more elaborately place this hour in amber. It was not enough that he chose to do a mean and monstrous action; the manner of his doing it was still meaner and more monstrous. The book had been for several years out of print. It was not in circulation. But in a drawer in the author's desk which stood in a room in the lower story of the Department building, there was a private copy rilled with pencilled interlineations, erasures, annotations—the revisions which prepare a text for future publication. This copy was the one over which Mr. Harlan pored in the still hours which followed the closing of the official day in the Department. But it was in his own office, in an upper story, that he pursued these secret studies. The book was always in its place in the author's desk when he went home in the afternoon, and it was always there when he returned the next morning. It was in the interim that it was upstairs. Who was it that edged along the shadowy passages of the huge building from the Secretary's apartment—that quietly slipped down the dim stairway—that crept, crawled, stole, sneaked into the deserted room of his illustrious fellow-officer—that tiptoed up to the vacant desk—that put a furtive hand into the private drawer and drew out the private volume—that glided back with it to the office of the Secretary? When the hours of gloating were over, and the building was darker and dimmer under its few funereal gaslights, turned murkily low, who crept back down the dead-house corridors and stair ways, with a volume in his hand, to the earlier visited apartment, stealthily replaced the volume in the desk, and softly slunk away? Was it Tartuffe disguised as Aminidab Sleek, or was it the rampant god Priapus masquerading as Paul Pry? Enough to know that these Department explorations and these sub-rosa examinations resulted in Mr. Harlan expelling Walt Whitman from his position for having once upon a time published a volume containing a little reference to some facts in universal physiology. This reference, it seems, shocked the Methodist virtue that had endured without flinching the daily conversation of Lincoln—Lincoln, under whom Mr. Harlan had accepted and held his Secretaryship—a President as soundly good and as frankly gross as Luther or Rabelais.

Mr. Harlan was the Secretary of the Department of the Interior. His charge included the public lands and the mines, the interests of the settlers and the diggers of ore, the fortune and fate of the red aborigines, the awards of the pensions and the tracts given in bounty to the soldiers and sailors, the promotion and safeguards of the myriad inventions through the issuance of their patents, the mighty task of the census when ordered, the care of the national insane and deaf and dumb, the supervision of vast territorial interests; in brief, an immense part of the ordinance, prosperity and development of the country. To execute the public business under his care, he had three thousand officers. As Secretary, his conduct of affairs could enhance the welfare of the nation; as statesman, his recommendation could mould the future. From all this lofty ministerial function, he stooped to the meanness and shame of the pick-pry inquisition, and the brutal and insolent expulsion described—his victim a poet illustrious in the verdict of the fittest of two worlds.

When I dealt with this abominable action as it deserved—although I no more than recognized it in its obvious character as an audacious assault upon the liberty of letters, and a flagrant and enormous breach of administrative propriety—although I merely flung the light upon it in its avowed intentions and proportions, and properly refuted the pretences upon which it claimed to be justified, by plainly bringing into opposition the superb purity and grandeur of the poem it attacked, as certified by the noblest minds of two continents, and the simple and sublime life of the poet it persecuted, as known to many of his countrymen—it was of course quite natural and logical that all the leading literary and many of the other journals in this country, which for years had been devoted to the defamation of which Mr. Harlan's conduct was the bright consummate flower, should respond by alleging that I was making mountains out of molehills, that my censure and my eulogy were alike inordinate; and that they should enter, as they did, into express extenuations and defences of the Secretary, coupled with their little sneers and scoffs at my vindication of the man he had wronged. You can judge of the force they brought to their task by the summary I offer of the points made upon me by the strongest article of all, the writer in this instance a prosperous and eminent man. By this literary magnate I was gravely reminded that Mr. Hawthorne lost his place in the Salem Custom House when the Whigs came into power, under our precious system of rotation in office, and hence in effect, that the Hon. Mr. Harlan's expulsion of Walt Whitman was quite a venial and normal act—as like the Whig dismissal of Hawthorne as one pea is like another pea. I was coldly informed that the gross wrong inflicted upon Mr. Whitman was "the mere loss of an office"—nothing more—nothing whatever; and I was made to feel that I had the assurance upon the honor of a refrigerator. Furthermore, that this "mere loss of an office" furnished no proper occasion for such a denunciation of the outrage, and such an apotheosis of its object, as were given in my pamphlet. For cool ignoring of all the circumstances of the case as set forth in my indictment, and for the simple and absolute frigidity of its belittling of Mr. Harlan's damnable action, I think this article in comparison makes Wrangel Land in the height of the Arctic winter an image of all that is bland and warm. Beside it, the icy sepulchre itself would seem a summer resort for consumptives. It never occurs to the dry light of mind of this just and intelligent critic, taking him on his own chosen ground, that there would have been some difference between Hawthorne civilly dismissed from office because of a change of administration, and Hawthorne brutally expelled with ignominy, because he had celebrated (some think covertly justified), in the sombre and splendid pages of the "Scarlet Letter," the adultery of Arthur Dimmesdale and Hester Prynne. It never occurs to this icily brilliant reviewer that expulsion for such a cause would be necessary to establish parity between Hawthorne's case and Walt Whitman's— and of course he never so much as glances side long at the consideration of the enormous uproar an expulsion on account of the "Scarlet Letter" would have created, though nobody knew this better than he. It never dawns for a moment on this prosperous and well-fed gentleman that to a poor man, hunted then by our literary ku-klux, almost outlawed at that time by the Kemper-county gang who carry out the shot-gun policy in our literature and journalism, "the mere loss of an office" might cut off the means of subsistence, and be no matter for whiffling away as a mere trifle. But why comment? Did he ever really think, or any of his tribe, that the expulsion of an author from a public employment on account of his book could be made to appear a small matter? While such as I are in the world, it can never be a small matter; it will always be a great matter, and among the greatest of great matters, in the lasting verdict of every man and woman who knows the relation of thought to life, of books to the fortunes of mankind. Suppose Chaucer had been ejected from his post of Comptroller of Customs under the third Edward, on account of some of that outrageous Gallo-Saxon license of conception and expression which so often wantons in his pages. Does any one fancy that our scholars and essayists, even at the distance of six centuries, would treat the incident coolly, or as of no importance? Suppose Defoe, on account of the broad pictures in "Moll Flanders," or the "Memoirs

of a Cavalier," had been deprived of any one of his employments under William or Anne. What sympathy or defence would the minister get that did it, from the biographers of the creator of "Robinson Crusoe"? Suppose Charles Lamb had been fired out of his clerkship in the India House, because of his defence of the fairy obscenities of Farquhar and Wycherly? Wouldn't there be heat in the blood of London in the Old World, and Boston in the New, over the record that such a thing had ever been done to sweet old Elia? Suppose Burns had been considered, in the holy name of virtue, chastity, decency, Christian civilization, morally unfit to measure Scotch malt forever, and turned out of his gaugership because of the ithyphallic audacities he showered on the Scotch Harlans in "Holy Willie's Prayer"! Wouldn't literature ring with the outrage? Yea, verily; and well do the literati know it, who tried to make out that Mr. Harlan's immortal disgrace was the merest bagatelle, and mocked at my pamphlet as one of the curiosities of literature because it denounced his action on the scale of its proper magnitude.

Enough said, both of him and them. "A dog's obeyed in office," but the next one the humor of politics dresses up for a Secretary's chair, like Toby in a Punch and Judy show, will think seriously before he gives an order for the expulsion of an author on account of the book he had once published. The prospect both for Mr. Harlan and his literary apologists grows steadily worse as time goes on, and the character and value of Walt Whitman's book become established. This is no case of an abuse of power practised upon an author of the grade of Chaucer, or Defoe, or Lamb, or Burns. The gross wrong done by Mr. Harlan was done to a poet whom all time and every land will remember, and the dimensions of the insult and the outrage will be gauged by the measure of that universal and eternal fame. Whatever basis the contemptible scribblers of the day gave it, steadily crumbles. It is not in the nature of things, it is not in the control of the whole Dunciad, that the vast and sane affirmations, the simple and gorgeous beauty, the biblical and demiurgic power of *Leaves of Grass*, can continue to be themes for the ass reviewer's blattering bray. All the literati that ever hee-hawed from the rick in their prior existence, before the metempsychosis which placed them in the chairs of criticism to continue their symphonies, cannot drown the omni-prevalent voice of a work of genius. I remember a scene long ago in Faneuil Hall, when an attempt was made to silence a matchless orator, the incomparable Wendell Phillips, then in the prime of his indescribable forensic powers. He stood that evening in the full relief of his severe grace and beauty upon the lighted platform of the historic hall—from brow to foot all noble, like those knights of Venice Ruskin describes; the vast floor and galleries before and around him densely thronged; and central in the audience was a mob of stevedores and truckmen, the hired Alsatia of that class of merchants whose truckling servility to the Slave Power nourished in it the strength for rebellion, and at length brought on our Civil War. The moment the orator began, this swarm of hirelings became a roaring mælstrom; they whirled around en masse without cessation in the middle of the concourse, yelling, howling, shouting, without a moment's intermission, and for some time the noise was deafening. But, gradually, amidst the tumult there was heard something marvellous. The orator had continued speaking with tranquil composure,—with his easy, almost careless grace,—with that memorable beauty of tone and demeanor veiling earnest feeling, as a Phidian vase might veil the Delphic fire within; and above the hoarse, unintermitted, tremendous uproar of the mob, in its preconcerted continuity, was heard his quiet voice ! I never can forget the thrill it gave me. Not a word, not an accent was lost. Even the mob heard it, and strained their bull-throats to drown it. In vain. Paramount over all the clamor, that sweet and penetrating tone was heard, silverly asserting itself in even and uninterrupted flow, as clear and alien as the notes of the nightingale above the brawl of a flooded gorge; and it went on until it conquered wholly, and in silence, broken only by the sublime roar of acclamations, the splendid fountain of that eloquence was streaming upward in full silver flower. So dominant above the animal tumult of its defamers, so conquering and to conquer, is the voice of the book we champion. Over the clamor of the whole menagerie it is heard by the minds it has enlightened, the hearts it has com forted, the souls it has deeply stirred, and this voiceless multitude is the van guard of the future.

Meanwhile the book has achieved the vantage-ground, hardly less valuable than its cordial recognition in certain quarters, of having been regularly bid for and issued by a business house, instead of being published, as previously, by its author only. It is an advance, which should, for the honor of our letters, be complemented by a corresponding change in the tone of criticism. But the welcome given the reappearance of the work proves, that, even after the lapse of twenty years, our reviews are in the same hands—that is to say, paws. The criticisms are, to be sure, somewhat improved since the former day when a filthy and malignant philistine in the London "Saturday Review" wrote that the author deserved to be scourged at the tail of the hangman's cart by the public executioner. Whoever seeks the missing link between the libidinous swell and the ferocious chimpanzee, might find it in this noble and decent criticaster. This amenity of criticism was prompted by the series of poems entitled "Children of Adam;" and you know what physiologic dignity, jyhat sanctities of purely human love and passion, what savor of natural sanity, what wealth of esoteric communication, what rapture of moral elevation, what adumbrations of holiness, are enshrined within those glorious verses, and give them their magnetic scope and fervor. They had the added honor some years afterward of causing one of Astor's gentlemen, who sometimes obscurely and feebly paddles in Castaly, to style their venerable author with fine scorn, "this swan of the sewers." I could retort upon Dr. Macnobody that he is a buzzard of the club-house kitchen, but this might be thought personal. Of the more recent notices it may be remarked that they are generally less poignant and more dull than their old prototypes. Some of them, as in the "Atlantic Monthly," show instinctively cordial perceptions quenched in abject cowardice. The review in the New York "Times," marked by great talent, is a singular example of stultification, the writer diplomatically annulling in one passage what he has just said in another, this process being pursued throughout with a mechanical uniformity which is simply comical. The one in the "Nation" is in artistic keeping with the tone of that chilly journal, and is otherwise only noticeable for its cold and brutal falsehoods. One of its in dictments appears again in an article in "The Woman's Journal," signed with the initials of the Rev. Thomas Wentworth Higginson. The exceeding value of this accusation warrants its reproduction, and also its rescue from the oblivion of the anonymous. What, think you, is this weighty finding? Actually, now—really, now—Mr. Higginson avers that Walt Whitman ought to become the focal point of million-fingered scorn for having served in the hospitals! It appears that the old poet performed a pathetic, a sublime, an immortal service—he tended the wounded and dying soldiers throughout the whole war, and for years afterward, until the last hospital disappeared. O, but this was infamous! Shame on such "unmanly manhood," yells the Rev. Mr. Higginson! He should have personally "followed the drum," declares this soldier of the army of the Lord, himself a volunteer colonel. In bald words, instead of volunteering for the ghastly, the mournful, the perilous labors of those swarming infernos, the hospitals, Walt Whitman should have enlisted in the rank and file. From all which, I gather that Mr. Higginson would have cast a stone at Jean Valjean for going down without a musket into the barricades. I beg leave to tell this reverend militaire that if Longfellow had gone from Cambridge to serve in the hospitals, as Walt Whitman served, the land would have rung from end to end, and there would have been no objurgations on his not enlisting in the army, from the pen of the Rev. Thomas Wentworth Higginson. I also beg leave to tell him, since he brings personalities into fashion, that Walt Whitman's work of comfort and charity beside the cots of the Union and rebel soldiers, will last as long, and stand as fair, as the military bungling and blundering which distinguished this clergyman turned colonel, and evoked such agonized curses from his commanding officer at Port Royal. Better be a good nurse like Walt Whitman, than a nondescript warrior like the Rev. Col. Higginson.

The remainder of his article is quite taken up with an attack upon a few erotic verses in Oscar Wilde's poems, about which Mr. Higginson, as badly read as badly bred, says there is "nothing Greek," because they do not "suggest the sacred whiteness of an antique statue," although, as Mr. Higginson ought to know, there is a mass of literature, ranging from Aristophanes, Anacreon, Sappho, Longus, etc., to such as Mimnermus and Alcman, which they do suggest, and which Mr. Higginson could hardly describe as having "nothing Greek," but which could give Mr. Wilde a good many points in erotic composition, if that has anything to do with making

him Hellenic. On the strength of these poetic audacities of Mr. Wilde, the Rev. Mr. Higginson lumps him in with Walt Whitman for reprobation, holding them both up in contrast with Sir Philip Sidney, whom he appears to consider the proper model of a poet, and calls (quoting Fulke Greville, I suppose), "a brave example of virtue and religion." I read this effusion with infinite amusement. Is it credible that the Rev. Mr. Higginson has never seen the "Astrophel and Stella" of that very Sir Philip Sidney he vaunts so roundly? He puts on the face of Nightgall the jailor, Sorrocold the torturer, Mauger the headsman, Mawworm the gospeller, and Moddles the weeper, all in one—he is dark, cruel, implacable, denunciatory, and disconsolate, all together—over the terrible fact that "the poems of Wilde and Whitman lie in ladies boudoirs." Does he think that the "Astrophel and Stella" of Sir Philip Sidney is the sort of poem that ought preferably to "lie in ladies boudoirs"? This work, a galaxy of songs and sonnets, some of them exquisite, was inspired, be it remembered, by a married woman, Lady Rich, who figures in it as Stella, and is addressed by Sidney as Astrophel. The husband, Lord Rich, is repeatedly mentioned in terms of the utmost contumely and insult. In one of the songs (the second) the fourth stanza of which is specially lascivious, the poet limns in glowing terms the lovely wife sleeping, steals a voluptuous kiss, and blames himself for not having taken the extremest advantage of her slumber ! In another song (the fourth) there is protracted and vehement amorous solicitation for her person to be yielded to him, ending with a strain of whimpering dejection because of her refusal! The eighth song is in a similar style. In the fifty-second sonnet he fables a contest between Virtue and Love for the possession of Stella, which he proposes to settle by letting Virtue have the lady on the condition that her voluptuous body be yielded to Love and him! In the tenth song his thought dwells in gloating anticipation of carnal enjoyment with her, and runs and revels in a rosy riot of amorous images, prolonged through half a hundred lines! These are specimens of the staple of the poetry this virtuous clergyman would seem to choose for the accompaniment of ladies boudoirs! Ah, Mr. Higginson! it will take the effacing memories of Zutphen—it will take some of the immortal water the dying Sidney yielded from his flask to the parched lips of the wounded soldier, to wash away, for some of us, from the fame of one of the last of England's chevaliers, the stain of these disgraceful poems—poems which dishonor the wife while they insult the husband, and whose author is nevertheless your chosen exemplar of manly excellence—brought forward to shame by contrast Oscar Wilde for the sin of publishing a few verses far less bold than the verses of the Rev. Dr. Donne, or the "Venus and Adonis" of Shakespeare—brought forward also to darken Walt Whitman because in a few of his lines he has celebrated with grave simplicity the noble amative impulse great Nature feels forever through all her immensity! So much for the criticism wherewith the Rev. Mr. Higginson decorates "The Woman's Journal."

As for the review in the "New York Tribune," it would seem to have been written, as Sir Walter Scott says "Amadis de Gaul" was written, in a brothel. The writer leads off by saying that the poems have "been read behind the door;" that "they have been vaunted extravagantly by a band of extravagant disciples, and the possessors of the books have kept them locked up from the family;" which makes you think that the critic is simply, as the Hon. Thomas H. Benton called Pettee, "a great liar and a dirty dog," until, reading further, you find him declaring that the book, which he has already elegantly called "the slop-bucket of Walt Whitman," has for a principle "a belief in the preciousness of filth," is "entirely bestial," full of "nastiness and animal insensibility to shame," and that the chief question it raises "is whether anybody, even a poet, ought to take off his trousers in the market place;" which makes you at once set down the reviewer as indubitably, in the phrase of the moralist Hawkesworth, "a lewd young fellow," and "a great liar and a dirty dog" besides. The whole article is thoroughly obscene. It is characterized throughout by what might be called the indecent exposure of the mind, and is a disgrace to even its author and to the journal in which it appears.

Better and worse than the stuff these scurrilous dreams are made of is an article by Mr. Clarence Cook, in the "International Review," which I have read with mingled feelings of regret and indignation. It is almost incredible to find this gentleman, who ought by his intellectual connections to be better informed, and who should have education enough to know the truth without information, asserting and assuming through his whole essay that *Leaves of Grass* is a derivation from the writings of Emerson. He says that the prose preface to the original edition of the poem shows "where the author came from intellectually;" that "Mr. Whitman had been for a long time milking the New England transcendentalists," and that "most of it is an echo of Emerson himself, minus his music and his wit." Furthermore, that Walt Whitman in his poetry" does nothing more than enlarge and exaggerate the Nature and the first volume of Essays, of his master." It was long ago published authentically in Mr. Conway's widely copied and circulated article, what is the fact, that Walt Whitman had never read Emerson at all until after the publication of his first edition; and he was quite as innocent of any knowledge of the papers in the "Dial," despite the preface which Mr. Cook fancies an echo of Emerson and Concord. But he *had* read Kant, Schelling, Fichte, and Hegel, as Mr. Cook, if he had taken the trouble to read the book he was reviewing, could have seen plainly, and the thought of that giant quaternion, which, in fact, is rather an expression of what is in the minds of all men in our age, than anything that has been communicated to them by the four philosophers, is precisely the thought of which Mr. Emerson, in this country, like Cousin in France, is, in his writings, without any derogation to his own proper originality, the carrier or interpreter; so that all the indebtedness Mr. Cook oracularly fancies, is referable to the German source both minds had drunk from, though in Walt Whitman's case it is easy to see that his own powerful and sensitive genius, naturally in rapport with the thought of his age, far better accounts for the ideas of his book than any acquaintance with the well-heads of modern philosophy. This ridiculous notion of *Leaves of Grass* as a sort of rowdy amplification of Emerson, began twenty years ago with some amusing persiflage in "Putnam's Magazine"—the harmless fancy of my old friend Mr. George William Curtis, who sometimes softly, sweetly, slips into ad captandums with irresponsible indolent grace. It was taken up again, and enforced, not at all harmlessly, but with malicious iteration, by Mr. Bayard Taylor, in a series of gratuitous and inappropriate editorials, published seven years ago in the "New York Tribune," with the object of breaking down a certain movement in behalf of Mr. Whitman, and it gave me then, in conjunction with some of his other representations, a new idea of what might be meant by the old saying that "a tailor is the ninth part of a man." Now it comes up again, with the pertinacity of wood-wax or the Canada thistle, among a lot of similar superstitions, in this "International Review" article, making me think of the Spanish proverb, "God sends meat, but the devil sends cooks." The meat is *Leaves of Grass*, and the aesthetic Clarence being *cuisinier*, a nice dish he makes of it, with his bogus recipes! Did it ever occur to any of these gentlemen who derive Walt Whitman's thought from Emerson's, to compare the two in their palpable and tremendous dissimilarities? Where, for one instance out of a hundred, is the pantheistic doctrine in the *Leaves*, which is the constant assertion and implication in the Essays? Where, for another instance, do you find in Emerson the haughty and rejoicing faith in the immortality of the personal soul, which peals from end to end of *Leaves of Grass* like the trumpet of the resurrection? It would be well for Mr. Clarence Cook's reputation as a critic, if the utter sciolism his dealing with this branch of his subject betrays, had no worse concomitants. But he goes on, and dropping into apologies in a friendly way, he slips in as their basis a string of defamations regarding the noble frankness of those passages of the book in which Emerson found "the courage of treatment which so delights us, and which large perception only can inspire." In the face of this imprimatur he has the Himalayan effrontery to represent that Emerson was originally "in the marble purity of his mind" very much shocked at these passages. "At first," says Mr. Cook, "he could not see the wood-god for his phallus." I beg to compliment Mr. Cook on the marble purity of this image, which does not, however, precisely remind one of the marble faun, nor of the good satyr the poet heard playing his flute in the heart of the twilight on Mount Janiculum.

But Mr. Cook's metaphors concern me less than his calumnies, and I would really like to know what evidence he has that Emerson was ever, first or last, shocked at Walt Whitman's volume. For in proof of his bold assertion he advances not one word. "Later," he continues, "Emerson wrote a letter to Whitman, in which he said, 'I greet you at the beginning of a great career' —" and the ice being thin here, he deftly skates away into an old worn-out impertinence about Mr. Whitman's "breach of

confidence," as he calls it, in printing this sentence from a communication not confidential "in letters of gold on the back of a new edition of his book," as it certainly deserved to be printed, and as Mr. Whitman had an unquestionable right to print it. But this letter of Emerson's in which he expressed his cool, deliberate judgment of *Leaves of Grass*, and told precisely how it affected him, what was it, and why did he not bring it forward? Here it is, and I invite you and your readers to decide whether it bears out, by any expression or implication, Mr. Clarence Cook's misrepresentations:

"I am not blind to the worth of the wonderful gift of *Leaves of Grass*. I find it the most extraordinary piece of wit and wisdom that America has yet contributed. I am very happy in reading it, as great power makes us happy. It meets the demand I am always making of what seemed the sterile and stingy nature, as if too much handiwork, or too much lymph in the temperament, were making our Western wits fat and mean.

"I give you joy of your free and brave thought. I have great joy in it. I find incomparable things said incomparably well, as they must be. I find the courage of treatment which so delights us, and which large perception only can inspire.

"I greet you at the beginning of a great career, which yet must have a long foreground somewhere, for such a start. I rubbed my eyes a little to see if this sunbeam were no illusion; but the solid sense of the book is a sober certainty. It has the best merits, namely, of fortifying and encouraging."

This was Mr. Emerson's judgment on *Leaves of Grass*, and never, to his undying honor, did he retract it. I call your attention to its scope, its absolute comprehensiveness. If there was anything in the book of which he disapproved he had the plain opportunity to say so, and it was his imperative duty to say so. On the contrary, he gives the poem—he gives the very edition of it Mr. Cook says had shocked him—the most unreserved, the most unqualified, the most unbounded approval. He calls it the most extraordinary piece of intellect and wisdom America has yet contributed; he congratulates the author on the liberty and valor of his thought; and he finds especial delight in the courage of treatment which marks the whole performance, and which, he says, and Walt Whitman's critics would do well to remember, large perception only can inspire.

This is the proof Mr. Cook shies from supplying, of the way *Leaves of Grass* "shocked" Mr. Emerson! He has no other, for the sentence he ascribes to Mr. Emerson as his judgment upon the book or its author—"Strange that a man with the brain of a god should have a snout like a hog"—was never uttered by Emerson at all. In a matter of this importance I insist upon the purity of the text, and Mr. Cook has reported this flashing moment of the wise wrong. The *mot* as it was really uttered ran thus, "Strange that a man should have the brain of a god and the snout of a hog," and in this shape it was said of Walt Whitman by Mr. E. P. Whipple in 1855 or thereabouts, and reported to me, with great glee, fresh from his lips, by one of his dear friends, who afterwards ran away with the trust funds and beggared the widow and the orphan—a natural consequence of his delight in such sarcasms. The habit of murder, De Quincey warns us, inevitably leads to procrastination and Sabbath-breaking, and a man who admires Mr. Whipple's wit may be expected, sooner or later, to make off with the cash of the community. I will only remark upon this particular *jeu d' esprit* that in its vitreous brilliancy, and the perfect moral absurdity of its antithesis, to say nothing of the falsehood of its application, it is entirely worthy of its true author, and I leave Mr. Cook to its continued enjoyment. But I assure him that his success in the correct ascription of epigram is not such as to inspire me with an unfaltering trust that Wendell Phillips uttered the pleasantry he attributes in turn to him. When I gratefully remember that Mr. Phillips wrote me that he placed Walt Whitman's "Democratic Vistas" in equal honor on the same shelf with his beloved Tocqueville, and when I recall with equal gratitude the glowing and ample welcome he gave my pamphlet defence of the slandered poet, I have little reason to assume on Mr. Cook's authority that that clear and generous voice expressed even the light disparagement the reviewer puts into currency. Still, Mr. Cook may claim something from my bounty, and I will give him this as a donation. Let me suppose that Mr. Phillips, in his own enchanting fashion, really did say of *Leaves of Grass*, as our gossip reports him—"here be all sorts of leaves except fig leaves"—but added with a graver modulation, "including those of the Tree of Life, whose leaves are for the healing of the nations"! That this is the true version, though a guess, I will

venture my last obolus, and go in debt to Charon!

Of Mr. Cook's remaining "International" excursions in criticism, it is not necessary to say anything. When he declares the poem destitute of beauty and proportion, and absolutely wanting in art, I might remind him that Ruskin, who is a tolerable authority in these respects, having forgotten considerably more of aesthetic law than Mr. Cook ever knew, has recently, if the public journals say truly, uttered a eulogium upon *Leaves of Grass*, which hardly sustains this weighty dictum. When he charges as the "worst fault of all" in the book "its absolute want of humor," I might venture to suggest that, although the rich mirthful temperament of the author, which all who know him know well, is evident enough in the opulent cheerfulness and the mellow tone of his work, *Leaves of Grass* is not, as Mr. Cook appears to fancy, an attempt at comedy, nor can it be considered the "worst fault of all" that we do not split our sides with laughter over the book of Isaiah. When he pronounces the work utterly "without taste," I could retort upon him that there are only ten baskets of taste let down from heaven for each generation, and he and nimble men like him have always got them all, which is probably the reason why none of the great geniuses in poetry ever had any, from Aristophanes to Moliere, or from Æschylus to Victor Hugo. But there is only one point upon which I care to offer a serious comment. In speaking of the first issue of *Leaves of Grass*, Mr. Cook says that in it was expressed "scorn of the conventions of society by one who never knew them, and was as ignorant of society as a Digger Indian." When I came upon this stroke of ignorant insolence I felt my blood stir, and Mr. Cook owes it to my forbearance if I do not make him feel what resources the English language has for the chastisement of offences of this description. What does he mean by publishing as a species of Yahoo a man who all his life has been the honor and ornament of society as good as Mr. Cook ever entered? whose high spiritual cultivation is as apparent in his personal manners as in his poetry; and who never, even in thought, could be guilty of such insufferable low-breeding as this sentence of his critic displays? I remember, years ago, the eminent son of the most eminent man in New England, at the very top of the highest and most exclusive Boston society, coming from his first interview with Walt Whitman, whom he had met with distrust and prejudice, and all we could get from him as to what had passed was the abstracted, iterated rejoinder, the expression of his prevailing impression—"He is a perfect gentleman." In his young man hood Walt Whitman was an intimate friend of Bryant, his companion in many long country rambles. He was a welcome guest, when I first knew him, at some of the best and wealthiest houses in New York, It was the same when he was with us here. It was the same when he was with me once in Providence. It was the same during his recent visit to Boston. It was the same when he was with you in Canada. Yet Mr. Cook prates of his ignorance of society and its conventions, and matches him, in reference, with the very lowest western savage. I used to think Mr. Clarence Cook, when I slightly knew him many years ago, a gentleman, although a somewhat super fine one, but one would think he desired to forfeit all claim to such consideration. He says, in the latter part of his article, that for much that Walt Whitman has written it would not be easy to repay him with grateful words. It is a sorry way to show gratitude, this reproduction of stale and shallow figments, most of them denied and refuted time and again; and this utterance of as brutal a personal insult, couched in utter falsehood, as one man could well offer to another.

Such, up to this date, is the best specimen we can offer in America of a review of *Leaves of Grass* in its new edition. Let me show you, in this connection, the kind of knave a literary editor can be. The New York "Tribune" reprinted this article of Clarence Cook's, in which, it is just to Mr. Cook to say, he had imbedded several paragraphs favorable in some degree to the work and its author; one praising its original typographical appearance, the poet's own get-up; another eulogizing some of the poems by name; and notably another, from which I give the following sentences: "It would be a thousand pities were the author judged by the few passages, perhaps not two pages in all, where his frankness pushes him to say things that are only coarse because they are said. Of indecency, of essential grossness, there is in the book really nothing. It is easy to believe the author as pure-minded, as incapable of doing or thinking evil, as any best man among us who would blush to be seen in his shirt-sleeves by a woman." These favorable paragraphs, the one quoted from being in direct opposition to the obscene review

previously published in the "Tribune," its literary editor suppressed in reproducing the article, sending it out thus shorn to a million of readers. The animus is evident. Such is the treatment received by the grandest book of poetry uttered in the English tongue for over two centuries. And it *is* grand! Well might Emerson greet its author at the beginning of a great career! Nothing equal to it has appeared in Celto-Saxon literature since Shakespeare.

I mean what I say, and I have considered my words. It is the first poetic work in the English language since Shakespeare—let them deny it who dare that sounds—the trumpet for a new advance; that is not merely original but aboriginal; that pours forth the afflatus for another movement; that is in its theory and purpose a new departure. "Solitary, singing in the West," the poet himself says, "I strike up for a New World."

Consider the cardinal poets since the age of Elizabeth. We all know the absolute high level, below that Elizabethan mountain range, constituted by Milton. Great and noble as he is, he is not even the poet of that Puritanism whose harsh spell left him, like the prince in the Arabian story, half breathing flesh and half marble. The lofty mood of Ann Hutchinson and Sir Harry Vane is not expressed in his poetry. What is Pope? The philosophy of Bolingbroke felicitously arrayed in facile iambics—a theism fit, as Heine says, to be the religion of watch-makers; a popular paraphrase, almost a court disguise, of Homer; some splendid intercolumniations of polished urban satire; these are his masterpieces. What is Dryden? A masterly satiric talent with out a conscience. What is Walter Scott? In his verse, only a superb story teller. In Wordsworth we have a strong but circumscribed intelligence. Once only, in his noble ode upon Immortality, he rose and broadened into the serene region of the great ideas. Below that, he is great only in a true perception of some common things—a stalk of celandine, a village rustic, a mountain cloud. But his kosmos is Westmoreland, and he is radically the centaur of the parson. In Burns there are true songs, wild gleams, immortal pulses, arrested by an early death. In Keats death also soon stopped that copious rich flowering into English verse of the Greek rose and asphodel. What leader of the nations might not the all-noble Byron have become, had he but lived to make ripe the continental promise which appears in the broad European picturings, the magnanimous intellections, the clarion blasts of rebellion, that fill "Childe Harold"; which appear still clearer in "Don Juan," whose fearless stripping of the veil from the monstrous hypocrisy of society, whose aggrandizement of humanity and liberty, and whose mines of liberal and revolutionary epigram, give it the rank of one of the greatest poems ever inspired by the pure moral sentiment! And Shelley—had he but grown to maturity, and gathered force and become intimate with rude life, what fire upon the altar of what gods would not have been pale beside that which sparkles in the ashes of his lines ! If Tennyson had continued as he began, the loyal outgrowth of Shelley and Byron, the developed poet of "Maud," of "Clara Vere de Vere," of "Ulysses" and "Locksley Hall".... but he soon learned that kind hearts are less than coronets, and simple faith than Norman blood;—he shrank back into aristocracy;—and now at the last analysis, what is he? An ethereal delight of poesy; no less; no more. I speak only of Celto-Saxon poetry, not of the mighty births of the French romantic movement. In my own country, in the United States, that poetry, aside from *Leaves of Grass*, has not appeared in a single racy specimen. The only possible exception, though in a minor key, is the weird and lovely lyric verse of Edgar Poe, perfectly distinctive, shrining a strange mythology of personal love and sorrow, and having its roots in certain parts of our southern life. But poetry such as his only influences, it does not emancipate or lead. Not one of our poets has had broad or deep aims. Longfellow, with exquisite literary grace and human benignity, yields only centos and distillations. Whittier makes local ballads. Emerson has produced a handful of mystic jewels, rose diamonds and white, a virtuoso's joy, like "the gems of Andrew Marvell or Vaughan. Bryant's fame rests on "Thanatopsis," a thing of faithless beauty, though a joy forever, but which internal evidence shows stolen, and which might have been written in Sherwood Forest, or by Omar Khayyam, so little does it smack of any particular soil. In fine, the last supreme performance in poetry, before any of the poets I have named, was Elizabethan. The last full signal for a great march—for an exodus out of old conventions, old dog mas, old ideas, old theories, was Shakespeare.

What is Shakespeare's new departure? It is this: He is the first poet that ever devoted the drama to the physiology of the human passions—the chief problem, Bacon says, of moral philosophy; the knowledge that philosopher proclaimed wanting in the antique past; the condition indispensable, he declares, to the human advancement. That initial body of natural history demanded by Bacon has been supplied by Shakespeare, in the interest of the human race. This is his cardinal distinction as a poet; this makes his greatness and his glory.

An old and valued friend of mine, whose opinions are entitled to deep respect, has lately said that the Greek dramatists, especially. Æschylus, excel Shakespeare in their treatment of the passions. I am sorry not to be able to think this true. Indeed, it seems to me it would be far nearer the truth to say that the Greek dramatists, in their colossal spectacular operas, never treated the passions at all. Much wisdom, much deep lore, much lofty morality, much fearful history, much dread theology, and questioning of that theology, expressed in tremendous passionate situation, these tragedies have indeed, but this is their whole staple. No one can better feel its majesty than

I, nor can any one more than I appreciate the sublimity of the appalling thunder-crash of fatal circumstance which bursts forth in pealing reverberations against that drama's religious and legendary depth of gloom, or the stupendous power of what must have been its lovely and mournful groupings, its horrible and magnificent denouements, its strange and supra-mortal living tableaux, as of gigantic animated sculpture, moving to breath-suspending music. But I affirm that never in a single instance did the Greek poets devote their tragedies to the exhibition of the passions in their evolution—in their circumstantial development from grade to grade of action—such as we see in "Hamlet," in "Othello," in "Lear." Indeed, the very conditions of their drama precluded such an exhibition. The theatre of Athens was built to accommodate thirty thousand spectators. To such a concourse the tragedy of "Macbeth," even with Kemble and Siddons in the chief parts, would have seemed a play of dwarfs—the tragic expression unseen, the gestures those of puppets, the voices almost lost, the sense incoherent, in the vastness of that stage and auditorium. In such a space nothing but a form of drama, of the nature of a spectacular opera, conceived in a gigantic mould, and suggesting the superhuman, would have been possible. Instead of the subtle passional metaphysics which Shakespeare, availing himself of the limits of the modern stage, can make dramatically evident— better still, can make by language alone even more evident to the solitary student of his pages—the Greek dramatist had to substitute such conceptions, ideas, conclusions, as might be broadly expressed in imposing stage effects, with adjuncts of scenic action and music. Hence actions rather than passions; hence a succession of tableaux; a tremendous, significant, sombre, sounding show. Hence upon the vast Athenian stage only two interlocutors at a time upon the scene, besides the choruses—Æschylus bayed at as an audacious innovator for introducing three; the stature of these actors raised to a supra-mortal height by the cothurnus; their size increased by voluminous draperies; their faces discharged of all but the one expression, by the awful and petrific mask; their voices augmented to thunderous or silver-shrilling tones by the brazen trumpet of the mouth-piece; and the verses of the tragedy intoned and sung by the duo or trio of histrions, or by the pealing voices of the choirs, ranged in dramatic sympathy with their action. In fact, if we can imagine an appalling and mysterious legend played by titanic statues of dreadful bronze and marble against a scene of eld, those statues become animate and vocal and resembling little that is human, we can gain some idea of the impression of a Greek tragedy. Something of its fearful and beauteous weird ness is suggested by that eerie line of Cowper, where, musing in his garden, he sees "a statue walk." Except to the evocation of the soul this form o-f supreme art is forever gone; the superb, the terrible, the enchanting spectacle, the astounding accumulation of catastrophes, the piled-up agonies, the marble loveliness, the celestial pathos, the horrent grandeurs, the Corybantic dances, the Eolian music, once ocular and auricular to the Greek audience, and surcharged with meaning not of this world, made evident through the senses to the souls of the auditors—all this can only be dimly recovered by the imagination; and of the august Greek tragedies (such as remain to us) we have nothing but the meagre and almost unintelligible librettos, no more to us than the librettos of great modern operas, except—a formidable exception indeed—that,

unlike the librettos of "William Tell," of "Don Giovanni," of "II Puritani," or the rest, they were written by mighty poets and in the pentecostal language of poetry. Still, they are but librettos, the broken fiery lines of a dying fire work of Promethean fire, the *caput mortuum*, the mere skeleton, the vacant framework of what was once in its enacting an orbicular and living drama, vital, glowing, sublime and enormous, the work of men like gods. As librettos—mere outlines which the representations are needed to complete—they cannot fairly be brought into comparison with the text of Shakespeare, a text as full to the reader as to the play-goer—fuller, indeed, so long as Shakespeare can be butchered to make a schoolboy's holiday by the gang of Barnums who run the modern stage, and mangle his dramas, and disembowel his meaning, with that brutish indifference to art and truth and human progress, which is fed by sole regard for fat receipts at the ticket-office. But, completed by the exercise of the conceptive power, the dry though mighty bones of these librettos, again clothed with their terrible and magnificent life, the Greek drama (although Æschylus has unquestionable features of resemblance) differs radically in form and motive from the drama of Shakespeare, and is intrinsically removed from comparison. I think Aristotle gives the full account of it when he says that its object was to move the soul with pity and terror; and the criticism that has been justly given in censure upon Aristotle as a philosopher in regard to his treatment of the human passions, namely, that he only considers the rhetorical or artificial means whereby they may be excited, and neglects to compile their natural history, may be made in no spirit of censure, but in simple descriptiveness, in regard to the Greek tragedies, inasmuch as their authors only regarded in their composition the means of exciting the passions of those who were to behold them played, and attempted in the works themselves no analysis or synthesis of any of the passions—not one. This undertaking was reserved for Shakespeare, and I affirm that the entire novelty of the conception and the scientific accuracy and massive comprehensiveness, as well as the supreme power and beauty of its execution, constitute his special and distinctive greatness as a poet. The main scope and purpose of the Shakespeare drama are definitely given by Lord Bacon in connection with his assertion that the compilation of the natural history of the human passions is the first duty of philosophy, and that it is particularly the province of poetry. In this connection he describes the Shakespearean work perfectly. Therein, he says, "we may find painted forth with great life how passions are kindled and incited; how pacified and refrained; and how again contained from act and further degree; how they disclose themselves; how they work; how they vary; how they gather and fortify; how they are inwrapped one within another; and how they do fight and encounter one with another; and other the like particulars." That is to say," remarks Dr. Kuno Fischer, quoting this passage: "Bacon desires nothing less than a natural history of the passions; *the very thing that Shakespeare has produced.* Is not," he says further, "the inexhaustible theme of Shakespeare's poetry the history and course of human passion? In the treatment of this special theme, is not Shakespeare the greatest of all poets, nay, is he not unique among them all?" Strange, I must remark, in passing, that the illustrious Kantian (and the observation applies to Gervinus as well) should have gone so far in this matter, and not taken the step that would seem inevitable! But the fact remains, admitted on all sides, its significance only remaining unperceived—Shakespeare is the poet of that particular knowledge of human nature which Bacon declares necessary "in order that the precepts concerning the culture and cure of the mind may be rightly concluded upon;" and no matter what the myriad-figured, many-millioned play of the imagination which attends his work—no matter how profuse and rich the pageant, wherein kings, lords, prelates, gentlemen, clowns, fairies, ghosts, trades, employments, wars, elements, cities, landscapes, antique and modern shows, appear in uni multiplex projection, and form in ensemble the immense profile of Europe from the view-point of the Elizabethan age—no matter how ample the pour of learning, wisdom, apothegm, axiom, wit, humor, literary felicity, dazzling metaphor, noble imagery, classic allusion, every verbal grace and grandeur, as from a cornucopia heaped with constellations—no matter how deep the summer of his verse, the purpose to present the physiology of the human passions runs through it all; and his drama stands the perfect suppliance of an immense

defect in ancient philosophy, and the foremost division of that scientific movement of his time for the relief of the human estate, the extension of the empire of man over Nature, the transformation of the world into Paradise, which still continues, and which we call Baconian. His main purpose does not, of course, prevent the inclusion of collateral purposes, only less vast—parables of a new philosophy, as in the "Tempest" and the "Midsummer Night's Dream;" special solutions of political problems, as in "Coriolanus" and "Julius Cæsar;" in one instance a complete epic of the Wars of the Roses—the series of historical plays which Bacon calls "history made visible." But the main purpose remains other than the special purposes of these.

To the historical plays, with their high-stomached lords, their dragon rancors, their stormy feudal splendor, I think Walt Whitman gives undue weight in his estimate of Shakespeare's world. He seems to derive from them his powerful generalization of Shakespeare as the poet of Feudalism. This would be true of Walter Scott, a man sounder and healthier in his moral nature than in his intellect, and who saw the horrible grandeur of the feudal past through a glamour of beauty: it would be measurably true of Tennyson; I doubt if it is true of Shakespeare. Certainly "King John," "Richard the Second," "Richard the Third" and the rest, do not affect the mind with the winsome charm of "Ivanhoe" or "The Talisman." Their atmosphere is one of barbarous and tumultuous gloom, and they do not make us love the times they limn. They seem simply and rudely historical in their motive, as aiming to give in the rough a tableau of warring dynasties, and carry to me a lurking sense of being in aid of some ulterior design, probably well enough understood in that age, which perhaps time and criticism will reveal. The literature of the Middle Ages, issued under the jealous eye of a military despotism, is extremely insidious; often needs to be read between the lines; and there is deep suggestion in Bacon's saying that "we ought to be much beholden to Machiavel, who writes what men do, and not what they ought to do." In Machiavel himself what dark nobility, when in "The Prince"—that hideous masterpiece—at the utter cost of his fair fame, at the price of giving his very name to become a byword among men—he teaches the tyrant so minutely, and with such perfect candor, all the arts by which a free people may be subjugated, that the people become masters of the trick too! "The ostent evanescent" has its application to much of the great literature of those times—at least to the penetrating eye that finds the ostent of that literature deceitful; and it is impossible to believe that the greatest of the Elizabethan men could have sought to indoctrinate the ages with the love of feudalism which his own drama in its entirety, if the view taken of it herein be true, certainly and subtly saps and mines. The only supreme tyrant is Ignorance. To destroy this, as the Shakespeare drama assists to destroy it—to destroy this by teaching man the science of his own nature—is to deliberately forelay for the destruction of the whole Olympus of lesser tyrants, feudal and other, of which Ignorance is the Jove. If I sought to express the Shakespeare drama in the image of a person, I would not choose the eidolon of any feudal emperor. My choice would be a man like Francis Bacon—so majestic in his presence, Osborne, his contemporary, says of him, that he awed all men upon occasion into reverence, and yet, continues Osborne, so much one of the commonalty that he could pass from talk with a lord about his hawks and hounds to out-cant a London chirurgeon in his slang, so that all sorts of men thought him one of themselves; Francis Bacon, wise with all the lore of all the ages, the companion and counsellor of princes, the familiar of gypsies and tinkers and sailors as well; deep-eyed with long insight into the minds of men of every degree; master of multiform experiences; travelled, elegant, courtly, august, intrepid, loyal, gentle, compassionate, sorrowful, beautiful; clothed from fondness for sumptuous apparel in purple three-piled velvet, rich laces and the hat with plumes, yet loving—another anecdote tells of him—to ride with bared head, in the warm and perfumed rains of spring, that he might feel upon him, he said, the universal spirit of the world! Such would be the image of the man I would choose to express the Shakespeare drama—an image, by the way, not much like the infamous caricature made of him by that brilliant thimble-rigging Scotch scoundrel, Macaulay, with the noble and honorable object of spiting Basil Montagu.

Still, let it be distinctly admitted, although the imputation of feudalism may be rejected, the point of view in the Shakespeare drama is always that of the court. The court perfume streams, like a necessity of authorship, less from choice than circumstance, through all this mighty and beneficent creation. For the plebeian point of view, maintained unconsciously throughout, despite the learning, despite the patrician themes or characters chosen, despite even the voluptuous dainty elegance and charm of some of the lyrics and epigrams, contrast the works of Ben Jonson. The son of the bricklayer appears throughout, and it is the bricklayer's son of the mournful age of Elizabeth and James, before the people was born. Strange grace of chance if, in that age, the patrician spirit, which may easily be the natural birthright of any farmer or mechanic now—at least in this country—should have animated one as lowly born as Shakespeare, so as to tincture all his works with an odor, clinging as the musk of Nepaul! But the fact cannot be unperceived—the outlook of the Shakespeare drama is from the court; the sympathy, though universal, is from the social above, never from the below; the implied life of the author is that of the gently born and bred, not of the tradesman or the laborer. In every page we feel the superior social grade. It is the best spirit of the best Elizabethan noble. One would say the author was a lord. Truly—but a lord as Buddha was a prince.

The times have gone by when the court was the generalization of the nation, and the typical man, either as person or poet, was necessarily of the aristocracy. The change has come to pass which the great Elizabethan men darkly toiled to accomplish, in an age when the new was stirring in the old—the dawn of which appeared for a little while a few years after they had passed away, in the Commonweal of Vane and Hampden, which Cromwell quenched in cloud. In every country in Christendom the people has been born, and in this has come to sovereignty. That democratic sovereignty, a political fact here to-day, will be a social fact here to-morrow, and of that fact in its present and its future, and of that New World which is the arena of its evolution, Walt Whitman is the poet, and *Leaves of Grass* is the poem. The very resistance to the work, as when a foreign journal denounced "its rank republican insolence," proves its democratic scope and character; the very criticism of its foes, who "cannot dispraise but in a sort of praise," supports its claim. Next in the order of intellectual succession to Shakespeare, its author appears in his typical mechanic's garb, as the portrait in the book shows him, a work man sprung from a race of workmen, a representative poet of the people; such here specifically, and collaterally throughout the world. "The people—the poor," says a recent reviewer, sympathetically defining. Alas! no: the poor are not the people! "The poor," says Victor Hugo, "are the mournful commencement of the people!" The people are the inhabitants of the country when political organization has secured for them the power of the sceptre, and social organization has endowed them with the opulence of the crown. From power and wealth in equitable distribution results the great spiritual patrician race worthy to be called the people. That race in its mighty infancy is here—a baby Hercules, who in its cradle has strangled monsters, and whose manhood and the labors of whose manhood are to come.

I have gazed for years into this grand orb of poetry; I have mused upon its wild elegance and splendor, its tranquil and candid reproduction of things gross and delicate as they are in the sphere of the great Pan, its august masculine and feminine ideals, its teeming shows of historic and current life, its magic changing palingenesis of the populous cities, the diversified landscapes, the picturesque solitudes, the genré male and female figures, the infinite fauna and flora, the skies, mountains, streams, prairies of our Continental West, all recreated here in their several idiosyncrasies, under every diversity of times and seasons, vital and magnetic, a scenic whole exhaling delicious natural odors, swept by free winds, alive and moving in harmony to the marching measures, the glorious rolling music of a rhythmus, caught, one might divine, from the movements, copious and unequal, of the surf sweeping in forever upon the beaches where the poet wandered as a child. I have brooded long upon it all, and I have compared it with the famous poems of the supreme men of all ages, and found it in no wise inferior to the best, as many besides me have felt, and the near future will declare; but I should shrink, faint-hearted in my conscious inferiority, from any effort at its adequate interpretation. It spreads before us all, a superb cosmorama of the West, populous, colossal and golden, under the ascending race of the rejoicing sun. Who am I that I should unfold the mystic reminiscences of this Universal Poem, reveal its oracular suggestions, comment upon its sublime annunciations, interpret its prophetic voices, declare anything of what it is to

every reader with an awakened soul?

Sometimes I think it might be considered the poem of embodiment. It indicates the august kosmic fact of numberless material entities held in cohesion by spirit, which in time loosens and departs. In a more restricted consideration, it appears as the poem of the embodied human soul. Other writers have celebrated the body, others the spirit, until we feel them almost in disconnection. Take, as opposing poles, Rabelais and Shelley. In Rabelais there is a creation, gross, enormous, carnal, full-blown, laughing, obscene, alimentative, bibulous, excrementitious, loathsome and magnificent. It is the fearful apotheosis of the flesh, the monstrous apocalypse of the abdomen become lord paramount—man submerged in his lusts and appetites. The conception could only have proceeded from a mighty intellect and a great moral nature. In Shelley there is evolved an image, phantasmal, super-celestial, inessential, divinely wan and lovely, the ghost become consubstantial with a music unearthly and wandering, a shape of woven perfume, an odic force grown palely visible, a perceived pneuma, an apprehended essence, an ethereal apparition, the presence of the violet-breathing night- wind of the spring. The eidolon of his poetry is as incredible in its beauty as in its utter removal from carnality. It is like a dream of the soul remembered in a dream. Its extreme sublimation will forever make it incomprehensible to any but the most imaginative minds—to aught but the clairvoyant sense that comes into rapport with thought clinging to the dim boundaries of the world: and Shelley can never have the fame his genius deserves, so far is his work removed from the reality and passion of our lives. His merits as a poet are inexpressible. Not least among them is the altogether new ideal of woman, radiant, heroic, noble, and exalte, which appears in his pages. His poetry suggests in its furthest rapt remove from realization, almost from apprehension, the unbodied soul. The athletic spirituality of *Leaves of Grass* has no kinship to the spirit of the "Gargantua," and it is far nearer to the divine afflatus of the "Epipsychidion." But the creation of the book is its author's own—as original as *sui generis*—and that creation is, within the limits of the present reference, the strongest, amplest, most definite projection of the soul incarnate—of the representative human being—which has ever been thrown into literature. In it the spirit and the flesh appear as a unit, in perfect equilibrium, in the mutual interpenetration and consubstantiality appropriate to the ideal Adam. Were humanity to disappear from the globe, and this poem alone to remain, the being of an other species than ours, finding it among the ruins, could recover from its pages full knowledge of what manner of man had inhabited here, as surely as Lamarck or Owen from the fossil vestiges can reconstruct the vanished mastodon. The great affirmation which pervades the whole conception is the veracity of consciousness. Let us bow down before this supreme word! Behind it there is nothing. It indicates the true finality, and in it is the entire proof of life. To be aware is all. To be aware is to be. Memory—the personal past—is consciousness retained: anticipation—the personal future—is consciousness projected. It is this divine fact that the poet, as he himself says, sings in so many ecstatic songs, and out of it has emerged his transcendent conception of the incarnate soul—the human creature, male or female, the female equal to the male—the being, dual and unitary at once, like the globe of two hemispheres—the insulated identity, type of all human identities, the woman, the man. A creature of substantial body, parts and passions; divine in every organ and attribute, not one of which is to be omitted or contemned in celebration, since each and all are intermutual in their adaptation, as they must be in an organic whole; infinite and omnigenous in character, without origin and without end, and grown and growing through sympathy by the accrument of myriad experiences; shaped, propelled, developed alike by good and evil, as under the mechanical law of the composition of rival forces, effects are resultant; prepared for in the earthly advent by all the cyclic preparations of the globe, and continued in endless course by all the operations of things; eternal in personal identity, the phases at once merged and retained, as infancy is both lost and kept in childhood, childhood in youth, youth in maturity, and so on forever; fathomless, abysmal, immense and interminable as Nature, to which he or she is related as a constant vital influence forever influenced; representative, at any given stage of his or her evolution, of the innumerable lower beings, progressing to that level, to sink in turn that level, and continue on; representative, in the best estate, of the intrinsic spiritual greatness and majesty of each and all of the rest through whatever the pitiable, grotesque or vile disguises of appearance incident to the processes of transformation; heir to an omnific personal destiny which is alike the destiny of each and all; governed through all the nature by the egoistic pride, and by love and the necessity for love, as by two paramount vital springs; conscious at the summit of the highest knowledge of the eternal mystery in which all beings must remain to each, and of the eternal mystery one must be to one's self; and, from that lofty summit, joyous, haughty, transfigured in the sense of the democratic constitution of the Universe, in which all between the worm and the god are equal, being all organically necessary to the whole, and of which perpetual ascension, perpetual transfer and promotion, is the law. Such, in my apprehension, and in a crude, didactic account of it, is this majestic conception, which, in the poet's work, is expressed in a thousand magnetic and eloquent sentences, in a thousand vivid and wondrous verbal pictures, and with a power of alto-relievo statement and illustration which the fancy-dealers in letters can never deal in. It is far enough removed from the conception wherewith Mr. Harlan's Messiah, Wesley, startled England, when he defined man as "half brute and half devil." The body is the temple of the Holy Ghost, says the rapt apostle; and of this text Walt Whitman's book is, within the limitations of this view of it, the ample, the electric, the robust and unrivalled commentary. As such it offers a new foundation for our philosophy, our politics, our life, above all for our religion—a religion to be greater than the world has ever seen, and worthy of these shores.

To others better equipped for the grateful labor, I will leave it to descant upon what is correlated to the conception I have so imperfectly touched—the matchless presentation of the representative man and woman of this country. In Shakespeare there are no ideals in the sense of exemplars of human excellence, or if so to any degree, it is in artistic and moral subordination to what seems his main aim, namely, to create types or models showing the operation of the perturbations or tempests of the mind. In *Leaves of Grass* the ideals are distinct, and nothing could be more resplendent or commanding. They will haunt the imagination of this country, they will haunt the imagination of the world, until they are realized in "the life that shall be copious, vehement, spiritual, bold," which the poet prophesies—in "the great individuals, fluid as Nature, chaste, affectionate, compassionate, fully armed"—in "the breeds of the most perfect mothers"—"the myriads of youths, beautiful, gigantic, sweet-blooded"—"the race of splendid and savage old men"—" the hundred millions of superb persons," which appear in his sublime annunciation as belonging to the future of America. Women have especial cause to be grateful to Walt Whitman. The noblest ideal of woman ever contributed appears in his pages. His supreme presentation of her in the natural privilege of her motherhood—in her all-enclosing, all-determining and divine maternity, is of more than any former majesty, and is unparalleled in philosophic depth and truth, as it is in august and tender beauty, I would fain dwell upon this feature of his book, as I would upon the crowded and splendid cartoon of the United States, in all their diversified truth of essence and appearance, in all their multiplicity and variety of life, which his pages offer broadly to contemplation. There are few national works which have so fully imaged the distinctive form of a land and its people. Homer has given to the ages a wondrous picture of the old Pelasgic civilization; Rome, when the city was the world, glows in the tragic light of dying liberty and virtue in the mighty pages of Juvenal; amidst the great fulgurations of the laughter of Rabelais, we see the gross swarming life of old Paris and Touraine; and France, as in the magic mirror of Agrippa, in all the horror and grandeur of the feudal past, the revolutionary combat and the anguish of the present, the superb promise of the future, and the supreme glory of compassion which streams from the poet's own mighty heart, lives in the poetry, the drama, the romance of the illustrious Victor Hugo; but in what poem have all the things which make up the show of a people's life appeared with such comprehensive and vivid reality, such national distinctiveness and such strength of charm, as in *Leaves of Grass*? Above all, the wonder of it is, to me, the marvel that what was thought commonplace and prosaic is restored in the book to the superbest poetry by the revelation of its intrinsic significance—by the establishment of its mystical relation. The common objects as well as the most beautiful and striking—the ordinary events and incidents as well as those of the greater

series—the rude, plain, simple, unlettered people, as well as the elevated and heroic—all appear in the poem in an equality of consideration, unrobbed of the deep interior value which truly belongs to every figure, to every object and emblem in the divine procession of life. Such mighty and democratic handling of a theme, without rejection or evasion, reveals the great master, just as the true sculptor is seen, when, after you have gazed at a number of the stone dolls which adorn our Capitol, in which the fact of the genre costume is commonly sought to be dodged by the artifice of a marmoreal cloak, you turn to David's noble bronze of Jefferson, in which the grace, the strength, the fire, the life of the figure are fused into every detail of the frankly rendered old colonial garb. The great master is equally revealed in the poems of the war for the Union, around which the orbit of the book is now arranged. Of these poems it may be said that they alone of all the song born from that struggle are in the true key. Apart from their clear, fresh and vital picturing—the sad and stormy truth and color of their scenery—they are surcharged with the peculiar tragic pathos which civil war must always inspire in hearts deeply noble, and will be accepted in all our latitudes, North and South alike, since they can be read without unmanly exultation by the victor, and without humiliation by the vanquished. The word "Reconciliation" spans them all:

Word over all, beautiful as the sky;
Beautiful that war and all its deeds of carnage must
  in time be utterly lost,
That the hands of the sisters Death and Night
  incessantly softly wash again, and ever
  again, this soiled world;
For my enemy is dead, a man divine as myself is
  dead,
I look where he lies white-faced and still in the
  coffin—I draw near,
Bend down and touch lightly with my lips the white
  face in the coffin.

A few years ago there was an old man in this city, an eminent officer of the government, formerly a judge, with whom I sometimes conversed, and the idol of whose thought and life was Jefferson. He set great value upon *Leaves of Grass*, but the works and life of the author of the Declaration of Independence made his central theme, of which he never wearied, nor, indeed, made others weary, he discoursed upon it so eloquently well. He has passed from among us; but I can still see in memory, his old, wrinkled, earnest, smiling face, and dark, sunken eyes tinged around with black, and hear his low, eager voice, as with the ardor of a boy he unrolled his dissertation upon some sentence of the sage of Monticello, or, kindling into some magian gloss upon his text, foretold in a sort of measured ecstasy the complete ultimate triumph of the democratic principle, and the transfiguration of government and society in the operation of the ideas of his master. But always as the climax of his rapt argument, or at the close of any stage thereof, before it mounted to a higher proposition, he would say, bending his old head forward, his voice trembling with intensity, his face glowing into a deeper wizard smile, his dark eyes shining in their swarthy circles—"and here," he would exclaim, "here is where our glorious Walt comes in and confirms Jefferson!" No description could convey a sense of the tone of utter satisfaction and triumph in which he announced his prophet confirmed by his poet, nor of the tremulous fervor, the supreme unction with which the words "our glorious Walt" were uttered. I take the remembrance of those words, as I would a wild flower from the kind old scholar's grave, and lay it on our poet's book as my latest offering, worth more than the little tribute I have ever brought, or all that I could ever bring. "Our glorious Willy" was the phrase the author of the "Faery Queen" threw, like a star, upon the name of Shakespeare, in the days when the term "a willy" was simply a euphuism for "a poet," and no more. "Our glorious Walt," the utterance of lips that fondly loved the name of Jefferson, and yielded the words in homage to the bard who has carried into literature earth's greatest dream, is at least an honor equal to that Spenser gave, and goes to an object no less worthy of such honor. For to have conceived and written *Leaves of Grass*—to have been of the old heroic strain of which such books alone are born— to have surcharged the pages with their world of noble and passionate life—to have done all this, to have dared all this, to have suffered for all this is to be the true brother of Shakespeare.

Pardon my imperfect contribution to your volume. You know how hastily I have written, using the little time left by the pressing tasks of the Life-

Saving Service. And with cordial wishes for the success of your book,

Believe me, Dear Sir,
Faithfully yours,
WILLIAM DOUGLAS O CONNOR.

[4]Bucke, Richard Maurice, M.D. *Walt Whitman.* Philadelphia, David McKay, 1883.

[A.21]

THE GOOD GRAY POET.
A VINDICATION.

Washington, D. C., Sept. 2, 1865.

NINE weeks have elapsed since the commission of an outrage, to which I have not till now been able to give my attention, but which, in the interest of the sacred cause of free letters, and in that alone, I never meant should pass without its proper and enduring brand.

For years past, thousands of people in New York, in Brooklyn, in Boston, in New Orleans, and latterly in Washington, have seen, even as I saw two hours ago, tallying, one might say, the streets of our American cities, and fit to have for his background and accessories their streaming populations and ample and rich facades, a man of striking masculine beauty—a poet—powerful and venerable in appearance; large, calm, superbly formed; oftenest clad in the careless, rough, and always picturesque costume of the common people; resembling, and generally taken by strangers for some great mechanic or stevedore, or seaman, or grand laborer of one kind or another; and passing slowly in this guise, with nonchalant and haughty step along the pavement, with the sunlight and shadows falling around him. The dark sombrero he usually wears was, when I saw him just now, the day being warm, held for the moment in his hand; rich light an artist would have chosen, lay upon his uncovered head, majestic, large, Homeric, and set upon his strong shoulders with the grandeur of ancient sculpture. I marked the countenance, serene, proud, cheerful, florid, grave; the brow seamed with noble wrinkles; the features, massive and handsome, with firm blue eyes; the eyebrows and eyelids especially showing that fulness of arch seldom seen save in the antique busts; the flowing hair and fleecy beard, both very gray, and tempering with a look of age the youthful aspect of one who is but forty-five; the simplicity and purity of his dress, cheap and plain, but spotless, from snowy falling collar to burnished boot, and exhaling faint fragrance; the whole form surrounded with manliness as with a nimbus, and breathing, in its perfect health and vigor, the august charm of the strong.

We who have looked upon this figure, or listened to that clear, cheerful, vibrating voice, might thrill to think, could we but transcend our age, that we had been thus near to one of the greatest of the sons of men. But Dante stirs no deep pulse, unless it be of hate, as he walks the streets of Florence; shabby, one-armed soldier, just out of jail and hardly notice, though he has amused Europe, is Michael Cervantes; that son of a vine-dresser, whom Athens laughs at as an eccentric genius, before it is thought worth while to roar him into exile, is the century-shaking Æschylus; that phantom whom the wits of the seventeenth century think not worth extraordinary notice, and the wits of the eighteenth century, spluttering with laughter, call a barbarian, is Shakespeare; that earth-soiled, vice-stained ploughman, with the noble heart and sweet bright eyes, abominated by the good and patronized by the gentry, subject now of anniversary banquets by gentlemen who, could they wander backward from those annual hiccups into time, would never help his life or keep his company—is Robert Burns; and this man, whose gravel perhaps, the next century will cover with passionate and splendid honors, goes regarded with careless curiosity or phlegmatic composure by his own age. Yet, perhaps, in a few hearts he has waked that deep thrill due to the passage of the sublime. I heard lately, with sad pleasure, of the letter introducing a friend, filled with noble courtesy, and dictated by the reverence for genius, which a distinguished English nobleman, a stranger, sent to this American bard [stopping en route at Cambridge, the bearer of this letter was informed by one of its most distinguished resident authors, that Walt Whitman was "nothing but a low New York rowdy," "a common street blackguard," and he accordingly did not venture to present the letter]. Nothing deepens my respect for the beautiful intellect of the scholar Alcott, like the bold sentence "Greater than Plato," which he once uttered upon him. I hold it the surest proof of Thoreau's insight, that after a conversation, seeing how he incarnated the immense and new spirit of the age, and was the compend of America, he came away to speak the electric sentence, "He is Democracy!" I treasure to my latest hour, with swelling heart and springing tears, the remembrance that Abraham Lincoln, seeing him for the first time from the window of the east room of the White House as he passed slowly by, and gazing at him long with that deep eye which read men, said, in the quaint, sweet tone, which those who have spoken with him will remember, and with a significant emphasis which the type can hardly convey, "Well, he looks like a MAN!" Sublime tributes, great words; but none too high for their object, the author of *Leaves of Grass*, Walt Whitman, of Brooklyn.

On the 30th of June last, this true American man and author was dismissed, under circumstances of peculiar wrong, from a clerkship he had held for six months in the Department of the Interior. His dismissal was the act of the Hon. James Harlan, the Secretary of the Department, formerly a Methodist clergyman, and president of a Western college.

Upon the interrogation of an eminent officer of the Government, at whose instance the appointment had, under a former Secretary, been made, Mr. Harlan averred that Walt Whitman had been in no way remiss in the discharge of his duties, but that, on the contrary, so far as he could learn, his conduct had been most exemplary. Indeed, during the few months of his tenure of office, he had been promoted. The sole and only cause of his dismissal, Mr. Harlan said, was that he had written the book of poetry entitled *Leaves of Grass*. This book Mr. Harlan characterized as "full of indecent passages." The author, he said, was "a very bad man," a "free lover." Argument being had upon these propositions, Mr. Harlan was, as regards the book, utterly unable to maintain his assertions, and, as regards the author, was forced to own that his opinion of him had been changed. Nevertheless, after this substantial admission of his injustice, he absolutely refused to revoke his action. Of course, under no circumstances would Walt Whitman, the proudest man that lives, have consented to again enter into office under Mr. Harlan; but the demand for his reinstatement was as honorable to the gentleman who made it as the refusal to accede to it was discreditable to the Secretary.

The closing feature of this transaction, and one which was a direct consequence of Mr. Harlan's course, was its remission to the scurrilous, and in some instances libellous, comment of a portion of the press. To sum up, an author, solely and only for the publication, ten years ago, of an honest book, which no intelligent and candid person can regard as hurtful to morality, was expelled from office by the Secretary, and held up to public contumely by the newspapers. It only remains to be added here, that the Hon. James Harlan is the gentleman who, upon assuming the control of the Department, published a manifesto, announcing that it was thenceforth to be governed "upon the principles of Christian civilization."

This act of expulsion, and all that it encloses, is the outrage to which I referred in my opening paragraph.

I have had the honor, which I esteem a very high one, to know Walt Whitman intimately for several years, and am conversant with the details of his life and history. Scores and scores of persons, who know him well, can confirm my own report of him, and I have therefore no hesitation in saying that the scandalous assertions of Mr. Harlan, derived from whom I know not, as to his being a bad man, a free lover, etc., belong to the category of those calumnies at which, as Napoleon said, innocence itself is confounded. A better man in all respects, or one more irreproachable in his relations to the other sex, lives not upon this earth. His is the great goodness, the great chastity of spiritual strength and sanity. I do not believe that from the hour of his infancy, when Lafayette held him in his arms, to the present hour, in which he bends over the last wounded and dying of the war, anyone can say aught of him, which does not consort with the largest and truest manliness. I am perfectly aware of the miserable lies which have been put into circulation respecting him, of which the story of his dishonoring an invitation to dine with Emerson, by appearing at the table of the Astor House in a red shirt, and with the manners of a rowdy, is a mild specimen. I know too the inferences drawn by wretched fools, who, because they have seen him riding upon the top of an omnibus; or at Pfaff's restaurant; or dressed in rough clothes suitable for his purposes, and only remarkable because the wearer was a man of genius; or mixing freely and lovingly, like Lucretius, like Rabelais, like Francis Bacon, like Rembrandt, like all great students of the world, with low and equivocal and dissolute persons, as well as with those of a different character, must needs set him down as a brute, a scallawag, and a criminal.

Mr. Harlan's allegations are of a piece with these. If I could associate the title with a really great person, or if the name of man were not radically superior, I should say that for solid nobleness of character, for native elegance and delicacy of soul, for a courtesy which is the very passion of thoughtful kindness and forbearance, for his tender and paternal respect and manly honor for woman, for love and heroism carried into the pettiest details of life, and for a large and homely beauty of manners, which makes the civilities of parlors fantastic and puerile in comparison, Walt Whitman deserves to be considered the grandest gentleman that treads this continent. I know well the habits and tendencies of his life. They are all simple, sane, domestic, worthy of him as one of an estimable family and member of society. He is a tender and faithful son, a good brother, a loyal friend, an ardent and devoted citizen. He has been a laborer, working successively as a farmer, a carpenter, a printer. He has been a stalwart editor of the Republican party, and often, in that powerful and nervous prose of which he is master, done yeoman's service for the great cause of human liberty and the imperial conception of the indivisible Union. He has been a visitor of prisons, a protector of fugitive slaves, a constant voluntary nurse, night and day, at the hospitals, from the beginning of the war to the present time; a brother and friend through life to the neglected and the forgotten, the poor, the degraded, the criminal, the outcast, turning away from no man for his guilt, nor woman for her vileness. His is the strongest and truest compassion I have ever known. I remember here the anecdote told me by a witness, of his meeting in a by-street in Boston a poor ruffian, one whom he had known well as an innocent child, now a fullgrown youth, vicious far beyond his years, flying to Canada from the pursuit of the police, his sin-trampled features bearing marks of the recent bloody brawl in New York, in which, as he supposed, he had killed some one; and having heard his hurried story, freely confided to him, Walt Whitman, separated not from the bad even by his own goodness, with well I know what tender and tranquil feeling for the ruined being, and with a love which makes me think of that love of God which deserts not any creature, quietly at parting, after assisting him from his means, held him for a moment, with his arm around his neck, and, bending to the face, horrible and battered and prematurely old, kissed him on the cheek, and the poor hunted wretch, perhaps for the first time in his low life, receiving a token of love and compassion like a touch from beyond the sun, hastened away in deep dejection, sobbing and in tears. It reminds me of the anecdotes Victor Hugo, in his portraiture of Bishop Myriel, tells, under a thin veil of fiction, of Charles Miolles, the good Bishop of Digne. I know not what talisman Walt Whitman carries, unless it be an unexcluding friendliness and goodness which is felt upon his approach like magnetism; but I know that in the subterranean life of cities, among the worst roughs, he goes safely; and I could recite instances where hands that, in mere wantonness of ferocity, assault anybody, raised against him, have of their own accord been lowered almost as quickly, or, in some cases, have been dragged promptly down by others; this, too, I mean, when he and the assaulting gang were mutual strangers. I have seen singular evidence of the mysterious quality which not only guards him, but draws to him with intuition, rapid as light, simple and rude people, as to their natural mate and friend. I remember, as I passed the White House with him one evening, the startled feeling with which I saw a soldier on guard there—a stranger to us both, and with something in his action that curiously proved that he was a stranger—suddenly bring his musket to the "present" in military salute to him, quickly mingling with this respect due to his colonel, a gesture of greeting with the right hand as to a comrade, grinning, meanwhile, good fellow, with shy, spontaneous affection and deference, his ruddy, broad face glowing in the flare of the lampions. I remember, on another occasion, as I crossed the street with him, the driver of a street-car, a stranger, stopping the conveyance, and inviting him to get on and ride with him. Adventures of this kind are frequent, and "I took a fancy to you," or "You look like one of my style," is the common explanation he gets upon their occurrence. It would be impossible to exaggerate the personal adhesion and strong, simple affection given him, in numerous instances on sight, by multitudes of plain persons, sailors, mechanics, drivers, soldiers, farmers, sempstresses, old people of the past generation, mothers of families—those powerful, unlettered persons, among whom, as he says in his book, he his gone freely, and who never in most cases even suspect as an author him whom they love as a man, and who loves them in return.

His intellectual influence upon many young men and women—spirits of the morning sort, not willing to belong to that intellectual colony of Great Britain which our literary classes compose, nor helplessly tied, like them, to the old forms—I note as kindred to that of Socrates upon the youth of ancient Attica, or Raleigh upon the gallant young England of his day. It is a power at once liberating, instructing, and inspiring.—His conversation is a university. Those who have heard him in some roused hour, when the full afflatus of his spirit moved him, will agree with me that the grandeur of talk was accomplished. He is known as a passionate lover and powerful critic of the great music and of art. He is deeply cultured by some of the best books, especially those of the Bible, which he prefers above all other great literature, but principally by contact and communion with things themselves, which literature can only mirror and celebrate. He has travelled through most of the United States, intent on comprehending and absorbing the genius and history of his country, that he might do his best to start a literature worthy of her, sprung from her own polity, and tallying her own unexampled magnificence among the nations. To the same end, he has been a long, patient, and laborious student of life, mixing intimately with all varieties of experience and men, with curiosity and with love. He has given his thought, his life, to this beautiful ambition, and, still young, he has grown gray in its service. He has never married; like Giordano Bruno, he has made Thought in the service of his fellow-creatures his *bella donna*, his best beloved, his bride. His patriotism is boundless. It is no intellectual sentiment; it is a personal passion. He performs with scrupulous fidelity and zeal the duties of a citizen. For eighteen years, not missing once, his ballot has dropped on every national and local election day, and his influence has been ardently given for the good cause. Of all men I know, his life is most in the life of the nation. I remember, when the first draft was ordered, at a time when he was already performing an arduous and perilous duty as a volunteer attendant upon the wounded in the field—a duty which cost him the only illness he ever had in his life, and a very severe and dangerous illness it was, the result of poison absorbed in his devotion to the worst cases of hospital gangrene, and when it would have been the easiest thing in the world to evade duty, for though then only forty-two or three years old, and subject to the draft, he looked a hale sixty, and no enrolling officer would have paused for an instant before his gray hair—I remember, I say, how anxious and careful he was to get his name put on the enrolment [sic] lists, that he might stand his chance for martial service. This, too, at a time when so many gentlemen were skulking, dodging, agonizing for substitutes, and practising every conceivable device to escape military duty. What music of speech, though Cicero's own—what scarlet and gold superlatives could adorn or dignify this simple, antique trait of private heroism?—I recall his love for little children, for the young, and for very old persons, as if the dawn and the evening twilight of life awakened his deepest tenderness. I recall the affection for him of numbers of young me, and invariably of all good women. Who, knowing him, does not regard him as a man of the highest spiritual culture? I have never known one of greater and deeper religious feeling. To call one like him good seems an impertinence. In our sweet country phrase, he is one of God's men. And as I write these hurried and broken memoranda— as his strength and sweetness of nature, his moral health, his rich humor, his gentleness, his serenity, his charity, his simple-heartedness, his courage, his deep and varied knowledge of life and men, his calm wisdom, his singular and beautiful boy-innocence, his personal majesty, his rough scorn of mean actions, his magnetic and exterminating anger on due occasions—all that I have seen and heard of him, the testimony of associates, the anecdotes of friends, the remembrance of hours with him that should be immortal, the traits, lineaments, incidents of his life and being—as they come crowding into memory— his seems to me a character which only the heroic pen of Plutarch could record, and which Socrates himself might emulate or envy.

This is the man whom Mr. Harlan charges with having written a bad book. I might ask, How long is it since bad books have been the flower of good lives? How long is it since grape-vines produced thorns or fig-trees thistles? But Mr. Harlan says the book is bad because it is "full of indecent passages." This allegation has been brought against *Leaves of Grass* before. It has been sounded long and strong by many of the literary journals of both continents. As criticism it is legitimate. I may contemn the mind or deplore the moral life in which such a criticism has its source; still, as criticism it has a right to existence. But Mr. Harlan, passing the limits of opinion, inaugurates

punishment. He joins the band of the hostile verdict; he incarnates their judgment; then, detaching himself, he proceeds to a solitary and signal vengeance. As far as he can have it so, this author, for having written his book, shall starve. He shall starve, and his name shall receive a brand. This is the essence of Mr. Harlan's action. It is a dark and serious step to take. Upon what grounds is it taken?

I have carefully counted out from Walt Whitman's poetry the lines, perfectly moral to me, whether viewed in themselves or in the light of their sublime intentions and purport, but upon which ignorant and indecent persons of respectability base their sweeping condemnation of the whole work. Taking *Leaves of Grass*, and the recent small volume, "Drum-Taps" (which was in Mr. Harlan's possession), there are in the whole about nine thousand lines or verses. From these, including matter which I can hardly imagine objectionable to any one, but counting everything which the most malignant virtue could shrink from, I have culled eighty lines. Eighty lines out of nine thousand! It is a less proportion than one finds in Shakespeare. Upon this so slender basis rests the whole crazy fabric of American and European slander and the brutal lever of the Secretary.

Now, what by competent authority is the admitted character of the book in which these lines occur? For, though it is more than probable that Mr. Harlan never heard of the work till the hour of his explorations in the Department, the intellectual hemispheres of Great Britain and America have rung with it from side to side. It has received as extensive a critical notice, I suppose, as has ever been given to a volume. Had it been received only with indifference or derision, I should not have been surprised. In an age in which few breathe the atmosphere of the grand literature—which forgets the superb books and thinks Bulwer moral, and Dickens great, and Thackeray a real satirist—which gives to Macaulay the laurel due to Herodotus, and to Tennyson the crown reserved for Homer, and in which the chairs of criticism seem abandoned to squirts, and pedagogues, and monks—a mighty poet has little to expect from the literary press save unconcern and mockery. But even under these hard conditions the tremendous force of this poet has achieved a relative conquest, and the tone of the press denotes his book as not merely great, but illustrious. Even the copious torrents of abuse which have been lavished upon it have, in numerous instances, taken the form of tribute to its august and mysterious power, being in fact identical with that still vomited upon Montaigne and Juvenal. On the other hand, eulogy, very lofty and from the highest sources, has spanned it with sunbows. Emerson, our noblest scholar, a name to which Christendom does reverence, a critic of piercing insight and full comprehension, has pronounced it "the most extraordinary piece of wit and wisdom that America has yet contributed." How that austere and rare spirit, Thoreau, regarded it may be partly seen by his last posthumous volume. He thought of it, I have heard, with measureless esteem, ranking it with the vast and gorgeous conceptions of the Oriental bards. It has been reported to me that unpublished letters, received in this country from some of Europe's greatest, announce a similar verdict. The "North American Review," unquestionably the highest organ of American letters, in the course of a eulogistic notice of the work, remarking upon the passages which Mr. Harlan has treated as if they were novel in literature, observes: "There is not anything, perhaps (in the book), which modern usage would stamp as more indelicate than are some passages in Homer. There is not a word in it meant to attract readers by its grossness as there is in half the literature of the last century, which holds its place unchallenged on the tables of our drawing-rooms." The London "Dispatch," in a review written by the Rev. W. J. Fox, one of the most distinguished clergymen in England, after commending the poems for "their strength of expression, their fervor, their hearty wholesomeness, their originality and freshness, their singular harmony," etc., says that, "in the unhesitating frankness of a man who dares to call simplest things by their plain names, conveying also a large sense of the beautiful," there is involved "a clearer conception of what manly modesty really is than in anything we have in all conventional forms of word, deed, or act, so far known of," and concludes by declaring that "the author will soon make his way into the confidence of his readers, and his poems in time will become a pregnant text-book, from which quotations as sterling as the minted gold will be taken and applied to every form of the inner and the outer life." The London "Leader," one of the foremost of the British literary journals, in a review which more nearly approaches perception of the true character and purport of the book than any I have seen, has the following sentences:

"Mr. Emerson recognized the first issue of the *Leaves*, and hastened to welcome the author, then totally unknown. Among other things, said Emerson to the new avatar, 'I greet you at the beginning of a great career which yet must have had a long foreground somewhere for such a start.' The last clause was, however, overlooked entirely by the critics, who treated the new author as one self-educated, yet in the rough, unpolished, and owing nothing to instruction. The authority for so treating the author was derived from himself, who thus described in one of his poems, his person, character, and name, having omitted the last from the title-page,

'Walt Whitman, an American, one of the
roughs, a kosmos,
Disorderly, fleshy, and sensual,—

and in various other passages confessed to all the vices, as well as the virtues, of man. All this, with intentional wrong-headedness, was attributed by the sapient reviewers to the individual writer, and not to the subjective-hero supposed to be writing. Notwithstanding the word 'kosmos,' the writer was taken to be an ignorant man. Emerson perceived at once that there had been a long foreground somewhere or somehow;—not so they. Every page teems with knowledge, with information; but they saw it not, because it did not answer their purpose to see it . . . . . . The poem in which the word 'kosmos' appears explains in fact the whole mystery—nay, the word itself explains it. The poem is nominally upon himself, but really includes everybody. It begins:

'I celebrate myself,
And what I assume, you shall assume;
For every atom belonging to me, as good
belongs to you.'

In a word, Walt Whitman *represents the kosmical man—he is the ADAMUS of the Nineteenth century-not an individual, but MANKIND.* As such, in celebrating himself, he proceeds to celebrate universal humanity in its attributes, and accordingly commences his dithyramb with the five senses, beginning with that of smell. Afterwards, be deals with the intellectual, rational, and moral powers, showing throughout his treatment an intimate acquaintance with Kant's transcendental method, and perhaps including in his development the whole of the German school, down to Hegel—at any rate as interpreted by Cousin and others in France and Emerson in the United States. He certainly includes Fichte, for he mentions the egotist as the only true philosopher, and consistently identifies himself not only with every man, but with the universe and its Maker; and it is in doing so that the strength of his description consists. It is from such an ideal elevation that he looks down on Good and Evil, regards them as equal, and extends to them the like measure of equity . . . . Instead, therefore, of regarding these *Leaves of Grass* as a marvel, they seem to us as the most natural product of the American soil. They are certainly filled with an American spirit, breathe the American air, and assert the fullest American freedom." The passages characterized by the Secretary as "indecent" are, adds the "Leader," "only so many instances adduced in support of a philosophical principle, not meant for obscenity, but for scientific examples introduced, as they might be in any legal, medical, or philosophical book, for the purpose of instruction."

I could multiply these excerpts; but here are sufficient specimens of the competent judgments of eminent scholars and divines, testifying to the intellectual and moral grandeur of this work. Let it be remembered that there is nothing in the book that in one form or another is not contained in all great poetic or universal literature. It has nothing either in quantity or quality so offensive as everybody knows is in Shakespeare. All that this poet has done is to mention, without levity, without low language, very seriously, often devoutly, always simply, certain facts in the natural history of man and of life, and sometimes, assuming their sanctity, to use them in illustration or imagery. Far more questionable mention and use of these facts are common to the greatest literature. Shall the presence in a book of eighty lines, similar in character to what every great and noble poetic book contains, be sufficient to shove it below even the lewd writings of Petronius Arbiter, the dirty dramas of Shirley, or the scrofulous fiction of Louvet de Couvray? To lump it in with the anonymous lascivious trash spawned in holes and sold in corners, too witless and disgusting for any notice but that of the police; and to entitle its author to treatment such as only the nameless wretches of the very sewers of authorship ought to receive?

If, rising to the utmost cruelty of conception, I can dare add to the calamities of genius a misery so degrading and extreme as to imagine the great authors of the world condemned to clerkships under Mr. Harlan, I can at least mitigate that dream of wretchedness and insult by adding the fancy of their fate under the action of his principles. Let me suppose them there, and he still magnifying the calling of the Secretary into that of literary headsman. He opens the great book of Genesis. Everywhere "indecent passages." The mother hushes the child, and bids him skip as he reads aloud that first great history. It cannot be read aloud in "drawing-rooms" by "gentlemen" and "ladies." The freest use of language, the plainest terms, frank mention of forbidden subjects; the story of Onan, of Hagar and Sarai, of Lot and his daughters, of Isaac, Rebekah, and Abimelech, of Jacob and Leah, of Reuben and Bilhah; of Potiphar's wife and Joseph; tabooed allusion and statement everywhere; no veils, no euphemism, no delicacy, no meal in the mouth anywhere. Out with Moses! The cloven splendor on that awful brow shall not save him.

Mr. Harlan takes up the Iliad and the Odyssey. The loves of Jupiter and Juno, the dalliance of Achilles and Patroclus with their women; the perfectly frank, undraped reality of Greek life and manners naively shown without regard to the feelings of Christian civilizees-horrible! Out with Homer!

Here is Lucretius: Mr. Harlan opens the "De Rerum Natura," and reads the vast, benign, majestic lines, sad with the shadow of the intelligible universe upon them; sublime with the tragic problems of the Infinite; august with their noble love and compassion for mankind. But what is this? "Ut quasi transactis soepe omnibus rebus," etc. And this: "More ferarum quadrupedumque magis ritu." And this: "Nam mulier prohibet se consipere atque repugnat," etc. And this: "Quod petiere, premunt arcte, faciuntque dolorem," etc. Enough. Fine language, fine illustrations, fine precepts, pretty decency! Out with Lucretius! Out with the chief poet of the Tiber side!

Here is Æschylus; a dark magnificence of cloud, all rough with burning gold, which thunders and drips blood! The Greek Shakespeare. The gorgeous and terrible Æschylus! What is this in the "Prometheus" about Jove and Io? What sort of detail is that which, at the distance of ten years, I remember amazed Mr. Buckley as he translated the Agamemnon? What kind of talk is this in the "Choephori," in "The

Suppliants," and in the fragments of the comic drama of "The Argians"? Out with Æschylus!

Here is the sublime book of Ezekiel. All the Hebrew grandeur at its fullest is there. But look at this blurt of coarse words, hurled direct as the prophet-mouth can hurl them—this familiar reference to functions and organs voted out of language—this bread for human lips baked with ordure—these details of the scortatory loves of Aholah and Aholibah. Enough. Dismiss this dreadful majesty of Hebrew poetry. He has no "taste." He is "indecent." Out with Ezekiel!

Here is Dante. Open the tremendous pages of the "Inferno." What is this about the she-wolf Can Grande will kill? What picture is this of strumpet Thais?—ending with the lines:

> "Taida e, la puttana che rispose
> At drudo suo, quando disse: Ho io grazie
> Grandi appo te? Anzi meravigliose."

What is this also in the eighteenth canto?

> "Quivi venimmo, e quindi gui nel fosso
> Vidi gente attuffata in uno sterco
> Che dagli uman privati parea mosso:
> E mentre ch' io la giu con l'occhio cerco,
> Vidi un col capo si di merda lordo,
> Che non parea sera laico o cherco."

What is this line at the end of the twenty-first canto, which even John Carlyle flinches from translating, but which Dante did not flinch from writing?

> "Ed egli avea del cul fatto trombetta."

And look at these lines in the twenty-eighth canto:

> "Gia reggia, per mezzul perdere o lulla
> Com' io vidi on, cosi non si pertugia
> Rotto dal mento insin dove si trulla."

That will do. Dante, too, has "indecent passages." Out with Dante!

Here is the book of Job: the vast Arabian landscape, the picturesque pastoral details of Arabian life, the last tragic immensity of Oriental sorrow, the whole overarching sky of Oriental piety, are here. But here also the inevitable "indecency." Instead of the virtuous fiction of the tansy bed, Job actually has the indelicacy to state how man is born—even mentions the belly; talks about the gendering of bulls, and the miscarriage of cows; uses rank idioms; and in the thirty-first chapter especially, indulges in a strain of thought and expression which it is amazing does not bring down upon him, even at this late date, the avalanches of our lofty and pure reviews. Here is certainly "an immoral poet." Out with Job!

Here is Plutarch, prince of biographers, and Herodotus, flower of historians. What have we now? Traits of character not to be mentioned, incidents of conduct, accounts of manners, minute details of customs, which our modern historical dandies would never venture upon recording. Out with Plutarch and Herodotus!

Here is Tacitus. What statement of crimes that ought not to be hinted? Does the man gloat over such things? What dreadful kisses are these of Agrippina to Nero—the mother to the son? Out with Tacitus! And since there are books that ought to be publicly burned [Mr. Harlan had said that *Leaves of Grass* ought to be publicly burned], by all means let the stern grandeur of that rhetoric be lost in flame.

Here is Shakespeare: "indecent passages" everywhere—every drama, every poem thickly inlaid with them; all that men do displayed, sexual acts treated lightly, jested about, mentioned obscenely; the language never bolted; slang, gross puns, lewd words, in profusion. Out with Shakespeare!

Here is the Canticle of Canticles: beautiful, voluptuous poem of love literally, whatever be its mystic significance; glowing with the color, odorous with the spices, melodious with the voices of the East; sacred and exquisite and pure with the burning chastity of passion, which completes and exceeds the snowy chastity of virgins. This to me, but what to the Secretary? Can he endure that the female form should stand thus in a poem, disrobed, unveiled, bathed in erotic splendor? Look at these voluptuous details, this expression of desire, this amorous tone and glow, this consecration and perfume lavished upon the sensual. No! Out with Solomon!

Here is Isaiah. The grand thunder-roll of that righteousness, like the lion-roar of Jehovah above the guilty world, utters coarse words. Amidst the bolted lightnings of that sublime denunciation, coarse thoughts, indelicate figures, indecent allusions, flash upon the sight, like gross imagery in a midnight landscape. Out with Isaiah!

Here is Montaigne. Open those great, those virtuous pages of the unflinching reporter of man; the soul all truth and daylight, all candor, probity, sincerity, reality, eyesight. A few glances will suffice. Cant and vice and sniffle have groaned over these pages before. Out with Montaigne!

Here is Hafiz, the Anacreon of Persia, but more; a banquet of wine in a garden of roses, the nightingales singing, the laughing revellers high with festal joy; but a heavenly flame burns on every brow; a tone not of this sphere is in all the music, all the laughter, all the songs; a light of the Infinite trembles over every chalice and rests on every flower; and all the garden is divine. Still when Hafiz cries out, "Bring me wine, and bring the famed veiled beauty, the Princess of the brothel," etc., or issues similar orders, Mr. Harlan, whose virtue does not understand or endure such metaphors, must deal sternly with this kosmic man of Persia. Out with Hafiz!

Here is Virgil, ornate and splendid poet of old Rome; a master with a greater pupil, Alighieri—a bard above whose ashes Boccaccio kneels a trader, and arises a soldier of mankind. But he must lose those fadeless chaplets, the undying green of a noble fame; for here in the "Æneid" is "Dixerat; et niveis hinc atque hinc Diva lacertis," etc., and here in the "Georgics" is "Quo rapiat sitiens Venerem, interiusque recondat," etc., and there are other verses like these. Out with Virgil!

Here is Swedenborg. Open this poem in prose, the "Conjugial Love," to me, a temple, though in ruins; the sacred fane, clothed in mist, filled with moonlight, of a great though broken mind. What spittle of critic epithets stains all here? "Lewd," "sensual," "lecherous," "coarse," "llicentious," etc. Of course these judgments are final. There is no appeal from the tobacco juice of an expectorating and disdainful virtue. Out with Swedenborg!

Here is Goethe: the horrified squealing of prudes is not yet silent over pages of "Wilhelm Meister;" that high and chaste book, the "Elective Affinities," still pumps up oaths from clergymen: Walpurgis has hardly ceased its uproar over Faust. Out with Goethe!

Here is Byron: grand, dark poet; a great spirit—a soul like the ocean; generous lover of America; fiery trumpet of liberty; a sword for the human cause in Greece; a torch for the human mind

in "Cain;" a life that redeemed its every fault by taking a side, which was the human side; tempest of scorn in his first poem, tempest of scorn and laughter in his last poem, only against the things that wrong man; vast bud of the Infinite that Death alone prevented from its vaster flower; immense, seminal, electrical, dazzling Byron. But Beppo—O! But Don Juan—O, fie! Not to mention the Countess Guiccioli—ah, me! Prepare quickly the yellow envelope, and out with Byron!

Here is Cervantes: open "Don Quixote," paragon of romances, highest result of Spain, best and sufficient reason for her life among the nations, a laughing novel which is a weeping poem. But talk such as this of Sancho Panza and Tummas Cecial under the cork trees, and these coarse stories and bawdy words, and this free and gross comedy—is it to be endured? Out with Cervantes!

Here is another, a sun of literature, moving in a vast orbit with dazzling plenitudes of power and beauty; the one only modern European poet and novelist worthy to rank with the first; permanent among the fleeting; a demigod of letters among the pigmies; a soul of the antique strength and sadness, worthy to stand as the representative of the high thought and hopes of the Nineteenth century— Victor Hugo. Now open "Les Miserables." See the great passages which the American translator softens and the English translator tears away. Open this other book of his, "William Shakespeare," a book with only one grave fault, the omission of the words "a Poem" from the titlepage; a book which is the courageous arch, the comprehending sky of criticism, but which no American publisher will dare to issue, or if he does will expurgate. Out with Hugo, of course!

Here is Juvenal, terrible and splendid fountain of all satire; inspiration of all just censure; exemplar of all noble rage at baseness; satirist and moralist sublimed into the poet; the scowl of the unclouded noon above the low streets of folly and of sin. But what he withers, he also shows. The sun-stroke of his poetry reveals what it kills. Juvenal tells all. His fidelity of exposure is frightful. Mr. Harlan would make short work of him. Out with Juvenal!

Open the divine "Apocalypse." What words are these among the thunderings and lightnings and voices? Is this a poem to be read aloud in parlors? (for such appears to be the test of propriety and purity). At least, John might have been a little more choice in language. Some of these texts are "indecent." Yes, indeed! John must go!

Here is Spenser. Encyclopædic poet of the ideal chivalry. It is all there. Amadis, Esplandian, Tirante the White, Palmerin of England, all those Paladin romances were but the leaves; this is the flower. A lost dream of valor, chastity, courtesy, glory—a dream that marks an age of human history—glimmers here, far in these depths, and makes this unexplored obscurity divine.1 "But is the 'Faery Queen' such a book as you would wish to put into the hands of a lady?" What a question! Has it not been expurgated? Out with Spenser!

Here is another, a true soldier of the human emancipation; one who smites amid uproars of laughter; the master of Titanic farce; a whirlwind and earthquake of derision—Rabelais. A nice one for Mr. Harlan! One glimpse at the chapter which explains why the miles lengthen as you leave Paris, or at the details of the birth and nurture of Gargantua, will suffice. Out with Rabelais—out with the great jester of France, as Lord Bacon calls him!

And here is Lord Bacon himself, in one of whose pages you may read [*Novum Organum*; Aphorism CXX.], done from the Latin by Spedding into a magnificent golden thunder of English, the absolute defence of the free spirit of the great authors, coupled with stern rebuke to the spirit that would pick and choose, as dastard and effeminate. Out with Lord Bacon!

Not him only, not these only, not only the writers are under the ban. Here is Phidias, gorgeous sculptor in gold and ivory, giant dreamer of the Infinite in marble; but he will not use the fig-leaf. Here is Rembrandt, who paints the Holland landscape, the Jew, the beggar, the burgher, in lights and glooms of Eternity; and his pictures have been called "indecent." Here is Mozart, his music rich with the sumptuous color of all sunsets; and it has been called "sensual." Here is Michelangelo, who makes art tremble with a new and strange afflatus, and gives Europe novel and sublime forms that tower above the centuries, and accost the Greek; and his works have been called "bestial"! Out with them all!

Now, except Virgil, for vassalage to literary models, and for grave and sad falsehood to liberty; except Goethe for his lack of the final ecstacy of self-surrender which completes a poet, and for coldness to the great mother, one's country; except Spenser for his

remoteness, and Byron for his immaturity, and there is not one of those I have named that does not belong to the first order of human intellect. But no need to make discriminations here; they are all great; they have all striven; they have all served. Moses, Homer, Lucretius, Æschylus, Ezekiel, Dante, Job, Plutarch, Herodotus, Tacitus, Shakespeare, Solomon, Isaiah, Montaigne, Hafiz, Virgil, Swedenborg, Goethe, Byron, Connotes, Hugo, Juvenal, John, Spenser, Rabelais, Bacon, Phidias, Rembrandt, Mozart, Michelangelo—these are among the demi-gods of human thought; the souls that have loved and suffered for the race; the light-bringers, the teachers, the lawgivers, the consolers, the liberators, the inspired inspirers of mankind; the noble and gracious beings who, in the service of humanity, have borne every cross and earned every crown. There is not one of them that is not sacred in the eyes of thoughtful men. But not one of them do the rotten taste and morals of the Nineteenth century spare. Not one of them is qualified to render work for bread under this Secretary! Do I err? Do I exaggerate? I write without access to the books I mention (it is fitting that this piece of insolent barbarism should have been committed in almost the only important American city which is without a public library!)—and with the exception of three or four volumes which I happen to have by me, I am obliged to rely for my statements on the memory of youthful readings, eight or ten years ago. But name me one book of the first order in which such passages as I refer to do not occur! Tell me who can—what poet of the first grade escapes this brand "immoral," or this spittle "indecent"?

If the great books are not, in the point under consideration, in the same moral category as *Leaves of Grass*, then why, either in translation or in the originals, either by a bold softening which dissolves the author's meaning, or by absolute excision, are they nearly all expurgated? Answer me that. By one process or the other, Brizeux, Cary, Wright, Cayley, Carlyle, everybody, expurgates Dante; Langhorne and others expurgate Plutarch; Potter and others expurgate Æschylus; Gifford, Anthon and others expurgate Juvenal; Creech, Watson and others expurgate Lucretius; Bowdler and others expurgate Shakespeare; Nott (I believe it is) expurgates Hafiz; Wraxall and Wilbour expurgate Hugo; Kirkland, Hart and others expurgate Spenser; somebody expurgates Virgil; somebody expurgates Byron;

the Oxford scholars dilute Tacitus; Lord Derby expurgates Homer, besides making him as ridiculous as the plucked cock of Diogenes in translation; several bands expurgate Goethe; and Archbishop Tillotson in design expurgates Moses, Ezekiel, Solomon, Isaiah, St. John, and all the others a job which Dr. Noah Webster executes, but, thank God, cannot popularize. What book is spared? Nothing but a chain of circumstances, which one might fancy divinely ordained, saves us the relatively unmutilated Bible. Nearly every other great book bleeds. When one is not expurgated, the balance is restored by its being cordially abused. Thanks to the splendid conscience and courage of Mr. Wight, we can read Montaigne in English without the omission of a single word. Thanks also to Smollett, Motteux and others, Cervantes has gone untouched, and we have not as yet a family Rabelais. Neither have we as yet a family Mankind nor a family Universe; but this is an oversight which will, doubtless, be repaired in time. God's works will also, doubtless, be expurgated whenever it is possible. Why not? One step to this end is taken in the expurgation of Genius, which is His second manifestation, as Nature is His first! Go on, gentlemen! You will yet have things as "moral" as you desire!

I am aware that as far as his opinion, not his act, is concerned, Mr. Harlan, however unintelligently, represents to some extent the shallow conclusions of his age, and I know it will be said that if the great books contain these passages, they ought to be expurgated. It is not my design to endeavor to put a quart into people who only hold a gill, nor would I waste time in endeavoring to convert a large class of persons whom I once heard Walt Whitman describe, with his usual Titanic richness and strength of phrase, as "the immutable granitic pudding-heads of the world." But there is a better class than these; and I am filled with measureless amazement, that persons of high intelligence, living to the age of maturity, do not perceive, at least, the immense and priceless scientific and human uses of such passages, and the consequent necessity, transcending and quashing all minor considerations, of having them where they are. But look at these sad sentences—a complete and felicitous statement of the whole modern doctrine—in the pages of a man I love and revere: "The literature of three centuries ago is not decent to be read; we expurgate it. Within a hundred years,

woman has become a reader, and for that reason, as much as, or more than, anything else, literature has sprung to a higher level. No need now to expurgate all you read." He goes on to argue that literature in the next century will be richer than in the classic epochs, because woman will contribute to it as an author—her contribution, I infer, to be of the kind that will not need expurgating. These, I repeat, are sad sentences. If they are true, Bowdler is right to expurgate Shakespeare, and Noah Webster the Bible. But no, they are not true! I welcome woman into art; but when she comes there grandly, she will not come either as expurgator or creator of emasculate or partial forms. Woman, grand in art, is Rosa Bonheur, painting with fearless pencil the surly, sublime Jovian bull, equipped for masculine use; painting the powerful, ramping stallion in his amorous pride; not weakly nor meanly flinching from the full celebration of what God has made. Woman, grand in art, will come creating in forms, however novel, the absolute, the permanent, the real, the evil and the good, as Æschylus, as Cervantes, as Shakespeare before her; with sex, with truth, with universality, without omissions or concealments. And woman, as the ideal reader of literature, is not the indelicate prude, flushing and squealing over some frank page; it is that high and beautiful soul, Marie de Gournay, devoutly absorbing the work of her master Montaigne, finding it all great, greatly comprehending, greatly accepting it all; fronting its license and grossness without any of the livid shuddering of Puritans, and looking on the book in the same universal and kindly spirit as its author looked upon the world. Woman reading otherwise than thus—shrinking from Apuleius, from Rabelais, from Aristophanes, from Shakespeare, from even Wycherley, or Petronius, or Aretin, or Shirley—is less than man, is not ideal, not strong, not nobly good, but petty, and effeminate, mean. And not for her, nor by her, nor by man, do I assent to the expurgation of the great books. Literature cannot spring to a higher level than theirs. Alas! it has sprung to a lower.

The level of the great books is the Infinite, the Absolute. To contain all, by containing the premise, the truth, the idea and feeling of all, to tally the universe by profusion, variety, reality, mystery, enclosure, power, terror, beauty, service; to be great to the utmost conceivability of greatness—what higher level than this can literature spring to? Up on the highest summit stand such works, never to be surpassed, never to be supplanted. Their indecency is not that of the vulgar; their vulgarity is not that of the low. Their evil, if it be evil, is not there for nothing—it serves; at the base of it is Love. Every poet of the highest quality is, in the masterly coinage of the author of *Leaves of Grass*, a kosmos. His work, like himself, is a second world, full of contrarieties, strangely harmonized, and moral indeed, but only as the world is moral. Shakespeare is all good, Rabelais is all good, Montaigne is all good, not because all the thoughts, the words, the manifestations are so, but because at the core, and permeating all, is an ethic intention—a love which, through mysterious, indirect, subtle, seemingly absurd, often terrible and repulsive, means, seeks to uplift, and never to degrade. It is the spirit in which authorship is pursued, as Augustus Schlegel has said, that makes it either an infamy or a virtue; and the spirit of the great authors, no matter what their letter, is one with that which pervades the Creation. In mighty love, with implements of pain and pleasure, of good and evil, Nature develops man; genius also, in mighty love, with implements of pain and pleasure, of good and evil, develops man; no matter what the means, that is the end.

Tell me not, then, of the indecent passages of the great poets! The world, which is the poem of God, is full of indecent passages! "Shall there be evil in a city and the Lord hath not done it?" shouts Amos. "I form the light, and create darkness; I make peace, and create evil; I, the Lord, do all these things," thunders Isaiah. "This," says Coleridge, "is the deep abyss of the mystery of God." Ay, and the profound of the mystery of genius also! Evil is part of the economy of genius, as it is part of the economy of Deity. Gentle reviewers endeavor to find excuses for the freedoms of geniuses. "It is to prove that they were above conventionalities." "It is referable to the age." "The age permitted a degree of coarseness," etc. "Shakespeare's indecencies are the result of his age." Oh, Ossa on Pelion, mount piled on mount, of error and folly! What has genius, spirit of the absolute and the eternal, to do with the definitions of position, or conventionalities, or the age? Genius puts indecencies into its works, because God puts them into His world. Whatever the special reason in each case, this is the general reason in all cases. They are here, because they are there. That is the eternal why.—No; Alphonso of Castile thought

that, if he had been consulted at the Creation, he could have given a few hints to the Almighty. Not I. I play Alphonso neither to genius nor to God.

What is this poem, for the giving of which to America and the world, and for that alone, its author has been dismissed with ignominy from a Government office? It is a poem which Schiller might have hailed as the noblest specimen of naive literature, worthy of a place beside Homer. It is, in the first place, a work purely and entirely American, autochthonic, sprung from our own soil; no saver of Europe nor of the past, nor of any other literature in it; a vast carol of our own land, and of its Present and Future; the strong and haughty psalm of the Republic. There is not one other book, I care not whose, of which this can be said. I weigh my words and have considered well. Every other book by an American author implies, both in form and substance, I cannot even say the European, but the British mind. The shadow of Temple Bar and Arthur's Seat lies dark on all our letters. Intellectually, we are still a dependency of Great Britain, and one word— colonial—comprehends and stamps our literature. In no literary form, except our newspapers, has there been anything distinctively American. I note our best books—the works of Jefferson, the romances of Brockden Brown, the speeches of Webster, Everett's rhetoric, the divinity of Channing, some of Cooper's novels, the writings of Theodore Parker, the poetry of Bryant, the masterly law arguments of Ly.sander Spooner, the miscellanies of Margaret Fuller, the histories of Hildreth, Bancroft and Motley, Ticknor's "History of Spanish Literature," Judd's "Margaret," the political treatises of Calhoun, the rich, benignant poems of Longfellow, the ballads of Whittier, the delicate songs of Philip Pendleton Cooke, the weird poetry of Edgar Poe, the wizard tales of Hawthorne, Irving's "Knickerbocker," Delia Bacon's splendid sibyllic book on Shakespeare, the political economy of Carey, the prison letters and immortal speech of John Brown, the lofty patrician eloquence of Wendell Phillips, and those diamonds of the first water, the great clear essays and greater poems of Emerson. This literature has often commanding merits, and much of it is very precious to me; but in respect to its national character, all that can be said is that it is tinged, more or less deeply, with America; and the foreign model, the foreign standards, the foreign ideas, dominate over it all.

At most, our best books were but struggling beams; behold in *Leaves of Grass* the immense and absolute sunrise! It is all our own! The nation is in it! In form a series of chants, in substance it is an epic of America. It is distinctively and utterly American. Without model, without imitation, without reminiscence, it is evolved entirely from our own polity and popular life. Look at what it celebrates and contains! Hardly to be enumerated without using the powerful, wondrous phrases of its author, so indissoluble are they with the things described. The essences, the events, the objects of America; the myriad varied landscapes; the teeming and giant cities; the generous and turbulent populations; the prairie solitudes, the vast pastoral plateaus; the Mississippi; the land dense with villages and farms; the habits, manners, customs; the enormous diversity of temperatures; the immense geography; the red aborigines passing away, "charging the water and the land with names;" the early settlements; the sudden uprising and defiance of the Revolution; the august figure of Washington; the formation and sacredness of the Constitution; the pouring in of the emigrants; the million-masted harbors; the general opulence and comfort; the fisheries, and whaling, and gold-digging, and manufactures, and agriculture; the dazzling movement of new States, rushing to be great; Nevada rising, Dakota rising, Colorado rising; the tumultuous civilization around and beyond the Rocky Mountains, thundering and spreading; the Union impregnable; feudalism in all its forms forever tracked and assaulted; liberty deathless on these shores; the noble and free character of the people; the equality of male and female; the ardor, the fierceness, the friendship, the dignity, the enterprise, the affection, the courage, the love of music, the passion for personal freedom; the mercy and justice and compassion of the people; the popular faults and vices and crimes; the deference of the President to the private citizen; the image of Christ forever deepening in the public mind as the brother of despised and rejected persons; the promise and wild song of the future; the vision of the Federal Mother, seated with more than antique majesty in the midst of her many children; the pouring glories of the hereafter; the vistas of splendor, incessant and branching; the tremendous elements, breeds, adjustments of America—with all these, with more, with everything transcendent, amazing, and new, undimmed by the pale cast of thought, and with the very color and brawn of actual life, the whole gigantic epic of our continental being unwinds in all its magnificent reality in these pages. To understand Greece, study the "Iliad" and "Odyssey;" study *Leaves of Grass* to understand America. Her democracy is there. Would you have a text-book of democracy? The writings of Jefferson are good; De Tocqueville is better; but the great poet always contains historian and philosopher—and to know the comprehending spirit of this country, you shall question these insulted pages.

Yet this vast and patriotic celebration and presentation of all that is our own, is but a part of this tremendous volume. Here in addition is thrown in poetic form, a philosophy of life, rich, subtle, composite, ample, adequate to these great shores. Here are presented superb types of models of manly and womanly character for the future of this country, athletic, large, naive, free, dauntless, haughty, loving, nobly carnal, nobly spiritual, equal in body and soul, acceptive and tolerant as Nature, generous, cosmopolitan, above all, religious. Here are erected standards, drawn from the circumstances of our case, by which not merely our literature, but all our performance, our politics, art, behavior, love, conversation, dress, society, everything belonging to our lives and their conduct, will be shaped and recreated. A powerful afflatus from the Infinite has given this book life. A voice which is the manliest of human voices sounds through it all. In it is the strong spirit which will surely mould our future. Mark my words: its sentences will yet clinch the arguments of statesmen; its precepts will be the laws of the people! From the beams of this seminal sun will be generated, with tropical luxuriance, the myriad new forms of thought and life in America. And in view of the national character and national purpose of this work—in view of its vigorous re-enforcement and service to all that we bold most precious—I make the claim here, that so far from defaming and persecuting its author, the attitude of an American statesman or public officer towards him should be to the highest degree friendly and sustaining.

Beyond his country, too, this poet serves the world. He refutes by his example the saying of Goethe, one of those which stain that noble fame with baseness, that a great poet cannot be patriotic; and he dilates to a universal use which redoubles the splendors of his volume, and makes it dear to all that is human. I am not its authorized interpreter, and can only state, at the risk of imperfect expression and perhaps error, what its meanings and purpose seem to me. But I see that, in his general intention, the author has aimed to express that most common but wondrous thing-that strange assemblage of soul, body, intellect—beautiful, mystical, terrible, limited, boundless, ill-assorted, contradictory, yet singularly harmonized—a Human Being, a single, separate identity—a Man—himself; but himself typically, and in his universal being. This he has done with perfect candor, including the bodily attributes and organs as necessary component parts of the creation. Every thinking person should see the value and use of such a presentation of human nature as this. I also see— and it is from these parts of the book that much of the misunderstanding and offence arises—that this poet seeks in subtle ways to rescue from the keeping of blackguards and debauchees, to which it has been abandoned, and to redeem to noble thought and use, the great element of amativeness or sexuality, with all its acts and organs. Sometimes by direct assertion, sometimes by implication, he rejects the prevailing admission that this element is vile; declares its natural or normal manifestation to be sacred and unworthy shame; awards it an equal but not superior sanctity with the other elements that compose man; and illustrates his doctrine and sets his example by applying this element, with all that pertains to it, to use as part of the imagery of poetry. Then, besides, diffused like an atmosphere throughout the poem, tincturing all its quality, and giving it that sacerdotal and prophetic character which makes it a sort of American Bible, is the pronounced and ever-recurring assertion of the divinity of all things. In a spirit like that of the Egyptian priesthood, who wore the dung-beetle in gold on their crests, perhaps as a symbol of the sacredness of even the lowest forms of life, the poet celebrates all the Creation as noble and holy—the meanest and lowest parts of it, as well as the most lofty; all equally projections of the Infinite; all emanations of the creative life of God. Perpetual hymns break from him in praise of the divineness of the universe; he sees a halo around every shape, however low; and life in all its forms inspires a rapture of worship.

How some persons can think a book of this sort bad, is clearer to me than it used to be. Swedenborg says that to the devils, perfumes are stinks. I happen to know that some of the vilest abuse *Leaves of Grass* has received, has come from men of the lowest possible moral life. It is not so easy to understand how some persons of culture and judgment can fail to perceive its literary greatness. Making fair allowance for faults, which no great work, from "Hamlet" to the world itself, is perhaps without, the book, in form as in substance, seems to me a masterpiece. Never in literature has there been more absolute conceptive or presentative power. The forms and shows of things are bodied forth so that one may say they become visible, and are alive. Here, in its grandest, freest use, is the English language, from its lowest compass to the top of the key; from the powerful, rank idiom of the streets and fields to the last subtlety of academic speech—ample, various, telling, luxuriant, pictorial, final, conquering; absorbing from other languages to its own purposes their choicest terms; its rich and daring composite defying grammar; its most incontestable and splendid triumphs achieved, as Jefferson notes of the superb Latin of Tacitus, in haughty scorn of the rules of grammarians. Another singular excellence is the metre—entirely novel, free, flexible, melodious, corresponsive to the thought; its noble proportions and cadences reminding of winds and waves, and the vast elemental sounds and motions of Nature, and having an equal variety and liberty. I have heard this brought into disparaging comparison with the metres of Tennyson; the poetry also disparaged in the same connection. I hardly know what to think of people who can talk in this way. To say nothing of the preference, the mere parallel is only less ludicrous and arbitrary than would be one between Moore and Isaiah. Tennyson is an exquisite and sumptuous poet of the third, perhaps the fourth order, as certainly below Milton and Virgil as Milton and Virgil are certainly below Æschylus and Homer. His full-fluted verbal music, which is one of his chief merits, is of an extraordinary beauty. But in this respect the comparison between him and Walt Whitman is that between melody and harmony—between a song by Franz Abt or Schubert and a symphony by Beethoven. Speaking generally, and not with exact justice to either, the words of Tennyson, irrespective of their sense, make music to the ear, while the sense of Walt Whitman's words makes a loftier music in the mind. For a music, perfect and vast, subtle and more than auricular—woven not alone from the verbal sounds and rhythmic cadences, but educed by the thought and feeling of the verse from the reader's soul by the power of a spell few hold—I know of nothing superior to "By the Bivouac's Fitful Flame," the "Ashes of Soldiers," the "Spirit Whose Work is Done," the prelude to "Drum Taps," that most mournful and noble of all love songs, "Out of the Rolling Ocean, the Crowd," or "Out of the Cradle Endlessly Rocking," "Elemental Drifts," the entire section entitled "Song of Myself," the hymn commencing "Splendor of Falling Day," or the great salute to the French Revolution of '93, entitled "France." If these are not examples of great structural harmony as well as of the highest poetry, there are none in literature. And if all these were wanting, there is a poem in the volume which, if the author had never written another line, would be sufficient to place him among the chief poets of the world. I do not refer to "Chanting the Square Deific," though that also would be sufficient, in its incomparable breadth and grandeur of conception and execution, to establish the highest poetic reputation, but to the strain commemorating the death of the beloved President, commencing "When Lilacs Last in the Dooryard Bloomed," a poem whose rich and sacred beauty and rapture of tender religious passion, spreading aloft into the sublime, leave it unique and solitary in literature, and will make it the chosen and immortal hymn of Death forever. Emperors might well elect to die, could their memories be surrounded with such a requiem, which, next to the grief and love of the people, is the grandest and the only grand funeral music poured around Lincoln's bier.

In the face of works like these, testimony of the presence on earth of a mighty soul, I am thunderstruck at the low tone of the current criticism. Even from eminent persons, who ought to know how to measure literature, and who are friendly to this author, I hear, mingled with inadequate praises, the self-same censures—the very epithets even which Voltaire not more ridiculously passed on Shakespeare. Take care, gentlemen! What you, like Voltaire, take for rudeness, chaos, barbarism, lack of form, may be the sacred and magnificent wildness of a virgin world of poetry, all unlike these fine and ordered Tennysonian rose-gardens which are your ideal, but excelling these as the globe excels the parterre. I, at any rate, am not deceived. I see how swiftly the smart, bright conventional standards of modern criticism assign Isaiah or Ezekiel to the limbo of abortions. I see of bow limited are the wit and scholarship of these "Saturday Reviews" and "London Examiners," with their *doopelgangers* on this side of the Atlantic, by the treatment some poetic masterpiece of China or Hindustan receives when it falls into their hands for judgment. Anything not cast in modern conventional forms, any novel or amazing beauty, strikes them as comic. Read Mr. Buckley's notes, even at this late day, on a poet so incredibly great as Æschylus. Read an Æschylus illustrated by reference to Nicholas Nickleby, Mrs. Bombazine, and Mantalini, and censured in contemptuous, jocular or flippant annotations—this, too, by an Oxford scholar of rank and merit. No wonder *Leaves of Grass* goes underrated or unperceived. Modern criticism is Voltaire estimating the Apocalypse as "dirt," and roaring with laughter over the leaves of Ezekiel. Why? Because this poetry has not the court tread, the perfume, the royal purple of Racine—only its own wild and formless incomparable sublimity. Voltaire was an immense and noble person; only it was not part of his greatness to be able to see that other greatness which transcends common sense as the Infinite transcends the Finite. These children of Voltaire, also, who make the choirs of modern criticism, have great merits. But to justly estimate poetry of the first order is not one of them. "Shakespeare's 'Tempest' or 'Midsummer Night's Dream,' or any such damned nonsense as that," said one of this school to me a month ago. "Look at that perpendicular grocery signboard, the letters all fantastic and reading from top to bottom, a mere oddity: that is *Leaves of Grass*," said another, a person of eminence. No, gentlemen! you and I differ. I see, very clearly, the nature of a work like this, the warmest praise of which, not to mention your blame, has been meagre and insufficient to the last degree, and which centuries must ponder before they can sufficiently honor. You have had your say; let me have at least the beginning of mine: Nothing that America had before in literature rose above construction; this is a creation. Idle, and worse than idle, is any attempt to place this author either among or below the poets of the day. They are but singers; he is a bard. In him you have one of that mighty brotherhood who, more than statesmen, mould the future; who, as Fletcher of Saltoun said, when they make the songs of a nation, it matters not who makes the laws. I class him boldly, and the future will confirm my judgment, among the great creative minds of the world. By a quality almost incommunicable, which makes its possessor, no matter what his diversity or imperfections, equal with the Supremes of art, and by the very structure of his mind, he belongs there. His place is beside Shakespeare, Æschylus, Cervantes, Dante, Homer, Isaiah—the bards of the last ascent, the brothers of the radiant summit. And if any man think this estimate extravagant, I leave him, as Lord Bacon says, to the gravity of that judgment, and pass on. Enough for me to pronounce this book grandly good and supremely great. Clamor, on the score of its morality, is nothing but a form of turpitude; denial of its greatness is nothing but an insanity; and the roar of Sodom and the laughter of Bedlam shall not, by a hair's breadth, swerve my verdict.

As for those passages which have been so strangely interpreted, I have to say that nothing but the horrible inanity of prudery, to which civilization has become subject, and which affects even many good persons, could cloud and distort their palpable innocence and nobleness. What chance has an author to a reasonable interpretation of such utterances in an age when squeamishness, the Siamese twin-brother of indelicacy, is throned as the censor of all life? Look at the nearest, the commonest, and homeliest evidences of the abysm into which we have fallen. Here in my knowledge is an estimable family which, when the baby playing on the floor kicked up its skirts, I have repeatedly seen rush en masse to pull down the immodest petticoat. Here is a lady whose shame of her body is such that she will not disrobe in the presence of one of her own sex, and thinks it horrible to sleep at night without being swaddled in half her garments. Everywhere you see women perpetually glancing to be sure their skirts are quite down; twisting their heads over their shoulders, like some of the damned in Dante, to get a rear view; drawing in their feet if so much as a toe happens to protrude beyond the hem of the gown, and in various ways betraying a morbid consciousness which is more offensive than positive immodesty. When I went to the hospital, I saw one of those pretty and good girls, who in muslin and ribbons ornament the wards, and are called "nurses," pick up her skirts and skurry away, flushing hectic, with averted face, because as she passed a cot the poor fellow who lay there happened, in his uneasy turnings, to thrust part of a manly leg from beneath the coverlet. I once heard Emerson severely censured in a private company, five or six persons present, and I

the only dissenting voice, because in one of his essays he had used the word "spermatic." When Tennyson published the "Idyls of the King," some of the journals in both America and England, and several persons in my own hearing, censured the weird and magnificent "Vivien," one of his finest poems, as "immoral" and "vulgar." When Charles Sumner, in the debate on Louisiana, characterized the new-formed State as "a seven months' child, begotten by the bayonet, in criminal conjunction with the spirit of caste "—a stroke of absolute genius—he was censured by the public prints, and reminded that there were ladies in the gallery! Lately the "London Observer," one of the most eminent of the British journals, in a long and labored editorial on the bathing at Margate, denounced the British wives and matrons in the severest terms for sitting on the beach When men were bathing in "slight bathing-dresses" (it was not even pretended that the men were nude)—and even went the length of demanding of the civil authorities that they should invoke the interference of Parliament to stop this scandal! These are fair minor specimens of the prudery, worse than vice, but also the concomitant of the most shocking vice, which prevails everywhere. Its travesty is the dressing in pantalettes the "limbs" of the piano; its insolent tragi-comedy is the expulsion of Shakespeare from office because he writes "indecent passages "; its tragedy is the myriad results of wrong, and crime, and ruin, carried into all the details of every relation of life.

A civilization in which such things as I have mentioned can be thought or done is guilty to the core. It is not purity, it is impurity, which calls clothes more decent than the naked body—thus inanely conferring upon the work of the tailor or milliner a modesty denied to the work of God. It is not innocent but guilty thought which attaches shame, secrecy, baseness, and horror to great and august parts and functions of humanity. The tacit admission everywhere prevalent that portions of the human physiology are base; that the amative feelings and acts of the sexes, even when hallowed by marriage, are connected with a low sensuality; and that these, with such subjects or occurrences as the conception and birth of children, are to be absconded from, blushed at, concealed, ignored, withheld from education, and in every way treated as if they belonged to the category of sins against Nature, is not only in itself a contemptible insanity, but a main source of unspeakable personal and social evil. From the morbid state of mind which such a theory and practice must induce are spawned a thousand guilty actions of every description and degree. There is no occurrence in the vast and diversified range of sexual evil, from the first lewd thought in the mind of the budding child, the very suspicion of which makes the parent tremble, down to the last ghastly and bloody spasm of lust which rends its hapless victim in some suburban woodland, that is not fed mainly from this mystery and mother of abominations, to whose care civilization has remitted the entire subject. The poet who, in the spirit of that divine utility which marked the first great bards and will mark the last, seeks to make literature remediate to an estate like this, works in the best interests of his country and his fellow-beings, and deserves their gratitude. This is what Walt Whitman has done. Directly and indirectly, in forms as various as the minds he seeks to influence; in frank opposition to the great sexual falsehood by which we are ruled and ruined, he has thrown into civilization a conception intended to be slowly and insensibly absorbed, and to ultimately appear in results of good—the conception of the individual as a divine democracy of essences, powers, attributes, functions, organs—all equal, all sacred, all consecrate to noble use; the sexual part the same as the rest, no more a subject for mystery, or shame, or secrecy, than the intellectual, or the manual, or the alimentary, or the locomotive part—divinely commonplace as head, or hand, or stomach, or foot; and, though sacred, to be regarded as so ordinary that it shall be employed the same as any other part, for the purposes of literature—an idea which he exemplifies in his poetry by a metaphorical use which it is a deep disgrace to any intellect to misunderstand. This is his lesson, This is one of the central ideas which rule the myriad teeming play of his volume, and interpret it as a law of Nature interprets the complex play of facts which proceeds from it. This, then, is not license, but thought. It may be erroneous, it may be chimerical, it may be ineffectual; but it is thought, serious and solemn thought, on a most difficult and deeply immersed question—thought emanating from the deep source of a great love and care for men, and seeking nothing but a pure human welfare. When, therefore, any persons undertake to outrage and injure its author for having given it to the world, it is not merely as the pigmy incarnations of the depraved modesty, the

surface morality, the filthy and libidinous decency of the age, but it is as the persecutors of thought that they stand before us. It is no excuse for them to say, that such treatment of Walt Whitman is justifiable, because his book appears to them bad. Waiving every other consideration, I have to inform them that on this subject they should not permit themselves the immodesty of a judgment. It is not for such as they to attempt to prison in the poor cell of their opinion the vast journey and illumination of the human mind. No matter what the book seems to them, they should remember that an author deserves to be tried by his peers, and that a book may easily seem to some persons quite another thing from what it really is to others.

Here is Rabelais, a writer who wears all the crowns; but even Mr. Harlan would consider Walt Whitman white as purity beside him. "Filth," "zanyism," "grossness," "profligacy," "licentiousness," "sensuality," "beastliness"—these are samples of the epithets which have fallen, like a rain of excrement, on Rabelais for three hundred years. And yet it is of him that the holy-hearted Coleridge—an authority of the first order on all purely literary or ethical questions—it is of him that Coleridge says, and says justly: "I could write a treatise in praise of the *moral elevation* of Rabelais' work which would make the Church stare, and the Conventicle groan, and yet would be the truth, and nothing but the truth." The moral elevation of Rabelais! A great criticism, a needed word. It is just. No matter for seeming—Rabelais is good to the very core. Rabelais' book, viewed with reference to ensemble, viewed in relation, viewed in its own proper quality by other than cockney standards, is righteous to the uttermost extreme. So is the work of Walt Whitman, far other in character, and far less obnoxious to criticism than that of Rabelais, but which demands at least as liberal a judgment, and which it is not for any deputy, however high in office, to assign to shame.

I know not what further vicissitude of insult and outrage is in store for this great man. It may be that the devotees of a castrated literature, the earthworms that call themselves authors, the confectioners that pass for poets, the flies that are recognized as critics, the bigots, the dilettanti, the prudes and the fools, are more potent than I dream to mar the fortunes of his earthly hours; but above and beyond them uprises a more majestic civilization in the immense and sane serenities of futurity; and the man who has achieved that sublime thing, a genuine book; who has written to make his land greater, her citizens better, his race nobler; who has striven to serve men by communicating to them that which they least know, their own nature, their own experience; who has thrown into living verse a philosophy designed to exalt life to a higher level of sincerity, reality, religion; who has torn away disguises and illusions, and restored to commonest things, and the simplest and roughest people, their divine significance and natural, antique dignity, and who has wrapped his country and all created things as with splendors of sunrise, in the beams of a powerful and gorgeous poetry—that man, whatever be the clouds that close around his fame, is assured illustrious; and when every face lowers, when every hand is raised against him, turning his back upon his day and generation, he may write upon his book, with all the pride and grief of the calumniated Æschylus, the haughty dedication that poet graved upon his hundred dramas: TO TIME!

And Time will remember him. He holds upon the future this supreme claim of all high poets— behind the book, a life loyal to humanity. Never, if I can help it, shall be forgotten those immense and divine labors in the hospitals of Washington, among the wounded of the war, to which he voluntarily devoted himself, as the best service he could render to his struggling country, and which illustrate that boundless love which is at once the dominant element of his character, and the central source of his genius. How can I tell the nature and extent of that sublime ministration? During those years, Washington was a city in whose unbuilt places and around whose borders were thickly planted dense white clusters of barracks. These were the hospitals—neat, orderly, rectangular, strange towns, whose every citizen lay drained with sickness or wrung with pain. There, in those long wards, in rows of cots on either side, were stretched, in all attitudes and aspects of mutilation, of pale repose, of contorted anguish, of death, the martyrs of the war; and among them, with a soul that tenderly remembered the little children in many a dwelling mournful for those fathers, the worn and anxious wives, haggard with thinking of those husbands, the girls weeping their spirits from their eyes for those lovers, the mothers who from afar yearned to the bedsides of those sons, walked Walt Whitman, in the spirit of Christ, soothing, healing, consoling, restoring, night and day, for years; never failing, never tiring, constant, vigilant, faithful; performing, without fee or reward, his self-imposed duty; giving to the task all his time and means, and doing everything that it is possible for one unaided human being to do. Others fail, others flag; good souls that came often and did their best, yield and drop away; he remains. Winter and summer, night and day, every day in the week, every week in the year, all the time, till the winter of '65, when for a few hours daily, during six months, his duties to the Government detain him; after that, all the time he can spare, he visits the hospitals. What does he do? See. At the red aceldama of Fredericksburg, in '62-'3, he is in a hospital on the banks of the Rappahannock; it is a large, brick house, full of wounded and dying; in front, at the foot of a tree, is a cart-load of amputated legs, arms, hands, feet, fingers; dead bodies shrouded in army blankets are near; there are fresh graves in the yard; he is at work in the house among the officers and men, lying, unclean and bloody, in their old clothes; he is upstairs and down; he is poor, he has nothing to give this time, but he writes letters for the wounded; he cheers up the desponding; he gives love. Some of the men, war-sad, passionately cling to him; they weep; he will sit for hours with them if it gives them comfort. Here he is in Washington, after Chancellorsville, at night, on the wharf; two boat-loads of wounded (and oh, such wounded!) have been landed; they lie scattered about on the landing, in the rain, drenched, livid, lying on the ground, on old quilts, on blankets; their heads, their limbs bound in bloody rags; a few torches light the scene; the ambulances, the callous drivers are here; groans, sometimes a scream, resound through the flickering light and the darkness. He is there, moving around; he soothes, he comforts, he consoles, he assists to lift the wounded into the ambulances; he helps to place the worst cases on the stretchers; his kiss is warm upon the pallid lips of some who are mere children; his tears drop upon the faces of the dying. Here he is in the hospitals of Washington—the Campbell, the Patent Office, the Eighth Street, the Judiciary, the Carver, the Douglas, the Armory Square. He writes letters; he writes to fathers, mothers, brothers, wives, sweethearts; some of the soldiers are poor penmen; some cannot get paper and envelopes; some fear to write lest they should worry the folks at home; he writes for them all; he uses that genius which shall endure to the latest generation, to say the felicitous, the consoling, the cheering, the prudent, the best word. He goes through the wards, he talks cheerfully, he distributes amusing reading matter; at night or by day, when the horrible monotony of the hospital weighs like lead on every soul, be reads to the men; he is careful to sit away from the cot of any poor fellow so sick or wounded as to be easily disturbed, but he gathers into a large group as many as he can, and amuses them with some story or enlivening game, like that of "Twenty Questions," or recites some little poem or speech, or starts some discussion, or with some device dispels the gloom. For his daily occupation, he goes from ward to ward, doing all be can to hearten and revive the spirits of the sufferers, and keep the balance in favor of their recovery. Usually, his plan is to pass, with haversack strapped across his shoulder, from cot to cot, distributing small gifts; his theory is that these men, far from home, lonely, sick at heart, need more than anything some practical token that they are not forsaken, that some one feels a fatherly or brotherly interest in them; hence, he gives them what he can; to particular cases, entirely penniless, he distributes small sums of money, fifteen cents, twenty cents, thirty cents, fifty cents, not much to each, for there are many, but under the circumstances these little sums are and mean a great deal. He also distributes and directs envelopes, gives letter paper, postage stamps, tobacco, apples, figs, sweet biscuit, preserves, blackberries; gets delicate food for special cases; sometimes a dish of oysters or a dainty piece of meat, or some savory morsel for some poor creature who loathes the hospital fare, but whose appetite may be tempted. In the hot weather he buys boxes of oranges and distributes them, grateful to lips baked with fever; he buys boxes of lemons, be buys sugar, to make lemonade for those parched throats of sick soldiers; he buys canned peaches, strawberries, pears; he buys ice cream and treats the whole hospital; he buys whatever luxuries his limited resources will allow, and he makes them go as far as he can. Where does he get the means for this expenditure? For Walt Whitman is poor; he is poor, and has a right to be proud of his poverty, for it is the sacred, the ancient, the immemorial poverty of goodness and genius. He gets the means by writing for newspapers; he expends all he gets upon his boys, his darlings, the sick and maimed soldiers—the young heroes of the land who saved their country, the laborers of America who fought for the hopes of the world. He adds to his own earnings the contributions of noble souls, often strangers, who, in Boston, in New York, in Providence, in Brooklyn, in Salem, in Washington and elsewhere, have heard that such a man walks the hospitals, and who volunteer to send him this assistance; when at last he gets a place under Government, and till Mr. Harlan turns him out, he has a salary which he spends in the same way; sometimes his wrung heart gets the better of his prudence, and he spends till he himself is in difficulties. He gives all his money, be gives all his time, he gives all his love. To every inmate of the hospital something, if only a vital word, a cheering touch, a caress, a trifling gift; but always in his rounds be selects the special cases, the sorely wounded, the deeply despondent, the homesick, the dying; to these he devotes himself; he buoys them up with fond words, with caresses, with personal affection; be bends over them, strong, clean, cheerful, perfumed, loving, and his magnetic touch and love sustain them. He does not shrink from the smell of their sickening gangrene; he does not flinch from their bloody and rotten mutilations; he draws nigher for all that; he sticks closer; he dresses those wounds; he fans those burning temples; he moistens those parched lips; he washes those wasted bodies; he watches often and often in the dim ward by the sufferer's cot all night long; he reads from the New Testament, the words sweeter than music to the sinking soul; he soothes with prayer the bedside of the dying; he sits, mournful and loving, by the wasted dead. How can I tell the story of his labors? How can I describe the scenes among which he moved with such endurance and devotion, watched by me, for years?

Few know the spectacle presented by those grim wards. It was hideous. I have been there at night when it seemed that I should die with sympathy if I stayed;—when the horrible attitudes of anguish, the horizontal shapes of cadaver on the white cots, the quiet sleepers, the excruciated emaciations of men, the bloody bandages, the smell of plastered sores, the dim lamplight, the long white ward, the groans of some patient half hidden behind a screen, naked, shorn of both arms, held by the assistant upon a stool, made up a scene whose well-compounded horror is unspeakable. Now realize a man without worldly inducement, without reward, from love and compassion only, giving up his life to scenes like these; foregoing pleasure and rest for vigils, as in chambers of torture, among the despairing, the mangled, the dying, the forms upon which shell and rifle and sabre had wrought every bizarre atrocity of mutilation; immuring himself in the air of their sighs, their moans, the mutter and scream of their delirium; breathing the stench of their putrid wounds; taking up his part and lot with them, living a life of privation and denial, and hoarding his scanty means for the relief and mitigation of their anguish. That man is Walt Whitman! I said his labors have been immense. The word is well chosen. I speak within bounds when I say that, during those years, he has been in contact with, and, in one form or another, either in hospital or on the field, personally ministered to upward of one hundred thousand sick and wounded men. You mothers of America, these were your sons! Faithfully, and with a mother's love, he tended them for you! Many and many a life has he saved—many a time has he felt his heart grow great with that delicious triumph many a home owes its best beloved to him. Sick and wounded, officers and privates, the black soldiers as well as the white, the teamsters, the poor creatures in the contraband camps, the rebel the same as the loyal—he did his best for them all; they were all sufferers, they were all men.—Let him pass. I note Thoreau's saying, that he suggests something more than human. It is true. I see it in his book and in his life. To that something more than human which is also in all men—to the hour of judgment, to the hour of sanity, let me resign him. Not for such as I to vindicate such as he. Not for him, perhaps, the recognition of his day and generation. But a life and deeds like his, lightly esteemed by men, sink deep into the memory of Man. Great is the stormy fight of Zutphen; it is the young lion of English Protestantism springing in haughty fury for the defence of the Netherlands from the bloody ravin of Spain; but Philip Sidney passing the flask of water from his own lips to the dying soldier looms gigantic, and makes all the foreground of its noble purpose and martial rage; and whatever be the verdict of the present, sure am I that hereafter and to the latest ages, when Bull Run and Shiloh and Port Hudson, when Vicksburg and Stone River and Fort Donelson, when Pea Ridge and Chancellorsville and Gettysburg and the Wilderness, and the great march from Atlanta to Savannah, and Richmond rolled in flame, and all the battles for the life of the Republic against her last internal foe are gathered up in accumulated terraces of struggle upon the mountain of history, well-relieved against those bright and bloody tumultuous giant tableaux, and all the dust and thunder of a noble war, the men and women of America will love to gaze upon the stalwart form of the good gray poet, bending to heal the hurts of their wounded and soothe the souls of their dying, and the deep and simple words of the last great martyr will be theirs, "Well, *he* looks like A MAN."

So let me leave him. And if there be any who think this tribute in bad taste, even to a poet so great, a person so unusual, a man so heroic and loving, I answer, that when, on grounds of taste, foes withhold detraction, friends may withhold eulogy; and that at any rate I recognize no reason for keeping back just words of love and reverence when, as in this case, they must glow upon the sullen foil of the printed hatreds of years. To that long record of hostility, I am only proud to be able to oppose this record of affection. And with respect to the crowning enmity of the Secretary of the Interior, let no person misjudge the motives upon which I denounce it. Personally, apart from this act, I have nothing against Mr. Harlan. He is of my own party; and my politics have been from my youth essentially the same as his own. I do not know him; I have never even seen him; I criticise no attitude nor action of his life but this; and I criticise this with as little personality as I can give to an action so personal. I withhold, too, as far as I can, every expression of resentment; and no one who knew all I know of this matter could fail to credit me with singular and great moderation. For, behind what I have related, there is another history, every incident of which I have recovered from the obscurity to which it was confided; and, as I think of it, it is with difficulty that I restrain my just indignation. Instead of my comparatively cold and sober treatment, this transaction deserves rather the pitiless exposure, the measureless, stern anger, the red-hot steel scourge of Juvenal. But I leave untold its darkest details, and, waiving every other consideration, I rest solely and squarely on the general indignity and injury this action offers to intellectual liberty. I claim that to expel an author from a public office and subject him to public contumely, solely because he has published a book which no one can declare immoral without declaring all the grand books immoral, is to affix a penalty to thought, and to obstruct the freedom of

A22

letters. I declare this act the audacious captain of a series of acts, and a style of opinions whose tendency and effect throughout Christendom is to dwarf and degrade literature, and to make great books impossible, except under pains of martyrdom. As such, I arraign it before every liberal and thoughtful mind. I denounce it as a sinister precedent; as a ban upon the free action of genius; as a logical insult to all-commanding literature; and as in every way a most serious and heinous wrong. Difference of opinion there may and must be upon the topics which in these pages I have grouped around it, but upon the act itself there can be none. As I drag it up here into the sight of the world, I call upon every scholar, every man of letters, every editor, every good fellow everywhere who wields the pen, to make common cause with me in rousing upon it the full tempest of reprobation it deserves. I remember Tennyson, a spirit of vengeance over the desecrated grave of Moore; I think of Scott rolling back the tide of obloquy from Byron; I see Addison gilding the blackening fame of Swift; I mark Southampton befriending Shakespeare; I recall Du Bellay enshielding Rabelais; I behold Hutten fortressing Luther; here is Boccaccio lifting the darkness from Dante, and scattering flame on his foes in Florence; this is Bembo protecting Pomponatius; that is Grostate enfolding Roger Bacon from the monkish fury; there, covered with light, is Aristophanes defending Æschylus; and if there lives aught of that old chivalry of letters, which in all ages has sprung to the succor and defence of genius, I summon it to act the part of honor and duty upon a wrong which, done to a single member of the great confraternity of literature, is done to all, and which flings insult and menace upon every immortal page that dares transcend the wicked heart or the constricted brain. God grant that not in vain upon this outrage do I invoke the judgment of the mighty spirit of literature, and the fires of every honest heart!

WILLIAM DOUGLAS O'CONNOR.

[14]Folsom, Ed and Kenneth M. Price, editors. *The Walt Whitman Archive*. University of Nebraska–Lincoln, 2017, http://whitmanarchive.org/criticism/disciples/tei/anc.00170.html. Accessed February 26, 2017.

[A.22]

A poem by a young Abraham Lincoln about a boy marrying another boy, thought the first reference to same-sex marriage in U.S. History:

I will tell you a Joke about Jewel and Mary
It is neither a Joke nor a Story
For Rubin and Charles has married two girls
But Billy has married a boy
The girlies he had tried on every Side
But none could he get to agree
All was in vain he went home again
And since that is married to Natty
So Billy and Natty agreed very well
And mama's well pleased at the match
The egg it is laid but Natty's afraid
The Shell is So Soft that it never will hatch
But Betsy she said you Cursed bald head
My Suitor you never Can be
Beside your low crotch proclaims you a botch
And that never Can answer for me

ABRAHAM LINCOLN, 1829

[41]Segal, Mark. "The men behind the man: Abraham Lincoln's gay lovers." Bilerico Report, February 15, 2016. http://www.lgbtqnation.com/2016/02/the-men-behind-the-man-abraham-lincolns-gay-lovers/. Accessed February 26, 2017.

BAYARD TAYLOR

Bayard Taylor (1825-1878) was an American poet, translator, and travel author who wrote *Eldorado, or, Adventures in the Path of Empire* (1850). Born in the predominately Quaker village of Kennett Square, Pennsylvania, he was a household name in his time. Taylor considered his last novel, *Joseph and His Friend* (1870), to be his most successful. It was also his least popular book.

L.A. FIELDS

L.A. Fields is the author of the young adult Disorder Series (2009-2017), the short story collection *Countrycide* (2014), and the Lambda Literary Award finalists *My Dear Watson* (2013) and *Homo Superiors* (2016). She has a BA in English Literature, an MFA in Creative Writing, a calico cat, and a day job.

CPSIA information can be obtained
at www.ICGtesting.com
Printed in the USA
FSOW03n0834010218
43888FS

9 781590 216422